# Lecture Notes in Computer Science 4740

Commenced Publication in 1973
Founding and Former Series Editors:
Gerhard Goos, Juris Hartmanis, and Jan van Leeuwen

T0181278

Lizhuang Ma   Matthias Rauterberg
Ryohei Nakatsu (Eds.)

# Entertainment Computing – ICEC 2007

6th International Conference
Shanghai, China, September 15-17, 2007
Proceedings

 Springer

Volume Editors

Lizhuang Ma
Shanghai Jiao Tong University
Shanghai, China
E-mail: ma-lz@cs.sjtu.edu.cn

Matthias Rauterberg
TU Eindhoven
Eindhoven, The Netherlands
E-mail: g.w.m.rauterberg@tue.nl

Ryohei Nakatsu
Kwansei Gakuin University
Nishinomiya Hyogo, Japan
E-mail: nakatsu@ksc.kwansei.ac.jp

Library of Congress Control Number: 2007934519

CR Subject Classification (1998): H.5, H.4, H.3, I.2, I.3, I.7, J.5

LNCS Sublibrary: SL 3 – Information Systems and Application, incl. Internet/Web
and HCI

ISSN        0302-9743
ISBN-10     3-540-74872-5 Springer Berlin Heidelberg New York
ISBN-13     978-3-540-74872-4 Springer Berlin Heidelberg New York

Springer is a part of Springer Science+Business Media

springer.com

© IFIP International Federation for Information Processing, Hofstrasse 3, A-2361 Laxenburg, Austria 2007
Printed in Germany

Typesetting: Camera-ready by author, data conversion by Scientific Publishing Services, Chennai, India
Printed on acid-free paper      SPIN: 12121045       06/3180       5 4 3 2 1 0

# Foreword

Welcome to the proceedings of ICEC 2007

It is our honor to edit this volume of LNCS reporting the recent progress in entertainment computing. We are pleased with the solid work of all the authors who contributed to ICEC 2007. ICEC 2007 attracted 99 technical papers. Based on a thorough review and selection process by 87 international experts from academia and industry as members of the Program Committee, a high-quality program was compiled. The International Program Committee consisted of experts from all over the world: 6 from the UK, 3 from Singapore, 1 from Lebanon, 30 from China, 2 from The Netherlands, 9 from Japan, 6 from Germany, 1 form Greece, 3 from Canada, 11 from the USA, 3 from Korea, 2 from Austria, 1 from Hungary, 1 from Spain, 1 from Portugal, 2 from Italy, 2 from France, 1 from Switzerland, 1 from Sweden, and 1 from Finland. The final decision was made by review and conference Chairs based on at least three reviewers' feedback available online via the conference management tool and E-mail. As a result, 25 full papers and 23 regular papers were accepted as submitted or with minor revisions. For the remaining submissions, 16 were recommended to change according to the reviews and were submitted as posters. In all the papers, five were published in the *International Journal of Virtual Reality*, three were recommended to the *Journal of Computer Animation and Virtual Worlds*, and six were recommended to the *Journal of Computer Science and Technology*. This proceedings volume presents 64 technical contributions which are from many different countries: Singapore, China, Japan, Korea, The Netherlands, Czech Republic, Spain, USA, Germany, France, Australia, Canada, etc. The accepted technical papers are compiled and presented in this volume in the order they were presented at the conference. They are classified into the following presentation sessions: (1) Augmented, Virtual and Mixed Reality; (2) Computer Games; (3) Image Processing; (4) Mesh and Modeling; (5) Digital Storytelling and Interactive Systems; (6) Sound, Music and Creative Environments; (7) Video Processing; (8) Rendering; (9) Computer Animation and Networks; (10) Game-Based Interfaces; (11) Robots and Cyber Pets. All poster papers are listed separately and presented in a specific section of this book.

July 2007

Lizhuang Ma
Matthias Rauterberg
Ryohei Nakatsu

# Preface

Entertainment is playing a very important role in our life by refreshing our mind, activating our creativity and providing different media for expression. Recently, with the advances made in graphics, image processing, sensors, networks, and media technologies, new types of entertainment have been emerging such as video games, edutainment, robots, augment reality, and online games. Entertainment has been merged into different fields of science, society, economy as well as our daily life. It is valuable to enhance the efficiency of many aspects, such as teaching, learning, playing, working, communicating and exchanging knowledge. New forms of entertainment are emerging and are studied by many scientists and engineers from different research fields. Entertainment has become one of the major research areas in information technology. Since there are rapidly expanding industries and markets devoted to entertainment, new technologies and methodology must be laid out for these increasing demands.

The emerging forms of entertainment have been changing our lives, and it is urgent for us to discuss various aspects of entertainment, to analyze the principle and structure of entertainment and to promote entertainment-related research.

With this basic motivation, the General Assembly of the International Federation of Information Processing (IFIP) approved in August 2002 the establishment of SG16 to monitor and promote research and development activities related to entertainment computing throughout the world. One of the major activities of SG16 is to organize and support the International Conference of Entertainment Computing (ICEC). The ICEC is expected to bring together researchers, developers, and practitioners working on entertainment computing topics, such as theoretical studies, social and cultural aspects, new hardware/software development, integrated systems, integrated systems, human interfaces and interactions, and applications.

Let us briefly review the history of ICEC. The annual conference started in 2002 as the International Workshop on Entertainment (IWEC 2002), which was held May 14-17, 2002 in Makuhari, Japan. The workshop attracted more than 100 participants, and 60 papers were published in the proceedings by Kluwer. Based on the success of IWEC 2002, SG16 upgraded the workshop to a conference and organized ICEC 2003. ICEC 2003 was held May 8-10, 2003 at the Entertainment Technology Center of Carnegie Mellon University, Pittsburgh, USA. ICEC 2003 was also successful, with more than 100 attendees and 20 highly selected papers. All of the papers of ICEC 2003 were accepted by ACM for inclusion in their ACM online digital library. The following year, ICEC crossed the Atlantic Ocean to Europe, and ICEC 2004 was held September 1-3, 2004 at the Technical University of Eindhoven in The Netherlands. The conference attracted more than 150 attendees, and 27 full papers were published by Springer in the *Lecture Notes in Computer Science* (LNCS) series. In 2005, ICEC came back to

Japan, and was held at Kwansei Gakuin University, Sanda. In this conference the Committee selected more than 50 papers, and these papers are published in the LNCS volume. In 2006, ICEC was hosted by Microsoft Research and the University of Cambridge, in Cambridge, UK. In the conference the Committee selected more than 60 papers.

Finally, in 2007, ICEC was hosted for the first time in Shanghai, China, hosted by Shanghai Jiao Tong University, sponsored by the Natural Science Foundation of China, Autodesk and Microsoft Japan.

For the success of ICEC 2007, we express our special thanks to all the people who worked so hard to organize the conference: the Shanghai Jiao Tong University for the support and to all the individuals who supported the organization with the Local Organization Committee.

We are also grateful for the contribution of all the paper reviewers as well as the sponsors and cooperating societies.

Special thanks to the support of the joint laboratory of Intelligent Computing and Systems between Microsoft Research Asia and Shanghai Jiao Tong University, the special group of computer animation and digital entertainment of China Association of Images and Graphics, and the 973 Plan of China 2006CB303105.

July 2007                                                                    Lizhuang Ma
                                                                        Matthias Rauterberg
                                                                          Ryohei Nakatsu

# Committees

## General Conference Chairs

| | |
|---|---|
| Lizhuang Ma | Shanghai Jiao Tong University , China |
| Matthias Rauterberg | Technical University of Eindhoven, The Netherlands |
| Ryohei Nakatsu | Kwansei Gakuin University, Japan |

## International Steering Committee

| | |
|---|---|
| Andy Sloane | University of Wolverhampton, UK |
| Bill Swartout | University of Southern California, USA |
| Don Marinelli | Carnegie Mellon University, USA |
| Lizhuang Ma | Shanghai Jiao Tong University, China |
| Marc Cavazza | University of Teesside, UK |
| Matthias Rauterberg | Technical University of Eindhoven, The Netherlands |
| Peter Robinson | University of Cambridge, UK |
| Ryohei Nakatsu | Kwansei Gakuin University, Japan |
| Stéphane Natkin | CNAM, France |
| Tak Kamae | Tokyo Women's Medical University, Japan |

## Program Chairs

| | |
|---|---|
| Lizhuang Ma | Shanghai Jiao Tong University, China |
| Rynson W. H. Lau | Durham University, UK |
| Zhigeng Pan | Zhejiang University, China |

## Organizing Chair

| | |
|---|---|
| Lizhuang Ma | Shanghai Jiao Tong University,China |

## Scientific Program Committee

| | |
|---|---|
| Abdennour El Rhalibi | Liverpool JM University, UK |
| Adrian David Cheok | National University of Singapore, Singapore |
| Ahmad H. Nasri | American University of Beirut, Lebanon |
| Ajay Joneja | HKUST, Hong Kong |
| Anton Nijholt | University of Twente, The Netherlands |
| Baining Guo | Microsoft Research Asia |

| | |
|---|---|
| Ben Salem | Technical University of Eindhoven, The Netherlands |
| Caiming Zhang | Shandong University, China |
| Carsten Magerkurth | Fraunhofer IPSI, Germany |
| Changhe Tu | Shandong University, China |
| Chenglian Peng | Fudan University, China |
| Christian Bauckhage | Deutsche Telekom, Germany |
| Christian Reimann | C-Lab, Germany |
| Christos Bouras | University of Patras, Greece |
| Clark Verbrugge | McGill University, Canada |
| David Gu | SUNY Stony Brook, USA |
| David S. Ebert | Purdue University, USA |
| Deok-Soo Kim | Hanyang University, Korea |
| Dongxu Qi | MUST, Macao, China |
| Eng Wee Chionh | National University of Singapore |
| Enhua Wu | Macau University, China |
| Ernst A. Heinz | UMIT, Austria |
| Falai Chen | China |
| Fuhua Cheng | University of Kentucky, USA |
| Gabor Renner | Hungary |
| Gabriel Zachmann | University of Bonn, Germany |
| Gino Yu | Hong Kong Polytechnic University, China |
| Hanqiu Sun | Chinese University of Hong Kong, China |
| Haruhiro Katayose | Kwansei Gakuin University, Japan |
| Herb Yang | University of Alberta, Canada |
| Hong Qin | SUNY, Stony Brook, USA |
| Hua Li | Chinese Academy of Science, China |
| Huamin Qu | HKUST, Hong Kong |
| Hyeong-Seok Ko | Seoul National University, Korea |
| Issei Fujishiro | Tohoku University, Japan |
| Javier Jaen | Polytechnic University of Valencia, Spain |
| Joao Manuel R. S. Tavares | Universidade do Porto, Portugal |
| Kaihuai Qin | Tsinghua University, China |
| Lars Wolf | TU Braunschweig, Germany |
| Leonid Smalov | Coventry University, UK |
| Lief Kobbelt | RWTH Aachen, Germany |
| Lifeng Wang | Autodesk, China |
| Luca Chittaro | University of Udine, Italy |
| Marco Roccetti | University of Bologna, Italy |
| Marie-Paule Cani | INRIA, France, France |
| Michael Haller | Upper Austria University, Austria |
| Nadia Magnenat-Thalmann | University of Geneva, Switzerland |
| Naoko Tosa | Kyoto University, Japan |
| Norman I.Badler | University of Pennsylvania, USA |
| Oskar Juhlin | Interactive Institute, Sweden |
| Paolo Remagnino | Kingston University, Hong Kong |

| | |
|---|---|
| Pheng-Ann Heng | Chinese University of Hong Kong, China |
| Rynson W. H. Lau | Durham University, Hong Kong |
| Seungyong Lee | Pohang University of Sci.&Tech., Korea |
| Shimin Hu | Tsinghua University, China |
| Sidney Fels | University of British Columbia, Canada |
| Steven Furnell | University of Plymouth, UK |
| Taku Komura | City University of Hong Kong, China |
| Tsukasa Noma | Kyushu Institute of Technology, Japan |
| Ville-Veikko Mattila | Nokia, Finland |
| W.Y. Ma | City University, HongKong |
| Xin Tong | Microsoft Research Asia |
| Xiuzi Ye | Solidworks, USA |
| Yizhou Yu | University of Illinois, USA |
| Yoshihiro Okada | Kyushu University, Japan |
| Yuan-Shin Lee | N.Carolina State University, USA |
| Zesheng Tang | Macau University, China |
| ZhaoQi Wang | Institute of Computing Tech, China |
| Zhiyong Huang | National University of Singapore, Singapore |
| Zhigeng Pan | Zhejiang University, China |

## Sponsors

Natural Science Foundation of China
Autodesk
Microsoft, Japan

# IFIP TC14

SG16 (Specialist Group on Entertainment Computing) was established at the General Assembly of IFIP (International Federation on Information Processing) in 2001. On August 28, 2006 the General Assembly of IFIP decided to establish the new Technical Committee TC14 on Entertainment Computing. Therefore SG16 will convert into TC14:

## Aims

To encourage computer applications for entertainment and to enhance computer utilization in the home, the Technical Committee will pursue the following aims:

- To enhance algorithmic research on board and card games
- To promote a new type of entertainment using information technologies
- To encourage hardware technology research and development to facilitate implementing entertainment systems
- To encourage non-traditional human interface technologies for entertainment

## Scopes

(1) Algorithm and strategy for board and card games

- Algorithms of board and card games
- Strategy control for board and card games
- Level setup for game and card games

(2) Novel entertainment using ICT

- Network-based entertainment
- Mobile entertainment
- Location-based entertainment
- Mixed reality entertainment

(3) Audio

- Music informatics for entertainment
- 3D audio for entertainment
- Sound effects for entertainment

(4) Entertainment and human interface technologies

- Haptic and non-traditional human interface technologies
- Mixed reality human interface technologies for entertainment

(5) Entertainment robots

- ICT-based toys
- Pet robots
- Emotion model and rendering technologies for robots

(6) Entertainment systems

- Design of entertainment systems
- Entertainment design toolkits
- Authoring systems

(7) Theoretical aspects of entertainment

- Sociology, psychology and physiology for entertainment
- Legal aspects of entertainment

(8) Video game and animation technologies

- Video game hardware and software technologies
- Video game design toolkits
- Motion capture and motion design
- Interactive story telling
- Digital actors and emotion model

(9) Interactive TV and movies

- Multiple view synthesis
- Free viewpoint TV
- Authoring technologies

(10) Edutainment

- Entertainment technologies for children's education
- Open environment entertainment robots for education

## TC14 Members (2007)

**Chair**
Ryohei Nakatsu - Kwansei Gakuin University, Japan
**Vice-Chair**
Matthias Rauterberg - Technical University of Eindhoven, The Netherlands
**Secretary**
Ben Salem - Technical University of Eindhoven, The Netherlands
**Industrial liaison**
Claudio Pinhanez - IBM, USA

## National Representatives

- Austria: Peter Purgathofer
- Bulgaria: Galia Angelova
- Canada: Sidney Fels
- China: Zhigeng Pan
- Czech Republic: David Obdrzalek
- Denmark: (to be nominated)
- Finland: Ville-Veikko Mattila
- France: Bruno Arnaldi
- Germany: (to be nominated)
- Hungary: Barnabas Takacs
- Ireland: Richard Reilly
- Italy: Paolo Ciancarini
- Japan: Ryohei Nakatsu
- Korea: Hyun S. Yang
- The Netherlands: Matthias Rauterberg
- Norway: Geir Egil Myhre
- Portugal: Nuno Correia
- Singapore: Adrian David Cheok
- Spain: Pedro Gonzalez-Calero
- Thailand: Natanicha Chorpotong
- United Kingdom: Marc Cavazza
- USA-ACM: Donald Marinelli
- USA-IEEE: Nahum Gershon
- Zambia: Milner Makuni

## WG Chairs

- WG14.1 Chair: Marc Cavazza
- WG14.2 Chair: Hitoshi Matsubara (ex-officio member)
- WG14.3 Chair: Matthias Rauterberg
- WG14.4 Chair: Jaap Van Den Herik (ex-officio member)
- WG14.5 Chair: Andy Sloane (ex-officio member)
- WG14.6 Chair: Lyn Pemberton (ex-officio member)
- WG14.7 Chair: Naoko Tosa (ex-officio member)

# Working Groups (WG)

## WG14.1 - Digital Storytelling

Scopes

Storytelling is one of the core technologies of entertainment. Especially with the advancement of information and communication technologies (ICT), new types of entertainment called video games have been developed where interactive story development is the key that makes these games really entertaining. At the same time, however, the difference between interactive storytelling and conventional storytelling has not been studied well. Also, as the development of interactive storytelling needs a lot of time and human power, it is crucial to develop technologies for automatic or semiautomatic story development. The objective of this working group is to study and discuss these issues.

## WG14.2 - Entertainment Robot

Scopes

Robots are becoming one of the most appealing forms of entertainment. New entertainment robots and/or pet robots are becoming popular. Also, from theoretical point of view, compared with computer graphics-based characters/animations, robots are an interesting research object as they have a physical entity. Taking this into consideration, it was decided at the SG16 annual meeting that a new working group on entertainment robot is to be established.

## WG14.3 - Theoretical Basis of Entertainment

Aims

For the benefit of society, to promote visibility and to increase the impact of research and development in the entertainment computing area, especially in the fields defined in the scope of this working group.

- To promote the quality and relevance of academic and industrial research and development in the entertainment computing area.
- To promote ethical behavior and appropriate recommendations or guidelines for research-related activities, for example, submission and selection of publications, organization of conferences, allocation of grants and awards, and evaluation of professional merits and curricula.
- To promote cooperation between researchers and with other established bodies and organizations pursuing the above aims.
- To contribute to assessing the scientific merits and practical relevance of proposed approaches for entertainment technology and applications.

Scopes

Although there are already huge entertainment industries such as video games, toys, movies, etc., little academic interest has been paid to such questions as what is the core of entertainment, which technologies of entertainment can be applied to other areas such as education, learning and so on. The main objective of this WG is to study these issues.

## WG14.4 - Games and Entertainment Computing

Aims

To research and develop computing techniques for the improvement of computer games and other forms of computer entertainment.

Scopes

The scope of this workgroup includes, but is not limited to, the following applications, technologies, and activities.

Applications:

- Analytical games (e.g., Chess, Go, Poker)
- Commercial games (e.g., Action games, Role-playing games, Strategy games)
- Mobile games (e.g., Mobile phones, PDAs)
- Interactive multimedia (e.g., Virtual reality, Simulations)

Technologies:

- Search Techniques
- Machine-Learning Games
- Reasoning
- Agent Technology
- Human–Computer Interaction

## WG14.5 - Social and Ethical Issues in Entertainment Computing

Aims

- Foster the ethical design, development, implementation, applications and use of entertainment computing.
- Encourage surveys and studies on social, ethical, and cultural aspects of entertainment computing. Develop methodologies for studying social, ethical, and cultural implications of entertainment computing.
- Establish a global platform for interaction, exchange, joint initiatives, and co-operation between such groups as:
- the end users of entertainment computing
- industrial developers and designers of entertainment computing
- policy, decision making, social, and consultative bodies
- academics and scientists.

Scopes

The social and ethical implications of entertainment computing, including:

- Actual and potential human usefulness or harm of entertainment computing
- Social impact of these technologies
- Developments of the underlying infrastructure
- Rationale in innovation and design processes
- Dynamics of technology development
- Ethical development
- Cultural diversity and other cultural issues
- Education of the public about the social and ethical implications of entertainment computing, and of computer professionals about the effects of their work

WG14.5 explicitly focuses on the position of, and the potentials for, vulnerable groups such as children, the less-educated, disabled, elderly and non-employed people, cultural minorities, unaware users, and others.

## WG14.6 - Interactive TeleVision (ITV)

Aims

- To promote visibility and to increase the impact of research and development in the ITV field
- To bring together interdisciplinary approaches to ITV research and development issues (e.g., content production, computer science, media studies)
- To encourage cooperation between researchers and other established bodies and organizations, through the development of joint project proposals
- To facilitate the development of suitable academic and practical teaching programs

Scopes

- Alternative content distribution (mobile TV, peer-to-peer TV, IPTV)
- Interactive storytelling, user-contributed content
- Interactive and personalized advertising systems
- Applications for t-commerce, t-learning, t-health, entertainment
- Ethical, regulatory and policy issues
- Interoperability of middleware, standards, multimedia metadata
- Authoring, production, and virtual reality systems
- Content management, digital rights management
- Multimedia, graphics, broadcast, and video technology
- Content-enriched communication services, video conferencing
- Personalization, user modeling, intelligent user interfaces
- Usability, accessibility, universal access, multimodal interaction

## WG14.7 - Art and Entertainment

Scope

The influence of technology and scientific innovation is profoundly changing how we express ourselves. Arts and entertainment is a new field that represents the exciting convergence of technology with the established design discipline. The media arts and cinema offer a comprehensive approach to design that encourages innovation by media artists, scientists, and engineers. The working group will pursue the following activities:

Aims

- To explore the way art and cinema esthetics can play a role in different areas of computer science.
- One of its goals is to modify computer science by the application of the wide range of definitions and categories normally associated by making art and cinema.
- To go beyond the usual definition of art and cinema esthetics in computing, which most often refers to the formal, abstract qualities of such structures - a beautiful proof, or an elegant diagram.

- To research the broader spectrum of esthetics—from abstract qualities of symmetry and form to ideas of creative expression and pleasure—in the context of computer science.
- To prove the assumption behind art and cinema esthetic computing that the field of computing will be enriched if it embraces all of esthetics.

# Invited Speakers

## Nadia Magnenat-Thalmann

Professor Nadia Magnenat-Thalmann has pioneered research into virtual humans over the last 25 years. She obtained several Bachelor and Master degrees in various disciplines psychology, biology, and chemistry) and a PhD in quantum physics from the University of Geneva. From 1977 to 1989, she was a professor at the University of Montreal where she founded the research lab MIRALab.

She was elected Woman of the Year by the Grand Montreal Association for her pionnering work on virtual humans, and her work was presented at the Modern Art Museum of New York in 1988. She moved to the University of Geneva in 1989, where she founded the Swiss MIRALab, an internationally interdisciplinary lab composed of about 25 researchers.

She is author and coauthor of more than 200 research papers and a dozen of books in the field of modeling virtual humans, interacting with them, and living in augmented life. She has received several scientific and artistic awards for her work, mainly on the Virtual Marylin and the film Rendez-Vous a Montreal, but more recently, in 1997, she was elected to the Swiss Academy of Technical Sciences, and has been nominated as a Swiss personality who has contributed to the advance of science in the 150 years history.

She has directed and produced several films and real-time mixed-reality shows, among the latest are Dreams of a Mannequin (2003), The Augmented Life in Pompeii (2004) and Fashion in Equations (2005). She is editor-in-chief of the *Visual Computer Journal* published by Springer and Co-editor-in-chief of *Computer Animation and Virtual Worlds* published by John Wiley. She has also participated in political events such as the World Economic Forum in Davos where she was invited to give several talks and seminars.

## Qunsheng Peng

Qunsheng Peng is a professor of computer graphics at Zhejiang University. His research interests include realistic image synthesis, computer animation, scientific data visualization, virtual reality, and bio-molecule modeling. In the past few years, he published more than 100 papers concerned with shading models, real-time rendering, curved surface modeling, and infrared image synthesis in international journals and conferences. Among them, two papers won the Best Paper Award of *J. Computer and Graphics* 1988-1989 and the Best Paper Award of Eurographics 89. He has received a number of domestic scientific prizes and is the recipient of Chinagraph 2000 Achievements Award.

Professor Peng graduated from Beijing Mechanical College in 1970 and received a Ph D from the Department of Computing Studies, University of East Anglia in 1983. He currently serves as a member of the editorial boards of several international and Chinese journals.

## Matthias Rauterberg

Professor (G.W.) Matthias Rauterberg has held teaching and research positions at the Technical University of Hamburg-Harburg (Germany), University of Oldenburg (Germay), and Swiss Federal Institute of Technology (Switzerland). He was a senior researcher and lecturer for 'human – computer interaction' and 'usability engineering' in industrial engineering and computer science at the Swiss Federal Institute of Technology (ETH) and at the University of Zurich. He was the head of the Man – Machine Interaction research group (MMI) of the Institute of Hygiene and Applied Physiology (IHA) at the Department of Industrial Engineering (ETH). He holds a Diploma Degree (M Sc) in Computer Science, a Diploma Degree (M Sc) in Psychology, and a Bachelor Degree (B A) in Philosophy. He finished his PhD in Computer Science/Mathematics at the University of Zurich (Institute for Informatics). He is now full professor of Human Communication Technology and head of the research group 'Designed Intelligence' at the Department of Industrial Design of the Technical University Eindhoven (The Netherlands), and since 2004 has been visiting professor at the Kwansei Gakuin University (Japan).

## Ryohei Nakatsu

Ryohei Nakatsu received a B S, M S, and Ph D degree in electronic engineering from Kyoto University in 1969, 1971, and 1982 respectively. After joining NTT in 1971, he mainly worked on speech recognition technology. In 1994, he joined ATR (Advanced Telecommunications Research Institute) as the president of ATR Media Integration and Communications Research Laboratories. From the spring of 2002 he has been a professor at the School of Science and Technology, Kwansei Gakuin University. At the same time he established a venture company, Nirvana Technology Inc., and became president of the company.

His research interests include emotion extraction from speech and facial images, emotion recognition, nonverbal communications, and integration of multimodalities in communications. In 1978, he received, Young Engineer Award from the Institute of Electronics, Information, and Communication Engineers Japan (IEICE-J). In 1996, he was the recipient of the best paper award from the IEEE International Conference on Multimedia. In 1999, 2000, and 2001, he got the Telecom System Award from the Telecommunication System Foundation and the best paper award from the Virtual Reality Society of Japan. In 2000, he got the best paper award from the Artificial Intelligence Society of Japan. He is a fellow of the IEEE and the Institute of Electronics, Information, and Communication Engineers Japan (IEICE-J), a member of the Acoustical Society of Japan,

Information Processing Society of Japan, and Japanese Society for Artificial Intelligence.

## Lizhuang Ma

Lizhuang, Ma, was born in 1963, and received his B Sc and Ph D degrees at Zhejiang University, China in 1985 and 1991, respectively. He was a post-doctoral fellow at the Department of Computer Science of Zhejiang University from 1991 to 1993. Dr. Ma was promoted to an Associative Professor and Professor in 1993 and 1995, respectively. Dr. Ma stayed at Zhejiang University from 1991 to 2002. He was a Visiting Professor at Fraunhofer IGD, Darmstadt, Germany from July to Dec. 1998, and visiting Professor at Center for Advanced Media Technology, Nanyang Technological University, Singapore from September 1999 to October 2000. He is now a Professor, PhD tutor, and the head of Digital Media Technology and the Data Reconstruction Lab. at the Department of Computer Science and Engineering, Shanghai Jiao Tong University, China from 2002. He is also the Chairman of the Center of Information Science and Technology for Traditional Chinese Medicine at the Shanghai Traditional Chinese Medicine University.

Dr. Ma has published more than 100 academic research papers both domestic and international journals, for instance, *Science in China, Computer-Aided Geometric Design, and Computers & Graphics.* The Science Press of Beijing has published a monograph by Dr. Ma, *Techniques and Applications for Computer Aided Geometric Modeling.* Dr. Ma is the recipient of the China National Excellent Young Scientist Foundation Award, first class member of the China National Hundred-Thousand-Ten-Thousand Talent Plan, the China National Award of Science and Technology for Young Scientists, and Second Prize of the Science and Technology of the National Education Bureau. His research interests include computer-aided geometric design, computer graphics, scientific data visualization, computer animation, digital media technology, and theory and applications for computer graphics, CAD/CAM.

# Table of Contents

## Session 1: Augmented, Virtual and Mixed Reality

## Session 2: Computer Games

## Session 6: Sound, Music and Creative Environments

## Session 7: Video Processing

## Session 8: Rendering

## Session 9: Computer Animation and Networks

## Session 10: Game Based Interfaces

## Session 11: Robots and Cyber Pets

## Posters

# A Training Oriented Driving Simulator

Chao Sun, Feng Xie, Xiaocao Feng, Mingmin Zhang, and Zhigeng Pan

CAD&CG State Key Lab. Zhejiang University, Hang Zhou, China, 310027
{sunchao,xiefeng,fengxiaocao,zmm,zgpan}@cad.zju.edu.cn

**Abstract.** In today's China, a growing number of people have the opportunity to have their own cars. This creates tremendous requirement of training of new drivers. At the same time, recent advances in Computer Graphics and Virtual Reality system have brought the new opportunities for the development of driving simulation. This paper describes a driving simulator named TODS which is the acronym of training oriented driving simulator, developed for rigorous driving training and for Computer Graphics study. TODS is designed under the human-in-the-loop real-time simulation mode providing 120°horizontal FOV(Field of View) and realistic visual feedback to give the driver a realistic feeling of immersion similar to the feeling in a real moving vehicle. TODS utilizes state-of-the-art real-time rendering techniques in Vertex Shader and Pixel Shader [1] to make it more flexible to implement more real-time rendering algorithms in GPU (Graphic Processing Unit) so as to enhance the system function. TODS's scene model is designed and constructed according to the "Driving Test Specification" of China to meet the demands of rigorous driving training. And a kind of modular construction method is used in the work of scene authoring in TODS.

**Keywords:** Driving simulation, Real-Time Simulation, Real-Time Rendering, Computer Graphics, GPU, Shader, Dynamic Texture Mapping.

## 1 Introduction

A driving simulator is a virtual reality tool that supports a variety of training, research, and design applications. It has advantages over comparable vehicle testing in many aspects including economy, safety, reproducibility, convenience of changing vehicle models and ease of data acquisition. In China, more and more individuals have the opportunity to have a car in recent years. This increases the burden of the training school for drivers. On the other hand, recent advances in Computer Graphics and Virtual Reality system are leading to the new opportunities for the development of driving simulation. To meet the increasing demand of driving training, we develop a training oriented driving simulator named TODS which is the acronym of training oriented driving simulator, based on state-of-the-art CG and VR science and technology. In addition to the common features of general driving simulators, we also implement several distinct functions in our study -- 120°horizontal field of view, high-resolution visual system to provide realistic visual feedback, more authentic effect of mirror in the virtual environment, precise appearance and size of scene model according to the "Driving Test Specification" for rigorous training.

L. Ma, R. Nakatsu, and M. Rauterberg (Eds.): ICEC 2007, LNCS 4740, pp. 1–9, 2007.

In the following sections, this paper describes TODS from four aspects: real-time simulation system, visual system, system enhancement based on programmable GPU and scene authoring. In the final part of this paper, we make several conclusions.

## 2  Related Work

Driving simulation research was first conducted in aircraft simulation. The pioneering work in human-in-the-loop driving simulation [2, 3] in the 1970s by General Motors® and Virginia Polytechnic Institute and State University lasted for three decades and made great advances in this area of study. Our study is also based on the human-in-the-loop mode. We will discuss it in detail in next section.

In 1990s, several outstanding simulators were built. The Center for Computer Aided Design at the University of IOWA developed the IOWA Driving Simulator [4, 5]. It includes a large hexapod motion base and operational gauges and instruments. The driver receives haptic feedback through the steering wheel, accelerator, and brake pedal. Within the vehicle cab, high-resolution, textured graphics generated by an Evans & Sutherland ESIG 2000 are projected onto a screen in front of the cab and a smaller screen behind the cab visible through real rear-view mirrors. There is still further work that can be done to create more realistic visual feedback than IOWA with the help of the latest Computer Graphics science and technology. We propose our methods in the following sections of "visual system" and "system enhancement based on GPU" in this paper.

The rapidly increasing power of computers makes it possible to produce cheaper driving simulators. For example, Systems Technology Incorporated® (STI®) has developed a desktop configuration that uses personal computers for graphics and vehicle dynamics [6, 7]. They have done innovative work in this field. However, the visual fidelity is not very high in these simulators. Narrow FOV (Field of View) becomes a crucial limitation. This has been changed in our study. And it will be described in detail in the section of "visual system" in this paper.

## 3  Real-Time Simulation System

The essence of a driving simulation has two aspects. One is the simulator's feedback that a driver receives responding to his/her input commands, another is his/her subsequent control responses induced by that feedback. Therefore, the realness of a simulation mainly depends on the fidelity feedback of visual image displayed on the screens generated by the Visual System in real time and the correct new state of the whole scene including your own car, traffic aids, autonomous cars etc. The new state is generated by the Physics and AI module. According to this, we utilize a nested-control-loop real-time simulation system developed from human-in-the-loop mode [2, 3] in TODS.

Figure 1 illustrates a basic concept of TODS's real-time simulation system. As can be seen in the block diagram, there are 3 layers of loop in the system – Operation Loop, Rendering Loop and Physics Loop.

1. In the Operation Loop, driver inputs his/her control operations to the inner loops through the simulator controls – steering wheel, break, throttle, clutch, etc. and get the feedback through the visual system feedback. The period of Operation Loop – △T mainly depends on the driver's response speed.
2. In the Rendering Loop, GPU renders the 3-D scene to the Frame Buffer through its fixed pipeline for some normal purpose. And we also employ Vertex Shader and Pixel Shader to implement more advanced effects, such as dynamic texture mapping for some special purpose. We will give a detailed explanation in the following section. The period of Rendering Loop – $dt'$ of a typical scene in TODS is about 30ms on our system. That means the FPS of our system is about 33.
3. In the Physics Loop, the Physics module calculates the driving car's position, velocity, acceleration, and orientation. In the scenes which have autonomous cars and traffic aids, the AI module is in charge of those cars' behavior. The period of Physics Loop – $dt$ is 10ms, which is set by us. It's the shortest period among the three, because in every single period of Physics Loop the physical event is computed on CPU by linear differential equations, the shorter the time the more accurate the results.

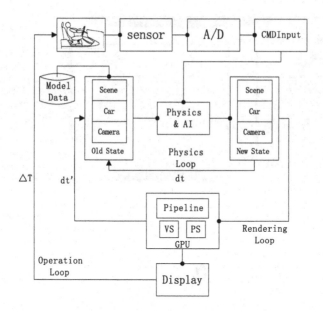

**Fig. 1.** Real-time simulation system of TODS is a human-in-the-loop mode. Human is in the outer loop operating the control equipments. GPU and CPU are in the inner loops engaged in the work of rendering, physical simulation and AI processing. In this diagram, triangle-arrows indicate control flow and point-arrows indicate data flow.

## 4  Visual System

For a driving simulator, it is most important to provide a realistic feeling of immersion similar to the feeling in a real moving vehicle. During driving, drivers' visual impression is the most significant cue for him/her to control the vehicle. Therefore, providing a realistic visual feel is the challenge to the visual system of a driving simulator. Since on the driver's seat of a real car, the front, left and right side are almost all in the driver's vision scope, providing a 120°horizontal field of view with high resolution graphics in the visual system is essential for the driver to have a realistic driving feel and react to the driving environment precisely.

In our study, Matrox® TripleHead2Go™ provides 3072×768 high-resolution images on three monitors which are arranged according to the form of an arc, and the specific frustums are designed to project precise images on each of the screens so that the images can be assembled seamlessly.

Figure 2 (a) shows the form of arranging the monitors and a typical driving scene of TODS. Figure 2 (b) illustrates how to set up the frustums that determine the projection matrixes.

At first, the angle of two contiguous screens - $\alpha$ , and the distance from driver's eye to screen – $d$, is preset. And then all of the parameters of these 3 frustums can be obtained by the following equations.

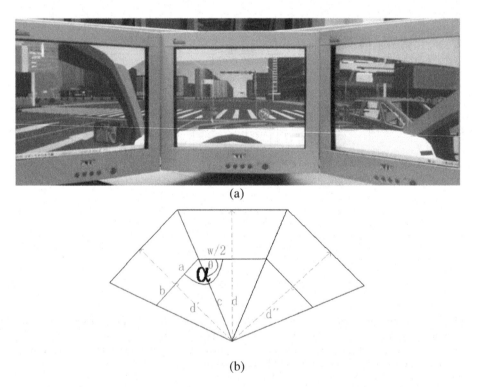

(a)

(b)

**Fig. 2.** A kind of display equipment and a typical running scene of TODS are shown in (a). Different display equipments e.g. projectors can be used for different occasions. The angle of two contiguous screens is preset, so as to provide a 120°horizontal FOV by 3 screens. The frustums' configuration is shown in (b). $W$ is the width of a screen.

$$c = \sqrt{(w/2)^2 + d^2} \; , \theta = \arctan(2d/w) \tag{1}$$

$$d' = \sin(\alpha - \theta) \times c \tag{2}$$

$$a = \cos(\alpha - \theta) \times c \, , b = w - a \tag{3}$$

Note that, the left and right frustums can be asymmetric projection. In other words, $a$ is unnecessarily equal to $b$.

## 5 System Enhancement Based on GPU

In our study, some real-time rendering techniques based on programmable Vertex Shader and Pixel Shader are utilized to make it more flexible to implement more real-time rendering algorithms in the GPU and relieve the burden of CPU at the same time. As we know, the rear-view mirror is an important tool for drivers to understand the situation of the rear and sides of his/her car. Therefore providing authentic effect of mirror in the virtual environment is essential for a driving simulator.

There are two kinds of rear-view mirrors on a real training car, planar mirror and convex mirror. Figure 3 presents the views in these two kinds of mirrors on a real training car.

**Fig. 3.** The views of these two kinds of mirrors on a real car are important for drivers

To simulate these rear-view mirrors, the method proposed by IOWA is to project rear scene of the car onto another small screen behind the cab which is visible through real mirrors [4, 5]. In our study, Dynamic Texture Mapping [8, 9, 10] technique based on the VS and PS is employed to solve this problem.

First, the whole scene is rendered to a Target Texture instead of Frame Buffer. We can regard it as an image on the near plane of a specific frustum. This specific frustum is mirror symmetrical with the frustum which is created as an imaginary driver's eyes looking at the virtual mirror. Second, the texture coordinates of the vertex $A$ and $B$ is calculated by Vertex Shader by projecting them onto the near plane. Third, in Pixel Shader, the correct image is mapped on the mirror in accordance with the texture coordinates acquired from previous step. Figure 4 illustrates a function diagram of this method in our study. $AB$ is the mirror plane; $C$ is the imaginary driver's eyes' position. $C'$ and $C$ are symmetrical with respect to the mirror plane. The whole scene is projected

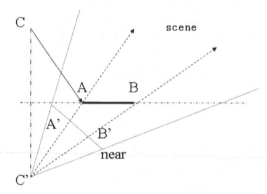

**Fig. 4.**The function diagram illustrates how to simulate the effect of training cars' planar rear-view mirrors in TODS

on the near plane and *A'B'* is the projection of *AB*. The dynamic texture is on the near plane and the texture coordinates of a point on *AB* is just the point's projection on *A'B'*.

For a convex mirror, the first step is the same as that of the planar mirror. However, the second and third step is different. Since the convex reflect more landscape, the *A'B'* has greater scope than that of a planar mirror. Figure 5 shows the function diagram of the method through which we simulate a convex mirror. In the second step, after the point *A* and *B* have been projected to *A'* and *B'* on the near plane, *A'* and *B'* will extend to *A''* and *B''* so as to involve more pixels in *A''B''* to approximate the visible scope of a real convex mirror, and now, *A''* and *B''* are the new texture coordinates of *A* and *B*. The stretch length-*A'A''* or *B'B''* is a projection of *AA''* or *BB''*. Note, the stretch length acquired by means of such projection is not strict. However, it becomes possible not only to reduce computing cost but also to provide sufficient accuracy in our experiment. All these treatments are performed in Vertex Shader. In the third step, before the image in the scope of *A''B''* is mapped on the mirror mesh, a normal map is utilized to modify the texture coordinates of each pixel (fragment) on the mirror so as to approximate the distortion effect on a real convex. All treatments in the third step are performed in Pixel Shader.

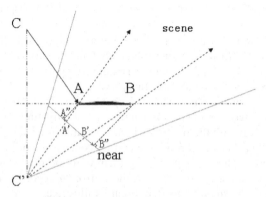

**Fig. 5.** The function diagram illustrates how to simulate the effect of convex rear-view mirrors on a training car in TODS

**Fig. 6.** The simulation of these two kinds of mirror in a virtual environment of TODS are shown in this figure

Figure 6 shows snapshots of two mirrors generated by TODS when the application is running.

## 6 Scene Authoring

Driving simulation requires scene databases of large geographic regions with properly constructed roads, highway, terrain, traffic aids, and appropriate culture features. Aside from those, as a training oriented driving simulator, TODS also focuses on the virtual practice scenes which aim at specialized driving exam items such as "Discus Road", "One Side Bridge", "Quarter Turn" and so on. As can be seen in figure 7, each leaf node of this dendrogram is a single scene of TODS. On the side of "Exam Practice", the appearance and size of every scene model is designed and constructed according to the "Driving Test Specification" of China. Figure 8 shows several scenes of Exam Practice in TODS.

On the other hand, the scenes of "Road Practice", including "City Road", "Mountain Road" and "Highway" are much larger than the scenes of "Exam Practice". At the same

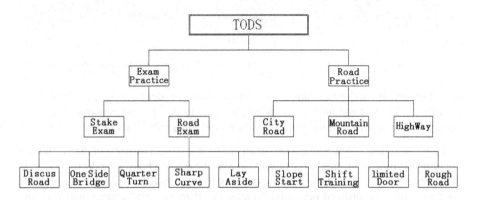

**Fig. 7.** Dendrogram of scenes in TODS

**Fig. 8.** Several scenes for Exam Practice in TODS, from left to right they are "Lay Aside", "Limited Door", and "One Side Bridge". They are designed and constructed according to the "Driving Test Specification" of China.

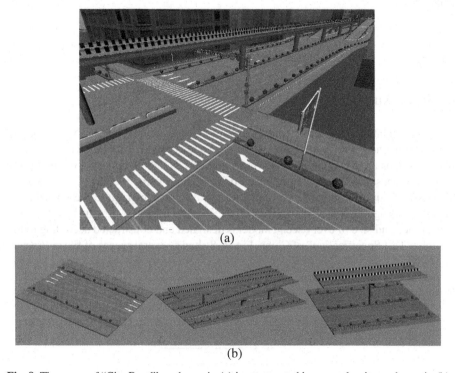

**Fig. 9.** The scene of "City Road" as shown in (a) is constructed by several units as shown in (b)

time, there exists no "specification" to restrict how to model these scenes. Therefore, we utilize a kind of modular construction method to design and construct the large scene with standardized units and dimensions. And this method has two purposes:

(1) By dividing a big scene into small units, we can give each of these units a bounding volume, and then we can only render the units whose bounding volume is within the view frustum. This increases the rendering efficiency. (2) If a big scene is designed with standardized units and dimensions, then we can "arrange and fix" this scene more easily. This increases the modeling flexibility.

Figure 9 demonstrates several units and a typical scene of "City Road".

# 7  Conclusions

A driving simulator named TODS based on state-of-the-art Computer Graphics and VR system technology has been developed.

TODS is designed under the human-in-the-loop real-time simulation system mode. Comparing to common driving simulators, it provides 120°horizontal FOV and realistic visual feedback to give the driver a realistic feeling of immersion similar to the feeling in a real moving vehicle. TODS utilizes state-of-the-art real-time rendering techniques in Vertex Shader and Pixel Shader to make it more flexible to implement more real-time rendering algorithms in GPU so as to enhance the system function. TODS's scene model is designed and constructed according to the "Driving Test Specification" of China to meet the demands of rigorous driving training. And a kind of modular construction method is used in the work of scene authoring in TODS.

There are still many visual and physical factors which have important influence on driving, e.g. weather, high light reflex, water on the front window, strong wind, should be simulated. Simulation of these kinds of phenomenon effecting on driving is the future research work of TODS.

TODS will be used for rigorous driving training and for Computer Graphics study. More research and study work on latest CG science and technology based on TODS are underway.

# References

1. Fernando, R., Kilgard, M.J.: The Cg Tutorial. The Definitive Guide to Programmable Real-Time Graphics. Addison Wesley, Reading (2003)
2. Wierwille, W.W.: Driving Simulator Design for Realistic Handling. In: Sachs, H.K., Swets, Zeitlinger. (eds.) Proceedings of the Third International Conference on Vehicle Systems Dynamics, B.V., Amsterdam (1975)
3. VPI-SU: (Accessed 2007.04), web site http://hci.ise.vt.edu/ vasl
4. Cremer, J., Kearney, J., Papelis, Y.: Driving Simulation: Challenges for VR Technology. IEEE Computer Graphics and Applications, 16–20 (September 1996)
5. Center for Computer Aided Design: (Accessed 2007), web site http://www.ccad.uiowa.edu/
6. Allen, R.W., Rosenthal, T.J., et al.: A Vehicle Dynamics Model for Low Cost. In: PC Based Driving Simulations Conference Proceedings DSC'97, pp. 153–164 (September 1997)
7. Systems Technology Incorporated: (Accessed 2007), web site
   http://www.systemstech.com/
8. Fernando, R., Kilgard, M.J.: The Cg Tutorial. The Definitive Guide to Programmable Real-Time Graphics. ch. 7: Environment Mapping. Addison Wesley, Reading (2003)
9. Ramamoorthi, R., Hanrahan, P.: An Efficient Representation for Irradiance Environment maps. In: Proceeding of SIGGRAPH 2001 (2001)
10. Bjorke, K.: Image-Based Lighting. In: GPU Gems: Programming Techniques, Tips, and Tricks for Real-Time Graphics, ch. 19. Addison Wesley Press, Reading (2004)

# Ghost Hunter:
# A Handheld Augmented Reality Game System with Dynamic Environment

Kyusung Cho, Wonhyoung Kang, Jaemin Soh, Juho Lee, and Hyun S. Yang

[1] Department of Computer Science, Korea Advanced Institute of Science and Technology,
373-1 Guseong-dong, Yuseong-gu, Daejeon 305-701, Republic of Korea
{qtboy,whkang,jmsoh,jhlee,hsyang}@paradise.kaist.ac.kr

**Abstract.** The progress of handheld devices has encouraged many researchers to make efforts to use handheld devices as an augmented reality platform. However, one of the important problems is a lack of immersion and reality due to small display. To overcome this problem, we introduce dynamic environment which consists of some movable structures and their controller that enable changes of virtual world to affect the real world. It has an effect on expanding the user's view limited by the small display of the handheld device. We have also developed the game content, 'Ghost Hunter', which is suitable for this platform.

**Keywords:** handheld augmented reality, dynamic environment, entertainment system.

## 1 Introduction

The technologies related to handheld devices have been developed rapidly in recent years, such as mobile phones, PDAs, portable game consoles and so on. These progresses have encouraged many researchers to make efforts to use handheld devices as an augmented reality platform [1], [2], [3], [4], [5]. It is called handheld augmented reality. Most handheld devices have a display and a camera. Those are convenient for carrying, and don't bother people like HMD so they are suitable for augmented reality. However, one of the important problems with it is a lack of immersion and reality compared with other augmented reality system due to small display of handheld devices.

To overcome this problem, we introduce dynamic environment which consists of some movable structures, and their controller that enable changes of virtual world to affect the real world. For example, the warning light could be turned on or the miniaturized building with a motor could move for representing the movements of the virtual world. It would expand the user's view limited by small display of devices into the real world beyond small display. We have also developed the game content, 'Ghost Hunter', which is suitable for a handheld augmented reality game system with dynamic environment.

L. Ma, R. Nakatsu, and M. Rauterberg (Eds.): ICEC 2007, LNCS 4740, pp.10–15, 2007.

## 2   A Handheld Augmented Reality Game System with Dynamic Environment

### 2.1   Dynamic Environment

As stated above, dynamic environment is the operating structures which allow the virtual world to have an effect on the real world. A user can easily see the outside of the display because most handheld devices just have small displays. For a user who plays a normal computer game, seeing outside of the display will break the immersed mood because the outside contains nothing related to the game. However, if there are some events related to the game in the outside of the display, the real world can become a part of the game (Fig 1).

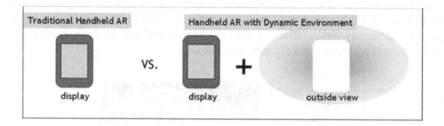

**Fig. 1.** Introduction of dynamic environment

Dynamic environment leads to a new experience beyond the limitation of small display of handheld devices. Such a new interaction immerse people in the game and increase the reality of the game.

### 2.2   Interactions in Dynamic Environment

In this research, we called the real world of traditional augmented systems as 'Static Environment'. Interaction between real world and virtual world in static environment just occurred by events in real world such as moving control markers. In this type of interaction, events in the real world affect some movement of virtual world, but the reverse process is impossible. That is a one-way interaction.

Compared with it, dynamic environment supports the interaction in static environment and above that, it is possible that events in virtual world can affect some movements of the real world. That is a two-way interaction. Dynamic environment enables a player to understand the state of virtual world more directly because it is able to represent virtual information by some movements in the real world such as turning on the warning light or operating the miniaturized building according to the movements of the virtual world.

# 3  Ghost Hunter

## 3.1  Scenario

One of the main characteristics of augmented reality is that while something is invisible through the naked eye, it is visible through a display device for augmented reality. So a handheld device plays a role such as 'Magic Lens', and that point became a motive of 'Ghost Hunter', the handheld augmented reality game that a player eliminates invisible ghosts which can be seen through AR Gun (Fig. 2. (left)).

We designed a miniaturized town like the Fig. 2 (right). Ghosts come out through tombs of the town. A game player can know that ghosts might exist in the town as seeing the opened tomb, but can't see ghosts through the naked eye. The player can take aim at and eliminate the detected ghost by AR Gun. If there exists a ghost which have intention of attack the player, the warning light which is closest to the ghost would be turned on, so the player becomes aware of the existence of the dangerous ghost. In Ghost Hunter, the tombs with the moving lid and the warning lights are dynamic environments which reflect changes in virtual world. Fig. 3 shows a user enjoying the ghost hunter game and the screen of AR Gun.

**Fig. 2.** (left) AR Gun and (right) Miniaturized Town

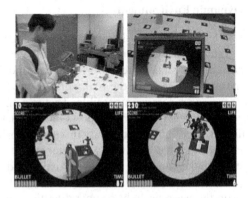

**Fig. 3.** Ghost Hunter

## 3.2   System Configuration

The fig. 4 represents the system configuration of Ghost Hunter. There are several miniaturized buildings, 3 tombs, and 8 warning lights on the game board (160cm x 120cm) with markers. The player enjoying Ghost Hunter wears the wearable computer connected to the AR Gun. The dynamic environment controller attached to the game board communicates with the wearable computer by blue-tooth wireless networking and controls dynamic environments such as the tombs and the warning lights.

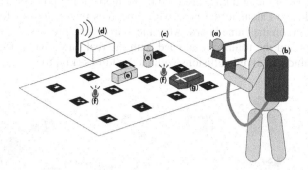

**Fig. 4.** System Configuration, (a)AR Gun, (b)Wearable Computer, (c)Game Board, (d)D.E. Controller, (e)Miniaturized Buildings, (f) Warning Lights, (g) Tomb

### 3.2.1   AR Gun
This research originally aimed at the development of an augmented reality game system suitable for handheld devices. It is difficult, however, to use pure handheld devices such as mobile phones and PDAs due to the performance limit. Therefore, we use the platform which consists of the AR Gun and the wearable computer like the fig. 5 instead of the mobile phone with a camera. Our platform has something in common with the latest mobile camera phone: a small display device, a camera, some buttons, the blue-tooth communication system, and the portability.

**Fig. 5.** (left)AR Gun and (right)Wearable Computer

### 3.2.2  Game Board and Map Editing Process

The game board is a background of the game like worlds of other computer games. The miniaturized buildings and tombs lay on the game board, and Ghosts move avoiding them. The markers are arranged at intervals of 20cm on the game board to calculate the pose with 6 degrees of freedom (3 for translation and 3 for rotation) of AR Gun.

The player can customize the positions of the buildings and the tombs through the map editing process that helps to avoid the monotonousness coming from the fixed arrangement of the miniaturized buildings and tombs. The pads with the same shapes of the bottom shapes of the buildings are used in the map editing process. The pads have their own marker to calculate the pose with 3 degrees of freedom (2 for translation and 1 for rotation) on the game board. After the map editing process, 3D CAD models of the buildings and the tombs are aligned with the real ones, and   ghosts can hide themselves behind and avoid collisions with the buildings (Fig. 6).

**Fig. 6.** Map Editing Process

### 3.2.3  Dynamic Environment Component and Controller

Dynamic environment components and their controller receive the events which are occurred by the changes in the virtual world, and represent it in the real world. Dynamic environment components may consist of various output devices such as motors, lamps, speakers, robots, and so forth. In Ghost Hunter, two types of dynamic environment component are used: RC-servo motors and LEDs. RC-servo motors are used in the tombs, and LEDs are used in the warning lights. The controller which controls dynamic environment components consists of a micro-controller and a blue-tooth module (Fig. 7).

**Fig. 7.** (left)Tomb, (center)Warning lights, (right)Controller

# 4 Conclusion

A handheld augmented reality system has less immersion and reality compared to other augmented reality systems due to its small display. To overcome this problem, we introduced dynamic environment, which has effects on real world from the changes in the virtual world. We expect a player to interact with the changing real world over the boundary of the small display of handheld device and feel more feel more immersion and reality.

Through the research, we have developed 'Ghost Hunter', the game content suitable for a handheld augmented reality game system with dynamic environment such as the tombs with the moving lid and the warning lights. In Ghost Hunter, the positions of the miniaturized buildings are customized through map editing process to reduce monotonousness, and game characters are able to interact with the miniaturized buildings aligned with 3D CAD models.

As a result of a user study, we found out that the introduction of dynamic environment in a handheld augmented reality helped players feel more reality and enjoyment.

In the future, the system will be used actively in theme parks or amusement halls. The players will hold their own mobile phones or special handheld devices and enjoy our system. We think that it has strong potential to contribute for amusement of modern people who want more realistic and tangible games.

**Acknowledgments.** This research was supported by the Ubiquitous Autonomic Computing and Network Project of the 21st Century Frontier R&D Program, which is sponsored by the Ministry of Information and Communication, and the Advanced Information Technology Research Center, which is sponsored by the Ministry of the Ministry of Science and Technology(MOST) Korea Science and Engineering Foundation(KOSEF).

# References

1. Azuma, R., Baillot, Y., Behringer, R., Feiner, S., Julier, S., MacIntyre, B.: Recent Advanced in Augmented Reality. Computer Graphics and Applications 21, 34–47 (2001)
2. Wagner, D., Pintaric, T., Ledermann, F., Schmalstieg, D.: Towards Massively Multi-User Augmented Reality on Handheld Devices. In: Proceedings of the Third International Conference on Pervasive Computing, Munich, pp. 209–219 (2005)
3. Henrysson, A., Billinghurst, M., Ollila, M.: Face to Face Collaborative AR on Mobile Phones. In: ISMAR2005. Proceedings of the International Symposium on Mixed and Augmented Reality, Vienna, pp. 80–90 (2005)
4. Wagner, D., Schmalstieg, D.: First Steps Towards Handheld Augmented Reality. In: Fensel, D., Sycara, K.P., Mylopoulos, J. (eds.) ISWC 2003. LNCS, vol. 2870, pp. 127–135. Springer, Heidelberg (2003)
5. Moehring, M., Lessig, C., Bimber, O.: Video See-Through AR on Consumer Cell Phones. In: ISMAR2004. International Symposium on Augmented and Mixed Reality, pp. 252–253 (2004)
6. Kang, W.: Handheld Augmented Reality Game System Using Dynamic Environment. Master thesis, KAIST (2007)

# Tea Table Mediator: A Multimodal Ambient Display on the Table Exploiting Five Senses Convergence

Hyun Sang Cho[1], Kyoung Shin Park[2], and Minsoo Hahn[1]

[1] Digital Media Laboratory, Information and Communications University,
51-10 Dogok-dong, Gangnam-gu, Seoul 135-854, S. Korea
haemosu@icu.ac.kr
[2] Multimedia Engineering, Dankook University,
San 29 Anseo-dong, Cheonan-si, Chungnam, 330-714, Korea

**Abstract.** In the past, many tabletop systems have used the traditional table augmented with digital technologies to enhance collaborative works such as face-to-face or remote meeting and working. In this paper, we describe the Tea Table Mediator, a multimodal ambient tabletop display designed for five senses convergence experience combined with tea drinking. This ambient display enhances a traditional tea table with multimodal interfaces forintimate small group interaction. This paper describes the design considerations, the details on system implementation, and the discussion of a preliminary user evaluation.

**Keywords:** Tabletop Display, Sense Convergence, Small Group Interaction.

## 1 Introduction

People traditionally have used a table for formal face-to-face meetings or private social interactions (such as family gathering, tea party and games). Recently the tabletop systems became a emerging research field in collaborative technology with pervasive intelligent objects and tangible interface [2][5][7][8][11]. Some of them are specifically designed for supporting intimate or entertaining activities, such as digital photo album [6][10], game [5] and private discourses or tea party [9][11]. However, all these systems force users to share information on the table display with exposed technology and hence it is difficult to keep a privacy and interest of intimate personal communication.

In this paper, we present Tea Table Mediator, a new ambient display system that fosters intimate group communication at the tea table. It provides a private display on the surface of a tea and gives a five senses convergence experience to promote small group intimate interaction during a tea party. The tea party is a moment when people can have casual social interactions and one of group entertainments. Gaver suggested several design assumptions for ludic engagement suggested by the drift table design [11]: promoting curiosity, exploration and reflection, de-emphasizing the pursuit of external goals, and maintaining the openness and ambiguity. In the Tea Table

L. Ma, R. Nakatsu, and M. Rauterberg (Eds.): ICEC 2007, LNCS 4740, pp. 16–21, 2007.
© IFIP International Federation for Information Processing 2007

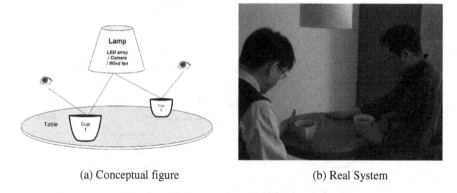

(a) Conceptual figure                                    (b) Real System

**Fig. 1.** The current prototype of Tea Table Mediator

Mediator system, we provide an abstract form of images and sounds. This system allows users keep their intimacy without any disgust from exposure of technology. The system works with any cup, i.e., no special electric hardware components required on the cup. As shown in Fig. 1, the tea itself acts as a private display for images from a lamp above the table, which is shared within a group around a table.

By drinking tea people can relax and feel they are sharing time with others [3] and there have been several tabletop systems designed for tea [5][11]. However, they were limited to a simple tangible cup interface with additional electric components on the cup or makers. In these systems, more than two senses (such as, visual-auditory, visual-touch or visual-auditory-touch) are combined to make more efficient user experience [4][8] with traditional cup and table. Recently there is a study on emphasizing holistic sense convergence to promote effective user communication [1]. Nonetheless, it is hardly found the systems that support smell and taste senses. Tea itself gives the sense of taste and smells which is difficult to represent with current technologies. Fig. 2 shows the relationship of five senses user interaction provided by the Tea Table Mediator system. In addition, we intended to expand individual sense experience to group experience by combining the dynamic images generated by the system and the static color on the surface of tea.

## 2   Design and Implementation

Single Display Groupware (SDG) has a great advantage – that is, it makes group members easily concentrate on group topics displayed on the shared display. In the Tea Table Mediator system, we wanted to provide the shared group display while maintaining the group's privacy even where they are in public place as like café or bar. The Tea Table Mediator system uses the surface of tea as a private group display. The concept of the display is based on the law of reflection; the angle of incidence equals the angle of reflection. The LED display patterns are shown on the cups of tea. The users (at the round table) can see the same display pattern at the same time. Theoretically, it works with the infinite numbers of cup on the table. We noticed that the

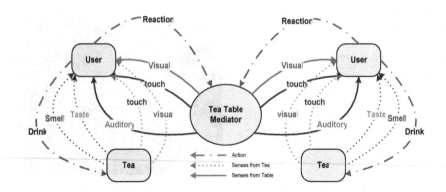

**Fig. 2.** The relation of five senses user interaction

tea also could satisfy some senses such as taste, smell and touch with temperature, which are difficult to serve conventional methods. The fusion of senses keeps users' interest.

For the intimate small group interaction such as friends and family, the privacy is a sensitive issue. Currently many tabletop systems display the information on the table surface. Such a public display disturbs people to keep concentration on their interaction topic and furthermore make people uncomfortable to use the system. It is a severe problem to play game or to enjoy entertaining rest with intimate members. While some applications served personalized display by mobile devices or directional view control film with multiple projectors [4][7]. The tea surface provides such private display and keeps the users' direction of sight on a virtual image in the cup to maintain users' concentration on their common topic. The holistic senses experience can enhance the emotional coziness.

Fig. 3 (a) shows the overall architecture of the Tea Table Mediator system. The system consists of a tea table with a lamp, and all the electric components are equipped in the lamp. In this system, any cup (preferably a large cup) can be used on the table and tea gives the private display surface for each user. Users can enjoy taste, smell and warm feeling while drinking tea. The system recognizes the kinds of tea that the user drinks (by detecting its color). It then displays additional visual, auditory and tactile patterns on the tea surface by the dynamic LED patterns and the wind generated by a fan embedded in the lamp. The LED patterns are reflected on the surface of tea in the cup. The lamp is composed of three main modules: the context recognition module, the interaction control module, and the display module. The main recognition module device is a camera module that detects the color of tea and the users' gesture. The camera continuously keeps watch over the cross-image marker area on the table. When a user places his/her cup on the marker, the changes of marker image is sent to a main PC. Then the image processing is performed by using the Video for Windows (VFW) library. It takes the 10×10 pixels marker-centered image as HSI data which is more robust for light intensity and the kinds of tea is classified by the data.

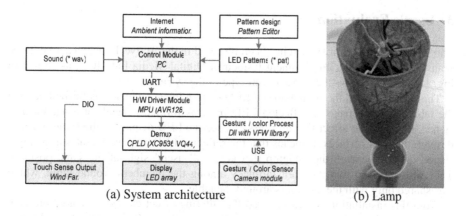

(a) System architecture                    (b) Lamp

**Fig. 3.** The Architecture of the Tea Table Mediator

The interaction session started when the color of idle marker is changed. Once the interaction session started, the camera also detects the users' gesture. When the control module receives the change of the marker color, it combines the user's context (such as, the kinds of tea and the user's gestures) with the environmental context (such as, ambient temperature, outside weather condition, and current time and season) gotten from the internet to determine the interaction scenario. The scenario includes predefined LED patterns (written by a LED pattern editor), sound effects, and winds.

The display module consists of a μ-controller hardware driver, a LED display array and a wind generation fan. Each LED on the array has three terminals for RGB colors. Fig. 3 (b) shows the structure of actual display module. The display module receives the interaction scenario from the control module through the RS-232C communication channel to the AVR128 micro controller. It sends the multiplexed LED pattern data to a demultiplex and latch module which consists of three XC9636 Xilinx Complex Programmable Logic Devices (CPLDs). Each CPLD was programmed by Verilog HDL as three-to-twenty four demultiplexer and latch. Users can see the reflected pattern of the LED array on the surface of tea. In addition, the micro controller directly operates a fan to generate ambient winds. The wind makes wave on the surface of tea to sway the reflected image on the surface of tea.

The first experience design was based on the tea colors. It consisted of simple scenarios, which gave different experiences by variation of host's sort (color) of tea. For example, when user put the green tea on the table, the green leave and moving caterpillar is reflected on the surface of tea. The LED patterns consisted of more than 15 images to show moving picture. Then the next experience included gesture detection. User could affect the image on LED array by their gesture to conduct simple game or interaction. They could push-pull their different colored area on the LED array. It could help to maintain and mediate their common attention.

## 3  User's Evaluation

The Tea Table Mediator system has been installed in the ActiveHome, an actual home scale ubiquitous living environment testbed in Digital Media Lab, ICU, as shown in Fig. 1. Fig. 3 (b) shows the current prototype of the system.

The users reported the immersion of LED pattern image, which was formed beyond the tabletop. The image of reflected LED patterns formed beneath of a tea surface. Hence, it shows the effect that all users can see the LED display at the same position through their tea surfaces. It means that the reflected LED display operates as a single shared display beneath the tabletop that keeps all users' sight at the same position. They also reported that they felt intimacy among the members around table, which was shared only with the members around the table.

From this installation, we discovered the filtering effect caused by tea color. That is, the blue color LED patterns was washed out on the surface of blue tea. Through this filtering effect, we can make different images on the display surface for users who had different tea colors – especially, it works well with pure red, green, or blue beverage. We believe that it shows another interaction possibility to multiple users with the same LED pattern source.

The patterns were designed to present the abstractive expression (i.e., not clear shapes) to promote user's imagination and curiosity. This strategy was somewhat successful to attract some user's attention. The results showed careful pattern design is still important to attract users' interest consistently if the patterns are not definite but abstractive and ambiguous.

## 4  Conclusion and Future Work

In this paper, we presented the Tea Table Mediator, a multimodal ambient tabletop display system that provides private small group display and five senses convergence experience. The system combined a traditional tea and a digital tea table. While most previous works focused on the development of functionally augmented objects in the ubiquitous environment, our approach simply added digital expression with additional visual, auditory, and tactile feedback onto tea that provides smell and taste. The passive sense information (such as smell and taste) from tea was combined with the dynamic and active sense information from the tea table.

This ambient display is designed for enhancing a traditional tea table with multimodal interfaces for intimate small group interaction. The system detects the user context (such as, the color of tea that the user drinks) and then creates the dynamic LED patterns which is reflected onto the surface of tea. It also provides ambient sound and wind effects to enrich user's sensation. In this system, we suggested several sense fusion scenarios affected by user's interaction. For example, when a user drinks a green tea, he/she can see the green leaf and pine tree caterpillar LED patterns on the surface of tea combined with the bird chirp sounds and wind (the degree of wind blowing is affected by outside weather condition).

The results of user test showed the effectiveness of the Tea Table Mediator system. The users showed the interest to their experience with the system providing five senses expression. We found that the system provided a shared display to all users at the tea table. That is, all users could see the LED display images at virtually the same position beneath the table. We also found the LED pattern filtering effect caused by the tea color that can be used for the personalized information display. The low resolution of the LED array will be enhanced with high resolution and high intensity LCD.

We could confirmed the effectiveness of reflect type private display and holistic senses experience to attract and to keep small group users' interest from user evaluation and encouraged to apply this system to other apply this system to other tasks include not only intimate but also formal collaborative works. We are applying the personal reflective display to a tabletop type Computer Supported Collaborative Work (CSCW) based digital storytelling system and scenario that uses the social intelligence from the results of web information retrieval for educational field trip of students. We expect to evaluate the system performance for the suggested methods by traditional evaluation method of education. The system can be used for virtual tour conduction for tour club in public café.

## Acknowledgement

This research was supported by the MIC (Ministry of Information and Communication), Korea, under the Digital Media Lab. support program supervised by the IITA (Institute of Information Technology Assessment).

## References

1. Schmitt, B.H., Simonson, A.: Marketing Aesthetics: The Strategic Management of Branding, Identity and Image. Simon & Schuster Inc., New York (1997)
2. Shen, C.: Multi-User Interface and Interactions on Direct-Touch Horizontal Surface: Collaborative Tabletop Research at MERL. In: TABLETOP'06 (2006)
3. Chung, H., Lee, C.-H.J., Selker, T.: Lover's Cups: Drinking Interfaces as New Communication Channels. In: CHI 2006 (April 2006)
4. Leikas, J., Strömberg, H., Ikonen, V., Suomela, R., Heinilä, J.: Multi-User Mobile Applications and a Public Display: Novel Ways for Social Interaction. In: PerCom 2006. 4th Pervasive Computing and Communications (2006)
5. Yoon, J., Oishi, J., Nawyn, J., Kobayashi, K., Gupta, N.: FishPong: Encouraging Human-to-Human Interaction in Informal Social Environments. In: CSCW'04 (November 2004)
6. Morris, M.R., Paepcke, A., Winograd, T., Stamberger, J.: TeamTag: Exploring Centralized versus Replicated Controls for Co-located Tabletop Groupware. In: CHI 2006 (April 2006)
7. Matsushita, M., Iida, M., Ohguro, T.: Lumisight Table: A Face-to-face Collaboration Support System That Optimizes Direction of Projected Information to Each Stakeholder. In: CSCW'04 (November 2004)
8. Ståhl, O., et al.: Information Exploration Using The Pond. In: CVE '02 (September 2002)
9. Stewart, J., Bederson, B., Druin: A Single display groupware: A model for co-present collaboration. In: CHI'99 (1999)
10. Apted, T., Kay, J., Quigley, A.: Tabletop Sharing of Digital Photographs for the Elderly. In: CHI 2006 (April 2006)
11. Gaver, W.W., et al.: The Drift Table: Designing for Ludic Engagement. In: CHI 2004 (April 2004)

# Measuring Game-Play Performance and Perceived Immersion in a Domed Planetarium Projection Environment

Timon Burney and Phillip Lock

Advanced Computing Research Centre, University of South Australia,
Mawson Lakes, South Australia 5095
Phillip Lock.phillip.lock@unisa.edu.au

**Abstract.** Game playing in immersive projection environments such as caves and domes is assumed to offer an enhanced experience but there is little quantitative research that measures this. This paper reports on a study of user performance statistics while playing a computer game projected onto a planetarium dome and compares these with similar measurements taken in a conventional projected flat screen environment. A survey of users' subjective impressions of immersion was also taken and used to compare these display modes. Analysis of users in each mode revealed differences in user experience and some aspects of performance. It was confirmed that dome projection enhanced the player's sense of immersion when compared with flat projection. Navigation speed was found to decline in the dome while other performance metrics showed no significant difference between the environments.

**Keywords:** Dome-projection, computer games, user interfaces, immersion, game-play performance.

## 1 Introduction

Planetariums have long been used to entertain, educate and excite their audiences. Digital projection systems have opened the full potential of a multi-media experience to planetarium audiences. The environment is dynamic and can now be interactive. Dome projection is perceived to offer significant advantages when used as a virtual reality display as its hemispherical nature engages the viewer's peripheral vision and more closely matches the natural world [1]. The migration of gaming into this environment is to be expected as players seek to enhance the game playing experience.

The cost of sophisticated dome projection equipment has been a barrier but a low cost dome projection system called "MirrorDome" [2] overcomes this to allow wider use of dome projection. MirrorDome uses a spherical mirror to reflect video from a single data projector onto a hemispherical surface. Content to be projected is first distorted in software so that the resulting projected image, after reflection from the

L. Ma, R. Nakatsu, and M. Rauterberg (Eds.): ICEC 2007, LNCS 4740, pp. 22–27, 2007.

mirror, appears undistorted on the dome surface.  The Cube[1] game engine was selected for this study, firstly, because it provides a fisheye viewing option which is required as the first distortion in MirrorDome. Secondly, the Cube source code is available. This allows us to interpose another layer of distortion before the image is displayed. The low cost of this system makes dome projection viable for gaming arcades, home theatres, as well providing a cheaper option for virtual reality labs and workplace visualisation suites. The attractions of dome projection in terms of its usability and the level of immersion and enjoyment are generally assumed, without being widely researched.  If possible, these should be measured to quantify the effectiveness of this mode of presentation for games.

Although these experiments were conducted using the first person shooter Cube game engine running on a Mirrordome projection system, we believe the results are applicable to any dome projection system running interactive content.

## 2  Background

### 2.1  Games in Cave/Dome Environments

Games are now joining simulations, visualizations and instructional presentations as content for immersive display environments. Immersive simulations/games such as low-end flight simulators, and sports games such as Golf[2], Grid-Iron Football[3] and Boxing games like 'Cyclone Uppercut' [3] fit somewhere in a continuum between serious training and pure entertainment. More commercial games such as Quake III (Cave Quake III) [4]and Unreal Tournament (CaveUT) [4] have also been produced in Cave and Dome display formats.  There have been quantitative studies into user performance in Cave and virtual environments in general [5], but studies specifically relating to the user experience of immersive gaming tends to be qualitative [6] whether in cave or dome environments [7]. Caves and domes have been used in museums to project instructional content but we speculate that the engagement with the user will less than is typically found in games where there is a competitive personal stake. As games are much more engaging it can be expected that user experience will be heightened when playing in the larger dome of a planetarium.

### 2.2  Usability

Studies of immersive environments have revealed psycho-physical impacts such as simulator sickness and balance problems related to wide fields of view, [8]. Immersive imaging affects on cognition have also been studied [9] revealing limits on cognitive benefits of environments. The advantage of spherical projection seems to be limited to providing an immersive and engaging user experience rather than optimally transferring information. It is reasonable to expect these physiological responses and

---

[1] http://www.cubeengine.com/cube.php4
[2] http://www.sports-coach.com
[3] http://www-vrl.umich.edu/project/football/index.html
[4] http://www.visbox.com/cq3a/

cognitive factors to result in differences in user performance when games are played in different visual environments.

## 2.3 Immersion

Immersion is a subjective sensation that is more difficult to define and therefore less amenable to quantitative measurement. Immersion is said to be "the degree of involvement in a game" [7]. Studies into the use of game engines for visualisation of virtual environments report positively on user engagement when using wider fields of view [10]. It is reasonable to expect a similar response when playing games.

# 3 Experimental

## 3.1 Experimental Method

Twenty participants were recruited to measure performance and perceived immersion when playing the game in the dome and then with a flat screen. Males and females from age 18-34 (average age 22), with a broad range of skill levels at playing first person shooter (FPS) console games, took part. Each participant undertook two trials, each of two rounds. They first navigated a 3D maze built in the Cube virtual space. In the second trial they played Cube as a FPS game in a controlled virtual space. The first round of each trial used dome projection; the second used flat screen projection. Quantitative data was gathered by automatic logging of times and events when the maze was traversed and the game was being played. This data was extended by qualitative responses collected from the participants in a post experimental survey. The participants were divided into two groups of ten to perform the trials in each environment. The first group began the trial in the conventional display environment while the other group used the dome projection first. This was done because it was expected that they would become better at performing the task at the second attempt no matter what the environment.

Four metrics werecaptured by instrumentation of the program and logging of user scores. These four are abstracted under the heading 'game-play performance'

The performance metrics were;

1. **Navigation** (n),  measured by the time taken to navigate the maze.
2. **Accuracy**  (a),  measured by the ratio of opponents hit (h) to the number of shots (s) fired by the player, expressed as a percentage.
3. **Dodging ability** (d), measured by the ratio of the number of hits (h) suffered by the player, divided by the shots (s) fired at the player by opponents, then subtracted    from    one.This    is    expressed    as    a    percentage.
   $$d = 100(1 - h/s)$$
4. **Number of opponents destroyed** (Frags) Opponents destroyed by the player.

## 3.2 Projection Environments

Two display environments were used in this study. The first used the MirrorDome projection system with an 8m diameter dome in a small planetarium. The second environment was in the same location but with a rectangular image projected onto the side of the dome instead of covering the entire surface. This method of rectangular projection was chosen because it made the image closer in size and orientation to that of dome projection. All other environment variables were kept constant (e.g. sound system, ambient lighting, seating position, and computer and projection hardware). This was done to limit the degrees of freedom in the experiment to one, the display mode.

The Cube game was instrumented to collect game-play statistics while the participants played, and data was also gathered from a questionnaire completed by the participants after the tests.

Each participant was told that their accuracy was being logged and was instructed to be as accurate as possible to discourage them from firing continuously or randomly when not under threat, as this would have distorted this measurement.

The dodging factor measures a player's ability to avoid being hit by opponents. This factor is less meaningful than the accuracy as the participant had no control over the accuracy of the opponents. It also depended on their movement through the task.

## 3.3 Measurement of Usability

**Navigation.** In the first trial users traversed a maze to test navigation speed. The maze was identical for all users and in both modes. Arrow images were placed on the walls to act as visual cues. The instrumented game engine logged the time taken to reach the end of the maze.

**The Death Match.** The remaining three metrics (Accuracy, Dodging and Frags) were measured in the second trial where the Cube game was played in a controlled virtual world containing wide corridors where the participant had to shoot, and avoid being shot by, opponents while moving to the end point.

A custom map was created within the game specifically for this trial, so that all users met the same opponents in about the same locations. The map consisted of three long, wide corridors with opponents spaced at even intervals on random sides of the corridor. The participant encountered the obstacles in sequence but, because of the width of the corridors, was still required to aim the gun at different areas of the map. This made the accuracy measurement more meaningful.

# 4 Results

## 4.1 Quantitative Measurements

The pairs of data sets for each of the measured quantities were analysed using the non-parametric Wilcoxon signed ranks test with 'Analyse-it' software. This was applied to identify any statistically significant differences in performance between modes in each of the four categories. The performance results of two participants were outside two standard deviations of the mean and were discarded as outliers. The results are shown in Table 1 below. Differences are calculated by subtracting the Flat screen measurement from the Dome measurement.

**Table 1.** Analysis of logged performance data

|  | Difference of means | W+ W- | 1 Tailed p | Better performance |
|---|---|---|---|---|
| **Navigation time** | 4.2sec | 102.5 33.5 | 0.034 | Flat $p<=0.05$ |
| **Accuracy** | 4.2% | 52 119 | 0.08 | Not sig $p>=0.05$ |
| **Dodging** | 3.27% | 69 102 | 0.25 | Not sig $p>=0.05$ |
| **Frags** | 0.167 | 41 37 | 0.45 | Not sig $p>=0.05$ |

The analysis reveals that navigation speed is significantly better in the flat screen mode. The other metrics showed no significant difference in performance between display modes.

### 4.2  Qualitative Survey Results

The participants were invited to provide a subjective evaluation of Navigation and Orientation, Sense of control and Sense of immersion in each environment. Each question was presented as a Likert scale. They also had the opportunity to make free text comments. A short summary of these

**Navigation and orientation.** Participants rated the ease of navigation and orientation to be higher in the flat screen environment. Some participants commented that they felt disoriented in the dome display.

**Sense of Control.** The overall feeling of navigation control confirmed that participants felt more in control on the flat display than on the dome display.

**Sense of Immersion.** The sense of immersion was reported to be higher in the dome display than in the flat display.

## 5  Discussion and Conclusion

This study confirms that dome environments do not hinder player performance in three of the four performance metrics. The exception of poorer navigation performance in the dome environment may be plausibly explained as the full surrounding visual space is more difficult to monitor during game play and navigation may suffer as a result. This conjecture is supported by some players who commented that a in a surround display, parts of the game action are necessarily out of view. It also suggests that games need to be designed specifically for immersive environments rather than simply modifying existing games that have been designed for a flat screen environment. Other comments concerned the placement of HUD information and the lower brightness and contrast levels in the Dome environment.

Participants reported the sense of immersion, to be much stronger in the dome than with the flat screen and that this contributed to the overall enjoyment of the experience. One participant commented that they felt closer to the dome display. The physical distance between displays was kept constant for all experiments but this comment was most likely a way of expressing the feeling of immersion experienced when viewing the dome display. The dome gives the illusion of drawing the user closer to the projection surface. This could be a result of either the wide field of view, the size of the display, the fact that the display surrounded the user or a combination of all these factors.

# References

1. Gaitatzes, A., Papaioannu, G., Christopoulos, D., Zyba, G.: Media Productions for a Dome Display System. In: Proceedings of the ACM symposium on Virtual reality software and technology, Limassol, Cyprus, pp. 261–264 (2006)
2. Bourke, P.: Spherical mirror: a new approach to hemispherical dome projection. In: Proceedings of the 3rd international conference on Computer graphics and interactive techniques in Australasia and South East Asia, pp. 281–284 (2005)
3. Sidharta, R., Cruz-Neira, C.: In: Proceedings of the 2005 ACM SIGCHI International Conference on Advances in computer entertainment technology, pp. 363–364 (2005)
4. Jacobson, J., Lewis, M.: Game engine virtual reality with CaveUT Virtual Worlds. Computer 38(4), 79–82 (2005)
5. Sutcliffe, A., Gault, B., Fernando, T., Tan, K.: Investigating Interaction in CAVE Virtual Environments. ACM Transactions on Computer-Human Interaction (TOCHI) 13(2), 235–267 (2006)
6. Sweetser, P., Wyeth, P.: Gameflow: A Model for Evaluating Player Enjoyment in Games (Article 3A). ACM Computers in Entertainment 3(3) (July 2005)
7. Brown, E., Cairns, P.: A grounded investigation of game immersion. In: CHI '04 extended abstracts on Human factors in computing systems, Vienna, Austria. ACM Press, New York (2004)
8. Lin, J.J.-W., Duh, H.B.L., Parker, D.E., Abirached, H., Furness, T.A.: Effects of field of view on presence, enjoyment, memory, and simulator sickness in a virtual environment. In: Virtual Reality, 2002. Proceedings. IEEE Computer Society Press, Los Alamitos (2002)
9. Fluke, C.J., Bourke, P.D., O'Donovan, D.: Future Directions in Astronomy Visualisation. Arxiv preprint astro-ph/0602448 (2006)
10. Fritsch, D., Kada, M.: Visualisation using game engines. Stuttgart, Geschwister-Scholl-Strasse (2002)

# Computer Game for Small Pets and Humans

Roger Thomas Kok Chuen Tan, Adrian David Cheok,
Roshan Lalintha Peiris, I.J.P. Wijesena,
Derek Bing Siang Tan, Karthik Raveendran,
Khanh Dung Thi Nguyen, Yin Ping Sen, and Elvin Zhiwen Yio

Mixed Reality Lab and Department of Biological Sciences,
National University of Singapore,
metazoa@mixedrealitylab.org
www.mixedrealitylab.org

**Abstract.** Interactive media not only should enhance human-to-human communication, but also human-to-animal communication. We promote a new type of media interaction allowing human users to interact and play with their small pets (like hamsters) remotely via Internet through a mixed-reality-based game system "Metazoa Ludens". To examine the systems effectiveness: Firstly, the positive effects to the hamsters are established using Body Condition Score study. Secondly, the method of Duncan is used to assess the strength of preference of the hamsters towards Metazoa Ludens. Lastly, the effectiveness of this remote interaction, with respect to the human users as an interactive gaming system with their pet hamsters, is examined based on Csikszentmihalyi's Flow theory [1]. Results of these studies have shown positive remote interaction between human user and their pet friends. This paper provides specific experimental results on the implemented research system, and a framework for human-to-animal interactive media.

**Keywords:** Human-animal interaction, mixed reality, multimodal interaction, computer gaming, communication.

## 1  Introduction

With the advancement of technology, longer working hours are expected in the professional world to match up with the higher level of efficiency [2]. Due to this change in the professional lifestyle [3] humans are out of the house for longer hours and pets are often neglected and taken for granted by their owners. With this negligence, pets will be deprived of love and care [4] as well as a good dose of exercise with suitable diet to ensure healthy living [5]. Thus there is a need to create an interface that is capable of allowing humans to shower their pets with attention locally or remotely; the element of exercise may be incorporated into the system to add yet another beneficial feature for small pets.

This new interface could give a different form of gameplay and connectivity between humans and small animals. In a mixed reality gameplay, different forms of interaction may be introduced where the small animals are allowed to "chase

L. Ma, R. Nakatsu, and M. Rauterberg (Eds.): ICEC 2007, LNCS 4740, pp. 28–38, 2007.

after" the human owners in a digital world (which is impossible in the physical world). Such gameplay may be extended to remote interaction over the Internet. Metazoa Ludens is therefore devised.

## 1.1 Objectives

Metazoa Ludens is a system that enables humans to play games with small animals in a mixed reality environment. This human-pet computer game system illustrates a way to reverse the trend of the increased lack of quality time between humans and pets. It creates a media interface capable of remote human-animal interaction and the way they may interact with the interface. The system will provide a way for human to interact remotely with their smaller pets and also provide health benefits to the pets.

In certain parts of the world, like Asia, where living spaces are smaller and larger animals like cats and dogs are not viable to be kept as pets, smaller animals like hamsters and fishes become a more popular choice. Therefore, smaller animals are the target pets for our research system Metazoa Ludens. For Metazoa Ludens, hamsters are specifically chosen for the following advantages:

- Domesticated hamsters' running spaces are normally within their cages. Therefore we would like to encourage a new media which will allow more variety of in-house-play for hamsters.
- Hamsters are a popular pet choice and the most popular of the smaller rodents [6]. They are economical and easy maintenance pets, kept by males and females as well as the rich and poor [7]. Therefore we can create a media which can be enjoyed by a wide range of society.
- Hamsters are naturally skillful intelligent runners, which is very suitable for fun gameplay with humans [8].
- Hamsters' natural habitat are burrows that have many tunnels and their natural behavior is to tunnel [6]. This feature is used to promote their attractive pleasure in the game play of our system.
- Hamsters have cheek pouches to store food. This is convenient for both humans and pets as they can to collect their reward from the attractor in our system [6].

It is noted that such an interface is meant to enhance human-animal interaction by allowing humans to continue interacting with their pet hamsters even in a remote situation, and is not meant to replace conventional human-animal interaction such as touch and hugging. A study showing that Metazoa Ludens system is beneficial to the hamsters based on Body Condition Scoring study (refer to section 4.1). In addition, a user survey is carried out to evaluate Metazoa Ludens system as a game by breaking down the system using features as described by Csikszentmihalyi's Flow theory [1]. The reason for using this theory for our experimental testing of our human-animal play system is substantiated by the academic GameFlow model [10] which states the appropriateness of using Flow theory to assess not just optimal performance condition but using it to assess the user's enjoyment of a game; the game in our case would be our system Metazoa Ludens. These studies were carried out based on these strong, dependent theoretical models as mentioned above to assess Metazoa Ludens in terms of the positive benefits to the hamsters and as an enjoyable interface to the human owners.

## 2   Related Works

Most interactions between pet owners and their pets typically involve simple games such as fetching objects or chasing squeaky toys. A more established tool-based interaction used for training dogs known as click training [11] uses a click sound as a signal before a treat is given to the pet. Augmenting these games with sophisticated technology (such as those seen in video game systems) could enrich the human-animal interaction experience. Poultry Internet [3] is a remote human-pet interaction system that allows owners to pet a chicken over the internet when they are away from home. Similarly, Petting Zoo [12] and Cat Toy [13] enable the pet owner to take care of their pet by monitoring it over the internet through a webcam. SNIF [15] is a system based on the concept of 'petworking' where owners can also learn about other animals (and their owners) that interact with their dog. Infiltrate [14] takes a different approach by displaying a virtual scene from the perspective of a fish in a fish tank. However, these systems only provide a one-way interaction with no means for the animals to directly interact with the human. Recently, Netband [16] is developing an internet based system for rearing a chick. Owners can tend to the pet by feeding them and cleaning them via tele robotic and sensor apparatus. This system purely functions as a remote means of rearing a chick and does not allow the owner to interact with the chick in an intimate manner. Thus, there is a need to create a system that is capable of enriching the interactivity between living animals and their owners by utilizing the power of advanced interactive media technologies. It is also important to note that owners spend many hours at work or on business trips, away from home and their pets. Rover@Home [11] is a system that uses common internet communication tools such as webcams, microphones and speakers to communicate with dogs over the internet. Therefore, there is a need to incorporate remote communication technology into a system to allow remote interactions between humans and their pets.

Mixed reality games allow remote/internet players to interact with each other in a more physical and ubiquitous manner. In Cricket-Controlled Pacman [18] , a human player can play the traditional computer game of Pacman with real live crickets in a variant of the standard mixed reality game. The crickets act as the ghosts and run in a real maze, while the human plays the part of the Pacman and controls his virtual character on a game screen. To make the game more enjoyable for humans, the crickets are constantly kept moving by vibrating the ground in the real maze with the help of motors. A negative motivation (fear from the vibration) is employed to ensure that the crickets appear to be chasing the human.

Metazoa Ludens extends previous human-animal interactive systems by allowing bidirectional interaction between humans and their pet hamsters via a

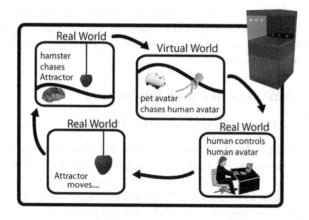

**Fig. 1.** System Overview

computer game. It should be noted that Metazoa Ludens is an interface meant for the benefit of small animals such as hamsters, as well as for the promotion of awareness of human-animal interaction. Positive motivation is employed so that hamsters play the game willingly and not out of fear or agitation. In addition, the game play ensures health exercise for the hamsters, which is beneficial for the well being of the pets.

## 3   Game Mechanics and Gameplay

Inside the structure a camera is placed at the top of the structure for tracking of the hamsters' movements on a mechanical driven arm that makes up the movable attractor. The surface which the pet hamsters scamper upon is a highly moldable latex sheet molded by sixteen actuators (electric motor driven) placed directly beneath them. Technical details regarding the subsystem are describe in previous works [19].

At the start of the game the pet owner moves a human avatar across the changing virtual terrain. This controls the mechanical attractor within the tank which then moves in correspondence to the human avatar. The latex surface changes in surface contour as molded by the actuators below, this in turn corresponds to the changing contours of the virtual terrain accordingly.

The hamsters chase after the mechanical attractor. The hamsters movements are tracked by the cameras at the top of the structure, mapping its positions and moving the pet avatar in the virtual world.

The basic game concept behind Metazoa Ludens game is a predator and prey chase game. However roles are reversed. The bigger human is now being chased by the physically small hamsters in the virtual world (pet avatar chases after human avatar). A general strategy of the pet owner is to try her best to evade the pet avatar (hamster). Getting caught will then deplete the human avatar's health points. As the game progresses the human avatar will have to evade the pet avatar within a certain time without depleting all her health. The game does not try to replace conventional human-pet interaction, but with the aid of a digital system it adds more variety to the way a pet owner may play with their small pets, especially remotely.

## 4 Evaluation, Results and Discussion

### 4.1 Study 1 - Health Benefits to the Hamsters

A trial test was carried out to assess the benefits of the system through regular exercise to the hamsters. All hamsters had their mean Body Condition Scoring (BCS) [9] taken at the first week of the experiment. For six weeks, each hamster is given one spoon of food daily [5]. The hamsters were allowed to play Metazoa Ludens for an hour each on every weekday for the period of six weeks. At the end of the sixth week their mean BCSs were taken again. The results are shown in Figure 2.

By using Wilcoxon signed-rank test, Metazoa Ludens was found to be able to change the BCS of the subject hamsters over the study period ($z = -3.8230$, $p = 0.0006$, Wilcoxon signed-rank test). Further statistical analysis of the mean BCS of the hamsters in the 6th week using Wilcoxon signed-rank test showed that the mean BCS of hamsters after 6 weeks of using Metazoa Ludens tend towards 3 ($z = -1.4154$, $p = 0.1586$, Wilcoxon signed-rank test), which is the optimal BCS score for hamsters. Hence it can be concluded that after 6 weeks of playing with Metazoa Ludens, the hamsters are getting healthier and their body condition tends to optimal. Further examinations are currently being carried out with a control group, to ensure that being in a large area was not the reason for the optimal BCS scores.

### 4.2 Study 2 - Hamsters' Positive Motivation to Play the Game

Besides studying the health benefits of hamsters, a separate study was carried out to measure the motivation of the hamsters to play Metazoa Ludens. In this study

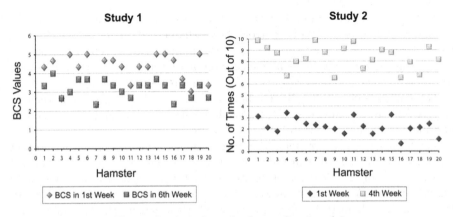

**Fig. 2.** Statistical results for studies 1 and 2

the method of Duncan [20] was adapted to assess the strength of preference of the hamsters towards Metazoa Ludens. The study was carried out for four weeks and the mean percentage for the number of times each hamster chose to play Metazoa Ludens in the 1st week was compared to that in the fourth week. It was shown that the mean number of times taken for the hamsters to play the game per day increased over the study period. Further statistical analysis showed that this increase was a 60% increment. As it is shown that the hamsters increasingly chooses to play Metazoa Ludens during the study period, we conclude that the hamsters have a positive desire to play Metazoa Ludens.

The results are given in Figure 2. By using the single-tailed Wilcoxon signed-rank test, it was shown that the mean number of times taken for the hamsters to play the game per day increased over the study period ($z = 3.9199$, $p$ equal to 1.0000, Wilcoxon signed-rank test). With the two-tailed Wilcoxon signed-rank test it was shown that this increase was by 6 times per day out of the 10 possible given chances ($z = 0.7467$, $p = 1.5468$, Wilcoxon signed-rank test), that is 60% increment. Hence based on study from Study 2 it may be concluded that with time, the number of times the hamsters chose to play the game of Metazoa Ludens increases even with the presence of a minor obstacle (as presented in the form of an additional tunnel). Based on the Method-of-Duncan, it could thus be shown that the hamsters are willing to play the game on its own free will.

### 4.3   Study 3 - Users' Enjoyment Based on Flow

For the users, a user survey was carried out to evaluate Metazoa Ludens system as a game. Game flow of the system was then broken down using features as described by Csikszentmihalyi's Flow theory [1] to evaluate the users' enjoyment of the game. Metazoa Ludens game flow is broken down as follows:

- **Concentration:** Concentration on the game is needed and players should be able to concentrate on the game.
- **Challenge:** The game should contain challenges that match the players' skill level.
- **Player Skills:** Player skill development and mastery should be supported in the game.
- **Control:** Player should be able to feel in control of their actions in the game.
- **Clear Goals:** Clear defined goals should be given to the players at appropriate times.
- **Feedback:** Appropriate feedback from the game at appropriate times is given.
- **Connection:** Players should feel deeply connected to the game and with little/no effort.
- **Social Interaction:** The game should support social interaction as well as create opportunities for it.

The original set of questions for the Flow model has been created for a generic task (like surfing the Internet) therefore some questions have been modified to

**Table 1.** User Evaluation Questions based on Flow model

| Element | Question |
|---|---|
| Concentration | 1) Did the game grab your attention and maintain your focus? |
|  | 2) Can you concentrate on the tasks at hand in the game? |
| Challenge | 3) Does the game skills needed match yours? |
|  | 4) Do you think the game provide different levels of challenge for different players? |
|  | 5) As the game progresses does it become more challenging? |
| Player Skills | 6) Are you able to play the game without spending too much time at the instructions? |
|  | 7) Is learning how to play the game fun? |
| Control | 8) Do you feel in control of your character in the game? |
|  | 9) Do you feel in control of the game shell (starting, stopping, saving etc.)? |
| Clear Goals | 10) Is the objective of the game clear and presented early? |
|  | 11) Are intermediate game goals clear and presented at appropriate times? |
| Feedback | 12) Do you have a clear picture of your progress to the game goals at any point of time? |
|  | 13) Does the game give you immediate feedback of your actions? |
|  | 14) Do you always know your health points and time remaining? |
| Connection | 15) During gameplay are you less aware of what is happening physically around you? |
|  | 16) Are you aware of the passing time during gameplay? |
|  | 17) Do you feel emotionally involved in the game? |
| Social Interaction | 18) Do you feel the competition against the pets and other players (if any)? |
|  | 19) Does the game support social communities (for both human players and pets) inside and outside the game? |
| Human-animal interaction | 20) Are you aware that you are playing with a hamster during gameplay? |
|  | 21) Do you feel more connected to the pets after gameplay? |

adapt to the Metazoa Ludens environment. Questions related to human-animal interaction are added as well. Table 1 illustrates the questions and the corresponding criterion and elements in the Flow model.

*Subjects:* 20 subjects from a local group of hamster lovers community were randomly selected with an average age of 25.4 years old (55% male and 45% female). Data collected from the survey after game play are expressed as mean and standard deviation unless otherwise specified. Results of the survey are given in Table 2. Of all elements explored with this survey, most of them performed positively in the survey as more than 50% selected the favorable choice to the questions posed. Nevertheless it is noted that the element Social Interaction did not score as well as the rest.

For Social Interaction, the majority agreed that they do feel the presence of social interaction at work, considering that the players are new to the game and having to cope with getting use to the controls and the game play in real-time, should be considered a positive result. A possible way to improve Social Interaction further would be to include video and voice feature which will then allow players to "see" and "speak" to the hamsters over the Internet as the hamsters may be able to recognize their owners' voice.

**Table 2.** Results of Survey

| Qn | Options | | | | |
|---|---|---|---|---|---|
| | Yes, very | Yes | Fairly | Not really | No |
| 1 | 75.00% | 25.00% | 0.00% | 0.00% | 0.00% |
| 2 | 70.00% | 10.00% | 20.00% | 0.00% | 0.00% |
| 3 | 65.00% | 20.00% | 15.00% | 0.00% | 0.00% |
| 4 | 70.00% | 30.00% | 0.00% | 0.00% | 0.00% |
| 5 | 60.00% | 20.00% | 20.00% | 0.00% | 0.00% |
| 6 | 95.00% | 5.00% | 0.00% | 0.00% | 0.00% |
| 7 | 85.00% | 15.00% | 0.00% | 0.00% | 0.00% |
| 8 | 95.00% | 5.00% | 0.00% | 0.00% | 0.00% |
| 9 | 65.00% | 20.00% | 10.00% | 5.00% | 0.00% |
| 10 | 95.00% | 5.00% | 0.00% | 0.00% | 0.00% |
| 11 | 70.00% | 5.00% | 20.00% | 5.00% | 0.00% |
| 12 | 65.00% | 15.00% | 20.00% | 0.00% | 0.00% |
| 13 | 65.00% | 15.00% | 15.00% | 5.00% | 0.00% |
| 14 | 85.00% | 5.00% | 10.00% | 0.00% | 0.00% |
| 15 | 95.00% | 5.00% | 0.00% | 0.00% | 0.00% |
| 16 | 60.00% | 40.00% | 0.00% | 0.00% | 0.00% |
| 17 | 40.00% | 50.00% | 10.00% | 0.00% | 0.00% |
| 18 | 15.00% | 70.00% | 10.00% | 5.00% | 0.00% |
| 19 | 15.00% | 55.00% | 20.00% | 10.00% | 0.00% |
| 20 | 60.00% | 10.00% | 15.00% | 15.00% | 0.00% |
| 21 | 65.00% | 30.00% | 5.00% | 0.00% | 0.00% |

## 5   Framework for Human-Animal Interaction System

A framework for describing human-animal interaction system and the interactions involved may be developed from the built of Metazoa Ludens. This can provide guidelines for future human-animal interaction systems to be based on, as well as provide possible insights for new human-animal interaction systems. Five design dimensions for human-animal interaction system are presented. Existing human-animal interaction systems are ranked upon these five dimensions. The dimensions are:

- **Habitat design:** The area of interaction should be safe, comfortable and suitable for the animal. Choices available for this dimension are - Native, where the environment used is where the animal normally resides; Recreated, where the environment is not where the animal normally can be found but yet not unsuitable for the animal to stay in; Unsuitable, where the environment is not suitable for the animal.
- **Ease of use:** The way to interact with the system should come naturally to the animal since it is not an easy task to teach the animal to for example use a keyboard or mouse as input. The natural behavior of animals thus needs to be studied and modeled. Choices available for this dimension are - Instinctive, where the actions required from the animal is instinctive to what the animal normally do; Learnt, where the animal requires certain learning process to perform the tasks required; Unsuitable, where the actions required are unsuitable to be performed by the animal.
- **Interactivity:** System should allow interaction between pet and owner via the human-animal interactive system. Choices available for this dimension are - None, where no interactivity is given between human and the animal; One-way where interaction is only one-way; Two-way where interaction is two-ways.
- **Pet's choice:** While the system allows users to play with their pets, such human-animal interactive system should consider giving the animals a choice

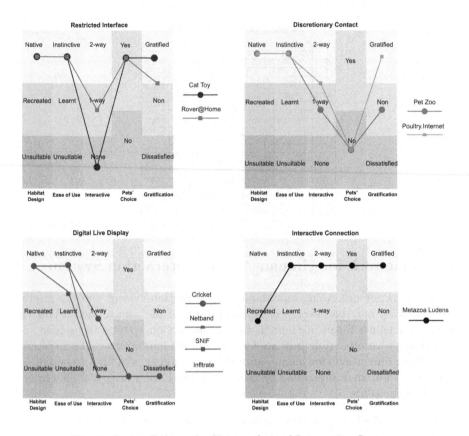

**Fig. 3.** Design Pattern for Human-Animal Interaction System

for interactivity. Choices available for this dimension are - Yes, where animals are given the choice to use the system; No, where animals are not given the choice to use the system.

- **Animal's Gratification:** There should be some form of gratification (be it health benefits or entertainment) for the animal in using the system, else it would be just a case of making the animal perform certain tasks for the entertainment of the human. Choices available for this dimension are - Gratified, where the animals are given some benefits or gratification from using the system; No, where animals are given gratification nor given dissatisfaction from using the system; Dissatisfied, where animals gets negative gratification from using the system.

Based on the clustering of systems, four design patterns for human-animal interaction system (after pattern language for architectural studies [21]) are obtained, see Figure 3. They are: Restricted Interface accounts for systems like Cat Toy. Such systems score fairly well in four of the dimensions except for Interactivity. Interaction is mostly one-way, from human to animal; the animal has no means to interact directly with the human. Such systems are mostly intended to have a restricted one-way interface focusing on the human's interaction with the animal. Discretionary Contact accounts for systems like Poultry.Internet and Pet Zoo, and are mostly intended for the human to interact with the animal at the human's discretion. Despite the animals having little choice in participating in this interaction, it is noted that gratification for the animal is high. Digital Live Display accounts for systems like Infiltrate. Such systems score very well in Habitual Design and Ease of Use while scoring very low for the remaining dimensions. These systems generally focus on being a means of digital live display for the human with little emphasis on the animal's choice to interact, their interaction with the human and their gratification from such systems. Interactive Connection accounts for systems like Metazoa Ludens. This archetype scores very well in all dimensions except for Habitual Design. This archetype focuses on bidirectional interaction as well as the animal's choice to play and its gratification, it also ensures the ease of use of the system by the animal. Such systems are mostly intended for equal emphasis on interaction between the human and the animal for connection. While the four presented system design can help designers in future design as model for development of new human-animal interaction systems, it does not represent the only possibilities for building such systems. More importantly will be the use of the five dimensions in consideration of the new design. In an ideal situation any such systems to be built should be high in all five dimensions.

## 6   Conclusion

Metazoa Ludens presents a mixed reality game which allows gameplay between humans and small animals (like hamsters) over the Internet. This system not only allows a novel game play but allows humans and hamsters to interact meaningfully and effectively with a mixed reality system. This type of interaction offered gives the enrichment and enhancement of the experience as brought about by digitalized system. While not trying to replace conventional interaction between humans and small animals, its aim is to offer remote interaction with the small animals as well as another way of interacting with the small animals through advanced digital technology. We not only showed detailed experimental verification and positive results, but deeply aimed this work to provide lessons and framworks for future human-animal media designs for the benefit of animal and human relations.

**Acknowledgments.** We would like to thank all members of Mixed Reality Lab, Singapore for all their help rendered.

## References

1. Csikszentmihalyi, M.: Beyond Boredom and Anxiety: Experiencing Flow in Work and Play. Jossey-Bass Inc., San Francisco, California (1975)
2. Kawakami, N., Haratani, T.: Epidemiology of Job Stress and Health in Japan: Review of Current Evidence and Future Direction. Industrial Health 37, 174–186 (1999)

3. Teh, K.S.J., Lee, S.P., Cheok, A.D.: Novel Uses of Existing Wearable Sensors Technology. In: ISWC, vol. 1(2), pp. 18–21. IEEE Press, Los Alamitos (2005)
4. Phaosavasdi, S., Thaneepanichskul, S., Tannirandorn, Y., Thamkhantho, M., Pruksapong, C., Kanjanapitak, A., Leong, H.: Journal of Medical Association of Thailand 88, 287–293 (2005)
5. Zim, H.S.: Golden Hamster. Morrow, New York (1951)
6. Pet Web Site (2007), Available Online http://www.petwebsite.com/
7. National Hamster Council (2007), Available Online http://www.hamster-uk.org
8. Hamster Land (2007), Available Online http://www.hamster.com/
9. Ullman-Cullere, M.H., Foltz, C.J.: Body Condition Scoring: A Rapid and Accurate Method for Assessing Health Status in Rodents. Laboratory Animal Science 49, 319–323 (1999)
10. Sweetser, P., Wyeth, P.: GameFlow: A Model for Evaluating Player Enjoyment in Games. Computers in Entertainment (CIE) 3(3), 14–27 (2005)
11. Resner, B.: Rover@home. MIT, Cambridge, Massachusetts, USA (2001)
12. CME (1999), Available Online from http://www.metahuman.org/web/pzoo1.html/
13. Mikesell, D.: Networking Pets and People. In: Adjunct Proceedings of Ubicomp, Seattle, USA, pp. 88–89 (2003)
14. Goldberg, K., Perona, P., Bender, J., Lobel, I., Chen, K.: On Exhibit: Neuro. Caltech336. Pasadena, CA, USA (2003)
15. Gips, J., Fields, N., Liang, P., Pilpre, A.: SNIF: Social Networking in Fur. In: CHI '05: CHI '05 extended abstracts on Human factors in computing systems, vol. 2(7), pp. 1391–1394. ACM Press, New York (2005)
16. Netband (1994), Available Online http://www.buitenland.org/
17. Behrens, D.: Keeping up with the Tamagotchis/ A Report on Virtual Pets and Knockoff Reality. Newsday, 6 (1997)
18. Cheok, A.D., Goh, K.H., Liu, W., Fabiz, F., Fong, S.W., Teo, S.L., Li, Y., Yang, X.: Human Pacman: a mobile, wide-area entertainment system based on physical, social, and ubiquitous computing. Personal and Ubiquitous Computing 8(2), 71–81 (2004)
19. Tan, K.C.R., Cheok, A.D., Teh, K.S.: Metazoa Ludens: Mixed Reality Environment for Playing Computer Games with Pets. The International Journal of Virtual Reality 5(3), 53–58 (2006)
20. Duncan, I.J.H., Kite, V.G.: Some investigations into motivation in the domestic fowl. Applied Animal Behavior Science 18, 387–388 (1987)
21. Alexander, C.: A Pattern Language: Towns, Buildings, Construction. Oxford University Press, Oxford (1977)

# Identification with the Player Character as Determinant of Video Game Enjoyment

Dorothée Hefner[1], Christoph Klimmt[1], and Peter Vorderer[2,*]

[1] Department of Journalism and Communication Research, Hanover University of Music and Drama, EXPO-Plaza 12, D-30539 Hannover, Germany,
Phone: +49.511.3100.451, Fax: +49.511.3100.400
hefner@ijk.hmt-hannover.de
[2] VU University Amsterdam, Center for Advanced Media Research Amsterdam (CAMeRA)

**Abstract.** In this paper, identification with a game character is discussed as mechanism of computer game enjoyment. Identification is explicated in terms of players' altered self-perception during game play: When identifying with a character or role offered by the game, players change their self-concept by adopting relevant attributes of the character, for instance, they perceive themselves as more courageous, heroic, and powerful during identification with a soldier. Theoretical arguments for the enjoyable quality of such temporary changes of the self-concept are introduced. Computer game interactivity is proposed as important facilitator of strong identification. Subsequently, a pilot experiment with players of "Battlefield 2" supports the assumptions on the relationships between interactivity, identification, and game enjoyment. Implications of the identification concept for research and applications in entertainment computing are discussed.

**Keywords:** Computer games, video games, enjoyment, identification, experiment.

## Introduction

The question of why computer games are enjoyable has been of major importance to entertainment computing [e.g. 1]. Video game enjoyment has only recently attracted notable attention in communication and media psychology [e.g. 2], but the number of studies on the fun of playing computer games is growing constantly. The explanation of video game enjoyment is crucial to understand the processes involved game-based human-computer interaction and to model the impact of technical properties of entertainment computing systems on user experience. Theories on (interactive) media entertainment are therefore helpful for research on entertainment computing and provide rich possibilities for interdisciplinary connections between the computer sciences and the social sciences.

In this paper, we introduce one mechanism of video game enjoyment, identification with a game character. Identification could be described as 'feeling like'

---

* The research presented in this paper was funded by the European Commission, project FUGA (NEST-PATH-28765). We thankfully acknowledge the Commission's support.

L. Ma, R. Nakatsu, and M. Rauterberg (Eds.): ICEC 2007, LNCS 4740, pp. 39–48, 2007.

or as creating the illusion to 'become' a key person within a computer game's universe; it is argued to be an essential element of game enjoyment. However, the notion of identification is widely used both in everyday and scientific contexts. In entertainment research, a controversy is still going on about users' identification with media characters (e.g., movie heroes or TV show protagonists). Part of the debate is the term and experiential quality of identification. Zillmann argues against identification and proposes that – at least in non-interactive entertainment such as watching television – media users keep a distance between themselves and a character on the screen [3]. In contrast to identification (which could be described scientifically as taking the media character's perspective), [4], people merely observe the actions of the characters, evaluate them from an observer's point of view, and develop empathic (or non-empathic) emotions with her/him. Such emotional bonds then drive entertainment experiences such as suspense (hoping that the liked character will face positive events while fearing that s/he could face negative events [5], [6]. Other lines of research suggest that identification can occur, at least in some people (especially children) and under certain conditions [4, 7, ]. However, none of these concepts has been applied to interactive video games, for which fundamentally different circumstances of exposure and user experience have to be expected [2]. The explication of identification with a video game character thus requires some preliminary theoretical work (section 2.) and some media-specific considerations on identification and game enjoyment (3.). We then report findings from a pilot experiment with players of the computer game "Battlefield 2" (4.) and outline future directions for thematic research based on the discussion of our findings (5.).

# 1 Identification Theory

Most theories on audience responses to media characters rely on the fundamental assumption that media users experience themselves and the media persona as two distinct social entities. Consequently, the theorized psychological responses to characters are grounded on processes of observation, evaluation (e.g., empathy), and (parasocial) dialogue [9, 10]. In spite of the empirical evidence for these concepts of dyadic user-character relationships, a different approach of a non-dyadic user-character relationship seems to be a necessary useful theoretical addition, especially for the understanding of the video game experience.

The proposed explication of identification resorts to conceptualizations of 'the self' advanced in social psychology. Current theories envision the "self" and self-concept not anymore as a stable construct but rather as state-sensitive and malleable depending upon the situation [11, 12]. People are able to integrate certain requirements not only into their actual behavior but also into their self-concept [13].

These advances in theories on the self-concept hold implications for the use of interactive media: Following Cohen's definition of identification, [4], we propose that for the moment of media exposure, users adopt (parts of) the identity of the target character. They perceive or imagine themselves to actually be the media character and thus alter their self-concept 'into the direction of' the media character. Identification with a media character is thus construed as a temporary alteration of media users' self-perception by inclusion of perceived properties of the target media character.

One argument for the enjoyable quality of such changes to users' self-concept is the recognition of escapism as important motivation to use entertainment [14, 15]. It is plausible that the desire to temporarily forget (or 'leave') one's real-life problems would be fulfilled more effectively if a viewer would not only enjoy the observation of media characters, but if s/he would experience to actually become a different person for the moment [16]. In respect to computer game play, game interactivity is considered as another important argument for the viability of the identification concept. This is because computer games present characters in similar, but also somewhat different modes as television and film do. Computer games do not only display mediated environments in which characters act (independently), they also enable and invite users to act by themselves in the environment and to become an integral part of the mediated world [17].

Most contemporary computer games include voluminous narrative elements that assign a certain role to players (Klimmt, 2003), such as the role of a sportsman, a military commander, or an ad-venture heroine such as 'Lara Croft'™. The way players 'fill in' the role offered to them shapes the properties and course of the game, which implies that players are not mere observers of the media environment (and of the media characters in it) as they are in television settings, but that they actively participate in the story unfolding on screen. Through interactivity, then, video games override the distance between media users and media characters: Players either control directly one specific character or take on a social role represented in the game world, [18]. In both cases, players do not observe autonomous social entities performing on screen, but they make characters perform or actually perform themselves. McDonald and Kim report that young video game players perceive no distance at all to their game protagonists, but "identify quite closely" with them [19].

Based on these considerations, we assume that identification processes within an interactive medium as video games differ from the empathy-driven kind of identification that is observable while watching a movie. The proposed monadic (i.e., non-dyadic) type of identification should accordingly apply particularly to interactive entertainment such as playing computer games.

## 2 Identification and Game Enjoyment

The described process of "monadic" identification is proposed to contribute to the fun of playing a computer game that is distinct from the fun entertainment experience of, for instance, watching an action movie on TV. Drawing back to escapism research, the understanding of identification as temporary change of media users' self-perception is assumed to frequently serve the desire to evade troublesome real-life circumstances [14]. Such problems frequently arise from people's recognition of themselves being different from the self they idealize or strive for (self-discrepancy, [20].

The enjoyment of identification with a game character can thus be grounded on the reduction of self-discrepancy for the time of media exposure. A media user who perceives himself as less courageous than he actually wants to be (high self-discrepancy on the dimension of courage) could reduce his self-discrepancy by identifying with a courageous game character such as James Bond by adopting the salient properties of him. For the period of identification with James Bond, the self-perception of the player is altered towards the characteristics of Bond, including an increased level of courage. Identification with James Bond thus leads to a higher self-ascribed value of courage, which consequently reduces or even eliminates the self-discrepancy (on this dimension). Such reductions or complete resolutions of self-discrepancies are accompanied by positive experiences, which would then become integral part of the overall game enjoyment.

However, interactivity might only be a necessary but not sufficient condition for identification. The role, the character that is "allowing" identification furthermore has to offer some appeal to the player. For example, a person that nauseates all war and battle aesthetics would probably not identify easily with the role of a soldier as it is offered by most first person shooter games. In contrast, a player who is attracted to war sceneries, conflict, and military stories, may find the same offer to identify with a soldier in a computer game most appealing and enjoyable, [18]. Thus the attractiveness and the personal desirability of the role that is offered to be occupied during game play must be given to a certain degree in order to facilitate monadic identification.

Hoffner and Buchanan refer to this phenomenon as "wishful identification", which is considered as constitutive for the playing motivation in young adults [7]. Jansz provides with his work about the emotional appeal of violent video games to adolescent males one reason why violent, strong, and hyper-masculine characters are attractive for wishful identification [21]. He compares a game playing session with an experiment in a private laboratory where the gamers can experience and practice certain roles and emotions related to these roles. Violent characters give especially male adolescents the possibility to experience a hyper-masculine role. "They can safely embrace the game heroes' violent performance of masculine identity without fearing moral reproach or ridicule by partners or peers." ([14], pp. 231-232).

Based on those considerations we assume that a given video game player is more willing to identify with a game protagonist if the offered role is attractive to him/her. For young males, this could especially be the case for (hyper-)masculine, dominant, and violent characters. To the extent that the vicarious experience of 'being' a game character (within the game world) is appealing to the player, identification with that character will turn into a major dimension of computer game enjoyment.

In addition to the personal appeal of the character-role, the dimension of performance and competence is relevant to the identification experience. Deci and Ryan declare "competence" one of the three fundamental needs of human being (alongside "relatedness" and "autonomy, [22]). Computer games may serve as an ideal area to experience this feeling of competence since their interactivity allows action, solving problems, etc. and thus the experience of self-efficacy [18, 23, 24]. If a player is attracted to the 'role offer' of a character but does not feel to fulfill the role adequately by means of accomplishing the missions attached to the role, identification with the character would probably not be enjoyable (the perception of 'being a bad soldier' is not attractive for players to like the idea of being a soldier, as it would lower their temporary self-esteem [25]), so identification is likely to decrease. In contrast, a good performance and the according experience of competence will prompt the player to occupy the role continuously. In other words: Players should tend to only identify with given characters if the identification will not harm their self but rather raise their self-esteem. In sum, a person playing a computer game is argued to find identification with a game protagonist (or the offered player role such as commander-in-chief) more enjoyable if the offered role is appealing to her/him and if s/he "does a good job" in carrying out the character's actions.

# 3  A Pilot Study on Identification with Computer Game Characters

## 3.1  Research Design

An experiment was conducted to explore the theorized relevance of identification with a game character for video game enjoyment. Specifically, the study was designed to answer the following research questions:

- Does game interactivity facilitate identification with the game character (see section 1.)?
- Does identification with the game character contribute to overall game enjoyment (section 2)?
- Does perceived competence facilitate identification with the game character (section 2)?

The research questions required a systematic comparison of interactive game play and non-interactive, passive game observation. Thus, the experiment compared participants who either played a game or only watched a recorded sequence of the same game. Identification with the game character was assumed to be much stronger for those participants actually playing by themselves. Moreover, a positive statistical correlation between the strength of identification and overall game enjoyment was hypothesized in respect to the second research question.

## 3.2  Participants and Procedure

30 voluntary male university students aged between 20 and 30 years (M = 24.37, SD = 2.66) took part in the experiment. 20 of them had some experience with the genre of the game used in the experiment,  first-person-shooters (FPS), 9 of them  had little experience, only one participant had never player FPS before.

Participants were randomly assigned to either play one level of "Battlefield 2" (Electronic Arts, Single-Player-Mode) or watch a video recording from the very same game level. A 32- inch LCD-TV was used as display for participants in both groups. After six minutes, the game session was interrupted or the video presentation was stopped in the non-interactive group, respectively. Participants were then asked to fill out a questionnaire regarding their enjoyment experience, state of presence during the game, current self-concept and identification with the game character. Moreover, respondents who had played the game were asked about their impression of competence during the game.

Identification with the game character was assessed with 8 items like "I have forgotten myself during the game", "I had almost the feeling of being the game character", and "the goals of the character became my own goals". Responses were measured on a five-point scale ranging from "I do not agree at all" to "I fully agree". The reliability of the scale was good (Cronbach's Alpha = .84), so a mean-index was used for further analyses. To assess the theorized quality of identification (i.e., changes in players' self-concept through adoption of game character's properties) in more detail, participants were also asked to describe themselves by rating the extent to which some verbal attributes were true for them. Among these rated attributes were some concepts immediately relevant to the soldier's role offered for identification by "Battlefield 2", namely "masculine" and "powerful". It was expected that stronger agreement to these attributes as valid self-descriptions would be correlated positively to video game enjoyment.

### 3.3 Results

An analysis of variance was computed to test the effect of interactivity on perceived identification. The results support our assumptions: Participants who actually played the game displayed a significantly higher mean score of identification (M = 2.72) than the participants assigned to the group who had only watched a recorded sequence from the game (M = 2.1; $F(1/28) = 5.43$; $p < .05$; $\eta^2 = .16$). Thus, interactivity was demonstrated to facilitate identification with the game character.

Furthermore, the second research question addressed the contribution of identification with the character to game enjoyment. To test this assumption, the correlation between the indices of identification and enjoyment was computed. In line with the theoretical assumption, identification correlated strongly with enjoyment (Pearson's $r = .57$; $p < .01$). Similar, although non-significant results were obtained for the relevance of game-related self-descriptions for identification (in the group who had played actively, n = 15): The agreement to "masculine" ($r = .61$, $p < .05$) and "powerful" ($r = .58$, $p < .05$) as valid self-descriptions also correlated with the index of identification. Thus, the extent to which players perceived key attributes of the game character valid for themselves was substantially correlated with identification.

Finally, we assumed that the perceived competence while playing the game was an important factor for identification. The correlation between the item "I felt competent during playing" and the identification index was significant in the player group ($r = .54$, $p < .05$), which supports the assumption that good performance when occupying a character role is crucial for the identification experience.

## 4  Discussion

The present pilot study has shed some light on identification processes. Based on theoretical assumptions, the role of interactivity on identification experience and the role of identification for game enjoyment were demonstrated in the experiment: Results confirm the interplay of interactive game use, identification and enjoyment. People playing the game and thus having the possibility to act efficiently within the character role identify with the game protagonist to a much larger extent than people do who could not interact with the game. The interactive use of the combat game "Battlefield 2" thus allowed for more intense, 'authentic' vicarious or simulated experiences of 'being' a soldier in a modern combat scenario, while such experiences were less accessible or less intensive in those participants who had only watched a recording of a game play session. Such identification with the soldier role was furthermore associated with a higher degree of enjoyment which indicates that identification is an important cornerstone for understanding game enjoyment. The findings on the self-descriptors "masculine" and "dominant", finally, suggest that the male players that had been invited to this study tend to find the role of a warrior attractive and thus engaged in identification with this role. This is in line with Jansz's (2005) theoretical argumentation of violent video gaming as experimentation environment for evolving (adolescent) masculinity. In sum, the pilot study supports the theoretical framework on narrative game enjoyment and provides empirical ground for the construal of playing video games as a simulated experience that allows to escape one's real-life environment and social contexts towards more interesting, attractive, suspenseful and/or otherwise rewarding worlds. Identification with the role offered by the game – be it a warrior, a corporate manager, a professional golfer or a gangster – thus opens the horizons for new experiences closely connected to player's self. By adopting those attributes of the game character that one finds attractive, players can perceive themselves as being more like they want to be. Identification is thus a path to temporary reduction of self-discrepancy [20], because it allows players to see themselves closer to their idealized identity. For (young) male players, identification with a soldier is likely to fulfill this function of coming close to one's ideal self (i.e., to feel more masculine, courageous, dominant and so on); for other player groups (e.g., girls), alternative characters may be more favorable in terms of identification-based reduction of self-discrepancy [23].

## 5  Conclusion

The present paper has investigated one component of computer game enjoyment, identification with the game character. Both theoretical argumentation and empirical pilot findings support the assumption that playing computer games is fun, (partly) because it allows to enter imagined worlds beyond one's real-life experiences and to perceive oneself in the way one wants to be. In this sense, the term "wishful identification" is most suitable to describe this facet of computer game enjoyment [26].

From the perspective of entertainment computing, our findings have several interesting implications. First, the concept of identification provides a theoretical foundation for the explanation why sophisticated interaction possibilities, intelligent agents and rich audiovisual representations of game worlds are directly linked to computer game enjoyment. In entertainment computing, these technical properties of computer games are constantly developed further and object of conceptual debate [27]. More advanced game technology can be argued to facilitate more intensive forms of identification with the game protagonist, for instance, by creating a more convincing spatial and social environment within which the player can perform the actions attached to his/her role ("Presence", [28]). Intelligent agents that interact with the player (or player character) in 'authentic ways' also support the capacity of the game to evoke identification, because the 'offer' for identification made to the player is more complete and more convincing if the player role is embedded in 'natural' social interaction within the game world [29]. In this sense, many more technical properties of advanced computer games could be linked to game enjoyment via the identification mechanism, and it remains a task for future research to investigate these connections systematically.

Second, the findings support the importance of narrative elements for successful computer games. A major part of the fun of playing comes out of identification processes that root back in the narrative framework of the game. If only a rudimentary background plot is available, the character or role that players could identify with may remain underdeveloped, which would result in lowered game enjoyment. Thus, the inclusion of rich narrative content is both a challenge for game development, but also an important advantage for the entertainment experience, [30].

Third, the entertainment valued of computer games can be improved if the games achieve to evoke the perception in players that they can occupy the role they identify with successfully. While it may be interesting to a given player to identify with the role of a corporate manager, our findings suggest that it is even more appealing to identify with a good manager, that is, to perform well within the role framework of the game. The importance of good performance in games has been highlighted in the game enjoyment literature, and the present paper links this factor of enjoyment to the issue of identification. So interactivity and game narrative should be intertwined in a way that enables simulated experiences of 'doing the character's job well' in order to maximize player enjoyment.

Finally, the importance of identification processes to game enjoyment holds implications for designing computer games that are appealing to different target groups. Different players will find different roles to identify with interesting and enjoyable. For instance, the gender gap in computer game involvement can be explained by the simple fact that most computer games today offer roles to identify with that are more interesting for boys and men than for girls and women [31]. Computer games for specific player segments will have to provide possibilities to identify with roles or characters whose properties resonate with the preferences and wishes of these players. The concept of identification may be helpful in thinking about and testing out game concepts that are intended to maximize enjoyment for such specified player groups.

# References

1. Vorderer, P., Hartmann, T., Klimmt, C.: Explaining the enjoyment of playing video games: The role of competition. In: Marinelli, D. (ed.) ICEC conference proceedings 2003: Essays on the future of interactive entertainment, pp. 107–120. Carnegie Mellon University Press, Pittsburgh (2003)
2. Vorderer, P., Bryant, J.: Playing video games: Motives, responses, and consequences. Lawrence Erlbaum Associates, Mahwah, NJ (2006)
3. Zillmann, D.: Dramaturgy for emotions from fictional narration. In: Bryant, J., Vor-derer, P. (eds.) Psychology of entertainment, pp. 215–238. Lawrence Erlbaum Associates, Mahwah (2006)
4. Cohen, J.: Defining identification: A theoretical look at the identification of audiences with media characters. Mass Communication and Society 4(3), 245–264 (2001)
5. Zillmann, D.: The psychology of suspense in dramatic exposition. In: Vorderer, P., Wulff, H.J., Friedrichsen (Hrsg.), M. (eds.) Suspense: Conceptualizations, theoretical analyses, and empirical explorations, pp. S. 199–231. Lawrence Erlbaum Associates, Mahwah, NJ (1996)

6. Klimmt, C., Vorderer, P.: Media Psychology is not yet there. Introducing theories on media entertainment to the Presence debate. Presence: Teleoperators and Virtual Environments 12(4), 346–359 (2003)
7. Hoffner, C., Buchanan, M.: Young adults' wishful identification with television characters: The role of perceived similarity and character attributes. Media Psychology 7, 325–351 (2005)
8. Oatley, K.: A taxonomy of the emotions of literary response and a theory of identification in fictional narrative. Poetics 23, 53–74 (1994)
9. Klimmt, C., Hartmann, T., Schramm, H.: Parasocial interactions and relationships. In: Bryant, J., Vorderer (Hrsg.), P. (eds.) Psychology of entertainment, pp. S. 291–313. Lawrence Erlbaum Associates, Mahwah, NJ (2006)
10. Konijn, E.A., Hoorn, J.F.: Some like it bad: Testing a model for perceiving and experiencing fictional characters. Media Psychology 7(2), 107–144 (2005)
11. Bracken, B. (ed.): Handbook of Self-concept: Developmental, Social, and Clinical Considerations. Wiley, New York (1995)
12. Hannover, B.: Das dynamische Selbst. Göttingen, Hogrefe (1997)
13. Goldstein, N.J., Cialdini, R.B.: The Spyglass Self: A Model of Vicarious Self-Perception. Journal of Personality and Social Psychology 92(3), 402–417 (2007)
14. Katz, E., Foulkes, D.: On the use of mass media for escape: Clarification of a concept. Public Opinion Quaterly 26, 377–388 (1962)
15. Henning, B., Vorderer, P.: Psychological escapism: Predicting the amount of television viewing by need for cognition. Journal of Communication 51, 100–120 (2001)
16. Vorderer, P.: Audience involvement and program loyalty. Poetics 22, 89–98 (1993)
17. Vorderer, P.: Interactive entertainment and beyond. In: Zillmann, D., Vorderer, P. (eds.) Media entertainment. The psychology of its appeal, pp. 21–36. Lawrence Erlbaum Associates, Mahwah, NJ (2000)
18. Klimmt, C.: Dimensions and determinants of the enjoyment of playing digital games: A three-level model. In: Copier, M., Raessens, J. (eds.) Level Up: Digital Games Research Conference, Utrecht: Faculty of Arts, Utrecht University, pp. 246–257 (2003)
19. McDonald, D.G., Kim, H.: When I die, I feel small: electronic game characters and the social self. Journal of Broadcasting and Electronic Media 45(2), 241–258 (2001)
20. Higgins, E.T.: Self-Discrepancy: A Theory Relating Self and Affect. Psychological Review 94(3), 319–341 (1987)
21. Jansz, J.: The emotional appeal of violent video games for adolescent males. Communication Theory 15(3), 219–241 (2005)
22. Deci, E.L., Ryan, R.M.: The "What" and "Why" of Goal Pursuits: Human Needs and the Self-Determination of Behavior. Psychological Inquiry 11(4), 227–268 (2000)
23. Klimmt, C., Hartmann, T.: Effectance, self-efficacy, and the motivation to play video games. In: Vorderer, P., Bryant, J. (eds.) Playing video games: Motives, responses, and consequences, pp. 133–145. Lawrence Erlbaum Associates, Mahwah (2006)
24. Ryan, R.M., Rigby, C.S., Przybylski, A.: The motivational pull of video games: A self-determination theory approach. Motivation and Emotion 30, 347–363 (2006)
25. Weiner, B.: An attribution theory of achievement motivation and emotion. Psychological Review 92(4), 548–573 (1985)
26. von Feilitzen, C., Linné, O.: Identifying with television characters. Journal of Communication 25(4), 51–55 (1975)
27. Kishino, F., Kitamura, Y., Kato, H., Nagata, N. (eds.): ICEC 2005. LNCS, vol. 3711. Springer, Heidelberg (2005)
28. Wirth, W., Hartmann, T., Böcking, S., Vorderer, P., Klimmt, C., Schramm, H., Saari, T., Laarni, J., Ravaja, N., Ribeiro Gouveia, F., Biocca, F., Sacau, A., Jäncke, L., Baumgartner, T., Jäncke, P.: A process model of the formation of Spatial Presence experiences. Media Psychology (in press)

29. Parise, S., Kiesler, S., Sproull, L., Waters, K.: Cooperating with life-like interface agents. Computers in Human Behavior 15, 123–142 (1999)
30. Lee, K.M., Park, N., Jin, S.-A.: Narrative and interactivity in computer games. In: Vorderer, P., Bryant, J. (eds.) Playing video games: Motives, responses, consequences, pp. 259–274 (2006)
31. Hartmann, T., Klimmt, C.: Gender and computer games: Exploring females' dislikes. Journal of Computer- Mediated Communication 11(4), Article 2.
http://jcmc.indiana.edu/vol11/issue4/hartmann.html

# Pass the Ball:
# Game-Based Learning of Software Design

Guillermo Jiménez-Díaz, Mercedes Gómez-Albarrán,
and Pedro A. González-Calero

Dept. de Ingeniería del Software e Inteligencia Artificial
Universidad Complutense de Madrid
C/ Prof. Jose Garcia Santesmases s/n. 28040. Madrid, Spain
gjimenez@fdi.ucm.es, {albarran,pedro}@sip.ucm.es

**Abstract.** Based on our experience using active learning methods to teach object-oriented software design we propose a game-based approach to take the classroom experience into a virtual environment.

The different pedagogical approaches that our active method supports, have motivated us to tailor an architecture that supports the creation of different variations of role-play environments, ranging from open-ended trial and error approaches to highly constrained settings where students can not get very far from the solution. We also describe a prototype that instantiates this architecture called ViRPlay3D2.

**Keywords:** Game-based learning, object-oriented design, role-play.

## 1 Introduction

Object-oriented software design requires a combination of abilities, which can not be easily transferred to the students in lecture sessions. We have tried a more active approach based on role-play sessions to teach software design. This way, the students have the chance to evaluate the consequences of a given design and test their ideas with the other students that intervene in the role-play. Our experience demonstrated its good results [5] and its empirical evaluation has concluded that participating in the play is more effective than just looking at it. Such good results have motivated the work presented in this paper: the construction of a virtual environment for teaching software design through role-play, that intends to maintain, and even reinforce, the benefits of role-play in the classroom. Using ideas from 3D sport games, the interface lets every student play her role while accessing to related information such as the underlying class diagram or previous steps of the use case execution.

Next Section describes the approach used for teaching software design in the classroom, as the starting point for the virtual environment. In Section 3 the features of different learning approaches supported by the teaching approach are presented. Section 4 describes an architecture for role-play virtual environments (RPVEs) that can be created taking into account the different approaches described in previous section. Section 5 details the proposed virtual environment for role-play and software design. Finally, Section 6 concludes the paper.

L. Ma, R. Nakatsu, and M. Rauterberg (Eds.): ICEC 2007, LNCS 4740, pp. 49–54, 2007.
© IFIP International Federation for Information Processing 2007

## 2  An Experience-Based Teaching Approach

During the last years, we have followed an active learning approach to teach object-oriented design. During each session, the instructor actively involves the students in the comprehension and development of a software application. The sessions are supported by two active learning techniques: CRC cards and role-play. A CRC card [1] represents a Class and it contains information about its Responsibilities –what a class knows and what it can do– and its Collaborators –classes that help to carry out a responsibility. CRC cards are combined with role-play activities in responsibility-driven design. The role-play activities [1] are employed to simulate the execution of a use case. Each participant performs the role of an object that intervenes in the simulation. The role-play simulation forces the participants to evaluate the design created using the CRC cards and to verify if they can reach a better solution.

Every session following this active approach runs in three stages:

1. Pre-simulation stage. The instructor selects a design scenario consisting of a case study (the design problem), an initial (and maybe incomplete) solution, and a set of use cases that will be used during the simulation. According to this scenario, the instructor binds each student to a specific role and provides her with the corresponding CRC card.
2. Cycle simulation-modification. Students are responsible for the message passing, modifying CRC cards and deciding when the simulation finishes. During the simulation, the instructor can help the students when a deadlock happens. Students can also communicate among them in order to know about their responsibilities. The instructor registers the simulation by constructing a Role-Play Diagram (RPD): a semi-formal representation of a scenario execution in an object-oriented application that capture objects' state [1].
3. Evaluation. The instructor evaluates the resulting design. If the design is appropriate, the practical session finishes. Otherwise, the instructor discusses with the students the pitfalls found in the design and analyses possible improvements. In this case, the practical session goes back to step 2.

## 3  Variations of the Learning Sessions

The analysis of the learning sessions has promoted the identification of a set of flexible aspects in the session pattern. These aspects allow us to define learning sessions with a common learning methodology and different pedagogical approaches. For each aspect, we have identified its degree of flexibility and how they affect to other aspects. Finally, we have classify them according to the stage that they affect. We have encountered the aspects listed below:

- **Scenario Selection.** This is a pre-simulation aspect that defines how the scenario is selected before starting the simulation.
- **Role assignment.** This pre-simulation aspect concerns how to assign the roles in the scenario to the students and what to do if there are not enough students to simulate the scenario previously selected.

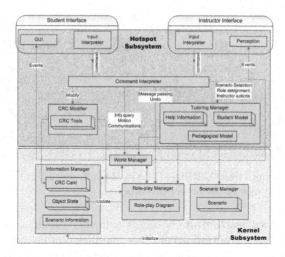

**Fig. 1.** RPVE Architecture

- **Student's degree of freedom.** This simulation-modification aspect determines when the instructor takes the control in order to provide help or to correct the wrong actions of the students.
- **Help provision.** This aspect is related to the previous one and it defines what the instructor does when it takes the control. It is classified as a simulation-modification aspect.
- **Modifications in the initial design.** This is a simulation-modification aspect that defines the modifications the students can do in the CRC cards provided with the scenario. It also concerns the tools and techniques employed to modify the CRC cards, who is responsible for doing the modifications and when they can be done.
- **Instructor.** This is an evaluation aspect that determines how and when the instructor interacts with the students. This aspect is strongly related with most of the previous aspects.

## 4   The RPVE Architecture

We have designed a high level architecture for RPVEs that gathers the variation aspects detailed in Section 3. The architecture is shown in Figure 1 and it clearly differs two subsystems:

- *Kernel subsystem.* It implements the behavior that is common to any RPVE. It is formed by several immutable modules and it is responsible for the management of the world entities (*World Manager*); the static information storage, such as the CRC cards (*Information Manager*) and scenario description (*Scenario Manager*); and the update of the dynamic information employed in the simulation, such as RPDs and the object state (*Role-play Manager*).

**Fig. 2.** Two screenshots from ViRPlay3D2. On the left, a student's point of view; on the right, the appearance of the object inventory

- *The Hotspot subsystem.* It contains the flexible modules within the architecture. Different instantiations of these modules produces different RPVEs. They are related to the communication interface between the users and the RPVE (*Student and Instructor Interface*); the translation of the user input to a set of commands that the rest of the modules understand (*Command Interpreter*); the management of the tools and strategies to modify the CRC cards (*CRC Modifier*); and the management of the tutoring tasks, such as the scenario selection and the role assignment strategies, how the instructor intervenes in the simulation and the help information storage and management (*Tutoring Manager*).

## 5   Transferring the Learning Sessions to a RPVE

Following this architecture, we are developing ViRPlay3D2 (see Figure 2), a multiplayer environment where the students mimic the classroom role-play sessions. The students are immersed using a first-person view that simulates the point of view of the objets that participate in the role-play. An aiming point in the center of the screen serves to interact with other entities in the virtual world and to throw a ball to represent the message passing. The user interface also displays a score that contains information about the current state of the role-play session.

The main elements and actions of a role-play session are represented in the RPVE according to the following metaphor:

**Objects and classes.** Each object is represented by an anthropomorphical avatar controlled by one student. In contrast, a wooden box represents a class. Each box carries a label showing the class name.

**CRC cards and inventory.** Every class and object in the virtual world has an inventory. An object inventory (see Figure 2) contains a CRC card with the object responsibilities and collaborators, and the current object state. A class inventory only displays information about the class constructors.

**Scenario description and role-play diagrams.** The virtual environment contains a desktop that contains the overall description of the played scenario. Moreover, the interface contains a score, which shows the number of role-play steps executed during the current simulation (see Figure 2, on the left). The student can enlarge this score and see the RPD.

**Active object and message passing.** In our environment, the active object is characterized by holding a ball. The execution control is transferred from one object to another by throwing the ball. This throwing represents the message passing and it is divided into three stages:

- Creating the message. When the active object is looking up the inventory of one of its collaborators (or her own inventory), the student can create a message by selecting a responsibility, filling in the actual parameters and clicking on the "Create message" button (see Figure 2 (right)). If an object can send a return message, the inventory contains a special responsibility called "Return". The student is responsible for providing the returned value. A new object is created using the class inventory of one of its collaborator classes.
- Throwing the ball. The avatar that owns the ball throws the ball in the direction that it is aiming. While the avatar throws the ball the environment displays a message with information about the message.
- Catching the ball. This action is available only when the avatar that wants to catch the ball is close to it and the object that represents is the receiver of the message created before throwing the ball. When an avatar catch the ball, it becomes the active object and the RPD and the score are updated with the message details.

**Information retrieval.** The "Look at" action allows the student to see the information related to the entity that her avatar is aiming. The action is executed aiming at an object and clicking with the right mouse button. "Look at" displays the avatar inventory and it contains information about the CRC card. The student can also look at the desktop and display the information about the current simulated scenario. Moreover, if she looks at the ball, detailed information about the current invoked method is displayed.

Furthermore, the student looks up her own inventory using the "My Inventory" tool. It displays the inventory of the object represented by the avatar. In this inventory, the student can see the CRC card and the object state. This inventory is also employed to create self-invoked messages.

**CRC modifications, Undo and Communication.** A CRC card Modifier tool is available through the object inventory (see the "Modify" button in Figure 2). Using this tool, a student can add, remove or modify the class responsibilities and collaborators. When the students consider that they have made a mistake when sending a message, the active object can undo this simulation step. When the "Undo" action is performed, the environment updates the state of the objects and the RPD according to the previous simulation step. The ball also returns to the right active object. Finally, the students discuss during the simulation using a chat-like communication tool.

# 6  Conclusions

In this paper we have described the transfer of a successful active learning methodology to teach object-oriented design into a virtual environment. Our own teaching experiences have revealed that this kind of techniques increases student motivation [5] and the students better assimilate concepts in object-oriented design after attending and participating in role-play sessions. CRC cards and role-play are commonly employed in computer science courses [1,6].

The good results of our experience have promoted to tailor a kind of virtual environments, where the students collaborate to create and evaluate an object oriented design using role-play. Although the use of simulation environments is well-known to teach object-oriented programming [2] we have not found this kind of environments for object-oriented design in the literature.

ViRPlay3D2 is a prototype of an RPVE that builds on our previous experience developing game-based learning environments [3,4]. After completing its development, we plan is to evaluate its impact in the students learning.

**Acknowledgments.** This work has been supported by the Spanish Committee of Education and Science project TIN2006-15202-C03-03 and it has been partially supported by the Comunidad de Madrid Education Council and Complutense University of Madrid (consolidated research group 910494).

# References

1. Börstler, J.: Improving CRC-card role-play with role-play diagrams. In: Companion to the 20th annual ACM SIGPLAN conference on Object-Oriented Programming, Systems, Languages, and Applications, pp. 356–364. ACM Press, New York (2005)
2. Dann, W., Cooper, S., Pausch, R.: Learning to Program with Alice. Prentice Hall, Harlow, England (2005)
3. Gómez-Martín, M.A., Gómez-Martín, P.P., González-Calero, P.A.: Dynamic binding is the name of the game. In: Harper, R., Rauterberg, M., Combetto, M. (eds.) ICEC 2006. LNCS, vol. 4161, pp. 229–232. Springer, Heidelberg (2006)
4. Jiménez-Díaz, G., Gómez-Albarrán, M., Gómez-Martín, M.A., González-Calero, P.A.: Software behaviour understanding supported by dynamic visualization and role-play. In: ITiCSE '05: Proc. of the 10th annual SIGCSE Conf. on Innovation and Technology in Computer Science Education, pp. 54–58. ACM Press, New York (2005)
5. Jiménez-Díaz, G., Gómez-Albarrán, M., González-Calero, P.A.: Before and after: An active and collaborative approach to teach design patterns. In: 8th International Symposium on Computers in Education, vol. 1, pp. 272–279, Servicio de Imprenta de la Universidad de León (2006)
6. Kim, S., Choi, S., Jang, H., Kwon, D., Yeum, Y., Lee, W.: Smalltalk card game for learning object-oriented thinking in an evolutionary way. In: Companion to the 21st annual ACM SIGPLAN conference on Object-Oriented Programming, Systems, Languages, and Applications, pp. 683–684. ACM Press, New York (2006)

# Comparison of AI Techniques for Fighting Action Games - Genetic Algorithms/Neural Networks/Evolutionary Neural Networks*

Byeong Heon Cho, Chang Joon Park, and Kwang Ho Yang

Digital Content Research Division, ETRI, Daejeon, 305-700 Korea
{bhcho,chjpark,khyang}@etri.re.kr

**Abstract.** Recently many studies have attempted to implement intelligent characters for fighting action games. They used genetic algorithms, neural networks, and evolutionary neural networks to create intelligent characters. This study quantitatively compared the performance of these three AI techniques in the same game and experimental environments, and analyzed the results of experiments. As a result, neural network and evolutionary neural network showed excellent performance in the final convergence score ratio while evolutionary neural network and genetic algorithms showed excellent performance in convergence speed. In conclusion, evolutionary neural network which showed excellent results in both the final convergence score ratio and the convergence score is most appropriate AI technique for fighting action games.

## 1 Introduction

Many AI techniques for computer games are being researched, from traditional techniques such as Finite State Machine (FSM) to new techniques such as Fuzzy State Machine (FuSM), artificial life, and neural networks [1,2,3]. Most of these AI techniques are for board games such as go, chess, and gomoku which must consider the overall situation when determining the action of each go stone or chessman. Recently, there are attempts to study how to tune up the overall strategy of grouped characters using neural network or artificial life [4,5,6]. The problem is, however, that it is difficult to apply the existing methods for establishment of overall strategy to fighting action games or online games. In such genres as fighting action games, it is more important to make the characters intelligent so that they can cope appropriately according to the location and action of surrounding opponents, rather than to tune up the overall strategy of the game. Due to this reason, many have carried out studies to implement intelligent characters in fighting action games [7,8,9,10]. They used genetic algorithms, neural networks, and evolutionary neural networks to create intelligent characters for fighting action games. Studies using genetic algorithms evolved intelligent characters by including the distance between characters, the action and step of the

---

* This work was supported by the IT R&D program of MIC/IITA. [2006-S-044-02, Development of Multi-Core CPU & MPU-Based Cross-Platform Game Technology].

L. Ma, R. Nakatsu, and M. Rauterberg (Eds.): ICEC 2007, LNCS 4740, pp. 55–65, 2007.

opponent character, and past actions in the chromosomes that express intelligent characters [10]. Studies using neural networks used the action and step of the opponent character and the distance between characters as the input for neural networks, and the difference of scores resulting from the actions of two characters as the reinforcement value so as to make the intelligent characters learn whether or not their current action is appropriate [8,9]. However, because neural networks that use the error backpropagation algorithm have such shortcomings as falling in local minima and slow convergence speed, methods to apply evolutionary neural networks were studied [7]. These studies expressed the weight of links in a neural network as a gene, and evolved chromosomes by expressing the weights of all links of intelligent characters in the form of one-dimensional array. As shown in the above examples, various AI techniques have been studied for fighting action games, but it is difficult to compare or analyze the performance of the different techniques because the applied games and experimental environments differed. Therefore, this study quantitatively compared the performance of these AI techniques in the same game and experimental environments, and analyzed the results of experiments. For experiments, We defined simple rules of fighting action game and the action patterns of characters, and evaluated by ratio of score whether the intelligent characters learned appropriate actions corresponding to the action patterns of the opponent character. As a result of this experiment, the evolutionary neural network showed the best performance from the aspects of final score ratio and convergence speed. This paper is structured as follows: Section 2 reviews the AI techniques that have been used in fighting action games. Section 3 describes the experiment on the AI techniques under the same game environment and analyzes the results. Lastly, Section 4 summarizes the conclusions.

## 2    AI Techniques for Fighting Action Games

### 2.1    Genetic Algorithms

Genetic algorithms are a searching process using the evolution theory of the natural ecosystem. Genetic algorithms can create various forms of entities through artificial selection, and performs evolution and learning by transmitting the best entities to the next generation. Genetic algorithms can be used when the searched space is very large or when it is difficult to define the given problem with accurate numerical expressions, and are appropriate when the optimal solution is not required [11,12]. Recently, there were studies to apply genetic algorithms to fighting action games [10]. In these studies, chromosomes included information on what action intelligent characters will show according to the distance between characters and the action of the opponent character. Therefore, the game must be created newly from scratch if the game changes or the method of character implementation changes. As shown in Table 1, in [10], the chromosomes that express intelligent characters included the distance between characters, the action and step of the opponent character, and past actions. These chromosomes are two dimensional, and the numbers in each cell express the action of the opponent character. For example, if the opponent character is in step 1 of down (5) action at the distance 10. The character gives down-punch (6) if the past action of the opponent character was idle, or up-punch (7) if it was forward.

**Table 1.** The structure of a chromosome

| action | idle (0) | forward (1) | backward (2) | guard (3) | jump (4) | down (5) | down-punch (6) | | up-punch (7) | | | ... |
|---|---|---|---|---|---|---|---|---|---|---|---|---|
| step \ distance | 1 | 1 | 1 | 1 | 1 | 1 | 1 | 2 | 1 | 2 | 3 | |
| 1 | | | | | | | | | | | | |
| 2 | | | | | | | | | | | | |
| 3 | | | | | | | | | | | | |
| ... | | | | | | | | | | | | |
| 10 | | | | | | | | | | | | |

| past action | idle(0) | forward (1) | backward (2) | guard (3) | jump (4) | down (5) | down-punch (6) | up-punch (7) | ... | ... | ... | ... |
|---|---|---|---|---|---|---|---|---|---|---|---|---|
| IC's action | 6 | 7 | 2 | 3 | 6 | 9 | 0 | 1 | ... | ... | ... | ... |

## 2.2 Neural Networks

Neural networks imitate the human neural system. They have a structure in which countless simple elements are connected, and outputs based on the recognition of the pattern of input data [13,14]. The highest benefit of the application of neural networks to games is that the intelligence can continually improve with the progress of the game because neural networks have learning ability. Consequently, there have been many studies to apply neural networks to games, but mostly board games such as gomoku and Tic-Tac-Toe [5]. One characteristic of board games is that you must be aware of the overall situation of the pieces on the board and determine their movement. Recently, there have been studies to apply neural networks to fighting action games [7,8,9]. These studies used the action and step of the opponent character and the distance between characters as the input for neural networks, and the difference of scores resulting from the actions of two characters as the reinforcement value so as to make the intelligent characters learn whether or not their current action is appropriate. [7,8,9] expressed the neural network to represent intelligent characters as Figure 1. In Figure 1, input is the information related to the opponent character, and PA(t) indicates the action of the opponent character at time "t", while T indicates the progress level of a particular action, and D indicates the distance between the intelligent character and the opponent character. The number of outputs of a neural network is equal to the number of actions of an intelligent character.

For example, if the opponent character is performing step 3 of "b" attack at the distance 2, and its past actions were (a1, a2, a3), the input of the neural network at this moment becomes PA(t)=b, T=3, D=2, PA(t-1)=a3, PA(t-2)=a2, PA(t-3)=a1 The determined input value is applied to the neural network and the output value is calculated. For the neural network, the feedforward neural networks are used which calculate the output in the same way as the general feedforward neural networks. Also, the reinforcement learning method is used for learning by neural networks [7,8].

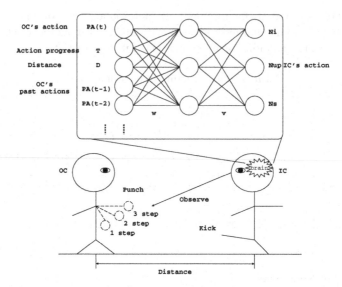

**Fig. 1.** The structure of the neural network

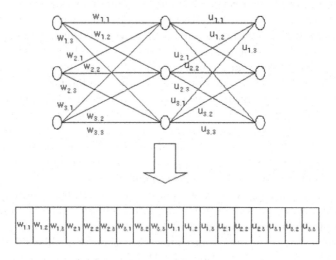

**Fig. 2.** The structure of a chromosome

## 2.3   Evolutionary Neural Networks

Past studies using neural networks mainly used the error backpropagation algorithm of multi-layer perceptiron to make intelligent characters learn [7,8]. However, it was pointed out that neural networks that use the error backpropagation algorithm have such shortcomings as falling in local minima and slow convergence speed [14]. To solve this problem, the methods to evolve the characters by expressing the weights of neural networks as chromosomes were researched so that the error backpropagation algorithm could be performed faster using the genetic algorithms. [7] proposed an evolutionary neural network to evolve intelligent characters expressed as neural networks. Genetic algorithms express the candidates of solutions to problems as chromosomes, usually as binary strings. However, binary strings are not appropriate for expression of neural networks. Therefore, as shown in Figure 2, the weight of links of a neural network was expressed as a gene, and chromosomes expressed the weights of all links in the form of one-dimensional array.

**Table 2.** Necessary time/Attack score/Effective range

| Action | Necessary time(clock) | Attack score | Effective range |
|---|---|---|---|
| idle | 1 | – | – |
| forward | 1 | – | – |
| backward | 1 | – | – |
| guard | 1 | – | – |
| down | 1 | – | – |
| jump | 1 | – | – |
| down-punch | 2 | 1 | 0~2 |
| up-punch | 4 | 2 | 0~2 |
| down-kick | 6 | 3 | 2~3 |
| up-kick | 8 | 4 | 2~3 |
| special | 10 | 5 | 3~5 |

# 3   Comparison of Performance

## 3.1   Fighting Action Games and Experimental Environment

To verify the three AI techniques described in Section 2 above, We developed a simple fighting action game. In this game, two characters attack and defend while moving in a one-dimensional game space, and acquire scores according to the result. The actions that the characters can make are as shown in Table 2, and all their actions are synchronized to the clock.

The characters can make three kinds of attack: punch attack, kick attack, and special attack that can be given from distance. The punch attack and kick attack is subdivided into down attack to the lower half of the opponent character and up attack to the upper half of the opponent character. Like the actual game, effective distance of each attack for getting the effect of attack and attack scores were set. Moreover, the down-punch and down-kick attacks cannot obtain a score if the other opponent makes up or guard, and up-punch and u-kick attacks cannot obtain a score if the opponent makes down or guard. The special attack acquires only 50 percent of the score if the opponent makes guard. This paper compares the performance of the three AI techniques by checking whether the intelligent character behaves appropriately by learning the action pattern of the opponent character in Table 3 in the fighting action game described above.

The performance of AI techniques was evaluated by the average score ratio of intelligent character against the opponent character after 10 experiments.

Table 3 Experimental action patterns and the optimal actions of intelligent characters against each pattern

**Table 3.** Experimental action patterns and the optimal actions of intelligent characters against each pattern

| No. | Action patterns of opponent characters | Initial distance |
|-----|----------------------------------------|------------------|
| A | forward, up-punch, backward, down-kick, backward, special, forward, up-kick | |
| B | forward, up-punch, backward, down-kick, forward, down-punch, backward, up-kick | 3 |
| C | backward, special, forward, down-kick ,backward, special, forward, up-kick | |

## 3.2   Experiments

To compare the results of the three AI techniques described above, we need to define criteria for fair evaluation of the three techniques. There may be many criteria such as the performance time of algorithm, but this paper adopted the number of matches with the opponent character to acquire the same score ratio for each intelligent character to which each AI technique was applied. The reason is because when AI techniques are applied to actual games, the number of learning is more important than the performance time which greatly depends on hardware.

**Genetic Algorithms.** Important parameters that must be considered when applying genetic algorithms are the size of population, the probability of crossover and mutation, and the crossover operator algorithm. In our experiment, the size of population was 30, the crossover probability 0.7, and the mutation probability 0.01. For crossover algorithm, the block crossover [10] was applied, and 10 was used for the number of block divisions which showed the best results from several prior experiments. For three action patterns in Table 3, the two cases where the intelligent character remembered one past action and two past actions of the opponent character were experimented, and shown in Figures 3 to 5. In the case where the character remembered two past actions, the size of chromosomes increases by the times of the number of actions (11) than the case where it remembers only one past action. Therefore, the evolution takes longer, but when the action pattern is long or complex, the character can make more appropriate response than the case where only one past action is remembered. However, as the number of generations for this experiment was limited to 1,000, the difference of learning performance between the two cases was not large.

**Neural Networks.** The neural network used in this paper has three layers as shown in Figure 1. There are four input nodes if one past action is remembered, five if two past actions are remembered, and the number of output nodes is 11 which is identical to the number of actions. For hidden nodes, 30 nodes which showed

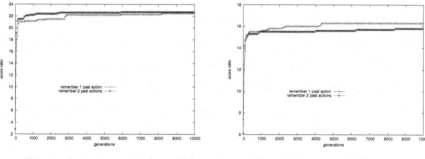

**Fig. 3.** Action pattern A          **Fig. 4.** Action pattern B

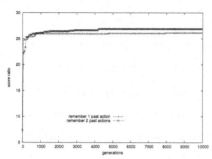

**Fig. 5.** Action pattern C

the best performance in several prior experiments were used. The representative learning ratio was set to 0.5. For the three action patterns, the two cases where the intelligent character remembered one past action and two past actions of the opponent character were experimented, and shown in Figures 6 to 8.

As a result of this experiment, the character learned responding action to the action of the opponent character much faster when it remembered two past actions than when it remembered only one past action, and the final score ratio was better. The reason that this result was different from that of genetic algorithms is because while the size of chromosomes becomes very large in order to memorize past actions, even if one input node is added, the complexity of neural networks does not increase.

**Evolutionary Neural Networks.** As described above, evolutionary neural network is a combination of genetic algorithm and neural network. Therefore, the same parameter values in section Genetic Algorithms and Neural Networks are applied to the main parameters of this experiment. In other words, for the neural network to express entities, the neural network that remembered two past actions which showed good results in the experiment in Neural Networks was used. For the parameters of genetic algorithm, the size of population was 30, the crossover probability was 0.7, and the mutation probability was set to 0.01. However, because the form of chromosome has changed, 5-point crossover operation was used instead of the prior crossover algorithm. For the three action

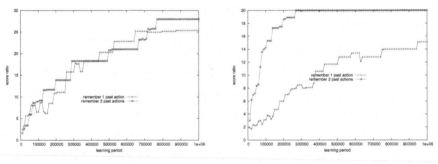

Fig. 6. Action pattern A                Fig. 7. Action pattern B

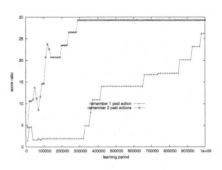

Fig. 8. Action pattern C

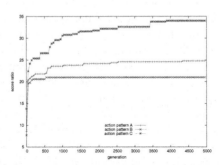

Fig. 9. Experimental result of evolutionary neural networks

patterns, the two cases where the intelligent character remembered one past action and two past actions of the opponent character were experimented, and shown in Figures 9.

Similar to the experiment in Genetic Algorithms, the score ratio rapidly increased initially, and then gradually converged.

## 3.3 Comparative Analysis of Results

As mentioned above, to compare the performance of three techniques, the experiment results were converted to the number of matches between the characters, which are shown in Figures 10 to 12. In the case of neural network, the learning time in the graph is the number of game matches. For genetic algorithm and evolutionary neural networks, the number of generations must be converted to the number of game matches. Further, to compare the performance during the early stage of learning, the initial section was enlarged and shown in Figures 13 to 15. In these figures, GA, NN, and Evolutionary NN indicate the results of each genetic algorithm, neural network, and evolutionary neural network, respectively.

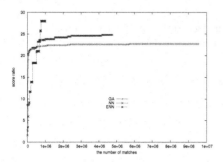

**Fig. 10.** Action pattern A

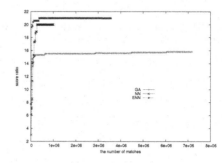

**Fig. 11.** Action pattern B

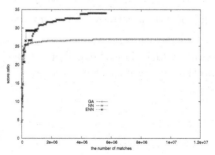

**Fig. 12.** Action pattern C

As shown in Figures 13 to 15, the final convergence score ratio is in the order of "neural network ≅ evolutionary neural network > genetic algorithm", and the convergence speed is in the order of "evolutionary neural network ≅ genetic algorithm > neural network". The reason that the final convergence ratio of genetic algorithm is lowest is because the chromosome size is considerably larger that that of the neural network or evolutionary neural network, it can attain a good score ratio only after evolution for a long time. Also, the reason that convergence speed of neural networks is the slowest is because due to the characteristics of reinforcement learning used as a learning method for neural network, the character needs experience about which action is good or bad in order to learn which actions are appropriate responses to action patterns. Furthermore, because the error backpropagation algorithm uses the gradient descent approach, the character needs to learn for a long time in order to output desired values. In conclusion,

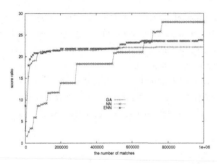

**Fig. 13.** Action pattern A - initial period

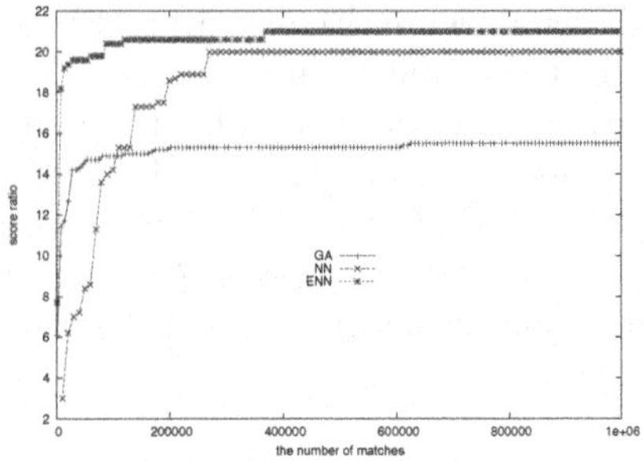

**Fig. 14.** Action pattern B - initial period

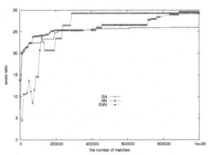

**Fig. 15.** Action pattern C - initial period

evolutionary neural network which showed excellent results in both the final convergence score ratio and the convergence score is most appropriate AI technique for fighting action games.

## 4    Conclusions

Recently there have been many studies on AI techniques for fighting action games. Studies using genetic algorithms evolved intelligent characters by including the distance between characters, the action step of the opponent character, and the action of the intelligent character for past actions in the chromosomes that express intelligent characters. Studies using neural networks used the action and step of the opponent character and the distance between characters as the input for neural networks, and the difference of scores resulting from the actions of two characters as the reinforcement value so as to make the intelligent characters learn whether or not their current action is appropriate. However, because neural networks that use the error backpropagation algorithm have such shortcomings as falling in local minima and slow convergence speed, methods to apply evolutionary neural networks were studied. These studies expressed the weight of links in a neural network as a gene, and evolved chromosomes by expressing the weights of all links of intelligent characters in the form of one-dimensional array. This study quantitatively compared the performance of these three AI techniques in the same game and experimental environments, and analyzed the results of experiments. The results of this experiment show that the final convergence score ratio is in the order of neural network ≅ evolutionary neural network > genetic algorithms, and the convergence speed is in the order of evolutionary neural network ≅ genetic algorithms > neural networks. In conclusion, evolutionary neural network which showed excellent results in both the final convergence score ratio and the convergence score is most appropriate AI technique for fighting action games.

# References

1. Fu, D., Houlette, R., Henke, S.: Putting AI In Entertainment: An AI Authoring Tool for Simulation and Games. IEEE Intelligent and Systems 17(4) (July/August 2002)
2. Johnson, D., Wiles, J.: Computer Games With Intelligence. In: IEEE International Fuzzy Systems Conference (2001)
3. De Loura, M.: Game Programming Gems 2. Charles River Media (2001)
4. Freisleben, B.: A Neural Network that Learns to Play Five-in-a-Row. In: 2nd New Zealand Two-Stream International Conference on Artificial Neural Networks and Expert Systems (1995)
5. Fogel, D.B.: Using Evolutionary Programming to Create Neural Networks that are Capable of Playing Tic-Tac-Toe. In: Intl. Joint Confrence Neural Networks, New York, pp. 875–880 (1993)
6. http://www.lionhead.com/bw2
7. Cho, B.H., Jung, S.H., Shim, K.H., Seong, Y.R., Oh, H.R.: Adaptation of intelligent characters to changes of game environments. In: Hao, Y., Liu, J., Wang, Y.-P., Cheung, Y.-m., Yin, H., Jiao, L., Ma, J., Jiao, Y.-C. (eds.) CIS 2005. LNCS (LNAI), vol. 3801, pp. 1064–1073. Springer, Heidelberg (2005)
8. Cho, B.H., Jung, S.H., Seong, Y.R., Oh, H.R.: Exploiting intelligence in fighting action games using neural networks. IEICE Transactions on Information and Systems E89-D(3), 1249–1256 (2006)
9. Cho, B.H., Jung, S.H., Shim, K.H., Seong, Y.R., Oh, H.R.: Reinforcement Learning of Intelligent Characters in Fighting Action Games. In: Harper, R., Rauterberg, M., Combetto, M. (eds.) ICEC 2006. LNCS, vol. 4161, pp. 310–313. Springer, Heidelberg (2006)
10. Lee, M.S., Cho, B.H., Jung, S.H., Seong, Y.R., Oh, H.R.: Implementation of Intelligent Characters adapting to Action Patterns of Opponent Characters. IEEK Transactions. 42(3(TE)), 32–38 (2005)
11. Bui, T.N., Moon, B.R.: On multi-dimensional encoding/crossover. In: International Conference on Genetic Algorithms, pp. 49–56 (1995)
12. Anderson, C., Jones, K., Ryan, J.: A two-dimensional genetic algorithm for the Ising problem. Complex system 5, 327–333 (1991)
13. Chin-Teng Lin, C.S.: George Lee. Prentice-Hall, Englewood Cliffs (1996)
14. Lippman, R.P.: An Introduction to Computing with Neural Nets. IEEE ASSP Magazine, 4–22 (April 1987)

# Theory to Practice: Generalized Minimum-Norm Perspective Shadow Maps for Anti-aliased Shadow Rendering in 3D Computer Games

Fan Zhang[1], Hanqiu Sun[1], Chong Zhao[1], and Lifeng Wang[2]

[1] Department of Computer Science and Engineering,
The Chinese University of Hong Kong, Shatin N.T., Hong Kong, China
{fzhang,hanqiu,czhao}@cse.cuhk.edu.hk
[2] Autodesk Software (China) Co., Ltd. (Shanghai Office),
399 Pu Dian Road, Shanghai Pudong District, Shanghai 200122, China
lifeng.wang@autodesk.com

**Abstract.** Shadow mapping has been extensively used for real-time shadow rendering in 3D computer games, though it suffers from the inherent aliasing problems due to its image-based nature. The aliasing errors in shadow mapping consist of perspective aliasing error and projection aliasing error. In this paper, we propose a novel shadow-map reparameterization to reduce perspective aliasing for varying viewer and/or light. This reparameterizing technique keeps the perspective aliasing distribution optimal in possible general cases. Our experiments have shown the enhanced shadow quality using our algorithm in dynamic scenes.

**Keywords:** Image-based rendering, shadow algorithms, computer games.

## 1 Introduction

Shadowing effects are very important for the realism of virtual scenes in 3D computer games, which significantly enhance players' perception of the surrounding environment with useful depth clues. For game developers, the reality that they are facing is that the commonly used shading models do not directly support the global illumination effects like shadows.

Shadow mapping[16] is one of the most popular dynamic shadowing techniques. This image-based approach doesn't require the knowledge of the scene's geometry, and requires only one extra rendering pass per light. Such generality and efficiency make shadow mapping extensively adopted in 3D games. There are two rendering passes involved in shadow mapping. In the first pass, the scene is rendered into the *shadow map* texture from the light's point of view. In the second pass, the scene is rendered from the eye's point of view. For each point being rendered, it is transformed into the light's coordinates again for depth comparison. If the corresponding depth value in shadow map is less than that of the transformed point, this point is shadowed.

When using shadow mapping, we need to handle aliasing problem which mainly resulted from insufficient shadow-map resolution (i.e. *under-sampling*).

L. Ma, R. Nakatsu, and M. Rauterberg (Eds.): ICEC 2007, LNCS 4740, pp. 66–78, 2007.

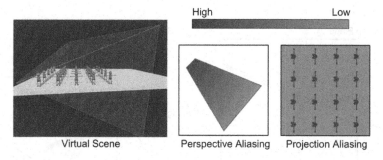

**Fig. 1.** Perspective aliasing v.s. projection aliasing. The blue frame in the virtual scene represents the view frustum.

Numerous approaches have been proposed to address this issue in different ways. Partitioning techniques[7][15][19][2][10][11] help the anti-aliasing in shadow mapping with multiple shadow maps, the performance cost is however increased due to extra rendering passes. Hybrid techniques[8][3][4][1] combine shadow mapping and *shadow volumes*[6] to achieve a better tradeoff of shadow quality and performance. For a thorough review of shadow rendering algorithms refer to [18].

The aliasing errors in shadow mapping are usually decomposed into *perspective aliasing errors* and *projection aliasing errors*[14], as visualized in Fig. 1. Projection aliasing depends on local geometry details such that reducing this kind of aliasing requires an expensive scene analysis at each frame. On the other hand, perspective aliasing comes from the foreshortening effect introduced by the perspective projection. Perspective aliasing is the only kind of aliasing that can be alleviated by warping the shadow plane using a perspective transform. This is based on the observation that the distribution of even-spaced texels on the warped shadow map plane better matches the distribution of even-spaced pixels on the screen. Hence, the sampling density at the light in the post-transformed space will better accommodate the requirements for the reconstruction of shadowed images (Fig. 2). This idea was first introduced in *perspective shadow maps* (PSMs)[14]. As pointed out by Wimmer et al[17], the optimal distribution of sampling points on the shadow map plane is a logarithmic function with respect to the depth value. However, this logarithmic reparameterization is not directly supported on current hardware because all input data are interpolated hyperbolically in the stage of rasterization[1]. For insightful analysis of perspective aliasing refer to [17][11].

This paper mainly addresses *perspective reparameterization* (PR) techniques that reparameterize the shadow map using a perspective transform as shown in Fig. 2. Perspective reparameterizations generate shadow maps in the post-perspective space of the warping frustum, to cancel out the foreshortening effect introduced by the view frustum. Since the perspective warping transformation enlarges the objects close to the viewer and shrinks the distant objects, perspective

---

[1] Strictly speaking, this reparameterization can be discretely approximated using multiple shadow maps[12]. However, the performance drop caused by extra rendering passes is not suited for complex scenes.

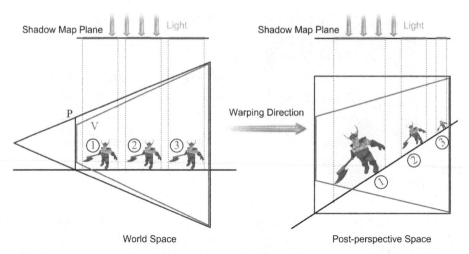

**Fig. 2.** A schematic illustration of perspective reparameterizations, where $V$ and $P$ stand for the eye's view frustum and perspective warping frustum respectively. Both $V$ and the light are transformed into $P$'s post-perspective space, in which the shadow map is generated.

aliasing is significantly reduced. Currently existing PRs[14][9][17][13][5][20] exploit two major factors: the near-plane distance of the warping frustum and the warping direction. The essential difference among perspective reparameterizations is the selection of the first factor, because the near plane distance of the warping frustum determines how strong the warping effect is. On the other hand, the selection of the second factor strongly influences the implementation complexity. With an inappropriate warping direction, the frequently changed types of lights after applying the perspective transform may cause mapping singularities. A smart choice of this factor is proposed in *light space perspective shadow maps* (LiSPSMs)[17], which use a warping direction in parallel with the shadow plane to avoid producing mapping singularities. It greatly simplifies the implementation and analysis of perspective reparameterizations.

In this paper, we propose the *generalized minimum-norm perspective reparameterization* (GMNPR) based on the generalized representation of aliasing errors proposed by Zhang et al.[20]. Our algorithm can be regarded as a generalization of LiSPSMs in non-ideal cases where the angle between the light and view directions are not orthogonal. A few advantages offered by our algorithm include:

- In comparison with most of prior reparameterizations in which the optimal aliasing distribution is achieved only in the ideal case, GMNPR keeps the aliasing distribution optimal in possible general cases. Such direction-invariant feature (partially) preserves the optimized shadow quality for dynamic scenes.
- GMNPR inherits the flexibility of LiSPSMs. The warping directions in both two methods are the same. We thus don't need special treatments such as

the "inverse perspective matrix" [9] for the mapping singularity problem in the post-perspective space.

The remainder of the paper is organized as follows: Section 2 briefly reviews the theory of perspective aliasing in shadow mapping. Section 3 derives our GM-NPR in detail. Section 4 presents the experimental results. Finally, the conclusion and further work go to Section 5.

## 2    Generalized Representation of Aliasing Errors

We first briefly review the aliasing problem in shadow mapping for the overhead light[14][17][11]. In Fig. 3, the light beams through a texel with the size $ds$ (in the $z$ direction) fall on a surface with the length $dz$ in world space. Here, the local parameterization of the shadow map $s(z)$ assumes that the shadow map is accurately focused on the view frustum and no resolution is wasted on invisible parts of the scene. The size of view beams $dp$ on the normalized screen projected from the surface is $dy/z\tan\phi$, where $2\phi$ is the field-of-view of the view frustum. $\alpha$ and $\beta$ denote the angles between the surface normal and vector to the screen and shadow map plane respectively.

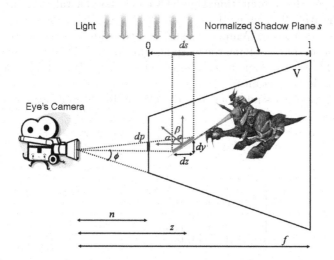

**Fig. 3.** Shadow map aliasing errors

By restricting the small surface on the $z$ direction, we have $dy \approx dz\cos\alpha/\cos\beta$. The aliasing error $\mathbf{E}$ for the small surface is then defined as

$$\mathbf{E} = \frac{dp}{ds} = \frac{1}{\tan\phi}\frac{dz}{z\,ds} \times \frac{\cos\alpha}{\cos\beta} \triangleq \mathbf{F} \times \frac{\cos\alpha}{\cos\beta} \tag{1}$$

The above shadow map aliasing consists of *perspective aliasing* $dz/zds$ and *projection aliasing* $\cos\alpha/\cos\beta$. Note that $\phi$ is a constant once given the view

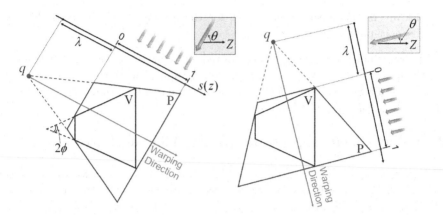

**Fig. 4.** The computational model. Left: $\phi \leq \theta \leq \pi/2$. Right: $0 \leq \theta \leq \phi$.

matrix. As we mentioned in the introduction, PRs focus on the reduction of perspective aliasing, i.e. reparameterizing $\mathbf{F}$.

For arbitrary lighting directions, Zhang et al.[20] derive a generalized representation of aliasing errors $\mathbf{F}$ for directional lights, which is adopted in this paper. Fig. 4 shows the computational model used by this generalized representation (all notations are self-explained), in which the warping frustum is constructed in the light space defined by Wimmer et al.[17]. The shadow map parameterization $s = s(z)$ is induced by applying the warping transform $P$. Note that we only need to consider $0 \leq \theta \leq \pi/2$ due to symmetry, where $\theta$ stands for the angle between the light and view directions.

With appropriate assumptions (e.g. directional lights and warping direction), $\mathbf{F}$ can be represented as

$$\mathbf{F}(\lambda, \theta, z) = \psi(\lambda, \theta) \frac{(z + \varphi(\lambda, \theta))^2}{z} \tag{2}$$

where,

$$\psi(\lambda, \theta) = \begin{cases} \dfrac{1}{\tan\phi} \dfrac{1}{\left(f - n + (f+n)\frac{\tan\phi}{\tan\theta}\right)\lambda(\lambda+1)} & \theta \in [\phi, \frac{\pi}{2}] \\[3ex] \dfrac{1}{\tan\phi} \dfrac{1}{2f\lambda(\lambda+1)} \dfrac{\tan\theta}{\tan\phi} & \theta \in [0, \phi] \end{cases}$$

$$\varphi(\lambda, \theta) = \begin{cases} \left(f - n + (f+n)\frac{\tan\phi}{\tan\theta}\right)\lambda + n\frac{\tan\phi}{\tan\theta} - n & \theta \in [\phi, \frac{\pi}{2}] \\[3ex] f(2\lambda + 1)\frac{\tan\phi}{\tan\theta} - f & \theta \in [0, \phi] \end{cases}$$

With the computational model shown in Fig. 4, $\mathbf{F}(\lambda, \theta, z)$ gives us a generalized representation of aliasing errors for arbitrary $\theta$ values in variant reparameterizations, in which the only free parameter $\lambda$ can be adjusted to produce appropriate warping effects according to specific requirements. For clarity, the detailed derivations for the above equations are ignored here. Refer to the original paper for more details.

## 3    The Algorithm

Because the perspective warping effect decreases as the light direction goes to parallel with the view direction, $\lambda$ should be *direction-adaptive* to satisfy the application-specific constraint as $\theta$ changes. With the representation expressed by Eq. (2), users are capable of designing the direction-adaptive $\lambda(\theta)$ to produce the expected warping strength in the general case. Although $\lambda_{\text{LiSPSM}}$ also takes into account $\theta$, as we explain later, it actually equalizes the aliasing distribution only in the ideal case. Based on the observations above, we proposed the *generalized minimum-norm perspective reparameterization* (GMNPR)[2] to satisfy the following two requirements,

- keep the optimal aliasing distribution in possible general cases.
- converge to standard shadow maps as the light direction goes to parallel with the view direction.

There's nearly no difference for implementing and applying GMNPR in comparison with LiSPSMs, except for the $\lambda$ selection in the warping frustum, to control the strength of the warping effect. In the following, we thus focus on deriving appropriate $\lambda$ values to produce the robust aliasing distribution for dynamic scenes.

In mathematical sense, we can define variant norms. Like LiSPSMs, GMNPR is designed to minimize the $\mathbf{L}^\infty$-norm of errors. Once given $\lambda$ and $\theta$, Eq. (2) shows that $\mathbf{F}(z)$ has a single positive local extremum (a minimum) at the location $z = n(1 - \frac{\tan\phi}{\tan\theta})(f - n + (f + n)\frac{\tan\phi}{\tan\theta})^{-1}$. Therefore, the maximum $\mathbf{L}^\infty(\mathbf{F})$ is achieved at the boundaries of the depth range. Let $\mathbf{L}^\infty_{\max}(\mathbf{F})$ be the maximum $\mathbf{L}^\infty(\mathbf{F})$ within $[n, f]$. Minimizing $\mathbf{L}^\infty_{\max}(\mathbf{F})$ requires that the errors at near and far planes are equal, or

$$\mathbf{F}(\lambda, \theta, n) = \mathbf{F}(\lambda, \theta, f). \tag{3}$$

The above maxima can be directly calculated from Eq. (2) as follows,

- **Case 1:** if $\phi \leq \theta \leq \pi/2$,

$$\mathbf{F}(\lambda, \theta, n) = \frac{\left(f - n + (f + n)\frac{\tan\phi}{\tan\theta}\right)}{n\tan\phi} \frac{(\lambda + \mu)^2}{\lambda(\lambda + 1)}$$

$$\mathbf{F}(\lambda, \theta, f) = \frac{\left(f - n + (f + n)\frac{\tan\phi}{\tan\theta}\right)}{f\tan\phi} \frac{(\lambda + \nu)^2}{\lambda(\lambda + 1)}$$

$$\mu = \frac{n}{(f - n)\frac{\tan\theta}{\tan\phi} + f + n} \qquad \nu = 1 - \frac{f}{(f - n)\frac{\tan\theta}{\tan\phi} + f + n}$$

- **Case 2:** if $0 \leq \theta \leq \phi$,

$$\mathbf{F}(\lambda, \theta, n) = \frac{2f}{n\tan\theta} \frac{(\lambda + \mu)^2}{\lambda(\lambda + 1)} \qquad \mathbf{F}(\lambda, \theta, f) = \frac{2}{\tan\theta} \frac{(\lambda + \nu)^2}{\lambda(\lambda + 1)}$$

$$\mu = \frac{1}{2} - \frac{f - n}{2f} \frac{\tan\theta}{\tan\phi} \qquad \nu = \frac{1}{2}$$

---

[2] To keep consistent with the naming convention in [20], we use the term "perspective reparameterization" instead of "perspective shadow maps" in this paper. Furthermore, the two terms are usually exchangeable in this research line.

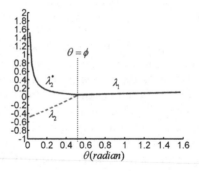

**Fig. 5.** Adjustment of the $\lambda_{\mathbf{GMNPR}}$ selection in practice

Leading the above results to Eq. (3) gives the optimal $\lambda$ selection,

$$\lambda = \frac{\nu - \mu}{\sqrt{f/n} - 1} - \mu = \begin{cases} \lambda_1(\theta) = \frac{(n+\sqrt{fn})-n\frac{\tan\phi}{\tan\theta}}{f-n+(f+n)\frac{\tan\phi}{\tan\theta}} & \theta \in [\phi, \frac{\pi}{2}] \\ \\ \lambda_2(\theta) = \frac{f+\sqrt{fn}}{2f}\frac{\tan\theta}{\tan\phi} - \frac{1}{2} & \theta \in [0, \phi] \end{cases} \tag{4}$$

Now let's consider the critical angle $\theta = \phi$. Fig. 5 plots $\lambda$ against $\theta$. We can see that $\lambda$ decreases slowly as $\theta$ goes from $\pi/2$ to $\phi$, thus the perspective warping effect becomes stronger. At the singularity $\theta = \phi$, $\lambda$ takes a nose-dive and rapidly plunges towards 0, which reaches well for $\lambda > 0$. But $\lambda = 0$ is obviously disastrous, as it practically concentrates the whole shadow map into one texel. Due to the fact that the perspective projection is a hyperbolic mapping, the depth region $[\lambda \leq z \leq 2\lambda]$ occupies about half of the depth range $[0 \leq s \leq \sim 0.5]$ in the post-perspective space. In practice, it's never a good idea to let $\lambda$ be too small in any perspective reparameterization, as this introduces strong warping such that the shadow-map texels are usually biased to few pixels in the near plane. Hence, the rapid decrease to zero for $\lambda$ makes Eq. (4) hard to be used in practice when $\theta < \phi$. To avoid this problem, we have to replace $\lambda_2$ by a positive function $\lambda_2^*$ which should satisfy two criteria,

- smooth transition of shadow qualities at $\theta = \phi$.
  Note the singularity at $\theta = \phi$ may result in the discontinuous transition of shadow qualities in practice. To avoid this problem, the continuous $\lambda$ transition at $\theta = \phi$ should be satisfied.

$$\lambda_2^*(\phi) = \lambda_1(\phi) \tag{5}$$

- convergence to SSM as $\theta$ goes to 0.
  When $\theta < \phi$, from Fig. 4, the warping frustum bounds two lines on the far plane of the view frustum. The available depth range distorted by the warping frustum is significantly narrowed. In such cases, perspective reparameterizations should weaken the warping strength in order to avoid the unbalanced distribution of shadow details on the screen. In particular, when $\theta = 0$, all perspective reparameteirzations converge to standard shadow maps.

$$\lim_{\theta \to 0} \lambda_2^*(\theta) = \infty \tag{6}$$

Many candidates can fulfill Eqs. (5) and (6). In our experiments, $\lambda_2^*$ is chosen to be

$$\lambda_2^*(\theta) = \lambda_1(\phi)/\tan(\frac{\theta}{4\phi}\pi) = \frac{\sqrt{fn}}{2f} \frac{1}{\tan(\frac{\theta}{4\phi}\pi)}. \tag{7}$$

Substituting Eq. (7) into Eq. (4) gives our final $\lambda_{\mathbf{GMNPR}}$ selection as follows,

$$\lambda_{\mathbf{GMNPR}} = \begin{cases} \lambda_{\mathbf{GMNPR}}^{(1)}(\theta) = \lambda_1(\theta) = \frac{n+\sqrt{fn}-n\frac{\tan\phi}{\tan\theta}}{f-n+(f+n)\frac{\tan\phi}{\tan\theta}} & \theta \in [\phi, \frac{\pi}{2}] \\ \\ \lambda_{\mathbf{GMNPR}}^{(2)}(\theta) = \lambda_2^*(\theta) = \frac{\sqrt{fn}}{2f}\frac{1}{\tan(\frac{\theta}{4\phi}\pi)} & \theta \in [0, \phi] \end{cases} \tag{8}$$

Eq. (8) gives us a direction-adaptive $\lambda$ selection for *minimum-norm* aliasing distribution, which essentially extends LiSPSMs to general cases. Note that all $\lambda$ values discussed in this paper are for the warping frustum $P$ with a normalized depth range, namely $P_f - P_n = 1$, where $P_f$ and $P_n$ represent $P$'s near-plane and far-plane values respectively. In LiSPSMs, the near-plane distance of the warping frustum $P_n$ in general cases is approximated as

$$P_n = \frac{n + \sqrt{fn}}{\sin \theta}$$

By normalizing the depth range of the warping frustum, we have

$$\lambda_{\mathbf{LiSPSM}}(\theta) = \frac{P_n}{P_f - P_n} = \begin{cases} \frac{n+\sqrt{fn}}{\sin\theta} \frac{1}{(n\frac{\tan\phi}{\tan\theta}+f-n+f\frac{\tan\phi}{\tan\theta})\sin\theta} & \theta \in [\phi, \frac{\pi}{2}] \\ \\ \frac{n+\sqrt{fn}}{\sin\theta} \frac{1}{2f\tan\phi\cos\theta} & \theta \in [0, \phi] \end{cases} \tag{9}$$

Refer to [20] for the derivation of $P_f - P_n$. Eq. (4) tells us that the above approximation is not optimal in non-ideal cases (at least for $\theta > \phi$). The $\lambda$ selection in LiSPSM makes $\mathbf{F}$ optimal only in the ideal case where $\theta = \pi/2$.

Other possible generalized PRs also can be derived from Eq. (2), such as the *generalized linear perspective reparamterization* (GLPR)[20] which requires $\mathbf{F}(z) \sim z$ for given $\lambda$ and $\theta$ values, where $\sim$ stands for the linear dependency. This reparameterization essentially extends PSMs to non-ideal cases. The main problem of GLPR is that the warping strength might be over-strong in some cases. We compare our GMNPR with GLPR in Section 4.

### Analysis of Aliasing Distribution

Fig. 6 plots the aliasing distributions in LiSPSM (top row) and GMNPR (bottom row) for the configuration $n = 1$, $f = 100$ and $\phi = \pi/6$. Due to the critical angle $\theta = \phi$ in Eq. (2), we compare them in the following two aspects.

- non-degenerate cases $\theta > \phi$.
  The aliasing distribution in GMNPR, $\mathbf{F}_{\mathbf{GMNPR}}$, is direction-invariant (in terms of minimum-norm) as the $\theta$ value changes. The aliasing errors at boundaries of the depth range remain equal for all possible $\theta$ values, while

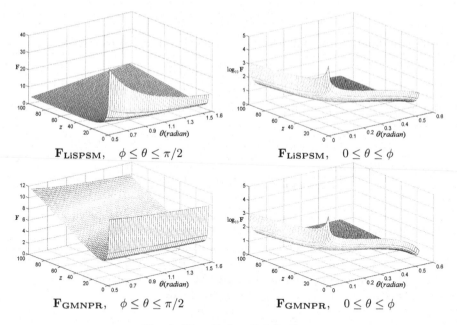

**Fig. 6.** The aliasing distributions

$\mathbf{F_{LiSPSM}}$ fluctuates with the varying of $\theta$. As $\theta$ decreases, the aliasing errors at near regions in LiSPSM increase, but the shape of $\mathbf{F_{GMNPR}}$ keeps unchanged for varying $\theta$ values. Such direction-invariant feature is very useful for shadow rendering in dynamic scenes, because the consistent transition of shadow quality should be preserved as possible during the user's navigation/interaction.

- degenerate cases $\theta \leq \phi$.

  The values of both $\mathbf{F_{LiSPSM}}$ and $\mathbf{F_{GMNPR}}$ become extremely large for small $\theta$ values. For better illustration, a $log_{10}$ scale is used in Fig. 6 now. As $\theta$ goes from $\phi$ to 0, all PRs can not make $\mathbf{F}$ optimal and converge to SSMs. The effectiveness of the perspective warping dramatically decreases such that no PR has any special advantage over others. This problem is well known as the *dueling frusta* case in which the anti-aliasing (using single shadow map with given resolution) still remains unsolved in computer graphics.

## 4   Results

We have developed our GMNPR using Microsoft DirectX SDK 9.0. We run the shadow rendering tests using 800*600 image resolution, and the performance is measured by an Intel Pentium 4 2.8GHz CPU with 1G RAM, a NVidia GeForce 6800Ultra GPU with 256M video memory. In addition, we have compared our algorithm with SSM, LiSPSM and GLPR[20]. Two virtual scenes are composed and tested in our experiments, as shown in Fig. 7. In our tests, a dynamic directional

**Fig. 7.** Testing scenes: Robots (11K) and Ceiling (23K)

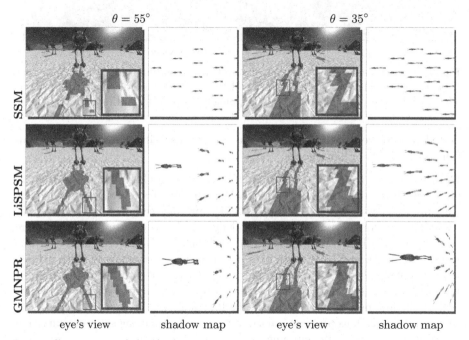

**Fig. 8.** Comparison of the shadow quality and associated shadow maps. The red rectangles zoom in the local shadow details.

lighting source and field of view $60°$ are set up. $n = 1m, f = 800m, \phi = \pi/6$ are configured for all of tests. All algorithms achieve real-time performance in our experiments.

**Robots:** to verify the theoretical results shown in Fig. 6, we compare different algorithms in this complex scene with a large number of triangles. Fig. 8 shows two views at $\theta = 55°$ and $35°$. As we can see, SSM produces the worst shadow quality for near objects. Since GMNPR preserves the optimal aliasing distribution in most general cases, the shadow quality in GMNPR is better than that in LiSPSM. The associated shadow maps are listed as well. As we can see, the shadow maps in

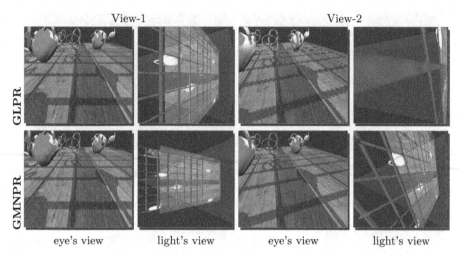

**Fig. 9.** Comparison of the shadow quality and corresponding light's views. Note that the extremely stretched shadow details in GLPR due to the over-strong warping effect. The optimization technique "unit cube clipping"[9] is used for both algorithms.

GMNPR preserves that near regions consume the majority of shadow map resolution as the viewer or light moves.

**Ceiling:** we use this scene to compare GMNPR with GLPR. Fig. 9 shows two views and corresponding light's views, where the blue frame represents the view frustum. In View-1, both GLPR and GMNPR produce satisfactory shadow quality at near regions. From the associated light's views, we can see the warping strength in GLPR is stronger than that in GMNPR. However, the over-strong warping strength in GLPR sometimes may cause the extremely unbalanced distribution of shadow details. When the viewer moves closer to the object, $\lambda_{\mathbf{GLPR}}$ becomes too small such that the warped object only occupies a very small portion of shadow map in practice. The shadow quality thus sharply decreases as shown in View-2. This problem is hard to be solved even using some optimization techniques like "unit cube clipping"[9].

## 5   Conclusion

In this paper, we have proposed the *generalized minimum-norm perspective reparameterization* (GMNPR) to enhance the shadow rendering in 3D computer games. Our algorithm preserves the optimal aliasing distribution in possible general cases. Such direction-invariant feature is very important for the consistent transition of shadow quality during user's interaction with dynamic scenes. Our experimental results have shown the improved shadow quality using our algorithm.

As the computational model used in this paper (Fig. 4) assumes that the warping direction is parallel to the shadow plane and lights are directional, we will further our work to derive other direction-adaptive reparameterizations using arbitrary warping direction, and extend our analysis to other types of lights. It would be interesting to take into account the errors in the $x$ direction [11] for better understanding of perspective reparameterizations.

## Acknowledgements

This work was supported by RGC research grant (NO. 415806). The Hugo robot model used in Fig. 1 was created by Laurence Boissieux at INRIA. The free 3D models used in our experiments are downloaded from *www.planetquake.com* and *www.3dcafe.com*.

## References

1. Aila, T., Akenine-Möller, T.: A hierarchical shadow volume algorithm. In: Proc. of Graphics Hardware 2004, pp. 15–23. Eurographics Association (2004)
2. Arvo, J.: Tiled shadow maps. In: Proc. of Computer Graphics International 2004, pp. 240–247. IEEE Computer Society Press, Los Alamitos (2004)
3. Arvo, J., Aila, T.: Optimized shadow mapping using the stencil buffer. Journal of Graphics Tools 8(3), 23–32 (2004)
4. Chan, E., Durand, F.: An efficient hybrid shadow rendering algorithm. In: Proc. of the Eurographics Symposium on Rendering 2004, pp. 185–195. Eurographics Association (2004)
5. Chong, H.Y., Gortler, S.J.: A lixel for every pixel. In: Proc. of the Eurographics Symposium on Rendering 2004, pp. 167–172. Eurographics Association (2004)
6. Crow, F.C.: Shadow algorithms for computer graphics. In: Proc. of SIGGRAPH '77, pp. 242–248. ACM Press, New York (1977)
7. Fernando, R., Fernandez, S., Bala, K., Greenberg, D.P.: Adaptive shadow maps. In: Proc. of SIGGRAPH '01, pp. 387–390. ACM, New York (2001)
8. Govindaraju, N.K., Lloyd, B., Yoon, S.-E., Sud, A., Manocha, D.: Interactive shadow generation in complex environments. ACM Trans. Graph 22(3), 501–510 (2003)
9. Kozlov, S.: Perspective shadow maps: care and feeding. In: GPU Gems, Addison–Wesley, Reading (2004)
10. Lefohn, A.E., Sengupta, S., Kniss, J., Strzodka, R., Owens, J.D.: Glift: Generic, efficient, random-access gpu data structures. ACM Trans. Graph 25(1), 60–99 (2006)
11. Lloyd, B., Tuft, D., Yoon, S., Manocha, D.: Warping and partitioning for low error shadow maps. In: Proc. of the Eurographics Symposium on Rendering 2006, pp. 215–226. Eurographics Association (2006)
12. Lloyd, B., Govindaraju, N.K., Tuft, D., Molnar, S., Manocha, D.: Practical logarithmic shadow maps. In: SIGGRAPH '06 Sketches, p. 103. ACM, New York (2006)
13. Martin, T., Tan, T.-S.: Anti-aliasing and continuity with trapezoidal shadow maps. In: Proc. of the Eurographics Symposium on Rendering 2004, pp. 153–160. Eurographics Association (2004)
14. Stamminger, M., Drettakis, G.: Perspective shadow maps. In: Proc. of SIGGRAPH '02, pp. 557–562. ACM Press, New York (2002)

15. Tadamura, K., Qin, X., Jiao, G., Nakamae, E.: Rendering optimal solar shadows with plural sunlight depth buffers. The Visual Computer 17(2), 76–90 (2001)
16. Williams, L.: Casting curved shadows on curved surfaces. In: Proc. of SIGGRAPH '78, pp. 270–274. ACM Press, New York (1978)
17. Wimmer, M., Scherzer, D., Purgathofer, W.: Light space perspective shadow maps. In: Proc. of the Eurographics Symposium on Rendering 2004, pp. 557–562. Eurographics Association (2004)
18. Woo, A., Poulin, P., Fournier, A.: A survey of shadow algorithms. IEEE Comput. Graph. Appl. 10(6), 13–32 (1990)
19. Zhang, F., Sun, H., Xu, L., Lun, L.K.: Parallel-split shadow maps for large-scale virtual environments. In: Proc. of the 2006 ACM international conference on Virtual reality continuum and its applications, pp. 311–318. ACM Press, New York (2006)
20. Zhang, F., Xu, L., Tao, C., Sun, H.: Generalized linear perspective shadow map reparameterization. In: Proc. of the 2006 ACM international conference on Virtual reality continuum and its applications, pp. 339–342. ACM Press, New York (2006)

# Kansei Games: Entertaining Emotions

Ben Salem

Department of Industrial Design, Eindhoven University of Technology, The Netherlands
also, School of Science and Technology, Kansai Gakuin University, Japan
mail@bsalem.info

**Abstract.** We introduce and describe the concept of Kansei Game as the implementation of Kansei Mediated Entertainment. In our current approach we translate the classical Zen story of ten Ox herding pictures into a game. We describe the features of such a game and we propose some guidelines for its design and development.

**Keywords:** Games, Kansei mediation, entertainment, Ox Herding, Zen.

## 1 Introduction

Essentially Kansei Games are a new concept of games that focus on delivering a constructive positive experience to the game player. We wish to do this by addressing the player needs, requirements and desires. Salem and Rauterberg [1] propose a Needs Requirements and Desires (NRD) model where the self is at the centre, and all needs requirements and desires radiate from it. It is an egocentric, egoistic and hedonistic model. In which, needs relates to the *essentials*, requirements to the *necessary* and desires to the *optional*. While playing a game, it is possible to assess its usage in terms of its effect on the player's NRD. We believe that the fulfillment of the NRD would yield a positive game experience. We would like to propose an approach that addresses user's NRD and results in enrichment, positive affect and inner balance for the user.

## 2 What Is Kansei

Originally, Kansei engineering was defined as the translating of a consumer feelings and image of a product into some of the design elements used to create that product [2]. Kansei Engineering is about addressing user's "real needs" through ergonomic technology that addresses feelings and sensations [3]. Furthermore it was defined as a consumer oriented technology for the creation of new products. It was subdivided into forwards and hybrid Kansei Engineering [4], [5]. In the first instance, subjective information from consumers is fed into the design process. In the second instance there is also a flow of information from the design process towards the consumer. Whereby design ideas and directions are tested and assessed by the consumers. Kansei Design is also about consumer subjective impressions [6]. It is an affective design approach that involves a mapping process between the consumer's affective needs and the designer's perceptual design elements. Kansei design addresses the optimisation of the affective

L. Ma, R. Nakatsu, and M. Rauterberg (Eds.): ICEC 2007, LNCS 4740, pp. 79–84, 2007.

description of a product. In contrast to addressing the emotional needs of a product user. In this perspective, Khalid [7] propose Hedonomics as the study of emotions in the valuation of products and Citarasa Engineering (CE) as engineering that addresses consumer emotional intent and aspirations. In a sense, CE is about designing products that will fulfil the consumer emotional needs. We aspire to go further and deal with the aesthetic of the user experience through the fulfilment of his/her objective (usability, ergonomics) and subjective (affect, experience) needs, requirements and desires.

Another approach into understanding Kansei Design is to look at the values it deals with. Kansei values are being subjective, multivocal and ambiguous [8]. They are subjective in that the information belongs to the thinking person rather than the object of thoughts. The values are multivocal in that they can have different meaning of equal probability and validity. They are ambiguous because they have several meanings and interpretations.

How could Kansei value and Design be relevant to the design of a game? Rather than move towards a mathematical modelling of Kansei Engineering, see for example [6], we would like to move towards a set of design rules and guidelines. We advocate this approach, because we believe that ultimately the design of an Kansei Game should be considered an end rather than a mean. A Kansei Game should deliver an experience that is effective, efficient and satisfactory. These are similar to the guidelines of ISO 9241 [9]. However, in that standard effectiveness is described as accuracy and completeness, efficiency relates to the expenditure of resources and satisfaction to the freedom from discomfort and the attitude towards usage. In our case we expend these definitions. Effectiveness relates to how good the system is at causing/achieving the desired results. Efficiency is about how minimal are the resources to achieve the desired results. As for user satisfaction relates to the user experience and its aesthetics (see [10]).

## 2.1  The Concept of Kansei Game

We propose a new concept of games that is based on Kansei. As such, a Kansei Game cannot be a game with clear objectives such as goals to reach or races to win. It has to have game mechanics that translate Kansei values into game rules and play. To help us in this direction we refer to popular stories of Zen culture such as the Ox Herding pictures that help explain how to reach Satori (a form of enlightenment). Furthermore, we have to investigate the selection of media and modalities that should be used within a Kansei Game to deliver an enriching user experience. Fig. 1, list some of the various media, modalities that are used for communication between humans. These are text, discourse, sound for explicit media. Voice tone, appearance, distance for implicit media. Body language, eye gaze, cultural references and wording of sentences for Kansei media.

Combined, explicit, implicit and Kansei media, form a rich channel of communication that should be implemented in Kansei Games as far as possible. This is even more important, because as human we are particularly sensitive to combination of media when building our perception. Human perception is a combination of sensory (what our senses tell us), synesthetic (the combination of senses), autonomic (what our guts tell us), motor (the quality of body movements) and cognitive (what our mind tells us) information.

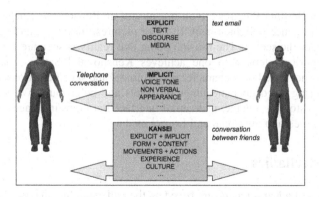

**Fig. 1.** Explicit, Implicit and Kansei Communication and Interface

Therefore a Kansei Game will rely on a combination of media, modalities and Kansei communication to deliver a rich positive user experience. However how to select the right combination of media, modalities and Kansei communication is an issue that need addressing during the development of the first proposed game.

## 3  Narrative

For the first implementation of a Kansei Game, we propose the story of the Ox Herding as a narrative for the game [11]. It is a well documented story that helps explain enlightenment and Satori.

This short story has ten steps:

1. Seeking the ox: Starting the journey, while being unaware that a dualist approach cannot lead to the understanding of the true nature of mind. There should not be a mind/body separation.
2. Seeing the ox tracks: Although the ox is still not seen, the tracks confirm its existence, and lead to way to it. Through self-discipline and training, it is possible to rediscover one's true self.
3. Seeing the Ox: The path to enlightenment has been seen. It is about finding one's true self, through trial and errors.
4. Catching the Ox: Although the ox has been seen, the difficulty now is to catch it.
5. Herding the Ox: Kencho is finally obtained after a long period of disciplinary training. However, the Kencho attained is only a stepping stone towards Satori.
6. Coming Home on the Ox Back: The efforts paid off. The ox and the herder move together effortlessly. This shows the state in which one completely finds one's true self, that is, the state in which one obtains Satori.
7. Ox is forgotten: The ox and the herder become one. Dualism has been overcome and the herder has no worldly attachments any more.
8. Both Ox and self-forgotten: The separation of reality from the mind is gone. Enlightenment is experienced and the mind has escaped.
9. Returning to the source: Back to square one. The world carries on as always.
10. Returning to help others: The enlightened has renounced all to selflessly help others.

The ten Ox Herding Pictures are an imagery of an illusion to be negated before a seeker can experience enlightenment. In these pictures, the ox symbolises the mind, while the herder the seeker. The illusion being that reality is separate from the mind. These metaphorical steps help one achieves Kensho and Satori. The story is a metaphor; it is not based on a character performing some specific actions. The story is about discovering the deeper meanings of events and behaviours. We would like to implement this story as a game made up of interface iterations/interface choreography based on multimedia, multimodal and Kansei media.

## 4   Game Mechanics

The mechanics of a Kansei game are based on the understanding that this is not a game with an end goal but a software toy. In similar fashion to SimCity and ATrainHX. The objectives are not competitive and the game is a form of interactive story. In our proposal the game is about relaxing and reaching inner balance, peace of mind and calmness. It is not about achieving a particular goal in terms of user actions and behaviour within the game. It is about nurturing a certain attitude and mood of quietness, calmness and inner balance. This implies a self-awareness and a selfcontrol from the user.

The mechanics proposed are those of a role-playing game, whereby the user is identified as the Ox-herder. But instead of the user having to play the role (behaviour) of the Ox-herder as if it were a fictional character, s/he has to control her/his attitude, mood and arousal levels (inner state) as if they were those for Ox-herder. In other words, with Kansei games it is not about adopting the behaviour of a fictional character but about transferring to the Ox-herder one's inner state. It is a transfer of inner state rather than a transfer of behaviour.

Furthermore, in line with role-playing games, the user will have to follow a story (in our case the 10 Ox-Herding pictures story). Within the framework of the story the players can improvise freely, however, the outcome and direction of the game will depend on their inner state rather than their actions.

## 5   Game Play

In essence the gameplay applicable to Kansei Games is that of a combination of adventure games and role-playing games. Both gameplays are very similar with the first focusing more on puzzle solving, and interaction with the game character (Oxherder).

In our case focusing on how to herd the Ox. In order to progress in the game narrative, the player has to help the character, the Ox-herder, achieve his aims, and thus catch and domesticate the Ox. Overall the game adventure can be treated as a finite state machine with transition conditions mainly related to the player inner state, emotions and moods. The game emphasis on the player's interpretation of the scenery and of the game mechanics make Kansei Games Puzzle adventures with plots that are not necessarily understood first time. Because the games are played from a first person perspective, the user is encouraged to decipher the game mechanics as soon as possible, and to map her/his actions and state to the game character attributes.

There are many attributes to the Ox-herder that are used as part of the story We call these attributes original ones. A second set of attributes of the Ox-herder are a result of the transfer of the player inner state, we call these acquired ones.

| Domain | Original | Acquired |
|---|---|---|
| Stamina | Necessary level to wander around the scenery | Increases with lower arousal levels as related to heart rate and blood pressure. |
| Dexterity | Close to none | Increases with better inner balance as related to body posture, and movements. |
| Effectiveness | Slow movement pace and irregular walking stride. | Increases with calmness as related to galvanic skin conductance. |

Within the game we propose three different reward systems for the player. Namely, level, skills and experience. The level reward is essentially about moving from one level of the game to the next. In this present context from one of the 10 Ox-Herder pictures to the next. The skills reward is linked to the improvement of the user inner state and is translated into a better (from the game perspective) set of attributes and resources of the Ox-herder. Finally the experience reward is related to the improvement of the positive experience the player is having, through a deeper and wider self-awareness and self control.

The game quest is about herding the Ox. It is a non-linear gameplay, in the sense that the game progresses regardless of the player either progressing towards herding the Ox or getting further away from achieving this. Furthermore, the game can be perceived as being about herding the Ox, reaching a better inner-balance, achieving a wider self-awareness or a deeper self-control, or any combination thereof.

The only one encounter there is in the game is that of crossing first the path of the Ox shadows, the Ox track and then encountering the Ox.

Regarding the interaction during gameplay, it will be based on both user actions on selected interaction devices (e.g. mouse, keyboard, gamepad...), as well as on the monitoring of the player physiological parameters (e.g. galvanic skin conductance, body heat, heart rate, blood pressure and body posture...).

## 6  Conclusion

Through this paper we have attempted to describe the development on a Kansei Game as the implementation of Kansei Mediated Entertainment. While only early stages of the game development are explained, we hope to show a clear direction in the development of this new game genre that is about encouraging player to attain a higher level of self-consciousness and a better inner balance. Furthermore, we would like to encourage the development of games that find inspiration in art and religious installations that have proven successful in influencing for the better people's minds.

# References

1. Salem, B., Rauterberg, M.: Multiple User Profile Merging: Key Challenges for Aware Environments. In: Harper, R., Rauterberg, M., Combetto, M. (eds.) ICEC 2006. LNCS, vol. 4161, pp. 103–116. Springer, Heidelberg (2006)
2. Nagamachi, M.: Kansei Engineering: A New Ergonomic Consumer-Oriented Technology for Product Development. International Journal of Industrial Ergonomics 15, 3–11 (1995)
3. Nagamachi, M.: Kansei Engineering and Comfort. International Journal of Industrial Ergonomics 19, 79–80 (1997)
4. Matsubara, Y., Nagamachi, M.: Hybrid Kansei Engineering System and Design Support. International Journal of Industrial Ergonomics 19, 81–92 (1997)
5. Nagamachi, M.: Kansei Engineering as a Powerful Consumer-Oriented Technology for Product Development. Applied Ergonomics 33, 289–294 (2002)
6. Jiao, J.R., Zhang, Y., Helander, M.: A Kansei Mining System for Affective Design. Expert Systems with Applications 30, 658–673 (2006)
7. Khalid, H.M.: Embracing Diversity in User Needs for Affective Design. Applied Ergonomics 37, 409–418 (2006)
8. Hashimoto, S.: Advanced Human-Machine Interface and Humanoid Robot for Kansei Communication. In: Proc. IECON 2000, pp. 493–498 (2000)
9. ISO: Ergonomic requirements for office work with visual display terminals (VDTs)- Part 11: Guidance on usability, ISO 9241-11:1998(E) (1984)
10. Jordan, P.W.: Human Factors for Pleasure in Product Use. Applied Ergonomics 29(1), 22–25 (1998)
11. Salem, B., Rauterberg, M., Nakatsu, R.: Kansei Mediated Entertainment. In: Harper, R., Rauterberg, M., Combetto, M. (eds.) ICEC 2006. LNCS, vol. 4161, pp. 103–116. Springer, Heidelberg (2006)

# An Algorithm for Seamless Image Stitching and Its Application

Jing Xing, Zhenjiang Miao, and Jing Chen

Institute of Information Science, Beijing JiaoTong University,
Beijing 100044, P.R. China

**Abstract.** Panoramic image stitching used to create virtual environments for many applications is crucial for IBR. In this paper, we introduce a four-step algorithm based on SIFT features which makes some improvements on large exposure difference, large scene motion or other misregistrations when stitching panoramic images. We introduce a new method that is to add the adjacent images according to a weight function to eliminate the seam in the transition region. As a result, we apply the panoramic image to a computer game to enhance the reality of the game environment. Through lots of analyses and experiments we find that our method is simple and effective. Because this method is not sensitive to ordering, orientation, scaling and illumination, its stitching precision is much higher than many other methods.

**Keywords:** Homography, game environment, SIFT features, panorama.

## 1 Introduction

Because of the limitation of geometry-based Rendering, Image-based Rendering (IBR) is becoming more and more important. Panoramic image stitching is to merge a sequence of images with limited overlapping area into one blended picture. As a result, the panoramic images are applied to construct virtual environment which can get higher reality. Satisfying image stitching results are crucial , which means a natural transition from one image to another, both in structure and intensity within and possibly beyond the overlapping region.

There are many algorithms to stitching panoramic images. Feature-based methods begin by establishing correspondences between points, lines or other geometrical entities. The approach based on area [2] calculates the difference of pixel values in the searching region between two adjacent images. This method is easy to implement but the results are related to the illumination and orientation of the input images. There is another approach based on feature seam [2] that is to search a seam where adjacent images can be stitched. In this method, better results are gotten, but the results are not reliable. In this paper, the algorithm based on SIFT features and a new approach to eliminate the seam between adjacent images are introduced.

L. Ma, R. Nakatsu, and M. Rauterberg (Eds.): ICEC 2007, LNCS 4740, pp. 85–90, 2007.

## 2 Algorithm Details of Images Stitching

It's a key to match features in the images stitching. Among the local descriptors compared, SIFT features generally perform the best [1] [4]. Our algorithm is divided four steps and the details are shown as follow.

### 2.1 Feature Matching

Because larger motions, or matching collections of images where the geometric relationship between them is unknown, it is a key and difficulty to attract features of the images. In our experiment, we use SIFT features [4] and get good results.

SIFT features provide a set of features of an object that are not affected by many of the complications experienced in other methods, such as object scaling and rotation. To aid the extraction of these features the SIFT algorithm applies a four-stage filtering approach [5]: (1). Scale-Space Extremum Detection; (2). Key point Localization; (3). Orientation Assignment; (4). Key point Descriptor.

### 2.2 Homography Calculating

As the above described, given two images taken from the same viewpoint but in different directions, the relationship of the two images can be described by a planar projective motion model which is Homography metrics denoted H. H is a matrix of 3×3, and we need four pairs matching points at least to calculate H. This projective transformation warps an image into another one using $x_i' \sim H x_i$. To calculate H correctly is crucial in the images matching. In our experiment, we use the method of direct linearity transformation (DLT) [3] and at least four pairs' interest points from image 2 to image 1 are needed.

### 2.3 Image Stitching

The third step is to stitch the images. After calculating H, image 2 is transformed into the same coordinate system as image 1 according the formulas introduces in section 2.2 [5]. Lots of information of image can be lost due to the transformation. In this experiment, we record the coordinates of the image 2 after transformation, and then stitch the two images directly. Described in formula is shown as follow:

$$\begin{bmatrix} x1 & x2 & x3 & x4 \\ y1 & y2 & y3 & y4 \end{bmatrix} \times H = \begin{bmatrix} x1' & x2' & x3' & x4' \\ y1' & y2' & y3' & y4' \end{bmatrix} \tag{1}$$

Where $\begin{bmatrix} x1 & x2 & x3 & x4 \\ y1 & y2 & y3 & y4 \end{bmatrix}$ is a matrix of four corners' coordinates of image 2 (shown clockwise), and then we can get the four corners' coordinates of image 2 after transformation $\begin{bmatrix} x1' & x2' & x3' & x4' \\ y1' & y2' & y3' & y4' \end{bmatrix}$.

According to the coordinates, we can stitch adjacent images exactly. Using this method, complex algorithm and unnecessary calculation are avoided. The illumination of the two original images is different, but the stitching result is not affected because of the SIFT features' insensitivities to illumination, oriental and scale.

## 2.4 Eliminating the Seam of the Image After Stitching

Although images can be stitched together exactly, a seam is still obvious in the transition region. There are many approaches to image stitching in the literature. Optimal seam algorithms [6] search for a curve in the overlap region on which the differences between image 1 and image 2 are minimal. Then, each image is copied to the corresponding side of the seam. However, the seam is visible when there is no such curve. Another approach is to minimize seam artifacts by smoothing the transition between the images. A related approach was suggested in [7], where a smooth function was added to the input images to force a consistency between the images in the seam curve. In case there are misalignments between the images [8], these methods leave artifacts in the mosaic such as double edges.

Our method is different from these methods: first, the camera parameters are not needed; second, our method can detect the seam between the two images correctly. Camera calibration is a complex work in big environment and the features are not easy to get. Our method avoids this problem. Because the algorithm based on SIFT features is adopted in our experiment, image 1 and image 2 are in the same coordinates system after image 2 multiplying H, where H is the homography of the two images. In the same way, the transition region can be located easily.

In order to make the image look no visible seam, process the transition region naturally stitch is important. Our method mainly processes the transition region. According this matrix $\begin{bmatrix} x1' & x2' & x3' & x4' \\ y1' & y2' & y3' & y4' \end{bmatrix}$ which is the coordinate matrix of image 2 after transformation, the transition region is computed correctly, shown in figure 1:

$(x1',y1)$ ⌐―⌐$(x2,y2)$

$(x4',y4)$ ⌐―⌐$(x3,y3)$

**Fig. 1.** The image after pasting two images (transition region in the red rectangle)

Because the transition region is the mix part of Image 1 and Image 2, we can assume a weight function and make the image after stitching smoothing. The image after stitching is noted as I. The left part of transition region is the image 1 and the right part is Image 2. Let the two images multiple a weight function $w(x)$ to eliminate the seam in transition region, and the transition region and weight function can be denoted as following formulas:

$$\begin{cases} S = (1 - w(x)) * I1(x, y) + w(x) * I2(x, y) \\ w(x) = \sin(x * \pi / (2 * d)) \end{cases} \qquad (2)$$

where $0 \leq w(x) \leq 1$ $0 \leq x \leq d$ $d$ is the width of transition region and it can be computed according to the figure 1.

## 3 Experiment Results and Application

In this experiment, the SIFT features are extracted from a pair of adjacent images. The features are matched using k-d tree, and the result is shown in figure 2. In figure 2, two original images are given which have overlapping region. And then, we detect the SIFT features of the two images and match them. After detecting the features and calculating the homography of two adjacent images, we stitch the images by recording coordinates of the image after transformation. Another result is also given that is obtained by the method based on area. Form these results compared, higher accuracy is gotten in our method. There is a visible seam in the transition area after stitching. The seam in transition region is eliminated by using our method and the result is shown in figure 3.

**Fig. 2.** Original images (the left two images) and SIFT feature matches extracted from a pair of images (right)

**Fig. 3.** the image after stitching using the method based on area [2] (the matching error is marked with red rectangle) and using the method based on SIFT features with obvious seam (middle) stitching result after smoothing the transition (right)

Some experiment results based on SIFT features are also shown as follow.

**Fig. 4.** Original images (left two images) and the image after stitching using our method (middle) and using software (right)

The original images with obvious illumination difference are shown in the left two images of figure 4. There are some commercial softwares to stitch panoramic images now in the market, so we also use one of them that can get good result to stitch the images to compare with ours, which is shown in the right image of figure 4. From these results we can see a higher graphics resolution is obtained by using our method than by software.

The main purpose of panorama is to construct virtual environment. We apply the panorama to a computer game we are now exploiting about tank war and get higher game environment reality. In figure 5, the two tanks are modeled by java3D and the environment is constructed by panorama that is stitched by a series of images with overlapping region.

**Fig. 5.** The left two images are the original images and the middle is the panorama and the right is the game environment using panorama

## 4   Conclusions

Some experiment results have been presented using SIFT feature-based algorithm in this paper. From these results, we can see that using SIFT features to transform images allows us to stitch them in an accurate way. In addition, because we stitch the images by using the coordinates of the image after transformation instead of interpolation, unnecessary calculation is avoided and the transition region is detected easily. Besides, the approach that is to add adjacent images by weight function is simple and effective.

## Acknowledgments

This work is supported by National 973 Key Research Program 2006CB303105, National 973 Key Research Program 2004CB318110 and University Key Research Fund 2004SZ002.

## References

1. Shum, H.Y., Szelishi, R.: Panoramic Image Mosaics. Technical Report, Microsoft Research (1998)
2. Kang, G.: Virtual Environment Touring based on image, master thesis, Nanjing Institute of Technology (2004)
3. Hartley, R., Zisserman, A.: Multiple View Geometry in Computer Vision. AnHui University Press (2002)
4. Lowe, D.: Distinctive image features from scale-invariant keypoints. Int. Journal of Computer Vision 60(2), 91–110 (2004)

5. Zhao, H.: Matching Technology based on SIFT Features, Shan Dong University, Institute of Information Science and Engineering (2006)
6. Efros, A., Freeman, W.: Image quilting for texture synthesis and transfer. In: Proc. SIGGRAPH, pp. 341–346 (August 2001)
7. Peleg, S.: Elimination of seams from photomosaics. Computer Graph Image Process. 16(1), 90–94 (1981)
8. Uyttendaele, M., Eden, A.: Eliminating ghosting and exposure artifacts in image mosaics. In: Proc. Conf. Computer Vision and Pattern Recognition, pp. II: 509–II: 516 (2001)

# A New Algorithm for Trademark Image Retrieval Based on Sub-block of Polar Coordinates

Bei-ji Zou[1], Lingzhi Li[1], Ling Zhang[2], and Yi Yao[1]

[1] School of Information Science and Engineering, Central South University
Changsha, 410083, China
[2] School of Computer and Communications, Hunan University
Changsha 410082, China

**Abstract.** The sub-block-based image retrieval method utilizes global and local image features to retrieve trademarks through separating individual an images into some blocks. This paper proposes a sub-block-based trademark image retrieval algorithm under the polar coordinate system. Experiment results show that our algorithm can keep excellent invariance in image translation, scaling and rotation and the retrieved results can satisfy human visual perception very well.

**Keywords:** trademark retrieval, sub-block image, mirror invariant performance.

## 1 Introduction

Trademark stands for reputation of enterprises and quality of products. For protecting the rights of the registered trademarks, we need to confirm the qualification of trademarks by checking the receptiveness and similarity between the trademarks that are being registered and those that have been registered. Due to the increase of the number of the registered trademarks, an accurate and effective automatic retrieving system needs to be established since the traditional method based on manual coding can hardly satisfy the real-time and accuracy requirement of retrieving.

Currently, there are many types of automatic trademark retrieving methods. Lam[1] used invariant moment and Fourier descriptor to describe the shape features of trademark images. The shape features such as comparative area, circularity and complexity were used to retrieve images by Eakins [2] and others. Kim [3] proposed an approach that retrieved image by using visual feature--the Zernike moment. Jau Ling Shih [4] described trademark images by using features such as deformation parameter, shape invariant moment and edge histogram, and he made the weighted computing to the general similarity. However, by these methods, only the overall features of images were considered but some special relations between individual images neglected.

Trademark image is firstly divided into several blocks through the way of quad-tree subdivision given by literature [5]. Then the image similarity is measured by extracting global features and features of every block. Compared to the approaches that extract only global features, the retrieval efficiency is enhanced by this method. However such method has to undergo rotation and it achieves invariance through

L. Ma, R. Nakatsu, and M. Rauterberg (Eds.): ICEC 2007, LNCS 4740, pp. 91–97, 2007.

matching the principal orientation of shapes. On the other hand experiment results show that after rotation and ratio alteration of images, certain discrepancy will occur to principal orientation of shapes, and the corresponding blocks of the related two images will not be identical in reality, which may seriously influence the retrieval effects. Furthermore, this method can't keep good image invariance. The problems above-mentioned are resolved perfectly by a new sub-block-based image retrieval algorithm under the polar coordinate system proposed by this paper through making the best use of the features of blocks. In addition, according to the fact that the edge patterns of trademarks are visually more perceptible than those in central parts, the power of the edge blocks are enlarged reasonably to improve the retrieval efficiency of the algorithm. Experiment results show that our algorithm can keep excellent invariance in image translation, rotation and scaling and the retrieved results match human visual perception very well.

## 2   The Sub-block-Based Retrieval Algorithm Under The Polar Coordinate System

The sub-block retrieval method under polar coordinate proposed in this paper will first normalize the trademark images, and set the minimum circumscribed circle of the object as the object region. Next, we will divide the image object into blocks under polar coordinate, calculate the shape histogram, and smooth it. Finally, the distances between images are computed by a new measurement of similarity so as to keep good image invariance.

### 2.1   The Method for Computing the Shape Principal Orientation and Object Region

Generally, differing from other images, the man made trademark image gives more importance to shape feature rather than color feature and texture feature. Therefore, in this paper only shape feature is utilized for data retrieval.

After pretreatment, a binary trademark image can be obtained. As shown in figure 1, the minimum circumscribed circle and shape principal orientation of object is computed, and the former is the object region of trademark image. Then a polar coordinate system is built up by considering the center of the minimum circumscribed circle as origin and shape principal orientation as polar pole. It can keep elementary invariance under translation and rotation processes. The steps are as follows:

1. Compute the minimum circumscribed circle
2. Compute the shape principal orientation ( $\alpha$ )

According to the angle ( $\beta$ ) between principal axis direction [7] and horizontal direction, it can be computed as below:

$$\beta = \arctan\left(\left(\mu_{02} - \mu_{20} + \sqrt{(\mu_{02} - \mu_{20})^2 + 4\mu_{11}^2}\right)\Big/2\mu_{11}\right). \tag{1}$$

$\mu_{pq}$ is the (p+q) step center moment of image. It is defined as

$$\mu_{pq} = \sum_x \sum_y (x - \overline{x})^p (y - \overline{y})^q f(x, y) \ . \tag{2}$$

$(\overline{x}, \overline{y})$ is the center of mass of image. The $\alpha$ can be computed as follows:

$$\alpha = \begin{cases} \beta + \pi, & u_{30} > 0 \\ \beta, & u_{30} \leq 0 \end{cases} \tag{3}$$

## 2.2 Division Method Under the Polar Coordinate System and Feature Extraction

First the coordinate $(r, \theta)$ of pixels in object region should be computed, then let the coordinate of center of minimum circumscribed circle be $(x_0, y_0)$, and radius be R

$$r = \sqrt{(x - x_0)^2 + (y - y_0)^2} \ , \quad 0 \leq r \leq R \ . \tag{4}$$

$$\theta = \left( \arctan \left( (y - y_0) / (x - x_0) \right) - \alpha + 2\pi \right) \bmod (2\pi), \quad 0 \leq \theta \leq 2\pi \ . \tag{5}$$

Figure 2 shows the blocking division of object region under polar coordinate. After dividing the object region into many blocks, the shape features of every block can be extracted. In this paper, the following two features are adopted to represent the shape of the divided block:

1) $e_i$ is denoted as the proportion of the object pixels in block which reflects the number of object pixels in No. i block, and the total pixels as $B_i$, then

$$e_i = \sum_{(x,y) \in B_i} f(x, y) \Big/ \sum_{(x,y) \in B_i} 1 \ . \tag{6}$$

2) $d_i$ is denoted as the distance between center of mass of block and origin, and $(x_{i0}, y_{i0})$ as the center of mass of block i, then

$$d_i = |(x_0, y_0), (x_{i0}, y_{i0})| / R \ . \tag{7}$$

The proportion histogram of pixels and distance histogram can be obtained by calculating the two shape features of every block and arranging these features according to their number. The histogram should be smoothed because the experiment results show that the shape principal orientations of two images have departure even though they are derived through rotating and scaling of the same image. The following is the smoothing method for the value of i in histogram

$$h_i = \sum_{j=i-k}^{j=i+k} h_j / (2k + 1) \tag{8}$$

$h_j$ and $h_i$ are neighbors in the same cirque.

**Fig. 1.** Compute the minimum circumscribed circle and shape principal orientation

**Fig. 2.** Division method under the polar coordinate system

### 2.3 Measurement of Comparability of Image

Comparability among images can be measured according to global features and the individual block features. First, we discuss the measurement of individual block features (shape histogram).

The histograms distance between sample image A and image Q need to be checked

$$D_1(A,Q) = \sum_n \sum_i \omega_n \mid h_{A,n,i} - h_{Q,n,i} \mid \tag{9}$$

$\omega_n$ is power of blocks on the nth cirque and $h_{A,n,i}$ is eigenvalue of image A in the ith block at the nth cirque. Besides, after mirror transformation, the order of each item in the histogram will be changed in relation to that of the original image. As shown in figure 3, the original anti-clockwise order is changed to clockwise one, and the distance between two histograms is

$$D_2(A,Q) = \sum_n \sum_i \omega_n \mid h_{A,n,i} - h_{Q,n,(8n+1-i)} \mid \tag{10}$$

And the distance of shape histogram is as below:

$$D(A,Q) = \min(D_1(A,Q), D_2(A,Q)) \tag{11}$$

The values of invariant moments in Hu invariant moment group are different. To give the same treatment to these invariant moments, internal normalization is required and Gauss normalization is the method generally adopted.

(a) The order of blocks of original image          (b) The order of blocks of mirror image

**Fig. 3.** The corresponding relations among sub-blocks of mirror images

$$\phi_i' = \begin{cases} 0, & \phi_i < \mu_i - 3\sigma_i \\ \dfrac{\phi_i - \mu_i + 3\sigma_i}{6\sigma_i}, & \mu_i - 3\sigma_i \le \phi_i \le \mu_i + 3\sigma_i \\ 1, & \phi_i > \mu_i + 3\sigma_i \end{cases} \tag{12}$$

Then the Euler distance of Hu invariant moment group and eccentricity distance of A and Q are computed. Now two shape histogram distances and two global feature distances are achieved. Before complex retrieval, the outer part of each distance should also be normalized. Next, compute the distance of every two images in database corresponding to one feature, then compute the excepted value and standard deviation of these distances, which should be normalized by Gauss normalization mentioned above. So the distance between sample image A and image Q that need to be checked is

$$D(A,Q) = \sum_{i=1}^{4} \omega_i D_i \,, \quad \sum_{i=1}^{4} \omega_i = 1 \tag{13}$$

$D_i$ is the distance of each feature after normalization. Experiment results show that retrieval outcome based on proportion histogram of pixels and distance histogram is more precise than that based on Hu invariant moment group and eccentricity. Therefore the power of two shape histograms should be a bit lager.

## 3 Experimental Results

To test the validity of algorithm in this paper, we performed several tests in trademark image database that contains 1000 binary trademark. The aim is to inspect the achieved geometry transform invariance of the algorithm proposed in this paper, and to see whether the retrieval effect satisfies visual requirement.

1) 50 trademark images belonging to different types from database are randomly chosen. Perform any combination of translation, rotation, scale, mirror and shape transformation to one of the selected image samples and we accordingly get four similar images to the original image. Then, we get a database including 250 trademark images that possesses 50 categories with each one containing five images. By taking any image from database as sample, the retrieval result returns the first 24 images arranged according to similarity.

As is shown in figure 4, it is clearly that other four images belonging to the same category with sample image are not arranged at the head of the range. And, the mirror image (the 12th and 14th in figure 4) is a bit far away from the first one (sample image).

Figure 5 shows the retrieval result of the same sample image by algorithm proposed in this paper. It shows that this algorithm can keep good geometry transformation invariance since images belonging to the same class with sample image are not only retrieved, but also arranged in the head of the range.

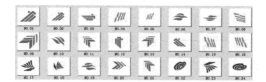

**Fig. 4.** The result of invariance experiment (based on quad-tree)

**Fig. 5.** The result of invariance experiment (under the polar coordinate)

3) Check the visual invariance of algorithm in this paper. In an image database that contains 1000 items, we choose anyone as sample and get the first 24 images arranged according to similarity. As is shown in figure 6 and 7, among images retrieved through quad-tree method (the 18th, 19th, 21st and 24th image), there are instances that differ from sample images obviously. But among the images achieved by algorithm in this paper, the construction and figure of most images are similar to the sample image. Furthermore, the more similar the images are, the nearer will they be arranged.

**Fig. 6.** The result of visual perception experiment (based on quad-tree)

**Fig. 7.** The result of visual perception experiment (under the polar coordinate)

## 4   Conclusion

The sub-block based trademark image retrieval method utilizes both global and local features, which is certainly more efficient than most of the existing retrieval methods.

Experiment results show that our method can keep good geometry transformation invariance and the human visual perception.

## Acknowledgement

This research was supported by National Natural Science Fund (60673093).

## References

1. Lam, C.P., Wu, J.K., Mehtre, B.: STAR - a system for Trademark archival and retrieval. In: Proceeding 2<sup>nd</sup> Asian Conf. On Computer Vision, vol. 3, pp. 214–217 (1995)
2. Eakins, J.P., Boardman, J.M., Graham, M.E.: Similarity retrieval of trademark images. IEEE Transactions on Multimedia 5(2), 53–63 (1998)
3. Kim, Y.S., Kim, W.Y.: Content-based trademark retrieval system using a visually salient feature. Image and Vision Computing 16(12-13), 931–939 (1998)
4. Shih, J.L., Chen, L.H.: A new system for trademark segmentation and retrieval. Image and Vision Computing 19, 1011–1018 (2001)
5. Guo, L., Huang, Y.Y., Yang, J.Y.: Using sub-block image features to retrieve trademark image. Journal of Computer-Aided Design and Computer Graphics 16(17), 968–972 (2004)
6. Preparata, F.P., Shamos, M.L.: Computational Geometry: an Introduction. Springer, New York (1985)
7. Wang, T., Liu, W.Y., Sun, J.g., Zhang, H.J.: Using Fourier descriptors to recognize object's shape. Journal of Computer Research and Development 39(12), 1714–1719 (2002)
8. Wu, J.K.: Digital Image Analysis (in Chinese), pp. 28–31. People's Posts and Telecommunications Press, Beijing (1989)

# Image Composition with Blurring Effect from Depth of Field

Hai Liu and Lizhuang Ma

School of Electronic, Information and Electrical Engineering,
Shanghai Jiao Tong University
No.800 Dongchuan Rd., Minhang, Shanghai, P.R. China
liuhai_xy@sjtu.edu.cn,
ma-lz@cs.sjtu.edu.cn

**Abstract.** This paper describes a new framework for image composition according to the blurring effect bred by changing depth of field from the target images. The framework involves two stages: a *learning phase*, in which the target image, with one part of the image purported to be "further" and another part "near", is presented as "learning data" and the learned filter is applied to some objects in source image; and a *composition phase*, in which those blurred objects of source image are composed into the "further" part of the target image. The framework is based on a simple multiscale Gaussian filter, inspired primarily by recent results in texture synthesis and image editing.

**Keywords:** Gaussian filter, texture synthesis, Markov random fields, texture transfer, image editing.

## 1 Introduction

Image composition is the process of creating a new image by pasting an object or a region from a source image onto a target image. Poisson image editing [10] has been proposed recently as an effective approach for seamless image composition. Lately, Drag-and-Drop pasting [7] optimizes the boundary condition for Poisson image editing to be more practical with a new objective function and a shortest closed-path algorithm.

By solving Poisson equations using the user-specified boundary condition, Poisson image editing [10] seamlessly blends the colors from both images without visible discontinuities around the boundary but may generate unnatural artifacts at places where the boundary intersects with salient structures in the target image. By optimizing the boundary condition for Poisson image editing and simplifying the interfaces of the system, Drag-and-Drop pasting [7] avoids as much as possible salient image structures on both source and target images and relieves users' operation. Although both the systems can obtain seamless composition, we observe that the composition results can not express the blurring effect bred by depth of field from focussing, i.e., the further objects of the imaging scenes gradually blurring in the images as the camera focuses on the near objects.

L. Ma, R. Nakatsu, and M. Rauterberg (Eds.): ICEC 2007, LNCS 4740, pp. 98–103, 2007.

In this paper, we propose a method to learn the blurring "filters" bred by focussing from the target images and to appropriately apply it to the composition process. With source images filtered by the learned "filters", we can use some approaches, e.g., Drag-and-Drop pasting, to obtain seamless composition. In this way, we can obtain the final composition results in which the objects from source images appear the same blurring effect in the target images context.

To learn the blurring "filters", we propose an optimized approach which uses Gaussian filter as the learning model in the given target image and matches features of pixel pairs based on the way proposed in Image analogies [1].

## 2  Related Work

In image composition, several different techniques have been used to seamlessly blend two different images, such as the multi-resolution spline technique [4] through interpolations at different levels of Laplacian pyramids and Poisson image editing [10] through Poisson equations with a guidance field and a user-specified boundary. Subsequently, Image stitching in the gradient domain[6][9] has also been proposed to reduce the artifacts caused by structure misalignment and to correct color discrepancy.

On the contrary, some techniques do the composition work by piecing together multiple image patches from a single image or from multiple images, such as Graph-cut textures [8] which stitch textures or natural images by finding the best seams using the graph-cuts algorithm [3] and Interactive digital photomontage [2] which combines different regions of a set of roughly aligned photos with similar content into a single composite using Graph-cuts and Poisson image editing.

In comparison with the previous work mentioned above, our work also build upon a great deal of previous work in several disparate areas, like Image analogies [1] including machine learning, texture synthesis, image editing, and image-based rendering. Generalizing from a set of known examples is a central problem in machine learning. Analogical reasoning is central to problem solving, learning, and creativity. Image analogies [1] proposed a novel statistical approach for finding analogies between images, from the perspective of modelling transformation that are mappings of one sort of object or relation into another. Their method differs from previous Markov random fields (MRFs) modelling techniques in that they do not require an iterative algorithm in order to apply the model.

## 3  Composition with Focussing Blurring Effect

Here,we describe a set of data structures and algorithms to support composition with blurring effect bred by focussing. To some extent, our description of data structures is similar to the way of Image analogies [1].

### 3.1  Definitions and Data Structures

As input, our algorithm takes a set of two images, the *source image A* and the *target image B* in which labelling areas indicate the different depth of field. It produces the *resulting image B'* as output and a secondary *filtered source image A'*. The *target image B* is preconditioned labelling image; that is, the further areas need to be labelled as $B_f$ according to the blurring effect bred by depth of field and the near areas as $B_n$, through manual or automatical manner, before the *target image B* and the *source image A* are combined into the final composition image $B'$.

Our approach assumes that the *target image B* and the *resulting image B'* are registered; that is, the colors at and around any given pixel $p$ in $B$ correspond to the colors at and around that same pixel $p$ in $B'$, through the composition process that we are trying to do. Thus, we will use the same index $p$ to specify both a pixel in $B$ and its corresponding pixel in $B'$. We will use a different index $q$ to specify a pixel in the source image $A$.

For the purposes of this exposition, we will assume that the various images contain not just an RGB color, but additional channels of information as well, such as luminance and various filter responses. Together, all of these channels (including RGB) comprise the *feature vector* for each pixel $p$ just as that of Image analogies [1]. We use $A(q)$ to denote the complete feature vector of $A$ at pixel $q$ and, similarly, $B(p)$ (or $B'(p)$) to specify the feature vector at pixel $p$.

### 3.2    Poisson Image Editing with Optimal Boundary

To obtain the *resulting image f* by pasting a region of interest from the *source image $f_s$* to the *target image $f_t$*, Poisson image editing [10] solves the following minimization problem using the guidance field $v = \nabla f_s$ given the exterior boundary $\partial \Omega_0$ condition defined on the user-drawn region of interest $\Omega_0$:

$$\min_f \int_{p \in \Omega_0} |\nabla f - v|^2 dp \ with \ f|_{\partial \Omega_0} = f_t|_{\partial \Omega_0}. \tag{1}$$

With the notation $f' = f - f_s$, the Laplace equation associated with the transformation of above equation is:

$$\triangle f' = 0 \ with \ f'|_{\partial \Omega_0} = (f_t - f_s)|_{\partial \Omega_0}. \tag{2}$$

The boundary conditions $(f_t - f_s)|_{\partial \Omega_0}$ determine the final results. A smoother boundary condition produces smaller variational energy in solving the Laplacian equations, thus improves the quality of the resulting composite. To reduce the color variance along the boundary, Drag-and-Drop pasting [7] minimize the following objective function or boundary energy:

$$E(\partial \Omega, k) = \sum_{p \in \partial \Omega} ((f_t(p) - f_s(p)) - k)^2, \tag{3}$$

where $k$ is a constant value to be determined and $(f(p) - f(q))$ is computed as the L2-norm in color spaces. $f_t(p) - f_s(p)) - k$ represents the color deviation of the boundary pixels with respect to $k$.

To obtain the optimal boundary, Drag-and-Drop pasting [7] proposes an iterative optimization algorithm in which a algorithm based on dynamic programming is employed to compute a closed shortest-path. However, the optimized boundary may intersect with the object with a fractional boundary and break up subtle and fine details. Thus, they also propose to incorporate an alpha matte in a blended guidance field for Poisson equations.

## 3.3 The Algorithm of Blurring Composition

Given above notation and basic algorithms, the composition algorithm of blurring effect is easy to describe. First, in an initialization phase, multiscale (Gaussian pyramid) representations of $A$ and $B$ is constructed, along with their feature vectors and some additional indices used for speeding the matching process as Image analogies [1] dose. The synthesis then proceeds from coarsest resolution to finest, computing a multiscale representation of *resulting image* $B'$, one level at a time. time. At each level $l$, the "blurring filter" is learned according to the Gaussian model, and then statistics pertaining to each pixel pair of $p$ in $B_f$ and $p'$ in $B_n$ are compared to obtain the relative difference of two filters. The feature vector $A'(q)$ is at last set according to the "blurring filter". The algorithm can be described more precisely in pseudocode as follows:

> **function** CREATEBLURRINGCOMPOSITION($A$, $B$):
>   Compute Gaussian pyramids for $A$ and $B$
>   Compute features for $A$ and $B$
>   Initialize the learning structures
>   **for** each level $l$, from coarsest to finest, **do:**
>     $filter_{B_f} \longleftarrow$ FILTERLEARNING($B_f$, $l$)
>     $filter_{B_n} \longleftarrow$ FILTERLEARNING($B_n$, $l$)
>     **for** each pixel pair $(p', p)$, $p \in B_f$ and $p' \in B_n$, **do:**
>       Match $p'$ and $p$ according to $B_n(p')$ and $B_f(p)$
>       $filter_{dif}(p') \longleftarrow filter_{B_f}(p) \ominus filter_{B_n}(p')$
>     $filter_A \longleftarrow$ FILTERLEARNING($A$, $l$)
>     **for** each pixel $q \in A$, in scan-line order, **do:**
>       Match $p'$ and $q$ according to $B_n(p')$ and $A(q)$
>       $filter_{A'}(q) \longleftarrow filter_A(q) \oplus filter_{dif}(p')$
>       $A'_l(q) \longleftarrow A_l(q) \otimes filter_{A'}(q)$
>     Composite $A'_l$ with $B_f$ within $B_l$ using Poisson equation
>   **return** $B'_L$

The heart of the image blurring composition algorithm is the FILTERLEARNING subroutine. This routine takes as input the complete image or an interesting area of an image, along with the feature vectors and other attributes of the image. It finds the filter of each pixel in the specified image that best describes the relations of feature between a pixel and its neighborhood using a Gaussian model. $filter_X$ is a set of Gaussian filter according to each pixel in the interesting image $X$. Given the different blurring effect bred by variant depth of field and other attributes, we need select the appropriate filter to blur each pixel of the *source image* $A$. Thus, we first find a pixel $p'$ that best match the pixel $p$ in terms of feature vector and other attributes within $B_n$ and $B_f$ of *target image* $B$ respectively and compute the filter variance $filter_{dif}(p')$ between them. Then we find a pixel $p'$ in $B_n$ that best match the pixel $q$ in $A$ and add the $filter_{dif}(p')$ to $filter_A(q)$. The *filtered source image* $A'$ can be obtained by applying appropriate $filter_{A'}$ to each pixel of *source image* $A$. The sign $\oplus$ indicates that each parameter of the Gaussian filter adds a value from $filter_{dif}$, $\ominus$ subtracts a value and $\otimes$ means to apply filter $filter_{A'}$ to all features of pixel $q$. At last, we implement composition between the *filtered source image* $A'$ and the *target image* $B$ using Poisson image editing with optimal boundary.

Here is a more precise statement of this algorithm:

> **function** FILTERLEARNING($A$, $l$)
> > **for** each pixel $p \in A$, in scan-line order, **do:**
> > > $N_p \longleftarrow$ Find the 8-neighborhood of the pixel $p$
> > > Compute the gradient between $p$ and $p' \in N_p$
> > > **if** existing salient border between $p$ and $p'$, **then**
> > > > **break**
> > > **else**
> > > > $\mu \longleftarrow$ fit the mean of $filter_A(p)$ from $p$ within $N_p$
> > > > $\sigma \longleftarrow$ fit the variance of $filter_A(p)$ from $p$ within $N_p$
> > > > Record $filter_A(p)$
> > **return** $filter_A$

Here, we use $filter_A(p)$ to denote the blurring filter coming from pixel $p$ within neighborhood $N_p$ and $filter_A$ the complete set of filter from each pixel of image $A$. The filter is the concatenation of all the feature vectors and other attributes from $p$ within $N_p$. We have used $5 \times 5$ neighborhoods in the fine level and $3 \times 3$ neighborhoods in the coarse level. The set $filter_A$ is not one pixel $p$ to one filter $filter_p$ because some pixels on the border of area in the image are not be dealt with.

During the computing process, we need match two pixels in different images or different areas of one image according to their feature vectors or other attributes. The matching subroutine we used is just as that used in Image analogies [1]. The selection and representation of feature used for matching is a large open problem and a crucial area of research. Using the RGB channels themselves is the most obvious choice. However, for some filters, it dose not contain enough data to match the pair well due to the well-known "curse of dimensionality".

An alternative is to compute and store the luminance at each pixel and use it in place of RGB in the distance metric. Luminance can be computed in a number of ways; we use the Y channel from the YIQ color space [5], where the I and Q channels are "color difference" components. After processing in luminance space, we can recover the color simply by copying the I and Q channels of the input image into the synthesized image, followed by a conversion back to RGB.

## 4    Conclusion and Discussion

Using the generic framework of image composition with blurring effect, we have introduced a novel method to composite the contents of an image selection with the blurring effect bred by depth of field. Compared with the original Poisson image editing and Drag-and-Drop pasting, our method is more practical and elegant for composition.

Our method uses filter learning from Image analogies and Poisson image editing with optimal boundary from Drag-and-Drop pasting to implement blurring effect and compositing respectively. The filter learning method is simpler and faster than that in Image analogies and the final composition is more practical in terms of the visual effect.

We propose future research directions are as follows: 1) Investigating the more appropriate filter model to learn the blurring effect bred by depth of field. 2) Investigating the degree of diffusion or color change controlled within the Poisson image editing framework.

**Acknowledgments.** This work was supported in part by the Chinese National Basic Research Program (973 Program) grant 2006CB303105.

# References

1. Aaron, H., Charles, E.J., Nuria, O., Brian, C., David, H.S.: Image analogies. In: Proceedings of ACM SIGGRAPH. ACM Press, New York (2001)
2. Agarwala, A., Dontcheva, M., Agrawala, M., Drucker, S., Colburn, A., Curless, B., Salesin, D., Cohen, M.: Interactive digital photomontage. In: Proceedings of ACM SIGGRAPH, vol. 23(3), pp. 294–302 (2004)
3. Boykov, Y., Jolly, M.P.: Interactive graph cuts for optimal boundary & region segmentation of objects in n-d images. In: Proceedings of ICCV (2001)
4. Burt, P.J., Adelson, E.H.: A multiresolution spline with application to image mosaics. ACM Transactions on Graphics 2, 217–236 (1983)
5. James, D.F., van Andries, D., Steven, K.F., John, F.H.: Computer Graphics, Principles and Practice, 2nd edn. Addison-Wesley, Reading (1990)
6. Jiaya, J., Chi–Keung, T.: Eliminating structure and intensity misalignment in image stitching. In: Proceedings of ICCV (2005)
7. Jiaya, J., Jian, S., Chi–Keung, T., Heung–Yeung, S.: Drag–and–Drop pasting. In: Proceedings of ACM SIGGRAPH. ACM Press, New York (2006)
8. Kwatra, V., Schodl, A., Essa, I., Turk, G., Bobick, A.: Graphcut textures: image and video synthesis using graph cuts. In: Proceedings of ACM SIGGRAPH, pp. 277–286. ACM Press, New York (2003)
9. Levin, A., Zomet, A., Peleg, S., Weiss, Y.: Seamless image stitching in the gradient domain. In: Pajdla, T., Matas, J(G.) (eds.) ECCV 2004. LNCS, vol. 3024, pp. 377–389. Springer, Heidelberg (2004)
10. Perez, P., Gangnet, M., Blake, A.: Poisson image editing. In: Proceedings of ACM SIGGRAPH, pp. 313–318. ACM Press, New York (2003)

# Temporal Color Morphing

Xuezhong Xiao and Lizhuang Ma

Department of Computer Science and Engineering
Shanghai Jiao Tong University, China

**Abstract.** Many natural phenomena usually appear in the scenes of movies. They are characterized by color changing smoothly following the time's advancement, e.g. day breaking, leaves' resurgence, foliage greening from yellow or yellowing from green. They are difficult to be captured wholly because of the long time span. Traditional methods for making these types of scenes are inefficient or makeshifts.
In this paper, we propose a semi-automatic temporal color morphing technique for the simulation of smooth color-changing phenomena. Our temporal color morphing method is based on histogram manipulation— histogram warping and histogram-based color transformation. For the simplicity of the calculation, we convert the input of the source sequence and target image to $l\alpha\beta$ color space. This way we split the three-dimensional problem to three one-dimensional problems. The coordinates are quantized in $l\alpha\beta$ space with a limited error condition. For customization of the results by the user, we introduce a timing mechanism for controlling the velocities of color morphing. Finally, we apply our temporal color morphing technique to the video clips of several representative natural phenomena to demonstrate the effectiveness of our method.

## 1 Introduction

There are many scenes of natural phenomena appeared in movies, e.g. day breaking, leaves' resurgence, foliage greening from yellow or yellowing from green, which behave as some processes and are characterized by color changing smoothly following the time's advancement. We call them *temporal color morphing*. These phenomena may last several hours or even several months whereas in movies these scenes just span several minutes or seconds.

Traditionally film makers have two types of methods to catch these scenes. One is that photographers take the whole process and film cutters cut and edit it to be a sequence with appropriate length, and another is that they shoot the initiative and terminative parts of the whole process respectively and produce the scene transiting from the initiative part to the terminative part by the use of cross-dissolves. The first method is inefficient and impractical in some situations, e.g., foliage yellowing which could cost several months. The second method is a makeshift, it can not produce image sequences showing the evolving process of these natural phenomena and to some extent its results just give audience some mental hints.

L. Ma, R. Nakatsu, and M. Rauterberg (Eds.): ICEC 2007, LNCS 4740, pp. 104–114, 2007.

In this paper, we propose a semi-automatic temporal color morphing technique for the simulation of smooth color-changing phenomena. We contend that there are three key points of the temporal color morphing algorithm:

- Availability: our algorithm needs input which can be gained easily. And it can produce plausible results. That is, the results look like the simulated natural phenomena visually.
- Adjustability: the algorithm should provide a way for users to impact the final results. Example properties are timing and target style selection.
- Efficiency: the algorithm acts on image sequences (or video clips), a several seconds' clip has over one hundred frames. So short processing times are very important.

Our algorithm takes an image sequence (called source sequence) and a static image (called target image) as inputs. The source sequence should contain the desired scene except the color alteration. So we commonly take the initiative or terminative part of the simulated phenomenon as the source sequence. Correspondingly, the target image can be the terminative or initiative photo of the simulated scene or other scene's photo which should have the target color characteristics. Obviously, we can conveniently capture the source sequence and target image. The algorithm then automatically creates the sequence with desired color alteration.

Our temporal color morphing technique is based on histogram manipulation in $l\alpha\beta$ color space. It is known that the histogram is an elaborate and useful image statistic which sums up the distribution of images' color. So we express the holistic effects of color alteration as histogram warping. After storing the intermediate states of histogram warping, a histogram-based color transformation algorithm is presented for generating the corresponding in-between frames. We also provide a parameter for users to control the color morphing speed.

Color histogram manipulation in $RGB$ color space is a difficult task because there exist correlations between the three channels' values and any histogram manipulation must operate on the three components simultaneously. $l\alpha\beta$ color space is developed to minimize correlations between the three channels for natural scenes [1]. After transforming to $l\alpha\beta$ space, we can manipulate the three channels' histograms separately. That is, the three dimensional problem is converted into three one-dimensional problems. The complexity of the problem is reduced greatly. We also quantize $l\alpha\beta$ coordinates to improve the algorithm's performance under a limited error condition.

## 2   Related Work

Our work is about color processing. Many color processing methods have been published recently, e.g. about colorization, color-to-gray, color transfer and color harmonization.

Colorization [2,3] is a technique for adding color to gray-scale images in order to increase the visual appeal of images. Welsh et al. describe a semi-automatic example-based technique for colorizing a gray-scale image by transferring color from an example color image [2]. Levin et al.'s method colorizes gray-scale images according to the scribbles marked by users using optimization [3].

Color-to-gray is an inverse procedure with colorization and a dimension reduction problem. Gooch et al. introduces a salience-preserving algorithm to convert color images to gray-scale [4]. The algorithm works in a perceptually uniform CIE $L^*a^*b^*$ color space. They use chrominance and luminance differences to create gray-scale target differences between nearby image pixels, and selectively modulate the gray-scale representation by solving an optimization problem. Simultaneous research by Rasche et al. on the color-to-gray problem transforms color to gray-scale preserving image detail by maintaining distance ratios during the reduction process [5,6]. They also extend it to aid color-deficient observers.

Reinhard et al. introduce a method for color transfer between images [7]. They convert pixel values in $RGB$ space to Ruderman et al's perception-based color space $l\alpha\beta$ [1], and scale and shift $l\alpha\beta$ values to produce very believable results using simple statistics—the mean and standard deviations. Our method works in the $l\alpha\beta$ space and is based on statistics too. However, the statistics used in our method are histograms that are more detailed than mean and standard deviations and are suitable for our applications. Also, our algorithm processes video clips.

Wang and Huang [8] proposed a color transfer method for image sequences. Their algorithm takes a single input image and three target images as inputs, so their resultant sequences keep a static scene while it exhibits color alteration. Our algorithm produces the results in which the scene and color can be changing simultaneously (Fig. 3 and Fig. 6). Furthermore, our method is based on the histogram manipulation which is more elaborate than the color moments (Fig. 5).

Cohen-Or et al.'s color harmonization method detects the best harmonic scheme for the color of a given image and enhances the harmony among the color while remaining faithful to the original color [9].

From the term "morphing", we naturally think of image morphing techniques. Image morphing is a powerful visual effects tool that creates a fluid transformation of one digital image into another [10]. It begins with feature correspondence, and then builds warp functions, and finally interpolates the positions and color to generate inbetween images [10]. Feature correspondence is a very important step for generating good effects, usually it is achieved by experienced animators. Our proposed color morphing is a semi-automatic method. The thing that users need to do is selecting the source sequence and target image for the input. Of course, users can also participate in the timing of color alteration. Another important point is that image morphing techniques cannot be used for simulating the natural phenomena which is our method's task.

Histogram warping and histogram-based color transformation are the core of our method. The correlation between three color components is always a intractable problem for color histogram manipulation. Grundland and Dodgson [12] selects $La''b''$ color space as their space for color histogram warping. But large numbers of experiments by Ruderman et al. [1], Reinhard et al. [7] and

Welsh et al. [2] indicate that $l\alpha\beta$ color space is an appropriate space for processing natural images. Grundland and Dodgson [11,12] interpolate histograms using piecewise rational quadratic splines and warp the interpolating splines to find the color correspondence. For the simplification of calculation, our method generates intermediate states by directly interpolating between two histograms.

Our histogram-based color transformation is very similar to histogram specification. Color histogram specification is a difficult problem because of three correlated dimensions. Gonzalez advised matching the color intensities and leaving the color themselves unchanged [13]. But his method results in dissatisfying results. Our method changes the three dimensional problem as three one-dimensional problems through converting $RGB$ values to the $l\alpha\beta$ color space.

## 3 The Algorithm

In this section, we describe in detail the temporal color morphing algorithm. Our goal is to construct a mapping function $f(\cdot)$ which defines a transformation that leads the source sequence's color from the beginning to the end to morph to the target image's characteristics.

The inputs (the source sequence and the target image) are RGB values. Firstly, they are converted to the decorrelated $l\alpha\beta$ color space. Then, there are two phases of processing performed on the three color components separately— histogram warping and histogram-based color transformation. After this process, we must transform the results back to $RGB$ space. The color space transformation procedures between $RGB$ and $l\alpha\beta$ follow directly from Reinhard et al. [7] except that the $l\alpha\beta$ data need to be quantized for higher performance. Figure 1 shows the framework of our algorithm.

The pixel values in an image may be viewed as random variables. We use random variables $s$, $r$ and $z$ to denote the source sequence, resultant sequence and target image, respectively, and their definition domain is $[C_{min}, C_{max}]$. Then histograms are represented by corresponding variables' probability density function that is one of the most fundamental descriptors of a random variable. Let $g_t(s)$, $p_t(r)$ and $h(z)$ denote the probability density functions of random variables $s$, $r$ and $z$, respectively, while $t$ denotes the $t$th frame in the source or resultant sequence. So the aforementioned mapping function can be formulized as $r = f(s, z)$.

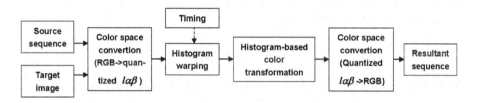

**Fig. 1.** The framework of temporally color morphing

## 3.1   Histogram Warping

For higher performance, we calculate the in-between histograms using the linear interpolation method. The speed of color alteration is controlled by a timing curve. Here is the formula of our histogram warping algorithm:

$$\int_{C_{min}}^{x} p_t(r)dr = \int_{C_{min}}^{x} g_1(s)ds + \left( \int_{C_{min}}^{x} h(z)dz - \int_{C_{min}}^{x} g_1(s)ds \right)$$
$$\cdot \frac{\int_0^t v(\omega)d\omega}{\int_0^N v(\omega)d\omega} \tag{1}$$

while N is the total number of frames in source sequence, $v(t)$ denotes the timing curve representing the speed of color changing and is the parameter for users' control. We define four velocity functions including three basic functions and their combination (Fig. 2).

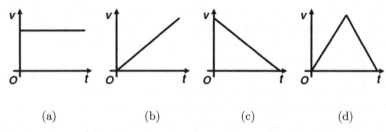

|     |     |     |     |
|:---:|:---:|:---:|:---:|
| (a) | (b) | (c) | (d) |

**Fig. 2.** Timing curves: (a) uniform speed, (b) uniform acceleration, (c) uniform deceleration, (d) combined curve

## 3.2   Histogram-Based Color Transformation

After histogram warping, we have two groups of histograms, one is the source sequence's and another is for the result sequence. They are $g_t(s)$ and $p_t(r)$, while $t = 1, 2, \ldots, N$, and $p_1(r) = g_1(s), p_N(r) = h(z)$. Each pair of $g_t(s)$ and $p_t(r)$ is the input of histogram-based color transformation algorithm.

Here, the goal is to find a transformation function which maps $s$ to $r$. We assume that the transformation function satisfies a condition: it is single-valued and monotonically increasing in $s$'s definition domain $[C_{min}, C_{max}]$.

A basic result from elementary probability theory is that, if $g_t(s)$ and the transformation function are known and satisfy the above single-valued and monotonically increasing condition, the probability density function $p_t(r)$ can be obtained using a rather simple formula [13]:

$$p_t(r) = g_t(s) \left| \frac{ds}{dr} \right|$$

We sort the data set in ascending order, so we get the following equation:

$$\int_{C_{min}}^{r} p_t(\omega)d\omega = \int_{C_{min}}^{s} g_t(\omega)d\omega$$

Let $P_t(r)$ and $G_t(s)$ denote the source and result images' cumulative distribution density functions respectively, then we obtain the equation of histogram-based color transformation as follows:

$$r = P_t^{-1}[G_t(s)] \tag{2}$$

while

$$P_t(r) = \int_{C_{min}}^{r} p_t(\omega)d\omega$$

$$G_t(s) = \int_{C_{min}}^{s} g_t(\omega)d\omega$$

After merging Eq. (1) into Eq. (2), we obtain the mapping function for temporal color morphing as follows:

$$r = f(s, z) = P_t^{-1}[G_t(s)] \tag{3}$$

while

$$P_t(r) = G_1(s) + [H(z) - G_1(s)] \cdot k$$

$$H(z) = \int_{C_{min}}^{z} h(\omega)d\omega$$

$$k = \frac{\int_0^t v(\omega)d\omega}{\int_0^N v(\omega)d\omega}$$

The procedure we develop for temporal color morphing is summarized as follows:

**Step 1:** Defining a timing curve which could be one of the three basic curves or their arbitrary combination (Fig. 2).

**Step 2:** Calculating the cumulative distribution density functions $H(z)$, $G_t(s)$ and $P_t(r)$.

**Step 3:** Interpolating $P_t^{-1}(\cdot)$ for each $x = G_t(s)$ but not within $P_t(r)$ and build a look-up table $s \rightarrow P_t^{-1}(\cdot)$.

**Step 4:** Finding the value from the look-up table $s \rightarrow P_t^{-1}(\cdot)$ for every pixel in $t$-th frame.

Running through the four steps once, the algorithm generates one frame.

### 3.3   Color Coordinate Quantization

Unlike the $RGB$ color having 256 regular values along each axis, each component of $l\alpha\beta$ color has over ten thousand values. This results in Step 3 in the above procedure to be the bottleneck of the algorithm. So the quantization of color coordinates in $l\alpha\beta$ space is very important.

In order to accelerate the algorithm, we quantize the coordinates' values of $l\alpha\beta$ according to allowable errors in different applications. We quantize the coordinate vectors using LBG algorithm [14] and set the terminate condition as

$$d(\{R, G, B\}, \{R^*, G^*, B^*\}) < e \tag{4}$$

**Fig. 3.** A woman and a man chatting through the caliginous early morning to the midday (Frames No.1, 60, 120, 180, 240 and 300, from left to right). The left column (a) is from the source sequence, the middle column (b) is the effect adjusted by the uniform speed timing curve in Fig. 2(a), and the right column (c) is adjusted by the combined timing curve in Fig. 2(d).

while $e$ denotes the allowable error, $\{R, G, B\}$ and $\{R^*, G^*, B^*\}$ are the original coordinate in $RGB$ space and the coordinate transformed from quantized $l\alpha\beta$ value, respectively. Namely, $\{R^*, G^*, B^*\}$ is obtained by the procedure of $\{l, \alpha, \beta\} = T(\{R, G, B\})$, $\{l^*, \alpha^*, \beta^*\} = Quantization(\{l, \alpha, \beta\})$ and $\{R, G, B\} = T^{-1}(\{l^*, \alpha^*, \beta^*\})$ while $T(\cdot)$ and $T^{-1}(\cdot)$ are the $RGB$ to $l\alpha\beta$ conversion and its inverse and $Quantization(\cdot)$ denotes a LBG algorithm.

# 4   Results

We apply our temporal color morphing technique to the video clips of several representative natural phenomena to demonstrate the effectiveness of our method. Fig. 3, 6 and 7 exhibit the selected frames produced by this technique. Fig. 4 shows the target images used in the paper.

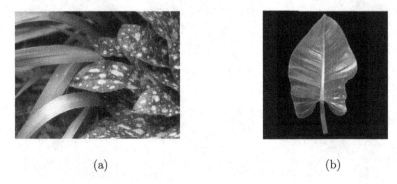

(a)                                         (b)

**Fig. 4.** The target images used in the paper. (a) Green leaves, used by Fig. 3; (b) Banana leaf, used by Fig. 6 and 7.

(a)                                         (b)

(c)                                         (d)

**Fig. 5.** Color transfor using our histogram-based color transformation and Reinhard et al.'s method: transferring (b)'s color into (a). (c) is the result by Reinhard's method and (d) is ours.

**Fig. 6.** Swinging branch is greening (Frames No. 1, 24, 48, 72, 96 and 120)

Fig. 3 shows a scene of chatting between a woman and a man through the caliginous early morning to the midday. The target image for them is Fig. 4(a). Fig. 3 also showcases the effects impacted by different timing curves. The left column is the selected frames from the source sequence, the middle column is the effect by a uniform speed timing curve (Fig. 2(a)), and the right column is resulted by the combined timing curve (Fig. 2(d)). The other examples are adjusted by the uniform speed timing curve.

The swinging branch in Fig. 6 is morphing its color to the color characteristics of Fig. 4(b).

When the frames of the source sequence are the same, they are decayed to be a static image. Fig. 7 is this type of examples. A dried leaf is resurgent in Fig. 7 when its color moves forward to fit the characteristics of Fig. 4(b).

Our histogram-based color transformation can be taken solely as an algorithm for color transfer between images. Fig. 5 shows the results produced by Reinhard et al.'s method and ours. The result by our method is more accordant with the target style (b). Reinhard et al.'s method is more efficient. So the users must leverage the efficiency and the effect to select an appropriate method.

Our experiments all run on a computer with Pentium 4 CPU (2.80GHz) and 1G Bytes memory. The running time of our implementation ranges from 1 second

**Fig. 7.** The resurgence of a dried leaf (Frames No. 1, 30, 60 and 90)

to 3 seconds per frame. The results shown here were all obtained by using a quantized $l\alpha\beta$ color space. The allowable error $e$ in Eq. 4 is 2 and the error for each component of $RGB$ color returned from quantized $l\alpha\beta$ color is less than 1 (while $R, G, B \in [0, 255]$).

## 5  Discussion and Conclusion

In this paper we present a temporal color morphing technique for producing the scenes of some natural phenomena in movies which are characterized by smooth color alteration along the time axis. While traditional methods accomplish this task by cutting and editing inefficiently or makeshifts, our approach generates plausible results and the needed inputs can be obtained conveniently.

This paper demonstrates that histogram warping can effectually represent the characteristics of temporal color morphing phenomena and that $l\alpha\beta$ color space's usefulness for color processing. We split the three-dimensional problem into three one-dimensional problems in $l\alpha\beta$ space and solve them more efficiently. We propose a quantized $l\alpha\beta$ color space under the condition of an allowable error.

**Acknowledgments.** This work is supported by National Science Fund for Creative Research Groups 60521002and national natural science foundation of China (Grand No. 60573147 and No. 60173035).

## References

1. Ruderman, D.L., Cronin, T.W., Chiao, C.-c.: Statistics of Cone Responses to Natural Images: Implications for Visual Coding. J. Optical Soc. of America 15(8), 2036–2045
2. Welsh, T., Ashikhmin, M., Mueller, K.: Transferring color to greyscale images. ACM Trans. Graph 21(3), 277–280 (2002)
3. Levin, A., Lischinski, D., Weiss, Y.: Colorization using optimization. ACM Trans. Graph 23(3), 689–694 (2004)
4. Gooch, A.A., Olsen, S.C., Tumblin, J., Gooch, B.: Color2Gray: salience-preserving color removal. ToG 24(3), 634–639 (2005)
5. Rasche, K., Geist, R., Westall, J.: Detail Preserving Reproduction of Color Images for Monochromats and Dichromats. IEEE Computer Graphics and Applications 25(3), 22–30 (2005)

6. Rasche, K., Geist, R., Westall, J.: Re-coloring Images for Gamuts of Lower Dimension. Computer Graphics Forum 24(3), 423–432 (2005)
7. Welsh, T., Ashikhmin, M., Mueller, K.: Transferring Color to Greyscale Images. In: SIGGRAPH 2002 Conference Proceedings, Annual Conference Series, pp. 277–280. ACM Press/ACM SIGGRAPH (2002)
8. Wang, C.-M., Huang, Y.-H.: A Novel Color Transfer Algorithm for Image Sequences. J. Inf. Sci. Eng. 20(6), 1039–1056 (2004)
9. Cohen-Or, D., Sorkine, O., Gal, R., Leyvand, T., Xu, Y.-Q.: Color harmonization. ACM Trans. Graph 25(3), 624–630 (2006)
10. Wolberg, G.: Image morphing: a survey. The Visual Computer 14(8/9), 360–372 (1998)
11. Grundland, M., Dodgson, N.A.: Automatic Contrast Enhancement By Histogram Warping. In: International Conference on Computer Vision and Graphics, Computational Imaging and Vision, vol. 32, pp. 293–300. Springer, Heidelberg (2004)
12. Grundland, M., Dodgson, N.A.: Color histogram specification by histogram warping. Color Imaging X: Processing, Hardcopy, and Applications. In: Proceedings of SPIE, San Jose, USA, 17-20 January 2005, vol. 5667, pp. 610–621, Society of Photo-Optical Instrumentation Engineers (2005)
13. Linde, Y., Buzo, A., Gray, R.M.: An algorithm for vector quantizer design. IEEE Trans. on Communications COM-28(1), 84–95 (1980)
14. Gonzalez, R.C., Woods, R.E.: Digital image processing, 2nd edn. Prentice-Hall, Englewood Cliffs (2002)

# A New Progressive Mesh with Adaptive Subdivision for LOD Models

Xiaohu Ma, Jie Wu, and Xiangjun Shen

School of Computer Science and Technology,
Soochow university, Jiangsu, 215006, China
xhma@suda.edu.cn

**Abstract.** Highly detailed models are becoming commonplace in computer graphics. Such models are often represented as triangle meshes, challenging rendering performance, transmission bandwidth, and storage capacities. This paper proposes a new scheme for constructing progressive meshes with adaptive subdivision. Besides, we introduce half-edge collapse simplification and present a new way to calculate error distance. Some experimental results show that our proposed method works well on various meshes.

## 1  Introduction

In order to meet the increasing needs on three-dimensional graphics, geometric models become highly detailed. However, these complex meshes are expensive to store, transmit, and render. In order to solve this problem, based on the mesh simplification algorithm, various level of detail (LOD) methods are created. Therefore people can first use the simplified meshes to replace the original meshes directly, or define a set of different levels of models, and then render them according to diverse scenes and view-points. However, if we use the general mesh simplification algorithm to construct the LODs, we have to build various simplified models, which usually requires lots of levels to assure the continuity among them. This makes effective storage and transmission impractical. Hoppe [1] proposed a progressive mesh (PM) scheme, which transform arbitrary mesh into a simplified one and stores all the necessary transform information for recovering the original mesh. This method can not only offer multiple LOD models, but also support progressive transmission in progressive mode. This paper proposes a new way to generate PM in a more appropriate way.

## 2  PM with Half-Edge Collapse

### 2.1  PM Model

The basic principle of Hoppe's PM is to iteratively collapse an edge from original mesh and lower the resolution gradually. At last, we may gain a coarse mesh and detailed collapse records. Based on these records, we may recover the original mesh through inserting vertices and triangles.

L. Ma, R. Nakatsu, and M. Rauterberg (Eds.): ICEC 2007, LNCS 4740, pp. 115–120, 2007.

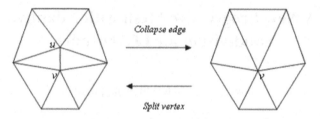

**Fig. 1.** Contraction of the edge (u, v) into a point

Figure 1 shows the edge collapse process. It shows that an edge collapse operation corresponds to a vertex split operation in an opposite action.

The problem with Hoppe's edge collapse method is that it needs to determine and create a new edge collapse point, which is time-consuming and memory-demanding. To resolve this problem, this paper adopts half-edge collapse scheme, which picks one of the two vertices on the given edge as the collapse point. Therefore, it can avoid complicated compute and massive storage requirement in creating a new collapse point.

### 2.2 PM Generating with Half-Edge Collapse Simplification

The mesh simplification algorithm plays a critical role in PM to reduce the number of faces while keeping original model's fidelity much. During the last decade, various mesh simplification algorithm have been proposed. The representative works include Vertex decimation algorithms [2], Re-tiling mesh algorithms [3], wavelet decomposition algorithms [4] and edge collapse algorithms [5-8].Garland [6] proposed an efficient and effective Quadric Error Metric to weigh the cost of edge collapse, in creating the new collapse point. The problem with QEM is that it only reflects the perpendicular distance from a point to a plane of triangle, not the real distance from the point to the triangle. Our method improves QEM by first applying sum of distances from the point to the triangle to control errors and adding the cost of sharp degree [8] to gain better effects.

As shown in Figure 2, assume the perpendicular projection from point $P$ to the plane is $P'$.

$$P' = aP_0 + bP_1 + cP_2 \tag{1}$$

where

$$a + b + c = 1 \tag{2}$$

Because $PP'$ is perpendicular to the line $P_0P_1$ and $P_0P_2$ respectively, there will be:

$$(aP_0 + bP_1 + cP_2 - P) \bullet (P_1 - P_0) = 0 \tag{3}$$

$$(aP_0 + bP_1 + cP_2 - P) \bullet (P_2 - P_0) = 0 \tag{4}$$

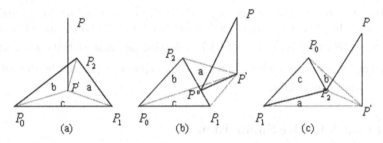

**Fig. 2.** Three kinds of distances from point to triangle. (a)when $P$ is closest to a point in the triangle (b)when $P$ is closest to an edge in the triangle (c)when $P$ is closest to one of three vertexes of a triangle.

Using the Gauss elimination method on expressions (2), (3) and (4) $a,b,c$ can be obtained easily.

In order to measure the real distance from the point $P$ to the triangle $P_0 P_1 P_2$, in term of the different values of $a,b$ and $c$, we divide it into three kinds of instances as shown in Figure 2.

(1) If $0 \leq a,b,c \leq 1, P'$ lies inside the triangle $P_0 P_1 P_2$ (as shown in Fig2a), where the distance from the point $P$ to the triangle is $|PP'|$.

(2) If one of $a,b,c$ is smaller than 0(assume $a<0$), $P'$ falls outside the triangle $P_0 P_1 P_2$ (as shown in Fig2b), where the distance from the $P$ to the triangle is $\sqrt{|PP'|^2 + |P'P''|^2}$.

(3) If two of $a,b,c$ are smaller than 0(assume $a<0$, $b<0$), $P'$ falls outside the triangle (as shown in Fig2c), where the distance from $P$ to the triangle is $|PP_2|$.

In order to better keeping the critical information in the original mesh, we adopt the sharp edge cost function which is ignored by Garland.

Sharp edge: Given a threshold $\theta$ and two triangles sharing a certain edge, if the angle between the two triangles shared is more than $\theta$, we mark the shared edge as a sharp edge. By default, we also regard the boundaries of the mesh as sharp edges. Based on this, we define the sharp degree of a vertex as the sharp edges associated with the vertex. In our cost function, we use $D(v)$ to denote $v$'s sharp degree. To avoid long and narrow triangles, we also consider the area cost of a vertex.

$$A(v) = \sum_{t \in N(v)} area(t) \tag{5}$$

where $N(v)$ is a set of the triangles which take $v$ as their vertex. Moreover, to prevent face-flipping phenomenon, we also check the change of the normal. If the normal is broken, we do not collapse this edge. In this paper, if the normal angle between new triangle's and former's exceeds 45 degrees, we define the normal as a broken one. In this way, our total cost function is shown as $Cost\ (v)$ $= \alpha Q(v) + \beta D(v) + \gamma A(v)$. Here $Q(v)$ is the distance cost of half-edge collapse; $\alpha, \beta, \gamma$ are set manually and the order of edge collapse is decided by the value of $Cost\ (v)$, from small to large.

## 3  PM with Adaptive Subdivision

As more and more 3D graphics transmit through the internet, the PM method mentioned above can implement multiple LODs better if there is enough bandwidth. However it can't fulfil the requirement when the bandwidth is limited and only a little latency time is allowed. In this paper, we adopt the subdivision algorithm to resolve the problem. The subdivision was proposed in 1970s and only received wide attention until 1990s.Various subdivision algorithms have been proposed since then. The representative researches include Catmull-Clark subdivision scheme, Loop subdivision scheme [9], Butterfly subdivision scheme and $\sqrt{3}$ subdivision scheme [10].

Among them, the Loop subdivision scheme and $\sqrt{3}$ subdivision scheme become popular in recent years due to adopting triangle mesh. We can apply the Loop subdivision mode in generating PM in a more effective way. If the network is not busy, we adopt the method mentioned above to get progressive mesh; if the network is busy, when the waiting time exceeds a given threshold $\alpha$, we use the loop subdivision way to obtain multiple LOD models at the clients.

Generally speaking, the number of triangles increases exponentially according to a given scale in the process of subdivision. For example, in the regular Loop scheme, the number of triangles in the mesh increases three times after one subdivision. Therefore it wastes massive resources to store the information of vertex, edge and face when dealing with large-scale meshes. It is also observed that, for most surfaces, there are regions that become reasonably smooth after a few levels of subdivision, and only certain areas of the surface, where there is a high curvature change, need more subdivisions to make it smooth. Therefore it is not ideal to have a global subdivision scheme applied at every level. Adaptive algorithm offers a way to take local subdivision, by striving to get high performance with fewer faces, and controlling the rapid increase of meshes, this enable the PM express more levels in detail.

## 4  Experimental Results and Discussions

We have implemented the proposed method for generating PM of 3D meshes using C++ and the OpenGL graphics library. For data storage, we adopt the data structure proposed by Stan Melax [11] for easy implementation. The results obtained on many different examples have highlighted strong benefits of our approach. Figure 3 shows the progressive meshes of footbones, it shows that our method can maintain the major sharps even there are only a few faces available. Figure 4 and Figure 5 compare

**Fig. 3.** The PM of footbones: the left model contains 1000 triangles, the middle one contains 2000 triangles and the right one contains 4204 triangles

**Fig. 4.** The PM of cow: the left model with 4000 triangles is initial control mesh, the middle one with 16000 triangles is the result after performing one step global Loop subdivision, the right one is the result after performing one step adaptive subdivision with sharp features

**Fig. 5.** The PM of mechanical part: the left model with 3808 triangles is initial control mesh, the middle one is the result after performing one step Loop subdivision, the right one is the result after performing one step adaptive subdivision with sharp features

**Table 1.** The comparison between the Loop subdivision and the adaptive algorithm after performing one step subdivision respectively

| Models | Loop subdivision | adaptive algorithm | Descendent rate of triangles |
|---|---|---|---|
| cow | 16000 triangles | 12872 triangles | 19.55% |
| mechanical part | 15232 triangles | 11412 triangles | 25.08% |

normal Loop subdivision and adaptive Loop subdivision which holds sharp degrees. Table 1 gives the descendent rate of faces after one subdivision while adopting adaptive algorithm. It indicates that adaptive subdivision can significantly reduce the number of faces while keeping the critical details.

## 5 Summary and Future Work

In this paper, we propose an efficient and effective way to generate progressive meshes based on half-edge collapse and the adaptive subdivision. Some experimental results show that our method can work well on various meshes. Main contribution of this paper is the new scheme to calculate error when collapsing the edge, and propose an adaptive subdivision method to produce PM. In the future work, we will explore to generate PM with color and texture attributes, which are important in some fields. Moreover, more systemic evaluation will be performed well.

**Acknowledgments.** The authors wish to acknowledge the support from the NaturalScience Foundation of Jiangsu Province under Grant 04KJB520142 and BK2007050.

# References

1. Hoppe, H.: Progressive meshes. In: Proceedings of the SIGGRAPH'96, pp. 99–108 (1996)
2. Schroeder, W.J., Zarge, J.A., Lorensen, W.E.: Decimation of triangle meshes. Proc. of the Computer Graphics 26(2), 65–70 (1992)
3. Turk, G.: Re-Tiling polygonal surface. Proc. of the Computer Graphics 26(2), 55–64 (1992)
4. Lounsbery, M., DeRose, T., Warren, J.: Multiresolution analysis for surfaces of arbitrary topological type. ACM Trans. on Graphics 16(1), 34–73 (1997)
5. Hoppe, H., DeRose, T., Duchamp, T., McDonald, J., Stuetzle, W.: Mesh optimization. Proc. of the Computer Graphics 27, 19–26 (1993)
6. Garland, M., Heckbert, P.S.: Simplifying surfaces with color and texture using Quadric Error Metrics. Proc. of the Computer Graphics 31, 209–216 (1997)
7. Ma, X.: New methods for triangle mesh simplification based on QEM. Computer Applications 21(12), 22–24 (2001)
8. Liu, X., Liu, Z., Gao, P., Peng, X.: Edge Collapse Simplification Based on Sharp Degree. Journal of Software 16(5), 669–675 (2005)
9. Loop, C.: Smooth subdivision surfaces based on triangles [M.S.dissertation]. Department of Mathematics of University of Utah (1987)
10. Kobbelt, L.: $\sqrt{3}$ -Subdivision. In: Proceedings of Computer Graphics, Annual Conference Series, ACM SIGGRAPH, New Orleans, pp. 103-112 (2000)
11. Melax, S.: A Simple, Fast, and Effective Polygon Reduction Algorithm. Game Developer 11, 44–49 (1998)

# Topology-Consistent Design for 3D Freeform Meshes with Harmonic Interpolation

Bin Sheng[1] and Enhua Wu[1,2]

[1] Faculty of Science and Technology, University of Macau, Macao, China
bsheng@sftw.umac.mo
[2] State Key Lab of Computer Science, Institute of Software, Chinese Academy of Sciences, Beijing, China
ehwu@umac.mo, enhua@iscas.cn

**Abstract.** One of the most exciting aspects of shape modeling is the development of new algorithms and methods to create unusual, interesting and aesthetically pleasing shapes. In this paper, we present an interactive modeling system for generating freeform surfaces using a 2D user interface. In this paper, we firstly interpret the given 2D curve to be the projection of the 3D curve that has the minimum curvature. Then we propose a topology-consistent strategy to trace the simple faces on the interconnecting 3D curves. By using the face tracing algorithm, our system can identify the 3D surfaces automatically. After obtaining the boundary curves for the faces, we apply *Delaunay* triangulation on these faces. Finally, the shape of the triangule surface mesh that follows the 3D boundary curves is computed by using harmonic interpolation. Solving Laplace's equations, we are able to construct simple and conceptual 3D models interactively. Although the incorporation of topological manipulation will introduce many new(and interesting) design problems that cannot be addressed in this paper, we show that automatically generated models are both beneficial and feasible.

## 1 Introduction

Nowadays, most designers still prefer to express their creative design idea through 2D sketches. However, space curve sketching using the 2D user interface has a challenging and active research problem of interpreting 2D sketches of curves and surfaces as a 3D entity. Obviously, this kind of reconstruction should need more information such as general assumptions or experiences, database of 2D-3D geometrical correlations or given models of reconstructed objects. it is well known that the fundamental difficulty is in choosing the appropriate one.

In this paper, we attempt to provide a physically sound and topologically elegant method of 3D model construction from 2D curves. Similar to the approach used in [1], we try to interpret the 3D curve corresponding to the given 2D curve to be the one that minimizes the maximum normal curvature in 3D. However, until now our construction of the 2D curves can only support the network of the 3D curves as the control profiles of smooth surfaces, and do not provide general

L. Ma, R. Nakatsu, and M. Rauterberg (Eds.): ICEC 2007, LNCS 4740, pp. 121–132, 2007.
© IFIP International Federation for Information Processing 2007

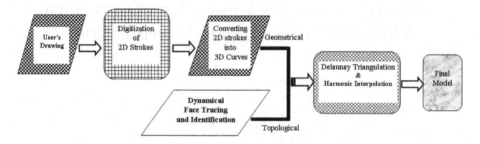

**Fig. 1.** The pipeline for Topology-consistent Design with Harmonic Interpolation

topology. In order to identify the faces on the mesh with topology consistency, we use topology graph operations which are similar to Euler's operations and based on graph embedding. The biggest advantage of our operations is that they are extremely simple and always guarantee topological consistency. We also developed a data structure, called *Bidirectional Face Table*(BFT), to support topological computation and identify the faces on the mesh efficiently.

The second issue we address in this paper is the generation of smooth surfaces on the above identified simple faces on the mesh. The 3D surface shape is generated in the form of a 3D parametric surface, which is obtained by transforming the 2D plane into 3D surfaces and automatically interpolating the mesh vertices of the 2D triangle mesh into 3D.

Primarily, there are four main contributions in this paper as follows:

- The topology of meshes can be updated automatically during the sketch process simply by adding or removing the key points and curves.
- Smooth free-form surfaces can be generated with simple user input, and adopt a face tracing algorithm for the simple face identification.
- Given the articulated sketches, we present an effective algorithm to generated shape of the surface mesh using a finite element method (FEM). All the internal vertices on the mesh are interpolated by using the harmonic functions.
- We developed an interactive modeling system to test a lot of drawings. It is proved that the system can create many reasonable shapes from the profile and silhouette sketches

## 2   Related Work

Some shape modeling systems are based on tensor product parametric surfaces such as tensor product B-spline [2]. However surfaces can only support quadrilateral meshes as control meshes for smooth surfaces and do not provide general topology [3]. And the restriction to quadrilateral meshes also makes the modeling process difficult for users. There have been significant efforts in solving this problem by still staying in the parametric surface realm [4].Recently, some papers have been presented on fitting surfaces to a network of curves.

On the other hand, three-dimensional shape modeling systems that use a volumetric data structure directly are relatively new [5,6] as compared with other popular modeling primitives, such as polygons, NURBS, and subdivision surfaces. Recently, a scripting language [7], octree [8], subdivision volume [9], and level set [10] have been used as volumetric modeling methodologies. Sketch-based modeling using standard mouse operations became popular in the past decade. One of the earliest sketching systems was Viking [11], which was designed in the context of prototypic CAD models. Later works include SKETCH [12] and Teddy [13]. The SKETCH system is intended to sketch a scene consisting of simple primitives, such as boxes and cones, while the Teddy system is designed to create rotund objects with spherical topology. Although improvements to the original Teddy system have been recently proposed [14,15], extending the topological variety of creatable models is still an unsolved problem.

## 3    Curve Construction

In our implementation, the given 2D curves are interpreted to be the projection of the 3D curve that has minimum curvature, by incorporating the idea from [1].In our implementation, the resulting 3D space curve, though a very close approximation of the curvature minimizing curve, has non-smooth, high frequency transitions of the depth values across the critical points. We use the *Laplacian filter* to obtain a final smooth space curve as it is extremely fast and simple as required by interactive sketching applications.

After transforming the 2D curers into 3D, our system also has the ability to form these curves into a network (graph). In this process, we call the end points of a curve to be the linkage points. And every point on the drawn curves could also be the linkage point, assigned by the users. Hence user could interactively specify the connectivity between the linguae points on the 2D interface. In this way, the curve network could be generated. Afterwards, we use an automatical recognition process of patch identification, where the the resulting network is the input. Once the patch boundary connectivity is known, the topological triangular mesh can be constructed, and then we can generates 3D surfaces by using Laplacian interpolation.

### 3.1    Conversion of 2D Curves to 3D Outlines

Usually, the 2D curves drawn freehand in sketching applications are not Bezier curves, but a sequence of edge connected points. Hence, we have to adapt the curvature minimizing scheme for the depth extraction for a generic 2D curve. Obviously, one way is to fit a Bezier curve to the input point sequence and interpolate the depth of this 2D Bezier curve. However, this is a computationally expensive operation and most importantly, the error in curve fitting will provide a distracting and unexpected feedback to the user.

In this subsection, we give a fast and simple method for finding the depth of the sketched 2D curve points that approximates the minimum curvature 3D curve. We assume that the depth values of the control points are equally spaced and the closest point on the curve from any control point has the same depth value as the control point. Hence if we identify these key points on the curve that are closest to the control points and space their depth values equally, we will have the first approximation of the space curve. Since we do not have these 3D Bezier curve control points and hence of its 2D projection, identifying even the correct number of key points is difficult.

Even though we do not have an explicit Bezier representation of the 2D sketched curve, the number of critical points in the curve is the lower bound on the number of control points of the hypothetical Bezier representation of the same curve. The critical point need not be the closest curve point (key point) to the corresponding control point. The fundamental source of approximation in our algorithm for curvature minimizing depth interpolation comes from the fact that we assume that these critical points are key points.

The second source of approximation comes from the fact that, there need not be a critical point corresponding to every control point. Hence all the required control points cannot be found by just one sequence of critical points. Differing from the previous approaches which hierarchically subdivide the curves, we solve this issue of selecting the key points, by simplifying the original 2D curve from the first point location. In practice, the hieratical method usually obtain the slow convergence, because that it takes many iterations to capture the key points, due to the local smoothness of the 2D curve. On the other hand, if we assume the starting point could be the key point, the alterative solution comes naturally and effectively. The basic idea of simplification is eliminating intermediate nodes in a straight boundary segment except two end nodes. Based on this idea, the algorithm inherently includes a routine for simplifying a curved boundary exactly made of many small segments. This is an artifact caused by the digitalizing the user's drawing. Meanwhile, what is important, is that if we perform the curve simplification to select the key points, we can easily apply curvature minimizing method to interpret the 2D curves, and the geometrical feature and the smoothness of curves still hold well for each curved segments.

Thus, the key points are extracted by the curve simplification. And the specific algorithm proposed here is based on the concept that newly simplified boundary segments are within a preset tolerance from original curve segments from 2D user's drawing. At first, two deviation tolerance schemes were examined. The one is limiting a maximum error between newly generated simplifying stroke segments and original stroke segments. The other is limiting a sum of errors between two different stroke segments. The latter scheme gave locally big deviations between the two boundaries although it limited a total accumulation of errors. So the former scheme was chosen for simplifying the curve from the original drawing. The summary of the algorithm for finding the key points by simplifying the curve is given as pseudo-codes in Algorithm 3-1.

---

**Algorithm 3-1.** KeyPointSelection(Curve $C$))

---

**Input**: Sample points of a 2D curve $C$.

**Procedure:**

Let $LS$ be {All the sample points of $C$}.
  {$v_0, v_1, v_2, ..., v_{n-1}$} is the point sequence from LS.
Let $KS$ be { point $v | v \in C \wedge$ v is a key point }.
Let $\tau$ be a preset tolerance to limit the difference between the original curve from $LS$
by and the simplified curve from $KS$.
Let $i$ and $j$ be the node indices of original curve.

$KS \leftarrow \{v_0, v_{n-1}\}$ , $i \leftarrow 0$ , $j \leftarrow 2$.
**Loop:**

  $KS = KS \cup \{v_i\}$

IF j==n-1 THEN
  **return**; {Break Looping.}
ELSE
Calculate a line, $L_{ij}$ , connecting $v_i$ and $v_j$.
Calculate the distances from the intermediate nodes,$v_k$, where $i < k < j$, to $L_{ij}$.
Let the distances be $d_k$ and the maximum among $d_k$ be $d_{max}$.
if $d_{max} > \tau$ then
  $KS = KS \cup \{v_{j-1}\}$;
  $i \leftarrow j - 1$.
end if
$j \leftarrow j + 1$.
END ELSE.

**END Loop.**

**return** $KS$.

---

## 3.2   Automatic Face Tracing and Identification

After transforming the 2D curves into 3D, our system also has the ability to form
these curves into a network (graph), which will directly control the generation
of the free-form surfaces on the curved boundaries. In this process, we call the
end points of a curve to be the linkage points. And any other point on a (already
drawn) curve could also be the linkage point, assigned by the users. Then user
could interactively specify the connectivity between the linkage points on the 2D
interface. In this way, the curve network could be generated. Afterwards, we use
an automatical recognition process of the face tracing and identification, where
the the resulting topology for the input control graph can have the on-the-fly
change.

## 3.3   Topological Operations on the Curve Networks

Our goal is to generate the 3D free-form surfaces from a network of input curves.
Hence, in our current implementation, once the user sketches the desired shape

of the object in the form of outline curves, the system should have some "intelligence" to help the user identify the face forming the surface. Please note that our system allows various models including smooth and sharp boundaries, and we consider the designed meshes can be divided into simpler surfaces, which are called *faces*. So the 3D curves here are nested to form the inter-connected boundaries of these faces.

Theoretically speaking, the face recognition is a face-tracing work in the graph represented by the network of curves. In order to make system automatically recognize the faces on the curve network and accelerate the further triangulation on the faces, we apply the graph rotation system [16] on the nested curves, as shown in Fig. 2. So that we can identify the following topological operations on the rotation systems as essential for the mesh modeling:

- **Face-Trace($f$)** outputs a boundary walk of the face $f$. This is related to reconstructing a "polygon"(face) in the curve graph and to triangulation of the faces on the mesh.
- **Vertex-Trace($v$)** outputs the edges incident on the vertex $v$ in the (circular) ordering of the rotation at $v$. This is useful when the constructed mesh needs reshaping.
- **Insert($v_1$,$v_2$,$e$)** inserts the new edge e between the face corners $v_1$ and $v_2$(a face corner is a subsequence of a face boundary walk consisting of two consecutive edges plus the vertex between them). This is used in revision of the curve network and triangulation of the face on the mesh, changing the topology of the mesh dynamically.
- **Delete(e)** deletes the edge $e$ from the current embedding. This is the converse operation of edge insertion and is also used in changing the topology of the mesh.
- **CoFacial($v_1$,$v_2$)** returns true if the two face corners $v_1$ and $v_2$ belong to the same face of the current embedding and false otherwise. This operation is useful in maintaining topological consistency of the mesh.

We have initiated the face tracing and identification algorithms on graph rotation systems in order to implement these operations efficiently. We have first observed that if a rotation system of a graph is represented in the edge-list form, which for each vertex $v$ contains the list of its incident edges, arranged in the order according to the rotation at $v$, the representation does not efficiently support the operations listed above. Here we introduce a new data structure and

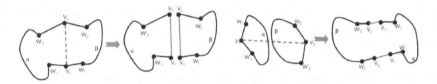

**Fig. 2.** Inserting an edge between two corners of the same face(*left*). Inserting an edge between two corners from two different faces.(*right*).

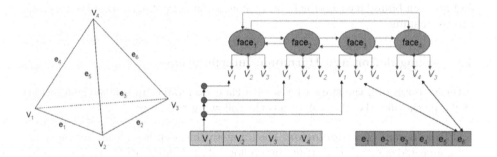

**Fig. 3.** An illustration of the BFT data structure for a tetrahedron

show that the new data structure efficiently supports all of the operations listed above.

Each face is given by a sequence of vertices corresponding to a boundary traversing of the face. The vertex appearances in the sequence will be called vertex nodes. Note that two consecutive vertex nodes in the sequence correspond to an edge side in the embedding. The sequence is represented by a cyclically concatenatable data structure. For specific discussion, we will use 2-3 trees for this concatenatable data structure. For readers' convenience, we recall 2-3 tree is a balanced tree whose depth is always logarithmic in the number of nodes in the tree. Moreover, operations on 2-3 trees such as inserting a node, deleting a node, splitting a 2-3 tree into two 2-3 trees, and concatenating two 2-3 trees into a single 2-3 tree, can all be done in logarithmic time.

**Definition 1.** Let $\rho(G)$ be an embedding of a graph $G = (V, E)$ with face set $F$. A *Bidirectional Face Table*(BFT) for the embedding $\rho(G)$ is a triple $L = <F, V, \epsilon >$, where the face list $F$ consists of a set of $|F|$ sequences. Each is given by a 2-3 tree and corresponds to the boundary walk of a face in the embedding $\rho(G)$. Moreover, the roots of the 2-3 trees are connected by a circular doubly liked list. The vertex array $V$ has $|V|$ items. Each $V[v]$ is a linked list of pointers to the vertex nodes of v in the 2-3 trees in $F$. The edge array $\varepsilon$ has $|E|$ items.Each $\varepsilon[e]$ is doubly linked to the first vertex nodes of the two edge sides of the edge $e$ in the 2-3 trees in $F$.

Figure 3 gives an illustration of the BFT data structure for a tetrahedron. It can be shown that the BFT structure and the BFT structure used in computational geometry can be converted from one to the other in the linear time. This implies that the computer space used by a BFT structure to represent a mesh modeling is linear in the size of the mesh, which is the best possible.

## 4   Surface Construction

Once the boundary connectivity for each face is known, our system constructs topological triangle mesh, and then generates a smooth freeform surface based on the given boundary curve network, using Laplacian interpolation followed by surface refining.

## 4.1  Triangulation and Harmonic Interpolation

After we obtain all the simple faces with their boundary curves, the generation of the meshes for the 3D profiles has the following two steps:

1. ***Topological Triangulation***-The input to this step is a closed sequence of connected curves. The output is a topology of the triangulation (with unrefined geometric coordinates for the vertices) that consists of input vertices on the curve and the newly introduced vertices in the interior of the identified face.
2. ***3D Interpolation of Surface Mesh***-The triangle mesh is automatically extended to the shape that represents the freeform surface by harmonic interpolation. Afterwards, mesh refining is processed to reduce the geometrical noise in generated mesh.

Specifically, in step 1, the boundary curves of the identified faces that are created in previous process are projected onto a plane that best approximates the curve points. Hence our triangulation method is applied on 2D domain, generally based on the *Delaunay triangulation*, where a triangles is created by joining nearest neighboring nodes as its edges. Since all the vertices having been projected onto the plane, such triangulation actually is a 2D Delaunay triangulation, called *topological triangulation*. Here,the input for mesh generation is a Planar Straight Line Graph (PSLG), including the vertices of the boundary curves projected onto the plane. Quality mesh generation for a PSLG is a standard computation involving two control parameters, a triangle size tolerance ($\mu$) and a minimum angle tolerance ($\theta$). A quality mesh generation program computes a constrained Delaunay triangulation that is a refinement of the input PSLG, with no triangle exceeding $\mu$ in size and no angle less than $\theta$, except possibly for small angles between constrained edges in the input PSLG. The modeler uses the freely distributed program program Triangle. As a result, the topological triangle mesh that is suitably fine for modeling the surface is obtained.

On the other hand, the nodes in the meshes which are obtained by triangulating the surface domain with the boundary curve constraints in 2D, are interpolated to give a 3D shape by using the transformed profiles in 3D. The surface mesh vertices are interpolated to conform to the profiles transformed in 3D using Laplacian interpolation. We seek to define the parametric surface by the function $f(r, s) = (x(r, s), y(r, s), z(r, s))$ representing the 3D surface mesh shape, where $r$ and $s$ are the parameters for a position in the 2D plane domain $\Omega$. We now specify $\partial\Omega$ be the outline of the faces projected onto the 2D plane, and let $\Gamma$ be the original 3D surface profiles which is interactively modeled and automatically captured before. There are two kinds of boundary conditions applied to the domain $\Omega$, the one is a *Neumann* boundary condition defined at $\partial\Omega$ because $\partial\Omega$ is considered as free, and the other is a *Dirichlet* boundary condition defined at $\Gamma$, which are illustrated in Figure 4. Let $g(r, s)$ be the forced boundary condition at $\Gamma$, which is

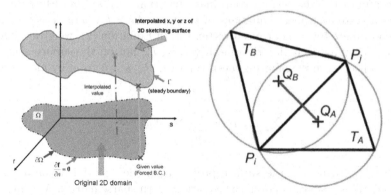

**Fig. 4.** Interpolation of 3D surface mesh coordinates(left), neighboring triangles of a Delaunay edge(right)

given by the 3D curves generated interactively as discussed previously. The interpolation problem is mathematically defined as follows.

$$\nabla^2 f = \frac{\partial^2 f}{\partial r^2} + \frac{\partial^2 f}{\partial s^2} = 0 \qquad \text{for } (r, s) \in \Omega \tag{1-1}$$

$$f(r, s) = g(r, s) \qquad \text{for } (r, s) \in \Gamma \tag{1-2}$$

$$\frac{\partial f}{\partial n} = 0 \qquad \text{for } (r, s) \in \partial \Omega \tag{1-3}$$

Functions that satisfy Laplace's equation, $\nabla F = 0$, are called *harmonic functions*. The Laplace's equation is interpreted as partial differential equations governing an elastic membrane problem. The function $f$ specified by Equations(1) can be viewed as 3 harmonic functions defined in $\Omega$ that interpolates $g(r, s)$ on $\Gamma$. Now the Laplacian interpolation problem of the surface mesh is solved by a *finite element method* (FEM) defined for the discretized domain. However, we do not need much of the apparatus of the FEM, because in this simple case, the linear equations for the coordinates, $x_k$, $y_k$, and $z_k$, can be formed from a single parameter, $\gamma_{ij}$, associated with the mesh edge between vertices $P_i$ and $P_j$, as shown in Figure 4. Because we are using a Delaunay triangulation, $\gamma_{ij}$ has a simple geometric description. For an edge internal to the mesh, let $T_A$ and $T_B$ be the mesh triangles that share the common edge between $P_i$ and $P_j$. Let $Q_A$ and $Q_B$ be the circumcenters of $T_A$ and $T_B$, then $\gamma_{ij} = \|Q_A - Q_B\| / \|P_i - P_j\|$; which is discussed in detail by [17].

If edge $P_i$ to $P_j$ is on the boundary of the surface, then $T_A$ has no neighbor $T_B$. In this case, $Q_B$ is the midpoint of edge $P_i$ to $P_j$ and $T_A$ must be acute so that $Q_A$ stays in $T_A$. This restriction on the triangles at the 3D surface boundary basically requires the mesh to be adequately fine and well shaped near the boundary.

To compute the discretized coordinate function, $x(r, s)$, the FEM method specifies a system of linear equations of the form $Ax = b$ where $x_k$ is the value of the coordinate function at mesh vertex Pk. In Equation (2), we give the form of the equation associated with a mesh vertex, $P_i$, not on the surface skeleton, that is connect to m neighboring mesh vertices, $P_{j_k}, k = 1$ to $m$ by mesh edges.

$$\left(\sum_{m}^{k=1} \gamma_{i,j_k}\right)x_i - \sum_{m}^{k=1} \gamma_{i,j_k} x_{j_k} = 0 \tag{2}$$

If $Pi = (r_i, s_i)$ lies on the surface profiles, then the equation is simply $x_i = x_{sk}(r_i, s_i)$. This is a system of linear equations with sparse matrix, A, which can be solved by most sparse matrix techniques or software.

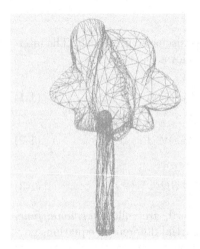

**Fig. 5.** Our system creates the mesh model for tree design(left). The textured tree model is rendered in the virtual environment(right).

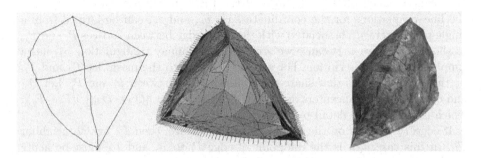

**Fig. 6.** One tetrahedron model generated by our system: the input sketches(left), the generated mesh(middle) and the texture-mapped appearance(right)

# 5   Experimental Results

We have tested our approach generating a number of simple models. Fig.5 and Fig.6 show some of the sketched-based models accursed using our interactive method. Most of the test cases are used with normally six to ten curves, producing a similar number of the simple faces on the model surface.

Our system provides a simple interface where the user can draw lines, rotate the view and continue drawing until the desired shape is achieved. Basic utilities like picking, moving and smoothing curves, or indicating corner points, are part of the interface. The identification of the simple faces on the mesh is automatically completed, but still needs the user's indication in some unusual cases. So the recognition work will be improved to be further self-acting and more interactive in future. In order to reduce the effect of the possible outliers in the surface fairing procedure, we damp the migration of vertices, only allowing displacements proportional to the length of surrounding edges. This way the relative movement of vertices is controlled by a user-defined parameter. The surface generated gives a coarse representation of the object and can be further refined using subdivision method.

# 6   Conclusions and Future Works

In this paper, we have also also proposed a conceptual framework for the development of systems for modeling topologically consistent meshes. We combine the graph rotation system representation and the harmonic interpolation scheme into one integrated system, in which the graph rotation system is used for an internal face recognition for models, while the harmonic interpolation is used for surface generation. We also provide efficient topological operations for edge insertion and deletion, and vertex and face tracing. In particular, we have also explored the physically-based method(FEM) to utilize the Laplacian interpolation to shape the mesh from the silhouette and profile curves.

Our planned future work includes more intelligent and automatic shape identification for surface generation, e.g., currently we are trying to use heuristics to determine the more plausible shape to be generated. In addition, future investigation will attempt to improve the surface reconstruction algorithm, including extensions to sketches that cannot be described by a connected graph. Finally, we believe that developing efficient ways to couple topology-guidance with geometrical optimization techniques is a fertile ground for future research.

# References

1. Das, K., Diaz-Gutierrez, P., Gopi, M.: Sketching free-form surfaces using network of curves. In: Proceedings of EUROGRAPHICS Workshop on Sketch Based Interfaces and Modeling (SBM05), Eurographics Association (2005)
2. Bartels, R.H., Beatty, J.C., Barsky, B.A.: An Introduction to splines for use in Computer Graphics and Geometric Modeling. Morgan Kaufmann, San Francisco (1987)

3. Loop, C., Rosa, T.D.: Generalized b-spline surfaces with arbitray topology. Computer Graphics 24, 101–165 (1991)
4. Loop, C.: Smooth spline surfaces over irregular meshes. Computer Graphics 28, 303–310 (1994)
5. Galyean, T.A., Hughes, J.F.: Sculpting: An interactive volumetric modeling technique. In: Proceedings of SIGGRAPH 1991. Computer Graphics Proceedings, Annual Conference Series, ACM, ACM Press / ACM SIGGRAPH, pp. 267–274 (1991)
6. Murali, T.M., Funkhouser, T.A.: Volume sculpting. In: Proceedings of ACM Symposium on Interactive 3D Graphics 1995, pp. 151–156. ACM Press, New York (1995)
7. Cutler, B., Dorsey, J., McMillian, L., Muller, R., Jagnow, R.: A procedural approach to authoring solid models. ACM Transactions on Graphics 21(3), 302–311 (2002)
8. Perry, R.N., Frisken, S.F.: Kizamu: A system for sculpting digital characters. In: Proceedings of SIGGRAPH, ACM, ACM Press / ACM SIGGRAPH, pp. 47–56 (2001)
9. McDonnell, K.T., Qin, H.: Dynamic sculpting and animation of free-form subdivision solids. The Visual Computer 18(2), 81–96 (2002)
10. Bærentzen, J.A., Christensen, N.J.: Interactive modelling of shapes using the level-set method. International Journal of Shape Modeling 8(2), 79–97 (2002)
11. Pugh, D.: Designing solid objects using interactive sketch interpretation. In: Proceedings of the 1992 symposium on Interactive 3D graphics, pp. 117–126. ACM Press, New York (1992)
12. Zeleznik, R.C., Herndon, K.P., Hughes, J.F.: Sketch: An interface for sketching 3d scenes. In: Proceedings of ACM SIGGRAPH 1996, pp. 163–170. ACM Press, New York (1996)
13. Igarashi, T., Matsuoka, S., Tanaka, H.: Teddy: A sketching interface for 3d freeform design. In: Proceedings of ACM SIGGRAPH, ACM, ACM Press / ACM SIGGRAPH, pp. 409–416 (2001)
14. Karpenko, O.A., Hughes, J.F., Raskar, R.: Free-form sketching with variational implicit surfaces. Computer Graphics Forum 21(3) (2002)
15. Karpenko, O.A., Hughes, J.F.: Smoothsketch: 3d free-form shapes from complex sketches. ACM Transaction on Graphics 25(3), 589–598 (2006)
16. Chen, J.: Algorithmic graph embeddings. Theoretical Computer Science 181(2), 247–266 (1997)
17. Letniowski, F.W.: Three-dimensional delaunay triangulations for finite element approximations to a second-order diffusion operator. SIAM Journal of Science and Statistical Computation 13, 765–772 (1992)

# Implementation and Optimization Issues of the Triangular Patch-Based Terrain System

Choong-Gyoo Lim*, Seungjo Bae, Kyoung Park, and YoungJik Lee

Electronics and Telecommunications Research Institute(ETRI)
161, Gajeong-dong, Yuseong-gu, Daejeon, 305-350, South Korea
{cglim,sbae,kyoung,ylee}@etri.re.kr
http://www.etri.re.kr

**Abstract.** A new dynamic LOD system is recently proposed to represent fairly large artificial terrains using hierarchical triangular patches[5]. Its mesh structure is unique from other conventional methods because it is designed to reduce the total number of draw primitive calls in a frame rather than the number of primitives. Another distinctive feature is its no-triangulation during the mesh adaptation by using its hierarchical layers and pre-constructed matching blocks. The purpose of the paper is to explain its implementation issues to make the new approach more understandable. Some of optimization issues are also discussed for better implementations.

**Keywords:** artificial terrain, fairly large terrains, level of details, triangular patches, hierarchical layers, terrain cell windowing, dynamic cell loading.

## 1 Introduction

Even with the high-end PCs, it is not easy to represent fairly large terrains in interactive applications because of the quite large number of mesh polygons involved. Dynamic LOD systems where a less number of polygons are used to represent remote areas and more polygons for close areas have been proposed in the literature such as ROAM(Real-time Optimally Adaptive Meshes)[2] and RQT(Restricted Quad-tree Triangulation)[6,8,9].

The mesh structure of ROAM is based on RTIN(Right Triangular Irregular Networks) which has a nice property that refining a triangle affects at most 2 triangles of each size in $[4.8^2]$ Laves nets[3]. ROAM optimizes re-triangulation by using the deferred lists of splitting and merging[2]. The mesh structure of RQT is based on quad-trees as its name implies. Each quad is refined according to the LOD value of the current area. This approach is well suited for texture allocation because of its rectangular shape while we need to enforce a block structure into a ROAM-based terrain system.

* This work was supported by the IT R&D program of MIC/IITA,[2006-S-044-02, Development of Multi-core CPU & MPU-Based Cross-Platform Game Technology].

L. Ma, R. Nakatsu, and M. Rauterberg (Eds.): ICEC 2007, LNCS 4740, pp. 133–138, 2007.

The new approach is proposed to take better advantage of the pipelined architecture of modern GPUs. Modern GPUs are known to perform better with a less number of draw primitive(DP) calls[7,1,?]. While conventional methods trying to reduce the total number of primitives, the new one try to reduce the total number of draw primitives.

## 2   Hierarchical Triangular Patches

One of the major components in conventional terrain systems is how to represent terrains in polygonal meshes. ROAM represents them in right triangles as it is a derivation of RTIN while RQT does it in quadtree-based triangles. The new approach represents terrains in triangular patches. Another component is how to adapt to the newly computed LODs and how to fill up the possible cracks between neighboring patches, which is called re-triangulation. A moving window system is critical to terrain systems because of the limited amount of system resources.

### 2.1   Mesh Structure

Modern GPUs use polygons, mostly triangles, to represent 3D meshes. The performance of a graphics system, thus, heavily depends on the number of polygons it has to draw in a single frame. That's why most traditional methods try to reduce the number of polygons. Modern GPUs are, however, known to work better with a less number of draw primitive calls due to their pipelined architectures. They are designed to perform better on a group of consecutive primitive inputs than on separate primitive inputs. One can reduce the number of draw primitive calls significantly if a set of triangles can be represented by a triangle which is just a single triangle of another triangle set as in Fig. 1.

Instead of trying to reduce the number of polygons, the newly proposed method utilizes a unique mesh structure to represent terrains. It constructs hierarchical layers of triangular patches where a patch can be represented by a single triangle at the next layer as in Fig. 1. A triangular patch $p_{0i}$ consists of $k \times k$ finest triangles from the given set of evenly spaced surface points, where $k$ is the number of grid in each triangular patch. Non-overlapping $p_{0i}$s collectively constitute the lowest layer of the hierarchy $P_0 = \bigcup p_{0i}$ and represent the whole terrain in LOD 0. The resulting patches $p_{ni}$ of layer $n$ becomes a triangle of a triangular patch $p_{(n+1)i}$ of the next layer that collectively constitutes the next layer of the hierarchy $P_{n+1} = \bigcup p_{(n+1)i}$

### 2.2   Re-triangulation

Once the camera moves, terrain systems re-compute LODs of each terrain area. There are possibly some changes in LODs so that they have to re-triangulate terrain meshes in order to keep terrains continuous. Conventional methods firstly re-triangulate whenever splitting or merging of triangles is required. Splitting or merging itself cause the re-structuring of the terrain mesh, that is re-triangulation.

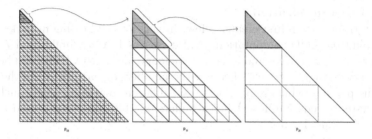

**Fig. 1.** A hierarchical layer of triangular patches when $k = 3$(from [5])

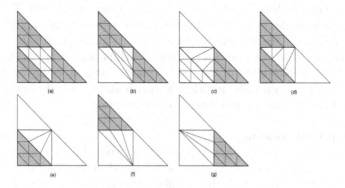

**Fig. 2.** 7 matching blocks(from [5])

This re-triangulation often leaves gaps between triangles. Another kind of re-triangulation is often carried out to fill up the gaps. As pointed out in Section 1, refinement of a triangle affects at most 2 triangles of each size in $[4.8^2]$ Laves nets.

The new system does not re-triangulate at all. Because it simply replaces the current patch with another patch from a higher or lower layer. If the LODs of 2 neighboring patches are different, then it replaces the current patch with one of 7 matching blocks. It identifies 7 matching blocks to stitch 2 neighboring patches of different LODs as shown Fig. 2. There are 7 different cases which are categorized by how the inner patch $p$ of level $i$ is surrounded by outer patches $p_h, p_l$, and $p_r$ of level $i + 1$, where the patch $p_h$ borders on the hypotenuse of the inner patch and the patches $p_l$ and $p_r$ on the left and right sides, respectively, facing the hypotenuse. The LOD difference of neighboring patches is 1 at most, which is not a rare practice[4].

## 3    An Implementation

There may be many various implementations for the new method. One can implement it with a few phases as follows.

– **Phase 1: Initialization**

The terrain system first creates a few threads for cell loading in background and multiple LOD computation. It also creates 1 vertex buffer and 7 index buffers to keep vertices and indices in memory. The vertex buffer can be used for every triangular patches because the numbers of vertices are all the same for the patches, which is 10. There are 7 different matching blocks such that the system needs 7 different index buffers of which one is also used for the original triangular patch.

– **Phase 2: Cell Loading**

The whole terrain is divided into equal-sized cells. For each cell. there is a heightmap which is a collection of height values for the cell. The terrain system reads in the height map for the visible cells and the candidate cells. After reading the heightmaps, it constructs the hierarchical layers of triangular patches. For the simplicity, it uses 3 layers only. 3 layers are enough to validate the feasibility of the new method. Using more layers, however, means bigger terrain cells. In other words, it means less flexibility for cell management because each cell needs more memory.

– **Phase 3: Cell Binding**

Now that the mesh structures have been constructed for the loaded cells, it needs to bind them together. Because it should propagate the LOD information on the boundary to the neighboring cells later during the phase of LOD computation

– **Phase 4: LOD Computation**

The system selects a single patch from 3 layers based on how much detail it needs to represent the area, which is the LOD value for the area. The current implementation determines LODs in proportion to the distances to the camera. Another way is to compute the sizes of the edges of the bounding box of the current patch[5].

– **Phase 5: Vertex Buffer Merger**

There is a severe penalty for the locking and transferring vertex buffers. The current implementation merges the whole vertex buffers of the current cell into a single one before transferring to the graphics pipeline. It saves the bandwidth of the AGP or PCI-express bus, thus improving the performance.

– **Phase 6: Rendering**

The terrain system renders each patch according to the LOD of the patch. If there is no neighboring patch of different LOD from the current patch, it is rendered with the patch from the layer of the current LOD. If not, it replaces the current patch with one of the 7 pre-constructed matching blocks. In order to generate realistic terrain images,

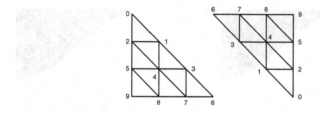

**Fig. 3.** Repeated uses of indices for the patches of different orientation

# 4  Optimization Issues

## 4.1  Re-use of Indexed Buffers

Indexed primitives are widely used in 3D applications as in [8] because of their smaller vertex buffers, which can maximize the use of the limited bandwidth of an AGP or PCI-express bus. Because of the same shape of triangular patches as shown in Fig. 3, the new system can transfers the indexed buffers at the beginning of the current cell and repeatedly use on all the patches, making better use of AGP or PCI-express buses. It transfers only the vertex buffers for the next patches.

A possible index list is $\{(0,1,2),(1,3,4),(1,4,2),\ (2,4,5),(3,6,7),(3,7,4),\ (4,7,8),(4,8,5),(5,8,9)\}$. It uses the fixed index lists for matching blocks as well with keeping the corresponding vertex buffers intact.

## 4.2  Dynamic Loading of Terrain Cells

The new terrain system uses a windowing system to avoid loading cells outside the viewing frustum. It loads the visible cells that move in the viewing frustum and off-loads the cells that move out.

There are, however, some IO delays when loading the cells that newly became inside of the viewing frustum. In order to avoid those delays which usually cause some popping artifacts, the new system load 2 rows and columns of neighboring cells using background threads. There is no popping artifacts, having the inside cells already loaded into the system.

It computes the LODs for inside patches before rendering. Those LODs of boundary patches are correct only if the LODs of candidate cells have been computed already. The system, thus, computes the LODs for candidate cells as well. The problematic situation occurs if the neighboring cells of a newly visible cell haven't been loaded yet and thus it can't compute the correct LODs for the patches of the new cell. The new system loads 4 more rows and columns of the candidate cells for correct LOD computation. 2 more rows and columns of candidate cells are enough if we allow some popping artifacts on the boundary cells, which can't be totally avoided because the LODs of the newly loaded candidate cells affects the LODs of the now visible cells.

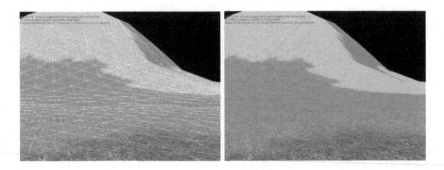

**Fig. 4.** A resulting surface in wireframe mode and in solid mode(from [5])

## 5    Conclusion

The implementation clearly shows that the newly proposed method can be used to represent fairly large terrains as some of screen shots are shown in Fig. 4.

## References

1. Ashida, K.: Optimising the graphics pipeline. In: China Joy 2004 (2004), http://www.chinajoy.net
2. Duchaineau, M., Wolinsky, M., Sigeti, D.E., Millder, M.C., Aldrich, C., Mineev-Weinstein, M.B.: ROAMing terrain: Real-time optimally adapting meshes. In: IEEE Visualization '97 Proceedings. IEEE Computer Society Press, Los Alamitos (1997)
3. Evans, W., Kirkpatrick, D., Townsend, G.: Right-triangulated irregular networks. Technical Report 97-09, University of Arizona, Computer Science (1997)
4. Herzen, B.V., Barr, A.: Accurate triangulations of deformed, intersecting surfaces. In: Proceedings SIGGRAPH 87, pp. 103–110. ACM SIGGRAPH, New York (1987)
5. Lim, C.-G.: A dynamic construction and representation scheme of multi-level LOD terrains using triangular patches. Submitted for Presentation to Pacific Graphics (2007)
6. Pajarola, R.: Overview of quadtree-based terrain triangulation and visualization. Technical Report UCI-ICS Technical Report No. 02-01, Department of Information & Computer Science, University of California, Irvine (2002)
7. Rege, A.: Optimization for DirectX9 graphics. In: Game Developers Conference 2004 (2004), http://www.gdconf.com
8. Snook, G.: Real-Time 3D Terrain Engines Using C++ and DirectX. Charles River Media (2003)
9. Szofran, A.: Global terrain technology for flight simulation. In: Game Developers Conference 2006 (2006)

# Deforming Surface Simplification Based on Feature Preservation

Shixue Zhang[1] and Enhua Wu[1,2]

[1] Dept. of Computer and Information Science, University of Macau, Macao, China
[2] State Key Lab. of Computer Science, Institute of Software,
Chinese Academy of Sciences, China
{ya57406,EHWu}@umac.mo

**Abstract.** In computer graphics, methods for mesh simplification are common. However, most of them focus on static meshes, only few works have been proposed for simplifying deforming surfaces. In this paper, we propose a new method for the multiresolution representation of time-varying meshes based on deformation area and feature preservation. Our method uses the famous QEM (quadric error metric) as our basic metric. The idea is to modify the edge collapse cost by adding the deformation and sharp feature weight to the aggregated quadrics errors when computing the unified edge contraction sequence, then adjust this sequence slightly for each frame to get a minimum geometry distortion. Our approach is fast, easy to implement, and as a result good quality dynamic approximations with well-preserved fine details can be generated at any given frame.

**Keywords:** Deforming mesh, LOD, Sharp feature, Mesh simplification.

## 1 Introduction

Nowadays more and more deforming meshes, also called time-varying surfaces or dynamic meshes, are widely used in many applications such as movies, games, simulations and so on. These surfaces are often represented by dense triangular meshes with high resolution, so sometimes we have to decimate the redundant details of the models for more efficient visualization processing, transmission and storage. Many mesh simplification methods have been proposed to simplify original models by repeatedly removing vertices, edges, or faces. However most of them are to deal with static meshes, and very little work has been made to address the problem on how to maintain accurate approximations of time-varying surfaces. In this paper, we propose an efficient method for generating progressive deforming meshes with high quality.

To simplify deforming meshes, one naive way is to simplify the models for each frame independently. This solution has the minimum error from the original model. However, since it does not exploit the temporal coherence of the data, it can involve the unpleasant visual artifact, causing the surface to vibrate and twitch. Moreover, this will waste a great deal of space.

L. Ma, R. Nakatsu, and M. Rauterberg (Eds.): ICEC 2007, LNCS 4740, pp. 139–149, 2007.

Some previous methods focus on preserving the static connectivity, i.e. the connectivity of the deforming surfaces remains unchanged for all frames. Such adaptations are inadequate and would cause arbitrarily bad approximations when deformation is highly non-rigid, since it does not take time-varying deformation into consideration.

We therefore propose a new method for simplifying deforming meshes based on feature preservation. Our method is a better tradeoff between the temporal coherence and mesh distortion, i.e. we try to maximize the temporal coherence while minimizing the visual distortion during the simplification process. Our idea is to first calculate the aggregated QEM error for each edge as DSD [26] method. We use the collapsing cost variation to measure the deformation degree of the deforming mesh. We calculate the sharp features the first and last frame according to the classification of the edges. By adding the deformation and sharp feature weight to the collapsing cost, we finally get the unified edge collapse sequence. For each of the frame we first do a majority of edge collapse operations based on this sequence to maintain the temporal coherence, and do the remainder operations based on the independent QEM sequence to minimize mesh distortion. We demonstrate that this provides an efficient means of multiresolution representation of deforming meshes over all frame of an animation.

The rest of this paper is organized as follows: Section 2 will review the previous works related in deforming mesh simplification. Section 3 will mainly introduce the procedure of our algorithm in detail and discuss its advantage. Section 4 will show the experimental results and compare our method with previous methods. Finally, conclusion will be made and some future work will be given in Section 5.

## 2  Related Work

**Simplification and LOD.** There are now extensive papers on the approximation of dense polygonal meshes by coarser meshes that preserve surface detail. These methods can be roughly divided into five categories: vertex decimation [1, 4, 33], vertex clustering [24, 29], region merging [8, 19, 27], subdivision meshes [6, 13, 23, 21], and iterative edge contraction [2, 3, 9, 10, 11, 12, 15, 16, 17, 18, 28, 32]. A complete review of the methods has been given in [7, 25]. Among these methods, the process of iteratively edge contraction is predominantly utilized. Representative algorithms include those from Hoppe [15] and Garland [9]. In such methods, a simple multiresolution structure is generated on the surface that can be used for adaptive refinement of the mesh [34, 16, 22]. Traditional mesh simplification algorithm works fine on a single static model, but it is unable to be directly applied to deforming meshes since no temporal coherence has been considered.

**Simplification of time-varying surfaces.** Shamir et al. [30, 31] are the pioneers to address the problem of simplifying efficiently deforming surfaces. They designed a global multiresolution structure named Time-dependant Directed Acyclic Graph (TDAG) which merges each individual simplified model of each frame into a unified graph. TDAG is a data structure that stores the life time of a vertex, which is queried for the connectivity updating. Unfortunately this scheme is very complex, and can not be easily handled.

Mohr and Gleicher [26] proposed a deformation sensitive decimation (DSD) method, which directly adapt the Qslim algorithm [9] by summing the quadrics errors over each frame of the animation. The result is a single mesh that attempts to provide a good average approximation over all frames. Consequently this technique provides a pleasant result only when the original surfaces do not present strong deformation.

DeCoro and Rusinkiewicz [5] introduced a method of weighing possible configuration of poses with probabilities. With articulated meshes, skeleton transformation is incorporated into standard QEM algorithm, and users must specify the probability distribution for each joint. This method works quite well, but is limited to a very specific class of deformations.

Kircher and Garland [20] proposed a multiresolution representation with a dynamic connectivity for deforming surfaces. By their method, the simplified model for the next frame is obtained by a sequence of edge-swap operations from the simplified model at the current frame. They treat a sequence of vertex contraction and their resulting hierarchies as a reclustering process [7]. This method seems to be particularly efficient because of its connectivity transformation.

Huang et al. [14] proposed a method based on the deformation oriented decimation error metric and dynamic connectivity update. They use vertex tree to further reduce geometric distortion by allowing the connectivity to change. Their method can provide a good approximation of deforming surfaces, but requires a complex structure.

# 3  Our Algorithm

Our algorithm consists of three parts: (1) Add the deformation information to the collapsing cost to preserve areas with large deformation. (2) Add the sharp feature weight to the cost to preserve the fine sharp features of the model. (3) Adjust the edge collapse sequence for each frame to reduce the approximation distortion. Next we will introduce the algorithm in detail.

## 3.1  Deformation Area Preservation

Our algorithm is based on the QSlim [9] which is now considered as one of the most efficient methods for static mesh simplification, so we should first have a quick review of it. Qslim iteratively selects an edge $(\mathbf{v}_i, \mathbf{v}_j)$ with the minimum contraction cost to collapse and replace this edge with a new vertex $\mathbf{u}$ which minimizes the contraction cost. For measuring the contraction cost of an edge, it utilizes the quadratic error metric (QEM) to measure the total squared distance of a vertex to the two sets of planes $\mathbf{P}(\mathbf{v}_i)$ and $\mathbf{P}(\mathbf{v}_j)$ adjacent to $v_i$ and $v_j$ respectively. A plane can be represented with a 4D vector $\mathbf{p},$ consisting of the plane normal and the distance to the origin. Hence, the squared distance of a vertex $\mathbf{v}$ to a plane $\mathbf{p}$ equals $\mathbf{v}^{\mathrm{T}}(\mathbf{pp}^{\mathrm{T}})\mathbf{v}.$ The QEM error function $ec_{ij}$ for a vertex $\mathbf{v}$ to replace the edge $(\mathbf{v}_i, \mathbf{v}_j)$ is

$$ec_{ij}(v) = \sum_{p \in P(v_i)} v^T(pp^T)v + \sum_{p \in P(v_j)} v^T(pp^T)v$$
$$= v^T Q_i v + v^T Q_j v$$

Garland also suggests using an area-weighted quadric error metric for better results [7] and defines the QEM error function as:

$$ec_{ij}(v) = v^T(w_iQ_i + w_jQ_j)v = v^TQ_{ij}v$$

where $w_i$ is the total area of triangles adjacent to $v_i$ and $w_j$ is defined similarly. Hence, the QEM cost $QEM_{ij}$ for contracting an edge $(v_i, v_j)$ is defined as $ec_{ij}(u_{ij})$, in which $u_{ij}$ is the vertex minimizing $ec_{ij}(v)$. QSlim simplifies a mesh by iteratively finding the edge $(v_i, v_j)$ with the minimum $QEM_{ij}$, performing an edge-collapse operation to replace $(v_i, v_j)$ with a new vertex $u_{ij}$ and updating the edge contraction costs related to $u_{ij}$ until the desired vertex count $m$ is reached.

To extend QEM to handle deforming meshes, a naive way is to use QEM to obtain an edge-collapse sequence for the first frame, and then apply this sequence to all frames. Since all frames use the same edge-collapse sequence, they have the same connectivity. The disadvantage of this approach is obvious. Features of other frames might be removed if they are not features in the first frame. The deformation sensitive decimation (DSD) algorithm addresses this problem by summing QEM costs across all frames [26]. The DSD contraction cost for an edge $(v_i, v_j)$ is defined as

$$DSD_{ij} = \sum_{t=1}^{f} QEM_{ij}^t = \sum_{t=1}^{f} u_{ij}^{t\,T} Q_{ij}^t u_{ij}^t$$

where $u_{ij}^t$ minimizes the QEM cost $QEM_{ij}^t$ for the edge $(v_i, v_j)$ at frame $t$. Hence, DSD tends to preserve edges that are geometric features more often in the animation.

We use the change of edge-collapse cost to measure the surface deformation degree. For areas with large deformation, the change of the collapsing cost must be prominent. On the other hand, collapsing cost may change slightly in areas with small deformation. We append additional deformation weight to the DSD cost, which can postpone the edge contraction in areas with large deformation. We define the deformation weight to be:

$$\sum_{t=1}^{f} \left| ec_{ij}^t - \overline{ec}_{ij} \right|$$

where $\overline{ec}_{ij}$ is the average collapse cost of edge $(v_i, v_j)$ over all of the frames. We add this cost to the DSD contraction cost:

$$cost_{ij}' = DSD_{ij} + k_1 * \sum_{t=1}^{f} \left| ec_{ij}^t - \overline{ec}_{ij} \right| = \sum_{t=1}^{f} ec_{ij}^t + k_1 * \sum_{t=1}^{f} \left| ec_{ij}^t - \overline{ec}_{ij} \right|$$

where $k_1$ is a user-specified coefficient to adjust the influence the deformation degree. In our experiment, we simply set $k_1$ to 1.

## 3.2 Sharp Feature Preservation

In order to preserve the sharp features of the original model, we should first define the sharp features. And this involves the classification of edges as Fig. 1 shows. The calculation of sharp features in each frame is obviously a time-consuming process, also wastes a lot of space. Our idea is to only compute the sharp features in the first and last frame, which can represent most of the characteristics of the animation. If the model is not much deformed during the animation, that is the first and last frame may have the identical sharp features, and these features are enhanced. On the other hand, if the deformation is totally non-rigid, that is the first and last frame may have totally different features, our method may possibly preserve most of the respective features during the animation. We implement the above by adding the feature weight into the collapse cost, as the follow equation shows:

$$cost_{ij} = (1 + k_2 * Feature\_Weight) \sum_{t=1}^{f} ec_{ij}^t + k_1 * \sum_{t=1}^{f} \left| ec_{ij}^t - \overline{ec}_{ij} \right|$$

where $k_2$ is between 0 and 1 to adjust the influence of the feature weight. If the user knows whether the deformation is rigid in advance, we can set more proper $k_2$ to get better result. Next we will discuss how to assign the value of *Feature_Weight*, and this involves the classification of edges [2]. We classify the edges into the following five types as Fig. 1 shows:

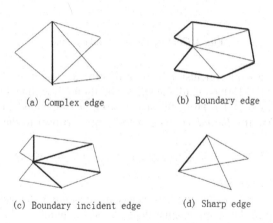

(a) Complex edge        (b) Boundary edge

(c) Boundary incident edge        (d) Sharp edge

**Fig. 1.** Classification of edges

① *Complex Edge*
Since shape changes of the 3D model due to contraction of complex edges could be severe, we give a large penalty on contracting the complex edges so that the contraction operation of complex edges can be conducted later relative to other types of edges. We can easily expect that the more incident triangles from the edge exist, the severer shape variation occurs. Hence, we define the *Complex_Weight* to be proportional to the number of incident triangles from the edge in the 3D model.

*Complex_Weight = (# of incident triangles − 3)*

② *Boundary Edge*
The shape variation of the 3D model becomes severe after contracting the boundary edges as well. Therefore, we must place a large penalty on contracting the boundary

edges. In addition, it would be more effective if we weigh differently according to the features in the 3D model.

We define θ as the angle between the incident boundary edge and itself, so a boundary edge may have two values of θ ($\theta_1$ and $\theta_2$) as Fig. 2 shows.

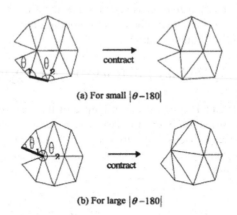

(a) For small $|\theta-180|$

(b) For large $|\theta-180|$

**Fig. 2.** Contraction of boundary edge

We have the following conclusion by investigating the variation after collapsing.

(1) If the value of |θ-180| is small, the shape variation of the model is limited.

(2) If the value of |θ-180| is large, the shape variation of the model is considerable.

Thus, we define the *Boundary_Weight* to be proportional to the maximum value of cosθ.

$$Boundary\_Weight = max\{cos\theta_1, cos\theta_2\}$$

③ *Boundary Incident Edge*

Contraction of boundary incident edges can yield substantial changes on the shape of the 3D model. Since the shape change depends on the number of incident boundary edges, we define the *Boundary_Incident_Weight* to be proportional to the number of incident boundary edges.

$$Boundary\_Incident\_Weight = (\# \ of \ incident \ boundary \ edges) / 4$$

④ *Sharp Edge*

Sharp edges connect two faces in the original mesh, and we define it as the angle (α) between the two neighboring faces should be smaller than a user-specified threshold (we set it to be 60°). Collapsing this kind of edges may cause large distortion of the model, so we define the *Shape_Weight* of it as sin α.

$$Sharp\_Weight = sin \ \alpha$$

⑤ *Interior Edge*

The rest of the edges are considered as interior edges. Since shape changes of the 3D model after contracting the interior edges is milder relative to any other types of edges, no penalty on contracting the interior edges would be reasonable.

Finally we define the *Feature_Weight* as follows:

$$Feature\_Weight = IsComplex * Complex\_Weight$$
$$+ IsBoundary * Boundary\_Weight$$
$$+ IsBoundaryIncident * Boundary\_Incident\_Weight$$
$$+ IsSharp * Sharp\_Weight$$

where *IsComplex, IsBoundary, IsBoundaryIncident* and *IsSharp* are Boolean variables. In other words, they can take 1 for TRUE or 0 for FALSE.

### 3.3 Distortion Adjustment

Based on the final collapse cost described above, we can finally get the overall edge-collapse sequence. This unified collapse sequence can maintain the connectivity of the whole mesh sequence unchanged. And also it has the optimal temporal coherence. However, since the unified order is applied, approximation can't be very satisfying on every frame. So our idea is to adjust this sequence slightly to get better approximation and preserve more fine details.

Considering the model in a certain frame, the independent QEM method can generate the optimal edge-collapse sequence. We can first do most of the collapse operation (we assume the proportion to be *P*, *P* is very near to 1) based on the previous calculated cost, then do the rest collapse based on the QEM cost. Since most of the operation is based on static connectivity, the temporal coherence is still maintained. We have tested different *P* during the animation, and we found that set *P* to around 96% can generate elegant result.

### 3.4 Algorithm Outline

Our algorithm can be summarized into the following steps:

1. Calculate the *QEM* collapsing cost of edges for each of the frame, to obtain the aggregate errors as the *DSD* method.

2. Based on the deforming sequence, measure the deformation degree to obtain the metric $cost_{ij}'$

3. Calculate the *Feature_Weight* of the first and last frame. Combined with previous cost, we get the destination cost $cost_{ij}$. Thus the final unified collapsing sequence is obtained.

4. For each of the frame, first do a majority of the edge collapse operations according to this sequence, and then do the rest of the operation following the QEM collapsing sequence to obtain the desired resolution.

## 4 Experimental Result

We test the result of our algorithm on a computer with Pentium4 3.2G CPU and 2G memory. We use OpenGL to render the models. The simplification of the horse gallop animation is shown in the Fig. 3. Compared to the upper full resolution models, the bottom shows our simplified results when 90% of its components are reduced. We could see that most of its features are preserved.

**Fig. 3.** Horse-gallops animation simplification with 48 frames. Original sequence: 8431v (upper), simplified models: 800v (bottom).

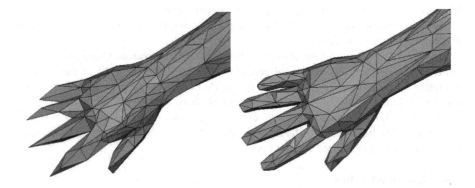

**Fig. 4.** Comparison of [20]'s method(left) and our method(right) of human's hand in horse-to-human morphing, the approximated versions contains 3200 vertices and 6396 triangles

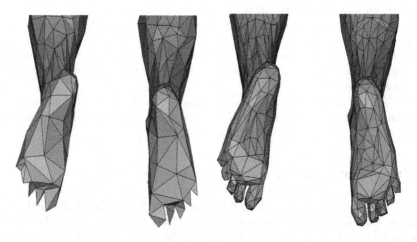

**Fig. 5.** Comparison of [20]'s method(left) and our method(right) of human's feet in horse-to-man morphing when 80% of its component is reduced

The next figures show the comparison of our method with the method in [20]. From Fig. 4 we could see that our method obviously preserves more details in the human's hand, also the distribution of triangle shape is more reasonable than [20]'s method. Since the features of the human's hands are not the features of the horse in the previous frames, and its deformation is totally non-rigid, our method can preserve such features much better than [20]. Another example shows the human feet approximation in Fig. 5. Our method also shows a much better simplification result than [20] with the toe details much better preserved. Since the deformation degree is so much in this area, the number of triangles in this area is much greater than [20]'s results.

An example of simplifying the whole sequence of horse-to-human morphing by using our method is shown in Fig. 6. Even the original model was reduced by 95%, our method can generate very faithful approximations.

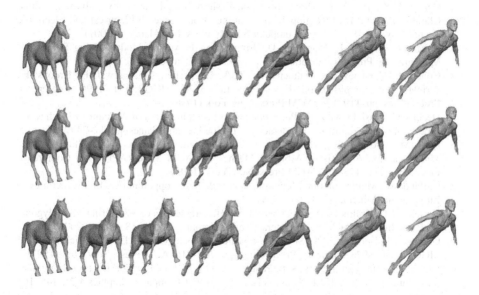

**Fig. 6.** A horse-to-human morphing animation with 200 frames. Top: The original sequence (17489 vertices). Middle: 3200-vertices approximation. Bottom: 800-vertices approximation.

## 5 Conclusion and Future Work

In this paper, we propose a simplification method for deforming surfaces based on deformation area and feature preservation. Given a sequence of meshes representing time-varying 3D data, our method produces a sequence of simplified meshes that are good approximation of the original deformed surface for a given frame. Our method extends the DSD formulation by adding deformation cost to preserve areas with large deformation. Feature weight is added to the collapse cost to preserve the sharp features of the original model. Finally, edge collapse sequence is adjusted for each frame to reduce the geometry distortion. Our method is easy to implement and produces better approximations than previous methods.

There are certainly further improvements that could be made to our algorithm. For example, we believe that there must be a way to extend our algorithm to be view-dependent.

**Acknowledgments.** We wish to thank Scott Kicher for providing the horse-to-man morphing sequence, Robert W. Sumner and Jovan Popovic for providing the horse-gallop data. The work has been supported by the Studentship & Research Grant of University of Macau.

# References

1. Ciampalini, A., Cignoni, P., Montani, C., Scopigno, R.: Multiresolution Decimation Based on Global Error. The Visual Computer 13(5), 228–246 (1997)
2. Chang, E.Y., Ho, Y.S.: Three-dimensional Mesh Simplification by Subdivided Edge Classification. In: IEEE Region 10 International Conference on Electrical and Electronic Technology, pp. 39–42. IEEE Computer Society Press, Los Alamitos (2001)
3. Cohen, J., Olano, M., Manocha, D.: Simplifying Polygonal Models Using Successive Mappings. In: Proc. Visualization '97, pp. 395–402 (October 1997)
4. Cohen, J., Varshney, A., Manocha, D., Turk, G., Weber, H., Agarwal, P., Brooks, F., Wright, W.: Simplification Envelopes. In: ACM SIGGRAPH 1996 Conference Proceedings, pp. 119–128. ACM Press, New York (1996)
5. Decoro, C., Rusinkiewicz, S.: Pose-independent Simplification of Articulated Meshes. In: Proceedings of Symposium on Interactive 3D Graphics and Games, pp. 17–24 (2005)
6. Eck, M., Derose, T., Duchamp, T., Hoppe, H., Lounsbery, M., Stuetzle, W.: Multiresolution Analysis of Arbitrary Meshes. In: ACM SIGGRAPH 1995 Conference Proceedings, pp. 173–182. ACM Press, New York (1995)
7. Garland, M.: Multiresolution Modeling: Survey & future opportunities. In: Proceedings of Eurographic, Milano, pp. 49–65 (1999)
8. Garland, M., Willmott, A., Heckbert, P.S.: Hierarchical Face Clustering on Polygonal Surfaces. In: Proc. ACM Symp. Interactive 3D Graphics, pp. 49–58 ( March 2001)
9. Garland, M., Heckbert, P.S.: Surface Simplification using Quadric Error Metrics. In: ACM SIGGRAPH 1997 Conference Proceedings, pp. 209–216. ACM Press, New York (1997)
10. Gieng, T.S., Hamann, B., Joy, K.I., Schussman, G.L., Trotts, I.J.: Constructing Hierarchies for Triangle Meshes. IEEE Trans. Visualization and Computer Graphics 4(2), 145–161 (1998)
11. Guéziec, A.: Surface Simplification with Variable Tolerance. In: Proc. Second Ann. Int'l Symp. Medical Robotics and Computer Assisted Surgery, pp. 132–139 (November 1995)
12. Guéziec, A.: Locally Toleranced Surface Simplification. IEEE Trans. Visualization and Computer Graphics 5(2), 168–189 (1999)
13. [GVS00] Guskov, I., Vidimce, K., Sweldens, W., Schroder, P.: Normal Meshes. In: SIGGRAPH '00 Conf. Proc., pp. 95–102 (2000)
14. Huang, F.C., Chen, B.Y., Chuang, Y.Y.: Progressive Deforming Meshes Based on Deformation Oriented Decimation and Dynamic Connectivity Updating. In: Proceedings of ACM SIGGRAPH/Eurographics Symposium on Computer Animation, pp. 53–62. ACM Press, New York (2006)
15. Hoppe, H.: Progressive meshes. In: ACM SIGGRAPH 1996 Conference Proceedings, pp. 99–108. ACM Press, New York (1996)
16. Hoppe, H.: View-dependent Refinement of Progressive Meshes. In: ACM SIGGRAPH 1997 Conference Proceedings, pp. 189–198. ACM Press, New York (1997)

17. Hoppe, H.: New Quadric Metric for Simplifying Meshes with Appearance Attributes. In: Proc. IEEE Visualization '99, pp. 59–66 (1999)
18. Hoppe, H., DeRose, T., Dunchamp, T., McDonald, J., Stuetzle, W.: Mesh Optimization. In: SIGGRAPH '93 Conf. Proc., pp. 19–25 (1993)
19. Kalvin, A., Taylor, R.: Superfaces: Polygonal Mesh Simplification with Bounded Error. IEEE Computer Graphics and Applications 16, 64–77 (1996)
20. Kircher, S., Garland, M.: Progressive Multiresolution Meshes for Deforming Surfaces. In: Proceedings of ACM SIGGRAPH/Eurographics Symposium on Computer Animation, pp. 191–200. ACM Press, New York (2005)
21. Lounsbery, M., DeRose, T., Warren, J.: Multiresolution Analysis for Surfaces of Arbitrary Topological Type. ACM Trans. on Graphics 16(1), 34–73 (1997)
22. Luebke, D., Erikson, C.: View-dependent Simplification of Arbitrary Polygonal Environments. In: ACM SIGGRAPH 1997 Conference Proceedings, pp. 199–208. ACM Press, New York (1997)
23. Lee, A., Moreton, H., Hoppe, H.: Displaced Subdivision Surfaces. In: SIGGRAPH '00 Conf. Proc., pp. 85–94 (2000)
24. Low, K.L., Tan, T.S.: Model Simplification Using Vertex-Clustering. In: Proc. ACM Symp. Interactive 3D Graphics, pp. 75–82 (1997)
25. Luebke, D., Reddy, M., Cohen, J.: Level of Detail for 3-D Graphics. Morgan Kaufmann, San Francisco (2002)
26. Mohr, A., Gleicher, M.: Deformation Sensitive Decimation. Tech. rep., University of Wisconsin (2003)
27. Mangan, A.P., Whitaker, R.T.: Partitioning 3D Surface Meshes Using Watershed Segmentation. IEEE Trans. Visualization and Computer Graphics 5(4), 221–308 (1999)
28. Popovic, J., Hoppe, H.: Progressive: Simplicial Complexes. In: SIGGRAPH '97 Conf. Proc., pp. 217–224 (August 1997)
29. Rossignac, J., Borrel, P.: Multi-Resolution 3D Approximations for Rendering Complex Scenes. In: Falcidieno, B., Kunii, T. (eds.) Modeling in Computer Graphics, pp. 455–465. Springer, Heidelberg (1993)
30. Shamir, A., Bajaj, C., Pascucci, V.: Multi-resolution Dynamic Meshes with Arbitrary Deformations. In: IEEE Visualization 2000 Conference Proceedings, pp. 423–430. IEEE Computer Society Press, Los Alamitos (2000)
31. Shamir, A., Pascucci, V.: Temporal and Spatial Level of Details for Dynamic Meshes. In: Proceedings of ACM Symposium on Virtual Reality Software and Technology, pp. 77–84. ACM Press, New York (2001)
32. Sander, P.V., Snyder, J., Gortler, S.J., Hoppe, H.: Texture Mapping Progressive Meshes. In: SIGGRAPH '01 Conf. Proc., pp. 409–416 (2001)
33. Schroeder, W.J., Zarge, J.A., Lorensen, W.E.: Decimation of Triangle Meshes. In: ACM Computer Graphics (SIGGRAPH 1992 Conference Proceedings), vol. 26(2), pp. 65–70 (1992)
34. Xia, J.C., Varshney, A.: Dynamic View-dependent Simplification for Polygonal Models. In: IEEE Visualization 1996 Conference Proceedings, pp. 327–334. IEEE Computer Society Press, Los Alamitos (1996)

# Procedural Modeling of Residential Zone Subject to Urban Planning Constraints

Liying Wang, Wei Hua, and Hujun Bao

State Key Lab of CAD&CG, Zhejiang University,
310027 Hangzhou, P.R. China
{huawei,wangliying,bao}@cad.zju.edu.cn

**Abstract.** Besides spatial elements, their spatial configuration is an important factor affecting urban image. In practice of urban planning, good designers do thoroughly consider goals of urban design and constraints of urban planning. In this paper taking the layout problems of a residential zone as background, a framework of procedural modeling and a constrained layout optimization approach is presented to simulate the design procedure of human. The approach represents design goals as cost function subject to planning constraints. We can obtain the design plan by minimizing the objective function. During optimization, we adopt heuristic algorithm to get solutions efficiently for elements layout. Experiments show this approach is able to achieve similar design of residential zone to human work, by using less human resources.

**Keywords:** Procedural modeling; urban planning; constrained layout optimization.

## 1 Introduction

### 1.1 Background

In recent years, many applications need highly efficient modeling for city model in both practical fields, such as digital city, national topography, urban planning and design, and virtual reality fields, such as digital entertainment, virtual learning, game and animation. So how to fast modeling city with highly realistic image becomes one promising research topic in many disciplines. New researches apply more interdisciplinary approach relating to urban planning and design, artificial intelligence, and computer graphics. Referring to the theory of urban planning and design, the basic elements forming urban image[1] consist of path, district, edge, node and landmark. Besides these spatial elements, their spatial configuration is an important factor affecting urban image through many combination ways which shows rich spatial texture, structure and human planning idea. Therefore visual design and spatial modeling for city involves these basic elements and their spatial configuration. However the spatial structure is so subtle that former researches mostly care for fast modeling elements and few combinations. Some works contribute to architecture modeling. Some deal

L. Ma, R. Nakatsu, and M. Rauterberg (Eds.): ICEC 2007, LNCS 4740, pp. 150–161, 2007.

with land use and functional zoning. Others focus on road network and building distribution. In this paper taking the layout problems of a residential zone as background, a framework of procedural modeling and a constrained layout optimization approach is presented. Layout problem is a kind of classical combinatorial optimization problem with a wide range of application. This problem means putting target objects into a bounded space or onto surface, satisfying some restrictions and reaching some optimal results. Layout problem has NP complete complexity for its geometrical and combinatorial features. Path planning is a key problem in fields of the intelligent robot and car navigator system. It also is a NPC hard problem.

## 1.2   Related Work

Nowadays Intelligent CAD research has been widely applied to achieve design goals semi-automatically in many fields, such as conceptual design, layout design, structural modeling for architecture and 3D scene modeling. Many modelers generate design by describing design intention as constraints and solving constraint satisfaction problem(CSP). Constraint description is classified to declarative and imperative method. From 1990's to today, there are many papers on declarative modeling. Several approaches have been attempted to solve CSP, for example mathematical programming, linear or non-linear equation solution, heuristic search of artificial intelligence. Ghassan[2] proposed hierarchical strength constraints of internal and external constraints to guarantee consistency of constraints. Coyne[3] constructed a WordsEye system to automatically convert text into representative 3D scenes. Generally CSP has many variables and iterative process need more time to get better solution, and during modeling users can intervene in an interactive and incremental way. But in general it is not suitable to generate results from a too vast search space.

Expert system tries to represent specific knowledge in abstract symbols and uses logical inference engine to get solution. Because inference process is limited to the specific problem, it rarely is adaptable to different situations. Grimsdale[4] expressed urban zoning and layout knowledge in pop-11 programming language and integrated inference engine with pop-11. It neither intervene the reference process directly nor support complex 3D models operation.

Grammar-based modeling approach has the advantage of rapidity and convenience by parameterization. Grammars such as L system, shape grammar, split grammar, are applied successfully to large-scale procedural modeling for plants, architecture and city. Parish[5] exploited extended-L system to model block partition, road network and simple building geometry. The highly abstract formalism of grammar had better include a small number of parameters, so grammar-based modeler does not show a bigger variety of urban patterns.

Object-oriented agent technique has well autonomous and extensible properties. Lechner[6] introduced agent technique to model urban zoning and road network. They avoided global rules manipulation, only processed local events and state query. Contrast to prior method, Guan[7] presented computer vision based registration method and imported augmented reality(AR) to planning residential zone. AR may reinforce people the sensibility to reality.

In the other hand, many researchers solved layout problems using AI algorithm to optimally place polygons on a bounded polygon without overlapping. Chen[8] used generic simulated annealing algorithm to search the placement order and orientation. A polygon spaces is filled with intervals data and heuristic search can exclude a lot of not good positions as earlier as possible and get an optimal layout. Particle swarm optimization is an efficient tool for non-linear and combinational and constrained optimization problems. Lei[9] et al presented a novel adaptive PSO based on multi-modified strategies to solve a layout problem of satellite cabins.

In general path planning method is heuristic search for its search space is too large and NP hard. Grid-based algorithm finds the best path by minimizing cost function. A-star algorithm[10] is a common approach to search a least cost path between a pair of grids, but it doesn't directly find a smooth path.

### 1.3 Contributions

Residential zone is the habitat of human being and one of important functional zones of city, its design often is a complex task of human. So a procedural modeling framework is presented to model the layout of its components following urban planning. Previous work used geometrical method for building distribution such as polygon subdivision and voronoi graph. Our former work introduced planning indices to control building density and height. Now we add spatial patterns to reinforce realistic and simulate the design procedure of human. Moreover parameterization makes it possible and controllable to fast modeling large scale scenes.

Secondly a constrained optimization approach is proposed to solve the layout problem. The approach represents design goals as cost function subject to planning constraints. The idea mainly comes from iterative adjustment and redesign during human design. Contrast to grammar-based method, the design plan is obtained by minimizing the constrained cost function. During optimization, we adopt heuristic algorithm to get solution efficiently.

Next we introduce the procedural modeling framework. Then constrained optimization approach, cost function and constraints are clarified. Solution including initial value decision and heuristic search are given in the following section. At last experiments are shown to conclude our method.

## 2    Procedural Modeling Framework

Fig.1 presents a hierarchical division in seven stages of city generation[11], we focus on two stages of lots and exteriors. We propose a procedural modeling framework shown in Fig.2 for residential zone with reference to a basic mode "patch-corridor-matrix" of modern landscape planning theory[12]. We specify components in a residential zone include residence, public facility, road, green land, tree, parking. Buildings (residence and public facility) within one patch

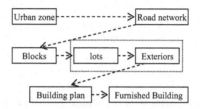

**Fig. 1.** Hierarchical division of city generation

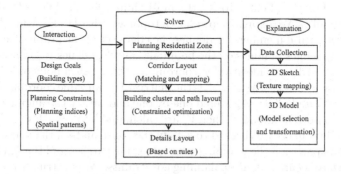

**Fig. 2.** Procedural modeling framework of residential zone

develop a building cluster. Road includes two grades which are corridor connecting patches and path connecting buildings to corridors. The framework consists of interaction layer, solver layer and explanation layer.

Interaction layer provides design goals and planning constraints. Design goals aim to put several kinds of buildings into the zone as many buildings and low costs as possible. Planning constraints include planning indices (building density, floor area ratio, the coefficient of sunshine spacing, green ratio) and spatial patterns shown in Fig.3. Spatial patterns describe the spatial structure of buildings and roads. The basic patterns of building are parallel and strew at random in different forms and the basic patterns of buildings group include determinant, centric, enclosed, symmetrical and dotted type. The basic patterns of paths have circle, direct and ending connection.

Explanation layer collects all components and outputs a 2D sketch with texture map and a 3D model whose elements are generated by transforming the selected basic models from a model library.

Solver layer solves three modeling sub-problems which are roads, building cluster and details layout. Details layout follows a certain rules, green lands are placed by searching plots in certain shapes subject to green ratio, trees are placed along road, parking facilities are beside roads.

Roads layout include corridor layout and path layout. For corridor, we reuse sample data and adapt them subject to the boundary and constraints of a planning zone. We use graph to express the boundary and corridor data. Given a planning graph($G'$) only with the boundary, the first step is to retrieve a matching sample

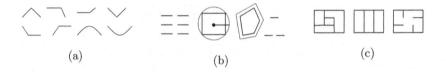

**Fig. 3.** Spatial basic patterns of (a) buildings (b)building groups (c)paths

graph($G$). We apply a polygon shape matching algorithm[13,14] and the correlation degree of area and entry to get the most similar graph. Then $G'$ adapts the corridor data of $G$. We express a graph as a topology with $\{V, E\}$, while $V$ defines the nodes set with $n$ members, $E$ defines the edges set of the graph. $V$ consists of two parts, $V_p$ defines $m$ nodes on the boundary, and $V_g$ defines $v - m$ nodes inside the graph. According to mean value coordinates theory[15] a polygon's $V_g$ can be formulated by $V_p$ as $V_g = M_p V_p$, $M_p$is the matrix of mean value coordinates. When $V_p$ and $V_p'$ of $G$ and $G'$ are registered one by one and satisfy the alignment of feature nodes on both boundaries, then $V_g'$ are calculated by $V_g' = M_p V_p'$. Finally the nodes and edges in $G'$ are checked to satisfy the constraints of the planning zone. The corridors partition the planning zone into some patches and the sample planning patterns of $G$ are reused as planning constraints. We construct a constrained optimization approach to layout buildings and paths within patches. Design goals are expressed as a cost function subject to planning constraints. By minimizing the cost function by heuristic algorithm buildings and paths are arranged efficiently.

## 3   Constrained Optimization Approach

Suppose we have the array of several types of buildings in a placement order, then what we optimize is to arrange the building position and orientation. The array is denoted as $\{B_i | i = 1..n\}$. A building $B$ can be represented by a vector $(A, h, v^b, p^g)$, where $A$ is the building's 2D projection on x-z plane represented by a polygon, $h$ is the height of building toward +y-axis, $v^b$ is the orientation of the building's balcony which is toward the south namely +z-axis. $p^g$ is the entrance to the building. The shape and the height of a building are determined by its type, but its position $p$ and its orientation $v^b$ is variable. Fig.4 shows a

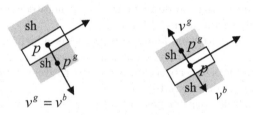

**Fig. 4.** The orientation relation between building's balcony and entrance,left is same, right is opposite

building's properties. The symbol $sh$ represents the shadow of the building, $v^g$ is the orientation of the entrance.

If one building is arranged a possible position, then it is constructed. What we solve for the array of buildings is a sequence of vectors $X = \{(p, v^b, s)_i | i = 1..n\}$, we use the building center to calculate $p$, $s$ is a boolean variable to identify whether the building is constructed. And the orientation of the entrance $v^g$ is from the center to the entrance. The exit path of the building is a sequence of path segments which connect the entrance to the exit $p^t$ on the corridor.

## 3.1   Cost Function of Buildings

We have mentioned that the design goals aim to put several kinds of buildings into the zone as many buildings and low costs as possible. So we propose a cost function of buildings is a weighted cost addition of constructing buildings and paths. The number of buildings is constrained by building density and floor area ratio. In order to put maximum buildings into the zone, we require the remainder building density and floor area ratio of the zone $S$ is minimum. It is known that grouping buildings together to be border upon influences the building cost. The longer the number of buildings in a group is, the lower the cost of gable is. But the length can't be too long[12]. We express the cost of a building group $C_t$ is a subsection linear function of the length and the total cost $C$ of all groups is their building costs addition. And $W$ is the cost of constructing paths. So we express the objective function is $f(X) = Min\{(w_1 S + w_2 C + w_3 W)/(w_1 + w_2 + w_3)\}$ subject to planning constraints.

To avoid the shadow occlusion, residences are separated by a reasonable sunshine spacing. The shadow of a building is calculated approximately according to its orientation and the coefficient of sunshine spacing. The occlusion distance of a building at the southern orientation equals its height multiples the coefficient. We suppose that the orientation of shadow opposites the orientation of the building's balcony and the shadow is a rectangle region within the occlusion distance, shown in Fig.4. Any residence does not in shadows. In addition, any building has an exit path. The constraints of building density and floor area ratio, sunshine spacing and path existence are checked while positioning buildings. Moreover the building layout follows a certain patterns. We require the pattern distance $P(X)$ of buildings is minimum. In order to solve the constrained optimal problem, we use penalty function method[16] which constructs an augmented objective function to solve an unconstrained optimal problem. Thus we need minimize the augmented objective function $O(X) = f(X) + MP(X), M > 0$ to solve the building layout problem.

## 3.2   Pattern Distance of Buildings

We use control lines to describe basic patterns of buildings. We organize the control lines as a tree, each leaf node can be used to search the building position while others are used to develop spatial patterns for paths. Each node includes the lines information data describing the start and ending, the building orientation and path pattern. After positioning buildings, the pattern distance of buildings includes building orientation and patterns cost. Residences had better orientate to south, so we define a subsection linear function to calculate the building orientation cost. We define a linear function for pattern costs to express the spatial structure and comfort degree of a building cluster.

### 3.3    Cost Function of Paths

Path cost includes the segments cost, exits cost and patterns cost. The minimum cost of the path segments of a building represents shortest, smoother and uniformly roomy, that is $G = L + N + E$, while $L$ is the length of the path segments of the building. When the directions of consecutive path segments are different, one turning occurs. So smooth degree is computed as the number of turnings $N$. Roomy degree $E$ expresses the space surrounding the path segments. We compute roomy degree as the cost of the distance before a point of path meets the boundary of buildings or the patch. Its first part is computed along the directions of path segments whose value is zero when the distance is far otherwise is 1. Its second part is calculated along upward, downward, leftward, rightward directions to show whether the space of both sides is uniform, whose value is 1 when a distance of four directions is near and a difference of two directions is large between up and down or between left and right, otherwise is zero. The exits on corridors are shared by many buildings and constructed using more costs. Additionally, a linear function for pattern costs is defined to express the spatial structure and comfort degree of paths.

## 4    Heuristic Algorithm

### 4.1    Building Placement

Building placement is a standard 2D polygons layout problem subject to constraints: (1) A building locates inside the zone with setback.(2)A building doesn't intersect with others. (3)Residence isn't in shadows. (4)A building has an exit path. (5) Buildings satisfy the building density and floor area ratio. (6)Buildings try to surround control lines of pattern. We construct polygons with a flag($> 0$ occupied by a residence, $= -1$ unavailable,$= -2$ shadow, $< -4$ occupied by a public facility).

Pairs of intersection develop internal intervals of a polygon, and we add a flag (flag$= 0$ available, $> 0$ occupied by a building, $= -1$ unavailable, $= -2$ shadow, $= -3$ setback space, $= -4$ shade) to manage the usage of a polygon's space.

Given an array of buildings in a placement order and patterns, we firstly solve the tree of control lines, collect background polygons filled with flags. Secondly we solve each of buildings position and orientation along control lines. When the building density and floor area ratio are not satisfied, or there isn't any space to place it, a building is not constructed and set its construction flag false. Otherwise the position on a line and the building orientation is used as the candidate value of the building. Next the building and its shadow polygons

**Table 1.** The Stages of optimal process

---

**Step1:** Set building patterns and solve control lines
**Step2:** Initiate background polygons
**Step3:** Create the array of buildings and the sequence of variable vectors
   $X = \{(p, v, c)_i | i = 0..n\}$
**Step4:** Calculate initial value $X_0$,and update background polygons,
   compute function value $O(X)$
**Step5:** Set iteration generation $G$, $0 \leq t < G$, set $t = 0$, $O(X(0)) = O(X_0)$
   **Step5.1:** Initiate background polygons,Set $t = t + 1$
      search descending direction $\triangle X(t) = (\triangle p_i, \triangle v_i, \triangle c_i)$ and
      max step $\lambda$, $X(t) = X_0(t) + \lambda \triangle X(t), \|\triangle X\| = 1$
   **Step5.2:** update background polygons, compute function value
      $O(X(t)$ as the fitness of $X(t)$
   **Step5.3:** Choose $X = \min\{O(X(t-1)), O(X(t))\}$
   **Step5.4:** When $t > G$ go to Step6.Else go to Step5.1
**Step6:** Search initial values for those buildings whose construction flags are false.
   If a building's construction flag is changed to be true, go to Step4.
**Step7:** Collect buildings' parameters, and change buildings from parallel
   to stew at random pattern.
**Step8:** Collect buildings' polygons and add to background polygons.

---

called foreground polygons are calculated and add to background after passing the placement constraints and exit path existence. Thereby the initial value of the building is decided by the candidate value, set its construction flag true. If there is any conflict, the candidate value is moved one step along its line and check again. If beyond its line, the candidate value is searched along next control line.

After getting initial values of all buildings, we need optimize the buildings' layout. Heuristic search may minimize the augmented objective function. We decide the descending direction through checking building groups one by one. If one building is border upon other and this group is too long then move tail part of the group to shorten it. When it is alone, move it along control line toward left or right neighbor to be border-upon other. The stages of optimal process are organized in table 1.

### 4.2   Path Planning

Building patterns and path patterns assist in our path planning. We plan paths in a building group to connect entrances each other and plan paths among groups to share the optimal exits. For a pair of points, path planning applies a modified A-star algorithm which can find a minimum cost path for a pair of grids. In order to obtain initial background grids, the background polygons are filled with scanning line shown in Fig.5(a). Pairs of intersection develop internal intervals of a polygon, and we add a flag ($= 0$ available, $> 0$ occupied by a building, $= -1$ unavailable, $= -2shadow$, $= -3$ setback space, $< -4$ occupied by a public facility) to manage the usage of a polygon's space. Then background intervals

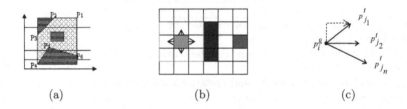

(a)                              (b)                              (c)

**Fig. 5.** Path planning (a) background polygons filled with scanning line (b)Modified A-star algorithm: green grid is the entrance, blue grid is the obstacle, red grid is the target. (c) Optimal exit search algorithm for a beginning grid.

are partitioned along vertical direction. The grids on corridor are exit grids. We modify A-star algorithm three points. First is to check whether a direct path exists between a pair of grids, second is path doesn't pass diagonal grids, which means current grid is not the parent of diagonal grids, shown in Fig.5(b). Third is to impose unfavorable cost on those grids which result in turning and narrow room, which adds extra cost to the $G$ part which has three items: path length, turning number and roomy degree. The process steps are shown in table 2.

**Table 2.** Optimal exit search algorithm for a beginning grid

| |
|---|
| **Step1:**Calculate the distance $d_j$ from $p_i^g$ to $p_j^t, j = 1..n$ then sort them to make $d_{j_1} < ... < d_{j_n}, j_1..j_n$ is the index of exits. |
| Shown in Fig.5(c), the worst case of the method is to search all exits |
| **Step2:** Set $d^r = \infty, m = 1$ |
| **Step3:** When $m < n$, get $j_m$, Else stop. if path exist from $p_i^g$ to $p_{j_m}^t$, and path length is $L_{j_m}$ and turning number is $N_{j_m}$ so the path cost $d_{j_m}^r = L_{j_m} + N_{j_m}$ |
| **Step4:** If $d_{j_m}^r < d^r$ then set $d^r = d_{j_m}^r$ otherwise set $m = m + 1$, go to Step3 |
| **Step5:** If $N_{j_m} = 0$ then $d^r$ is minimum (it is easy to prove). So stop and set $j = j_m$.Otherwise set $m = m + 1$, go to Step3 |

## 5   Experiments

We code the basic patterns of buildings and paths using numbers shown in table 3. And set the coefficient of sunshine spacing is 1 and the height of one

**Table 3.** Pattern definition

| Building pattern(sp) | Empty | Determinant | Centric | Enclosed | Symmetry | Dotted |
|---|---|---|---|---|---|---|
| Value | 0 | 1 | 2 | 3 | 4 | 5 |
| Path pattern(pp) | Circle connection | | Direct connection | | Ending connection | |
| Value | 1 | | 2 | | 3 | |
| Path direction(sp) | Same | Opposite | Inside | Outside | | |
| Value | 1 | 0 | 1 | 0 | | |

**Table 4.** Building types and pattern choices

| Demo | Name | Value | | | | | |
|---|---|---|---|---|---|---|---|
| 1 | Residence dimension(m) | 10.8,18,10.2 | 16,24,13 | 18.8,18,15.4 | 20,9,18 | | |
| | Facility dimension(m) | 30,9,30 | | 15,6,10 | | | |
| | Residence Pattern(sp/pp/pd) | 1/3/1 | 1/2/0 | 0/0/0 | /2/1/0 | 1/2/0 | 5/1/0 |
| | Facility Pattern(sp/pp/pd) | 1/2/0 | 1/2/0 | 1/2/0 | 0/0/0 | 1/2/0 | 1/2/0 |
| 2 | Residence dimension(m) | 16.3,60,12.3 | 13.9,36,13 | 13.8,60,14.5 | | | |
| | Facility dimension(m) | 15,6,10 | | | | | |
| | Residence Pattern(sp/pp/pd) | 1/3/0 | 1/2/0 | 2/2/1 | 2/2/1 | | |
| | Facility Pattern(sp/pp/pd) | 1/2/0 | 1/2/0 | 1/2/0 | 1/2/0 | | |

**Table 5.** Planning indices

| Main Indices (plot (100%)) | Planning Goals | | | Planning Results | | | | | | |
|---|---|---|---|---|---|---|---|---|---|---|
| | Floor area ratio | Building density (%) | Green ratio (%) | Floor area ratio | Building density (%) | Green ratio (%) | Residence plot (%) | Facility plot (%) | Path plot (%) | Parking ratio (%) |
| Demo1 | 1.1 | 28 | 40 | 1.06 | 18.1 | 22 | 15.2 | 2.9 | 17.7 | 4.5 |
| Demo1 | 1.8 | 25 | 40 | 1.6 | 13.4 | 26.4 | 9.5 | 3.9 | 14 | 2.1 |

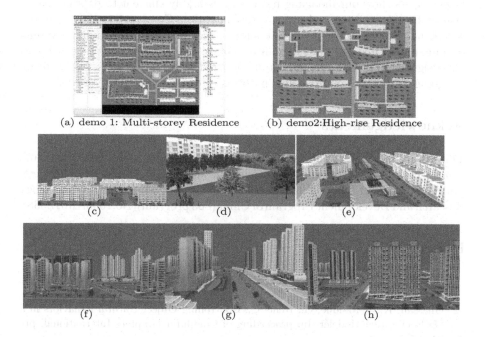

(a) demo 1: Multi-storey Residence    (b) demo2:High-rise Residence

(c)    (d)    (e)

(f)    (g)    (h)

**Fig. 6.** Experiments of 2D planning and 3D effect: (c-e)3D effect of demo 1 from different views (f-h)3D effect of demo 2 from different views

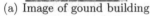

(a) Image of gound building        (b) Human detail building planning

**Fig. 7.** Comparison to human planning

floor is three meters, the dimension of a building is its length, height, width. We respectively use two patterns of corridors to partition the zone to plan the residential zone whose area is 108 thousand square meters. We give several types of buildings and pattern choices for each of patches, shown in table 4. We can get 2D sketch and 3D effect shown in Fig.6 in several minutes satisfying planning goals given in table 5.

# 6   Conclusion and Future Work

Experiments show our modeling framework is highly efficient to present spatial layout of residential zone subject to users' intention. Compared to the real image and human design shown in Fig.7, it is found that we can obtain similar planning to human work by using less human resources. Moreover our planning is useful for designers to improve incrementally and redesign more details. In future we are going to research more flexible patterns to do planning.

## Acknowledgements

This research work is supported by the 973 Program of China (No. 2002CB312102) and the Cultivation Fund of the Key Scientific and Technical Innovation Project, Ministry of Education of China (No.705027) and the National High Technology Research and Development Program of China(863 program)(No.2006AA01Z338).

## References

1. Wan Suzhen, et al.: Urban Spatial Structure Analysis. Scientific Publishing House (in Chinese) (2004)
2. Ghassan, K., Veronique, G., Rene, C.: Controlling Object Natural Behaviors in a 3D Declarative Modeler. In: proceeding of Computer Graphics International, pp. 248–253 (1998)
3. Coyne, B., Sproat, R.: WordsEye: An Automatic text-to-Scene Conversion System. In: proceeding of ACM SIGGRAPH, pp. 487–496. ACM Press, New York (2001)
4. Grimsdale, R.L., Lambourn, S.M.: Generation of Virtual Reality Environments using Expert Systems. In: proceedings of WSCG, pp. 153–162 (1997)

5. Parish, Y.I.H., Müller, P.: Procedural modeling of cities. In: proceeding of ACM SIGGRAPH, pp. 301–308. ACM Press, New York (2001)
6. Lechner, T., Watson, B., et al.: Procedural Modeling of Urban Land Use. In: proceeding of ACM SIGGRAPH. ACM Press, New York (2006)
7. Tao, G., Lijun, L.: The Application Research of Augmented Reality in Residential Area Planning. Journal of Engineer Graphics 5, 50–54 (2006) (in Chinese)
8. Yong, C., Min, T., Ruofeng, T.: Packing of Polygons Using Genetic Simulated Annealing Algorithm. Journal of Computer-Aided Design & Computer Graphics 15(5), 598–603 (2003) (in Chinese)
9. Kaiyou, L., Yuhui, Q.: A Study of Constrained Layout Optimization Using Adaptive Particle Swarm Optimizer. Journal of Computer Research and Development 43(10), 1724–1731 (2006)
10. Zixing, C., Guangyou, X., et al.: Artificial Intelligence and Application. QingHua University Publishing House (in Chinese) (1996)
11. Larive, M., Dupuy, Y., Gaildrat, V.: Automatic Generation of Urban Zones. In: proceeding of WSCG, pp. 9–12 (2005)
12. Dehua, L.: Urban Planning Theory. Chinese Architecture Industry Publishing House (in Chinese) (2001)
13. Arkin, M., Chew, L.P., et al.: An Efficiently Computable Metric for Comparing Polygonal Shapes. IEEE Trans. Pattern Analysis and Machine Intelligence 13, 206–209 (1991)
14. Ping, X., Xiaoyong, M., et al.: A New Fast Algorithm for Complex Polygons Matching. Computer Engineering 29(16), 177–181 (2003) (in Chinese)
15. Floater, M.S.: Mean value coordinates. Computer Aided Geometric Design 20(1), 19–27 (2003)
16. Yaxiang, Y., Wenyu, S.: Optimal Theory and Method. Scientific Publishing House (in Chinese) (1997)

# Concept and Construction of an Interactive Folktale System

Kozi Miyazaki, Yurika Nagai, Takenori Wama, and Ryohei Nakatsu

Kwansei Gakuin University, School of Science and Technology
2-1 Gakuen, Sanda 669-1337, Japan
miyazaki@nirvana.ne.jp,
{bfy68428,scbc0057,nakatsu}@ksc.kwansei.ac.jp

**Abstract.** In this paper as one example of a new edutainment system, we propose an "Interactive Folktale System," which makes it possible for people, especially children, to enjoy folktales in various ways. They can appreciate the generation of original tales and variations. Also they can interact with the story by communicating with its characters or by playing one of the characters. Moreover, they can easily create a new folktale by changing the original story or by describing a new story.

## 1 Introduction

Recently, extremely rapid progress in computer graphics (CG) technology has made it possible to virtually generate various kinds of objects in the real world. Such technologies are being widely applied to video games such as Role Playing Games (RPG). In RPGs, by controlling one of the game's computer graphic characters (CG characters), people can enjoy the development of fantasies, myths, and folktales. The problem with present RPGs is that their main focus is "fighting enemies," thus neglecting the original capability of fantasies or myths. On the other hand, the original function of fantasies, myths, and folktales was to influence the imagination of readers and cultivate creative capabilities.

There are several reasons why present RPGs avoid this important issue. One is that it is easier to sell and market games that directly appeal to such basic desires as fighting and conquering enemies rather than to highly sophisticated, imaginative, and/or creative capabilities. Another is that it is becoming increasingly difficult and time-consuming to develop/create contents and programs related to CG, and in this area non-professionals face barriers to develop entire systems from scratch.

Based on the above considerations, focusing on Japanese folktales we are developing an "Interactive Folktale System" with which people can enjoy various story developments. For example, they can enjoy original Japanese folktales as animation. Also using the system's interactive capabilities, they can interact with the characters in a story such as chatting with them. Also by controlling one of the characters as their avatar, they can enjoy the development of their own story. In addition users can reveal their own creative power by generating variations based on the original story, by creating a new story by combining multiple stories, and even by

L. Ma, R. Nakatsu, and M. Rauterberg (Eds.): ICEC 2007, LNCS 4740, pp. 162–170, 2007.

creating a completely new story that describes a new script using a script language supplied by the system. The last function of this system is crucial because the creation of new stories strengthens the people's creative capabilities.

We will first describe the basic concept of this system. Also we will explain the kinds of databases we are preparing. Since a key issue is an authoring system that makes it possible for an interactive folktale system to be realized, we will describe the details of the authoring system.

## 2 Related Works

One of the most important issues for interactive stories is controlling the development of interactive stories that have been actively studied as "Interactive Storytelling" [1][2][3][4]. The key issues in interactive storytelling include the generation of autonomous interactive characters and the emergence of storylines based on interactions between virtual characters and users and also among virtual characters. This is undoubtedly the final target of interactive storytelling. The problem with present interactive storytelling is that, since the generation of sophisticated autonomous characters is so complicated, it is difficult to maintain the consistency of the generated story for more than several minutes [4]. Game and e-learning users are expected to interact with the system for hours. Therefore, for these applications, developing a narrative based on a plot prepared beforehand is more realistic. If many story variations must be generated, our idea is to produce a story by connecting various short stories called 'segments.' In this case there must be an authoring system with which content creators can easily develop interactive contents.

## 3 Interactive Folktale System

### 3.1 Basic Concept

We are developing a system where having a database of Japanese folktales, it is possible to interactively regenerate original stories, generate wide variations based on the original stories, and even generate new stories [5]. For this purpose it is necessary to develop a model of folktale generation. To analyze and model folktales, V. Prop's study [6] is one of the best known. In this book, based on the analysis of old Russian magic folktales, he insisted that each folktale be considered a series of short story segments (hereafter, segments). Each segment could be classified into one of 31 categories called a "function" that corresponds to the kind of action of characters in the segment. Also he found that almost all folktales are constructed based on only one story line, in other words, one specific sequence of segments.

Studying whether this basic concept can be applied to other folktales and even to general stories is an interesting research theme. We applied his concept to Japanese folktales and also tried to develop an interactive folktale generation system.

Based on the concept of Prop, our hypothesis is the following:

(1) Each Japanese folktale can be segmented into a series of short story segments, as shown in Fig. 1.

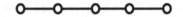

**Fig. 1.** Story as a sequence of story segments

(2) The sequence of these segments defines a specific story.
(3) Each segment is classified into one of several functions, each of which is defined based on the actions of the characters in it.

### 3.2 Analysis of Japanese Folktales

Based on the above hypothesis we analyzed fifty Japanese folktales and found that about fifty functions are enough to cover the stories in Japanese folktales. The number of functions is larger than in Prop's study because Japanese folktales cover wider areas than Russian magic folktales, and also some of them could be merged based on further research. We can treat Japanese folktales following the method proposed and adopted by Prop.

### 3.3 Functions of the System

Based on the above considerations, we are going to develop a system that can treat Japanese folktales in various ways. The major users of this system are children. As for video games we introduce the capability of interactive functions between the system and users to the system. We expect that users will enjoy the following methods of system interaction.

(1) Watching the generation of animation for each of the original Japanese folktales.
(2) Changing the characters as well as the backgrounds to enjoy wide variations of the original stories.
(3) Generating new stories. For example, it will be possible to create a new story by combining multiple original stories and to create a completely new story using a script language dedicated for the system.
(4) Watching the animations and talking to the characters in the stories or even controlling one as an avatar.

The interactive function described in (4) has been already realized in video games. For video games, however, all possible variations must be defined and involved in the system beforehand. So the development process of video games is time-consuming and expensive. We have developed an authoring system that supports the content development process of these interactive contents.

### 3.4 System Construction

The system consists of a folktale database and authoring system.

#### 3.4.1 Folktale Database
The database contains various kinds of data necessary to handle Japanese folktale generation based on three-dimensional computer graphics (3D-CG). It consists of the following sub-databases:

(1) Story segment database

This database stores a set of short segments extracted from Japanese folktales. Each segment defines an event in it and is expressed as a script using the script language dedicated to this system. Since the language makes it possible to develop an interactive story, users can interactively enjoy story development.

(2) Character/background database

Various characters, objects, and backgrounds that appear in Japanese folktales are stored here. Using this database, users can change characters or backgrounds and enjoy new sensations even if watching the same story. Also users can create a new story by combining the data and the script language.

(3) Animation database

In folktales, characters achieve different kinds of behaviors. It is very troublesome to prepare new animations that correspond to these behaviors when required by the story. Therefore by analyzing Japanese folktales we examine the kind of animations that can be generally used to create folktales and store these animations in the database. Thus users can create any kind of CG animation by simply choosing a character and animation from this database.

### 3.4.2 Authoring System

The authoring system has the following two functions:

(1) Event generation

Each segment corresponds to a scene in a movie or a play. Therefore the authoring system must have a function that generates any kind of event and character behaviors in the scene. For this purpose we developed a script language. One example of such a script language is TVML [7]. For TVML, users select characters and backgrounds stored in the database, and then they can create a CG scene by defining the actions of the characters using TVML. However, this system lacks an interactivity function. But since our developed script language has an interactivity function, users can describe interactive events in each segment.

(2) Story generation

The system must generate a story by selecting segments one by one and generating an event in each segment, Here the essential issue is the algorithm for selecting a sequence of segments to generate adequate story. The details will be described in the next section.

## 4  Story Generation Based on Segment Concatenation

### 4.1  Basic Concept

The sequence of selected segments obviously defines the story. Therefore developing an algorithm that defines the selection process is necessary. This is an essential problem in story generation and remains a difficult problem. In our study, so far the following basic methods have been adopted:

(1) Generation of an original story

As basic information, the sequence of segments for each original folktale is stored in the database. Using this information, users can enjoy the story development of each original Japanese folktale. Even in this case, users can enjoy variations by changing the characters and/or the backgrounds of the original story.

(2) Story transition from a story to a different story

Japanese folktales contain wider story variations than Russian magic folktales. However there are many cases where the short story within a segment resembles a short story from a different segment. For example, a scene where a boy called Momorato leaves his home to fight monsters resembles a scene where a boy called Issun-Bohshi leaves his home for the big city. In other words, these two segments have identical functions. Therefore we introduce a function that jumps from one story to another when these two stories have segments with identical functions. Figure 2 illustrates the story jump. This mechanism makes it possible to generate a huge amount of variety in story development.

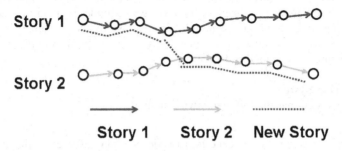

**Fig. 2.** Story transition

### 4.2  Segments and Stories

Let $\{S_i\}$ (i=1, 2, …) be a set of stories. Also let $\{SE_i\}$ (i=1, 2, …) be a set of story segments. Then each story can be expressed by a series of story segments:

$$S_i = SE_{i1}, SE_{i2}, SE_{i3}, \ldots \qquad (4.1)$$

### 4.3  Segment Index

We define each segment $SE_i$ by the following index:

Function: $F_i$ $\qquad (4.2)$

Main character: $(MC_{i1}, MC_{i2}, \ldots)$
Sub character; $(SC_{i1}, SC_{i2}, \ldots)$
The characters are listed based on order of importance.

### 4.4  Concatenation

(1) Let $D_{ij}$ be a distance between $SE_i$ (function: $F_i$) and $SE_j$ (function: $F_j$)

Example: $D_{ij} = 0$ (where $F_i = F_j$) $\qquad (4.3)$
$$D_{ij} = 1 \text{ (where } F_i \text{ does not equal } F_j)$$

(2) Let two stories $S_i$ and $S_j$ be
$S_i = SE_{i1}, SE_{i2}, \ldots, SE_{im}, \ldots\ldots$
$S_j = SE_{j1}, SE_{j2}, \ldots\ldots SE_{jn}, \ldots\ldots$

If the distance between $SE_{im}$ and $SE_{jn}$ is less than a predetermined threshold T, then story $S_i$ could jump to $S_j$ at $SE_{im}$ like:

$$SE_{im-1}, SE_{jn}, SE_{jn+1}, ...., \qquad (4.4)$$

Example: If the distance between two segments is defined by (4.3), then the threshold is set to T=0. This means that if there is a segment whose function is identical to another segment, then at this point, the story can jump to another story.

### 4.5 Maintaining Consistency in a Story

Consistent story development must be maintained even though a story jump might occur. Consistency contains various issues. For simplicity, however, here only the consistency regarding the CG models of characters is considered. If segment $SE_{im}$ is replaced by another segment $SE_{in}$, the consistency of the characters can be retained as follows. All the characters in $SE_{jn}$ corresponding to the number of characters in $SE_{im}$ are replaced. If several characters remain in $SE_{in}$, they remain unchanged. This operation is carried out both for main and sub characters.

## 5 Authoring System

We developed an authoring system that supports the realization of the interactive folktale system described above. In it, there are two kinds of files: object (Object.txt) and script (Script.txt). The system generates interactive narrative by interpreting these files.

Script.txt: A text file that defines the generation of each scene, the actions of each character, and the interactions between users and the characters and also among characters.

Objext.txt: A text file used for the basic definition and setting of 3D objects.

Figure 3 shows an example of the basic structure of Script.txt. An example of Object.txt is shown in Fig. 4. Since the details of this authoring system are described in [5], a detailed description is omitted here.

```
START HUMAN_SCRIPT
$count = $count + 1
IF $count > 1 THEN
@mes = $count
@mes    =    @mes    +    "times   you
visited."
MSG @mes
ELSE
MSG "Hello!"
END_IF
WAIT 0.5
END HUMAN_SCRIPT
```

**Fig. 3.** Basic structure of Script.txt

```
// Countryside
BACKGLOUND_01 {
// House
LOAD_MESH( "cottage01.x" );
MESH_SCALE( 1.2 );
// Ground
LOAD_MESH( "ground01.x" );
MESH_ROTATION( 0.0, 0.0, 0.0 );
MESH_SCALE( 1.0 );
}
```

**Fig. 4.** A description sample of Objext.txt

## 6  System Evaluation

We evaluated the functions of the Interactive Folktale System by selecting five representative folktales for experiments on which we carried out the following processes.

(1) Segmented each story into a set of short segments and generated a segment database.
(2) Generated CG models necessary to generate scenes and objects for all segments.
(3) Generated animation data necessary to generate actions and events that occur in each short story.

After the above preparation processes, we carried out story generation, which was confirmed in experiments.

(1) Generation of animation: All five classic tales were generated as an animated movie by concatenating segments based on the original story. Adding a slight variation to the animation by changing character models or backgrounds gave users a fresh feeling each time they observed the animation.
(2) Automatic story transition: Then we tested the story transition function described in Section 4. At certain segments when other segments with the same function are found, the story randomly transits to another segment, changing the story line. Although further study is still necessary, such story transition capability is very powerful and is a key function for the automatic generation of stories. Figure 5 illustrates an example of such a story transition. In one story, Princess 'Kaguya' who was born in a bamboo grows up to be a beautiful lady and attracts many noble men. In another story 'Momotaro' who was born in a peach grows up and leaves home to fight monsters. Since the maturation scenes match, the story starts as Kaguya and then changes to Momotaro. Figure 5 shows Princess Kaguya leaving her home to go to monster island.

**Fig. 5.** Example of a story transition

Figure 6 shows several other scenes in this story.

**Fig. 6.** Examples of scenes in the system

# 7  Conclusion

In this paper we proposed an Interactive Folktale System that can generate various types of Japanese folktales based on the concept of Prop. The system consists of an authoring system and three types of databases: story segment, CG, and animation. Taking Japanese folktales as an example, we constructed the system and carried out evaluation experiments that showed the system can generate original folktales, their variations, and also new stories by jumping from one story to another.

There are several issues to be pursued further. The most important one is to strengthen its interactive capability. Although the system basically has the function of interactivity, so far we have focused on the regeneration of original stories, generation of their variations, and the transition from one story to another. By extending these basic functions, we will develop the second prototype where story would change depending on the interaction between users and the system.

# References

1. Swartout, W., et al.: Toward the Holodeck: Integrating Graphics, Sound, Character and Story. In: Proceedings of the Autonomous Agents 2001 Conference (2001)
2. Mateas, M., Stern, A.: Socially Intelligent Agents: The Human in the Loop. In: AAAI Fall Symposium (2000)
3. Young, R.M.: Creating Interactive Narrative Structures: The Potential for AI Approaches. In: AAAI Spring Symposium in Artificial Intelligence and Interactive Entertainment. AAAI Press, Stanford, California, USA (2000)
4. Charles, F., Cavazza, M.: Exploring Scalability of Character-based Storytelling. In: Proceedings of ACM AAMAS'04 (2004)
5. Miyazaki, K., Nagai, Y., Bosser, A.G., Nakatsu, R.: Architecture of an Authoring System to Support the Creation of Interactive Contents. In: Harper, R., Rauterberg, M., Combetto, M. (eds.) ICEC 2006. LNCS, vol. 4161, pp. 165–174. Springer, Heidelberg (2006)
6. Prop, V.: Morphology of the Folktale. University of Texas Press (1968)
7. Douke, M., Hayashi, Makino, E.: A Study of Automatic Program Production Using TVML. In: Short Papers and Demos, Eurographics'99, pp. 42–45 (1999)

# Cultural Computing and the Self Concept: Towards Unconscious Metamorphosis

Tijn Kooijmans[1] and Matthias Rauterberg[2]

[1] Studio Sophisti, Amsterdam, The Netherlands
[2] Eindhoven University of Technology, The Netherlands

**Abstract.** We are exploring an application for a novel direction in human-computer interaction named 'cultural computing', which aims to provide a new medium for cultural translation and unconscious metamorphosis. The main objective of this project is to create an interactive experience that encourages people in Western culture to reflect on their self-concept. In Western culture the self-concept is generally based on conscious perception of the self. Over centuries the book 'Alice's Adventures in Wonderland' got continuous attention, and therefore seems to be a promising narrative to address issues like logic, rationality, and self. The user in the role of Alice will go through an interactive experience and meets a Caterpillar, who questions the participant's whereabouts of his/her self-concept. To determine the effect of this experience, we discuss a method that measures changes in a person's implicit self-concept for we predict that the experience will have an unconscious effect towards individual metamorphosis. Using the 'implicit association test' (IAT) we could find a significant effect in the hypothesized direction.

**Keywords:** cultural computing, interactive experience, unconscious, self-concept.

## 1 Introduction

Developments in the field of Human Computer Interaction (HCI) have opened up a new direction for the application of computer technology. After the introduction of personal computing, cooperative computing and social computing, a new paradigm named 'cultural computing' has emerged [22]. Cultural computing is based on what is called Kansei Mediated Interaction [18]. Kansei Mediation is a form of multimedia communication that carries non-verbal, emotional and even unconscious information. "Through the effects of psychology and psychotherapy, the unconscious became an optional ontology through which individuals could reframe their lives. As such, it has become one of the most powerful artefacts of psychology" [26].

First we have to introduce in our understanding and positioning of 'culture'. Westerners and East Asians perceive the world, think about it and act in it in very different ways [21]. Westerners pay primarily attention to some focal object, analyzing its attributes and categorizing it in an effort to find out what determinate its behavior. Determinates used mainly formal logic. Causal attributions tend to focus exclusively on the object and are therefore often mistaken. On the other side, East Asians pay

L. Ma, R. Nakatsu, and M. Rauterberg (Eds.): ICEC 2007, LNCS 4740, pp. 171–181, 2007.

primarily attention to a broad perceptual and conceptual field, noticing relationships and changes and grouping objects based on familiarities rather than categories. They relate causal attributions to the context instead of objects. Mainly social factors are directing the East Asians' attention. They live in complex social networks with determined role relations. Attention to the context is more important than to objects for effective functioning.

Westerners live independently in less constraining social worlds and attend to the object and their goals with respect to it. Physical 'affordances' of the environment can also influence perception but is assumed less important. The built environments of the East are more complex and contain more objects than do those of the West. In addition, artistic products of the East emphasize the field and deemphasize objects. In contrast, Western art renders less of the field and emphasizes individual objects and people [21].

The concept 'culture' has been defined and used in many ways throughout different contexts. More than one hundred different definitions for culture can be identified [15]. Anthropologists most commonly use the term culture to refer to the universal human capacity to classify, to codify and to communicate their experiences symbolically [32]. One of the most popular definitions of culture is a complex web of shifting patterns that link people in different locales and that link social formations of different scales. The integration and synchronization of human behavior in a particular cultural system can be achieved on very different time scales, called layers (from years to millennia; see Fig. 1). We do not discuss cultural development on the Y-layer (i.e., individuals, organizations, etc.), C-layer (i.e., societies, nations, etc.), but on the M- or even U-layer (see the concept of archetypes [10]). Over the last several thousands years (the M-layer) the peoples of four distinct regions of the civilized world created the religious and philosophical traditions that have continued to nourish humanity into the present day: (1) Confucianism and Daoism in China; (2) Hinduism and Buddhism in India; (3) monotheism in middle east; and (4) philosophical rationalism in Greece. 'Monotheism' and 'philosophical rationalism' is the religious and cultural foundation of the occident. We will use the term culture as the integration and synchronization of human behavior that includes attitudes, norms, values, beliefs, actions, communications and groups (ethnic, religious, social, etc.).

An important expansion of cultural theories can be discussed as falling into four focal areas [11]: (1) cultures as adaptive systems, (2) cultures as ideational systems, (3) cultures as socio-cultural systems, and (4) cultures as symbolic systems that are cumulative creations of mind. Conceiving culture as an ideational subsystem within a vastly complex system, biological, economical, social and symbolic, and grounding our abstract models and theories in the creation and usage of artifacts should make it possible to deepen the understanding of ourselves and our future. Whether the concept of culture has to be refined, radically reinterpreted, or progressively extinguished will probably not matter in the long run, unless we can not find a way to ask the right strategic questions, identifying connections that would otherwise be unseen, and therefore to enable us finding the best answers for our cultural development. Therefore ambient culture focuses nowadays on the development of open systems that understand and support the rituals of our living and adapt themselves to people through time and space [17].

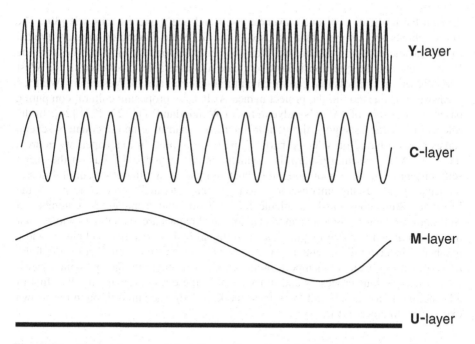

**Fig. 1.** The different layers and time frames for cultural developments (Y=year, C=century, M=millennium, U=universal)

Cultural computing is more than integrating cultural aspects into the interaction with computers. It is about allowing the user to experience an interaction that is closely related to the core aspects of his/her culture. In a way that let him/her engage with an augmented reality using the values and attributes of his/her own culture. As such it is important to understand one's cultural determinants and how to render them during the interaction [27]. In this paper we will describe two cultural computing projects, one from the Eastern World (prevailing in Japan) and one from the Western world (prevailing in England). It can be confirmed that Westerners are analytic, paying attention primarily to the object and the categories to which it belongs and using rules, including formal logic, to understand its behavior [20]. In contrast East Asians are more holistic, attending to the entire field and assigning causality to it, making relatively little use of categories and formal logic, and relying on 'dialectical' reasoning. These Western and Eastern types of cognitive processes are embedded in different naive metaphysical systems and tacit epistemologies. It can be speculated that the origin of these differences is traceable to markedly different social systems as part of the underlying cultural determinants [20].

In the Eastern application, cultural computing is defined as cultural translation that uses engineering methods to represent essential aspects of a culture [28] [29]. These engineering methods, such as artificial intelligence and mixed realities can give a person the sense of entering and participating in a different world. 'ZENetic Computer' is such an installation, which incorporates certain elements of the Japanese Zen culture (i.e., sansui paintings, poetry and kimonos). Through an interactive dialog with the system, users can experience the birth of self-awareness brought about through the unification of one's everyday self and one's unconscious self [30]. The Zen teachings and symbols that are used in the 'ZENetic Computer' are very typical for the Japanese culture and are not likely to be understood by most people from the West. Therefore the question is how to create a comparable experience in the West that is based on symbols that can touch cultural determinates of Westerners. We tried to answer this question in the project named ALICE by proposing cultural computing based on the story of 'Alice's Adventures in Wonderland' [1] [22] [23] [24]. In the role of Alice, the user goes through an interactive narrative and encounters several stages that are based on selected parts of the original plot. In this paper, we address the stage 'Advice from a Caterpillar', which centers around and focus on the user's self-concept [14]. To support individual metamorphosis and therefore cultural developments by addressing unconscious layers we have to make core concepts of the Western culture consciously available for reflection and disputation. A number of well-known cognitive, emotive and behavioral techniques are available to address our main objectives including disputation of irrational beliefs, emotive techniques and a number of behaviorally oriented assignments [12]. One of the main therapeutic functions of our approach is to support, in all meanings of the term, the symbolic expression of unconscious processes and to try to make these processes intelligible: first of all, intelligible to oneself and then, from the knowledge acquired through one's own experience, to others [16].

## 2 The Self

Throughout history, there have been wide varieties of theories about the self, coming from the fields of philosophy, psychology, and religion. This includes assertions that there is no self; that the idea is a logical, psychological, or grammatical fiction; that the sense of self is properly understood and defined in terms of brain processes; that it is merely a constructed sociological locus, or the centre of personal and public narratives, or that it belongs in an ineffable category on its own [6]. There is a significant difference in the construction of the self when comparing European/American culture and the Japanese culture [13] [21]. Western middle-class cultures are generally organized according to meanings and practices that promote the independence and autonomy of a self that is separate from other similar selves and from social context. This resulted in a prevalent self-esteem among western people with a tendency to self-enhancement. In contrast, many Asian cultures do not highlight the explicit separation of each individual, promoting the fundamental connectedness among individuals in a social group. The result of this on the construction of the self is that they are more likely to engage in self-criticism instead of self-enhancement [13]. Among contemporary researchers in social cognition, distinctions are drawn among self concept (cognitive component), self-esteem (affective component) and self-presentation (behavioral component) [3].

By addressing the Western individual self-concept, Alice's self is challenged in 'Advice from a Caterpillar'. After she entered the rabbit hole to follow the White Rabbit, she experienced a lot of transformations both physically and mentally. This brought her in an initial state of confusion, which is emphasized in her conversation with the Caterpillar: 'Who are YOU?' This challenging attitude of the Caterpillar makes Alice uncertain about herself, becoming vulnerable and open for persuasion [5]. Such a situation gives the possibility for a confrontation with and stimulates awareness of the self-concept. The character symbolized as a caterpillar is well chosen. One of the most important characteristic of caterpillars and butterflies is their unique life cycle. One of nature's most mysterious metamorphoses[1] occurs when a caterpillar changes from a slow-moving, fat and ugly creature to a colorfully winged, beautiful butterfly. This metamorphosis happens to a lot of insects, but not as dramatically as it does to a butterfly [9]. In this respect the 'caterpillar' character can unconsciously pursue the message to a human user not to be afraid of a fundamental metamorphosis in his or her self concept. This symbolic meaning can counterbalances the challenges intended by a conscious dialog next to it.

# 3   The Caterpillar Robot

Using an interactive installation, our goal is to make the participant question her/his own self-concept [14]. Our design strategy is thus to design the installation in such a way that the participant's experience is as consistent as possible with Alice's experience in the original story. Caused by the preliminary stages in the ALICE installation, the user will feel small and therefore confused about what happened (*criteria 1*). We also expect s/he wants to know what this entire means (*criteria 2*). Criteria (1) and (2) correspond with guidelines for timing persuasion [5]. Hence, it creates an opportune moment to question whether people are, and what they think they are. On entering the stage, the user will meet a Caterpillar, who has its back turned towards the user. He is humming softly and smoking a water pipe. When the user comes closer and enters the personal space of the Caterpillar, he suddenly wakes up, turns and bends towards the user. This should be a spontaneous movement to yield a surprise reaction. 'Who are YOU?' the Caterpillar asks first. This should initiate a dialog in which the Caterpillar is leading. During the dialog, the Caterpillar maintains eye contact with the user and supports its utterances with subtle body expressions. The question 'You? Who are YOU?' is repeated whenever the participant speaks with the words 'I', 'my', 'me' or 'mine' until s/he replies with a sentence like 'I don't know'. This will initiate a monologue of the Caterpillar about the transience of the self and his future metamorphosis into a beautiful butterfly. After that, he sends the user away.

## 3.1   Form and Movement

In order to make the Caterpillar prototype work as an unconscious symbol of metamorphosis, it is important that the form of the prototype matches with the archetypical form of a caterpillar. In moving from a natural form of a caterpillar towards an embodied artificial representation (further called 'robot'), there were several considerations taken into account. First of all, it demands for social abilities in order to become a persuasive character [5]. Since people have a basic tendency to project human beings onto animistic objects [25], there is no need for really adding a human face onto the robot to make it social [2]. We equipped our robot with only one eye and a mouth, to enable gaze and talk. Another aspect in achieving social abilities is lifelike behavior

---

[1] The Greek word 'metamorphosis' means 'change in form'.

[31]. We implemented this by means of a periodical wave motion of the robot's body that resembles the locomotive contractions and extractions of a real Caterpillar. Furthermore, the robot gazes at its dialog partner by aiming its body, eye and head. This gaze was implemented semi-contingent, which means that it combines random movements with reactive movements. A contingency factor of 60% (40% random, 60% reactive) will be perceived as most lifelike for communication robots [31].

To enable these required movements, we have equipped our robot with a number of servomotors that provide in total nine degrees of freedom. Four degrees of freedom are dedicated to the periodic motion of its body, two for horizontal and vertical rotation of its head, two for horizontal and vertical rotation of its eye, and one for the overall rotation of the body. To determine the position and distance of the participant, the robot has an array of nine motion detection sensors around its base and a rotating distance sensor. A limitation of this configuration is that it is impossible to measure the vertical size of a participant for proper gazing.

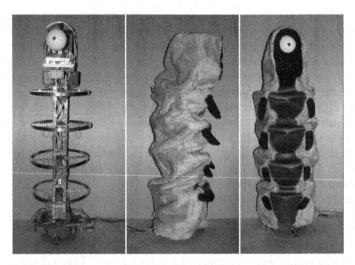

**Fig. 2.** The appearance of the caterpillar robot (skeleton,, side, front)

### 3.2 Dialog Management

Since the dialog between the Caterpillar and the participant is one of the crucial components of the interaction, we will address this in more detail. In order to engage the participant in a spoken dialog with the Caterpillar, there is a need for a system that facilitates speech input to understand the participant, speech output to talk to the participant and script control to steer the dialog in the right direction. The problem here is that every person will react differently to what the Caterpillar says; hence the dialog cannot be fully pre-programmed and should be constructed dynamically, we will outline the implemented technologies that deal with this. In choosing between a synthetic or recorded voice, it should be well taken into account that if a robot has a recorded (read: naturally human) voice, people feel easily tricked when the robot doesn't look human [19]. This argument made us choose for a synthetic voice for the

Caterpillar robot. A drawback of this decision is that it became difficult to give emotional expression or emphasis to utterances. In line with the earlier mentioned guidelines for persuasion, we have selected a voice that resembles a wise person. To pursue consistency with the original story, it is a male and bit languid, sleepy voice.

For speech input, the available technology is speech recognition. The current status of natural language recognition through speech is still of low quality and needs training time to let the system get used to a voice. To overcome this problem we have used a limited set of vocabulary to detect. When focusing only on a small set of key words, the accuracy of speech recognition can increase significantly. An advantage is that the Caterpillar steers the dialog and act as an agent. It can then predict the possible answers a participant is likely to give. To control the dialog, we implemented a script-based dialog management system. Input sentences are analyzed on the basis of decomposition rules, which are triggered by key words appearing in the input text. Responses are generated by reassembly rules associated with selected decomposition rules. The rules are stored in a script and can be edited to tailor the software for a specific application.

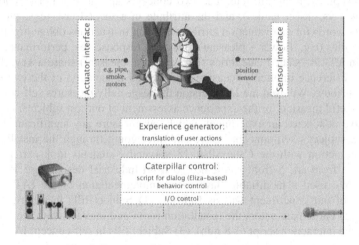

**Fig. 3.** System architecture and overall structure

Fig. 3 gives a global overview of the software framework of our prototype. The dashed-line boxes contain the following software components for the system:

- The main component is the *experience generator*. This takes care of the overall management of the installation and schedules the execution and transitions of the different states of the *interaction script*.
- The next component is in charge of the *Caterpillar control*, which manages the behaviors of the robot. It also incorporates a dialog manager that steers the conversation with the participant according to the predefined script, and deals with the speech input and output of the robot.
- The role of the *sensor interface* is to gather information about the participant in the installation. This is done by translating the retrieved data from the distance and mo-

tion sensors into higher-level information, such as the position of the participant in the area around the robot.
- The *actuator interface* controls the hardware part of the installation, which basically consists of the robot's motors. The actuators are activated through the experience generator and Caterpillar control components.

# 4 Experience Assessment

To measure the effect of our installation with respect to our objective, we need to test whether users experience any changes in self-concept when coming out of the test. We hypothesize that our installation will have mainly an *unconscious* effect on the self concept of our test subjects. We have to distinguish between conscious (explicit) and unconscious (implicit) cognition and the way they influence human responses [7]. The Implicit Association Test (IAT) focuses only on the implicit (unconscious) part of cognition [7] [8]. The IAT measures differential (unconscious) association of two target concepts with an attribute. The two concepts appear in a binary choice task (e.g., flower vs. insect names), and the attribute in a second task (e.g., pleasant vs. unpleasant words for an evaluation attribute). When instructions oblige highly associated categories (e.g., flower + pleasant) to share a response key, performance is faster than when less associated categories (e.g., insect + pleasant) share a key. This performance difference implicitly measures differential association of the two concepts with the attribute. We used the IAT version that especially measures self-concept [8]. This is a useful measure for the experience assessment of our test subjects.

We have conducted an experiment, which can measure any significant difference between a subject's self-concept before and after going through the installation and having interaction with the Caterpillar. 18 university students took part in this experiment (3 from art, 5 from medicine, 10 from industrial design; age 19-25; both genders). We used a modifiable flash-based implementation of the IAT [33]. The procedure of our experiment was as follows: (1) Subject fills in self-concept IAT (before). (2) Participant enters the installation room and interacts with the Caterpillar based on the interaction script (3-8 min). (3) Subject fills in self-concept IAT (after).

**Table 1.** Result of the MANOVA for the repeated measures of the IAT

| Measure | Mean (std) | |
|---|---|---|
| IAT before | 43.4 (± 24.5) | N=18 |
| IAT after | 21.3 (± 24.1) | N=18 |
| Main effect | Df=1, F=13.4, MS=4399.3 | P≤0.002 |

The results of these 18 test-subjects were gathered and analyzed using within-subject MANOVA (SPSS Vers. 12.01 for Windows). The average score of test A, on a scale of 0 to 100, significantly decreased from 43 to 21 (P≤0.002, see Table 1). This indicates that the measured unconscious self-concept changed significantly before and after the test in line with our hypothesis. Our test subject becomes less self confident and more separated from their original self concept. This can help to change the self-concept of Westerners to less individualism and egoism. If we assume that association strengths measured by the IAT are often not accessible to conscious inspection, then the difference between self-reports and IAT can be understood as a difference in their access to unconscious knowledge. Our experiment set out developing a theoretical integration of the important cognitive construct (self-concept) with its most important affective construct (self-esteem) to start investigating effects based on cultural computing.

An important limitation that one should take into account when assessing the individual experience of 'Advice form a Caterpillar' only, is that in the original story, there are a number of experiences such as 'falling down the rabbit hole' and 'shrinking and growing' that precede this encounter with the caterpillar. This could have a limiting or even enhancing effect on the unconscious impact of the experience. In addition, our experiment did not have a proper control group, so we can not claim any causal relationship. We are therefore looking forward to reassess the experience with the full installation in a later stadium of the ALICE project [34].

## 5  Conclusions

We have introduced and discussed an application for the new field named cultural computing, based on one particular part in the narrative 'Alice in Wonderland' [1]. This narrative addresses the individual self-concept of Westerners through an interactive experience of Alice's encounter with a caterpillar. Our installation can offer an experience that is similar and consistent with the original narrative. The encounter with our caterpillar robot had a significant influence on the self-concept of our test subjects in such a way, that these users get less attached to their self-concept. This can be seen as valuable contribution to cultural computing by providing access to the unconscious determinates of the Western culture: the self-concept as an individual. This can change Westerners to weaken their self-concept to become less individualistic and egoistic for the benefit of future societies [4].

**Acknowledgments.** This project is sponsored by Microsoft Research in Cambridge, UK. We want to thank D. van de Mortel, J. Hu, C. Seyfert, and J. Goldstein for their valuable contributions to our project.

## References

[1] Carroll, L.: Alice's adventures in Wonderland. Macmillan, London (1865)
[2] Bartneck, C.: Negotiating with an embodied emotional character. In: Forzlizzi, J., Hamington, B., Jordan, P.W. (eds.) Design for Pleasurable Products, pp. 55–60. ACM Press, Pittsburgh (2003)
[3] Brehm, S.S., Kassin, M.S., Fein, S.: Social psychology, 4th edn. Houghton Mifflin, Boston (1999)
[4] Deikman, A.J.: The observing self: mysticism and psychotherapy. Beacon Press (1983)
[5] Fogg, B.J.: Persuasive technology, using computers to change what we think and do. Morgan Kaufmann Publishers, San Francisco (2003)
[6] Gallagher, S., Shear, J. (eds.): Models of the self. Imprint Academic, Exeter (1999)

[7]  Greenwald, A.G., McGhee, D.E., Schwartz, J.K.L.: Measuring individual differences in implicit cognition: The Implicit Association Test. Journal of Personality and Social Psychology 74(6), 1464–1480 (1998)

[8]  Greenwald, A.G., Farnham, S.D.: Using the Implicit Association Test to measure self-esteem and self-concept. Journal of Personality and Social Psychology 79(6), 1022–1038 (2000)

[9]  Heiligman, D.: From caterpillar to butterfly. A Let's-Read-and-Find-Out Science Book (1996)

[10] Jung, C.G.: Man and his Symbols. Doubleday Garden City, New York (1969)

[11] Keesing, R.M.: Theories of culture. Annual Review of Anthropology 3, 73–97 (1974)

[12] Kinney, A.: The intellectual-insight problem: implications for assessment and Rational-Emotive Behavior Therapy. Journal of Contemporary Psychotherapy 30(3), 261–272 (2000)

[13] Kitayama, S., Markus, H.R., Matsumoto, H., Norasakkunkit, V.: Individual and collective processes in the construction of the self: self-enhancement in the United States and self-criticism in Japan. Journal of Personality and Social Psychology 72(6), 1245–1267 (1997)

[14] Kooijmans, T., Rauterberg, M.: Advice from a caterpillar: an application for cultural computing about the self. In: Harper, R., Rauterberg, M., Combetto, M. (eds.) ICEC 2006. LNCS, vol. 4161, pp. 5–8. Springer, Heidelberg (2006)

[15] Kroeber, A.L., Kluckhohn, C.: Culture: A critical review of concepts and definitions. Peabody Museum, Cambridge, Massachusetts (1952)

[16] Leclerc, J.: The unconscious as paradox: impact on the epistemological stance of the art psychotherapist. The Arts in Psychotherapy 33, 130–134 (2006)

[17] Marzano, S.: Ambient culture. In: Aarts, E., Encarnação, J. (eds.) True visions- the emergence of ambient intelligence, pp. 35–52. Springer, Heidelberg (2006)

[18] Nakatsu, R., Rauterberg, M., Salem, B.: Forms and theories of communication: from multimedia to Kansei mediation. Multimedia Systems 11(3), 304–312 (2006)

[19] Nass, C., Brave, S.: Wired for Speech: How voice activates and advances the human-computer relationship. MIT Press, Cambridge (2005)

[20] Nisbett, R.E., Peng, K., Choi, I., Norenzayan, A.: Culture and systems of thought: Holistic versus analytic cognition. Psychological Review 108(2), 291–310 (2001)

[21] Nisbett, R.E., Masuda, T.: Culture and point of view. PNAS 100(19), 11163–11170 (2003)

[22] Rauterberg, M.: From personal to cultural computing: how to assess a cultural experience. In: Kempter, G., von Hellberg, P. (eds.) uDayIV–Information nutzbar machen, pp. 13–21. Pabst Science Publisher, Lengerich (2006)

[23] Rauterberg, M.: Usability in the future –explicit and implicit effects in cultural computing. In: Heinecke, A.M., Paul, H. (eds.) Mensch & Computer 2006: Mensch und Computer im StrukturWandel, pp. 29–36. Oldenbourg Verlag, München (2006)

[24] Rauterberg, M.: How to assess the user's experience in cultural computing. In: Bosenick, T., Hassenzahl, M., Müller-Prove, M., Peissner, M. (eds.) Usability Professionals 2006, Fraunhofer Informationszentrum Raum und Bau, pp. 12–17 (2006)

[25] Reeves, B., Nass, C.: The Media Equation: How people treat computers, television, and new media like real people and places. Cambridge University Press, New York (1996)

[26] Shamdasani, S.: Unconscious. In: Odijk, E., Syre, J.-C., Rem, M. (eds.) PARLE 1989. LNCS, vol. 365, p. 1921. Springer, Heidelberg (1989)

[27] Tosa, N., Nakatsu, R.: Interactive Comedy: Laughter as the next intelligence system. In: Proceedings International Symposium on Micromechatronics and Human Science, pp. 135–138. IEEE Computer Society Press, Los Alamitos (2002)

[28] Tosa, N.: Interactive Comedy. Journal of the Institute of Image Information and Television Engineers 57(4), 454–455 (2003)

[29] Tosa, N., Matsuoka, S.: Cultural computing: ZENetic computer. In: ICAT'04. Proceedings of the 14th International Conference on Artificial Reality and Tele-existence, pp. 75–78, Korea Advanced Institute of Science and Technology, Korea (2004)

[30] Tosa, N., Matsuoka, S.: ZENetic Computer: Exploring Japanese Culture. Leonardo 39(3), 205–211 (2006)

[31] Yamaoka, F., Kanda, T., Ishiguro, H., Hagita, N.: Lifelike behavior of communication robots based on developmental psychology findings. In: Proceedings IEEE International Conference on Humanoid Robots, pp. 406–411. IEEE Computer Society Press, Los Alamitos (2005)

[32] Retrieved on (March 23, 2007) from http://en.wikipedia.org/wiki/Culture

[33] Test of Unconscious Identification (TUI):
http://jamiep.org/mod/tui/view.php?id=154&do=test

[34] The ALICE project: http://www.alice.id.tue.nl/

# A Role Casting Method Based on Emotions in a Story Generation System

Ruck Thawonmas[1], Masanao Kamozaki[1], and Yousuke Ohno[1]

Intelligent Computer Entertainment Laboratory
Graduate School of Science and Engineering, Ritsumeikan University
Kusatsu, Shiga, 525-8577, Japan
ruck@ci.ritsumei.ac.jp

**Abstract.** We first point out a problem in the role casting method of a story generation system called OPIATE and then propose a solution to this problem. The existing casting method does not take into account the emotions of a cast non-player character towards actions that it must perform in its role, leading to a miscast. In the proposed casting method, such emotions are considered, besides emotions towards other characters as done in the existing one. Evaluation results, using an online-game simulator, confirm the effectiveness of the proposed method over the existing one with respect to the number of miscasts.

## 1 Introduction

Storytelling pervades our daily life and has a large social impact through media such as novels, movies, dramas, and games. It thus plays a central role in an entertainment area.

In our research, we focus on a story generation system called OPIATE[1][2] oriented to online-games. In OPIATE, a story based on the Propp's morphology[3] is developed through interactions between a player character (PC) and non-player characters (NPCs). In an OPIATE's story, a quest is issued to the PC acting as the hero, and NPCs act according to their cast roles, such as the villain, princess, etc.

The main technology in OPIATE is case-based reasoning (CBR) [4] used for selection of a sub-plot (case) that defines a set of actions to be carried out by the corresponding characters, each cast a different role. At a given point in the story, a selected case is the one with the highest suitability of roles and actions.

In this paper, we point out a problem residing in role casting of OPIATE. We then propose a new casting method for solving the problem and evaluate its effectiveness.

## 2 Story Generation

According to the Propp's morphology, there are 31 functions, each for being carried out by a character cast one out of seven roles. These functions differ in

L. Ma, R. Nakatsu, and M. Rauterberg (Eds.): ICEC 2007, LNCS 4740, pp. 182–192, 2007.
© IFIP International Federation for Information Processing 2007

their effects on the sub-plot. Their examples are "trickery" carried out by the villain attempting deception to prepare for the act of villainy and "complicity" by the hero succumbing to the trickery. In OPIATE, two roles were additionally added, i.e., the family and the king. These 31 functions were thus divided into eight role groups of NPCs, and one role group of the PC, which is the hero. Henceforth, the term "character(s)" is used to represent both the PC and NPCs when there is no need to distinguish them.

An OPIATE's case is a script consisting of multiple lines. Each line represents a function and contains a maximum of three elements: the function name, an action that is carried out by the character cast the role corresponding to this function, and a character that is the objective of the action (henceforth, this kind of character is called objective character). Hence, a function involves up to two roles, depending on the presence of the last element.

## 2.1 Case Suitability

During case selection using CBR, the suitability of a case is computed as the average of the suitability of all functions in the case as follows:

$$Sn = \sum_{i=1}^{Ln} (Wr * Sri + Wa * Sai)/Ln \tag{1}$$

where $Sn$ denotes the suitability of case $n$, $Ln$ represents the number of functions in this case, $Wr$ and $Wa$ are the weights. $Sri$ is the sum of the relevance degrees to the role(s) in function $i$ of all available characters, where the relevance degree to a role of a character is decided based on the casting rules in Table 1. $Sai$ is the sum of the relevance degrees to the action in function $i$ of all available characters' actions, where the relevance degree of a character's action to a function's action is 1 if the latter action can be accomplished by the former action and is 0 otherwise.

## 2.2 Conflict Casting

In OPIATE, once a case with the highest suitability has been selected, all roles in that case are cast to characters according the casting rules in Table 1, where roles are filled from top to bottom. As can be seen from this table, casting is based mainly on NPCs' emotions towards other characters. Let us take Villain for example. The role of Villain consists of aggressive and/or villainous actions such as Attack, Capture, and Expel. Its casting rule is to cast Villain to an NPC who has a negative emotion towards the Hero. Suppose that there exists an NPC with the most negative emotion towards the Hero, but this NPC does not like to carry out such aggressive and/or villainous actions. According to the casting rule, Villain will be cast, however, to this NPC, which is conflicting to its personality.

As can been seen from the above example, existing casting rules sometimes cast roles to NPCs that confict their personalities.

**Table 1.** Casting rules

| Role | Rule |
|---|---|
| Hero | The player character |
| Villain | An NPC with a negative emotion towards the Hero |
| Donor | An NPC who has not met the Hero yet or<br>an NPC with a slightly positive emotion towards the Hero |
| Mediator | An NPC with a slightly negative emotion towards the Hero |
| Family | An NPC with a positive emotion towards the Hero |
| Princess | An NPC with a positive emotion towards the Hero<br>and a negative emotion towards the Villain |
| Helper | An NPC who has met Hero earlier and<br>has a positive emotion towards the Hero |
| King | An NPC with a positive emotion towards the Princess |
| False Hero | An NPC with a negative emotion towards the Hero |

### 2.3 Proposed Casting Method

Here, we propose a new casting method that considers also NPCs' emotions towards actions. In the proposed casting method, for each role, a number of candidate NPCs are selected from the remaining NPCs according to the casting rules in Table 1. Then from these candidates, the NPC with the most positive emotions towards the role's actions is selected for being cast. However, casting will not be done if there is no NPC with positive emotions towards the role's actions among the candidates.

For example, let us take the case of Villain again. First, all remaining NPCs with a negative emotion towards the Hero are raised as the candidates for this role. Then, among these candidates, the NPC with the most positive emotions towards Villain's actions is selected for being cast. Thereby, with the proposed casting method, role casting is done without any conflict to NPCs' personalities.

## 3 Implementation of Emotions

In this section, we describe EMAI (Emotionally Motivated Artificial Intelligence) [5][6] that we adopt for implementing NPCs' emotions.

### 3.1 Emotions in Appraisal Space

EMAI is a mechanism that decides agents' actions based on their emotions. There are two groups of emotions. One is a group of emotions related to internal desires of the agent (NPC) such as hungry or sleepy. The other one is a group of emotion towards other characters, objects, actions, and situations. Below we explain the implementation of the emotions towards other characters and actions because they are used in our research. Emotions in EMAI are defined by six orthogonal appraisal dimensions identified in [7]: *Pleasantness, Responsibility, Certainty, Attention, Effort,* and *Control*. Figure 1 shows typical emotions in the appraisal space spanned by *Pleasant* and *Control*.

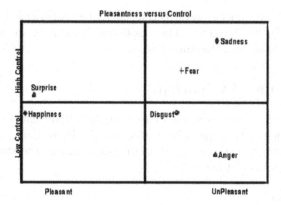

**Fig. 1.** Typical emotions in two dimensional appraisal space

## 3.2 Emotional State and Its Updating Rule

An event in the story occurs when a function in a selected case is carried out by the corresponding NPC, causing a change in the emotional state of the NPC towards each element of the event. In our system, an event $E$ is defined by at most two elements: an action and an objective character if this action acts upon someone. Let an element in $E$ be denoted by $e$. The NPC emotional state towards $e$, $\Omega_e$, is defined by the six orthogonal appraisal dimensions as follows:

$$\Omega_e = \{P_e, R_e, C_e, A_e, E_e, O_e\}, \tag{2}$$

where the value on each dimension is represented by the initial character of the corresponding dimension, except for *Control* represented by $O$.

When an event occurs at time $t$, the NPC emotional state can be described by the following formula.

$$\Omega_{E,t} = \sum_{e=1}^{n} W_e \Omega_{e,t}, \tag{3}$$

where $n$ is the number of elements in $E$ at time $t$ (either one or two), and $W_e$ is the weight of $e$. Let us denote the outcome of $E$ by $\Omega_F = \{P_F, R_F, C_F, A_F, E_F, O_F\}$ that is an emotion based on the action result and/or the feedback from the objective character. Because $\Omega_F$ indicates a right direction in the appraisal space that $\Omega_E$ should follow, the updating rule of each element in the NPC emotional state, henceforth called emotional element, can be given below as:

$$\Omega_{e,t+1} = \Omega_{e,t} + W_e \left( \Omega_{F,t} - \Omega_{E,t} \right) \tag{4}$$

Note that after the update, the direction of each emotional element will have been partly shifted to the direction of the event's outcome.

In Table 1, negative or positive emotions towards other characters are used for role casting. Such emotions are derived as follows. If the emotional element of an NPC towards a given character is nearer to Happiness than Sadness, then the

NPC has a positive emotion towards that character, otherwise it has a negative emotion towards the character. The emotional element of an NPC towards a given action is decided in the same fashion

# 4   Performance Evaluation

In our performance evaluation, we focused on the Villain that has several functions and the Helper that has a high effect on the Hero. Using an online-game simulator, we compare the proposed casting method and the existing one with respect to the number of miscasts.

## 4.1   Simulator

In this simulator, we implemented one PC and 19 NPCs. The PC was also simulated and thus not directly controlled by a human player. NCPs' actions, their success/failure conditions, and the probability of receiving each feedback are summarized in Table 2. For Attack, the objective character is randomly selected from all other characters, while for Heal it is randomly selected from all characters, i.e., an NPC can carry out Heal to heal itself. For Quest and Give, the objective character is the PC. Capture and Save are not carried out by NPCs, but the emotional states towards them of the NPC issuing a quest Abduction or Potion Procurement in Table 3 to the PC are indirectly updated when the PC completes the quest.

Each NPC has three parameters: the number of items, the number of quest types, and its power. The number of item shows the number of items that an NPC of interest is currently holding, and this number is decremented each time it carries out Give. The number of quest types indicates how many quest types an NPC can issue to the PC among four types shown in Table 3. The power of an NPC is decreased accordingly when it is attacked by another NPC or a monster, and its power will be resumed to the initial value if it is successfully healed. For each NPC, the number of items and quest types were randomly initialized to a value between 0 and 4 and a value between 0 and 2, respectively. The initial power was randomly initialized to a value between 50 and 150.

Among the four actions available, an NPC stochastically selects an action to carry out with the highest probability for the action towards which it has the most positive emotion and with the lowest probability for the action towards which it has the most negative emotion. For each NPC, each dimension of its emotional elements towards other characters and actions was initialized with a random value between -1.5 and 1.5. As described in 3.2, the emotional elements of an NPC are updated according the outcome of an event that is based on the action result (c.f. Table 4) and/or the feedback from the objective character (c.f. Table 5). NPCs who are attacked or healed also update their related emotional elements, i.e., for Attack the emotional elements of the objective NPC towards Attack and the character carrying out Attack are shifted to Sadness, and for Heal the emotional elements of the objective NPC towards Heal and the character carrying out Heal are shifted to Happiness provided that the heal is successful.

**Table 2.** List of NPCs' actions, their success (failure) conditions, and the probability of each feedback

| Action | Role | Success(Failure) Condition | Feedback Probability |
|---|---|---|---|
| Attack | Villain | The power of the objective character becomes zero (remains more than zero). | p(Sadness) = 0.5 and p(no feedback) = 0.5 |
| Heal | Helper | The power of the objective character is recovered to its initial value (does not change). | p(Happiness) = 0.5 and p(no feedback) = 0.5 when the heal is successful only |
| Quest | Donor | The PC accepts (refuses) to pursue the quest. | - |
| Capture | Villain | Not considered. | - |
| Save | Helper | Not considered. | - |
| Give | Donor | The NPC receives the Happiness (Sadness) feedback from the PC. | - |

**Table 3.** List of quests and their effects on the corresponding emotional elements

| Quest | Update direction when the PC completes (fails) the quest |
|---|---|
| Expedition | Shifted to Happiness (Sadness) the emotional elements of the NPC towards Attack and the PC |
| Abduction | Shifted to Happiness (Sadness) the emotional elements of the NPC towards Capture and the PC |
| Potion Procurement | Shifted to Happiness (Sadness) the emotional elements of the NPC towards Heal and the PC |
| Rescue | Shifted to Happiness (Sadness) the emotional elements of the NPC towards Save and the PC |

For updating emotional elements, the weight $W_e$ was set to 0.5. The appraisal vectors of the two emotions in use were set according to [7], i.e., Happiness = {-1.46, 0.09, -0.46, 0.15, -0.33, -0.21}, and Sadness = {0.87, -0.36, 0, -0.21, -0.14, 1.15}.

When an NPC carries out Attack, if the objective character is a monster, the NPC continues fighting against the opponent monster, initialized with the power of 100, until the power of either of them reaches zero. The amount of damage that the NPC gives to or receives from the monster was set to a random value between 30 and 40. If the objective character is another NPC, the NPC carrying out Attack gives the damage to the objective NPC with a random value between 30 and 40.

The probability that Heal, Quest, and Give are successful was set to 0.5. The probability that the PC successfully completes a quest was also set to 0.5. Note that a quest will cause the issuing NPC to update its emotions at most twice, i.e., when the PC accepts or rejects to pursue the quest (c.f. Table 4), and then when the quest is completed or failed by the PC (c.f. Table 3). The latter update is an indirect one because the PC carries out an issued quest, but it is the issuing NPC that updates its emotional elements towards the PC and the related action. The weight for this indirect update $W_e$ was set to 0.25.

**Table 4.** List of actions' effects on the corresponding emotional elements

| Action | Update direction when successful (failed) |
|---|---|
| Attack | Shifted to Happiness (Sadness) the emotional element of the NPC towards Attack |
| Heal | Shifted to Happiness (Sadness) the emotional element of the NPC towards Heal |
| Quest | Shifted to Happiness (Sadness) the emotional elements of the NPC towards Quest and the PC |
| Give | Shifted to Happiness (Sadness) the emotional elements of the NPC towards Give and the PC |

**Table 5.** List of feedbacks' effects on the corresponding emotional elements

| Action | Update direction when receiving a feedback |
|---|---|
| Attack | Shifted to Sadness the emotional element of the NPC towards Attack and the objective character |
| Heal | Shifted to Happiness the emotional elements of the NPC towards Heal and the objective character |

## 4.2   Results and Discussions

In each trail the simulator was run for 150 seconds. After this, role casting for the eight NPC roles was done based on NPCs' emotional states according to the proposed method and the existing one. For comparisons, the number of trials was set to 200, from which the number of miscasts of each method was obtained. Note that in the existing method, a miscast will occur if a cast NPC has negative emotions towards the actions of its role. In the proposed method, this type of miscasting does not occur, but there exist miscasts due to not able to cast a role to any candidate NPC if they all have negative emotions towards the role's actions.

Figures 2 and 3 show the time series of the distances to Happiness and Sadness from each emotional element of an NPC towards Player (the PC) and towards Attack and Villain, respectively, in a trail where the proposed method correctly cast Villain to this NPC. In our simulator, the emotional element towards Villain is the sum of the emotional elements towards the two related actions: Attack and Capture. Table 6 shows the action logs of this NPC.

The NPC received the Sadness feedback from the PC at $t = 7$ and 45. As a result, as shown in Fig. 2, the distance to Sadness of its emotional state towards Player decreased, while the distance to Happiness of this emotional state increased. This means that its emotion towards Player became more negative after these time steps.

In addition, the NPC successfully performed Attack at $t = 6, 30, 33, 34, 42, 83,$ 105, 148, and 150. As shown in Figure 3, these successes resulted in having more positive emotions towards Attack and Villain. Note that at $t = 6$ the distances to Happiness and Sadness of its emotional state towards Attack both decreased. However, because the decreasing amount of the former is larger than that of the

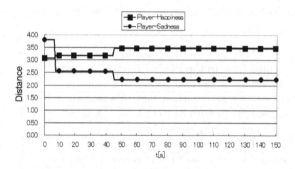

**Fig. 2.** Time series of the distances to Happiness and Sadness from the emotional element of an NPC towards Player

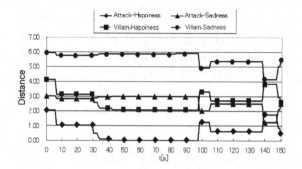

**Fig. 3.** Time series of the distances to Happiness and Sadness from the emotional elements of the NPC in Fig. 2 towards Attack and Villain

latter, this led to a more positive emotion towards Attack. At $t = 98$ the NPC was attacked by NPC 15, and at $t = 139$ its Attack was lost to a monster. As a result, after these time steps, its positive emotion towards Attack was decreased. It can be seen from these results that the NPC correctly updated its emotional states according to event outcomes.

Table 7 compares the existing casting method and the proposed casting method with respect to the number of miscasts. As can been seen from the table, the proposed method significantly outperforms the existing one. In both methods, the number of miscasts for Helper is more than that for Villain. This is due to the fact that Helper is cast after Villain because the casting rules in Table 1 are executed from top to bottom, which means that the number of NPCs available for Helper is less than that for Villain.

Table 8 shows results from a trial where the existing method miscast Villain to NPC 9, but the proposed method correctly cast Villain to NPC 6, where each number shows the distance to Happiness or Sadness of the emotional element of the corresponding NPC towards Player, Villain, or Helper. Because NPC 9 has the most negative emotion towards Player, Villain was cast to it in the existing method although it has a negative emotion towards the role. In the proposed

**Table 6.** Action logs of the NPC in Figs. 2 and 3

| Action | @Time (s) |
|---|---|
| Successfully performed Attack to a monster | 6 |
| Performed Give to the PC but received Sadness | 7 |
| Successfully performed Attack to a monster | 30 |
| Successfully performed Attack to a monster | 33 |
| Successfully performed Attack to a monster | 34 |
| Successfully healed by NPC 19 | 38 |
| Successfully performed Attack to a monster | 42 |
| Performed Give to the PC but received Sadness | 45 |
| Successfully performed Attack to a monster | 83 |
| Successfully healed by NPC 11 | 87 |
| Attacked by NPC 15 | 98 |
| Successfully performed Attack to a monster | 105 |
| Successfully healed by NPC 12 | 108 |
| Performed Attack to a monster but was lost to it | 139 |
| Successfully healed by itself | 146 |
| Successfully performed Attack to a monster | 148 |
| Successfully performed Attack to a monster | 150 |

**Table 7.** Comparison between the existing casting method and the proposed casting method with respect to the number of miscasts

| Role | The existing method | The proposed method |
|---|---|---|
| Villain | 25 | 2 |
| Helper | 28 | 4 |

**Table 8.** Results from a trial where the existing method miscast Villain to NPC 9, but the proposed method correctly cast Villain to NPC 6

| | Player | | Villain | | Helper | |
|---|---|---|---|---|---|---|
| | Happiness | Sadness | Happiness | Sadness | Happiness | Sadness |
| NPC1 | 2.26 | 3.73 | 3.04 | 4.06 | 3.45 | 4.37 |
| NPC2 | 1.81 | 2.53 | 3.63 | 2.39 | 2.07 | 4.36 |
| NPC3 | 1.44 | 2.69 | 1.90 | 4.55 | 1.97 | 4.21 |
| NPC4 | 3.27 | 1.55 | 4.27 | 2.84 | 2.26 | 3.61 |
| NPC5 | 1.89 | 2.24 | 3.64 | 2.07 | 2.50 | 3.99 |
| **NPC6** | **3.46** | **2.21** | **2.13** | **3.88** | 3.22 | 4.61 |
| NPC7 | 2.29 | 1.46 | 2.77 | 2.61 | 3.51 | 4.26 |
| NPC8 | 1.57 | 1.98 | 3.04 | 4.70 | 3.12 | 5.33 |
| **NPC9** | **3.61** | **1.04** | **4.07** | **2.84** | 2.87 | 4.95 |
| NPC10 | 1.81 | 1.71 | 2.26 | 3.88 | 3.30 | 3.63 |
| NPC11 | 2.03 | 1.62 | 2.57 | 3.53 | 3.16 | 4.48 |
| NPC12 | 3.07 | 1.65 | 4.39 | 2.97 | 2.44 | 4.45 |
| NPC13 | 2.27 | 1.67 | 3.27 | 4.14 | 3.65 | 4.43 |
| NPC14 | 1.31 | 2.90 | 2.61 | 3.41 | 2.43 | 3.11 |
| NPC15 | 1.49 | 2.95 | 2.70 | 3.19 | 3.18 | 4.11 |
| NPC16 | 2.27 | 1.46 | 2.66 | 2.63 | 2.01 | 4.42 |
| NPC17 | 2.98 | 2.75 | 4.51 | 2.90 | 3.85 | 5.25 |
| NPC18 | 2.09 | 4.30 | 3.70 | 2.18 | 3.95 | 3.53 |
| NPC19 | 2.08 | 2.41 | 2.87 | 3.32 | 1.94 | 5.18 |

**Table 9.** Results from a trial where the proposed method miscast Helper

| | Player | | Villain | | Helper | |
|---|---|---|---|---|---|---|
| | Happiness | Sadness | Happiness | Sadness | Happiness | Sadness |
| NPC1 | 1.61 | 2.45 | 3.13 | 4.04 | 2.16 | 4.57 |
| NPC2 | 2.78 | 1.80 | 2.40 | 3.25 | 2.07 | 3.95 |
| NPC3 | 1.73 | 2.28 | 1.86 | 4.77 | 1.76 | 4.05 |
| NPC4 | 1.93 | 1.77 | 2.56 | 3.63 | 3.08 | 4.15 |
| NPC5 | 2.32 | 1.41 | 4.60 | 2.33 | 2.66 | 4.46 |
| NPC6 | 3.81 | 3.08 | 4.25 | 3.03 | 3.17 | 4.56 |
| **NPC7** | **2.15** | **2.30** | 2.66 | 2.57 | **4.10** | **3.96** |
| NPC8 | 3.21 | 1.00 | 3.01 | 4.77 | 3.18 | 5.18 |
| NPC9 | 4.11 | 1.39 | 2.93 | 3.02 | 2.86 | 5.01 |
| **NPC10** | **2.05** | **2.49** | 2.91 | 3.68 | **3.30** | **3.26** |
| NPC11 | 1.81 | 2.32 | 3.49 | 2.82 | 1.75 | 4.05 |
| NPC12 | 3.07 | 1.65 | 4.02 | 3.16 | 2.50 | 4.49 |
| NPC13 | 2.27 | 1.67 | 3.50 | 3.45 | 3.65 | 5.36 |
| NPC14 | 2.11 | 1.83 | 4.47 | 2.86 | 2.45 | 3.64 |
| NPC15 | 3.33 | 1.65 | 4.07 | 2.49 | 2.37 | 4.40 |
| NPC16 | 2.60 | 1.17 | 3.28 | 2.15 | 2.07 | 4.39 |
| NPC17 | 3.30 | 1.56 | 4.56 | 2.91 | 1.84 | 4.36 |
| NPC18 | 2.53 | 4.12 | 3.48 | 2.16 | 3.95 | 3.84 |
| NPC19 | 3.61 | 3.13 | 2.67 | 3.98 | 2.68 | 4.17 |

method, Villain was cast to NPC 6 that has a negative emotion towards Player and a positive emotion towards this role.

Table 9 shows results from a trial where the proposed method miscast Helper. The remaining candidates for Helper are NPC 7 and NPC 10 that both have a positive emotion towards Player. However, both have a negative emotion towards this role, so no casting was performed leading to a miscast. All other miscasts in the proposed method occurred in a similar fashion.

## 5   Conclusions and Future Work

To reduce miscasts in a story generation system OPIATE, we have proposed a role casting method that considers the emotions of NPCs towards both characters and roles. EMAI was adopted for implementing those emotions. The proposed method was evaluated with an online-game simulator. According to the evaluation results, the proposed method had a much lower number of miscasts than the existing method used in OPIATE, and miscasts in the proposed method were due to the unavailability of candidate NPCs with positive emotions towards the corresponding character and role's actions.

As our future work, we plan to implement the proposed method into an online game under development at our laboratory and evaluate it through real test plays. In addition, we plan to improve the formula for computing the suitability of a case and evaluate it on the aforementioned online game.

## References

1. Fairclough, C.R., Cunningham, P.: A MULTIPLAYER OPIATE. International Journal of Intelligent Games & Simulation 3(2), 54–61 (2004)
2. Fairclough, C.R.: Story Games and the OPIATE System Using Case-Based Planning for Structuring Plots with an Expert Story Director Agent and Enacting them in a Socially Simulated Game World. Doctoral Thesis, University of Dublin - Trinity College (2004)

3. Propp, V.: Theory and History of Folklore. University of Minnesota Press (1984)
4. Aamodt, A., Plaza, E.: Case-Based Reasoning: Foundational Issues, Methodological Variations, and System Approaches. Artificial Intelligence Communications. 7(1), 39–52 (1994)
5. Baillie-de, B.P.: Programming Believable Characters for Computer Games. Charles River Media, pp. 385–392 (2004)
6. Baillie-de, B.P.: A Six Dimensional Paradigm for Generating Emotions in Virtual Characters. International Journal of Intelligent Games and Simulation. 2(2), 72–79 (2003)
7. Smith, C.A., Ellsworth, P.C.: Attitudes and Social Cognition. Journal of Personality and Social Psychology. 48(4), 813–838 (1985)

# A Novel System for Interactive Live TV

Stefan M. Grünvogel[1], Richard Wages[1], Tobias Bürger[2], and Janez Zaletelj[3]

[1] Cologne University of Applied Sciences, IMP, Betzdorferstr. 2,
50679 Cologne, Germany
`{richard.wages,stefan.gruenvogel}@fh-koeln.de`
[2] Salzburg Research Forschungsgesellschaft m.b.H., Jakob-Haringer-Strasse 5/III
5020 Salzburg, Austria
`tobias.buerger@salzburgresearch.at`
[3] University of Ljubljana, Trzaska 25,
1000 Ljubljana, Slovenia
`janez.zaletelj@ldos.fe.uni-lj.si`

**Abstract.** For the production of interactive live TV formats, new content and new productions workflows are necessary. We explain how future content of a parallel multi-stream production of live events may be created from a design and a technical perspective. It is argued, that the content should be arranged by dramaturgical principles taking into account the meaning of the base material. To support the production process a new approach for content recommendation is described which uses semantic annotation from audio-visual material and user feedback.

**Keywords:** interactive live television, recommender system, extraction of meaning, dramaturgical principle, content, multi-stream.

## 1 Introduction and Set-Up

Interactive digital television demands new kinds of content and new kinds of production workflows. TV-on-demand service providers (like "Zattoo" or "Joost") make it possible to watch any movie, series or news broadcast at any time, independent of the original broadcasting. But there are events (like e.g. elections or football matches), where the fascination of watching is based in the "live" character of the broadcast – anything can happen in the moment of the actual broadcast. Within the project "LIVE" [1] our aim is to enable the production of interactive live TV events.

There are already several approaches to create interactive live TV formats (e.g. BBC's interactive broadcasting of the 2004 Olympics). A successful example is multi-stream sports where the consumers at home are able to choose from different video channels. The streams could come from several cameras, filming the event from different angles (e.g. at a football stadium). But also the case where an event consists of several sub-events and each sub-event is filmed by its own cameras is possible.

In the LIVE project [1] it is the aim to support the parallel production of several multi-channels. The creation of the multi-channels is done by the "video conductor" (VC), who may be a single human or a whole team at the production site.

L. Ma, R. Nakatsu, and M. Rauterberg (Eds.): ICEC 2007, LNCS 4740, pp. 193–204, 2007.
© IFIP International Federation for Information Processing 2007

The content on which the work of the VC is based can come from live AV-streams or from the broadcasters archive. The VC has to combine and stitch the streams together to produce several AV-streams in real-time (cf. Figure 1) which can be received by the consumers. We term the viewers at home who interact with the iTV program as "consumers" and the people working at the production site as "professional users" or simply "users."

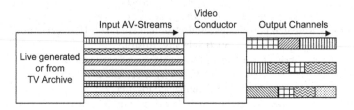

**Fig. 1.** Creation of multi-channels

Now the interaction issues come into this system in several ways, which distinguishes it from other systems.

The VC does not only produce the live AV-streams, but in addition he will also create transitions points, where the consumer is invited to switch to another channel (cf. Figure 2).

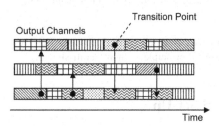

**Fig. 2.** Multi-channels with transition points

The aim is to prevent a mere "zapping" between channels and instead help the consumer to steer through the content such that an overall dramatic arc persists. How this can be achieved practically is explained in Section 2.

The second type of interaction works by involving both the consumer and the professional users. By using a backchannel from the consumers to the broadcaster, the VC will be able to adapt his style of content stitching, depending on the behaviour of the audience. The technical details of how this works is explained in Section 3.

## 2   How Will Future Interactive Content Look Like?

### 2.1   The Need for Dramaturgical Design Principles in Interactive Live TV

When thinking about future interactive content for iTV one has to consider current state-of-the-art approaches to this topic. These approaches can be categorized based on the interaction design including devices and on-screen interfaces and based on the genres or formats which are transported. As an example, the interaction of the consumer from BBC interactive is accomplished by using the "Red Button" on the remote control, to interact with the program. Various formats like quiz games or voting opportunities are already available.

A lot of work and research has been undertaken to optimize the on-screen consumer interface by e.g. using well-known metaphors from personal computers (like menus, buttons etc.) or to enable the viewer to have a multi-perspective view of an event (e.g. by using split screens, showing different camera views of an event). These approaches work well with almost any content, because they are created to work irrespective of the actual semantic essence of the video feeds.

But: there are currently almost no design principles available to connect different video streams in such a way that consumers have the possibility to switch between these channels *and* to have a consistent dramaturgical concept over all these channels. Thus for the most part current iTV formats fail to generate two consumer experiences: flow and immersion.

To explain this a little further, one example from another medium. In movies, beneath the underlying story, the camera work and the editing of the scenes and shots are crucial for the dramaturgical arc over the whole film. The editor is responsible to collect and compose the raw film material into a consistent entity depending on the story elements been told and the camera representation of these elements. As a result, good editing and storytelling lead to an *immersive* experience for the consumer. The semantic meaning and the representation are crucial for success. This has already been known since the beginning of beginning of the past century. In the famous Kuleshov experiment from 1919 two unrelated images have been shown in juxtaposition to the viewer. Kuleshov discovered, that the viewers interpreted both images as a part of a related sequence. In the experiment a face with neutral facial expression was shown after showing images with different moods. Depending on the preceding image, the same facial expression led to a completely different interpretation by the viewers.

## 2.2  Levels of Meaning

Thus as a consequence, iTV formats could be enhanced, if different live feeds are composed carefully depending on the *meaning* of content which is presented in this channel. Instead of allowing the consumer to switch randomly between different channels which are not related at all, switching should be stimulated at those points where it makes sense from a dramaturgical point of view. One has to be aware, that "dramaturgical" does not only mean "thrilling" or "exciting", also formats with funny elements need a dramaturgy.

Another important fact is, that one and the same video stream has different meanings for one and the same consumer depending on the context in which it is presented to the consumer. Thus by allowing the consumer to switch between different live channels, the meaning of each channel depends on the other channels. This makes it possible to stitch one live stream into different live formats, each time with at different meaning to the viewer.

In the LIVE project we distinguish between different levels of meaning, reaching from particle to universal statements. The information of the different levels of meaning is extracted from and assigned to the AV material relative to an abstract viewpoint (i.e. an ontology). The execution of this task will be done by an "Intelligent Media Framework" (cf. Section 3.3).

As a starting point we defined the different levels of meaning of an AV object relative to an observer perspective. The four levels are termed "Particle", "Local", "Global" and "Universal".

*Example 1.* Consider a clip where a ball in a football match crosses the goal line. We could assign the following levels of meaning to this clip:

- **Particle:** Ball crosses line, player kicks ball, goalkeeper misses ball
- **Local:** Team A wins football match, end of career of coach from team B
- **Global:** Sportive competition between opposing teams
- **Universal:** Success depends on skills

One could easily construct similar examples for all kind of situations of live event situations such as e.g. a folded piece of paper put into a box (at elections).

### 2.3  Dramaturgical Enhanced Interface

An important question is how the interface for such new content for live iTV may look like. It is well known, that the use of a classical "WIMP" (window, icon, menu, pointing device) interactions techniques easily destroys the immersion of a consumer. Thus, although indispensable for many iTV formats, these kinds of interfaces are not suitable for keeping a dramaturgical arc over a longer period of time. In computer games, a similar problem arises because good games should not pull out gamers from the cognitional state of "flow". Current solutions use in-game controls, which connote objects from the game world with a known in-game meaning with an additional meaning of the (real) players world. This technique can not be transferred directly to iTV, because in most cases it will not be possible to add real objects to the physical world of the filmed live events, which could be interpreted by the consumer as a meta object. But the content of a live stream could be used as is to provoke the consumer to switch to another channel. To give a very simple (but drastic) example: Showing an empty pool over minutes during a swimming championship most likely provokes the consumer to switch to another channel – or to switch off.

## 3  Extraction of Meaning and Content Recommendation

The creation of future interactive content needs (as stated in Section 2) new workflows and new tools. In this section a new workflow satisfying the demands of future interactive content creation is proposed. It is based on the extraction of meaning of content and content recommendations for the video conductor. Also a first prototypical interface for the recommendation system is shown.

### 3.1 The Concept of Content Recommendations in TV Production

The introduction of interactive digital TV [2], [3] brings new challenges to the existing world of TV production. One of the important new features of digital and interactive technologies is the possibility to produce and transmit programs which are composed of several sub-channels. The exploitation of this feature is a big challenge, because this means that some proven concepts of classical TV production have to be transformed. It requires new tools and new workflows to support the parallel production of several multi-channels. A vital requirement to the tools and workflows is that it should be possible to combine live audio-visual material and also to enable the reuse of already existing content in video archives for live production.

To reuse archived TV material a new content workflow for iTV production has been developed in the LIVE project (cf. Figure 3). This workflow addresses the issue of on-the-fly content selection from broadcaster archives and its reuse during live production. For implementing the content workflow, several items have to be realized:

- Adapt the production workflow so that the professional user (the editor) will be able to search and retrieve material on-the-fly.
- Properly annotate the TV content so that an intelligent search at the fine level of content granularity will be possible (for example, at the level of shots).
- Establishing a digital TV archive in which the content is instantly available for play-out.
- The development of a suitable personalized content selection algorithm.

The recommender system prototype of the LIVE project is aiming at providing a first implementation of the production support system. This system will enable live personalized content selection for the TV production. We have to stress the fact, that the system will recommend content for a professional user (the video conductor) at the production site. Still (and presumably also in the long run) we believe, that humans will have to be responsible for the *creative* assembly of the different streams.

We will now explain the workflow in more detail (cf. Figure 3).

First, the AV content is processed to extract semantic information. This can be done in two ways: either automatically or by human annotation. With human annotation higher levels of meaning (e.g. at universal or global level) can be generated. The results of both approaches are "semantic content annotations" of the audio-visual material. The extracted information enables the generation of "content recommendations". The video conductor receives content recommendations in the form of a list of audio-visual segments matching the search query. Items from this list of AV material are included into the final program by the video conductor. The resulting TV streams are sent to the consumers.

The crucial requirement to produce content recommendation is that the meaning is extracted from raw audio-visual material first and is represented within the predefined ontology.

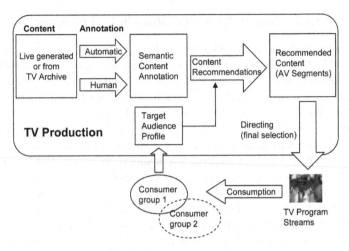

**Fig. 3.** The content workflow

## 3.2   Extraction of Meaning from Videos

Extraction of meaning is the process of analysis of videos and in turn the semantic enrichment of the metadata that accompanies its binary representation. Semantics and the interpretation of the content is important to make content machine-processable. This semantic enrichment of content can be done manually, which is expensive, or automatically, which is error-prone. In particular, automatic semantic enrichment must be aware of the gap between the semantics that are directly retrievable from the content and those which can be inferred within a given interpretative context (the "Semantic Gap"). Semantic machine readable metadata of content is beneficial in many ways. Based on earlier investigations [4], semantic descriptions of content can enhance fast and easy navigation through audio-visual repositories for example. It can be used to create content recommendations for a video conductor, who can make decisions based on these recommendations which AV-stream will be played out and which of the streams will be interlinked.

Some of the recent research projects in the area of semantic (or symbolic) video annotation try to derive the semantics from the low level features of the audiovisual material or from other available basic metadata, e.g. by audio-classification of classification of camera movement. Some of the projects aim at highly automated indexing using the results of automatic speech recognition however error-prone they may be. Most of these approaches are - as also pointed out in [5] - not capable to derive the semantics of multimedia content because in many cases the results of the analysis cannot be related to the media context [6]. For humans the construction of meaning is an act of interpretation that has much more to do with pre-existing knowledge (the "context") than with the recognition of low-level-features of the content. This situation is commonly referred to as the "semantic gap" [7].

Two solution paths have emerged for this problem: The first one is to provide rich annotations created by humans as training data for the system to learn features of videos for future automatic content-based analysis. The second approach does not rely on training, but purely on analysis of the raw multimedia content. The training approach is not well suited for scenarios in which a great amount of content has to be annotated before any training and automation can be done or in which the application domain is very broad. The second approach usually only works well in settings where the relevant concepts can easily be recognized. However, most content based services demand richer semantics. As pointed out in section 4, popular examples on the Web show that there are currently many service-based platforms that make use of their users' knowledge to understand the meaning of multimedia content.

We differentiate between three levels of knowledge to refer to this semantic enriched information about content: This distinction is based on the organization of so-called Knowledge Content Objects [8], a semantic model for the trade of information goods: (1) There is the resource or the video file itself which can uniquely be identified by URIs, then (2) traditional metadata attached to the content like frame rate, compression type or colour coding scheme, and (3) semantic knowledge about the topics (subject) of the content as interpreted by an actor which is realized by the video. The semantic knowledge is further divided into particle, local, global, and universal knowledge (cf. Section 2). This distinction refers to the validity of the knowledge.

In the following section we explain how knowledge comprising to these different levels can be extracted from the raw content with the Intelligent Media Framework.

## 3.3 Real-Time Extraction of Meaning with the Intelligent Media Framework for the Staging of Live Media Events

In the terminology of the project, "staging live media events" is a notion for the creation of a non-linear multi-stream video show in real-time, which changes due to the interests of the consumer (end user). From a technical viewpoint, this requires a transformation of raw audiovisual content into "Intelligent Media Assets", which are based on the Knowledge Content Object that were already introduced above in Section 3.2. To extract knowledge on all levels (e.g. particle, local, global, universal) the development of a knowledge kit and a toolkit for an intelligent live content production process including manual annotation and automated real-time annotation is needed (cf. Figure 3).

To design this knowledge kit we applied lessons learnt from automatic approaches to overcome the weaknesses of automatic metadata extraction. We started to design an "Intelligent Media Framework" (IMF) that is taking into account the requirements of real-time video indexing to combine several automatic and manual annotation steps in order to enrich content with knowledge on different levels. The Intelligent Media Framework thereby integrates the following sub-components into one consistent system:

The "Intelligent Media Asset Information System" (IMAIS) provides access to services for the storage of media, knowledge models and metadata relevant for the live staging process. It also provides services for the creation and management and delivery of intelligent media assets. The IMAIS will be the central component of the Intelligent Media Framework and will semantically enrich incoming metadata streams with help of incoming manual and automatically derived annotations. The semantic enrichment process in LIVE is twofold: An application for automatic analysis delivers typical video metadata like close-ups, shots, faces, camera-motion, colour schemes, scenes and artists. This information is enriched in a manual step done by an human agent in the Intelligent Media Framework that has knowledge about the context of the analysed media item, and in the Recommender System (cf. below) which has the knowledge about the user preferences.

The *"Recommender System"* provides content recommendations for the video conductor based on previous user feedback, making use of knowledge. In Section 3.5 the functionalities of the Recommender System for the Video Conductor are presented in more detail.

In the next section (Section 3.4) we will explain how the components of the Intelligent Media Framework work together.

### 3.4  Content Recommendations Within the TV Production

Content selection within LIVE will primarily focus on the selection of audio-visual materials which may come from the TV archives or from a loop server where the live created material we be stored directly after been annotated by humans. The content selection is made according to the preferences of the target audience.

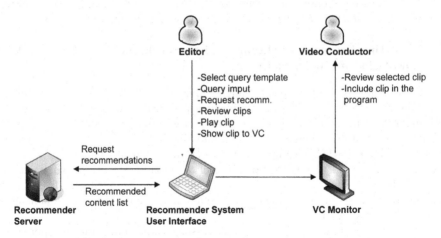

**Fig. 4.** The Recommender System setup and actions performed by the users

In Figure 4 the proposed components of the content selection workflow are shown. Content selection within LIVE is done in two stages. First, the archived content is processed and recommended within the production workflow. The editor receives "Archive Content Recommendations" in form of a list of audio-visual segments found in the TV archives. Items from this list of AV material are included into the final program by the video conductor. The resulting TV stream is sent to the Consumers.

### 3.5  Recommender System Functionalities for the Video Conductor

The video conductor and members of his team will be able to benefit from content recommendation functionalities by using the Recommender System user interface. The Recommender System user interface was implemented as a standalone Java

**Fig. 5.** The Recommender System user interface

application. The user interface connects to the "Recommender Server" and retrieves a recommended content list. This content (AV material) is then displayed in the Recommender System user interface. The editor is able to review the content and prepare a final selection for the video conductor.

The main functionalities of the Recommender System user interface (cf. Figure 5) are the following:

- **Search specification.** The editor is able to select search terms in event-specific fields, for example athlete name, venue, etc. Selected or entered keywords are combined into a query, which is sent to the Recommender Server.
- **Search Templates.** The editor can select a more specific search template which has some predefined knowledge already built in. For example, he can search for interviews, and the single parameter of this search would be the athlete name.
- **Loading of event information.** Pre-existing event information such as athlete lists is retrieved from IMF or loaded from XML file, so that the input fields already contain possible search terms.
- **Display of the recommended clips.** Recommended material can be previewed in low resolution and selected for play-out on the professional equipment.

The editor is using the user interface (cf. Figure 5) to search and retrieve audio-visual materials. The search capabilities apply to all AV material which is properly annotated and available through the Intelligent Media Asset Information System (IMAIS). This might include TV archive content (if it has been annotated in advance) and also live content which is annotated on-line. We now explain the typical workflow for an editor by example.

*Example 2.* Suppose that the editor is looking for additional background material on the two leading athletes named Bettini and Hasselbacher. Then the following steps are made:

(1) First, he needs to select a suitable search template which he will use to enter the search terms. Different search templates are available for typical editor's queries. For example, he might select a template named "Sportsman Background":

```
Content Type = {"Portrait", "Interview"}
```

This template already includes pre-specified terms to search for. The only parameter that needs to be specified is the names of the athletes.

(2) The editor now enters an athlete name or selects his name from the start list.

(3) He selects a target audience profile. This means that he is able to select a specific profile of the target group of TV consumers. The audience profile includes preferences of the TV consumers towards different types of content. The effect of the profile is that the resulting list of content will be personalised to the needs of target audience.

(4) The editor requests a content recommendation. The search query is compiled within the user interface and sent to the Recommender Server, which will return a list of matching content (cf. Figure 4). In our example the recommendation query is composed of the following information

```
Recommendation Query = {
        AudienceProfile = "General Austrian audience"
        SearchTemplate = "Sportsman Background"
        SearchTerms = {
           AthleteName = "Bettini"
           AthleteName = "Hasselbacher"
        }
}
```

(5) Finally, the editor will show the selected content to the video conductor, who will preview clip on the professional video monitor (cf. Figure 4). The video conductor will make the final decision if the clip shall be included into the TV program or not.

### 3.6 Computation of Content Recommendations Within the Recommender System

The goal of the Recommender System is to compile a list of suitable content based on the query and return it to the user interface. This is done in a sequence of steps where different information is added in each step. The proposed method is essentially a content-based filtering approach where content items are selected according to their metadata description.

*Example 3.* To explain the different steps for the compilation of a list suitable content we explore the search template from Example 2 in more detail.

(1) The search template information is added to the search terms and an `IMF_Query` is generated. This means that the `IMF_Query` now contains the information on the content type, where `ContentType` = {`Portrait`, `Interview`}. The final `IMF_Query` is:

```
IMF_Query = {

            { "Bettini" AND "Portrait" }         OR

            { "Bettini" AND "Interview" }         OR

            { "Hasselbacher" AND "Portrait" }     OR

            { "Hasselbacher" AND "Interview" }

    }
```

(2) The `IMF_Query` is sent to the IMAIS, which returns the list of matching AV segments and corresponding annotations.

(3) The list of matching segments is analysed according to the target audience profile. This means that returned segments are ranked according to their metadata annotations and how they fit with the audience preferences. If the selected audience profile has a preference value of 0.8 for Bettini and 0.3 for Hasselbacher, then clips which are annotated as "Bettini" are sorted on the top of the returned list.

(4) The final ranked list of audio-visual segments is returned to the user interface where clips can be previewed by the editor.

## 4 Conclusion

We depicted how future content for interactive live TV consisting of multi-channel programs may look like. The key element for the production of this content is the exploitation of the semantic meaning of the AV clips in the production process. A new content workflow was proposed in which semantic annotations of AV objects are integrated into an intelligent media framework. To support the VC, a recommender system is described together with a first prototype of a user interface.

**Acknowledgments.** The LIVE project is a joint research and development effort of the following academic and commercial institutions: Fraunhofer IAIS, Cologne University of Applied Sciences, Salzburg Research Forschungsgesellschaft m.b.H., University of Ljubljana, ORF – Austrian Broadcasting, Atos Origin s.a.e., Academy of Media Arts Cologne, University of Bradford and Pixelpark AG.

This work was partially funded by the European Commission within the 6th Framework of the IST under grant number FP6-27312. All statements in this work reflect the personal ideas and opinions of the authors and not necessarily the opinions of the European Commission.

# References

1. LIVE – Live Staging of Media Events (last visit 09.07. 2007), project website: http://www.ist-live.org/
2. Hartmann, A.: Producing Interactive Television, Charles River Media, Inc., Hingham, MA (2002)
3. ITV Production Standards Committee, iTV Standards Links (last visit 09.07.2007), http://itvstandards.org /iTVPublic/standards.aspx
4. Bürger, T., Gams, E., Güntner, G.: Smart Content Factory - Assisting Search for Digital Objects by Generic Linking Concepts to Multimedia Content. In: Proceedings of the Sixteenth ACM Conference on Hypertext and Hypermedia (HT '05). ACM Press, New York (2005)
5. Bloehdorn, S., et al.: Semantic Annotation of Images and Videos for Multimedia Analysis. In: Gómez-Pérez, A., Euzenat, J. (eds.) ESWC 2005. LNCS, vol. 3532. Springer, Heidelberg (2005)
6. Bürger, T., Westenthaler, R.: Mind the gap - requirements for the combination of content and knowledge. In: Proceedings of the first international conference on Semantics And digital Media Technology (SAMT), Athens, Greece (December 6-8, 2006)
7. Smeulders, A.W.M., et al.: Content-Based Image Retrieval at the End of the Early Years. IEEE Transactions on Pattern Analysis and Machine Intelligence 22(12) (December 2000)
8. Behrendt, W., Gangemi, A., Maass, W., Westenthaler, R.: Towards an Ontology-Based Distributed Architecture for Paid Content. In: Gómez-Pérez, A., Euzenat, J. (eds.) ESWC 2005. LNCS, vol. 3532, pp. 257–271. Springer, Heidelberg (2005)

# Using Narrative Cases to Author Interactive Story Content

Ivo Swartjes

University of Twente, Human Media Interaction group
Enschede, The Netherlands
i.m.t.swartjes@ewi.utwente.nl

**Abstract.** Interactive storytelling is a rapidly emerging field that tries to reconcile story-like experiences with user control. These forces oppose each other, as story implies predetermination and author intent, and interactivity implies freedom and variability. This paper focuses on unscripted (emergent) narrative and addresses the authoring problem resulting from bringing story development into free form interaction. It discusses the possibility of writing story pieces as input knowledge, portraying both believable character behaviour and interesting story situations. It also discusses how such input knowledge can be a source of inspiration for agents in an emergent narrative simulation to improve its potential for story development.

## 1 Introduction

The computer forms a new medium to convey stories. Other than in traditional media, such as books and television, computation can be used to bring *interactivity* into these stories. In this paper, we consider such interactive stories to be stories where a (human) participant can influence the course of the story. Writing an interactive story is a design problem, asking for an investigation of story construction: where can the story offer choices to this participant, and how is the course of the story influenced by these choices?

A traditional way of introducing interactivity to stories is to use branching story lines [11]. However, using branching story lines results in an 'explosion of endings': each choice point theoretically introduces a different ending to the story. An added disadvantage is the fact that the whole story is pre-written and therefore has a limited replay value.

The construction of interactive stories beyond the traditional branching story lines calls for more generative descriptions of story content. However, generating an interesting story-like experience is potentially in conflict with generating believable character behaviour [9]. A character must appear consistent and personally motivated for the audience to suspend their disbelief, but personally motivated action does not necessarily help the story forward. The same sort of potential conflict arises when a human participant gains a more central role in the story and can impact its course of events. A user who has freedom of interaction can make choices that conflict with the story intended by the author. This conflict is often referred to as the *narrative paradox* [1].

L. Ma, R. Nakatsu, and M. Rauterberg (Eds.): ICEC 2007, LNCS 4740, pp. 205–210, 2007.

Ideally, an author of an interactive story should be able to write content that satisfies both sides. An author should be afforded to put his specific ideas about the story into the system, but these ideas should also be represented in a way suitable for use in story-generative processes. This paper proposes an authoring paradigm in which example story pieces are used to influence the event sequence of the story. These pieces are expressed using a semantic representation that enables generative processes to use them. In section 2, some authoring paradigms in the context of interactive storytelling are discussed. In section 3 I propose the use of example story pieces as an alternative paradigm, and discuss the knowledge contained in such story pieces from two perspectives: that of character and that of plot.

## 2    Authoring Paradigms in Interactive Storytelling

Several approaches have been made to address the narrative paradox, each with their own advantages and disadvantages. These approaches can be placed on a spectrum between focusing on autonomous character behaviour on one side, and focusing on engaging plot on the other side.

On one end of the spectrum is a practice to define character behaviour with the aim to make story emerge from it. Two notable projects that follow this approach are the I-Storytelling project [2] and the FearNot! project [1]. The I-Storytelling project uses planning formalisms (Hierarchical Task Networks and Heuristic Search Planning) to define character behaviour. The hierarchical definition of tasks and methods roughly corresponds with episodic structures present in simple stories [6] and thus allows for authoring goal-based story content where the real-time interaction of the character's goals allow story variability under the assumption that alternative plans of action are also authored. The focus on character behaviour is even more prevalent in the emergent narrative approach [1]. The FearNot! project is an example, using an affective agent architecture to generate character behaviour portraying bullying scenarios in a primary school setting. The emergent narrative paradigm has no focus on plot whatsoever and the authoring is focused on instantiating the affective models controlling the behaviour of the characters to suit a particular story domain.

At the other end of the spectrum are approaches that use plot requirements to determine the character behaviour necessary to satisfy them. One approach involves constructing a plot using planning operators, and addresses the question how to place character behaviour believably in service of this plot. The authoring focus here is on defining operators that determine a search space for plans in which certain plot goals (e.g., "a bomb goes off") are reached. The (non-interactive) plot planning approach is described in [9]; subsequent effort has shown its applicability in the Interactive Storytelling domain [10]. The preconditions of the planning operators enable the off-line creation of alternative plots for each possible violation of these preconditions by the user.

There seems to be a trade-off between expressiveness and generativity of a particular interactive storytelling system, whereas both seem important. Expressiveness is needed to for the system to satisfy the artistic, educational or entertainment goals of the author whereas generativity is important to be able to offer a flexible interactive narrative without the need for hand-authoring many possible plot developments. Highly generative systems require access to the semantics of story content. However, current AI formalisms do not offer the semantics necessary to for instance represent the specific character behaviour of James Bond. Capturing James Bond in a general cognitive architecture seems like a daunting psychoanalytic venture, if at all possible. In designing an interactive storytelling system, a middle ground must therefore be found between generating character behaviour using generic personality models that can respond flexibly to many situations, and writing specific characters with specific behaviours in specific situations. Michael Mateas coins the term *Expressive AI* to refer to the endeavour of building AI systems that can generate expressive content that conveys the intent of an author [7]. The Façade system [8] is a good example of this; its behaviour language allows interactive drama to be authored at beat level. A beat is the smallest unit of dramatic action, i.e., action that helps the story forward. This paper argues for a similar (but more declarative) architectural entity in the form of a *narrative case*: a semantic representation of an example story piece that portrays believable character behaviour in the context of an interesting story situation. A narrative case aims at representing expressive content with generative semantics.

## 3   Narrative Inspiration from Example Story Pieces

The practice of using examples to capture and reuse knowledge in a certain domain, rather than a full specification of the domain knowledge, is referred to as Case Based Reasoning (CBR). Up till now, CBR is used only sporadically in interactive storytelling or story generation projects. The interactive storytelling system OPIATE uses CBR to achieve morphological plot variation [3], similar to [4]. MINSTREL [14] is model of story generation using CBR to modify and recombine predefined episodic knowledge structures to construct stories. Its story generation process is guided by author goals, such as illustrating an intended theme, or fixing consistency problems in a story under construction.

Now, the core value of CBR is that knowledge is captured in terms of *examples* (rather than extensive domain knowledge). From the standpoint of Expressive AI, it offers *authorial affordances*, in that these examples can express the intentions of the author, and can as such be used as inspiration by a system that tries to deliver a story-like experience. If example story pieces are formulated in terms of elements that can also be generated[1] and as such be incorporated in the emergent unfolding of a story, we allow a framework that has the flexibility to produce narrative on the spot to be infused with authorial intent, a process I would like to call *narrative inspiration* [13].

When the narrative cases (expressing example story pieces) are authored with two principles in mind, namely (1) that they express believable behaviour, and

---

[1] When using affective architectures as in emergent narrative, these are elements like emotions, goals, actions, events and beliefs.

(2) that they portray interesting specific situations as desired by the author, a collection of such cases can be used as information source for interactive storytelling applications. To this end, my aim is to integrate the use of narrative cases with the emergent narrative approach of the Virtual Storyteller [12]. The Virtual Storyteller simulates affective character agents and uses a plot agent to manage the unfolding narrative, trying to steer it in a promising direction. The semantics of our narrative case representation is based on *causality* between story elements [13]. The unfolding narrative is also represented in terms of causality. Rather than using the narrative cases as (partial) solutions to author goals (as done in MINSTREL), I want to integrate the causal knowledge that these cases contain with the processes that the agents in the Virtual Storyteller already run. I will briefly discuss such processes from both perspectives (from a generative point of view), and show how these processes can be informed by narrative cases. When using narrative cases as knowledge sources, I hope to end up with narrative that is still believable and more interesting than can be achieved without the use of these cases.

### 3.1    The Character Perspective

In the Virtual Storyteller, we follow the work that has been done by Bryan Loyall on designing believable characters [5]. Some of the requirements for believable characters are that they express personality and emotions, appear self-motivated, change by experience, form social relationships, are consistent and portray the 'illusion of life'. I will address the causal aspects of two of these believability requirements: self-motivation and emotion.

It is important that character actions appear motivated by their own personal goals or emotions [9]. When a character tries to achieve goals, the question is what actions or subgoals it should choose to achieve them. The aim of 'standard' AI task planning algorithms (intended for effective and efficient achievement of intentions) does not necessarily match the aim of dramatic task planning, where ways to achieve goals are determined by a dramatic perspective. For instance, James Bond might have a very specific way to dismantle a villainous organization, a high-level goal that is not only awkward to express in primitive planning operators, but is also typically something an author might want to have specific control over. Narrative cases can express how these high-level goals might decompose; the lower-level physical details lend themselves better for planning approaches using means-end reasoning, since they arguably exist mainly to afford the dramatic action.

The second process that contributes to character believability is that of emotional reactions to events. Within the affective agent architecture of the Virtual Storyteller, a character first adopts beliefs based on perceptions which will then result in emotional states that affect how it proceeds to act. Such processes are currently based on realism, but can also be informed by what the story needs. For instance, in Shakespeare's "Romeo and Juliet", when Juliet sees Romeo faking his death, her belief in his death (a believable reaction) has dramatic consequences (i.e., she commits suicide). A more realistic but maybe less interesting response might have her check his pulse. By modelling the relationship between perceptions, beliefs and emotional reactions from an author perspective, a character's internal world can be enriched by a case base of dramatically fertile experiences. This also makes it possible for characters to make quick assumptions about other characters' internal worlds. They can make plans to affect each other's beliefs without complicated adversarial reasoning.

A narrative case effectively defines specific character behaviour within a certain narrative context that makes it believable and helps the story forward. If this context is met, a character can respond according to the case rather than according to the result of its own deliberative processes, thus contributing to the emerging story.

### 3.2   The Plot Perspective

The plot agent is responsible for helping the story forward where necessary. Within the emergent narrative simulation, the unfolding narrative can be influenced without breaking the autonomy of the characters, when environmental control is used. Two ways of environmental control that can be inspired by narrative cases, are the following: making events occur that (possibly) affect the plans of characters, and real-time construction of the story world.

The first way of environmental control raises the question which events will contribute to an interesting plot. These are for instance events that thwart or help a character's goals and plans, or cause an emotional reaction. Narrative cases can express how character action results in events (e.g., James Bond cuts himself when he breaks through a window), and how these events can cause interesting or desired character reactions. Both might form a basis for the drama manager to select and introduce them in the story.

The second way of environmental control involves filling in the details of the story world setting, which does not need to be fully fixed from the start. Theoretically, only information conveyed to a user at a certain point in time constrains the possible setting the story world can be in. This allows the introduction of characters, objects and such when needed for plot development (this idea has been explored in a story planning domain [9]). The drama manager can use the narrative cases as inspiration to decide what knowledge to introduce at a certain point in time: certain cases will become applicable for the unfolding of the story (e.g., introducing a window in the house of the villain when James Bond arrives makes it possible for him to break in). The idea here is that the setting exists in *service* of the plot, rather than as a cause of it.

On the assumption that a narrative case expresses a course of events as the author intends it, trying to achieve this course of events is a high priority for the plot agent. The plot agent keeps track of the unfolding story and can opportunistically detect a context in which these cases can apply, or try to achieve such contexts more actively.

## 4   Conclusion

This paper puts forward the idea of having an author express his intent for the unfolding of an emergent narrative by combining representations of believable character behaviour with interesting narrative situations, resulting in a knowledge structure called the narrative case. Authoring such cases is less awkward than specifying high level domain knowledge, and integrating them with an emergent narrative architecture increases the potential of the author's intent being reflected in the actual simulation. A more detailed description of the use of narrative cases for the Virtual Storyteller is given in [13]; subsequent research will focus on actual experiments to investigate the effects of offering narrative inspiration to the processes that the agents of the Virtual Storyteller already run.

# References

1. Aylett, R., Louchart, S., Dias, J., Paiva, A., Vala, M., Woods, S., Hall, L.: Unscripted narrative for affectively driven characters. IEEE Computer Graphics and Applications 26(4), 42–52 (2006)
2. Cavazza, M., Charles, F., Mead, S.J.: Character-based interactive storytelling. IEEE Intelligent Systems 17(4), 17–24 (2002)
3. Fairclough, P., Cunningham, C.R.: AI structuralist storytelling in computer games. Technical report, University of Dublin, Computer Science Department (2004)
4. Gervás, P., Díaz-Agudo, B., Peinado, F., Hervás, R.: Story plot generation based on CBR. Knowledge-Based Systems 18(4-5), 235–242 (2004)
5. Loyall, A.B.: Believable Agents: Building Interactive Personalities. PhD thesis, Carnegie Mellon University, Pittsburgh, PA (1997)
6. Mandler, J.M., Johnson, N.S.: Remembrance of things parsed: Story structure and recall. Cognitive Psychology 9, 111–151 (1977)
7. Mateas, M.: Expressive AI. Leonardo: Journal of the International Society for Arts, Sciences, and Technology 34(2), 147–153 (2001)
8. Mateas, M., Stern, A.: Façade: An experiment in building a fully-realized interactive drama. Technical report, Literature, Communication and Culture and College of Computing, Georgia Tech. (2003)
9. Riedl, M.O.: Narrative Generation: Balancing Plot and Character. PhD thesis, North Carolina State University (2004)
10. Riedl, M.O., Stern, A.: Believable Agents and Intelligent Story Adaptation for Interactive Storytelling. In: Technologies for Interactive Digital Storytelling and Entertainment (TIDSE) (2006)
11. Riedl, M.O., Young, R.M.: From linear story generation to branching story graphs. IEEE Computer Graphics and Applications 26(3), 23–31 (2006)
12. Swartjes, I., Theune, M.: A Fabula Model for Emergent Narrative. In: Technologies for Interactive Digital Storytelling and Entertainment (TIDSE) (2006)
13. Swartjes, I., Vromen, J., Bloom, N.: Narrative inspiration: Using case based problem solving to support emergent story generation. In: Proceedings International Joint Workshop on Computational Creativity (2007)
14. Turner, S.R.: The creative process: a computer model of storytelling. Lawrence Erlbaum Associates, Hillsdale, NJ (1994)

# Multi-track Scratch Player
# on a Multi-touch Sensing Device

Kentaro Fukuchi

Graduate School of Information Systems
The University of Electro-Communications
Choufu-shi, Tokyo , Japan 182-8585
fukuchi@megaui.net

**Abstract.** Scratching with turntables is a popular sound generation technique in today's music scene, especially in hip-hop culture. A conventional turntable system consists of two turntables (record players) and an audio mixer, but the proposed system requires a computer and a multi-touch sensing device, so it is smaller and portable. Moreover, the proposed system enables the use of various novel scratching techniques that are difficult or impossible to perform on existing systems. In this paper we describe the implementation of the proposed system and introduce some scratching techniques that can be used with it.

## 1 Background

Scratching on a turntable is a popular sound generation technique in today's music scene. Scratching usually involves the use of two turntables and an audio mixer for scratching. A player (known as a *DJ* or *turntablist*) manipulates these with his hands (Figure 1). A scratching sound is generated by rotating a record on the turntable back and forth by hand, while the other hand moves a cross fader or volume slider[7][8]. Therefore, both hands are busy in scratching so the records cannot be changed during a scratching motion and scratching two or more records is not possible. This limitation is considered to be an important problem in scratching, especially for the "no-tricks" style of scratching performance whereby a player performs music by scratching alone.

A simple solution to this problem is the use of more turntables, but they are too large (at least 12 inches square) to allow manipulation of multiple turntables by hand. There are a number of software-based scratching applications, but these employ conventional pointing devices or a dedicated external input device which has two rotary encoders to simulate a pair of turntables. They do not allow scratching of two or more soundtracks.

We developed a computer-aided scratching system that enables simultaneous multi-track scratching by using a multi-touch sensing device. The system is small and portable, and enables the use of various novel scratching techniques that are difficult or impossible to perform on existing systems.

## 2 Related Work

Audiopad[11] allows multitrack audio mixing by Phicons that contain RFID tags. By attaching a soundtrack to a Phicon and moving them, the user can control the volumes of the soundtracks concurrently, but scratching is not possible.

L. Ma, R. Nakatsu, and M. Rauterberg (Eds.): ICEC 2007, LNCS 4740, pp. 211–218, 2007.

**Fig. 1.** Scratching using a turntable

KORG KAOSS PAD[10] is a commercial product that allows scratching by moving a finger on an embedded touch sensor. The sensor does not detect multiple touches so it is not possible to scratch multiple soundtracks.

Skipproof[6] allows a scratch performance with various input devices such as MIDI interfaces or gesture sensors. The user can scratch a single 1.8 second long audio sample with an input device. In addition, the user can trigger a pre-recorded (readymade) scratching technique instead of manual scratching.

Jeff Han introduced a multi-touch sensing technique that utilizes an internal reflection in a clear acrylic board[5]. They also developed a software-based musical application on it.

## 3   System Architecture

### 3.1   Multi-touch Sensing Device

We employed SmartSkin[13], a human-body sensing device based on capacitive sensing. The sensor recognizes multiple hand or finger positions and shapes, and calculates the distance between the hand and the surface. We used a tablet-sized SmartSkin that has $32 \times 24$ grid cells and each cell is 9 mm$\times$9 mm.

We used a pair of tablet-sized SmartSkin sensors to create a larger input surface that is 47 cm$\times$31 cm. Both SmartSkins are connected to a computer via USB 1.1, and the computer estimates the motion of the fingertips from the sensor data from the input data then generates sound. The resolution of finger positions is $1504 \times 992$.

### 3.2   Display

A projector is located above the input surface, and the projector displays the screen on the surface. The resolution of the screen is $1504 \times 992$, which is the same as the resolution of the input system. Figure 2 shows an overview of the system.

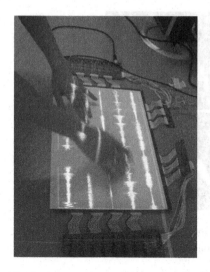

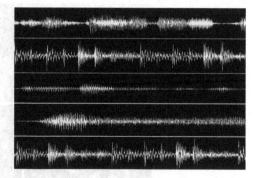

**Fig. 3.** Screenshot of the multi-track scratch player. Five soundtracks are shown, and each waveform is displayed horizontally. The performer touches the waveform with his fingers directly and performs scratching. The speed and

**Fig. 2.** An overview of the multi-track scratch player

direction of playback is synchronized to the motion of the finger.

### 3.3 Finger Tracking

A multipoint input system was implemented on SmartSkin[4][3]. With this system, the user touches an input surface by his fingers directly. The sensing range of tablet-sized SmartSkin is 5 mm, which means that the system can distinguish whether or not a finger is touching the surface. As a result, a touch-panel-like multipoint input surface was developed. In this section, we describe the algorithm of the finger tracking.

First, the system scales up the sensor values by bicubic convolution interpolation. As shown in Figure 4, fingertips can clearly be seen in the interpolated image (bottom right). The system then detects the fingertips from the interpolated values. The values below a threshold are omitted to detect only contact or very close presence to the input surface parts. The bottom right section of Figure 4 shows a filtered image. Next, the system divides the values into several continuous regions by using the segmentation algorithm. If the number of pixels of a region is within a certain range, the system recognizes the region as a fingertip and calculates its centroid as the position of the fingertip.

SmartSkin cannot identify which finger of whose hand is on the grid. Therefore, in order to track the motions of the fingers, the system has to estimate the motions by comparing the current positions of fingers and their previous positions. A cost minimization analysis technique was employed for motion tracking. The details are as follows.

In frame $t$, let $F_{i,t}(i = 1, 2, \ldots, n_t)$ be positions of detected fingertips. When $F_{j,t+1}(j = 1, 2, \ldots, n_{t+1})$ is given as their positions in the next frame $t + 1$, the system calculates a *candidate set* of corresponding points $S_{i,t}$ for every $F_{i,t}$: when a cut-off value $R$ is given, $S_{i,t}$ consists of points of $F_{j,t+1}$ which satisfies $|F_{i,t} - F_{j,t+1}| < R$.

In the same way, the system calculates $S_{j,t+1}$ for $F_{j,t+1}$, which consists of points of $F_{i,t}$, which satisfies $|F_{i,t} - F_{j,t+1}| < R$. If $F_{i,t}$ has no candidate ($S_{i,t} = \emptyset$), it

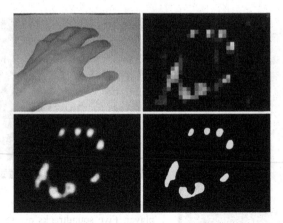

**Fig. 4.** Step of fingertip detection: A hand on the SmartSkin (top left), sensor values (top right), interpolated values (bottom left), after the segmentation process (bottom right)

is considered that the corresponding finger is released, and it is eliminated from the remaining process. If $F_{j,t}$ has no candidate ($S_{j,t+1} = \emptyset$), it is considered that the finger is newly detected, and it is eliminated as well.

Next, in order to determine a corresponding point for the rest of $F_{i,t}$, the system checks all of the combinations. Let a matrix $T$ be a combination of $F_{i,t}$ and $F_{j,t+1}$. Its cost is calculated by following equation:

$$\sum_{i,j} T_{i,j} |F_{i,t} - F_{j,t+1}|^2$$

Then, the system compares all of the costs of $T$ and choose the minimum cost. If the number of combinations is too large, the system aborts the tracking and treats all of fingers as being released. In this implementation, the cut-off value $R$ is 200 pixels, and the limit of the number of combinations is $10^6$.

Finally, the system uses a Kalman filter to absorb small shaking. However, because the scan rate of SmartSkin is as slow as per 20 scan/sec, its response became worse when the filter was applied naively. In order to avoid this, the system does not apply the filter when the motion length is longer than five pixels. In addition, the system does not use a Kalman filter to estimate the motion.

Figure 5 shows an increase in computational time for finger tracking. The computational time is averaged over frames of every number of fingers. The light gray area represents the time required to read the sensor values and interpolate them. The dark gray are represents the time required to detect and track the fingers from the interpolated data. As shown in the graph, the current implementation is sufficiently fast for one or two users for real-time processing.

### 3.4 Multi-track Scratching

Figure 3 shows a screenshot of the screen that is overlaid on the input surface, as shown in Figure 2. Current implementation enables five sound tracks to be played, and the

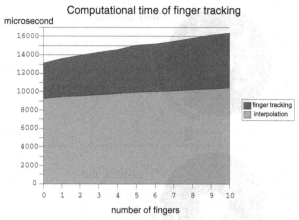

**Fig. 5.** Average computational time of finger tracking

sound wave from each track is shown horizontally. Each sound track is the same length as the PCM wave data.

If a track is not touched by a finger, the track is not played. When it is touched by a finger, the application plays the waveform that the finger passes over, as if the finger was a needle and the soundtrack was the groove of a vinyl record. The vertical motion of the finger controls the volume of the sound (optional for advanced use). This manipulation can be performed in parallel on all sound tracks, and the result is mixed down to the computer's audio output. Even when a sound track is touched by two or more fingers, it acts in the same manner.

### 3.5  Audio Processing

The motion of a finger is used to make a scratching sound. When a new finger position is acquired, the application plays the waveform that the finger passes over within the interval of scanning.

The length of each soundtrack is 2–3 seconds. In order to play a soundtrack at normal speed, it is necessary to move a finger at 16–28 cm/s, because the width of the input surface is 47cm. The sampling rate of soundtracks is 44.1KHz. Therefore, a soundtrack contains 88200–132300 samples and a horizontal step of finger motion plays 88 samples at most. In order to play the waveform within a certain time, the waveform data must be resampled. At present, the application resamples the data discretely, which results in loss of the sound quality. Several techniques by which to avoid quality loss are known, such as Sinc-based resampling[14][1]. However, these techniques were not tested on our system.

## 4  Simulation of Known Scratching Techniques

There are several scratching techniques for conventional turntables and audio mixers. A scratching technique consists of a pattern of motion of a turntable and a cross fader. DJs and turntablists use these techniques sequentially in a performance.

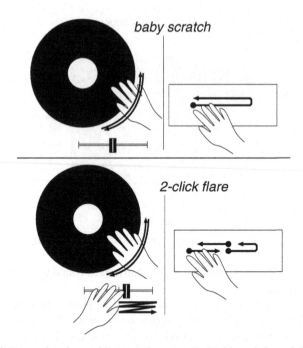

**Fig. 6.** Conventional scratching techniques on the Multi-track Scratch Player

As well as enabling the use of known scratching techniques, the proposed scratching system is also designed to allow novel scratching techniques that cannot be performed on conventional systems.

Figure 6 shows two major scratching techniques on a turntable and the corresponding procedures for the proposed system. The technique shown at the top of the figure is known as the "baby scratch". This is the simplest type of scratching, in which the player rotates the turntable back and forth repeatedly. This scratching can be performed by repeatedly moving a finger on a track horizontally.

The bottom figure shows the "two-click flare" technique, which requires concurrent manipulation of the turntable and cross fader. The player rotates the turntable back and forth using one hand, while the other hand quickly slides the cross fader between the min and max positions twice. By this fading motion, the player can cut the sound to make beats. In order to simulate this scratching technique in the proposed system, the player must release the finger from the input surface twice while moving his finger repeatedly. However, it is difficult to perform this motion quickly. To perform a rapid click, the player can play the first click with one hand then the second click with the other hand.

## 5   Discussion

This system was tested and a sound delay was found to be a significant problem. The SmartSkin sensor scans at 20 Hz but because the application plays a soundtrack between the current and previous positions of a finger, a 50 millisecond playback delay is generated. In music performance, this delay is unacceptable. In order to avoid this problem, we plan to alter the multi-touch sensing device such as iGesturePad[9].

Generally, a turntable rotates at a constant speed when a player does not touch it. The speed can be controlled by a slide volume. Moreover, it can be slowed down by touching the surface of the record softly, or increased by pushing it in the direction of rotation. At this time, the proposed system does not support this kind of manipulation. Some DJs have reported that these manipulations are very important for scratching. Therefore, in order to realize these existing scratching techniques, these manipulations should be supported.

Turntablists use a cross fader to click the sound (see Figure 6). In order to simulate this technique, our system requires the performer to move his fingers up and down very quickly, and this is not as easy as the fader action. We plan to add fader widgets next to the tracks. This idea is inspired by Vestax QFO[12], a turntable system with a built-in mixer, designed by a professional turntablist, Q-BERT.

## 6   Future Work

We have developed a multiple pointing input system based on camera-tracked laser pointers[2]. This input system allows users to point to multiple positions on a screen using laser pointers. We plan to implement the multi-track scratch player on the laser-based input system. In this case, we hypothesize that the problem of latency will be reduced because the laser based system scans positions at 30 scans per second. In addition it allows multi-user interaction of scratch playing.

We plan to use low-latency input devices and evaluate our multi-track scratch player to prove that our approach is useful for advanced DJ-style music. To evaluate these devices, we are using a high-speed camera to analyze the motion of a scratch play.

## 7   Conclusion

We developed a software scratching system with a multi-touch sensing device, which enabled concurrent scratching of multiple soundtracks. The proposed system allows some new scratching techniques as well as conventional ones to be used on turntables.

At this time, the proposed implementation causes a 50 millisecond delay, which is unacceptable for musical performance.

The proposed approach was well-received by DJs. Therefore, the scan rate of the multi-touch input device should be improved and the delay should be decreased. Finally, more new scratching techniques should be developed for the system.

## References

1. Secret Rabbit Code: http://www.mega-nerd.com/SRC/
2. Fukuchi, K.: A Laser Pointer/Laser Trails Tracking System for Visual Performance. In: Costabile, M.F., Paternó, F. (eds.) INTERACT 2005. LNCS, vol. 3585, pp. 1050–1053. Springer, Heidelberg (2005)

3. Fukuchi, K.: Concurrent Manipulation of Multiple Components on Graphical User Interface. PhD thesis, Tokyo Institute of Technology (2006)
4. Fukuchi, K., Rekimoto, J.: Interaction Techniques for SmartSkin. In: Proceedings of UIST'02 (2002)
5. Han, J.Y.: Low-Cost Multi-Touch Sensing Through Frustrated Total Internal Reflection. In: UIST '05. Proceedings of the 18th annual ACM symposium on User interface software and technology, pp. 115–118. ACM Press, New York (2005)
6. Hansen, K.F., Bresin, R.: The Sounding Object. In: Complex Gestural Audio Control: The Case of Scratching, Mondo Estremo, pp. 221–269 (2003)
7. Hansen, K.F., Bresin, R.: Analysis of a genuine scratch performance. In: Camurri, A., Volpe, G. (eds.) GW 2003. LNCS (LNAI), vol. 2915, pp. 519–528. Springer, Heidelberg (2004)
8. Hansen, K.F., Bresin, R.: Mapping strategies in DJ scratching. In: Proceedings of NIME 2006, pp. 188–191 (2006)
9. iGesturePad: http://www.fingerworks.com/igesture.html
10. KORG KAOSS PAD: http://www.korg.co.jp/Product/Dance/KPE1/
11. Patten, J., Recht, B., Ishii, H.: Audiopad: A Tag-based Interface for Musical Performance. In: Proceedings of the 2002 International Conference on New Interfacefor Musical Expression (NIME02), pp. 11–16 (2003)
12. QFO: http://www.vestax.com/v/products/players/qfo.html
13. Rekimoto, J.: SmartSkin: An Infrastructure for Freehand Manipulation on Interactive Surfaces. In: Proceedings of CHI2002, pp. 113–120 (2002)
14. Smith, J.O., Gossett, P.: A flexible sampling-rate conversion method. In: Proceedings of the International Conference on Acoustics, Speech, and Signal Processing, vol. 9, pp. 112–115 (1984)

# PanoMOBI: Panoramic Mobile Entertainment System

Barnabas Takacs[1,2]

[1] MTA SZTAKI, Virtual Human Interface Group, Hungarian Academy of Sciences,
Kende u. 11-13, 1111 Budapest, Hungary
[2] Digital Elite Inc.
415 Washington Blvd, 90292 Marina del Rey, CA, USA
Btakacs@sztaki.hu

**Abstract.** This paper presents a panoramic broadcasting system for mobile entertainment using 3G network or WIFI where multiple viewers share an experience but each having full control of what they see independent from other viewers. Our solution involves a compact real-time spherical video recording setup that compresses and transmits data from six digital video cameras to a central host computer, which in turn distributes the recorded information among multiple render- and streaming servers for personalized viewing over 3G mobile networks or the Internet. In addition, using advanced computer vision, tracking and animation features, our architecture introduces the notion of Clickable Content (CC) where each visual element in the image becomes a source for providing further information, educational content or advertising. Therefore the PanoMOBI system offers a low-cost and economical solution for personalized content management and it can serve as a unified basis for novel applications.

**Keywords:** PanoMOBI, PanoCAST, Clickable Content, Telepresence, Immersive Spherical Video, Mobile Broadcast Architecture (MBA).

## 1 Introduction

The dream of achieving panoramic broadcasting and subsequently delivering immersive content for tele-operators of robotic- or surgical equipment as well as for security and defense purposes, has been in the focus of research for many decades. In addition, the notion of telepresence as implemented with the tools of virtual-reality for entertainment and education (edutainment) have also long intrigued scientists and developers of complex systems alike. Our current research focuses on presenting visual and auditory stimuli to multiple viewers at the same time and allowing them to share their experience. Video-based telepresence solutions that employ panoramic recording systems have recently become an important field of research mostly deployed in security and surveillance applications. Such architectures frequently employ expensive multiple-head camera hardware and record data to a set of digital tape recorders from which surround images are stitched together in a tedious process. These cameras are also somewhat large and difficult to use and do not provide full spherical video (only cylindrical), a feature required by many new applications. More recently new advances in CCD resolution and compression technology have created

L. Ma, R. Nakatsu, and M. Rauterberg (Eds.): ICEC 2007, LNCS 4740, pp. 219–224, 2007.
© IFIP International Federation for Information Processing 2007

the opportunity to design and build cameras that can capture and transmit almost complete spherical video images [1], but these solutions are rather expensive and can stream images only to a *single viewer*. For the purposes of entertainment, however, many of these systems are too complex for the every-day user and also costly for operators and content providers to deploy. Therefore in our current research we focused on presenting visual and auditory stimuli to multiple users who share the same experience using their mobile-phone or IP-based digital delivery mechanisms. To address this technical challenge we have designed and architecture that can redistribute spherical video to multiple independent viewer each having control over their own respective point of view with the help of an advanced virtual reality environment, called the *Virtual Human Interface (VHI)* [2][3].

## 2   PanoMOBI System Architecture

PanoMOBI stands for *Panoramic Mobile Broadcasting*. The technology is the extension of our earlier solution for telepresence and Internet-based services, called *PanoCAST* (Panoramic Broadcasting). To record and stream high fidelity spherical video we employ a special camera system with six lenses packed into a tiny head-unit. The images captured by the camera head are compressed and sent to our server computer in real-time delivering up to 30 frames per second, where they are mapped onto a corresponding sphere for visualization. The basic server architecture, then employs a number of virtual cameras and assigns them to each user who connects from a mobile phone, thereby creating their own, personal view of the events the camera is seeing or has recorded. The motion of the virtual cameras is controllable via TCP/IP with the help of a script interface that assigns camera motion and pre-programmed actions to key codes on the mobile device. The host computer then generates the virtual views each users sees and streams this information back to their location using RTSP protocol. This process is demonstrated in Figure 1 in the context of a rock concert. The spherical camera head (left) is placed at the remote site in an event where the user wishes to participate. The camera head captures the entire spherical surroundings of the camera with resolutions up to 3K by 1.5K pixels and adjustable frame rates of maximum 30 frames per second (fps). These images are compressed in real-time and transmitted to a remote computer over G-bit Ethernet connection or using the Internet, which decompresses the data stream and remaps the spherical imagery onto the surface of a sphere locally. Finally, the personalized rendering engine of the viewer creates TV-like imagery and sends it to a *mobile device* with the help of a *virtual camera* the motion of which is directly controlled by the actions of the user.

The key idea behind our *PanoMOBI* solution is based on distributing each user only what they currently should see instead of the entire scene they may be experiencing. While this reduces the computational needs on the receiver side (essentially needing only to decode streamed video and audio data) and send tracking information and camera control back in return, it places designers of the server architecture in a difficult position. To overcome these limitations we devised an architecture as follows: The *panoramic camera head* is connected via an optical cable to a *JPG compression* module, which transmits compressed image frames at video rates to a distributions server using IEEE firewire standard. The role of the

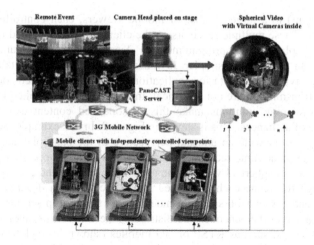

**Fig. 1.** Overview of the PanoMOBI system used for interactive mobile entertainment

*distribution server* is to multiple the data video data and prepare it for broadcast via a server farm. To maximize bus capacity and minimize synchronization problems, the distribution server broadcasts its imagery via *UDP protocol* to a number of *virtual camera servers*, each being responsible for a number of individually controlled cameras. Video data is then first encoded in MPEG format and subsequently distributed among a number of *streaming servers* using RTSP (Real-time Streaming Protocol) before sent out to individual clients over 3G mobile networks (or the Internet for WIFI service). Assuming 3Gbit/sec connection a streaming server is capable of servicing up to 100 simultaneous clients at any given moment. Again, the number of streaming servers can be scaled according to the need of the broadcast. Finally, independent image streams are synchronized with audio and arrive at the user site ready to be decoded and displayed. In the *PanoMOBI* entertainment system interaction occurs by key action on the mobile device whereas the user controls the orientation and field of view of the camera to observe the remote concert event taking place.

## 3   Panoramic Recording and Broadcasting

One of the key elements of our mobile broadcasting solution is the *PanoMOBI* recording system that comprises of a compact and portable 360 degree panoramic video recording system that was designed to minimally interfere with the scene while providing maximal immersion for the viewer. Since practically the entire spherical surround environment is recorded working with such a camera is rather difficult from a production's point of view. Specifically, the basic rules and the concept of frames here become obsolete, both lighting, microphones as well as the staff remains visible. To provide as much immersion as possible, the camera head is placed on the end of a long pole carried by the cameraperson. To enhance the functionality of our broadcasting solution we have enabled our server-architecture to create multiple live streams of the panoramic imagery and redistribute them in real-time (or from recorded content) to a large number of mobile viewers, each controlling their own point of view. These multiple receivers on the client side were created in the form of a *PanoMOBI* player and programmed in *Symbian* for maximum speed and performance. In addition, a simpler Java-based client is also available, which is capable of receiving video data for applications where synchronized sound and high speed image transmission are not as critical. In addition to the mobile player different Web-based streaming solutions make this personalized content available to even broader range of audiences. This is shown in Figure 2. In this example the camera was placed on stage to provide an unusual perspective of the band playing. The six raw images from the panoramic recording head are shown in the upper left corner. From these streams a full spherical view of the scene was created and a number of virtual cameras image the scene each controlled independently by a different user. In the upper right hand corner with six independent views stacked up serving as examples. The streaming server then encodes and distributes these streams to individual viewers in different formats, such as RTSP on 3G mobiles (shown lower left) or web-based clients (lower right). In the former case, the rotation and field of view of the camera may be controlled from the keypad of the mobile phone, while in the latter case HTML-embedded keys and Java script commands serve the same purpose. Finally, in both situations the user may click on the screen the result of which the *PanoMOBI* system computes which object was selected and sends back information and web-links for later use. This provides added value for services based on this technology not only for entertainment, but e-commerce, education and many other fields of application. In the next section we briefly discuss how the functionality of *Clickable Content* was achieved using resources of the GPU and our advanced real-time image processing pipeline.

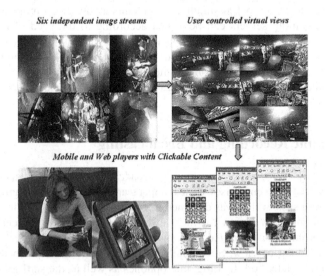

*Six independent image streams*          *User controlled virtual views*

*Mobile and Web players with Clickable Content*

**Fig. 2.** Panoramic imagery is passed from the camera head to individual users who view and interactively control their viewpoint as well as the content using mobile- and web clients

# 4  Real-Time Image Processing and Clickable Content

To enhance the functionality and the utilization of the basic panoramic viewing experience we have incorporated a set of real-time image processing algorithms that help with compression, correct artifacts, produce effects and finally, but most importantly allow for tracking different elements as they move in the scene or measure displacements as a result of camera motion (Handy-Cam mode). The high resolution raw image that contains six independent images) enters the stream and first passed through a real-time image processing module. This module was built on top of *OpenCV*, a computer vision library that offers basic image processing and enhancement algorithms as well as advanced tracking solutions and 3D reconstruction methods. These processes run on the CPU and are used for non-linear noise filtering (not only to improve overall image quality, but also to allow the better compression of the image stream). Due to the very high resolution of the raw images, the average performance rate (for decoding the video frames and processing them) drops render performance to approx. 15 to 24 fps. As a function of lighting conditions and scene complexity, which is still sufficient to stream images live to the mobile devices at a rate of 15 fps. These CPU-based algorithms are also useful for extracting the information needed for *Clickable Content*, as automated face detection algorithms and other object recognition modules are used to identify and track the apparent motion of elements of interest. The processed images are mapped onto surfaces (a sphere in our case) using a dynamic texture mapping algorithm that was optimized for minimizing the bottleneck between the CPU and the Graphics Card (GPU) present on the computer bus that connects them. Finally, once the textures are uploaded onto the graphics card, the parallel image processing algorithms may be constructed to further enhance the image itself in the form of pixel shaders. We use a single pass method whereas the shader code and parameters correct color, find edges and/or filter out noise using kernels. The main advantage of processing images at this stage comes from the distributed nature of the architecture. According to our experiments the GPU-based image enhancement algorithms we implemented caused practically no slow down in the overall rendering performance.

*Clickable Content* (*CC*) means that whenever the user clicks on the scene the rendering engine "fires a search ray" from the viewing camera and orders each visual elements as a function of their distance along this ray to find the closest one. Then the algorithm returns the object's name, the exact polygon it is intersected at, and the texture coordinates of the intersection point itself. The final output of such algorithms is a set of tracked regions with actions, text information and web pages assigned on each of which *PanoMOBI* viewers can click on during a performance and learn more about the event or simply educate themselves.

# 5  Conclusion and Future Work

In this paper we have introduced a multi-casting application for mobile phones where each viewer is allowed to individually control their own perspective while sharing this experience with others. We used a high resolution panoramic camera head placed at an entertainment event to create a real-time spherical video. We devised a rendering architecture to map virtual views of this scenery with multiple cameras and augmented the basic capabilities of our solution with real-time image processing pipeline running both on the CPU and the graphics card. This allows for balanced performance and personalized effects viewers may want. Finally, with the help of built-in tracking algorithms a content management solution, called *Clickable Content* (CC) was developed in order to turn an every day video into a rich source of information and commercial tool. Using this *PanoMOBI* architecture we developed intuitive user controls and multiple applications that involve this special form of telepresence. Specifically, we recorded music concerts, real-estates, scenery and travel-sites to demonstrate the usability of our system in real-life applications. The broadcasting system been tested in a number of digital networks including 3G mobile with multiple carriers for phone devices and PDA's, WIFI connection and even wired-Internet for desktop solutions. Test results showed that a single server computer can deliver services to up to 50 clients with reasonable 1-2 seconds delay. We argue that such a technical solution represents a novel opportunity for creating compelling content.

**Acknowledgments.** The research described in this paper was partly supported by grants from MTA SZTAKI, *VirMED Corporation*Budapest, Hungary (www.VirMED.net), and *Digital Elite Inc.,* Los Angeles, California, USA (www.digitalElite.net).

# References

1. Immersive Media: http://www.immersive-video.eu/en
2. Takacs, B.: Special Education and Rehabilitation: Teaching and Healing with Interactive Graphics. IEEE Computer Graphics and Applications 25(5), 40–48 (2005)
3. Takacs, B.: Cognitive, Mental and Physical Rehabilitation Using a Configurable Virtual Reality System. International Journal of Virtual Reality 5(4), 1–12 (2006)

# Application MDA in a Collaborative Modeling Environment

Wuzheng Tan[1], Lizhuang Ma[1], Zhiliang Xu[1], and Junfa Mao[2]

[1] Department of Engineering and Computer Science, Shanghai Jiao Tong University,
200240, China
[2] Department of Electronic Engineering, Shanghai Jiao Tong University, 200240, China
tanwuzheng@yahoo.com.cn, ma-lz@cs.sjtu.edu.cn,
{xuzhiliang,jfmao}@sjtu.edu.cn

**Abstract.** This paper proposes a modeling environment that intends to support service collaboration. In this platform, technology independence is a very important goal to be achieved. Model Driven Architecture and metamodels are some of the resources to provide such independence. Based on [1] and [2], this article offers a modified software development process that would leverage MDA, and studies a web application case of conceptual innovation modeling system.

**Keywords:** MDA, Collaborative Modeling, Collaborative Modeling Platform, Web Application.

## 1 Introduction

Building enterprise-scale software solutions has never been easy. The difficulties of understanding highly complex business domains are typically compounded with all the challenges of managing a development effort involving large teams of engineers over multiple phase of a project spanning many months. In addition to the scale and complexity of many of these efforts, there is also great complexity to the software platforms for which enterprise-scale software are targeted.

For a successful conception design initiative, an open and evolutionary platform must be considered in order to provide means to enable the old world of the legacy systems accessible to the new facilities brought by Internet. The Web Service (WS) architecture delivers standards for such collaborative environment. Although a good reference, the WS specifications, and the technologies to implement them, are still in evolution. To preserve the development efforts, at least minimal technology independence is desirable at the legacy integration and at the services design and compositions.

To meet these needs, we propose the construction of conception design platform, which main objective is to provide an effective and consistent approach to manage metadata and a service-oriented architecture for the cooperation among disparate administrative units in a collaborative environment.

Figure 1 shows n N-tier architecture for the platform. In the conception design logic, the service tier is responsible for the service management and the integration tier provides an integrated approach to the existing legacy systems.

L. Ma, R. Nakatsu, and M. Rauterberg (Eds.): ICEC 2007, LNCS 4740, pp. 225–230, 2007.

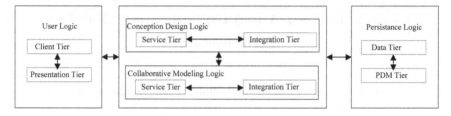

**Fig. 1.** Platform n-tier architecture

In [2], it introduced some related works about models and meta models, mapping between models and legacy integration.

In [14], it propose a sugarcane harvester modeling framework based on the commonly available communication platform and illustrate it with the implemented software that can be used as a core part for different real life applications. It is possible to perform their collaborative interactive modifications with concurrent synchronous visualization at each client computer with any required level of detail. The platform provides a product modeling and assembling environment and changes paradigms between I_DEAS, Smarteam(PDM software) and Conceptual Innovation Design System (CIDS). The platform is illustrated for sugarcane harvester modeling and assembling analysis as an example, and provides a collaborative intelligent environment for the model of products, aiming at integrating people, process and data in the model development.

The remainder of this paper is organized as follows. In section 2, we present key concepts related to MDA and Web Services. In section 3, we present an outline of MDA-Compatible conception design development process. Section 4 and section 5 deploy a case study of the conception design environment and MDA of web application.

## 2 Outline of MDA-Compatible Collaborative Modeling Development Process

The following twelve modified process steps based on [1][2], taken together, offer a simple robust way to incorporate MDA into a software development project for CIDS.

1. Establish the domains of interest, and the requirements within those domains.
2. Establish the connection between requirements and target platform.
3. Identify a set of target platforms.
4. Identify the metamodels that we want to use for describing models for conception design platform, and also the modeling language/profile in which we will express our models.
5. To Find or select the proper abstracting metamodels.
6. Establish the connection between abstracting metamodels and their instances.
7. Define a model as an instance of a metamodel.
8. Define the mapping techniques that we will use with our metamodels  so that there are full paths form the most abstract metamodels to the metamodels of all of our target platforms.

8.1  Define mapping Language Requirements.

8.2  Define the functional requirements

8.3  Define the usability requirements.

8.4  Define the transfering requrements.

8.5  Define the collaborating modeling requirements.

9.  Define the annotation models that these mapping techniques require.

10.  Implement the mapping techniques either by using tool support or by describing the steps necessary to manually carry out the technique.

11.  Modelling: use ArgoUML [6] to build an executable specification, or Platform-Independent Model(PIM) for each of the new domains/steps to be developed.

12.  Conduct iterations of the project. Each iteration will add detail to one or more models describing the system at one or more levels of abstraction. We will map the additional details all the way down to the target platforms

The transformation language in these steps must be able to accord with the rules[2].

## 3  Case Study-The Collaborative Modeling System

We study a simplified example independent model (PIM) and its transformation into three different platform-specific models (PSM), in this paper, we select the three platform specific model (PSM).

In our work, we adopt the tool of TUPI [3] (Transformation from PIM to IDL)- that does an automatic transformation from a PIM to the corresponding specification in CORBA IDL [4]. TUPI receives as input a XMI (XML Metadata Interchange Format) [5] file that contains the meta-model description of the PIM model. ArgoUML [6] is used to produce the PIM Model. The PIM Model follows the syntax proposed by the UML profile for EDOC [7]. The PIM-PSM conversion rules are described in XSLT (eXtensible StyleSHeet Language Transformations) [8] and they produce a specific model to the CORBA platform represented in IDL (Interface Definition Language).

The project had two main objectives.

It provides a stable application interface between PDM framework layer, a configuration model layer, a functional model layer, a fuzzy reasoning layer, an integration layer for I-DEAS and CIDS, Service-Oriented Conception Design (SOCD) Model layer, design evaluation layer, a computer methods layer and a personal Web Graphical User Interface (GUI).

It provides organizational use of access control and collaborative services, and allows users to access to the CIDS.

### 3.1  Requirements and Domains

The requirements for access control and collaboration could be traced into the UML models. We build and test UML models. It was configured using the requirements schema in Fig.2 below, and represented as a UML class diagram.

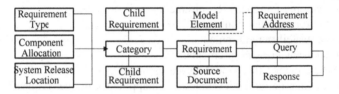

**Fig. 2.** Requirement Schema

These requirements can be categorized, arranged into parent-child hierarchies, traced back to their source, or forward into the models, as illustrated in Fig.2.

Each requirement also went through a set of life cycle phase, as shown in the state chart diagram in Fig.3 below, that is represented using the Moore formalism as described in [12] and [13].

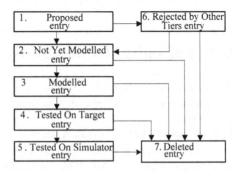

**Fig. 3.** Requirement State Machine

## 3.2  The Components (Domains)

To formalize the conceptual content of the requirements and the behavior they define; models were designed to lend themselves to ongoing modification. We can combine generic modeling and isolate volatile issues in separate domains, which nonetheless offer a stable interface to the rest of the system layers.

We define several inter-related domains to capture and control the complexity of the overall system.

This domain model diagram in Fig.4 shows the various components (domains) comprising the proposed solution.

In order to address these models, we got the conclusion that , the first step was to identify the different conceptual tiers involved in the development of an application using DAOP platform [10]. The following list of models was produced.

The Computational Model focuses on the functional decomposition of the system into objects which interact at interface, exchanging messages and signals that invoke operations and deliver service responses-but without detailing the system precise architecture, or any of its implementation details. This model basically corresponds to an ODP computational viewpoint model of the system, or to Zachman's Framework for Enterprise Architecture Row3[11]. Entities of this model are objects

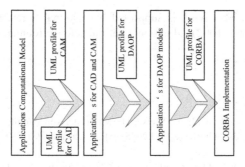

**Fig. 4.** The stack with the different models and the MDA transformations between them

(implementing interfaces) and operations. To which we have added some constraints for expressing extra-functional requirements (such as security or persistence, for instance).

The component and aspect model (CAM) and the component and aspect design model (CAD) define the basic entities and the structure of the system form an architectural point of view. In our case, components and aspects are the basic building blocks, following our goal of integrating CBSD and AOCD approaches.

The DAOP platform implements the concepts of the CAM model in a particular way. This level is still technology-independent, since it just deals about the way components and aspects are weaved, and how the abstract entities of the CAM model can be represented form the computational and engineering viewpoints-but still independently form the middleware platform (CORBA, EJB,.NET) or programming language used implement them.

The middleware platform provides a description of the system form a technology viewpoint. In this model we decide whether we want to implement the DAOP platform using Java/RMI, CORBA, EJB, or .NET, using their corresponding services and mechanisms.

## 4  Model Driven Architecture of Web Application

The proposed platform supports the design of collaborative services using the MDA concepts and the Web Services composition techniques. The services are first developed platform independent, by means of the ArgoUML [6] profile and thereafter transformed to platform specific model like Web Service(WS-PSM).

In order to define a Web application System, [9] proposes a Web application view model that is made up 8 views, grouped into three: requirements, functional and architectural viewpoints. This viewpoint includes a logical architectural view and a physical architecture view. The logical architectural view gathers the set of logical components (subsystems, modules and/or software components) and relations among them. While the physical architecture view describes the physical components that integrate the lower level specification of the application (clients, servers, networks, etc.). [9] defines a process that can shift one view to the other.

**Acknowledgments.** This work is supported by National Science Fund for Creative Research Groups (60521002)and national natural science foundation of China (Grand No. 60573147).

# References

1. Mellor, S.J., Scott, K., Uhl, A., Weise, D.: Model-Driven Architecture. In: Bruel, J.-M., Bellahsène, Z. (eds.) OOIS 2002. LNCS, vol. 2426, pp. 290–297. Springer, Heidelberg (2002)
2. Tan, W., Ma, L., Li, J., Xiao, Z.: Application MDA in a Conception Design Environment. In: International Multi-Symposiums on Computer and Computational Sciences(IMSCCS'06) (2006)
3. Nasciminto, T., Batista, T., Cacho, N.: TUPI: Transformation from to IDL. In: Meersman, R., Tari, Z., Schmidt, D.C. (eds.) CoopIS 2003, DOA 2003, and ODBASE 2003. LNCS, vol. 2888, pp. 1439–1453. Springer, Heidelberg (2003)
4. Tari, Z., Bukhres, O.: Fundamentals of Distributed Object Systems- The CORBA perspective. John Wiley & Sons, Chichester (2001)
5. OMG: XML Model Interchange (XMI) OMG Document ad/98-10-01 (1998)
6. Ramirez, A., Vanpeperstraete, P., Rueckert, A., Odutola, K., Bennett, J., Tolke, L.: ArgoUML, - a Tutorial and Reference Description (2000), Available at argouml.tigris.org/
7. OMG: UML Profile for Enterprise Distributed Object Computing Specification(EDOC), OMG Document ad/01-08-18 (2001)
8. W3C: XSL Translations Specification W3C (1999), Available at www.w3.org /TR/xslt
9. Beigbeder, S.M., Castro, C.C.: An MDA Approach for the Development of Web Applications. In: Koch, N., Fraternali, P., Wirsing, M. (eds.) ICWE 2004. LNCS, vol. 3140, pp. 300–305. Springer, Heidelberg (2004)
10. Fuentes, L., Pinto, M., Vallecillo, A.: How Can Help Designing Component-and Aspect-based Applications. In: EDOC'03 (2003)
11. Zachman, J.A.: The Zachman Framework: A primer for enterprise Engineering and Manufacturing. Zachman International (1997), http://www.zifa.com
12. Shlaer, S., Mellor, S.J.: Object Lifecycles: Modelling the World in States. Yourdon Press Computing Series (April 1991)
13. Raistrick, C., et al.: Model Driven Architecture with Executable UML. Cambridge University Press, Cambridge (2004)
14. Tan, W., Ma, L., Li, J., Mao, J.: A Platform for Collaborative Modeling. Journal of Computer Science and Technology (submitted)

# Age Invaders: User Studies of Intergenerational Computer Entertainment

Eng Tat Khoo[1], Tim Merritt[2], Adrian Cheok[1], Mervyn Lian[1], and Kelvin Yeo[1]

[1] Mixed Reality Lab, National University of Singapore
[2] Jyvaskyla University
http://www.mixedrealitylab.org

**Abstract.** The design goal of the Age Invaders[1] system is to make a mixed reality interaction platform that can facilitate meaningful social interaction with players, from many backgrounds and demographics, at appropriate levels of physical exertion for their age. This paper discusses a multidisciplinary approach to analyzing the user experience and re-assessment of the context of use of the Age Invaders system. This paper tests the effectiveness of the system in promoting the intended design goals and the results show strong support for intergenerational interaction using digital technology. Additionally, the results of the study help to focus the refinements of the existing platform and development of further novel games and interactive applications for this mixed reality system, and provide insights into the user in complex mixed reality experiences.

**Keywords:** Mixed reality entertainment, social computing, family entertainment, game play, user-centered design.

## 1 Introduction

The research reported here aims to show the user acceptance of the Age Invaders (A-I) game system [4] by players of various ages. As a design goal, Age Invaders aims to provide engaging physical and virtual play for elderly and young together in a novel mixed reality entertainment system. Unlike standard computer systems, A-I requires whole body movements over a large play area rather than constraining the user to sit in front of the computer for long periods of time. Age Invaders provides family entertainment that is attractive to, and inclusive of, all family members including the elderly and young. The system encourages and promotes human interaction at the physical, mental and emotional level. A-I provides a means to re-connect family members in shared activities across locations, thus increasing cross-generational interaction. The research situation aimed to better understand the users of the A-I system and to take inventory of

---

[1] Videos and photos of the work can be accessed via the website
http://ageinvaders.mixedrealitylab.org
Email address: contact@mixedrealitylab.org

L. Ma, R. Nakatsu, and M. Rauterberg (Eds.): ICEC 2007, LNCS 4740, pp. 231–242, 2007.

recurring user experience issues. The methods include questionnaires and other qualitative data analysis borrowing from the grounded theory approach [2]. Our selection of users varied in many respects including age, physical ability, familiarity with computers and electronic games, and level of education in order to gain as much relevant input as possible.

## 2    System Description

The system consists of a game server which is connected to the Internet through a router, large floor display platform with embedded RFID tags, online virtual client for real time remote game play, Bluetooth display, controller and special slipper with embedded RFID reader for tracking of players. The system's inter-devices communication is completely wireless.

### 2.1    Age Invaders Game Play

The concept of the Age Invaders game is shown in Figure 1, two children are playing with two grandparents in this interactive physical space while up to two parents can join into the game via the internet as virtual players, thus increasing the intergenerational interaction. The grandchildren form a team and the grandparents form another. The parents' role is to balance the game between the two teams.

Grandparents and grandchildren put on lanyard-style Bluetooth LED display for the purpose of displaying some game events. The players then wear the special slippers and pick up the Bluetooth controller.

Each game lasts for up to 2 minutes. The players gain points by picking up bonus items and avoiding laser beams. The player is out of the game when his or her energy level drops to zero. The game ends prematurely if the energy level of

**Fig. 1.** Age Invaders: An inter-generational, social and physical game. Players are wearing cute RFID tracking slippers and holding Bluetooth controllers.

both players of the same team became zero. Otherwise, at the end of 2 minutes, the team with the highest score wins.

During the game play, as the player presses a button on the handheld device, a laser beam image is displayed on the game board and heads towards the opponent. If the grandparent launches the laser, its speed is fast so that the grandchild has to react quickly. On the other hand, the grandparent has more time to react to the much slower laser beams launched by the grandchild. This balances the game difficulty between the ages.

In order to make the difficulty of the game strike a balance between the young and the elderly, Age Invaders imposes some challenges in an innovative way for the invader players (the young and more dextrous). The invader footprint is one of these challenges. In the game, the invaders have to physically follow the footprints and have to remain in the squares with footprints indicated with a pattern of lights which they see on the floor square. Each invader has two footprints from which to select as their next step. In any case that they are not stepping in the square that has their footprint indicated for a certain period of time, their energy is deducted. This period is determined by the invaders' footprint speed which can also be adjusted by the virtual players at any time. To be fair to these players, they are rewarded with one bonus health point by following the footprints correctly ten times in a row.

The parents as virtual players, can drag-and-drop barriers or energy on the virtual player interface which appears almost immediately on the physical game board rendered in patterns of lights. The physical players can pick up the bonus to gain extra energy and barriers will block laser beams. Parents can also adjust the game parameters as mentioned previously including: laser speed and the speed of the dance step patterns for the young players to follow. All the actions in the virtual environment are translated to the physical game board in real time. This provides a seamless game interaction between the real world players and the parents in the virtual world.

The game play challenges and aids are summarized below:

*Young Player*

— Must follow the dance steps as they appear
— Speed of laser beam is slower
— More difficult to collect power-ups unless intended for the player, due to need to constantly follow dance steps

*Older Player*

— Can move freely on the game board
— Speed of laser beam is faster
— Power-up hearts can be collected easily

*Virtual Player*

— Placing power ups and barriers
— Balancing the play experience by adjusting the step speed and laser speed

# 3   Method

## 3.1   Design

Games play sessions were conducted in a controlled laboratory setting. Users answered questionnaires before and after game play sessions to gather levels of enjoyment, contributing and detracting factors on the game play, and social aspects of the experience.

Additionally, case studies of other sources of data were reviewed using a grounded theory approach borrowing from the methods offered by Glaser [1]. We conducted focus group discussions with users immediately following a two hour session of game play and began the note-taking process.

As more of the themes emerged, some categories of issues affecting user experience provided a framework to organize the concepts. Subsequent review of data gathered from open ended questions from the same user group helped to confirm these categories and in some cases provided candid feedback that respondents in a group situation chose to withhold. For the older adults, we also conducted a follow up focus group session 5 weeks after the first focus group session. In this later focus group, we probed the issues of the gameplay experience to understand the lasting impressions and the issues that were most memorable for positive and negative aspects of the game play. The design team then reviewed the categorized data and wrote summaries of the observations. The researchers were also encouraged to reflect on the observations and user statements of players and spectators engaged in the system during the conference exhibitions and to compare against the more structured game play sessions. With the categories defined and researcher notes gathered, the process of producing the theory of the user experience issues in the form of linear and coherent statements was undertaken.

## 3.2   Data Sources

Among the data sources reviewed were video recordings from platform demonstrations at conferences, structured game play observation of 49 players in a structured format, questionnaires involving closed and open-ended questions, 3 focus group discussions involving the 49 players immediately after the gameplay and 7 of the older adults 5 weeks after the game play, and 4 semi-structured interviews with the design team and gameplay facilitators.

# 4   Results

## 4.1   Profile of Users

The data from the users came from observations made at various conferences and exhibitions including CHI 2006 (Canada), Interactive Tokyo 2006 (Japan), Greenfield 2006 (Singapore), Singapore Science Center i-Future 2007 (Singapore), NUS Arts Festival 2007 (Singapore).

In the first focused gameplay sessions, there were 2 groups from the Ngee Ann Polytechnic in Singapore, taking part in a study module about electronic games were invited. These initial sessions involved a total of 37 total participants. The average age of the participants was 19 years old. The gender of these participants was 24 males and 13 females.

An additional gameplay session was organized involving the intended age disparity of the players. There were 10 students from the Hougang Primary School, with average age of 11.7 years. There were 7 females and 3 males. The opponents were the older players who were invited from a community center in the Jalan Basar area of Singapore. The ages of these players ranged from 58 to 80, and an average age of 68.7 years made up of 7 females and 3 males. It is worthy of note that a majority of the older adults self reported that they are illiterate. The older players spoke Hokkien or Cantonese, yet understood Mandarin that was spoken by the children. The children spoke in the Chinese dialects of the older players, but also Malay and English amongst themselves.

## 4.2  Teen Player Study

The first formal studies were aimed at showing the acceptance and enjoyment of the Age Invaders game by younger players that have familiarity with contemporary electronic gaming. Prior to game play, the respondents were asked to rate themselves in experience level with electronic games choosing between the categories Newbie, Casual User, Moderate User, and Hardcore User. The results showed that 78% of the players were casual to hardcore users. All of the users reported that they do play some kind of electronic games.

After the game play sessions, the users answered additional questions pertaining to the game experience. Most importantly, the respondents were asked to rate their enjoyment level with the game. Overwhelmingly, the respondents enjoyed the game play as shown in and would recommend it to be used for encouraging social interaction within families. The users were asked to indicate their level of agreement with the statement, "I enjoyed the gamplay experience." As shown in Figure 2a all respondents chose "Agree or Strongly Agree."

Players were also asked to rate their agreement with the statement, "I would recommend this game to be used to encourage social interaction within a family." The strength of their positive sentiment is shown in Figure 2c. Only one of the players disagreed with the statement.

The players were asked to indicate their level of agreement with the statement, "The skills required by the game were well matched to my skills and experience." The responses showed that 84% Strongly Agree to Somewhat Agree that the game play experience was well matched to their skill level and experiences. The responses are represented in Figure 2d.

The users showed preference to the four-player configuration compared to the two-player format according to their responses. The responses showed again that 84 % Strongly Agree to Somewhat Agree that the four-player game was more enjoyable. This is shown in Figure 2b. In the focus group discussions, the users

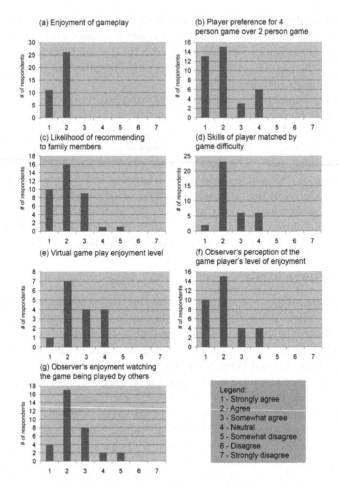

**Fig. 2.** Responses to questions based on a Likert scale. 1-Strongly Agree to 7-Strongly Disagree.

explained that the four-player games were more exciting and having a team member to engage in cooperative competition

Most players also had a chance to take part in the game as a player in the Virtual role. The level of enjoyment was less, but showed positive sentiment towards the virtual play. In this case, the players were asked to indicate their agreement with the statement, "Playing via the virtual player was fun." The results of the satisfaction levels are shown in Figure 2e.

In order to determine what was enjoyable vs. not enjoyable, we discussed the virtual game play in the focus group discussions and some themes emerged and were reinforced. These themes are discussed in the Emergent Themes section.

Because the game system may have spectators, we also asked questions about the experience as an observer. Respondents were asked to indicate their agreement with the statement, "The game seemed fun to play from the observer's point of view" This data is represented in Figure 2f. Additionally, the spectators agree that watching the game is enjoyable as shown in Figure 2g.

### 4.3   Young and Elderly Player Study

With a general understanding that the game is enjoyable to play from the younger audience point of view, the more critical study came when conducting the play sessions for the older generation playing with a younger generation as shown in Figure 3.

**Fig. 3.** Age Invaders players taking part in a gameplay session

The questionnaires were made in simpler language and with fewer questions in general to avoid overloading their first experience with electronic games. An important assumption to test first was our thought that the older players were not familiar with electronic games. Responses showed that 80 % of the children reported playing computer games, while the adults all reported never having played electronic games.

In order to determine their habits with their families, all players were asked if they play any games non-electronic or otherwise with their families. 60 % of the young reported that they play some type of game, while only 30 % of the older players reported playing games with their families. Those that do play games with their families reported similar types of games regardless of age. The older generation reported playing chess and cards with their families, while the children reported cards and board games.

In order to "break the ice" and to get the two generations of players to interact and converse, players were organized into 5 teams of 4 players each. Each team was made up of 2 young players and 2 older players. These players made name tags for each other, introduced their teams and the children were designated as the scribes of the teams and would help the older players to fill out the questionnaires in English. Each team was also designated a game studies facilitator from our lab who helped to ensure that the questionnaires were filled out appropriately and honestly. The game sessions were conducted similarly to the previous studies mentioned earlier. Again, overwhelmingly the players enjoyed the game experience with all respondents reporting a positive sentiment with nearly all respondents showing positive experience and only one reporting a neutral experience.

The user's were also asked, "Can you imagine your family enjoying the game?" The overwhelming response showed a high motivation to play the game with their families. All of the young people reported that the game would be appropriate for family play, while 80 % of the older players answered positively. In order to understand the differences in the age, we discussed this in the focus group and found that the respondent who did not imagine playing the game with her family did not previously consider extended family members when answering the question. In the focus group she mentioned that she discussed the game with her niece and felt that she would enjoy playing the game in a family setting.

### 4.4    Focus Group Session with Older Players

Five weeks after we conducted the initial user study for the elderly and young, we went back to the senior center to conduct a follow up focus group session with 7 of the elderly players. Our aim was to investigate the longer lasting impact of the Age Invaders game. When prompted the most memorable thing about the game, all of them mentioned the launching of lasers, avoiding lasers and chasing after the hearts on the game board. "This is a fresh idea and it was my first time playing" quoted by a few of the elderly. They are all excited about this new entertainment platform. Two elderly have shown some interest to understand what technology is behind the platform. Many related Age Invaders to the popular arcade game, Dance Dance Revolution. In almost identical questions, there were two older adults that stated, "I suppose there are computers controlling the shoes, controller and floor display, but how?" More detailed technical explanations were given, and we then asked if they have an increased interest in trying out other electronic/computer based games as a result of their experience with A-I. To this question, all of them gave a negative answer. Some of the reasons given were the fact that they are illiterate and they have no prior experience with operating computers. It seems as though the older adult players see the game system as being so different from traditional computer systems that the relative level of comfort with traditional computer platforms is unchanged after playing the A-I game.

Among other issues, a consensus was made amongst the elderly that the sound was too soft in the game and they strongly suggested that the new version of the game incorporate louder sounds and music to accompany the play session in addition to the sound effects already present. More specifically, most of the players expressed a desire for a sound event indicating the game outcome and a larger screen for displaying the game score. "We do not understand words, so just display the numbers like those in a basketball tournament", was suggested by one of the elderly.

When asked what skills were involved in playing the game and about the difficulty level, all agreed that the game was easy to learn, and that the game speed was fine, but a few mentioned that the pace could be a little slower in order to play for longer amounts of time. However, they emphasized that the game speed cannot be too slow otherwise it would become boring. The current game pace is exciting for them. This was well stated by one of the players, "The game gives me good exercise. When you see heart, you have to run to collect it. If a laser is approaching, you have to avoid it quickly. The game is very engaging and can we play it again?" This supports the design goal of providing a game that challenges the elderly in terms of visual-motor coordination and physical activity level.

When asked about how much fun was the game you played, they all gave the maximum rating. "Thinking about it now, we can't wait to play again!" said one of them. It is obvious that the elderly players have enjoyed the game and have high motivation to play the game again. Of particular interest is the fact that the users don't see a strong connection between this system and traditional electronic gaming and computing in general. This high motivation level is valuable in and of itself as confirmation that older adults can be engaged in new technologies and have high enjoyment levels.

### 4.5    Emergent Themes

As the data coding process continued, the themes developed into to two main categories. These categories were related to the Physical Player and Virtual Player. Issues that were reported by user statements and supported by additional observation are now presented.

**Physical Player Issues.** Regarding the physical game space and player activities, there were Four issues that emerged: Strategies were developed, Stepping action was enjoyable, The smart slipper should be user friendly, and the handheld device and personal display should have more features.

*Strategies Developed*

Through demos, exhibitions, and user studies, the researchers observed many interesting strategies employed by the defender team. The defender team member, knowing that the invader only has two boxes to stand in, blocks one of the spaces. This prevents the invader from moving in any direction. The defender can then trigger the laser beam and the invader loses a heath level. The aspect that makes an activity a game is the need to make decisions [3] [6]. Defenders derive satisfaction from the game play as they claim direct responsibility for winning the game due to their strategies in the game. On the other hand, the invaders have less freedom of movement as they have to constantly follow the flashing patterns on the floor. Failure to do so means losing a health level.

*Stepping Action is Enjoyable*

The invaders often enjoy following the dance step-like patterns on the game board despite being limited to two squares at any one time. This could be affected by the presence of audience members who are spectators to the performance. In traditional computer games, the audience passively watches the player exploring the game. However the performance play elements introduced by the dance step-like movements give the invaders an expressive visibility which encourages acting by the player and more audience support. We observed that the audience is continually shouting to the invaders as to where he or she should step next. This is especially useful when the patterns are behind the invaders and the audiences give a timely cue to power up. Following the step patterns requires some level of physical exertion that brings the invaders to a highly energetic game play. The audience's support and feedback also gives invaders a sense of responsibility for the performance that they put up. Some invaders are overwhelmed by the tasks of following the step patterns, avoiding the approaching laser beams and trying to launch one at the same time.

It turns out that the footprint makes the game more interesting and challenging to the young and easier for the elderly. The young players have to constantly search in all directions for the footprint patterns on the floor and at the same time try to launch laser beams towards the opponents and avoid the opponents' laser beams. Furthermore, the young players' laser beams are, by default, significantly slower than their older counterpart. This has encouraged great team work between the elderly and young player as the older team player always alerts the young player for approaching laser beams.

*The Smart Slipper Should Be Easy To Use*

The usability of the smart slippers presented a particular challenge to the older players most likely due to their reduced mobility and dexterity. All of the adult players agreed that easily adjustable slippers are needed. One generally accepted feature change idea by the older players was to use an adjustable velcro strap to adjust tightness of fit. Otherwise, the use of the slipper was enjoyable and its cute styling was well received.

*Performance Aspect*

This theme came up in many aspects which have been mentioned in most other topics. This may be a parallel to human nature as seen in professional sports. The "happening" itself is a large portion of the experience. The players often responded to the cheers and shouts from the audience and reacted to suggestions and hints. The audience helped to raise the awareness of which team was winning and losing and also seemed to raise the excitement level of the players. Some of the younger players were shy at the beginning of the game, however, they would loosen up quickly and the shouts from the audience were encouraging them to play freely. Some of the younger players adopted a special finesse to their play which was accompanied by their playing off the audience and making exaggerated gestures when facing challenges and scoring points.

**Virtual Player Issues.** The players were briefed about the design goal of having a parent fill the virtual player role. In the proposed user scenario, grandparents and children would play in the physical space and the parent would join in as a virtual player while away from the home. Users of all roles were asked to describe their impression of the family interaction scenario and most imagined that their family would enjoy this interaction. The players that had also played in the physical space also had a chance to play in the virtual player role. The most prevalent issues that arose regarding the virtual player were as follows:

*Virtual Player Role Is Currently Not As Much Fun As The Physical*

Although the players enjoyed the virtual role, the sense of connectedness and ability to take part in the gameplay was not as enjoyable.

*More Features Desired For The Virtual Player Experience*

Most of the suggestions offered included a desire for more and varied power-ups and obstacles as a way to expand the sense of presence in the game play.

*Balancing Gameplay For Other Players Was An Interesting Concept*

The virtual players took on a sense of balancing the game play between invaders and defenders, not focused solely on helping just one team. Being in the constantly switching team position, one instant helping the invaders, but in the next moment helping defenders, the virtual players often did not identify themselves with either the winning or losing team but agreed that the interaction was rewarding as an activity of facilitator of fun. In this sense the virtual player has to follow the game progress closely and provide assistance where it best contributes to the overall game experience for all players. Suggestions for improvement include having a virtual helper for each team in the competition scenario. During the game play, the physical players can communicate in the physical space by eye contacts, body gestures, speech and laughter which introduce a high level of engaging and immersive game play. However when translated to the virtual player's interface only the coordinates of the physical players are represented and the emotional connection is not as firmly established. In the future developments, web cam and voice over IP could be introduced to facilitate better coordination and interaction amongst all players and within teams.

## 5   Conclusion

Our play based user studies support the claim that the Age Invaders system is engaging for the physical and virtual players of all ages. We have identified key areas that contribute and detract from the experience.

The older players have shown a high motivation to play the game again immediately after the game play and even after considerable time has past since they have played the game. Players have given feedback that physical movements and skills needed in the game, such as collecting hearts, avoiding lasers and launching lasers, and the aspect of performance made for very exciting and enjoyable play. It may be that the introduction into the computing world using this game system may help to reduce the fear of technology and therefore reduce the social barrier between the generations. This may be more fully explored with future user studies over a longer period of time and with more game configurations for the platform.

Playtesting of game iterations is especially important for the elderly because their familiarity with gaming technology is limited. Mere interviews and surveys attempting to gather feedback from the elderly can not gather useful results.

These players confirmed that it is more appropriate to offer a prototype to evaluate by experience.

The familiarity with electronic games and computers in general is an important factor in the player experience. Those most familiar with contemporary computer games can enjoy more simplified game graphics such as in the Age Invaders prototype, but the challenges need to be presented at appropriate levels to hold the player interest and motivation.

Unlike conventional computer games, Age Invaders encourages large physical movements over a wide area. The user study results support our claim that the Age Invaders game is a form of exercise for the elderly. Participation in such an activity helps the elderly feel healthier and encourages movements that may promote health [5]. In the future, user studies will be conducted to investigate to what degree the elderly visual-motor reaction time improves through playing the A-I game on a regular basis.

Social interaction has been identified as the key factor that attracts the elderly and young to play the game harmoniously. 84% of the players enjoyed the experience of playing the four-player over the two-player game. The elderly and young gave feedback that the game should be played with many spectators.

Another strong point indicated was the performance aspect of playing the game. We will explore this more closely to determine how the audience affects the game experience and search for limits and optimum scenarios of interaction.

It is our hope that this project will encourage more future works aimed at fusing art and digital games to fulfill the scientific objective of improving the welfare of older people and the entire family.

## 6    Special Thanks

Our sincere gratitude for Peace Center, Hougang Primary School, Ngee Ann Polytechnic and all of the players who came to the user studies with an open mind and a willingness to have fun and share their experiences!

## References

1. Glaser, B.G.: Doing Grounded Theory: issues and discussions. Sociology Press, Mill Valley, CA (1998)
2. Glaser, B.G., Strauss, A.L.: The Discovery of Grounded Theory. Aldine de Gruyter (1967)
3. Huizinga, J.: Homo Ludens. Roy Publishers, New York (1950)
4. Khoo, E.T., Cheok, A.D.: Age Invaders: Inter-generational Mixed Reality Family Game. The International Journal of Virtual Reality 5(2), 45–50 (2006)
5. Matsuo, M., Nagasawa, J., Yoshino, A., Hiramatsu, K., Kurashiki, K.: Effects of Activity Participation of the Elderly on Quality of Life. Yonago Acta medica 46(1), 17–24 (2003)
6. Salen, Zimmerman: Rules of Play: Game Design Fundamentals. The MIT Press, Cambridge (2004)

# Dynamic Texture Synthesis in the YUV Color-Space

Leilei Xu[1], Hanqiu Sun[2], Jiaya Jia[3], and Chenjun Tao[4]

Department of Computer Science and Engineering
The Chinese University of Hong Kong, Shatin, Hong Kong
{llxu,hanqiu,leojia,cjtao}@cse.cuhk.edu.hk

**Abstract.** Dynamic textures are representations of such textured surfaces that exhibit certain stationarity properties in time. These include sea-waves, smoke, foliage, whirlwind, dense crowds, and traffic scenes. We address the problem of *dynamic color texture* synthesis which is a natural extending of the state-of-art *Linear Dynamic System* to the YUV color space by analyzing the intrinsic relationship between the color channels and intensity channel. Our experimental results have shown good performance for the testing examples, which remodel short dynamic texture videos into infinite time domain with similar dynamic behaviors.

## 1 Introduction

With the fast developing of computer hardware, especially on graphics cards, realistic rendering of dynamic textures are more commonly used in computer games, special effects in TV/film producing, and rich-media digital entertainment to create virtual environments which photo-realistically simulate the natural phenomenon.

### 1.1 Related Work

Dynamic Textures can be defined as repetitive patterns exhibiting both spatial and temporal coherence intrinsic in the process. The methods for dynamic texture synthesis in vision can be mainly categorized into two classes: *nonparametric* and *parametric*. The nonparametric methods directly sample the original information from the input image or sequence of images. Wexler's method [1] copies the patches from the input sequence and solves the synthesis process as a global optimization process. In [2], the author also copies the appropriate 2D patches or 3D voxels to synthesize by finding the optimal seam for blending using the state-of-art Graph Cut technique. Unlike the prior two methods, Video Textures [3] chooses a whole image from the sampling sequence and copy it to the suitable location to preserve temporal continuity. These nonparametric methods usually provide high quality visual effect but yield a limited amount of information for the intrinsic property of textures.

On the other hand, parametric models provide better generalization and understanding of the perceptual process, thus these models are natural choices

L. Ma, R. Nakatsu, and M. Rauterberg (Eds.): ICEC 2007, LNCS 4740, pp. 243–248, 2007.
© IFIP International Federation for Information Processing 2007

for analysis and controlling of textures. In [4], images and videos are treated as a superposition of image or video basis which are called *texton* and *movton*. Szummer and Picard's work [5] models the interaction of pixels within a local neighborhood over both space and time using the spatio-temporal auto-regressive (STAR) model. Dorrto's model [6] provides an auto-regressive random process (specifically, a *linear dynamic system*, LDS, also known as Kalman filter model) which forms the basic model for the following papers in this area.

The most related work to ours is Filip's [7] which addresses the problem of synthesizing dynamic color textures by analyzing the eigen-system of dynamic texture images and subsequent preprocessing and modelling of temporal inter-polation eigen-coefficients using a causal auto-regressive model in RGB color space. But the results turn out to be not so satisfying for some of the dynamic textures. Blurring effects can be easily observed. Doretto [6] suggests a way to synthesize color videos by applying LDS model in the combined three unfolded RGB channels ordered one after the other. The synthesized result is satisfying, but when the size of the input image sequence is large, the method will become time consuming and even cannot solve the problem because of complex matrix operations on a very large matrix.

### 1.2 Overview

The main goal of this paper is to provide a novel approach for dynamic color texture synthesis in the YUV color space using the LDS model by analyzing the intrinsic connection between color channels and intensity channel. In Section 2, the LDS model is briefly outlined, and based on it our proposed approach in the YUV space for dynamic color texture synthesis (or *DCTS* for short) is described in details in Section 3. The experimented results are presented in Section 4, and conclusion goes to Section 5.

## 2  Dynamic Texture Model

The basic model we are working with is a second-order stationary process represented by a discrete time LDS with white, zero-mean gaussian noise [8] [10]. The observation or input of the system is a sequence of $\tau$ images represented by matrix $Y = [y(1) \ldots y(\tau)] \in \mathcal{R}^{m \times \tau}$ with each image represented by column vector $y(t) \in \mathcal{R}^m$; $X = [x(1) \ldots x(\tau)] \in \mathcal{R}^{n \times \tau}$ with $x(t) \in \mathcal{R}^n$ stands for the hidden state vector at time $t$ encoding the evolution of the image sequence and the initial condition $x(0)$ known. Typically, $m \gg n$ and with values of $n$ in the range of 10 to 50. Both the observation and state variables are corrupted by additive gaussian noise, which is also hidden. The basic generative model can be written as:

$$\begin{cases} x(t+1) = Ax(t) + v(t) \ v(t) \sim \mathcal{N}(0, Q) \\ y(t) = Cx(t) + w(t) \quad w(t) \sim \mathcal{N}(0, R) \end{cases} \tag{1}$$

where $A \in \mathcal{R}^{n \times n}$ is the state transition matrix and $C \in \mathcal{R}^{m \times n}$ is the observation matrix which encodes the appearance information. $v(t)$ and $w(t)$ are random variables representing the state evolution noise and observation noise, respectively, which are independent of each other and the values of $x$ and $y$.

Learning of the LDS model is to learn the model parameters $\Theta = \{A, C, Q, R, x(0)\}$ given the sequence of images in matrix form $Y$. Assumptions are adopted to solve the degeneracy in the model: $m \gg n; rank(C) = n$ and choose a realization that makes $C$ orthonormal: $C^T C = I_n$ to maximum likelihood $\arg\max_\Theta \log p(y(1) \cdots y(\tau))$. A suboptimal *closed-form* solution for the model parameters can be learned by using principal component analysis (PCA).

Once the model parameters $\Theta$ are learned from the original sequence of images, we can synthesize new dynamic textures with infinite length by starting from a given initial state $x(0)$ and the driven noise covariance $Q$ to calculate $x(t)$ step by step, and finally obtain the synthesized sequence $y(t)$.

## 3   Dynamic Color Texture Synthesis

We work in the $YUV$ color space, commonly used in image and video processing. $Y \in \mathcal{R}^{m \times \tau}$ (Here we use the same $Y$ as in LDS model in most cases, it stands for intensity) is the monochromatic luminance channel, which we refer to simply as intensity, while $U \in \mathcal{R}^{m \times \tau}$ and $V \in \mathcal{R}^{m \times \tau}$ are the chrominance channels, encoding the color [11]. The framework of our DCTS model in Figure 1 outlines the processes of LDS model and the linear-evolution model between intensity channel (the intrinsic factor) and color channels (the extrinsic appearance).

In human perception, the most important clue is the intensity which gives most informative signals, and color signals can be regarded as evolving with intensity value. Because $Y, U, V$ values are all gaussian distributed [6], we can assume that there is an *linear-evolution* process with gaussian noise driven

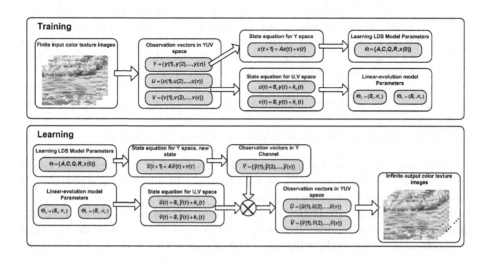

**Fig. 1.** The framework of our DCTS model

between intensity and color: color changes according to the underlying change of intensity. (We only concern $U$ channel from now on, as $V$ channel behaves the same as $U$).

$$u(t) = Sy(t) + k(t) \tag{2}$$

where $u(t) \in \mathcal{R}^m$ is the column vector of $U$ channel, $y(t) \in \mathcal{R}^m$ the column vector of $Y$ channel. $S \in \mathcal{R}^{m \times m}$. The m-vector $k(t) \sim \mathcal{N}(\mu, \Sigma)$ is random variables representing the driven noise. We call this model the *linear-evolution* model between intensity and color channels. The parameters of the model are $\Theta_u = \{S, k(t)\}$ for $U$ channel.

There are two problems in the solution of equation 2: First, the size of matrix $S$ is too large to be computed and stored even for a small sized video; Second, the equation is under-constrained, so there are many solutions which satisfy the requirements. Thus, we need to make reasonable assumption to uniquely define the solution which has $S$ small in size.

### 3.1   Learning of Dynamic Color Texture

In order to solve the problems shown in above, we employ the theory in [13] which justifies that there is a linear relation between color and intensity. Formally, it assumes that color $u_r$ and $v_r$ at a pixel $r$ is a linear function of intensity $y_r$: $u_r = s_r y_r + k_r$. The assumption intuitively tells that when the intensity is constant the color should be constant, and when the intensity is an edge the color should also be an edge (although the values on the two sides of the edge can be any two numbers). Rewritten the linear relation in matrix form we get:

$$u(t) = S(t)y(t) + k(t) \tag{3}$$

where $S(t) \in \mathcal{R}^{m \times m}$ is the diagonal matrix of corresponding $s_r$ for each pixel, and $k(t) \in \mathcal{R}^m$ is the column vector for parameter $k_r$. We observe that if we suppose for all $t$, the matrix $S$ is the same, $S(1) = \cdots = S(\tau)$. Then Equation 3 will become a special case of Equation 2 where $S$ is diagonal matrix which is small in storage and easy for matrix computation. Then model 2 becomes:

$$u(t) = Sy(t) + k(t) \ k(t) \sim \mathcal{N}(\mu, \Sigma) \tag{4}$$

with $S$ the diagonal matrix, and others the same as Equation 2.

**Closed-form solution for Linear-evolution model.** The first observation in Equation 4 is that the choice of $S, \Sigma$. We want to find a unique closed-form solution which is easy for computation.

In order to make sure that the resulted $k(t)$ is gaussian distributed, in our tests, we generate a random m-vector distributed as $\mathcal{N}(0, 1)$ to be the diagonal elements in $S$ which is distributed independently with $U$ and $Y$. This ensures that $k(t)$ is also gaussian distributed. Then $\mu, \Sigma$ can be easily calculated given $U, Y$, and $S$.

## 3.2   Synthesizing of Dynamic Color Texture

Given the LDS model parameters $\Theta$ and linear-evolution model parameter $\Theta_u$ and $\Theta_v$, we can easily generate new image sequences in the infinite time domain, by first applying LDS model to generate the new intensity images, and then given the new intensity value and $\Theta_u$ and $\Theta_v$, linear-evolution model can calculate the new corresponding $U, V$ channels.

## 4   Experimental Results

Using the model we developed, we have tested a set of dynamic color textures from [9] which provides sample dynamic textures, for learning and synthesizing DC textures in the infinite time domain.

In Figure 2, some blurring effects can be seen in the generated video frames from Filip's method, while ours has shown the better visual quality in comparison with Filip's results and similar dynamic behavior as the original input video. Our synthesized result is comparatively the same with the LDS model in [6] applied to color video sequence. But the size of the processed matrix size is much smaller than that: for a commonly $200 \times 150 \times 100$ input color video, the largest size of matrix to be dealt with is 3 times larger than the video size. If video size grows bigger, there will be not enough memory to store all the data which will make the task impossible or really time consuming to be finished. For our DCTS model, the largest matrix size to be dealt with is only the size of the video which takes a much smaller memory. Figure 2 compares the synthesized result of our DCTS model with the ones by Filip's method ( [7]) and the input short video. It is clear that there is blurring effects in the image sequence generated by Filip's method, while ours is fine with better visual quality also comparable dynamic behavior as to the input video.

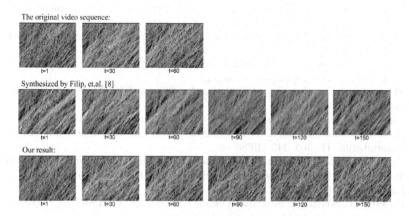

**Fig. 2.** The grass video sequence. The original video size is $m = 200 \times 150$, $\tau = 100$. Feom top down, row 1 shows the selected frames of input video; row 2 shows the synthesized result of Filip's method; row 3 shows the synthesized result of our DCTS model in corresponding frames as row 2.

## 5   Summary

In this paper, we have proposed and developed the novel approach to synthesis dynamic color textures by taking the advantage of Linear Dynamic Systems and its sub-optimal solution. We analyzed the intrinsic connection between color channels and intensity channel, and establish the relation between color information and state transition vector for the intensity channel. Our proposed DCTS approach is fast and can compress the data significantly.

Further efforts can be directed in the shifting of the control probabilities [14] of gray-level LDS model into our DCTS model to manipulate the speed, size and other characters of the dynamics. Also, feedback controls on pole distributions, presented in [15] can be employed into our model to further optimize the synthesized DCTS video results.

## References

[1] Wexler, Y., Shechtman, E., Irani, M.: Space-Time Video Completion. In: CVPR, pp. 120–127 (2004)

[2] Kwatra, V., Schödl, A., Essa, I., Bobick, A.: Graphcut textures: image and video synthesis using graph cuts. In: ACM SIGGRAPH 2003, vol. 22, pp. 277–286. ACM Press, New York (2003)

[3] Schödl, A., Szeliski, R., Salesin, D.H., Essa, I.: Video textures. In: Proceedings of Siggraph'00 (2000)

[4] Wang, Y., Zhu, S.: Analysis and synthesis of textured motion: Particle, wave and cartoon sketch. IEEE Trans. on Pattern Analysis and Machine Intelligence 26, 1348–1363 (2004)

[5] Szummer, M., Picard, R.: Temporal texture modeling. In: Proceedings of IEEE International Conference on Image Processing (ICIP 96). IEEE Computer Society Press, Los Alamitos (1996)

[6] Doretto, G., Chiuso, A., Wu, Y.N., Soatto, S.: Dynamic textures. International Journal of Computer Vision 2, 91–109 (2003)

[7] Filip, J., Haindl, M., Chetverikov, D.: Fast Synthesis of Dynamic Colour Textures. In: Proceedings of the 18th IAPR Int. Conf. on Pattern Recognition, pp. 25–28 (2006)

[8] Ljung, L.: System Identification -Theory for the User. Prentice Hall, Englewood Cliffs, NJ (1987)

[9] Péteri, R., Huiskes, M.: A comprehensive database of dynamic textures, http://www.cwi.nl/projects/dyntex/

[10] Shumway, R., Stoffer, D.: Time Series Analysis and Its Applications. Springer, Heidelberg (2000)

[11] Jack, K.: Video Demystified, 3rd edn. Elsevier, Amsterdam (2001)

[12] Roweis, S., Ghahramani, Z.: A Unifying Review of Linear Gaussian Models. Neural Computation 11, 305–345 (1999)

[13] Zomet, A., Peleg, S.: Multi-sensor super resolution. In: Proceedings of the IEEE Workshop on Applications of Computer Vision. IEEE Computer Society Press, Los Alamitos (2002)

[14] Doretto, G., Soatto, S.: Editable dynamic textures. In: ACM SIGGRAPH Sketches and Applications. ACM Press, New York (2002)

[15] Yuan, L., Wen, F., Liu, C., Shum, H.-Y.: Synthesizing Dynamic Texture with Closed-Loop Linear Dynamic System. In: Pajdla, T., Matas, J(G.) (eds.) ECCV 2004. LNCS, vol. 3024. Springer, Heidelberg (2004)

# Video Affective Content Recognition
# Based on Genetic Algorithm Combined HMM

Kai Sun and Junqing Yu

Computer College of Science & Technology, Huazhong University of Science & Technology,
Wuhan 430074, China
sunkai@smail.hust.edu.cn, yjqing@hust.edu.cn

**Abstract.** Video affective content analysis is a fascinating but seldom addressed field in entertainment computing research communities. To recognize affective content in video, a video affective content representation and recognition framework based on Video Affective Tree (VAT) and Hidden Markov Models (HMMs) was proposed. The proposed video affective content recognizer has good potential to recognize the basic emotional events of audience. However, due to Expectation-Maximization (EM) methods like the Baum-Welch algorithm tend to converge to the local optimum which is the closer to the starting values of the optimization procedure, the estimation of the recognizer parameters requires a more careful examination. A Genetic Algorithm combined HMM (GA-HMM) is presented here to address this problem. The idea is to combine a genetic algorithm to explore quickly the whole solution space with a Baum-Welch algorithm to find the exact parameter values of the optimum. The experimental results show that GA-HMM can achieve higher recognition rate with less computation compared with our previous works.

## 1 Introduction

Intensive research efforts in the field of multimedia content analysis in the past 15 years have resulted in an abundance of theoretical and algorithmic solutions for extracting the content-related information from audiovisual information [1]. However, due to the inscrutable nature of human emotions and seemingly broad affective gap from low-level features, the video affective content analysis is seldom addressed [2]. Several research works have been done to extract affective content from video. One method is to map low-level video features into emotion space. Hanjalic and Xu found in literature connections between some low level features of video data streams and dimensions of the emotions space and made algorithmic models for them [2]. Although this method can be used to locate video affective content or highlights effectively, the recognition of specific affective category is beyond its ability. Another method is using HMMs to recognize video affective content [3]. In this method, empirical study on the relationship between emotional events and low level features was performed and two HMM topologies were created. However, it can't measure the affective intensity and discriminate fear and anger due to the lack of proper low level features (e.g. audio affective features). Taking these results into account, we proposed

L. Ma, R. Nakatsu, and M. Rauterberg (Eds.): ICEC 2007, LNCS 4740, pp. 249–254, 2007.
© IFIP International Federation for Information Processing 2007

a novel video affective content representation and recognition framework based on VAT and HMMs [4]. Firstly, video affective content units in different granularities are located by excitement intensity curve and then mapped to be a Video Affective Tree (VAT). The affective intensity of affective content units in VAT is quantified into several levels from weak to strong (e.g. weak, median and strong) according to the intensity of excitement curve. Video affective content can be conveniently represented by VAT at different granularities. Next, low level affective features that represent emotional characteristics are extracted from these affective content units and observation vectors are constructed subsequently by combining these features. Finally, HMMs-based affective recognizer are trained and tested to recognize the basic emotional events (joy, anger, sadness and fear) using these observation vector sequences.

Our HMMs-based affective recognizer used Baum-Welch algorithm to estimate the model parameters. Expectation-Maximization (EM) methods like the Baum-Welch algorithm are known to converge to an optimum of the solution space, but nothing proves that this optimum is the global one. In fact, these algorithms tend to converge to the local optimum which is the closer to the starting values of the optimization procedure. The traditional remedy to this problem consists in running several times the EM algorithm, using different sets of random starting values, and keeping the best solution. More advanced versions of the EM algorithm (ECM, SEM, ...) can also be used, but they do not constitute a definitive answer to the local optima problem [5]. In this paper, we presented a Genetic Algorithm combined HMM (GA-HMM) to address this problem.

## 2  Genetic Algorithm Combined HMM (GA-HMM)

A HMM is fully described by three sets of probability distributions: a initial distribution $\pi$ of the hidden variable $X$, a transition matrix $A$ describing the relation between successive values of the hidden variable $X$ and a transition matrix $B$ used to describe the relation between successive outputs of the observed variable $O = \{O_1, O_2, ..., O_T\}$ ($T$ is the number of the observation vectors). Therefore, the computation of HMM involves three different problems: the estimation of the log-likelihood of the data given the model, the estimation of $\pi$, $A$ and $B$ given the data and the estimation of the optimal sequence of hidden states given the model and the data. Due to the structure of the HMM, there is no direct formula to compute the log-likelihood. The problem is solved using an iterative procedure known as the forward-backward algorithm. The estimation of the model parameters is traditionally obtained by an Expectation-Maximization (EM) algorithm known in the speech recognition literature as the Baum-Welch algorithm. Finally, the optimal sequence of hidden states is computed using another iterative procedure called the Viterbi algorithm [6].

GA-HMM is presented here to estimate the model parameters more precisely and efficiently, which is an iterative procedure computing simultaneously several possible solutions (the population). At each iteration, a new population is created by combining the members of the current population using the principles of genetics, i.e., selection, crossover and mutation [7]. This new population has a better probability to come close to the global optimum than the previous population had. This method presents the advantage to allow the exploration of a large part of the solution space, with a very high probability to find the global optimum. On the other hand, once the region of the solution space containing the global optimum has been determined, the robustness of GAs is balanced by the large number of iterations required to reach this optimum.

---

**Algorithm 1.** Estimation of a HMM.

---

```
Random initialization of the population.
Computation of the log-likelihood of each member of the population.
for iterga = 1:IterGA do {Iterations of the genetic algorithm.}
   Computation of the new population.
   Recomputation of the log-likelihood of each member of the population.
   for iterbw = 1:IterBW do {Iterations of the Baum-Welch algorithm.}
      for pop=1:PopSize do {Loop on the population size.}
         Reestimation of π, A, and B for the pop-th member of the population.
         Recomputation of the log-likelihood of the pop-th member of the population.
      end for
   end for
end for
Computation of the optimal sequence of hidden states (Viterbi algorithm).
```

---

**Fig. 1.** Estimation of a HMM

After each iteration of the genetic algorithm, the members of the population are improved through several iterations of a Baum-Welch algorithm. This method is summarized in Algorithm 1 (Fig. 1). *IterGA* is the number of iterations of the genetic algorithm. *IterBW* is the number of iterations of the Baum-Welch algorithm. *PopSize* is the size of the population used by the genetic algorithm.

---

**Algorithm 2.** Computation of the new population.

---

```
Binary coding of each member of the old (current) population.
for pop = 1:PopSize do
   Selection: Random selection of a member of the old population (based on
   the value of its log-likelihood), to become a member of the new
   population.
   if pop is even then
      Crossover: Exchange a part of the binary vectors describing the last two
      members included in the new population with probability PCross.
   end if
end for
for pop=1:PopSize do
   Mutation: Change 0s to 1s and vice-versa in the binary vector describing
   the pop-th member of the new population with probability PMut.
end for
if the best member of the old population is not included in the new population then
   Elitism: Replace the first member of the new population by the best
   member of the old population.
end if
Decoding of the binary vectors into real parameters form.
```

---

**Fig. 2.** Computation of the new population

The computation of the new population using the genetic algorithm follows the steps given in Algorithm 2 (Fig. 2). Note that the parameters are recoded in binary form at the beginning of the procedure so that each member of the population is described by a vector of zeros and ones. Members of the old population are selected to be part of the new population according to their log-likelihood. This implies that best members of the old population have a greater probability to be chosen. *PCross* is the probability of crossover (exchange of a part of the parameter values) between two members of the population. *PMut* is the probability of mutation, which is the probability with which a 0 is replaced by a 1, and vice versa, in the binary writing of a member of the new population.

## 3   GA-HMM Based Video Affective Content Recognizer

We aim to utilize GA-HMM in two distinct ways for video affective content recognition: (*i*) given a sequence of observations extracted from an affective content unit, to determine the likelihood of each model (every basic emotion has its own GA-HMM model) for the input data, (*ii*) given the observation sequences, to train the model parameters. The first problem can be regarded to score how well a given model matches a given observation sequence. The second problem is attempting to optimize the model parameters in order to best describe how a given observation sequence comes about. The observation sequence used to adjust the model parameters is called a training sequence since it is used to "train" the GA-HMM. The training problem is the crucial one for our GA-HMMs based affective recognizer, since it allows us to optimally adapt model parameters to observed training data, i.e., to create best models for real phenomena.

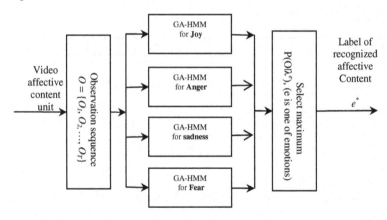

**Fig. 3.** GA-HMM based affective recognizer

Therefore, in order to recognize affective content, our affective recognizer contains two components: training and recognizing. For each basic emotion $e$, we build an ergodic 2-state GA-HMM $\lambda^e$. We must estimate the model parameters $(A, B, \pi)$ that optimize the likelihood of the training set observation vectors for the basic emotion

$e$. For each affective content unit which is to be recognized, the processing listed in Fig. 3 should be carried out, namely measurement of the observation sequence $O = \{O_1, O_2, ..., O_T\}$ ($T$ is the number of the shots within a affective content unit); followed by calculation of model likelihoods for all of possible models, $P(O \mid \lambda^e)$, $e \in \{joy, anger, sadness, fear\}$ ; followed by selection of the basic emotion type whose model likelihood is the highest, i.e., $e* = \underset{e \in \{joy, anger, sadness, fear\}}{\arg\max} \{p(O \mid \lambda^e)\}$ . The probability computation step is performed using the Viterbi algorithm (i.e., the maximum likelihood path is used).

## 4 Experimental Results

We made a data set from ten feature films such as "Titanic", "A Walk in the Clouds", "Love Letter", "Raiders of the Lost Ark", "Con Air", "Pirates of the Caribbean", "Scary Movie", "Spider-Man", "Lord of the Rings" and "the Lion King". Firstly, the excitement intensity curves for all the films were computed. Next, we utilized these excitement intensity curves to construct the Video Affective Tree for each film [4]. The ground truth for the four basic affective events (joy, anger, sadness and fear) was manually determined within the extracted video affective units at different levels. To compute color features, we transformed RGB color space into HSV color space and then quantized the pixels into 11 culture colors such as red, yellow, green, blue, brown, purple, pink, orange, gray, black and white [8]. For a key frame of each shot, we computed the histogram of 11 culture colors. We also computed the saturation(S), value (V), dark colors, and bright colors. So, 15 color features were extracted from each shot. The motion phase and intensity for each shot were also computed. The audio features, such as speech rate, pitch average, pitch range and short time energy, were computed using MPEG-7 XM software [9]. By fusing all of these audio and visual features, observation vectors are generated by vector quantization.

Our experimental results are shown in Table. 1. From the results, it can be easily found that GA-HMM can achieve higher recognition rate compared with classic HMM, which was adopted by our previous works [4].

**Table 1.** Experimental results

| Results \ Affective events | | Joy | Anger | Sadness | Fear |
|---|---|---|---|---|---|
| Number of Affective content units | | 87 | 105 | 152 | 213 |
| HMM | Recognized | 76 | 78 | 124 | 153 |
| | Recognition Rate | 87.4% | 74.3% | 81.6% | 71.8% |
| GA-HMM | Recognized | 81 | 85 | 131 | 167 |
| | Recognition Rate | 93.1% | 81.0% | 86.2% | 78.4% |

# 5  Conclusion and Future Work

Hidden Markov model (HMM) is a powerful tool for characterizing the dynamic temporal behavior of video sequences. In this paper, we propose an improved HMM called GA-HMM to design a video affective content recognizer. The experimental results show that GA-HMM can achieve higher recognition rate with less computation compared with our previous works.

Affective content is a subjective concept which relies on audience's perceptions. Talking about affect (feeling, emotion and mood) inevitably calls for a discussion about subjectivity. There are many implementation issues for our proposed video affective content recognizer. For example, finding a representative training data set in the affective domain is a crucial task for us. Moreover, the comparison criteria of models (HMM and GA-HMM) should be further investigated in the real world applications.

**Acknowledgments.** We gratefully acknowledge the granted financial support from China Postdoctoral Science Foundation (20060400847) and Huawei Foundation (YJCB20060471N).

# References

1. Hanjalic, A.: Extracting Moods from Pictures and Sounds: Towards truly personalized TV. IEEE Signal Processing Magazine 3, 90–100 (2006)
2. Hanjalic, A., Xu, L.-Q.: Affective video content representation and modeling. IEEE Trans. Multimedia 2, 143–154 (2005)
3. Kang, H.-B.: Affective Content Detection using HMMs. In: Proceedings of the eleventh ACM international conference on Multimedia, pp. 259–262 (November 2-8, 2003)
4. Sun, K., Yu, J.: Video Affective Content Representation and Recognition Using Video Affective Tree and Hidden Markov Models. LNCS. Springer, New York (to appear, 2007)
5. McLachlan, G.J., Krishnan, T.: The EM Algorithm and Extensions. Wiley, New York (1997)
6. Rabiner, L.: A tutorial on hidden Markov models and selected applications in speech recognition. Proc. IEEE 77(2), 256–286 (1989)
7. Coley, D.A.: An introduction to genetic algorithms for scientists and engineers. World Scientific Press, Singapore (1999)
8. Goldstein, E.: Sensation and Perception. Brooks/Cole (1999)
9. Information Technology—Multimedia Content Description Interface—Part 4: Audio, ISO/IEC CD 15938-4 (2001)

# Video Processing and Retrieval on Cell Processor Architecture

Junqing Yu and Haitao Wei

Computer College of Science & Technology,
Huazhong University of Science & Technology, Wuhan, 430074, China
yjqing@hust.edu.cn, whtaohust@163.com

**Abstract.** A multi-level parallel partition schema and three mapping model – Service, Streaming and OpenMP model – are proposed to map video processing and retrieval (VPR) workloads to Cell processor. We present a task and data parallel partition scheme to partition and distribute intensive computation workloads of VPR to exploit the parallelism of a sequential program through the different processing core on Cell. To facilitate the VPR programming on Cell, OpenMP programming model is loaded to Cell. Some effective mapping strategies are also presented to conduct the thread creating and data handling between the different processors and reduce the overhead of system performance. The experimental results show that such parallel partition schema and mapping model can be effective to speed up VPR processing on Cell multi-core architecture.

## 1 Introduction

Nowadays, with the rapid development of multimedia and network technologies, digital video information has grown exponentially. Digital video rapidly becomes an important source for information, education and entertainment. It is much easier to access video content via network than ever. How to help people conveniently and fast retrieve the interested video content is becoming more and more important. To this aim, content-based video processing and retrieval (VPR) is extremely needed. VPR has been an international research focus in multimedia domain. However, the intrinsic features of video, such as rich and non-structured data, intensive computing, and complex algorism, have prohibited VPR's further development. VPR programming is challenging and real-time processing and parallelization are expected.

Multi-core chip architecture is becoming the mainstream solution for next generation microprocessor chips. Cell processor, developed by IBM/Sony/Toshiba, provides an efficient high performance computation platform, with 9 cores one PowerPC Processor Element (PPE) and eight Synergistic Processor Elements (SPE). In order to meet the intensive computation and the real-time processing, we port VPR to Cell multi-core processor, with each core performs a part of VPR processing. A multi-level parallel partition schema and three mapping model (Service, Streaming and OpenMP model) are proposed to map VPR workload to the 9 cores of Cell.

L. Ma, R. Nakatsu, and M. Rauterberg (Eds.): ICEC 2007, LNCS 4740, pp. 255–262, 2007.
© IFIP International Federation for Information Processing 2007

The rest of this paper is organized as follows. In section 2, we try to use Service and Streaming model to map VPR workloads to Cell. It is proposed to map OpenMP programming model to Cell in section 3. Section 4 concludes this paper.

## 2  Video Processing and Retrieval on Cell

As digital video data becomes more pervasive, mining information from video data becomes increasingly important, but the huge computation prohibits its wide use in practice. Accelerating the video processing application by exploiting multi-level parallelism on Cell would be a promising way to boost the performance and provide more functionality for VPR.

### 2.1  Cell Architecture Overview

The first-generation Cell processor consists of a 64-bit multithreaded Power PowerPC processor element (PPE) and eight synergistic processor elements (SPE) connected by an internal, high-bandwidths Element Interconnect Bus (EIB) [1]. The PPE contains two levels of globally coherent cache and also supports Vector/SIMD Multimedia Extension (VMX) instruction set to accelerate multimedia and vector application [2]. The major powerful computation ability derives from the eight SPEs. Each SPE contains non-coherent local store for instructions and data.

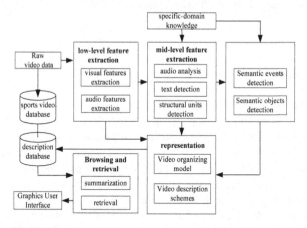

**Fig. 1.** Overview of video processing and retrieval framework

### 2.2  Video Processing and Retrieval Framework

Video processing and retrieval aims to help users to search, browse and manage video contents easily. The key components include low-level feature extraction such as visual and audio features, shot boundary detection, scene segmentation, video structural summary, high level semantic concept detection, annotation, indexing and content-based video retrieval [3]. We propose an efficient framework for indexing, browsing, abstracting and retrieval of sports video. As illustrated in Fig. 1, the framework consists of five stages: low-level feature extraction, mid-level feature extraction, high-level feature extraction, representation, browsing and retrieval as well. In these five stages, there exist multi-level parallelisms, such as feature extraction, indexing and retrieval, which can be exploited intensively.

## 2.3 Service and Streaming Programming Model for VPR on Cell

The key characteristics of VPR application are variety of tasks and intensity of computation. Therefore, the Service Model and the Streaming Model are proposed to be the best candidates.

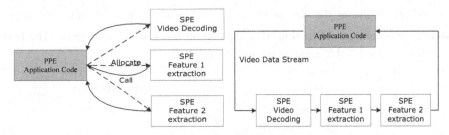

**Fig. 2.** Service Model of Video Processing     **Fig. 3.** Stream Model of Video Processing

Fig. 2 shows the Service Model in video processing. The processor assigns different services to different coprocessors, and the processor's main process calls upon the appropriate coprocessor when a particular service is needed. It is well known that feature extraction is a basic and important step in video processing. Here, each feature extraction is regarded as a service, which is assigned to one or more coprocessors and the processor's main process call upon these coprocessors' services needed. Fixed static allocation of coprocessors' services is avoided. These services are virtualized and managed on a demand-initiated basis.

Fig. 3 illustrates the Streaming Model, the main processor acts as a stream controller, and the coprocessors act as stream-data processors in either a serial or parallel pipeline. In video processing, each procedure has inherent computing stage which is mapped to one coprocessor. Here, the first coprocessor decodes the input raw video data stream and outputs decoded video data stream. The second coprocessor takes the decoded video data stream as input and extracts the feature 1 in stage 2. Finally, the third coprocessor extracts feature 2 and output the result data to the main processor. Under the control of the main processor, all the coprocessors work together in a pipeline to speed up the computation performance.

## 2.4 Block Matching Algorithm on Cell Using Parallel Partition

### 2.4.1 Block Matching Algorithm

Block matching algorithm is an important step of motion compensation algorithms for inter-frame predictive coding, which is used to eliminate the large amount of temporal and spatial redundancy that exists in video sequences and helps in compressing them. These algorithms estimate the amount of motion on a block by block basis, i.e. for each block in the current frame $i$, a block from the previous/after frame $j$ is found, that is said to match this block based on a certain criterion.

Here, the block matching criteria is the sum of absolute differences and the algorithm is Full Search or the Exhaustive Search. As Fig.4 shown, each block within a given search window in frame $j$ is compared to the current search block $g(x,y)$ in frame $i$. At each search step, the sum of absolute differences between the search block and the given block f(x,y) is evaluated using the following criterion.

$$AE = \sum_{i=1}^{K} \sum_{j=1}^{K} \left| f(i, j) - g(i - d_x, j - d_y) \right| \qquad (1)$$

Where, $K$ means the size of the block, $d_x$ and $d_y$ refers to the motion vector, which means amount of motion from the current block to the aim block. The best match is obtained if $AE$ achieves the minimum.

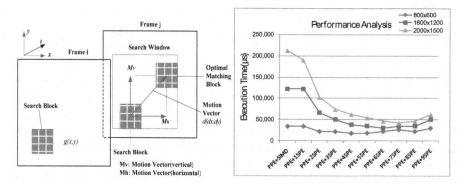

Fig. 4. Illustration of Block Matching    Fig. 5. Performance Analysis on Block Matching

### 2.4.2 Parallel Scheme of Block Matching Algorithm

The sequential algorithm uses four nested loops to evaluate the minimum $AE$. As the program following, array *Block[8][8]* and *Frame[M][N]* are allocated for the current search block and search window respectively, and variable *diff* preserves the absolute difference at each searching step. The minimum absolute difference and corresponding motion vector are stored in variable *min, x* and *y* respectively.

```
...
For(i=0;i<M-7;i++)
    for(j=0;j<N-7;j++){
        for(l=0;k<8;l++)
            for(m=0;l<8;m++)
            diff+=abs(Block[k][l]- Frame[k+i][l+j]);
    if(diff<min)
    {min=diff;x=i;y=j;}
    }
...
```

In order to contrast the performance improvement and communication overhead generated by different level parallelism, a step by step parallel scheme is adopted on

Cell. In the first step, we SIMDize the code for PPE to attain the data level parallelism, and then port the PPE code to multiple SPEs to achieve the task and data level parallelism. Finally, the overhead of communication is measured by setting the number of thread to one.

**Scheme 1: SIMDize the code for execution on PPE**
The main idea in this scheme is to utilize the VMX instruction set to accelerate the data computation. VMX instructions-*vec_perm, vec_abs, vec_add, and vec_sums*-are used to execute the vector absolute evaluation by allocating the array *block[8][8]* and *frame[M][N]* into one dimension array of vector. By this way, computation complexity is reduced by about 8 times and the number of loops is decreased to 3.

**Scheme 2: Parallelize Code for Execution across Multiple SPEs**
PPE initializes to partition and distribute the task to each SPE. It divided the search window into some sub-windows, and then maps the matching procedure in each sub-window to each SPE to evaluate the local minimum of AE and correlative local motion vector. In the end, PPE reduces the global AE and correlative global motion vector comparing all the local AE. SPEs receive the sub-window and current block from PPE, search the best local match to get the local minimum of AE and correlative motion vector, and sends the results to PPE to evaluate the global AE and motion vector.

The different instruction set between PPE and SPE makes the program running on Cell partitioned into two sections – PPE code for PPE and SPE code for SPE. The following *PPE Code* shows that the subroutine *spe_create_thread* creates a group threads running on SPE, the address of the data can be transmitted through the parameter `ctx`. After the threads are created, subroutine *spe_wait* is called to wait all the SPE threads to finish. At last, PPE gets the global result from local result returned from the SPE. In the *SPE Code*, each SPE gains the data from PPE through DMA transform, and then evaluates local minimum *AE* and the coordinate motion vector with SIMD instruction in SPE. After matching, each SPE sends the result to PPE by DMA.

**PPE Code:**

```
...
//correspond to 'fork' in OpenMP
For(i=0,offset=0;i<SPE_THREADS;i++,offset+=P){
// Create SPE thread of execution passing the context
as a parameter.
spe_ids[i]  =  spe_create_thread(0,  &match_multi_spu,
&ctx[i], NULL, -1, 0);      }
...
// correspond to 'join' in OpenMP
 for(i=0;i<SPE_THREADS;i++){
(void)spe_wait(spe_ids[i],&status,0);   }
//find the globe minimum, coordinate x,y
for (i=0; i<SPE_THREADS;i++){
  if(diff[i]<globemin)
    {globemin=diff[i];x=posx[i];y=posy[i];}
 }
```

**SPE Code:**

```
...
//gain the  data from ppe
spu_mfcdma32(…, MFC_GET_CMD);
...
//compute the absolute and the local minimum and
//the coordinate x,y with SIMD instruction in spu.
...
uschRowAbs_v[k]=spu_absd(model_v[k],uschRow_v[k]);
if(diff[k]<localmin)
    {localmin=diff[i];x=posx[k];y=posy[k];}
...
spu_mfcdma32(…, MFC_PET_CMD); //return the resulte
```

**Scheme 3: Set 1 thread to Measure the Communication Overhead**
Comparing to the program only running on PPE without communication with SPE, the program is ported to one SPE to measure the communication overhead setting the MARO *SPE_THREADS* of the SPE thread to one.

### 2.4.3  Experimental Results
The experiment of block matching algorithm was realized on IBM Cell simulator v2.0, using the language of PPE SPE C/C++ language extension (Intrinsics), with the SDK v2.0 [4]. As Fig. 5 shows, parallelization boosts the performance dramatically with the resolution accreting. Here, approximate 5x speedup is achieved referring to the resolution  of $2000 \times 1500$ contrasting to $2x$ speedup referring to resolution of $800 \times 600$. The performance achieves a peak with SPE increasing, but over parallelization deteriorates the performance. Referring to the resolution of $800 \times 600$, $1600 \times 1200$, and $2000 \times 1500$, the number of SPE to achieve the best performance is 4, 6, 7, respectively. It is illustrated that with the SPE increasing, the computation ability is strengthened, but the communication overhead is expanding as well. Only when the balance point reaches, the best performance is achieved.

## 3  Loading OpenMP Programming to Cell

Cell provides an efficient computation resource for application of intensive computation with the data and the task level parallelism. But, programming on Cell for VPR is not an easy job, e.g., the block matching algorithm in section 3, programmer has to be acquainted with the Cell architecture, PPE and SPE instruction sets, DMA transfer, and register files, etc. Although suit for VPR, Service and Streaming models are low level and inconvenient. All of these constrain the improvement of facility and performance for programming. OpenMP is an industrial standard for shared memory parallel programming agreed on by a consortium of software and hardware vendors [5]. It consists of a collection of compiler directives, library routines, and environment variables that can be easily used for VPR programming on Cell [6].

### 3.1 Loading Strategy

The parallel computation needs to be split among PPE and SPE processors. The parallelism is represented in OpenMP using "parallel" directive. PPE and SPE processors can be viewed as a group of "threads". Through data allocation PPE tells each SPE processor to execute specific regions in parallel. PPE executes the region as the master thread of the team. At the end of a parallel region, PPE waits for all other SPE to finish and collect the required data from each SPE [7, 8].

### 3.2 Exploitation Locality

The shared data is allocated in the main storage of PPE, and can be accessed exclusively through the atomic operation on Cell. Operation on shared data, each SPE needs to translate the local address to the effective address. The solution is to keep a copy of the shared data in the local storage of each SPE instead of the direct accessing to main storage when reading/writing the shared data. Then, if the local copy of the shared data is updated, the changed data will be written through DMA transfers back to the main storage after the end of parallel section.

### 3.3 Parallel Synchronization

The parallel synchronization is implemented with the mechanisms of memory tag polling and event trigger on Cell. The first method is to allocate a tag memory for each SPE with values initialized to "0" and each SPE polls the tag to wait the task assigned by PPE. PPE wakes up each SPE by setting the tag to "1". If detecting the tag set to "1", then each SPE runs the computation immediately, and after the computation is completed, the tag is set to "2" to notice PPE. At the same time, the PPE polls the tag until all of them are set to "2" by the SPEs, and then the PPE cleans the tag to "1" to resume the SPE execution. The second method is to utilize the mailbox and signal mechanism for parallel synchronization. The PPE deploys the task to each SPE by sending signal, once receiving the "start" signal each SPE does the work from PPE. And at the time of barrier, each SPE will send "completion" event to PPE by mailbox and then sleep. Once receiving all the events from SPEs, PPE will resume the SPEs to continue to work.

## 4  Conclusion

This paper presents a parallel partition schema and three mapping model to load video processing and retrieval (VPR) workloads to Cell multi-core processor. By means of partition and distributing the intensive computation workload to PPE and SPEs, the VPR processing is accelerated notably and a remarkable speedup is achieved. The proposed Service and Streaming models which use the mode of allocating-calling and data-streaming pipeline, are suitable and efficient, but somewhat of inconvenient. In addition, OpenMP programming model is presented on Cell to facilitate mapping VPR to Cell. Some effective strategies for data distribution and processor synchronization are also proposed by comparing the different approaches of data distribution and processor synchronization. And the overhead of the strategies for data sharing and processor synchronization are tested.The proposed partition schema and mapping model are reasonable for VPR on Cell, but there is a lot of work left to do, for example, the effectiveness of VPR mapping and the improvement of data distribution and synchronization mechanism between the PPE and the SPEs.

## Acknowledgements

We gratefully acknowledge the financial supports received from Intel Corporation for a study of multi-core programming environment.

## References

1. Pham, D., Asano, S., Bolliger, M., Day, M.N., Hofstee, H.P., Johns, C., Kahle, J., Kameyama, A., Keaty, J., Masubuchi, Y., Riley, M., Shippy, D., Stasiak, D., Suzuoki, M., Wang, M., Warnock, J., Weitzel, S., Wendel, D., Yamazaki, T., Yazawa, K.: The Design and Implementation of a First-Generation CELL Processor. In: Proc. IEEE International Solid-State Circuits Conference, pp. 184–185. IEEE Computer Society Press, Los Alamitos (2005)
2. IBM Microelectronics Division: PowerPC Microprocessor Family: AltiVec Technology Programming Environments Manual. IBM Corporation, pp. 282–308 (2004)
3. Li, E., Li, W., Wang, T., Di, N., Dulong, C., Zhang, Y.: Towards the Parallelization of Shot Detection – a Typical Video Mining Application Study. In: Proc. 35th International Conference on Parallel Processing (2006)
4. IBM Corporation: IBM Full-System Simulator User's Guide version 2.0. IBM Corporation (2006)
5. OpenMP Architecture Review Board: OpenMP C and C++ Application Program Interface Version 2.0. (2002), http://www.openmp.org
6. Liu, F., Chaudhary, V.: Extending OpenMP for Heterogeneous Chip Multiprocessors. In: Proc. 32nd International Conference on Parallel Processing (2003)
7. Eichenberger, A.E., O'Brien, K., O'Brien, K., Wu, P., Chen, T., Oden, P.H., Prener, D.A., Shepherd, J.C., So, B., Sura, Z., Wang, A., Zhang, T., Zhao, P., Gschwind, M.: Optimizing Compiler for a CELL Processor. In: Proc. 14th International Conference on Parallel Architectures and Compilation Techniques (2005)
8. Wei, H., Yu, J.: Mapping OpenMP to Cell: A Effective Compiler Framework for Heterogeneous Multi-Core Chip. In: Proc. International Workshop on OpenMP (to appear, 2007)

# A Hybrid Image Coding in Overdriving for Motion Blur Reduction in LCD

Jun Wang, Kyeongyuk Min, and Jongwha Chong

Hanyang University, Seoul, Korea, 133-791
junmei0073@hotmail.com, kymin@hanyang.ac.kr,
jchong@hanyang.ac.kr

**Abstract.** Overdriving technique enlarges the desired change of the pixel value, the error in general compression methods is enlarged at the same time. Therefore, we propose a novel Adaptive Quantization Coding (AQC) to reduce the error in compression for overdriving technique reducing motion blur. Considering hardware implementation, we develop a hybrid image coding which uses color transform first, and then uses AQC to compress luminance data as well as Block Truncation Coding (BTC) to compress chrominance data. The simulation results shown that the average PSNR was improved 5.676dB as compared with the result of BTC, and the average SD of error was reduced 50.2% than that in the BTC. The proposed algorithm is implemented with the verilog HDL and synthesized with the synopsys design compiler using 0.13μm Samsung Library.

**Keywords:** LCD, Motion blur, Overdriving, Compression, Block Truncation Coding, Adaptive Quantization Coding.

## 1 Introduction

Nowadays, Liquid Crystal Displays (LCDs) have been widely considered to have many advantages over Cathode Ray Tube (CRT) displays in the respects of resolution, power consumption, size, thickness, and other critical parameters. However, LCDs have a drawback of motion blur in TV applications and desktop for entertainment. One of the causes of motion blur is the sample-and-hold characteristic of the LCD panel, i.e. the image during the frame time is continuously shown. This type of motion blur can be reduced with a flashing or scanning backlight as in [1]. Another cause of motion blur is the slow reaction of the liquid crystal (LC) cell to a change in the pixel value as in [2]. Strong user demand for a high performance display creates the need to rapidly improve the liquid crystal response time and minimize the motion blur. Therefore, a lot of efforts have been put into speeding up the response of LC materials. This can be done by applying better materials, or by improving LC cell design as in [3]. There is also a well known method for response time improvement based on video processing called overdrive as in [4]. The technique of overdrive reduces motion blur by enlarging the desired change in the pixel value in order to force the LC material to react faster as in [5].The illustration of overdrive mechanism in LCD is shown in figure 1.

L. Ma, R. Nakatsu, and M. Rauterberg (Eds.): ICEC 2007, LNCS 4740, pp. 263–270, 2007.

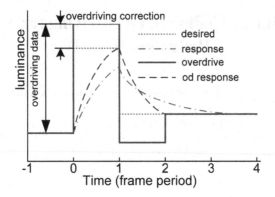

**Fig. 1.** Illustration of overdrive mechanism in LCD

Since overdrive compensates for a non-linear effect of the LCD panel it should preferably be placed at the end of the video processing chain, right before the LCD panel as in [2]. According to the pixel values of the current frame and the previous frame, the look-up table (LUT) provides the overdriving data to the LCD panel. The frame memory stores the pixel values of the current frame and give an output of the pixel value of the to the lookup table. A simple block diagram of general overdriving circuit is shown in figure 2.

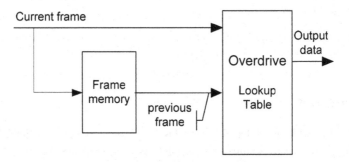

**Fig. 2.** Block diagram of overdrive

However, the conventional overdriving technique stores the current frame in the dynamic random access memory (DRAM) which is large and expensive. It is desired to reduce the cost of the system by compressing the data stored in the DRAM as in [6] and [7]. The errors in the decompressed image cause the errors in the amount of overdriving correction and have an effect on the reduction of motion blur. It is necessary to develop an effective compression method to reduce the errors in the decompressed image by the general compressing methods such as quantization, sub-sampling and block truncation coding (BTC). Therefore, we propose a novel hybrid image coding (HIC) to reduce the errors in decompressed image for the reduction of frame memory in LCD overdriving. The proposal uses a color space transform first, and then the proposed adaptive quantization coding (AQC) to compress the luminance data as well as the BTC to compress the chrominance data.

This paper will describe the background of the BTC techniques in Section 2.1. A novel proposal for the adaptive quantization coding (AQC) techniques is introduced in Section 2.2. In Section 2.3, a hybrid image coding method which integrates the advantages of the AQC and the BTC is introduced. In Section 3, the simulation result is described. This paper will be concluded in Section 4.

## 2 Proposal

### 2.1 The Background of the BTC

Block Truncation Coding (BTC) is a type of lossy compression technique for grayscale images. It divides the original images into small sub-images and then uses the quantization method, which adapts itself to the image statistics to reduce the number of gray levels in the image.

The compression procedure is as follows:

An image is divided into blocks of 4 x 4, 4 x 2, 4 x 1 or 2 x 2 pixels. For each block, the mean is computed; the value changes from block to block. Then a two-level quantization in the block is made as follows: If the value of a pixel is greater than the mean it is offered at a value of "1"; otherwise, it will be "0". By this way, the block is divided into two groups: upper group and lower group. The mean of the upper group and the mean of the lower group are computed. The image is reconstructed with the upper group mean, the lower group mean and the bit-plane which is made up of "1" or "0".

### 2.2 The Proposed Adaptive Quantization Coding (AQC)

The proposed coding method Adaptive Quantization Coding (AQC) is also a type of lossy image compression technique for grayscale images. It divides the original images into small sub-images and then uses an adaptive quantization, which adapts itself to the image statistics to reduce the number of gray levels in the image.

The compression procedure is as follows:

An image is divided into blocks of 4 x 4, 4 x 2 or 2 x 2 pixels. For each block, the minimum and the maximum are computed; these values change from block to block. Then an eight-level quantization in the block is made and the quantization step adapts itself to the difference of the block. So the value of the pixel is offered from "000" to "111" according to the level which the pixel belongs to. The image is reconstructed with the minimum, the quantization step and the bit-plane which is made up of three binary bits.

### 2.3 The Hybrid Image Coding Method

The block diagram of overdriving circuit using compression is shown in figure 3. The current frame in 24bit/pixel is compressed by the encoder and conserved in frame memory. The decoder gets data from frame memory and gives an output of decompressed previous frame. The module of overdriving lookup table uses the

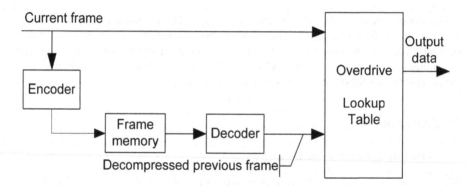

**Fig. 3.** Block diagram of overdriving circuit using image compression

lookup table and gives an output of overdriving data according to the pixel value of the current frame and the decompressed previous frame.

The human visual system (HVS) is less sensitive to color than to luminance (brightness), so that we have proposed an algorithm of HIC. The HIC converts RGB color space into YCbCr color space, first. Then it uses an efficient coding method of the proposed AQC to compress the luminance data which is more sensitive to HVS than color as well as the conventional simple method of BTC to compress the chrominance data. The YCbCr sampling format is 4:2:0 which is exactly half times as many samples as R: G: B video. The block diagram of the encoder and the decoder in the HIC is shown in figure 4.

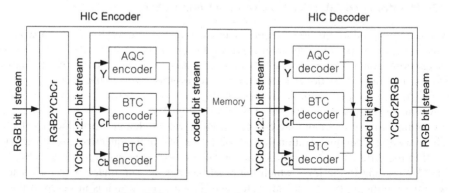

**Fig. 4.** Block diagram of encoder and decoder in the HIC

In the *HIC encoder* shown in figure 4, there are 4 modules: *RGB2YCbCr* module, the *AQC encoder* module and two *BTC encoder* modules. In *RGB2YCbCr* module, it converts the frame data from RGB color space into YCbCr color space, and gives us an output of YCbCr 4:2:0 bit stream in the YCbCr sampling format. In the *AQC encoder* module, it uses the AQC to encode the luminance component *Y*. In the two *BTC encoder* modules, they use the BTC to encode the chrominance component *Cr* and *Cb*, respectively. The output of the AQC and the BTC modules are stored in the reduced frame memory.

In the *HIC decoder* shown in figure 4, there are 4 modules: *AQC decoder* module, two *BTC decoder* modules and *YCbCr2RGB* module. In the *AQC decoder* module, it uses the AQC to decode the luminance component *Y*. In the two *BTC decoder* modules, they use the BTC to decode the chrominance component *Cr* and *Cb*, respectively. In *YCbCr2RGB* module, it converts the frame data from YCbCr color space into RGB color space, and gives us an output of RGB bit stream which will be supplied to the overdriving lookup table module.

The block size can affect not only the coding performance but also the compression ratio. So, to determine the block size, we must investigate the relationship among the coding performance, the compression ratio and the block size. The coding performance and the compression ratio of the AQC and the BTC in different block sizes in case of luminance data Y are shown in table 1. The PSNR and the SD of error are used to evaluate the image coding performance. The test image is "Lena" which is used generally.

**Table 1.** Compare the AQC coding performance and the compression ratio with the BTC in different block sizes in case of luminance component Y

| Lena | PSNR (dB) | | SD | | Compression ratio | |
|---|---|---|---|---|---|---|
| Block size | BTC | AQC | BTC | AQC | BTC | AQC |
| 8 x 8 | 31.385 | 41.060 | 6.858 | 2.242 | 6.40 | 2.49 |
| 8 x 4 | 32.289 | 42.320 | 6.177 | 1.935 | 5.30 | 2.33 |
| 4 x 4 | 34.608 | 45.100 | 4.724 | 1.392 | 4.00 | 2.06 |
| 4 x 2 | 36.089 | 47.133 | 3.983 | 1.100 | 2.67 | 1.68 |
| 2 x 2 | 41.266 | 52.053 | 2.191 | 0.622 | 1.60 | 1.23 |
| 4 x 1 | 37.624 | 49.153 | 3.343 | 0.875 | 1.60 | 1.23 |

From table 1, three trends can be seen in the following:

1. The coding performance of the AQC and the BTC become better and better when block size becomes smaller and smaller.

2. The compression ratio of the AQC and the BTC become smaller and smaller when block size becomes smaller and smaller.

3. The AQC gains a much better coding performance in case of every block size.

Before coding by the AQC and the BTC, the data is transformed from RGB format to YCbCr 4:2:0 format, and the compression ratio in the course of color transformation is 2. The preferred option is to compress the data of YCbCr 4:2:0 with compression ratio slightly more than 1.5 in order to get better image quality. Furthermore, to reduce the system cost by using one line buffer memory in hardware implementation, the blocks of 4 x 2 AQC, 2 x 2 BTC and 4 x 1 BTC are the preferred candidates, and the performances of these are descended in turn in case of similar compression ratio.

To apply the 4 x 2 block AQC which is the best of the three candidates to the more sensitive luminance data, the chrominance data Cr and Cb must be compressed in 4 x 1 block BTC considering the hardware implementation. As the image data is converted from RGB format into YCbCr 4:4:4 format, the YCbCr 4:4:4 format data are subsampled to YCbCr 4:2:0 format data. In YCbCr 4:2:0 sampling format, the chrominance data Cr and Cb have only half as many samples as Y. For chrominance data, therefore, the 4 x 2 block AQC or the 2 x 2 block BTC can not be used and the only available candidate is to use 4 x 1 block BTC. Finally, the HIC can gain a compression ratio of 3.31.

The proposed algorithm is implemented with software in C language and with hardware in the verilog HDL and synthesized with the synopsys design compiler using 0.13μm Samsung Library. The delay of encoder is 34 clocks and the delay of decoder 11 clocks.

## 3   Results

If image compression is used to reduce the image data stored in the frame memory, the reconstructed image will contain errors. In the configuration shown in Figure 3, the encoded image data is used only to detect the amount of temporal change between the current frame and previous frame and the encoded image data is never displayed directly. Errors caused by reducing the image data become errors of the overdriving correction, and lead to the insufficient or excessive correction of response time. Therefore the performance of overdriving with memory reduction can be evaluated to investigate the amount of errors in the decompressed image. We can evaluate the total error by the PSNR which is well known as an evaluation method of image coding, but we also care for the distribution of the error. That can be evaluated by the SD of the error.

To evaluate the proposed algorithm of the AQC and the HIC, the following general test images are used for simulation: 'Airplane', 'Baboon', 'Lena', 'Sailboat', 'Tiffany'. The simulation has been carried out in three coding methods: the BTC uses the BTC of 4 x 2 block with compression ratio of 2.67 to compress the RGB data; the TBC uses 2 x 2 BTC to replace 4 x 2 AQC basing on the HIC; the HIC is the proposed algorithm. The compression ratios are 2.67, 3.2 and 3.31, respectively. The figure 5 shows the simulation result of PSNR, and the figure 6 shows the simulation results of SD of error.

In figure 5, we can see that the PSNR of the HIC is higher than that of the TBC and the PSNR of the TBC is higher than that of the BTC in case of every test image, though the PSNRs of each method are different in these images. The average PSNRs of these samples are 30.864dB, 33.611dB and 36.540dB for the BTC, the TBC and the HIC, respectively. It is said that the TBC which uses the BTC to compress the data of converted YCbCr 4:2:0 color space can gain an improvement of 2.746dB in PSNR as compared with the BTC which compresses the data of RGB color space. The performance can improve 2.929dB in PSNR than the TBC using 4 x 2 AQC to replace 2 x 2 BTC in case of the HIC. Totally, the PSNR of image compressed in the HIC is improved as much as 5.676dB than that of the BTC.

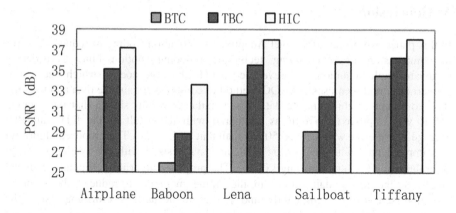

**Fig. 5.** The PSNR of various test images

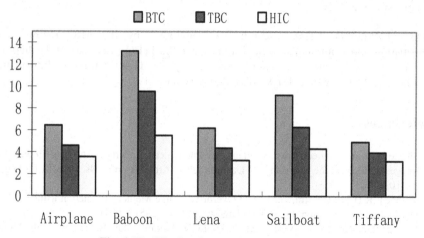

**Fig. 6.** The SD of various test images data error

In figure 6, we can see that the SD of error in decoded image used the HIC is smaller than that of the TBC and the SD of the TBC is smaller than that of the BTC in case of every test image, though the SD of each method are different in these images. The average SDs of these samples are 8.006, 5.756 and 3.987 for the BTC, the TBC and the HIC, respectively. It is said that the TBC which uses the BTC to compress the data of converted YCbCr 4:2:0 color space can reduce 28.1% in SD comparing with the BTC which compress the data of RGB color space. Because of using 4 x 2 AQC to replace 2 x 2 BTC in the HIC, the performance can reduce 30.7% in SD than the TBC. Totally, the SD in the HIC can reduce 50.2% than that in the BTC.

# 4 Conclusion

In this paper, we proposed a novel Adaptive Quantization Coding to reduce the error in compression for overdriving technique reducing motion blur. Considering hardware implementation, we developed a hybrid image coding which uses color convert first, and then uses the AQC method to compress luminance data and uses the BTC to compress chrominance data. The simulation results shown that the average PSNR was improved 5.676dB as compared with the result of the BTC, and the average SD of error was reduced 50.2% than that in the BTC. The proposed algorithm was implemented with the verilog HDL and synthesized with the synopsys design compiler using 0.13μm Samsung Library. The proposed algorithm efficiently reduced 30.2% of the image data stored in the frame memory. It reduced the error in decompressed image significantly and got more accurate overdriving data. The technique can be used to reduce the motion blur in TV applications and desktop for entertainment. In the future we will study the relationship between image features and errors using image samples such as graphic images and evaluate some other image compression methods.

**Acknowledgments.** "This research was supported by the MIC (Ministry of Information and Communication), Korea, under the ITRC (Information Technology Research Center) support program supervised by the IITA (Institute of Information Technology Assessment)" (IITA-2006-C1090-0603-0019).

# References

1. Shimodaira, Y.: Invited Paper: Fundamental Phenomena Underlying Artifacts Induced by Image Motion and the Solutions for Decreasing the Artifacts on FPDs. In: SID. 03 Digest, pp. 1034–1037 (2003)
2. Wubben, R.H.M., Hekstra, G.J.: LCD Overdrive Frame Memory Reduction using Scalable DCT-based Compression. In: SID. 04 Digest, pp. 1348–1351 (2004)
3. Klompenhouwer, M.A., Velthoven, L.J.: LCD Motion Blur Reduction with Motion Compensated Inverse Filtering. In: SID. 04 Digest, pp. 1340–1343 (2004)
4. Okumura, H.: A new Low-image-Lag Drive Method for Large Size LCTVs. Journal of the SID 1(3), 335–339 (1993)
5. Hartman, R.A., et.al.: Fast Response Electro-Optic Display Device. United States Patent US5, pp. 265–495
6. Someya, J., et al.: Reduction of Memory Capacity in Feedforward Driving by Image Compression. In: SID. 02 Digest, pp. 72–75 (2002)
7. Someya, J., et al.: A new LCD Controller for Improvement of Response Time by Compression FFD. In: SID. 03 Digest, pp. 1346–1349 (2003)

# See, Hear or Read the Film[*]

Carlos Teixeira[1] and Ana Respicio[2]

[1] Lasige/DI/Universidade de Lisboa, Portugal
cjct@di.fc.ul.pt
[2] CIO/DI/Universidade de Lisboa, Portugal
respicio@di.fc.ul.pt

**Abstract.** Films have been the most entertaining art form during the past century. Sometimes they were inspired in written novels; sometimes they have inspired new written novels. Film scripts are halfway between the film in the screen and the pure world of written imagination. Real time is one of the dimensions lost in the script, breaking the anchors to the time signals of what films are made. This paper presents a full approach for merging these two worlds in the real time dimension. Using subtitles time stamping and a new parallel text alignment algorithm, a time stamped script is produced. This is used to create new enriched narrative films, also presented in the paper.

## 1 Introduction

A film script is usually available as a separated text document which can be read apart from the film visioning. It is structured into scenes and includes information from both the dialogue and the action. The dialogue lines are usually very close from what can be found in the subtitles, sometimes even closer to what was actually spoken in the audio signal. Each dialogue line begins with the identification of the corresponding character. Usually a description of the character behavior (visual expression and type of speech, etc.), for specific parts of the discourse, is described within the dialogue lines. Action information includes scene and shots identification, and several descriptions of the visual and audio scenario as well as the position of the characters. Often camera directions as well as shot boundaries are also included. Most of the above mentioned information is not explicitly available in the film itself. One aim of the present study is to explore contexts where this information will be helpful to be presented synchronously. However, there is no explicit link between the script and the video, as the first one does not include references to the precise time of the signal.

Nowadays, together with the video and audio signals, many programs and films are distributed including subtitles. Not matching exactly the speech transcription, as it would be done with an idealistic automatic speech recognizer (ASR), these are manual transcriptions often done by human transcriber, which main concern is to keep the subtitle semantic value according to the available slot of time and visual space. Including subtitles serves mainly as a suitable form of presenting language translation or as a

---

[*] This work was partially supported by FCT through the Large-Scale Informatic Systems Laboratory and Centro de Investigação Operacional – POCTI/ISFL/152.

L. Ma, R. Nakatsu, and M. Rauterberg (Eds.): ICEC 2007, LNCS 4740, pp. 271–281, 2007.

substitute of the audio signal in any conditions where audio is not available. These conditions include problems with the availability of the audio signal, channel transmission, environment of the listener (i.e. noisy or bad sound propagation) or the listener himself (i.e. deaf). On the other hand, if for some reason the access to visual information is not allowed, translated subtitles could be used by a text to speech (TTS) system to replace those subtitles by audio. Additional real-time information can also be useful for the above mentioned restrictions in visual or audio access. If time synchronization is made possible between the available text streams, script extra information can be used revealing advantages comparable to the use of subtitles.

Obtaining a time synchronous script allow us to envisage two main types of applications. The first type will rely on the audio as a substitute for the video signal, in any conditions where video is not physically available. Similarly, as it was mentioned for audio, these conditions include problems with the availability of the video signal, channel transmission, environment of the viewer (i.e. driving) or the viewer himself (i.e. blind). In such cases, information from the script could be helpful if transmitted synchronously with the use of TTS technology. The second type of applications aims to provide an integrated view of the process of film production, namely about what was originally in the mind of the scriptwriter. Current technology allows foreseeing alternative views of the script as well as other texts, namely the possibility to access these documents synchronously with the visioning of the concerning film.

The present work proposes an approach for the automatic alignment of the script with the video signal, producing a synchronized script, and its integration in the visual domain together with extended browsing and querying facilities over the film. The paper is organized as follows. Next section summarizes previous related work. Section 3 describes the general approach for obtaining the time stamped script, and the methodology used for parallel text alignment, focusing on the preprocessing of the text pieces and on the alignment algorithm. Preliminary experimental results are given. Section 4 presents the tool developed for an enriched visualization of video. Finally, some conclusions and perspectives of future work are presented.

## 2    Previous Related Work

In the past some approaches have been published for aligning texts close related with video. TV programs are sometimes transcribed for documentation on web sites. Gibbon [2] proposes an approach to use this type of transcriptions aligned with the video signal to create improved hypermedia web pages for those programs. The time alignment is found by doing parallel text alignment of the transcripts with the subtitles of the same program. Gibbon refers difficulties arising at many-to-one sentence mappings. Text alignment is first done at the word level using a dynamic programming (DP) procedure. At a second stage, an alignment at the sentence level is searched for.

A framework for aligning and indexing movies with their scripts is proposed by Ronfard and Thuong [6]. They propose a grammar for the script of a given movie. Structural entities, such as shots, scenes, actions and dialogs are extracted. Subtitles are extracted from the video stream using optical character recognition, producing a stream of time-stamped short texts. The alignment is performed by searching for the longest increasing subsequence of matched shots and subtitles.

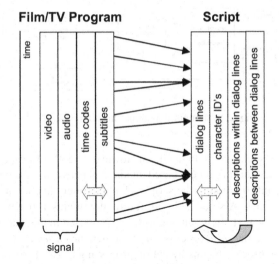

**Fig. 1.** Aligning a film/TV program with the script

Aligning the script dialogues with closed captions is the basis to address character/speaker identification in [8]. A DP procedure finding the "best path" across a similarity matrix allows for defining an alignment at the word level. The approach combines the text alignment with audio segmentation to accomplish audio speaker identification.

Martone et. al. [4] propose the off-line generation of closed captions by synchronizing program transcripts with the texts (subtitles) produced by an ASR system. A DP procedure similar to the one used by Gibbon [2] is applied to perform text alignment at the word level. More recently, Martone and Delp presented two systems based on the alignment of program transcripts with ASR results [3]. One of them allows for locating speakers in news program, while the other one generates DVD chapter titles using the information of the closed captions.

MUSA IST Project(2002-2004) aimed the creation of a multimodal multilingual system that converts audio streams into text transcriptions, generates subtitles from these transcriptions and then translates the subtitles in other languages. MUSA operated in English, French and Greek. When the audio transcripts are available, the ASR MUSA module aligns the audio with the transcript and provides time codes. This is effective if no large omissions are found in the audio, as is the case in many TV productions [5]. The algorithm presented in this paper can help to overcome such difficulties.

## 3  Obtaining Time Stamped Scripts

In this section an approach is proposed for obtaining the time stamped script (TSS). The description of the global approach must consider two main blocks of information which are represented in figure 1: time synchronized information (video and subtitles); and the textual information structured according to the time line but without any detailed anchors to the real time of the movie (script). The arrows intent to represent the above mentioned anchors. In the present work, these time anchors are built exclusively

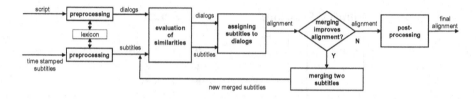

**Fig. 2.** System for obtaining time aligned scripts

between the subtitles and the dialogue lines. However, we also foresee future developments that will enrich this alignment based on anchors between the video and the audio and the remaining information in the script - character identification as well as the descriptions of the scenes. Also considering future alignments with texts with different time structures, a new text alignment algorithm is proposed in this paper.

Figure 2 displays a pictorial description of the new proposed algorithm for parallel text alignment. The process begins by the preprocessing of two texts in order to obtain two streams of word sets: dialogs and subtitles. Then, the core alignment follows including two main phases. In first phase, the algorithm computes a heuristic assignment of subtitles to dialogs that maximizes the global similarity. The second phase searches iteratively for merging pairs of consecutive subtitles that produce local improvements. The last iteration occurs when no further improving merge can be found. In the end, due to several reasons explained in section 3.3, a small set of subtitles and dialogue lines remain unassigned or out of expected time order. A final post-processing phase (third phase) is used to assign these subtitles with unassigned dialogue lines. Each of these dialogue lines should be surrounded by already assigned dialogue lines that encompass the time order where the concerned subtitle occurs. Finally, the resulting assignment is used to link time codes to the dialogs in the script providing the TSS.

### 3.1   Texts Preprocessing

The alignment process begins by preparing the texts to align: script and time stamped subtitles. Both texts are converted to a common standard format. A token is a sequence of alphanumeric characters (letters or digits) occurring between white spaces or a white space and a punctuation mark. Punctuation characters, as well as non-alphanumeric characters are removed in both texts. Additionally, all the letters are converted to lower-cases. This means that every word, number, acronym, etc. will be coded into a lexicon as a token. A single lexicon is build which will allow referring to every token with an unique index.

Each dialog line in the script is represented by a sequence of tokens. Descriptions of an emotion to be expressed by the character or a special setting of the scene, frequently appear as text between parentheses in the script. These may occur within and between dialog lines and are ignored in the alignment. However, they remain linked to the corresponding dialog lines as they are essential to be displayed in the final enriched browsing video. In the same way, the character ID, although not considered in the alignment, remains assigned to each dialogue line. Each subtitle is also converted to a sequence of tokens. Additionally, subtitles are labeled with their time codes (not used in the alignment) that will make possible, afterwards, to produce the synchronized script.

Thus, each subtitle or dialogue line can now be represented by the respective set of indexes. Actually, as the vector space model will be used (subsection 3.2), the order of the tokens is not considered, and this set is represented in a vector with same size as the total number of tokens in the lexicon. Accordingly, each element of this vector contains the number of repeated tokens occurring for a specific lexicon entry. Each token is weighed according to its length. In such way, in the core alignment, more weight is given to longer tokens.

## 3.2  Text Alignment Algorithm

To produce synchronized scripts, a correspondence between single subtitles or subsequences of consecutive subtitles, and dialog lines in the script, must be established. Furthermore, many to one assigning of subtitles to dialog lines must be produced. The algorithm proposed here uses the similarity measure of the vector space model [7] which has been adopted for many applications in the information retrieval area. This model achieved special relevance in the text retrieval area where the it proves to be relatively language independent. One of the characteristics that can be seen as a problem is the fact that this model does not take into account the order of the tokens inside a document. However this did not seem to compromise the success of this model with such linear structures such as language.

Similarities between subtitles and dialog lines are ranked by evaluating the deviation of angles between the related token vectors. This is equivalent to compute the cosine of the angle between the corresponding vectors. Consequently, the similarity between the $i$-th subtitle and the $j$-th dialog line is given by:

$$S(i,j) = \frac{st_i.dl_j}{\|st_i\|\|dl_j\|},\qquad(1)$$

where $st_i$ is the vector representing the $i$-th subtitle and $dl_j$ is the vector representing the $j$-th dialog line. A formal pseudo-code description of the core alignment procedure is given in figure 3. The algorithm aligns two lists: $m$ sets of tokens from subtitles $st[i]$ and $n$ sets of tokens from dialogue lines $dl[j]$ – typically $m > n$. The similarity of each subtitle with each dialog line is kept in a $m \times n$ similarity matrix denoted by $sim$.

The result of the core alignment procedure is the assignment of subtitles to dialogs given in a list denoted by $assigned$. $assigned[i]$ contains the index of the dialog to which the $i$-th subtitle is assigned. Some subsequences of subtitles are eventually merged during the execution of the process and the current list $st$ is updated accordingly.

In first stage, one-to-one assignment is performed by a greedy heuristic. The matrix of similarities $sim$ is computed using equation (1). The values in this matrix are ranked building a list of ordered pairs (subtitle, dialog) sorted by decreasing order of the corresponding similarities.

Then, iteratively, assignments are made by looking first for the pairs with higher similarity values. The matching is done only if both elements of the pair were not previously assigned and if their similarity value is greater than a given threshold $\alpha$. In that

1: **function** $one2one\_assignment(st, dl, sim)$

2:     $pairs \leftarrow sort(sim)$ {sort pairs (i,j) in decreasing order of sim[i,j]}

3:     $k \leftarrow 1$

4:     **repeat**

5:         **if**     $is\_free?(st\_in\_pair(k))$     $\wedge$     $is\_free?(dl\_in\_pair(k)$     $\wedge$
$sim[st\_in\_pair(k), dl\_in\_pair(k)] > \alpha$ **then**

6:             $assigned[st\_in\_pair(k)] \leftarrow dl\_in\_pair(k)$

7:         $k \leftarrow next\ k$

8:     **until** $all\ pairs\ were\ analyzed$
$\{k = m \times n \vee sim[st\_in\_pair(k), dl\_in\_pair(k)] \leq \alpha\}$

9:     **return** $assigned$

10: **main** ()

11:     $Input\ st[1..m]$ {list of subtitles }

12:     $Input\ dl[1..n]$ {list of dialogs }

13:     $assigned[1..m] \leftarrow 0$ {assignments of subtitles}

14:     {first phase}

15:     $sim[1..m, 1..n] \leftarrow compute\_similarities(st, dl)$ {matrix of similarities }

16:     $assigned \leftarrow one2one\_assignment(st, dl, sim)$

17:     {second phase}

18:     **repeat**

19:         $improvement \leftarrow false$

20:         $i \leftarrow 1$

21:         **while** $i \leq m \wedge \neg improvement$ **do**

22:             $max\_sim \leftarrow max\{sim[k, assigned[k]], k = i, i + 1\}$

23:             $best\_s \leftarrow s : max\_sim = sim[s, assigned[s]], s = i, i + 1$

24:             $merged\_s \leftarrow merge(st[i], st[i + 1])$

25:             **if** $max\_sim < compute\_similarities(merged\_s, assigned[best\_s])$ **then**

26:                 $st[i] \leftarrow merged\_s$ {merge two consecutive subtitles}

27:                 $st \leftarrow remove\_subtitle(i + 1)$ {update subtitles list}

28:                 $sim \leftarrow update\_similarities(st, dl, i)$

29:                 $assigned \leftarrow one2one\_assignment(st, dl, sim)$

30:                 $improvement \leftarrow true$

31:             $i \leftarrow next\ i$

32:     **until** $\neg improvement$

**Fig. 3.** Core alignment procedure

case, the *assigned* list is updated accordingly. This cycle continues until a pair with a similarity value lower or equal to the threshold is found or all the pairs have been analyzed.

The number of subtitles is usually greater than the number of dialogs and, consequently, in the end, many subtitles remain unassigned. Giving a minimum value of similarity to accomplish a matching also contributes to this output. Also, potentially, in the result, two consecutive subtitles may be linked to two dialogs located apart.

On the other hand, the process described above does not take into account the order of subtitles and dialogs in their respective streams. Considering these order restrictions in the time neighborhood of each subtitle, and to overcome the above mentioned problems, an improvement phase is executed. Iteratively, the algorithm searches for pairs of consecutive subtitles that can be merged together leading to an increased value of local similarity. This is done by going through each subtitle $i$ and evaluating the impact of merging it with its successor. The merging of two subtitles is considered if it leads to a local improvement. In that case, the list $st$ is updated, replacing the two sets of tokens by the concatenation of both into a single set. Finally, a similarity matrix is updated for another one-to-one assignment run. The whole process repeats until no eligible merges can be found.

### 3.3 Experimental Results

The approach has been tested with episodes of a series produced by RTP[1], one of the Portuguese major television channels. The episodes have 45 minutes of duration. The script of each episode includes an average of 3500 words, comprising an average number of 200 dialogue lines. The average number of subtitles for each episode is around 300. The algorithm presented above was coded in the C programming language and preliminary experiences revealed very promising results.

Figure 4 illustrates the evolution of the alignment between subtitles and dialogs during the execution of the algorithm for a given episode. The first plot is the result of the initial one-to-one assignment. Each point represents for each subtitle, in the X axis, the dialog to which an alignment was obtained, in the Y axis. The second plot displays the alignment at iteration 50 of the second phase. Most of the subtitles analyzed in this second phase are now assigned. The third plot corresponds to the last merging iteration (107). A few subtitles are still unassigned and a very few were wrongly assigned. Two situations leading to non assignment of subtitles were found. One relates with texts that do not exist in the script as, for instance, the first 21 subtitles referring to a summary of the previous episodes as well as a flashback to a specific scene in a previous episode (164-170.) Also, it happened that a single word subtitle reinforced its predecessor, although absent in the script, as for instance, in subtitles 274, 275 – "Anda, vamos embora." (Come on, let's go.); "Vamos!". The information about the authoring of the adaptation and edition of the subtitles also appeared at the end of the episode (297-299). Another situation concerned audio information that appeared transcribed in subtitles, as these were conceived for deaf people (subtitles 263 to 270).

The few false alignments, which occurred in less than 1% of the cases, were due to detached situations where the subtitles editor included in the same subtitle speech from

---

[1] Rádio Televisão Portuguesa.

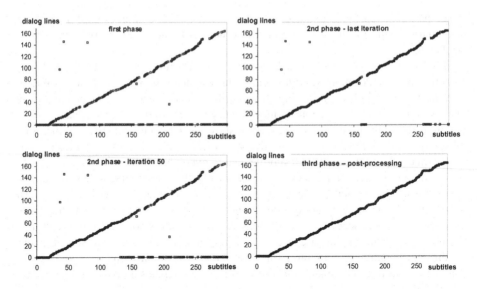

**Fig. 4.** Evolution of the alignment - assignment of subtitles to dialog lines

different dialog lines. In these cases, the dialogs were very short, for instance subtitle 44 – "Adeus! Adeus." (Bye! Bye) – referring to two different characters saying goodbye to each other, was assigned to a later dialog line including the word "adeus" (bye).

Final alignment, found after post-processing is presented in the last plot. The outlier cases described above, although specific for this episode, are similar to those found in other experiences.

The average number of aligned subtitles was around 87%. In this case, all the subtitles were accounted for. Excluding the situations where the subtitles texts do not exist in the script (flashbacks and extra audio information), and, therefore, that could not be solved by the algorithm, the average number of aligned subtitles was greater than 98%. The merging phase contributed with an improvement of 60%, as the initial one-to-one assignment could only find 51%. The average global similarity reached values around 82% when considering all subtitles and 95% excluding those non-assigned. Above all, the detected unassigned subtitles and dialogue lines were found to be useless and probably confusing for the expected applications.

## 4   Towards an Enriched Narrative Film Player

This section describes how to play and browse the narrative films integrating each of the pieces of information contained in the TSS. These pieces can be very useful after being converted to the audio domain, specially in situations in which vision can not be used - already detailed in section 1. The use of the audio domain can be done with TTS systems. Audio synthesized dialogue lines sound necessarily very unnatural when compared to the original audio dialogues or to the traditional output from dubbing. However, the remaining information from the script (character ID, scene descriptions, etc.) is actually the main novel addition to consider and can be synthesized with lower quality requirements. Namely, emotional speech aspects which are essential for the dialogues, such as prosody, are not so crucial for this type of information. Actually, if a real speaker should pronounce this, his speech should be even less emotive than narrator. In order to be efficiently discriminated, each piece of information in the TSS can be assigned to different audio spatial channels and, preferably, to different speaker voices. However, reducing a demonstration of this approach to the audio representation was found not very convincing, since it does not allow an easy evaluation for users who are not really restricted to the audio input. Considering this, at the present stage of this work and after implementing a robust algorithm for text alignment, the second concern is actually to provide a visual integration of the TSS with the film in order to provide a convincing demonstration of the use and efficiency of the approach. The integration and navigation of video and other media is the central aspect in hypervideo, where video is not regarded as a mere illustration, but can also be structured through links defined by spatial and temporal dimensions [1].

A small video demonstration of the present work is available in:"http://www.di.fc.ul. pt/~cjct/ICEC2007/". It shows 80 seconds of a scene from an episode of the television series "Quando os Lobos Uivam" (when the wolves howl), an adaptation of the novel of Aquilino Ribeiro with the same name made by Francisco Moita Flores for the RTP. In this scene, a couple of peasants (Rosa and Jaime) collect some brushwood from an area they were recently forced to sell to a capitalist. A national guard named Modesto founds and menace them. The original titles are in Portuguese, they were translated just for a better illustration in the present paper.

Figure 5 was obtained from the same portion of this film. The video is shown in the upper left corner and the name of the speaking character is shown right below. The subtitles are also presented bellow the video just according to common standards. Further bellow, a description about the specific shot can be found. All the right side of the display area was used for the script. This is shown as a scrolling text with new dialogue lines and related comments coming from below shortly after the corresponding subtitle was shown. It seems like the subtitles feed the scrolling script but, as mentioned before, these are often different from the dialogue lines and can sometimes include extra information about the actor expected behavior. Together with the dialogue lines, the corresponding shot description is included – the same way as it appears in the script and it was previously shown the bottom left corner.

Each of these text streams have different showing times. However, all these timing sequences were built from the subtitles time codes. Table 1 shows the adopted time shifts for each piece of information taking the corresponding subtitle time code as reference.

The integration of all the text elements in a single video allows browsing capabilities where the player can do fast forward, backward or accessing directly a specific shot while all the elements appear synchronously, namely the scrolling TSS. More than that, simple query facilities will be integrated which will allow to directly access a particular shot given some words spoken by a specific character. Other than character ID and subtitles or dialogue lines, other queries can be made based on the shot description, scene names, expected character behavior and any combinations between these.

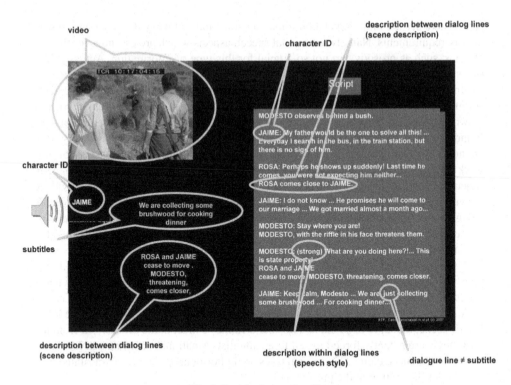

**Fig. 5.** Enriched narrative film

**Table 1.** Selected delays (in seconds) for the script units with regard to the subtitles time code

| Text unit | character ID | subtitle | shot description | dialogue line |
|-----------|--------------|----------|------------------|---------------|
| begin     | -1           | 0        | -2               | +1            |
| end       | +5           | 0        | +6               | +6            |

## 5  Conclusions

This paper proposes an approach to create enriched narrative films. The central idea is to enrich the experience of watching films by providing synchronized textual information from the script. The approach relies on aligning the script with the subtitles and a new text alignment algorithm is presented. The alignment is made at sentence level and avoids some differences between sentences, such as those resulting from word ordering as well as structural differences between documents. This is a novelty regarding other text alignment algorithms from the literature, that are mainly based on dynamic programming procedures working at the word alignment level [2,4,3]. This feature also provides flexibility to deal with more complex alignments allowing the integration of other related textual contents, as well as to consider flashbacks and flash forwards of scenes. Moreover the algorithm is almost language independent and robust enough to deal with other complex alignments.

Future work will concentrate on applying the proposed algorithm to a broad collection of English films and upon further testing by comparing it with other text alignments algorithms from the literature. Experiments will also consider other related texts namely behind the scene documents. An envisage application is to use a text to speech system to convert the script and produce contents specially designed to visual-impaired people. The presented approach could have a high impact on next generation multi-media retrieval, digital content management or entertainment electronics for the home environment.

## Acknowledgments

The authors want to thanks RTP, namely João Sequeira and the RTP Multimedia Director Francisco Teutónio Pereira for providing the videos and scripts used in the present publication; as well as the anonymous reviewers for the useful comments.

## References

1. Chambel, T., Guimarães, N.: Context perception in video-based hypermedia spaces. In: Proc. ACM Hypertext'02, College Park, Maryland, USA. ACM Press, New York (2002)
2. Gibbon, D.C.: Generating hypermedia documents from transcriptions of television programs using parallel text alignment. In: Proc. Eighth Int. Workshop on Research Issues In Data Engineering, Continuous-Media Databases and Applications, pp. 26–33 (1998)
3. Martone, A., Delp, E.: An overview of the use of closed caption information for video indexing and searching. In: Proc. CBMI Fourth International Workshop on Content-Based Multimedia Indexing (2005)
4. Martone, A., Taskiran, C., Delp, E.: Automated closed-captioning using text alignment. In: Proc. SPIE International Conference on Storage and Retrieval Methods and Applications for Multimedia, pp. 108–116 (2004)
5. Demiros, I., Prokopidis, P., Vanroose, P., Hoethker, A., Daelemans, W., Sklavounou, E., Konstantinou, M., Piperidis, S., Karavidas, Y.: Multimodal multilingual resources in the subtitling process. In: LREC. Proc. of the 4th International Language Resources and Evaluation Conference, Lisbon, Portugal (May 2004)
6. Ronfard, R., Thuong, T.T.: A framework for aligning and indexing movies with their script. In: Proc. IEEE International Conference on Multimedia and Expo. (ICME 2003), vol. 1, pp. 121–124. IEEE Computer Society Press, Los Alamitos (2003)
7. Salton, G., Wong, A., Yang, C.S.: A vector space model for automatic indexing. Communications of the ACM 18(11), 613–620 (1975)
8. Turetsky, R., Dimitrova, N.: Screenplay alignment for closed-system speaker identification and analysis of feature films. In: Proc. IEEE International Conference on Multimedia and Expo (ICME 2004), vol. 3, pp. 1659–1662. IEEE, Los Alamitos (2004)

# A Practical Framework for Virtual Viewing and Relighting

Qi Duan, Jianjun Yu, Xubo Yang, and Shuangjiu Xiao

Digital Art Laboratory,
School of Software
Shanghai Jiao Tong University
{duanqi1983,jianjun-yu}@sjtu.edu.cn, {yangxubo,xsjiu99}@cs.sjtu.edu.cn

**Abstract.** Recently many practical applications have concerned with observing objects that have specular reflection properties. They intend to know how the specular reflections and other details vary according to different lighting conditions and view positions. In this paper, we propose an innovative framework combining the novel view synthesis algorithm and the relighting algorithm to fulfill these requirements. Another important feature of this framework is that all the algorithms are based on image without acquiring any 3D model which may contain some high confidential secrets. Meanwhile an image measurement criterion is proposed to verify the feasibility and effectiveness of the framework.

**Keywords:** Novel View Synthesis, Image-based Relighting, Image Measurement.

## 1 Introduction

Recently, the technique that can render images of products under arbitrary illuminations and view points became increasingly important in movie, museums, and electronic commerce applications. Various special lights will be placed in certain positions to augment the effects of details on product surface; meanwhile the observation position and angle also influence the display result. The position of viewpoints and the condition of luminance are two key factors that influence the effects. To determine the best luminance condition and view point position, it is very helpful to design a tool that can precisely observe the target with specular propertities under various light conditions and in some arbitrary view positions. Considering that the product may contain some highly confidential secrets, those requirements can be summarized as follows:

- A method to simulate the result of the objects under various light conditions, for example, different numbers, sizes, types, colors of light resources and different distances between objects and light. And we need to get the best result with the minimal cost.
- A technique to synthesize novel images of the objects. Considering the objects may relate to commercial confidential secrets, the less 3D information of the target we calculate, the better.

L. Ma, R. Nakatsu, and M. Rauterberg (Eds.): ICEC 2007, LNCS 4740, pp. 282–287, 2007.

## 1.1  Related Work

Two main algorithms employed in this framework are the image-based relighting and the novel view synthesis.

**Image-Based Relighting(IBL)** attracts a lot of attention recently. It can be classified into three categories: reflectance function based relighting, basis function-based relighting and plenoptic function-based relighting. Reflectance Function-based Relighting techniques explicitly estimate the reflectance function at each visible point of the object, which is known as the Anisotropic Reflection Model[1] or the BSSRDF[2]. Basis Function-based Relighting techniques take advantage of the linearity of the rendering operator with respect to illumination. Relighting process is accomplished via linear combination of a set of pre-rendered "basis" images. Nimeroff et al. [3] used a technique of combining images to relight a scene. Debevec et al.[4] describes a Light Stage in which an object can be placed. Plenoptic Function-based Relighting techniques are based on the computational model-the Plenoptic Function[5]. It extracts out the illumination component from the aggregate time parameter, and facilitate relighting of scenes.

**Novel image synthesis** has been studied in the last decade. The work can be divided into two main classes roughly: image-based modeling and rendering(IBMR) and image-based morphing and rendering. The first class is designed to reconstruct 3D models from photographs. Debevec et al.[6] have shown a method of modeling and rendering architecture from a small number of photos. Criminisi et al.[7] create 3D texture-mapped models relying solely on one single image as its input. Byong Mok Oh et al.[8] take a single photo as input and model the scene. The second class does not calculate any 3D information of the scene. It use various methods to synthesis the novel image such as image warping[9], image interpolation[10], image extrapolation and so on. For example, Seitz and Dyer[11] interpolate along the base line of image pairs to obtain novel images. Levoy and Hanrahan[12] and Gortler et al.[13] interpolate between a dense set of several thousand-example images to obtain novel view images. Peleg and Herman[14] relax the fixed camera constraint to synthesis results. Avidan and Shashua[16] introduce the concept of trilinear tensor space and use trilinear tensor to synthesize the novel view images.

However, the image-base relighting approach and novel view synthesis method can only satisfy one of the two requirements. Our framework integrates the two algorithms closely, which can render images of products under arbitrary illuminations and view points.

In the following section 2 we introduce the framework in detail. Image measurement criterion and framework performance are described in section 3. Finally, we conclude and present the idea for future work in section 4.

## 2  Algorithms

### 2.1  Framework Architecture

The most significant feature of the framework is that it can satisfy the specified requirements and is totally based on images. The framework integrates two important algorithms above as two modules. The structure is shown in Figure 1. Firstly in image-based relighting module, the camera position is fixed and the relighting process is performed, then the result image is obtained under arbitrary luminance situation as the "source image". After that the camera position and orientation are moved in a little range and a picture of the object is captured as the "reference image". Using source image and reference image as the input of novel view synthesis module, the final novel image can be synthesized. Once the light environment changes, the relighting result is recalculated and the source image is updated, leaving reference image unmodified. Then the novel image is synthesized again. Employing this framework, we can observe the target of various luminance situations under arbitrary viewpoints.

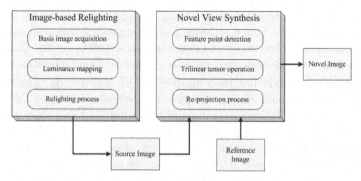

**Fig. 1.** Framework Architecture.The architecture contains two main algorithm modules. The source image is the output of relighting module, and the input of the second module, as well as the reference image. The novel image is the final result as the output of the novel module.

## 2.2   Image-Based Relighting

Our image-based Relighting (IBL) can synthesize realistic images without a complex and long rendering process as in traditional geometry-based computer graphics. The algorithm detail is divided into three parts-basis image acquisition,luminance mapping and relighting process.

To acquire the basis image,we design a spherical light stage with prepared "standard" point light source as "directional light source" attached on it. The light moves around the surface of sphere and for each light position and a corresponding basis image of objects placed at the center is captured. This process is repeated until the entire sphere of incident illumination is sampled at a predefined resolution.

To accelerate our whole process, we map the sphere map to a latitude-longitude map. Each region in the map has different scalaring factors because it has different impact on the final result, which can be determined by the following equation 1:

$$A_i = \frac{1}{4\pi} \int_{\left(\phi_i - \frac{\Delta\phi}{2}\right)}^{\left(\phi_i + \frac{\Delta\phi}{2}\right)} \int_{\left(\phi_i - \frac{\Delta\theta}{2}\right)}^{\left(\phi_i + \frac{\Delta\theta}{2}\right)} \sin(\theta)\, d\theta\, d\phi \tag{1}$$

To render the target under arbitrary illumination, the virtual light is mapped onto the sphere map first. Then the sphere map is converted to the Longitude-Latitude map. So the relighting problem can be solved by linear combination of the basis images.

### 2.3 Novel View Synthesis

The novel view synthesis algorithm is employed to synthesize the image under arbitrary view position. This technique is based on two or three sample images and the primary process is the tirlinear tensor operation, which is quite fit to our application.

To accelerate the process, we take two sample images, extract the putative match points[15] and then calculate a 3 × 3 × 3 basis trilinear tensor matrix $T_i^{jl}$[16]. To acquire novel image of the object, a 3 × 3 rotation homography $R$ and a 3 × 1 translation vector $t$ should be specified, and the new tensor $G_i^{jk}$ will be calculated in equation 2 [16]:

$$G_i^{jk} = R_l^k T_i^{jl} + t^k a_i^j \qquad (2)$$

Using new tensor and sample images, the new novel image can be rendered.

## 3   Experiments

Regarding to the two different algorithms, diverse verification experiments are carried out separately according to different modules in this section.

To verify the accuracy of this relighting algorithm, we design a new approach that compare the histograms of the $R, G, B$ channel as well as the luminance channel. In addition, the mean value and variance of the two images are calculated. Here we show the analysis results of a example relighting result and the real image in Table 1. The range of error between image pair is limited to a very small fraction. This experiment proves the method used for image-based relighting is extremely accurate and efficient.

**Table 1.** Statistical result of the image pair

| Channel | Mean Value | | Variance | | Error |
|---------|------------|------------|----------|------------|-------|
|         | Our Method | Real Photo | Our Method | Real Photo | |
| Red | 127 | 128 | 89.16 | 93.29 | 0.03% |
| Green | 115 | 115 | 89.08 | 94.54 | 0.03% |
| Blue | 120 | 122 | 90.81 | 95.77 | 0.02% |
| Luminance | 119 | 119 | 81.94 | 88.04 | 0.02% |

Considering the interpolation and extrapolation characteristic of novel view algorithm, the criterion is that the result satisfies people's vision effect and the physical distortions of the target object occur in an acceptable range. Figure 2 shows the experiment result of this module, which is also the final novel result of this framework.

**Fig. 2. Novel View Results.** The left above image is the reference image and the left below image is the generated new source image. The other images are the synthesized novel view images that we specify the camera move around the Z-axis of the target from left to right.

## 4   Conclusion and Future Work

In this paper we present a framework to satisfy practical requirements of observing objects in various environments, especially the specular and shadow details on the surface. And we choose the image-based methods to avoid calculating 3D information or model. In the future, we will still do some researches in these aspects: accelerating the process of relighting, improving the accuracy of novel view methods, extending the novel view algorithm that can observe the target globally.

**Acknowledgments.** This research is sponsored by 863 National High Technology R&D Program of China (No. 2006AA01Z307), National Natural Science Foundation of China (No. 60403044) and partially sponsored by Omron company.

## References

1. Kajiya, J.T.: Anisotropic reflection models. In: SIGGRAPH '85. Proceedings of the 12th annual conference on Computer graphics and interactive techniques, pp. 15–21. ACM Press, New York (1985)
2. Jensen, H.W., Marschner, S.R., Levoy, M., Hanrahan, P.: A practical model for subsurface light transport. In: SIGGRAPH '01. Proceedings of the 28th annual conference on Computer graphics and interactive techniques, pp. 511–518. ACM Press, New York (2001)
3. Nimeroff, J., Simoncelli, E., Dorsey, J.: Efficient rerendering of naturally illuminated environments. In: Eurographics Rendering Workshop 1994, Darmstadt, Germany. Springer, Heidelberg (1994)

4. Debevec, P., Hawkins, T., Tchou, C., Duiker, H.-P., Sarokin, W., Sagar, M.: Acquiring the reflectance field of a human face. In: SIGGRAPH '00. Proceedings of the 27th annual conference on Computer graphics and interactive techniques, pp. 145–156. ACM Press/Addison-Wesley Publishing Co., New York (2000)
5. Adelson, E.H., Bergen, J.R.: The plenoptic function and the elements of early vision. Computational Models of Visual Processing, 3.20 (2001)
6. Debevec, P.E., Taylor, C.J., Malik, J.: Modeling and rendering architecture from photographs: A hybrid geometry and image-based approach. In: Proc. SIGGRAPH'96, pp. 11–20. ACM Press, New Orleans, LS, USA (1996)
7. Criminisi, A., Reid, I., Zisserman, A.: Single View Metrology. International Journal of Computer Vision 40, 123–148 (2000)
8. Oh, B.M., Chen, M., Dorsey, J., Durand, F.: Image-based modeling and photo editing. In: SIGGRAPH '01. Proceedings of the 28th annual conference on Computer graphics and interactive techniques, pp. 433–442. ACM Press, New York (2001)
9. Beier, T., Neely, S.: Feature-Based Image Metamorphosis. In: ACM SIGGRAPH Computer Graphics, vol. 26, pp. 35–42. ACM Press, New York (1992)
10. Seitz, S.M., Dyer, C.R.: Physically-Valid View Synthesis By Image Interpolation. In: IEEE Workshop on Representation of Visual Scenes, p. 18. IEEE Computer Society Press, Los Alamitos (1995)
11. Seitz, S.M., Dyer, C.R.: View Morphing. In: SIGGRAPH '96. Proceedings of the 23rd annual conference on Computer graphics and interactive techniques, pp. 21–30. ACM Press, New York (1996)
12. Levoy, M., Hanrahan, P.: Light field rendering. In: SIGGRAPH '96. Proceedings of the 23rd annual conference on Computer graphics and interactive techniques, pp. 31–42. ACM Press, New York (1996)
13. Gortler, S.J., Grzeszczuk, R., Szeliski, R., Cohen, M.F.: The lumigraph. In: SIGGRAPH '96. Proceedings of the 23rd annual conference on Computer graphics and interactive techniques, pp. 43–54. ACM Press, New York (1996)
14. Peleg, S., Herman, J.: Panoramic Mosaic by Manifold Projection. In: IEEE Computer Society Conference on Computer Vision and Pattern Recognition, p. 338. IEEE Computer Society Press, Los Alamitos (1997)
15. http://www.cs.unc.edu/~blloyd/comp290-089/fmatrix/
16. Avidan, S., Shashua, A.: Novel View Synthesis by Cascading Trilinear Tensors. In: IEEE Transactions on Visualization and Computer Graphics (TVCG), vol. 04, pp. 293–306. IEEE Computer Society Press, Los Alamitos (1998)

# Interactive Image Based Relighting with Physical Light Acquisition

Jianjun Yu, Xubo Yang, and Shuangjiu Xiao

Department of Computer Science and Engineering
Shanghai Jiao Tong University, Shanghai, China 200240
{jianjun-yu,yangxubo,xsjiu99}@sjtu.edu.cn

**Abstract.** We present an interactive image-based technique to relight real scene with physical light sources acquisition. Firstly, basis images of the real scene are acquired from a fixed viewpoint. Secondly, light direction is estimated and physical light image is captured. Thirdly, measurement image between the reference light image and the novel light image is computed for relighting scene. We demonstrate the technique by interactively relighting a pre-captured real scene using a hand held spotlight projecting light on a white paper.

**Keywords:** Interactive, Image-based Relighting, Physical Light Acquisition, Lighting Sensitive Display.

## 1  Introduction

Image-based relighting(IBL) techniques attract more and more research interest recently. It combines appropriate multiple images and generates novel illuminations in synthesized images[5]. Applications of IBL techniques range from real-time global illumination, digital arts, entertainment computing, light design to mixed reality.

In many applications, virtual scene is required to respond to physical light source or real world environment illuminations. For example, in augmented reality games, if the virtual scene is sensitive to the physical light sources and their change, the game content will integrate closely to the physical environment and enhance the immersiveness of the player. However current IBL techniques usually relight objects or scenes under virtual illuminations or natural/synthetic environments. Few works have addressed the issue of relighting real scenes with physical light source acquisition, and rarely for interaction purpose. Hašan et al[1] presented a fixed view-point interactive relighting. Sun et al[2] described an interactive relighting technique with dynamic BRDFs. Nayer et al proposed a concept of lighting sensitive display, called LSD, which measures the incident illumination and modified its content accordingly[7]. They needed a specially designed camera for acquiring environment light.

In this paper, we present a cheap approach to interactively relighting real scenes based on physical light source acquisition. It can reconstruct realistic appearances of the scenes, and is efficient enough to respond to the hand held

L. Ma, R. Nakatsu, and M. Rauterberg (Eds.): ICEC 2007, LNCS 4740, pp. 288–293, 2007.

light changes in real time. Our work is somewhat similar to LSD, however our method for light acquisition and tracking is much easier and cheaper.

## 2   Related Works

Relighting is not a new topic in computer graphics and considerable research has already been done in this field. In article [5], IBL technique was classified into three categories, namely: Reflectance-based, Basis Function-based and Plenoptic Function-based technique.

IBL techniques require no geometry at all. Nimeroff et al[10] used a technique of combining images to relight a scene. Due to the linearity of illumination, objects can be relit by creating a weighted sum of basis images. The weights are calculated using steering functions. Debevec et al[3] address a human face relighting technique, can acquire the reflectance field of a human face and use these measurements to render the face under arbitrary changes in lighting and viewpoint. Masselus et al[4] presents a Free-form Light Stage, a system that captures the reflectance field of an object using a free-moving hand-held light source. And the relighting image is created as a linear combination of basis images with the weights.

Verbeck and Greenberg figure out that "to correctly describe the physical characteristics of light sources, three attributes must be modeled: (1) the light source geometry, (2) the emitted spectral distribution, and (3) the luminous intensity distribution". While these attributes may be necessary and sufficient, they rarely lead to useful models of complex three-dimensional light sources. The problem is common to all point source models: the geometries and photometric distributions of most physical light sources are simply too complicated to describe accurately. The field-theoretic approach[9][6][8] that can be used to model arbitrarily complex three-dimensional light sources. Goesele at el[8] develop a method for dealing with complex light sources from acquisition to global illumination rendering by measuring real-world light sources using an optical filters.

## 3   Data Acquisition

To obtain basis data for relighting, Debevec et al describes a series of Light Stages, Masselus et al[4] represent a Freeform Stage and use four diffuse spheres to estimate light directions. We have designed equipment for data acquisition. Our setup of acquisition system (see Fig. 1) is a computer controlled semicircle arm with reference light sources attached to it. We use a Nikon D80 digital camera for acquiring data and 8 Watt white LED as point light sources. The subject is placed in the center of the stage and illuminated by the controlled light sources. For each light source position an image is captured. This process is repeated until the entire sphere of incident illumination is sampled at some resolution. Fig. 1 also displays several images, from the full set of images, illuminated from different directions.

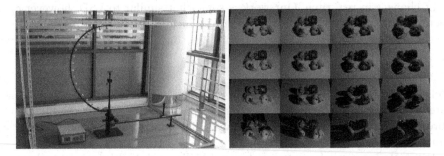

**Fig. 1.** Light stage and Basis images set

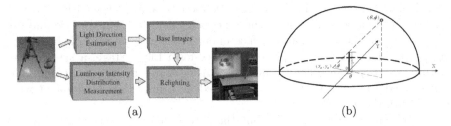

(a)                                                              (b)

**Fig. 2.** System overview and equipment & Light direction estimation

## 4    Interactive Relighting

We use a webcam camera to capture the physical light sources luminous intensity
distribution. Also we use a pole on the paper for estimating the light direction.
Then we employ an image-based relighting method to relight the scene under
arbitrary physical illumination. The main modules of our system is shown in
Fig. 2(a).

### 4.1    Light Direction Estimation

We detect the shadow of pole by using Canny edge detector. The direction of
light can be computed with the two vertices of the shadow and the position of
the pole. Fig. 2(b) and Equation 1 show how to estimate the light direction.

$$\theta = \begin{cases} \pi - \arctan(x_s/y_s) \text{ if } x_s \geq 0 \\ \pi + \arctan(x_s/y_s) \text{ if } x_s < 0 \end{cases}$$

$$\phi = \arctan\left(L/\sqrt{x_s^2 + y_s^2}\right) \tag{1}$$

### 4.2    Luminous Intensity Distribution Measurement

**Theoretical Framework.** We first introduce the mathematical notation used
throughout this document. This notation is summarized in Table 1.

**Table 1.** Mathematical Notation

| Symbol | Meaning |
|---|---|
| $L_{di}(x,y)$ | reference light source radiance passing through pixel $(x,y)$ from $di$ direction |
| $\hat{L}_{di}(x,y)$ | novel light source radiance passing through pixel $(x,y)$ from $di$ direction |
| $I_{L,di}(x,y)$ | irradiance caused by $L_{di}(x,y)$ on diffuse plane |
| $\hat{I}_{L,di}(x,y)$ | novel irradiance caused by $\hat{L}_{di}(x,y)$ on diffuse plane |
| $I_{O,di}(x,y)$ | irradiance caused by $L_{di}(x,y)$ on object |
| $\hat{I}_{O,di}(x,y)$ | novel irradiance caused by $\hat{L}_{di}(x,y)$ on object |
| $LT_{di}(x,y)$ | diffuse plane's basis function at pixel $(x,y)$ |
| $OT_{O,di}(x,y)$ | object's basis function at pixel $(x,y)$ under $L_{di}(x,y)$ |
| $M_{L,di}(x,y)$ | measurement image between reference and novel light source at pixel $(x,y)$ |

According to Levin's Field Theory[9], which can accurately predict the direct illuminance at any point on any surface anywhere within the surrounding three dimensional space without requiring any knowledge of the geometry of the source or its distance from the surface being illuminated, the light distribution in region of interesting can be described as Fig.3. So we can represent a light source image by Equation 2.

$$I_{L,di}(x,y) = LT_{di}(x,y) \cdot L_{di}(x,y)$$
$$I_{O,di}(x,y) = OT_{O,di}(x,y) \cdot L_{di}(x,y) \tag{2}$$

So, Equation 3 describes object image with different direction incident illuminations:

$$I_O(x,y) = \sum_{di=1}^{N} OT_{O,di}(x,y) \cdot L_{di}(x,y) \tag{3}$$

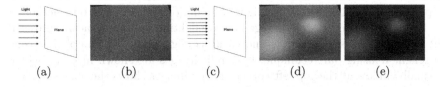

| (a) | (b) | (c) | (d) | (e) |

**Fig. 3. Reference and Physical Light.** (a),(c): show the distribution of reference incident and physical incident; (b),(d): show the distribution of incident in light image;(e)shows measurement image for visualization purposes.

### 4.3   Image-Based Relighting

Relighting is the process of rendering the captured reflection data as illuminated by some novel lighting conditions. Ray Tracing method traces rays of light from the eye back through the image plane into the scene. It assumes that there is one backward light ray belonging to each pixel and the color of the pixel is decided by the light ray. So, if we can measure the difference between the reference light image and the novel light image, then we can relight the object under novel light source. While we denote novel physical light source using $\hat{L}_{di}(x, y)$ and an object image under $\hat{L}_{di}(x, y)$ by $\hat{I}_O(x, y)$. We can get our relighting equation (see Equation 4) by employing the ray tracing idea. Then we get Equation 4:

$$
\begin{aligned}
\hat{I}_O(x, y) &= \sum_{di=1}^{\hat{N}} OT_{O,di}(x, y) \cdot \frac{\hat{I}_{L,di}(x, y)}{I_{L,di}(x, y)} \cdot L_{di}(x, y) \\
&= \sum_{di=1}^{\hat{N}} OT_{O,di}(x, y) \cdot L_{di}(x, y) \cdot M_{L,di}(x, y) \qquad (4)
\end{aligned}
$$

Equation 4 shows that we can use the basis images and measurement weights to relight object under novel light sources. Then, a measurement image (see Fig.3) between the reference light image and physical light image is calculated for relighting. In order to remove the effects of pole's shadow, we use an interpolation algorithm for compensation.

**Fig. 4.** System outputs with different illuminations

## 5 Experiments

In our experiment, we achieve real time performance using 2.8GHz CPU and the appearance of the scene including shadows and specularities is represented with the position of the hand held spotlight. The major advantage of our method is that it can handle successfully image-based relighting under interactive physical light illumination using a simple and cheap configuration. We sampled a scene and relight it using our technique. Four relit images are shown in Fig.4, where the small window at the top-left corner of each images shows the corresponding projected light on the white paper. We also use a paper with texture instead of the white paper which the hand held spotlight project on. The interesting result shows our light acquisition method is insensitive to the background. It means that we can implement system in more nature environment.

## 6 Conclusion and Future Work

In this paper we have presented a simple and cheap interactive image-based technique to relight real world scenes interactively with physical light acquisition. Our solution makes it possible to relight surfaces with complex material properties under interactive light illuminations using simple equipments.

Our algorithm may be improved in several ways. Since we only handled the linear relationship, light acquisition can be refined by a more efficient manner. To achieve more natural interactions, we can improve on the compensation technique as well.

**Acknowledgments.** This work is sponsored by 863 National High Technology R&D Program of China (No. 2006AA01Z307) and National Natural Science Foundation of China (No. 60403044) and partially by Omron company.

# References

1. Hašan, M., Pellacini, F., Bala, K.: Direct-to-indirect transfer for cinematic relighting. In: ACM SIGGRAPH, pp. 1089–1097. ACM Press, New York (2006)
2. Sun, X., Zhou, K., Chen, Y.Y., Lin, S., Shi, J.Y., Guo, B.N.: Interactive Relighting with Dynamic BRDFs. In: ACM SIGGRAPH. ACM Press, New York (2007)
3. Debevec, P., Hawkins, T., Tchou, C., Duiker, H.P., Sarokin, W., Sagar, M.: Acquiring the Reflectance Field of a Human Face. In: ACM SIGGRAPH, pp. 145–156. ACM Press, New York (2000)
4. Masselus, V., Dutre, P., Anrys, F.: The Free-form Light Stage. In: Eurographics Workshop on Rendering, pp. 26–28 (2002)
5. Choudhury, B., Chandran, S.: A Survey of Image-based Relighting Techniques. In: The Proceedings of the International Conference on Computer Graphics Theory and Applications (GRAPP) (2006)
6. Ashdown, I.: Near-Field Photometry: Measuring and Modeling Complex 3-D Light Sources. In: ACM SIGGRAPH '95 Course Notes - Realistic Input for Realistic Images, pp. 1–15 (1995), citeseer.ist.psu.edu/ashdown95nearfield.html
7. Nayar, S.K., Belhumeur, P.N., Boult, T.E.: Lighting Sensitive Display. In: Proceedings of ACM SIGGRAPH, Technical Sketch, vol. 23(4), pp. 963–979 (October 2004)
8. Goesele, M., Granierd, X., Heidrich, W., Seidel, H.P.: Accurate Light Source Acquisition and Rendering. ACM Transactions on Graphics 22(3), 621–630 (2003)
9. Levin, R.E.: Photo metric characteristics of light-controlling apparatus. Illuminating Engineering 66(4), 205–215 (1971)
10. Nimeroff, J., Simoncelli, E., Dorsey, J.: Efficient Rerendering of Naturally Illuminated Environments. IEEE Computer Graphics and Applications (1994)

# Real-Time Rendering of Daylight Sky Scene for Virtual Environment

Changbo Wang

Software Engineering Institute of East China Normal University, Shanghai, China
cbwang@cad.zju.edu.cn

**Abstract.** Realistic rendering of sky scene is important in virtual environment. Traditional methods are mostly based on skybox, thus failing to realistically simulate the change of sky scene under different weathers and conditions. In this paper, a new sky light model under different weathers for virtual environment is proposed. We first analyze the atmosphere characters of sky scene, and calculate the light path and light intensity into eyes through the atmosphere considering atmospheric scattering and refraction. Then for different weathers, by adapting a path tracing algorithm, the intensity distribution of sky light is gained. we also adopt the scattered volume model and GPU techniques to accelerate the calculation. Finally, various sky scenes in sunny day, foggy day, raining day and that with rainbow under different conditions are realistically rendered in real time.

## 1 Introduction

Real-time rendering of outer-scene has always been a hotspot in virtual environment. Although the sky is one of the most common scene in virtual rendering systems, the sky scenes are quite difficult to be modeled and rendered realistically due to the complex mechanisms of interactions among the molecules, particles, light and the environment. A realistic sky scene will greatly improve the reality of the virtual environment when walkthrough.

Recently skybox technique is mainly used in virtual environment when rendering sky scene, but due to the simpleness of skybox, it could not show the realistic changes of sky scene in different weathers, such as sunny day, foggy and raining day, snowing day, et al. In order to simulate the dynamic changes of the sky scene, we must consider the physical character of light and particles in atmosphere, especially the scattering and refraction of sky light. For atmospheric scattering, in 1986, Max et al [1]introduced a single scattering model for light diffusion to generate haze in the atmosphere. in 1993, Nishita et al [2] proposed a metaball model to render the scattering effect of atmosphere which is based on the change of atmosphere density. Later, they introduced a method taking into account the multiple anisotropic scattering to render clouds and sky. In 2000, Dobashi et al [3] proposed an easy method for rendering shadows of clouds and shafts of light. Dobashi et al [4] proposed a fast rendering method for atmospheric scattering effects by using graphics hardware. Jackel et al. [5] simulated

L. Ma, R. Nakatsu, and M. Rauterberg (Eds.): ICEC 2007, LNCS 4740, pp. 294–303, 2007.

the Mie Scattering in 1997, and Nishita [6] used an improved sky illumination model to render the fog scene. But this approach of calculating the scattering effect for air particles is quite time-consuming. Nakamae et al.[7] proposed a continuous tone representation of the illuminated object by sky light. Sun et al. [8] proposed practical analytic method to render the single scattering in fog, mist and haze in real time. Nseda and Volksan [9] have calculated the atmosphere refraction and compared with experimental data, but they could not simulate it. By now little works have been reported about the real-time rendering of sky scene under different weather conditions.

In this paper, we propose a new physically based approach to model and render the sky scene under different weathers. We first analyze the character of atmosphere in sky scene, and establish a spacial sky light model considering atmospheric scattering and refraction. For different weathers, by adapting a path tracing algorithm, the intensity distribution of sky light into eyes is calculated. Finally, various sky scenes in sunny day, foggy day, raining day and that with rainbow under different conditions and different viewpoints are realistically rendered in real time.

The reminder of this paper is organized as follows: the next section we describe the sky light model considering the scattering and refraction. In section 3, we calculate the sky light and rendering different sky scene under different weathers. The implementation details are described in section 4. Experimental results with dynamic real-time rendering of sky scene are presented in section 5. Conclusions and discussion for future works are given at last.

## 2   Modeling of Sky Scene

### 2.1   The Character of Atmosphere in Sky Scene

The earth's atmosphere is categorized into 4 layers - troposphere, stratosphere, mesosphere and thermosphere. The earth's atmosphere is composed of many gases. Gravity holds the atmosphere close to the earth's surface and explains why the density of the atmosphere decreases with altitude. The density and pressure of the atmosphere vary with altitude and depends on solar heating and geomagnetic activity.

In addition to the various gases, atmosphere also contains water vapor, dust particles, etc. The molecules and particles absorb energy at discrete wavelengths, which are determined by their internal properties. In addition to absorption, molecules and particles also scatter energy out from its original direction. Suns white light is scattered into the viewing ray as shown in Figure 1. The scattered light is received at the earths surface from all directions as diffuse skylight or daylight.

On rainy environment, there are an enormous number of particles floating in the air. The density of raindrops is decreased exponentially as the increase of the raindrops' size. Although big raindrops account for only a small portion in rainfall, their effects on the scattering of lighting in the whole scene are apparent.

We adopt the following statistical model for numerous raindrops in a rain[11]:

$$F(r) = [1 - e^{-(\frac{r}{a})^m}] \tag{1}$$

where $F(r)$ is the accumulated mass of raindrop with radius from zero to $r$, $r$ is the radius of a raindrop, $m$ is the exponent, for rain, $m$ is equal to 2.25, $a$ is the parameter about the amount of auriferous intensity, and its value depends on the rainfall amount. In this way, we are able to generate the spatial distributions of raindrops with different radii, and simulate different sizes of particles in the virtual environment.

## 2.2    The Atmosphere Scattering and Refraction

For a clear sky, various types of atmospheric particles are responsible for the scattering. There are mainly two kinds of scattering: Rayleigh scattering and Mie scattering.

Particles smaller than the wavelength and usually less than 0.1 times the wavelength of light exhibit Rayleigh scattering [3]. Rayleigh scattering is observed by molecules in the earth's atmosphere. The amount of scattering for such particles is inversely proportional to the 4-th power of the wavelength.

Larger particles scatter strongly in the forward direction and this scattering phenomenon is called Mie scattering. The scattering is inversely proportional to the second order of the size of the particles and is independent of wavelength. When foggy or raining day, there are more Mie scattering.

For different weathers, the particles is changed great, so we should extend the conventional single particle scattering model to accommodate the multiple particle scattering.

Above the light is taken as line when they travel through atmosphere. But in fact they are curve. Atmospheric refraction is responsible for the bending of light-rays in the atmosphere. It is a result of the continuous decrease in the refractive index of the air as a function of altitude. A well-known consequence of this phenomenon is the apparently elliptic shape of the setting or rising sun, and the color of sun is also more red when rising.

The refractive index of air of the Earth is very close to 1, and depends slightly on its pressure and temperature following Edlen's semi-empirical law [10], as shown in Eq. (2):

$$n = 1 + 10^{-6}(776.2 + 4.36 \times 10^{-8}\nu^2)\frac{P}{T} - 0.1127\frac{e}{T} \tag{2}$$

In the above formula, $\nu$ is the wave-number of the light in $cm^{-1}$. $P$ is the pressure in $kPa$ , $e$ is vapor and $T$ the temperature in $K$. Since the pressure and temperature varies within the atmosphere, we get a refractive index gradient which is responsible for atmospheric refractions. Although the variations in n are quite small, the large distances travelled by light-rays in the atmosphere makes refraction effects observable and sometimes important.

We can derive the quantitative formula of refraction index in the term of air pressure, temperature, and vapor along with the attitude under different weather conditions, and then calculate the refractional track of light through the atmosphere to simulate the sky scene. In order to improve the calculate speed, we can divide the earth attitude into several layer. These layers have slightly different refractive indices.

## 2.3    Calculation of Light Intensity

Figure 1 shows the path of a single beam of sky light to the eyes of the viewer. All particles distributed along the sight ray will transmit the scattered light to the eye and these intensities are integrated by the following equation:

$$I_v = \int_0^{2\pi} \int_{-\frac{\pi}{2}}^{\frac{\pi}{2}} \int_{s_{cp}=s}^{s_v} I_\alpha(S_{cp}) \sum_{i=0}^{N_s-1} (D_{\alpha,i}[\lambda, \theta] * p_i(S_{cp}))$$

$$*exp[-\sum_{i=0}^{N_s-1} \gamma_i \int_{s_{cp}}^{s_p} p_i(S_b)dS_b]dS_{cp}d\alpha d\delta \tag{3}$$

where $D_{\alpha,i}[\lambda, \theta]$ is the phasic function of direction $\alpha$, $p_i(s_{cp})$ is the density of particle $i$ at the position $s_{cp}$, $\lambda_i$ is the scattered coefficient of particle $i$, and $N_s$ is the number of scattered particles in the sky. The first term of the interior integral shows the summed intensity of scattered light by all particles located within the interval of the sight ray from $S_{cp}$ to $S_v$ with respect to the sky light in direction $\alpha$ interacting with the second term of the interior integral shows the energy attenuation from $s_{cp}$ to to $S_v$. Exterior integral account for skylights from all direction in the sky. When $N_s = 1$, Eq.(3) is reduced to the single particle scattering model.

In Eq.(3), $I_\alpha(s_{cp})$ is the intensity of the directional skylight. For different weathers, it can take different values.

Then we can calculate the light scattering through the whole ray path. Here we adopt the skylight model proposed by Nishita [1]. The sky is divided into several

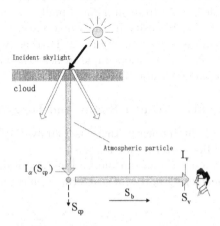

**Fig. 1.** The path of a single beam from the sun to the viewer's eye

light straps, the intensity of each light strap is determined by the intensity of a sampling ray. Because the calculation of skylight is time-consuming, we simply assume the magnitude of the intensity of skylight at an arbitrary point as a function of height. Therefore, we pre-calculate the intensity at every height, then establish a lookup table.

Nevertheless, Eq.(3) does not present a direct solution and may cost much computation. it is then necessary to simplify this formula. Considering the diffuse illumination of the sky scene, we can ignore the direction of the skylights and regard the skylight uniformly from various directions as a diffuse light source and apply the sky luminance model directly. Then we can get the entire incident intensity of skylight at an arbitrary point to account for sky rays from different directions, and adopt a uniform phase function.

To avoid calculating the scattered light at each particle, we employ the concept of scattered volume [5]. Because the density of each kind of particles varies slowly. We piecewise sample the atmosphere by concentration of particles in the visual direction with respect to the distribution of the sky luminance. For each segment, we adopt the average value of the same kind of particles. The number of segments can be adjusted according to the precision. Finally, we can get the total intensity received by the viewer's eye.

## 3    Rendering of Sky Scene

### 3.1    Rendering Algorithm of Path Tracing

Since it is in outer-door and the atmosphere space is so big, the traditional rendering methods such as ray tracing and radiosity methods are not fit for. Here we propose a novel rendering algorithm: path tracing algorithm consider refraction.

The main idea of this algorithm is: firstly one ray is shot out from viewpoint to one sample point in the rendering screen plane, then conversely tracing this ray, which is along the refraction path $L(OP)$. For each point $S$ in the path, we can gain the refraction path $L(SP_s)$ from sunlight. Finally by the method in section 3.2, calculate the scattering intensity in the whole path, that is integral along this path. The algorithm is shown in Figure 2. Further, we can use adaptive sample algorithm, that is more subtle sample in near the viewport, and coarse sample at the screen plane for these blue sky areas.

### 3.2    Rendering Sky Scene Under Sunny and Foggy Day

When calculating the light intensity, there is mainly Rayleigh scattering for sunny day, and more Mie-scattering for foggy sky.

For simplification, we use a uniform phasic function of direction, $D(g, \theta)$, to show both Rayleigh scattering and Mie scattering, which is used in Eq.(3) [5]. That is:

$$D(g, \theta) = \frac{(3(1 - g^2)}{(2(2 + g^2))} \frac{(1 + \cos^2(\theta)}{(1 + g^2 - 2g\cos(\theta))^{3/2}} \tag{4}$$

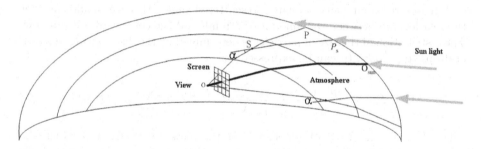

**Fig. 2.** Rendering algorithm of path tracing

Where $g = \frac{5}{9}u - (\frac{4}{3} - \frac{25}{81}u^2)x^{-1/3} + x^{1/3}$, $x = \frac{5}{9}u + \frac{125}{729}u^3 + (\frac{64}{27} - \frac{325}{243}u^2 + \frac{1250}{218}u^4)^{1/2}$. When $g = 0$, the above equation is the Rayleigh scattering, and $u$ depends on the weather conditions, changing among $[0.7, 0.85]$.

### 3.3  Rendering Sky Scene Under Raining Day

Unlike clear-days, there is normally no-direct solar light in raining scenes. Previous works mainly focus on calculation of light scattering by small particles in clear days, but the scattering mechanism in raining days is more complex due to the existence of different kinds of particles, such as raindrops, mists, aerosols, etc.

During raining days, the sky illumination is caused mainly by diffuse sky light rather than the direct solar light. All particles should interact with the sky light coming from different directions. Considering the diffuse property of the rainy sky, we can regard the skylight as a uniform light casting in from different directions within semi-sphere. Then we can express the entire incident intensity of skylight from different directions at an arbitrary point with a uniform phase function.

Just as in Eq.(3), for rainy day, the intensity $I_v$ should be attenuated through the path $S_{cp}$ to $S_v$, before the light is received by the viewer. This attenuation includes the scattering of small atmosphere particles and the refraction attenuation caused by encountering raindrops. The final intensity reaching the viewer's eye is:

$$\acute{I}_v = I_v R^{N(SV)} \tag{5}$$

Where $N(SV)$ is the number of segments along the path. Here $R^{N(SV)}$ is the attenuation of raindrops, $R$ is the average refraction index of raindrops, $N(SV)$ is the number of rain streaks through the path $S_{cp}$ to $S_v$.

### 3.4  Rendering Rainbow in Sky Scene

Rainbow is a beautiful phenomenon that happens immediately after raining in sky scene. But it is not easy to realistically render in real time.

To render the rainbow, here we adopt the formula of light scattering discussed previously. However, in this case the incident light now is the parallel sunbeam and the scattered intensity is related to scattered angle. Also, we should consider the relationship between the amount of rainfall and the color width of rainbow. The distribution of the size of particles is determined by the distributing function of drops [10]. So Eq.(6)can be expressed as:

$$I_s^j = I_\alpha^j \frac{1 - exp[-(s_{j+1} - s_j)\sum_{i=0}^{N_s-1} p_{i,j}\lambda_i]}{\sum_{i=0}^{N_s-1} p_{i,j}\lambda_i} \times \sum_{i=0}^{N_s-1} p_{i,j}D_i[\lambda, \theta] \qquad (6)$$

where $I_\alpha^j$ is the intensity of sunbeam, $\theta$ is the phasic angle from at which the sunbeam interact with the particles to transmit the color rays to the viewer's eye. We can produce the different effects of rainbow with respect to different amount of rainfall by adjusting the parameter $p_{i,j}(s_v)$.

As the scattering property is related to the size of a particles, we need to sample the atmosphere subtly, which would cost a lot of time. To balance our computing source and the final effect, we perform a fine sampling from $129°$to $138°$(scattered angle). This method not only accelerates the speed of rendering, but also seamlessly blends rainbow and the sky together well. At the same time, we can simulate the dynamic process of rainbow from appearing to vanish by adjusting the density of particles in the atmosphere.

## 4   Implementation

### 4.1   Implementation Steps

The implementation of our algorithm can be described as follows: (1) According to the weather type of sky scene, we set up the certain sky light propagation model. (2) For each sample point, we use the method discussed in Section 3.1 to calculate the trajectory and the light intensity of the light ray that passes through both the view point and that point, considering the refraction and scattering. (3) After rendering the scenes of the sea, landscape or building, and synthesizing them with the sky scene, we also render the raining and snowing based on particle systems, then we get the whole realistic dynamic sky scene under different weathers in virtual environment. (4) By adjusting the sky light model and the related parameters, we can simulate various dynamic processes of sky scenes.

### 4.2   Luminance Transform

By now, we have calculated the spectral intensity distribution of light incident into the eyes of an observer taking into account the interaction between light and various kinds of particles in virtual environment. But if we want to render the scattering effect realistically, we should transform the energy of spectrum to luminance perceived by the eyes.

According to the theory of human vision system(HVS), when perceiving an image, human eyes are more sensitive to the regions of moderate intensity than those of higher or lower intensity. Conventional linear transform method between the light energy and illumination is less adequate. Here we propose a new HVS based transform model as follows, which is in some extent like the form of bi-logarithmic curve, that is:

$$\begin{cases} 255*(log_{10}(x-a)+b)(x \geq a+1) \\ 255*(-log_{10}(-x+a+2)+b)(x < a+1) \end{cases} \tag{7}$$

where x is the intensity,a b is the curvilinear transformative parameters, which satisfies:$10^b = a+2$; $10^{1-b} = I_{max} - a$($I_{max}$ is the maximum intensity).

In this way, the effect of light scattering in virtual environments can be interpreted more realistically conformed to the optical characteristic of human eye.

### 4.3   Other Acceleration Techniques

In the before, we have used the scattered volume model and the path tracing algorithm to accelerate the calculation.

We also utilize GPU techniques to accelerate our scene rendering by storing the information of light etc. as texture in graphics card, and update it every frame. This greatly improve the rendering speed. The highlight on the car, rain splash effect on road and the other special effects in virtual environment are also generated with GPU acceleration.

## 5   Results

Based on the above models, we achieve the real-time rendering of sky scene on a PC with PIV3.0GHZ, 2.0GB, NVIDIA GeForce FX7900 graphics card, the average rendering speed reaches 20 frames per second.

Figure 3 shows the sky scene under sunny day. From it, we can see that the sky scenes are different between sea scene and landscape scene, that is because the vapors different, so atmosphere refraction is different and sky scene show different color. Figure 4 shows foggy and raining sky scenes with light scattering.

**Fig. 3.** Simulated sky scenes at sunny day

**Fig. 4.** Simulated sky scene under foggy and raining day

**Fig. 5.** Simulated snowing sky scene and the sky scenes with rainbow

The effect of light scattering is much better than that by directly applying the fog function of OpenGL. Figure 5 shows the snowing sky scene and the sky scene with rainbow after raining, we also can simulate the appear and disappear of rainbow. From these results, we can get that our simulated results is realistic.

## 6   Conclusions

we propose a new method to render the sky scene under different weather conditions for virtual environment. Firstly we consider the atmosphere scattering and refraction, build the sky light calculation model of sky scene. Then we use several methods to accelerate the rendering speed, including using the scattered volume model to simplify the calculation of scattering light intensity, and adapting a path tracing algorithm considering refraction to calculate the intensity distribution of sky light. Finally, various sky scenes in sunny day, foggy day, rainy day, and that with rainbow under different conditions and different viewpoints are realistically rendered in real time.

Future works include: real-time rendering of cloud to improve the reality of sky scene; simulating the scene under different weathers and further accelerating the rendering speed by exploiting the power of the techniques of GPU.

## Acknowledgements

This research was supported in part by 973 Program of China under Grant No. 2002CB312101, Natural Science Foundation of China under Grant No. 60603076.

## References

1. Max, N.: Atmospheric Illumination and Shadows. Computer Graphics, 117–124 (1986)
2. Nishita, T., Takao, S., Tadamura, K., et al.: Display of the earth taking into account atmospheric scattering. In: Computer Graphics(ACM SIGRAPH'93), vol. 27(4), pp. 175–182 (1993)
3. Dobashi, Y., Kaneda, K., Yamashita, H., Okita, T., Nishita, T.: A simple, efficient method for realistic animation of clouds, pp. 19–28 (2000)
4. Dobashi, Y., Yamamoto, T., Nishita, T.: Interactive rendering method for displaying shafts of light, pp. 31–37 (2000)
5. Jackel, D., Walter, B.: Modeling and rendering of the atmosphere using mie-scattering. Computer Graphics Forum 16(4), 201–210 (1997)
6. Nishita, T., Dobashi, Y., Nakamae, E.: Display of clouds taking into account multiple anisotropic scattering and sky light, pp. 379–386 (1996)
7. Nishita, T., Nakamae, E.: Continuous tone representation of three- dimensional objects illuminated by sky light. Computer Graphics 20(3), 125–132 (1986)
8. Sun, B., Ramamoorthi, R., Narasimhan, S., Nayar, K.: A practical analytic single scattering model for real time rendering. Computer Graphics 24(3), 1040–1049 (2005)
9. Neda, Z., Volkan, S.: Flatness of the setting Sun. Journal of Physics 1, 379–385 (2002)
10. U.S. Standard Atmosphere 1976, U.S. Government Printing Office, Washington D.C. (1976)
11. Best, A.: The size distribution of raindrops. Quarterly Journal of the RoyaMeteo-rological 76(16), 16C36 (1950)

# Robust Dense Depth Acquisition
# Using 2-D De Bruijn Structured Light

Zhiliang Xu, Lizhuang Ma, and Wuzheng Tan

Department of Computer Science & Engineering
Shanghai Jiaotong University
No. 800, Dongchuan Rd., Shanghai 200240, P.R. China
{xuzhiliang,ma-lz,tanwuzheng}@sjtu.edu.cn

**Abstract.** We present a new dense depth acquisition method using 2-D
De Bruijn structured light, which is robust to various textures and is
able to reconstruct dense depth maps of moving and deforming objects.
A 2-D binary De Bruijn pattern is emitted to the target object by an
off-the-shelf projector. Fast dynamic programming based stereo matching is performed on images taken from two different views. The depth
is obtained by robust least square triangulation. The advantages include
that we do not need to take image sequences with different illumination
patterns and do not assume that the surface for reconstruction has uniform texture. Experimental results show that shapes can be efficiently
obtained in good quality by the proposed approach. We believe that our
approach is a good choice in applications of acquiring depth maps for
moving scenes with inexpensive equipments.

**Keywords:** Depth acquisition, range sensing, 3-D model reconstruction,
De Bruijn sequence.

## 1 Introduction

### 1.1 Related Work

Scene depth acquisition is a rapidly expanding field, with applications in robotics,
modeling and virtual reality. Among them, binocular stereo [1], [2] is a convenient
and inexpensive approach. It is also a hot field of recent researches.

Traditional passive stereo suffers from ambiguities in large textureless areas.
To solve this problem, structured light is projected onto the object to endow it
with a coded pattern, which is referred to as active stereo [3]. To obtain dense
depth maps, time multiplex schemes are commonly used, such as Rusinkiewicz et
al. [4] and Scharstein and Szeliski [5]. In their works, since a series of patterns are
projected sequentially, the objects to be reconstructed is either still or restricted
to only slow motion, compared to the patterns cycled in 60Hz.

Generally, in active stereo, it is assumed that the surfaces to be reconstructed
have uniform texture. Otherwise, the pattern received by the camera is hard to
decode. To deal with the texture problem in active stereo scheme, Scharstein and
Szeliski [5] project a series of black and white stripes as well as their inverses,

L. Ma, R. Nakatsu, and M. Rauterberg (Eds.): ICEC 2007, LNCS 4740, pp. 304–314, 2007.
© IFIP International Federation for Information Processing 2007

which requires about 20 patterns to be projected sequentially to obtain the dense depth map with $1024 \times 768$ resolution.

Other related works include Lavoie et al. [6] and Pagès et al. [7]. Their methods are similar to ours in that they use only one light pattern and take a single image of the illuminated object. However, Lavoie et al. [6] encode the structured light on the intersections of a grid pattern, and match the code only where reliable decoding is available. Thus a sparse reconstruction is obtained as the result. Pagès et al. [7] use 1-D color De Bruijn sequences so that the length of the pattern can cover the whole image and more information can be retrieved, and thus give a dense reconstruction. But color patterns are very sensitive to the textures on the surface.

## 1.2   Overview of Our Approach

In this paper, we propose a dense depth acquisition method which needs only a single image pair taken simultaneously, and avoids the difficulty in decoding the structured light pattern. As a result, our method is able to acquire depth maps of moving and deforming objects.

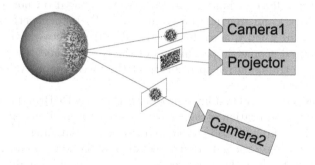

**Fig. 1.** Equipment setup of the dense depth acquisition system. The projector emits a 2-D binary De Bruijn pattern to the target object (a sphere). Camera #1 (optional) is placed closely above the projector. Camera #2 is located at an angle (about $20°$) of the projector.

For hardware, we only require one off-the-shelf projector and at least one off-the-shelf camera. Another camera is needed optionally if the user is unwilling to calibrate the projector. The experiment setup is shown in Fig. 1. The projector emits a 2-D De Bruijn pattern onto the target object. One camera (the optional one) is located above the projector, as close as possible. Another camera is placed at an angle (typically $20°$) with respect of the first camera. From now on, we assume that two cameras are used. The alternative system using only one camera is only a simple modification, which will be discussed in section 3.2. In our experiments, these two cameras are synchronized. Stereo matching and triangulation is then performed on the two images taken simultaneously to acquire the depth of the object.

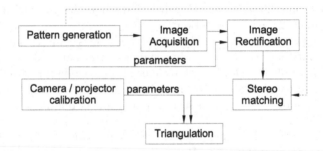

**Fig. 2.** The flow chart of our system. Two images are needed for stereo matching. The dotted line means that the projected pattern can be substituted by the image taken by Camera #1.

The flow chart of our system is shown in Fig. 2. We first generate a binary 2-D De Bruijn pattern and emit it onto the target object. In the image acquisition step, two images of the target object are taken. These images are then rectified so that camera's radial distortion effect is removed and epipolar lines correspond to horizontal scanlines of images. Stereo matching based on normalized cross correlation (NCC) and dynamic programming (DP) is then performed on the stereo image pair. Finally, according to the disparities between the image pair and the recovered geometric parameters of the cameras and the projector, we use least square triangulation to reconstruct the metric depth values for every pixel of the object.

In the following, we will first introduce our 2-D binary De Bruijn pattern in section 2. Geometry calibration of cameras and projector is discussed in section 3. We will introduce our NCC and DP based dense stereo matching algorithm in section 4, and least square triangulation in section 5. In section 6, some experimental results are given to show the effectiveness of our approach. Finally, the paper is ended with a conclusion and discussion in section 7.

**Notations.** In this paper, we refer to the image taken by the first camera, which is placed just above the projector as $I_1$, the image taken by another camera as $I_2$, and the image emitted by the projector $I_p$. The projection matrices of the cameras are denoted as $\mathbf{M}_1$ and $\mathbf{M}_2$ respectively.

## 2   2-D De Bruijn Sequences

To reduce the ambiguities in stereo correspondence to the greatest extent, we need an illumination pattern with the property that every small local window appears only once in the whole pattern. Moreover, the pattern should be binary-colored so that it is robust to various surface textures. Traditional structured light patterns based on 1-D binary De Bruijn sequences are not enough, since they are limited on the length. In theory, the length of a 1-D De Bruijn sequence with unique sub-window size of 5 is only 32 $(= 2^5)$, which is too short to cover

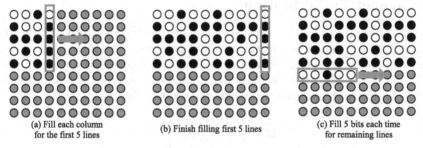

(a) Fill each column
for the first 5 lines

(b) Finish filling first 5 lines

(c) Fill 5 bits each time
for remaining lines

**Fig. 3.** Our algorithm for generating 2-D De Bruijn sequences

**Fig. 4.** A part of 2-D binary De Bruijn sequence with $64 \times 48$ resolution. The pattern is enlarged to make every code bit distinguishable to the reader. Note that there is no repeated $5 \times 5$ sub-window in this pattern.

the whole image. However, if we use 2-D De Bruijn sequence with $5 \times 5$ (5 rows by 5 columns) unique windows, the size becomes $2^{5 \times 5}$ ($\approx 5792 \times 5792$), which is adequately large for our application.

Although theoretically there exist 2-D De Bruijn sequences of $5 \times 5$ unique sub-windows with a large size, it is rather difficult to search for a valid one in practice. Here, we use a new algorithm for searching valid 2-D De Bruijn sequences, which is a modification of Morano et al. [8]. Suppose that the size of unique sub-windows is $5 \times 5$, as illustrated in Fig. 3, the algorithm starts with randomly assigning the first 5 bits of the first column. We choose to fill 5 bits each time to avoid early termination and save the memory for back-tracking. For filling a new 5-bit group, we randomly generate a 5-bit code (we call it test bits, in contrast to those currently determined bits), and check whether $5 \times 5$ windows containing the test bits collide with all currently determined bits. If not, the 5 test bits are reserved and become determined bits, and then we go on to fill another 5-bit group. Otherwise, we generate another random 5-bit code, and test for collision again. If all the 32 possible 5-bit codes have been tested, the algorithm comes to a failure. Then another trial should be aroused from scratch. After the first 5 rows are filled, each following rows are filled 5-bit by 5-bit in the same manner. Generally, about 5 to 8 trials are needed before obtaining such a part of valid 2-D De Bruijn sequence of size $512 \times 384$. A valid sequence can be obtained in about 5 minutes, which is satisfactory. A typical part of the pattern is shown in Fig. 4.

## 3  Geometric Calibration

In order to obtain the metric reconstruction of the object's depth, both intrinsic and extrinsic parameters of cameras and projector (optionally) are needed. Intrinsic parameters include focal length $f$, principal point $p_0 = (u_0, v_0)$, skew coefficient $\alpha$ and distortions $\mathbf{k}$. In practice, we only consider the first order distortion $k_1$. Extrinsic parameters include the rotation matrix

$$\mathbf{R} = \begin{pmatrix} r_{11} & r_{12} & r_{13} \\ r_{21} & r_{22} & r_{23} \\ r_{31} & r_{32} & r_{33} \end{pmatrix}, \tag{1}$$

and translation vector $T = (T_x, T_y, T_z)'$ of camera with respect to the world coordinate, which is defined by a reference object, such as a checkerboard.

### 3.1  Camera Calibration

Camera geometric calibration has been well studied by Tsai [9], Zhang et al. [10], and Heikkilä and Silvén [11], etc. In this paper, we employ the four-step approach of Heikkilä and Silvén [11], which is more convenient. Actually, other calibration methods and even self-calibration [12] can also be adopted. The only additional equipment needed for camera calibration is a checkerboard. Omitting the skew effect, the relationship between world coordinate $P_w = (X_w, Y_w, Z_w, 1)'$ and the pixel coordinate of its projection on the image $p = (u, v, 1)'$ can be represented by

$$(1 + k_1 r^2)u = f\frac{r_{11}X_w + r_{12}Y_w + r_{13}Z_w + T_x}{r_{31}X_w + r_{32}Y_w + r_{33}Z_w + T_z}, \tag{2}$$

$$(1 + k_1 r^2)v = f\frac{r_{21}X_w + r_{22}Y_w + r_{23}Z_w + T_y}{r_{31}X_w + r_{32}Y_w + r_{33}Z_w + T_z}. \tag{3}$$

where $r^2 = u^2 + v^2$. After we have estimated all the 14 unknowns using the method of [11], we rectify the radial distortion of the camera according to $k_1$, after which the camera model becomes a linear projection one, which can be written in matrix form as

$$Z_c \begin{bmatrix} u \\ v \\ 1 \end{bmatrix} = \begin{bmatrix} f & 0 & u_0 & 0 \\ 0 & f & v_0 & 0 \\ 0 & 0 & 1 & 0 \end{bmatrix} \begin{bmatrix} \mathbf{R} & T \\ \mathbf{0} & 1 \end{bmatrix} \begin{bmatrix} X_w \\ Y_w \\ Z_w \\ 1 \end{bmatrix} = \mathbf{M} \begin{bmatrix} X_w \\ Y_w \\ Z_w \\ 1 \end{bmatrix}, \tag{4}$$

where

$$Z_c = r_{31}X_w + r_{32}Y_w + r_{33}Z_w + T_z, \tag{5}$$

and

$$\mathbf{M} \overset{\Delta}{=} \begin{bmatrix} m_{11} & m_{12} & m_{13} & m_{14} \\ m_{21} & m_{22} & m_{23} & m_{24} \\ m_{31} & m_{32} & m_{33} & m_{34} \end{bmatrix} = \begin{bmatrix} f & 0 & u_0 & 0 \\ 0 & f & v_0 & 0 \\ 0 & 0 & 1 & 0 \end{bmatrix} \begin{bmatrix} \mathbf{R} & T \\ \mathbf{0} & 1 \end{bmatrix}. \tag{6}$$

This rectification is crucial, since the computational cost in stereo matching and triangulation can be dramatically reduced if we use linear projection models for camera and projector.

## 3.2 Projector Calibration

If only one camera is used in the system, as in many active stereo systems, stereo matching is performed between the image taken by camera and the pattern image emitted by the projector. That is, the role of image $I_1$ is replaced by $I_p$. In such a case, the projector has to be geometrically calibrated. Projector calibration is a tough task since the projector cannot take images of the scene. We solve this problem taking the advantage of our calibrated camera.

The projector is considered as the "reversed" camera, which projects the image on "CCD plane" *back* to the scene. We can use the same projection model for projector calibration. But unlike the camera, the world coordinates of the points projected into the scene have to be obtained with the help of the calibrated camera. We make the projector emit a checkerboard pattern onto the $Z_w = 0$ plane. The other two coordinate components ($X_w$ and $Y_w$) of the projected points on the plane are computed according to the pixel coordinates in the image taken by the calibrated camera. Formally, we solve for $X_w$ and $Y_w$ in the following linear equation set:

$$Z_c \begin{bmatrix} u \\ v \\ 1 \end{bmatrix} = \mathbf{M}_2 \begin{bmatrix} X_w \\ Y_w \\ 0 \\ 1 \end{bmatrix}, \tag{7}$$

where $u$ and $v$ are the homogeneous pixel coordinates of the point's projection on the image taken by camera, and $\mathbf{M}_2$ is the projection matrix of the calibrated camera. $u$, $v$ and $\mathbf{M}_2$ are already known to us by corner extraction and camera calibration. Now that we have the world coordinates of the points corresponding to the projected pattern, projector calibration can be continued in the same manner as camera calibration. Here we assume that the projector has no radial distortion and skew effect.

The advantages of using one calibrated camera and one calibrated projector in stereo matching include saving one camera, and avoiding the efforts to synchronize two cameras. But the disadvantages are that the projector calibration is more complicated, and there exists no self-calibration technique for recovering the geometry parameters of the projector. Additionally, we need to ensure that the scaled images $I_2$ and $I_p$ have similar pattern sizes. Otherwise, the stereo matching algorithm will be confused.

## 4 Stereo Matching

Although the original structured light pattern has the unique sub-window property, new ambiguities are aroused after camera's re-sampling and distortion caused by different view angles. So we cannot directly decode the images. On the contrary, NCC based robust stereo matching is used instead.

For sake of efficiency, the two stereo images $I_1$ and $I_2$ are further rectified using the method of Loop and Zhang [10], so that each epipolar line corresponding to horizontal scanlines of the images, and the disparities between two views only resides in the horizontal direction.

We use NCC as the basic match metric, thus the cost for matching pixel $p$ in $I_1$ with pixel $p + d$ in $I_2$ is

$$C_{NCC}(p,d) = \frac{\sum\limits_{q \in W_p} (I_1(q) - \bar{I}_1(p)) \cdot (I_2(q+d) - \bar{I}_2(p+d))}{\sqrt{\sum\limits_{q \in W_p} (I_1(q) - \bar{I}_1(p))^2 \cdot \sum\limits_{q \in W_p} (I_2(q+d) - \bar{I}_2(p+d))^2}}, \qquad (8)$$

where $d = (d_x, 0)'$ is the disparity, $W_p$ is the local aggregation window centered at pixel $p$, $\bar{I}_k(p)$ is the average intensity value of the pixels within the aggregation window centered at $p$. The effect of aggregation window size is twofold. The larger the aggregation window, the more robust the matching. But on the other hand, the aggregation window has to be small enough to avoid covering pixels from different depth levels. So we choose $5 \times 5$, which is moderate, to be the size of aggregation window throughout the paper. Equation (8) requires to compute the intensity differences between all the pixels in the local window and the average intensity for each $(pixel, disparity)$ pair, which is too computationally expensive. So we use the fast NCC algorithm proposed by Lewis [14] in our system.

The NCC cost is then reversed and normalized into the range of $[0, 1]$, with lower costs for more likely matches:

$$Cost(p,d) = \frac{1 - C_{NCC}(p,d)}{2}. \qquad (9)$$

Since the images are taken from different view points, and are possibly with different sample quality, even each small local window has a unique intensity encoding in the original light pattern, error matches between $I_1$ and $I_2$ will still occur, especially where the surface curvature is large. So global stereo matching algorithms such as dynamic programming (DP) [15] have to be utilized for depth optimization. We find that DP is an effective approach to solve the problem of error matches caused by pixel sampling and noise.

The DP algorithm is processed along each scanline from left to right. For each $(pixel, disparity)$ pair $(p, d)$, the accumulated cost is stored in the array $S$. Formally,

$$S(p,d) = Cost(p,d) + \min(S(p-(1,0)',d), S(p-(1,0)',d+(1,0)') + P_1,$$
$$S(p-(1,0)',d+(-1,0)') + P_1, \min_k S(p-(1,0)',k) + P_2)), \qquad (10)$$

where cost $Cost(p,d)$ is the NCC-based cost for matching pixel $p$ in $I_1$ to pixel $p + d$ in $I_2$. Discontinuities are not prohibited, but discouraged in our system. $P_1$ and $P_2$ are respectively the constant penalties for disparity discontinuity of 1 pixel and above 1 pixel. We empirically set $P_1$ to 0.2 and $P_2$ to 1.5 throughout our experiments.

After minimal total matching cost of the scanline is found, the disparity of each pixel p is taken as the one on the minimal cost path.

Since the disparities obtained from stereo matching are in pixel unit, the reconstructed shape will appear ladder-like if the disparities are directly used in triangulation. To solve this problem, for each pixel, we smooth its disparity value to sub-pixel accuracy by fitting a quadric surface within a $21 \times 21$ local window. Pixels that have far different disparity values with the center one are excluded in the fitting process. Outlier matches have less depth supports in their neighborhood, so they are easily detected and eliminated in the same process. The smoothed and outlier-free disparity map is then used as input in triangulation.

## 5   Robust Least Square Triangulation

Now we have corresponded any pixel $\mathbf{u}_1 = (u_1, v_1, 1)'$ in $I_1$ with a particular pixel $\mathbf{u}_2 = (u_2, v_2, 1)'$ in $I_2$. We can obtain the world coordinate $(X, Y, Z)'$ corresponding to $\mathbf{u}_1$ by solving the following linear equations:

$$
\begin{cases}
Z_{c1} \begin{bmatrix} u_1 \\ v_1 \\ 1 \end{bmatrix} = \mathbf{M}_1 \begin{bmatrix} X \\ Y \\ Z \\ 1 \end{bmatrix} = \begin{bmatrix} m_{11}^1 & m_{12}^1 & m_{13}^1 & m_{14}^1 \\ m_{21}^1 & m_{22}^1 & m_{23}^1 & m_{24}^1 \\ m_{31}^1 & m_{32}^1 & m_{33}^1 & m_{34}^1 \end{bmatrix} \begin{bmatrix} X \\ Y \\ Z \\ 1 \end{bmatrix} \\[2em]
Z_{c2} \begin{bmatrix} u_2 \\ v_2 \\ 1 \end{bmatrix} = \mathbf{M}_2 \begin{bmatrix} X \\ Y \\ Z \\ 1 \end{bmatrix} = \begin{bmatrix} m_{11}^2 & m_{12}^2 & m_{13}^2 & m_{14}^2 \\ m_{21}^2 & m_{22}^2 & m_{23}^2 & m_{24}^2 \\ m_{31}^2 & m_{32}^2 & m_{33}^2 & m_{34}^2 \end{bmatrix} \begin{bmatrix} X \\ Y \\ Z \\ 1 \end{bmatrix}
\end{cases} . \tag{11}
$$

By eliminating $Z_{c1}$ and $Z_{c2}$, we will get four linear equations concerning about $X, Y,$ and $Z$:

$$
\begin{cases}
(u_1 m_{31}^1 - m_{11}^1)X + (u_1 m_{32}^1 - m_{12}^1)Y + (u_1 m_{33}^1 - m_{13}^1)Z = m_{14}^1 - u_1 m_{34}^1 \\
(v_1 m_{31}^1 - m_{21}^1)X + (v_1 m_{32}^1 - m_{22}^1)Y + (v_1 m_{33}^1 - m_{23}^1)Z = m_{24}^1 - v_1 m_{34}^1 \\
(u_2 m_{31}^2 - m_{11}^2)X + (u_2 m_{32}^2 - m_{12}^2)Y + (u_2 m_{33}^2 - m_{13}^2)Z = m_{14}^2 - u_2 m_{34}^2 \\
(v_2 m_{31}^2 - m_{21}^2)X + (v_2 m_{32}^2 - m_{22}^2)Y + (v_2 m_{33}^2 - m_{23}^2)Z = m_{24}^2 - v_2 m_{34}^2
\end{cases} . \tag{12}
$$

This is an over-determined linear equation set. So $(X, Y, Z)$ is solved using least square error method [16], which is corresponding to finding the point with smallest sum of distances to the rays of two cameras.

## 6   Experimental Results

Our experimental setup consists of an NEC LT 245+ projector working at $1024 \times 768$, two Olympus C-5060 cameras at $2592 \times 1944$, and a standard PC. Due to the depth blurring effect of the projector, although the resolution of our projector is $1024 \times 768$, we only use half its resolution in practice. A 2-D binary De Bruijn pattern with size $512 \times 384$ is scaled to fill the screen of projector, and thus every $2 \times 2$ square pixel unit represents a code bit. All the images taken by cameras are scaled to Video Graphics Array (VGA) size ($640 \times 480$) for the processing followed. The algorithm is implmented in C++ and run on a PC with 2.6GHz CPU and 1GB memory. The depth acquisition process takes about $3 \sim 4$ seconds for each image pair.

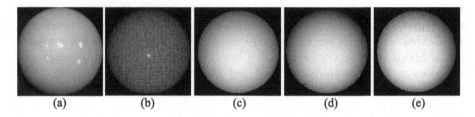

**Fig. 5.** (a) real object, (b) object illuminated by structured light pattern, (c, d) acquired depth maps and (e) reconstructed meshes of the experiment on a ball

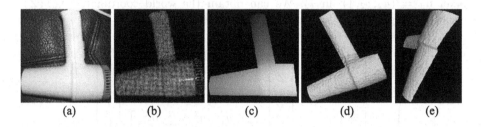

**Fig. 6.** (a) real object, (b) object illuminated by structured light pattern, (c) acquired depth maps and (d, e) two different views of the reconstructed meshes of the experiment on a hair drier

Firstly, the depth maps of a ball and a hair drier are reconstructed using our system. The real objects are shown in Fig. 5a and Fig. 6a, and the objects illuminated by the structured light are shown in Fig. 5b and Fig. 6b. The recovered depth maps using two calibrated cameras are shown in Fig. 5c and 6c. Fig. 6d shows the ball's depth map obtained by the alternative system using a calibrated projector and only one camera. There are more stereo matching errors near the object boundary, since in these regions, image $I_p$ and $I_2$ have much different pattern intensities and distortion. The reconstructed mesh of the ball is shown in Fig. 5e, and two different views of the reconstructed hair drier are shown in Fig. 6d and 6e.

We find that the reconstructed meshes appear to be a little rough, especially where depth changes rapidly in Fig. 6d and 6e. The main cause is that our stereo matching algorithm is based on pixel as searching unit. It is worthwhile to note that these results are obtained from only a single image pair.

In another experiment, a rotating cup is taken as the target object, which illustrates the system's ability to recover depth maps for moving objects. Due to space limitation, we only show two frames from the video sequence and their experimental results in Fig. 7. There are some characters in dark color (see Fig. 7b). Other structured light approaches base on pattern decoding such as 2-D binary grid [5] and colored De Bruijn sequence [7] will fail on such regions. On the contrary, our method gives robust reconstruction in such regions. The matching error to the right of the cup handle is caused by pattern occlusion in the other view.

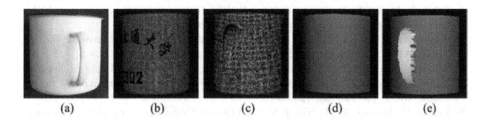

**Fig. 7.** (a) real object, (b, c) two frames of the object illuminated by structured light pattern and (d, e) acquired depth maps of the experiment on a rotating cup

## 7   Conclusion and Discussions

In this paper, we have proposed a new active stereo approach based on 2-D De Bruijn sequences. It has the advantage of handling the texture problem and acquiring depth maps of moving and deforming objects. 2-D De Bruijn sequences are emitted to the target object so that every small local window on the image is endowed with a unique code. But the difficulty of decoding these codes after camera's re-sampling is avoided by the use of NCC-based dense stereo matching. So there are few erroneous matches in the stereo matching stage.

Both the systems of using two calibrated cameras and one un-calibrated projector, and that using one calibrated camera and one calibrated projector are implemented. For geometrically calibrating the projector, we have proposed a novel reverse calibration method, which is validated by our experimental results. Good depth reconstruction results are obtained with both the systems.

A drawback of our system is the restriction to working only for indoor environments, due to the limitation of the energy emitted by the projector. This is a common limitation of active stereo.

In our current implementation, the processing speed is relatively slow for real time applications. By now, we can only record the moving objects with fixed cameras and reconstruct the depth maps offline. Hardware implementation of a real time online system is a challenging future work.

**Acknowledgments.** This work was supported in part by funds from China National Basic Research Program (973 Program 2006CB303105), Natural Science Foundation of China 60573147, and the collaboration research project with Omron Corporation, Japan.

## References

1. Scharstein, D., Szeliski, R.: A Taxonomy and Evaluation of Dense Two-Frame Stereo Correspondence Algorithms. Int. J. Computer Vision 47(1-3), 7–42 (2002)
2. Brown, M.Z., Burschka, D., Hager, G.D.: Advances in Computational Stereo. IEEE Trans. Pattern Analysis and Machine Intelligence 25(8), 993–1008 (2003)

3. Salvi, J., Pagès, J., Batlle, J.: Pattern Codification Strategies in Structured Light Systems. Pattern Recognition 37(4), 827–849 (2004)
4. Rusinkiewicz, S., Hall-Holt, O., Levoy, M.: Real-Time 3D Model Acquisition. In: SIGGRAPH 2002 Conference Proceedings, pp. 438–446 (2002)
5. Scharstein, D., Szeliski, R.: High-Accuracy Stereo Depth Maps Using Structured Light. In: IEEE computer society conference on computer vision and pattern recognition, vol. 1, pp. 195–202 (2003)
6. Lavoie, P., Ionescu, D., Petriu, E.M.: 3-D Object Model Recovery from 2-D Images Using Structured Light. IEEE Trans. Instrum. Meas. 53(2), 437–443 (2004)
7. Pagès, J., Salvi, J., Forest, J.: A New Optimised De Bruijn Coding Strategy for Structured Light Patterns. In: 17th Int. Conf. Pattern Recognition, vol. 4, pp. 284–287 (2004)
8. Morano, R.A., Ozturk, C., Conn, R., Dubin, S., Zietz, S., Nissanov, J.: Structured Light Using Pseudorandom Codes. IEEE Trans. Pattern Anal. Mach. Intell. 20(3), 322–327 (1998)
9. Tsai, R.Y.: A Versatile Camera Calibration Technique for High-Accuracy 3D Machine Vision Metrology Using Off-the-Shelf TV Cameras and Lenses. IEEE Trans. Robotics and Automation 3(4), 323–344
10. Zhang, Z.: A Flexible New Technique for Camera Calibration. IEEE Trans. Pattern Anal. Mach. Intell. 22(11), 1330–1334 (2000)
11. Heikkilä, J., Olli Silvén, O.: A Four-step Camera Calibration Procedure with Implicit Image Correction. In: IEEE Conf. Computer Vision and Pattern Recognition, pp. 1106–1112. IEEE Computer Society Press, Los Alamitos (1997)
12. Zeller, C., Faugeras, O.: Camera Self-calibration from Video Sequences: The Kruppa Equations Revisited. Research Report 2793, INRIA (February 1996)
13. Loop, C., Zhang, Z.: Computing Rectifying Homographies for Stereo Vision. In: Proc. IEEE Computer Science Conference on Computer Vision and Pattern Recognition, pp. 125–131 (1999)
14. Lewis, J.P.: Fast Normalized Cross-Correlation. In: Proceedings of Vision Interface (VI '95), pp. 120–123 (1995)
15. Cox, I.J., Hingorani, S.L., Rao, S.B., Maggs, B.M.: A Maximum Likelihood Stereo Algorithm. Computer Vision and Image Understanding 63, 542–567 (1996)
16. Press, W.H., Teukolsky, S.A., Vetterling, W.T., Flannery, B.P.: Numerical Recipes in C: The Art of Scientific Computing, 2nd edn., pp. 59–70. Cambridge University Press, Cambridge (1992)

# Semiautomatic Rule Assist Architecture Modeling

Hua Liu, Hongxin Zhang, and Hujun Bao

State Key lab of CAD&CG, Zhejiang University, Hangzhou, China
{sun_day,zhx,bao}@cad.zju.edu.cn

**Abstract.** This paper presents a novel rule-driven architecture modeling technique. Different from grammar based procedural modeling approaches, our proposed method, called *rule assist architecture modeling (RAAM)*, tends to integrate user interactions with implied modeling rules. Construction rules, configure rules and constrain rules are introduced in our method to minimize user interactions and enhance modeling efficiency. The experimental results demonstrate the efficiency and flexibility of our method to generate villas and skyscrapers.

## 1 Introduction

Architecture models are widely used in many computer graphics applications. Commonly, people use commercial modeling software [9,10] to build 3D architecture models with high details. It is a tedious task to model thousands of different buildings, which are often used in virtual cities and urban reconstruction. Recent years, grammar based procedural modeling methods are introduced to model buildings [6,8] and synthesize virtual cities [7] efficiently. Unfortunately, aforementioned methods are only good at modeling virtual buildings in similar style. To model buildings in different styles, the user has to define rules for each of them, which turns out to be inefficient. Moreover, writing desirable production rules is only possible for professional users. Although the priority can be assigned to each rule in [8], grammar based methods do not allow enough control mechanisms over the architecture modeling process.

In this paper, we present an interactive architecture modeling approach which is assisted by rules, called *rule assist architecture modeling (RAAM)*. Different from existing grammar based modeling approaches, the modeling process of our RAAM is mainly controlled by user interactions. The assist rules maintain construction information, default configuration data and modeling constrains of the target models. In our modeling system, rules are activated and executed automatically to reflect user interaction and commands. Construction rules are utilized to reduce user interactions and help users to complete the nonsignificant part. Additionally, the RAAM also allows users to modify predefined rules. Our proposed approach can help users to control the architecture modeling process more efficiently than previous method.

The rest of the paper is structured as follows. After reviewing procedural modeling methods in section 2, we introduce the assist rules in section 3. Then the

L. Ma, R. Nakatsu, and M. Rauterberg (Eds.): ICEC 2007, LNCS 4740, pp. 315–323, 2007.

user interface are presented in section 4. In section 5, implementation details are provided and several modeling examples are demonstrated by using our prototype system. At last, we draw conclusions and discuss future work in section 6.

## 2    Relate Works

Rule and grammar based modeling techniques were developed in the first years of 20th century, such as L-System and parameter L-System, which are mainly used in plant modeling [2,3,4,5].

In recent years, several researchers extended the rule based techniques and leveraged them in other modeling domains. In  [7], an extended L-System is applied to generate streets of a virtual city. Population density, height map and water map are employed as the input parameters that influenced the generation of the streets. After that, split grammar [6], which is a subset of the shape grammar [1], is proposed to describe the rules of shape splitting. Control grammar is also introduced in that paper, which is used to distribute the attributes of the modeling rules and selecting the next executed rule by matching attributes. The modeling process started from a bounded simple shape, and then split it recursively to form a complex shape with many details progressively. By using the splitting rules, [16] can produce a class of models automatically. More recently, [8] addressed application related details in the context of procedural modeling of buildings, such as the definition of the context sensitive shape rules and the concise notation. It also address the intersection problem of the architecture modeling process.

As formalizing knowledge of architecture construction is the essential part of our method, we would recommend starting with books that emphasize structure of architecture, such as a visual dictionary [11], the Logic of Architecture by Mitchell [12], Space Syntax [13], Design Patterns [14], and studies of symmetry [15].

## 3    Assist Rules

Comparing with the traditional modeling systems, our *RAAM* has assist rules between users and operation commands. For users, they only need to tell the system where and what components they want to create. Then the assist rules will translate their designs into real operation commands. Additionally, assist rules also detect the correction of modeling results and call the corresponding commands automatically, when it is necessary. Obviously, the key part of *RAAM* is the assist rules, which formalize the knowledge of architecture construction. The assist rules work with a configuration of components and operation commands. Here, we introduce them first:

*Component*: A component consists of a symbol, geometry (geometric attributes) and numeric attributes. Components are identified by their symbols which is either a *terminal symbol* (e.g., door or window) or a *non-terminal symbol* (e.g., hall or veranda). The corresponding components are called terminal components and non-terminal components. The most important geometric attributes are the center position $P$ and a size vector $S$. These attributes define an oriented bounding box of component in space. All the result models are constructed by terminal components non-terminal components.

*Operation Commands*: An operation command is described as $C()$, which can be a transform function, a creating function or a editing function etc. Operation commands exactly define the action on the components.

The assist rules not only describe the construction information, but also include the default configuration and modeling constrains. So we divide the assist rules into three categories: *construction rules*, *configure rules* and *constrain rules*.

## 3.1 Construction Rules

A class of buildings with similar style are always consist of a set of finite components. The generation of the components are described by the construction rules, which are defined as a set $R$ in our paper. Similar as the production rules presented in [8,16], for each $r$, $r \in R$ is represented as Equation. 1,

$$\alpha \rightarrow C_1(\beta_1)C_2(\beta_2)\cdots C_i(\beta_i), \tag{1}$$

where $\alpha$ and $\beta_i$ are components. $C_i$ are operation commands. Terminal components are created by simple shapes or loaded directly from the component library, such as [17]. For example, the window component, which is loaded from the library, is described by the construction rule: $window(s,p) \rightarrow Load(name, s, p)$, where *name* indicates which component to be loaded and $s, p$ are attributes of the window. Body components are created by blocks which are represented as: $body(s,p) \rightarrow T(CreateBlock(s), p)$, where $T$ is a transform function.

Non-terminal components, such as hall, veranda etc., consist of terminal components or non-terminal components. Here, we will show how a veranda component is constructed. The related rules are shown as follow:

**Table 1.** Rules for generate a veranda

| id | construction rules |
|---|---|
| 1. | $veranda(s,p) \rightarrow vB(V_{bottom}(s,p))vL(V_{left}(s,p))vR(V_{right}(s,p))vF(V_{front}(s,p))$ |
| 2. | $vB(s,p) \rightarrow T(CreateBlock(s), p)$ |
| 3. | $vL(s,p) \rightarrow T(CreateBlock(s), p)$ |
| 4. | $vR(s,p) \rightarrow T(CreateBlock(s), p)$ |
| 5. | $vF(s,p) \rightarrow T(railing(s), p)$ |
| 6. | $railing(s) \rightarrow Repeat(pillar(R_s(s)), R_n(s))railing_{top}(R_{top}(s))$ |
| 7. | $pillar(s) \rightarrow CreateCylinder(P_{top}(s))CreateCylinder(P_{bottom}(s))$ |
| 8. | $railing_{top}(s) \rightarrow CreateBlock(s)$ |

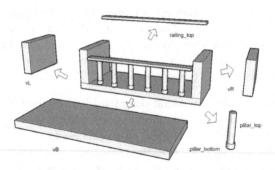

**Fig. 1.** Construction of veranda

Here, $V_{bottom}, V_{left}, V_{right}, V_{front}, R_s, R_n, R_{top}, P_{top}, P_{bottom}$ are configure rules which will be introduced in the next subsection. $CreateBlock$ and $CreateCylinder$ are both operation commands, which will create a parameterized basic shape immediately. $Repeat(s, n)$ is also an operation command, which make a component cloned $n$ times. As shown in Fig. 1, we can see how a veranda is built up. In this process, users only need to specify parameters of a veranda and the whole generation work is done automatically by assist rules.

## 3.2   Configure Rules

In our modeling process, the user do not need to specify all modeling parameters. Most of them can be calculated by the corresponding components. For example, a window or a door component always has a same dimension value of $p$ with the wall, which it belongs to. The bottom of a roof component always has the same size with the top of the corresponding body component. The others can be determined by domain knowledge, e.g., the width and height of each step of a stair component always has a fixed scale.

At some time, if the default value generated by configure rules conflicts with users' purpose, we also allow them to edit the default configure rules or utilize the interaction tools to set the value directly. If most of the configure rules have satisfied users' purpose, it could be great helpful to improve the modeling efficiency.

A configure rule consists of a symbol (string) and a function $F(X)$. The symbol indicates which component the configure rule is related to and $X$ is the input parameter. The function $F$, which is commonly a linear function or a constant, indicates the default value of the component's attribute. In the previous subsection, we mentioned some configure rules in the modeling of a veranda component. For instance, the configure rule $V_{bottom}$ is written as:

$$V_{bottom}(s, p) : \begin{cases} scale_{bottom} = 0.2 \\ s_{bottom} = (s_u, scale_{bottom} * s_v, s_w) \\ p_{bottom} = (p_x, p_y - 05 * s_v(1 - scale_{bottom}), p_z) \end{cases} \tag{2}$$

where $scale_{bottom}$ is a constant, which may be changed by users. As shown in Equation. 2, $V_{bottom}(s,p)$ returns the size vector $s_{bottom}$ and center position $p_{bottom}$ of the component $vB$(veranda bottom). The configure rule will be activated when the related component is created, which is always invoked by construction rules. Here, we should notice that the input of users have the higher priority than the configure rules. If the user has specified the attributes, the corresponding configure rule will not be used anymore.

### 3.3   Constrain Rules

As the modeling process is semiautomatic and is controlled by users, we cannot know the sequence beforehand. The new added component probably influence the existing ones and cause bad results and vice versa. Traditionally, the correction is confirmed by user themselves. But in our method, it is automatically done by the constrain rules.

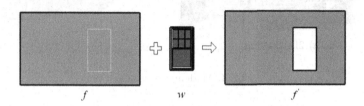

$$f \qquad\qquad w \qquad\qquad f'$$

**Fig. 2.** Constrain rules

As shown in Fig. 2, a new added window $w$ will intersect an existing wall $f$, if we directly load the window component and put it in the scope, which is indicated by the yellow rectangle. In general, users will add a hole in the wall before they put a window on it. This task is not the purpose (creating a window on the wall) of the user, But it is essential. We call this type of tasks as *additional tasks* and make them done automatically by constrain rules as many as possible. The constrain rules are defined as:

$$T(s,o) : con \rightarrow C(X) \tag{3}$$

where $T$ is a function which detect the constrains between current scene($s$) and the new added object($o$). The sign $con$ indicates the condition value. When the return value of $T()$ is equal to $con$, the operation command $C(X)$ is executed:

$$Intersect(f,w) : true \rightarrow hole(f,rec) \tag{4}$$

For example: as shown in equation 4, this constrain rule is activated when a new window is added into the scene.It detects intersections between walls and window and add a hole on the wall when the detection result is matched. The result is shown in Fig.2.

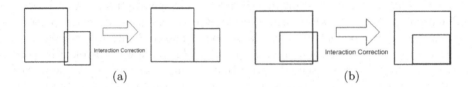

(a)                                      (b)

**Fig. 3.** Automatic correction

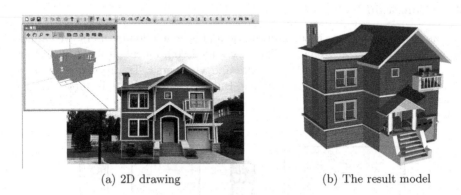

(a) 2D drawing                          (b) The result model

**Fig. 4.** Modeling of a villa

## 4   User Interface

In our prototype system, we use simple 2D user interface. Users may paint from front, back, up, left and right, five directions totally. The only painting tool used here, is a rectangle drawing tool. A rectangle from one view side determines two dimensions of the position $p$ and the size vector $s$. And the left dimension value will be determines by a rectangle from the other view sides or directly from the configure rules.

*Automatical Correction*: As we choose 2D painting as the interaction, rectangles maybe not express the user's input exactly. As shown in Fig. 3, two rectangles drawn by the user in the left side are intersected. It will be error if the coordinates of input rectangle are parameterized directly. To solve this problem, an automatical correction step is performed before the parameterized step. The new added component is detected with the related components which exist already. If the dimension error is in a given threshold, the new added component will be resized and aligned to the exist corresponding one, as shown in Fig. 3(a) and Fig.3(b).

## 5   Implementation and Results

We implement the rule assist approach for modeling villas and high buildings. Fifteen components and ten operation commands are defined in our implementation. As all user interaction are in 2D, referenced photos may be used to help users to determine the position of components and also it is helpful to get material and texture images directly from photos, especially in the application of urban reconstruction. The interface of our application is illustrated in Fig. 4(a). And Fig.4(b) shows the result villa model, which is modeled referring to the left photograph.

## 5.1    Material and Textures

As the result model is combined by predefined components and all the components are well oriented, we can easily assign material and calculate texture coordinates automatically. When selecting a piece of the referenced photo and the corresponding component, image quilting [18] is applied to synthesize texture for filling the faces of component.

## 5.2    Results

In this paper, we implemented the rules assist modeling approach to model villas and skyscrapers. Each model is created in less than one minute including the generation of textures. The generated models (Fig. 5,   6 and   7 ) are exported

(a) Referenced Photo                     (b) Virtual building

**Fig. 5.** Building Reconstruction

(a) Villa Model A                         (b) Villa Model B

**Fig. 6.** Villa models

(a) Whole view                              (b) Local view

**Fig. 7.** Dorm Building Model

from our application and rendered by 3DSMax. Fig.5(a) is the referenced photo of the virtual building (see Fig.5(b)). From this example, we can see that the rules assist method not only suits for the virtual architecture modeling but also can be applied to reconstruct real buildings.

## 6   Conclusion and Future Work

In this paper, we present a rule assist architecture modeling method. Different from the existing grammar based ones, the assist rules are activated and executed according to the user interactions. Our proposed assist rule set consists of three types of rules, including construction rules, configure rules and constrains rules. Construction rules are used to model the non-terminal components automatically, which are similar to the existing production rules [8]. Configure rules represent the default value and relationship of components' attributes. Constrain rules are activated when the corresponding components are added. Then additional commands are executed automatically to help modeling. All these assist rules are leveraged to generate modeling commands automatically from user interactions. It is worth mentioning that our RAAM also allows users to modify the predefined rules which can provides additional flexibility for modeling different styles of buildings.

In near future, we plan to integrate 2D matching algorithms in our prototype system. Then the selection of terminal-components can be done automatically instead of being chosen by users. We will also explore the possibilities for modeling and quantitating architecture styles. For different purpose, the requirement of geometry resolution is not same. For example, in game applications, for rendering fast the geometry resolution of 3D models is always in a low resolution and details are represented by textures. But in the application of computer aided architecture design(CAAD), users require more geometry details. In the future, we can define a set of construction rules in different resolutions for one component and choosing them according to users' requirement.

# Acknowledgements

This research work is supported by the 973 Program of China (No. 2002CB312102), NSFC (No. 60505001), the Cultivation Fund of the Key Scientific and Technical Innovation Project, Ministry of Education of China (No. 705027), and the 863 program Program of China (No. 2006AA01Z338).

# References

1. Stiny, G.: Introduction to shape and shape grammars. Environment and Planning B 7, pp. 349–351. Pion Ltd., London, England (1980)
2. Prusinkiewicz, P., Lindenmayer, A.: The algorithmic beauty of plants. Springer, New York (1990)
3. Prusinkiewicz, P., James, M., Radom: Synthetic topiary. In: Proceedings of ACM SIGGRAPH 1994, pp. 351–358. ACM Press, New York (1994)
4. Měch, R., Prusinkiewicz, P.: Visual models of plants interacting with their environment. In: SIGGRAPH '96. Proceedings of the 23rd annual conference on Computer graphics and interactive techniques, pp. 397–410. ACM Press, New York (1996)
5. Przemyslaw, P., Mndermann, L., Karwowski, R., Lane, B.: The use of positional information in the modeling of plants. In: Proceedings of ACM SIGGRAPH 2001, pp. 289–300. ACM Press, New York (2001)
6. Wonka, P., Wimmer, M., Sillion, F., Ribarsky, W.: Instant Architecture. In: ACM Transactions on Graphics, vol. 22(3), pp. 669–677. ACM Press, New York (2003)
7. Parish, Y.I.H., Müller, P.: Procedural modeling of cities. In: Proceedings of ACM SIGGRAPH 2001, pp. 301–308. ACM Press, New York (2001)
8. Müller, P., Wonka, P., Haegler, S., Ulmer, A., Van Gool, L.: Procedural Modeling of Buildings. In: Proceedings of ACM SIGGRAPH 2006. ACM Press, New York (2006)
9. Autodesk 3ds Max software: 3D studio Max, Autodesk Inc., http://usa.autodesk.com
10. Sketchup Software: Sketchup. Google Inc., http://www.sketchup.com
11. Ching, F.D.K.: A Visual Dictionary of Architecture. Wiley, Chichester (1996)
12. Mitchell, W.J.: The Logic of Architecture: Design, Computation, and Cognition. MIT Press, Cambridge (1990)
13. Hillier, B.: Space Is The Machine: A Configurational Theory Of Architecture. Cambridge University Press, Cambridge (1996)
14. Alexander, C., Ishikawa, S., Silverstein, M.: A Pattern Language: Towns, Buildings, Construction. Oxford University Press, New York (1977)
15. Shubnikov, A.V., Koptsik, V.A.: Symmetry in Science and Art. Plenum Press, New York (1974)
16. Liu, H., Hua, W., Zhou, D., Bao, H.: Building Chinese Ancient Architectures in Seconds. In: Sunderam, V.S., van Albada, G.D., Sloot, P.M.A., Dongarra, J.J. (eds.) ICCS 2005. LNCS, vol. 3515, pp. 248–255. Springer, Heidelberg (2005)
17. Google 3D Warehouse, Google Inc., http://sketchup.google.com/3dwarehouse/
18. Efros, A.A., Freeman, W.T.: Image Quilting for Texture Synthesis and Transfer. In: Proceedings of SIGGRAPH 2001, pp. 341–346. ACM Press, New York (2001)

# Online Expression Mapping for Performance-Driven Facial Animation

Hae Won Byun

School of Media & Information, Sung Shin Woman's University,
169-1 Dongsun-dong 2, Sungbuk-gu, Seoul, Republic of Korea
hyewon@sungshin.ac.kr

**Abstract.** Recently, performance-driven facial animation has been popular in various entertainment area, such as game, animation movie, and advertisement. With the easy use of motion capture data from a performer's face, the resulting animated faces are far more natural and lifelike. However, when the characteristic features between live performer and animated character are quite different, expression mapping becomes a difficult problem. Many previous researches focus on facial motion capture only or facial animation only. Little attention has been paid to mapping motion capture data onto 3D face model.

Therefore, we present a new expression mapping approach for performance-driven facial animation. Especially, we consider online factor of expression mapping for real-time application. Our basic idea is capturing the facial motion from a real performer and adapting it to a virtual character in real-time. For this purpose, we address three issues: facial expression capture, expression mapping and facial animation. We first propose a comprehensive solution for real-time facial expression capture without any devices such as head-mounted cameras and face-attached markers. With the analysis of the facial expression, the facial motion can be effectively mapped onto another 3D face model. We present a novel example-based approach for creating facial expressions of model to mimic those of face performer. Finally, real-time facial animation is provided with multiple face models, called "facial examples". Each of these examples reflects both a facial expression of different type and designer's insight to be a good guideline for animation. The resulting animation preserves the facial expressions of performer as well as the characteristic features of the target examples.

## 1 Introduction

Recently performance-driven facial animation has become popular for on-line animation. Its basic idea is capturing the facial motion from a real performer and adapting it to a virtual character. The performance animation not only makes it possible to acquire highly natural facial motion but also automates facial motion generation with little help from animators. Being difficult with conventional approaches, one can generate time-varying expressions such as lip-synch and eye-blink effectively with performance animation.

In on-line performance-driven facial animation, it is required to capture facial expressions in real time. For a live performer to feel comfortable in making expressions, it is also desirable, if not required, to avoid any devices such as a head-mounted camera

L. Ma, R. Nakatsu, and M. Rauterberg (Eds.): ICEC 2007, LNCS 4740, pp. 324–338, 2007.

and face-attached markers. These constraints on facial expression capture enforce additional difficulties: The performer naturally moves his/her head to express emotions while making facial expressions according to an animation script. Without a head-mounted camera, one needs to track the position and orientation of performer's head for more accurate facial expression capture. Moreover, without any markers attached on the face, extra effort is needed to track the features of the face that characterize facial expressions. The final difficulty comes from the real-time constraint, that is, to capture facial expressions in real time while addressing the former two difficulties.

The previous approaches for facial expression capture have tried to track the position of markers attached on a face performer [9,24]. To promote the convenience of face performer, facial feature extraction techniques without markers have been proposed in computer vision [6,7,22]. These researches are mostly used for face detection, face recognition, or facial expression analysis. Thus, they must cope with large variations in the appearance of facial features across rather general subjects as well as the large appearance variability of a single subject caused by changes in lighting. In this field, the real time constraint is not at issue. However, in the case of facial expression capture for performance-driven animation, it is required to track the facial features, in real time, for only a small number of specific persons who are employed as face performers.

Real-time facial animation is essential for on-line performance-driven facial animation. Multiple face models, called facial examples, are widely used for real-time facial animation. Those facial examples comprise a facial expression database from which we select appropriate face models to blend and to deform. However, a facial example consists of a set of vertices with few handles to control such geometric operations except the vertices themselves. To achieve smooth local deformation and non-uniform blending without any tools, one would have to deal with every vertex of facial examples involved in these operations. Due to its capability of local control on facial features, "wires"[20] is known as a popular tool for facial animation. However, we cannot expect that a designer does necessarily employ wire deformation to model a example of facial expression.

Those facial examples have been hardly used in conjunction with performance-driven facial animation. In order to combine an example-based facial animation and expression capture approach, we should address how to blend the facial examples according to the expression of face performer. The combined approach has the advantage that leverages the usefulness of facial examples, while gaining the efficiency of facial expression capture. The method is effective even when the size and characteristics of the face of performer is quite different from that of face model. Furthermore, attenuating or exaggerating an expression is also possible by making artificial facial examples with those expressions.

In this thesis, we present a new scheme for on-line performance-driven facial animation. As depicted in Figure 1, we address following three issues: First, we present a comprehensive solution for real-time facial expression capture from a stream of images without any special devices. The performer is allowed to move the head as long as all the facial features are observable from a camera. Next, in order to facilitate real-time expression mapping, we address how to blend facial examples with a set of wires

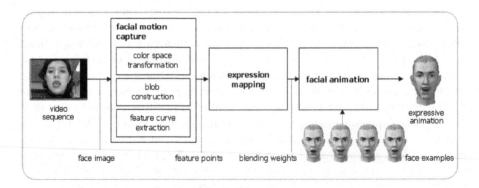

**Fig. 1.** The overall structure of on-line performance-driven facial animation

and deformation parameters extracted from a facial example. Finally, we propose a novel approach for real-time facial animation with facial examples represented by wire curves.

The remainder of this thesis is organized as follows: In Chapter 2, we explain the overall structure of on-line performance-driven facial animation. In Chapter 3, we introduce the first step in detail, that is, how to extract facial expression. To adopt facial examples for real-time facial animation, we present an expression mapping scheme for facial examples and their effective representation in Chapter 4. The step for facial animation is described in Chapter 5. We demonstrate some experimental results in Chapter 6. Finally, conclusion and future works are given in Chapter 7.

## 2   Related Work

There are rich results on facial expression capture. We specifically refer those that are directly related to our work. Williams[24] proposed an approach to capture the facial features with markers attached to the feature points on the face of a live performer. Due to its efficiency and robustness, this approach is widely used in practice. However, the markers not only cause discomfort to the performer but also are hard to attach on some facial features such as eyelids.

Terzopolous and Waters[22] adopted an active contour model called "snakes" presented by Kass *et. al.*[13] to track the outlines of facial features highlighted with special makeup. Thalmann *et. al.*[8] and Oliver *et. al.*[16] extracted facial features directly from an input image without any markers. Exploiting anthropometric knowledge, they were able to obtain geometric information such as the width, height, and area of a feature region. This type of approaches is simple and efficient. Instead of finding the outlines of the facial features, Essa *et. al.*[7] proposed a 3D model-based approach for tracking facial features. They used the optical flow field to displace the vertices of 3D models. DeCarlo *et. al.*[6] deformed a 3D facial model to produce a least-squares optical flow solution while relaxing constraints with an extended Kalman filter. Black and Yacoob[2] used locally parametrized models for recovering and recognizing the non-rigid and articulated motions of human faces.

For real-time facial animation, blending multiple face models with different expressions is popular [3,17,10,19,26,5]. Blanz et al.[3] and Pighin et al.[17] proposed an automatic face modeling technique by linearly blending a set of example faces from a database of scanned 3D face models. To avoid unlikely faces, they restricted the range of allowable faces with constraints derived from the example set. For local control on each facial feature, those approaches allow interactive segmentation of a face into a set of regions to assign a proper blending factor to every vertex. Joshi et al.[10] adopted an automatic segmentation method to learn the local deformation information directly from the multiple face models. Chuang et al.[5] extends blendshape retargetting technique to include subsets of morph targets.

Other alternatives are based on deformation techniques. Thalmann et al.[12] employed FFD to simulate the muscle action on the skin surface of a human face. Kahler et al.[11] and Terzopoulos et al.[14] proposed a physically-based method for skin and muscle deformation to enhance the degree of realism over purely geometric techniques. Guenter et. al.[9] and Zhang et. al. [25] used facial motion data captured from real actors to deform face models. Marschner et al.[15] computed the displacements of control points for a specific face model from the movements of sample points on a face performer by solving a system of linear equations in the least squares sense.

## 3   Facial Motion Capture

We describe how to track the facial features in real time without any devices such as face-attached markers and head-mounted cameras. We assume a stream of images is captured from a single camera with known parameters located at a given position with a fixed orientation. Feature tracking consists of three major tasks: color space transformation, blob construction, and feature curve extraction. Considering that each feature appears in an image as a blob[1,16], that is, a set of pixels with similar properties, we track the movement of the blob to extract the feature. The first task is for enhancing the features for robust tracking. In the second task, we first exploit anthropometric knowledge to confine a blob within a rectangle and then explore the rectangle for the blob. This accelerates constructing the blob, from which we extract its outline in the final task using snakes[13]. The outline is represented as a cubic Bezier curve with small number of control points. We describe each of these tasks in detail.

### 3.1   Color Space Transformation

For robust feature extraction, we transform the color space of the input image from the RGB model to a model in which the facial features such as eyelashes, eyebrows, nostrils, and lips are significantly distinguishable from their background, that is, the skin. Color spaces including the chromatic color model were employed for robust facial expression capture[1,16]. Based on statistical learning, this model is useful to detect the lips and the skin robustly.

To enhance the facial features, we design a new color transformation function from RGB values to gray-scale values(see Figure 2). By making observation of the face performers, we conceive that the skin has low values of the magenta (M) and black (K) channels in the CYMK color model. A low intensity (V) value of the HSV color model

**Fig. 2.** Proposed color transformation:(left)Original Image (right)The image obtained by color transformation

is observed for the pixels in dark features such as eyebrows, eyelashes, and nostrils. Moreover, the portion of the hue (H) band occupied by the color of lips is fairly different from that of the skin. Therefore, we use those four components to emphasize the features in an image.

With our transformation function, the intensity $I(u, v)$ of a pixel $(u, v)$ is defined as follows:

$$I(u,v) = w_1 M(u,v) + w_2 K(u,v) + w_3 V(u,v) + w_4 G(H(u,v)). \tag{1}$$

Here, $G$ is a function which has high values at a range of hue values which are similar to those of lips, and has very low values, otherwise. The terms, $w_i$, $1 \le i \le 4$ are weights for four components, M, K, V, and H. Here, $w_3$ is negative while the others are positive, since pixels in features have lower V values compared to those in the skin. We may further emphasize the features by a contrast enhancement function $C$. This function is used to amplify lighter pixels and to attenuate dimmer pixels. Thus, by applying this function on the intensity, that is, the result of Equation, we can make the pixels in the feature regions brighter and those of the skin darker.

The weights $w_i$, $1 \le i \le 4$ are varied according to both lighting condition change and skin color variation. In order to estimate the weights, we employ a three-layered neural network . A neural network which has learned several patterns of facial images can estimate the weights for the four color components M, K, V, H in Equation (1) from the RGB color values of facial features in the captured image. The input layer of neural network gets 11 representative intensity values for subareas of each facial feature(skin, eyes, eyelids, nostrils, a mouth, and so on). Each representative value is computed as the average of all the pixel values in the subarea which contains each facial feature in the image. The output layer consists of 4 units specifying the weights that we wanted to estimate in Equation (1). The hidden layer has 10 units, decided empirically, of a sigmoid function to effectively model the non-linear capacity. Once trained for each puppeteer, the training data can be used for other sessions of the same puppeteer without re-training. Whenever we capture facial motion, we can obtain the weights in real time by evaluating the trained neural network with back propagation.

### 3.2 Blob Contruction

A blob is said to be a set of connected pixels in an image that share similar visual properties such as color and intensity. Facial features such as eyes, lips, eyebrows, and etc. are normally projected onto the image as distinct blobs. By constructing those blobs properly, we can estimate the facial features from the image at each frame. In order to accelerate blob construction, we confine a blob in a rectangle using anthropometric knowledge such as the relative positions of facial features and their size. A similar idea is used in Thalmann *et al.*[23]. Under the assumption that head movement is allowed as long as no blobs disappear in an image, we empirically determine the size of the rectangle for each feature. Initially, the edges of the rectangle are parallel with either the $x$-axis or $y$-axis of the global coordinate.

Given the rectangle containing a feature, we employ a blob growing algorithm in [1,16] to construct the blob. Initially, we sample a small number of pixels in the rectangle, of which intensities are above a threshold, as the seed points for blob growing. From each of those seeds, the algorithm searches an area within a given radius and collects the neighborhood pixels which have greater intensity than the threshold. For each collected yet not expanded pixel, this process is repeated until no such pixels remain. Ideally, these pixels would comprise a single connected component. However, in practice, the pixels give multiple connected components due to threshold and noise. Each of those components form a region that is either a false blob or a subset of a blob. To reduce the influence of threshold and noise, we apply morphological operations such as dilation and erosion[18] to connect the separate regions and eliminate their protrudent features. We finally take the largest region within each rectangle as a feature blob.

### 3.3 Feature Curve Extraction

In order to extract the outlines of features, we employ snakes as proposed by Kass *et al.*[13]. Snakes are energy-minimizing spline curves under the influence of three (possibly conflicting) forces: internal force, image force, and constraint force. Due to its high degrees of freedom, the snake may snap to unwanted boundaries. To avoid this problem, we need to design the constraint force carefully. Therefore, we remove the internal force from our formulation, differently from the original version of snakes. Instead, we employ cubic Bezier curves with a small number of control points to represent snakes. The outlines of facial features are so simple that they can be well represented by such curves. Moreover, the Bezier curve is infinitely differentiable within itself, and is therefore continuous to any degree. The property of Bezier curve guarantees its smoothness. This simplification increases time efficiency and robustness while sacrificing some flexibility that is not necessarily required for our purpose. In practice, we employ cubic Bezier curves with four control points.

The energy function of our contour model consists of two terms:

$$E(\mathbf{v}) = \int_0^1 E_{image}(\mathbf{v}(\mathbf{s})) + E_{con}(\mathbf{v}(\mathbf{s})) ds, \tag{2}$$

where $E_{image}$ and $E_{con}$ are respectively the energies due to the image force and the constraint force, and $\mathbf{v}(s)$ is a 2D cubic Bezier curve representing the contour of the feature. Therefore, by minimizing $E(\mathbf{v})$, we compute the unknown control points of the 2D curve $\mathbf{v}$.

The energy $E_{image}$ is an edge detecting function, that is,

$$E_{image}(\mathbf{v}(\mathbf{s})) = -w_1 |\nabla I(u, v)|^2. \tag{3}$$

**Fig. 3.** Two candidates and offset curves:(a)Two candidate contours of the upper lip (b)Offset curves

Here, $w_1$ is a constant weight value. Large positive values of $w_1$ tend to make the snake align itself with sharp edge in the image. $(u, v)$ is a point on a 2D cubic Bezier curve $\mathbf{v}(s)$ and $\nabla I(u, v)$ is the gradient at a point $(u, v)$, that is, $\nabla I(u, v) = (\frac{\partial I(u,v)}{\partial u} \quad \frac{\partial I(u,v)}{\partial v})$, and $I(u, v)$ is obtained from Equation (1). This energy function makes the curve $\mathbf{v}$ be attracted to the contour of a blob with large image gradients, or the outline of a feature. However, using only image gradients may cause an unwanted result. For example, as shown in Figure 3, we cannot discriminate the upper curve (A) and lower curve (B) with image gradients alone.

We resolve this problem by employing the constraint energy together with simple upper and lower offset curves as illustrated in Figure 3. Suppose that we want to extract the upper curve (A). Provided with the up-vector of the head, for example, we make those offset curves by slightly shifting the pair of middle control points of each feature curve of lips in the opposite directions with respect to the up-vector. For each feature curve, one of its offset curves is supposed to lie inside the feature while the other outside. An offset curve of a feature curve $\mathbf{v}(s)$ is said to be its inner curve $\mathbf{v}_{in}(s)$ if it is supposed to lie in the corresponding feature. Otherwise, it is said to be its outer curve $\mathbf{v}_{out}(s)$ (see $\mathbf{v}^1$ in Figure 3). Let $I(\mathbf{v}_{out}(s))$ and $I(\mathbf{v}_{in}(s))$ be the intensity of $\mathbf{v}_{out}(s)$ and that of $\mathbf{v}_{in}(s)$, respectively. Because of the color transformation in Section 3.1, a point in a feature region has a high intensity value, and that in the skin has a low value. Given $I(\mathbf{v}_{out}(s))$ and $I(\mathbf{v}_{in}(s))$, the constraint energy of the feature curve $\mathbf{v}(s)$ is defined:

$$E_{con}(\mathbf{v}(s)) = w_{out}I(\mathbf{v}_{out}(s)) - w_{in}I(\mathbf{v}_{in}(s)), \qquad (4)$$

where $w_{out}$ and $w_{in}$ are positive constants providing the relative weighting of the intensity terms. As illustrated in Figure 3, with $w_{in}$ sufficiently greater than $w_{out}$, $E_{con}$ is positive for a curve ($\mathbf{v}^2$ in the figure) that is not properly located, but negative for a properly located one ($\mathbf{v}^1$).

To make an initial guess of the outline of a feature, we first scale the bounding box of each feature, so that it tightly bounds the feature blob. We use the boundary of this box as the initial guess of the feature curve at the current frame. To minimize the total energy function $E(\mathbf{v})$, we adopt the downhill method which uses the gradient of the energy function. The local minimum problem can be alleviated by blurring the image intensity.

## 4   Expression Mapping

We extracted time-varying movements of feature points from a face performer in the previous capture stage. In this section, given the movements of feature points, our objective is to generate a facial motion for a 3D face model in real time, so as to mimic the expression of performer. To create facial animation, we adopt an example-based approach to blend facial examples in accordance with their contributions to synthesize the resulting expression[4,10,19,26]. Each of facial example reflects both expressions of different types such as happiness, sadness, and anger and designer's insight to be a good guideline for animation. With the advantages of this approach that preserve the characteristic features of examples and reflecting a designer's intention accurately, it becomes a popular method for various shape modeling and animation. However, it is rarely used in combination with performance-driven facial animation. Our contribution is to present a realtime example-based scheme for facial motion synthesis in conjunction with facial motion capture.

Given the displacements of feature points, our problem is to find the best blend of examples at each frame to resemble the facial motion of a performer. Provided with the source examples and corresponding target examples, in the pre-processing, all the target examples are parameterized by using the corresponding source examples to apply multidimensional scattered data interpolation. We provide a simple, elegant parameterization scheme for effective expression blending. Provided with the parameterized target examples, the next step is for computing the contribution of every target example to the new expression using cardinal basis functions. The final step is to blend the corresponding target examples in accordance with their contributions to synthesize the resulting expression.

### 4.1 Parameterization

We parameterize the target examples based on the displacements between the source examples. In the capture step, the displacements of feature points are extracted from a face performer. Concatenating these displacements, the displacement vector of each source example is formed to parameterize the corresponding target example. Most individual parameter components tend to be correlated to each other. Thus, based on PCA (principal component analysis), the dimensionality of the parameter space can be reduced by removing less significant basis vectors of the resulting eigenspace.

The displacement vector $\mathbf{v}_i$ of a source example $\mathbf{S}_i$ from the source base model $\mathbf{S}_B$ is defined as follows:

$$\mathbf{v}_i = \mathbf{s}_i - \mathbf{s}_B, \ 1 \le i \le M, \tag{5}$$

where $\mathbf{s}_B$ and $\mathbf{s}_i$ are vectors obtained by concatenating, in a fixed order, the 3D coordinates of feature points on $\mathbf{S}_B$ and those on $\mathbf{S}_i$, respectively, and $M$ is the number of source examples. As shown in Figure 4, $\mathbf{v}_i$ places each target example $\mathbf{T}_i$ in the $N$-dimensional parameter space, where $N$ is the number of components, that is, three times the number of feature points.

Since the dimensionality $N$ of the parameter space is rather high compared to the number $M$ of examples, we employ PCA to reduce it. Given $M$ displacement vectors of dimension $N$, we first generate their component covariance matrix, which is an $N \times N$ square matrix, to compute the eigenvectors of the matrix and the corresponding eigenvalues. These eigenvectors are called the *principal components* representing the principal axes that characterize the distribution of displacement vectors. The dimensionality of the parameter space can be reduced by removing less significant eigenvectors, which have small eigenvalues. In our experiments, we use an empirical threshold

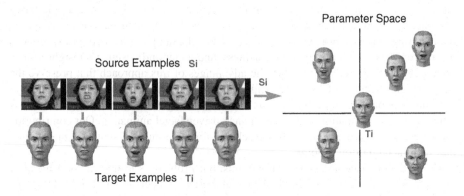

**Fig. 4.** The displacement vector of each source key-model $\mathbf{S}_i$ is used for parameterizing the corresponding target key-model $\mathbf{T}_i$

value of 0.00001 to remove those eigenvectors. The removal of such eigenvectors may cause some characteristics of the examples not to be parameterized. With our choice of the threshold, we have observed that the effect is negligible. In experiments, the dimensionality of the parameter space can be reduced from 60 to 18 without any difficulty.

Let $\mathbf{e}_i, 1 \leq i \leq N$ be the eigenvector corresponding to the $i$th largest eigenvalue. Suppose that we choose $\bar{N}$ eigenvectors as the coordinate axes of the parameter space, where $\bar{N} < N$. To transform an original $N$-dimensional displacement vector into an $\bar{N}$-dimensional parameter vector, an $\bar{N} \times N$ matrix $\mathbf{F}$ called the *feature matrix* is constructed:

$$\mathbf{F} = [\mathbf{e}_1 \, \mathbf{e}_2 \, \mathbf{e}_3 \ldots \mathbf{e}_{\bar{N}}]^\top, \tag{6}$$

Using the feature matrix $\mathbf{F}$, the parameter vector $\mathbf{p}_i$ corresponding to the displacement vector $v_i$ of a target example $\mathbf{T}_i$ is derived as follows:

$$\mathbf{p}_i = \mathbf{F}\mathbf{v}_i, \; 1 \leq i \leq M, \tag{7}$$

which reduces the dimensionality of the parameter space from $N$ to $\bar{N}$. This is equivalent to projecting each displacement vector $\mathbf{v}_i$ onto the eigenspace spanned by the $\bar{N}$ selected eigenvectors. We later use this feature matrix $\mathbf{F}$ to compute the parameter vector from a given displacement vector.

## 5   Facial Animation

With the target 3D face examples thus parameterized, our problem is how to blend the examples so as to resemble the input expression extracted from a face performer. Our problem is essentially one of scattered data interpolation, as we have very sparse target examples in a relatively high dimensional parameter space. To solve the problem, we predefines an weight function for each target example based on cardinal basis functions [21], which consist of linear and radial basis functions. The global shape of weight function is first approximated by linear basis functions, and then adjusted locally by radial basis functions to exactly interpolate the corresponding example.

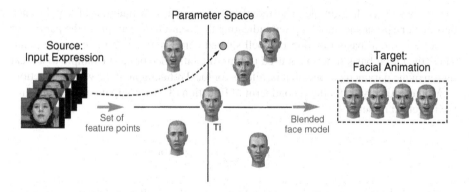

**Fig. 5.** Generating a new face model by blending target key-models

## 5.1 Weight Function

The weight function $w_i(\cdot)$ of each target example $\mathbf{T}_i, 1 \leq i \leq M$ at a parameter vector $\mathbf{p}$ is defined as follows:

$$w_i(\mathbf{p}) = \sum_{l=0}^{\bar{N}} a_{il} A_l(\mathbf{p}) + \sum_{j=1}^{M} r_{ji} R_j(\mathbf{p}). \tag{8}$$

where $A_l(\mathbf{p})$ and $a_{il}$ are the linear basis functions and their linear coefficients, respectively. $R_j(\mathbf{p})$ and $r_{ij}$ are the radial basis functions and their radial coefficients. Let $\mathbf{p}_i, 1 \leq i \leq M$ be the parameter vector of a target example $\mathbf{T}_i$. To interpolate the target examples exactly, the weight of a target example $\mathbf{T}_i$ should be one at $\mathbf{p}_i$ and zero at $\mathbf{p}_j, i \neq j$, that is, $w_i(\mathbf{p}_i) = 1$ for $i = j$ and $w_i(\mathbf{p}_j) = 0$ for $i \neq j$.

## 5.2 Linear Approximation

Our scheme first approximates the global shape of weight function by finding the hyperplane through the parameter space that best fists each example. Formally, in Equation (8), we would like to solve for the linear coefficients $a_{il}$ to fix the first term. By ignoring the second term, we obtain the following Equation 11:

$$w_i(\mathbf{p}) = \sum_{l=0}^{\bar{N}} a_{il} A_l(\mathbf{p}). \tag{9}$$

The linear bases are simply $A_l(\mathbf{p}) = \mathbf{p}^l, 1 \leq l \leq \bar{N}$, where $\mathbf{p}^l$ is the $l$th component of $\mathbf{p}$, and $A_0(\mathbf{p}) = 1$. Using the parameter vector $\mathbf{p}_i$ of each target example and its weight value $w_i(\mathbf{p}_i)$, we employ a least squares method to evaluate the unknown linear coefficients $a_{il}$ of the linear bases.

## 5.3 Radial Basis Function

Given the linear approximation, there still remain residuals between the examples and the approximated hyper-planes. To correct for the residuals, we associate radial basis functions with each example. The radial basis function is a function of the distance between one point and another point indicating the location of example in the parameter space. The radial basis function is a bell shaped curve centered at the example point. Thus, the radial basis function is used to limit the influence of each example to a local region of the parameter space, that is, allows for local refinement of the weight function.

Mathematically, to fix the second term of Equation (8), we compute the residuals for the target examples:

$$w_i'(\mathbf{p}) = w_i(\mathbf{p}) - \sum_{l=0}^{\bar{N}} a_{il} A_l(\mathbf{p}) \text{ for all } i. \tag{10}$$

The radial basis function $R_j(\mathbf{p})$ is a function of the Euclidean distance between $\mathbf{p}$ and $\mathbf{p}_j$ in the parameter space:

$$R_j(\mathbf{p}) = B\left(\frac{\|\,\mathbf{p} - \mathbf{p}_j\,\|}{\alpha}\right) \text{ for } 1 \le j \le M, \tag{11}$$

where $B(\cdot)$ is the cubic B-spline function, and $\alpha$ is the dilation factor, which is the separation to the nearest other example in the parameter space. The radial coefficients $r_{ij}$ are obtained by solving the matrix equation,

$$\mathbf{r}\mathbf{R} = \mathbf{w}', \tag{12}$$

where $\mathbf{r}$ is an $M \times M$ matrix of the unknown radial coefficients $r_{ij}$, and $\mathbf{R}$ and $\mathbf{w}'$ are the matrices of the same size defined by the radial bases and the residuals, respectively, such that $\mathbf{R}_{ij} = R_i(\mathbf{p}_j)$ and $\mathbf{w}'_{ij} = w_i'(\mathbf{p}_j)$.

### 5.4 Runtime Expression Synthesis

Given the input expression captured from a face performer, the application computes a novel output model at runtime by blending the target examples as illustrated in Figure 5. The resulting expression are produced so as to resemble the input expression. Our scheme consists of three steps. The first, as an input, the displacement vector of feature points on a face performer is given. The next step is to derive the parameter vector from the displacement vector by using the Equation 13. Finally, the predefined weight functions are computed at this parameter vector to produce the weight values, and the output model is generated by blending the target examples with respect to those weight values.

First, we form the $N$-dimensional displacement vector $\mathbf{d}_{in}$ by concatenating, in a fixed order, the 3D displacements of feature points captured from a face performer. N is three times the number of feature points for X, Y, and Z coordinates.

Next, given this $N$-dimensional displacement vector $\mathbf{d}_{in}$, we then obtain the corresponding $\bar{N}$-dimensional parameter vector $\mathbf{p}_{in}$ as follows:

$$\mathbf{p}_{in} = \mathbf{F}\mathbf{d}_{in}, \tag{13}$$

where $\mathbf{F}$ is the feature matrix defined in Equation (6).

Finally, using the predefined weight functions for the target examples $\mathbf{T}_i$ as given in Equation (8), we estimate the weight values $w_i(\mathbf{p}_{in})$ of all target examples $\mathbf{T}_i, 1 \leq i \leq M$ at the parameter $\mathbf{p}_{in}$ to generate the output face model $\mathbf{T}_{new}(\mathbf{p}_{in})$:

$$\mathbf{T}_{new}(\mathbf{p}_{in}) = \mathbf{T}_B + \sum_{i=1}^{M} w_i(\mathbf{p}_{in})(\mathbf{T}_i - \mathbf{T}_B), \tag{14}$$

where $\mathbf{T}_B$ is the target base model corresponding to the source base model $\mathbf{S}_B$ with the neutral expression.

## 6   Experimental Results

To evaluate effectiveness and performance of the proposed method, we performed experiments on a PC with Pentium IV 1.2 GHz CPU and 512 MB memory. Face images were captured with a single digital camera and sent to the PC through a video capture board at 30 frames per second. To illuminate the puppeteer's face, we used two desktop lamps each of which has a single 13W bulb. As shown in Figure 6, neither any markers were attached to performer's face nor any head-mounted camera was employed. The head was allowed to move and rotate during facial expression capture on condition that all facial features were visible.

Figures 6 (a), (d) and (g) show the captured face images of nine puppeteers. Face images after color space transformation are given in Figures 6 (b), (e), and (h). Here,

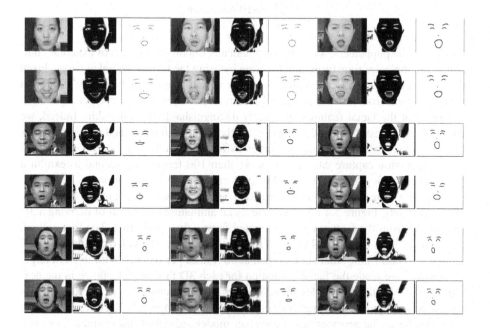

**Fig. 6.** Original images, color-transformed images, and extracted curves

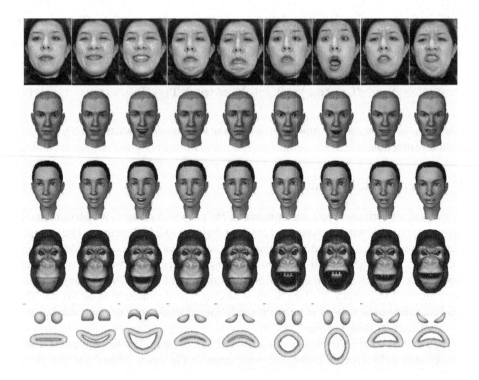

**Fig. 7.** Facial Animation

for each of the puppeteers, we could automatically obtain the weights of the color components in the color transformation function by using the trained neural network. From those images, we can observe that the intensity values of pixels in the region of the skin are so different from those of the facial features such as eyelashes, eyebrows, nostrils, and lips that the facial features are clearly distinguishable from the skin. Indeed, we were able to extract the facial features robustly from the transformed images. Figures (c), (f), and (i) exhibits the feature curves extracted from the images.Our method for facial expression capture can process more than 100 frames per second to exhibit a sufficient efficiency for real-time on-line performance-driven animation.

To demonstrate the final facial animation, we create several examples for various 3D face models. Figure 5.4 illustrates the facial animation as a result of deriving a 3D face model from the feature curve, extracted from a face performer. The first column of Figure 6 shows the original video of the face performer. The video comprises a total sequence of 800 frames that are recorded at 30 frames per second. With thirteen target key-models, we made the facial animation for each 3D face model, shown in the next four rows. Four different styles(Man, Woman, Monkey, and Toy) of 3D face models were used to show the usefulness of our example-based approach. Each result of facial animation keeps the personalities of each face model and reflects the designer's original intention. We can observe that our approach works well even though the shape of the performer's face and 3D face model largely differ.

# 7  Conclusion

In this paper, we have proposed online expression mapping method for performance-driven facial animation, reflecting the animator's creativity and imagination for a face model, by using a combination of facial expression capture and example-based animation. Our method is useful to overcome the characteristic differences between the performer's face and the target face model. Our solution consists of three major steps: facial motion capture, expression mapping, and facial animation. Our approach extracts facial expression from a performer in real time without employing a head-mounted camera or markers. With facial example-based approach, we adapt the captured motion of a performer to a specific face model, even if it is a anthropomorphized animal, in an on-line manner. Moreover, we achieve real-time facial animation by blending facial examples with their wire curves. As shown in the experimental results, our approach has achieved very convincing and lifelike facial animation following the expression of face performer, while reflecting an animator's intention, with great efficiency.

One limitation of our method require animators to prepare a set of facial examples. At the same time, it can be an advantage that it allows for human control of animation results so that the characteristics of examples are fully reflected. However, even for skilled artists, it is time consuming work to create a number of facial examples with extreme expressions. Automatic construction of facial examples from the captured expression or animator's sketch will be a good future research topic on facial animation. For more realistic facial animation, we would like to extend our scheme to incorporate subtle movements in addition to verbal and emotional expressions, such as eyeballs rolling and tongue movement.

# References

1. Basu, S., Oliver, N., Pentland, A.: 3D modeling and tracking of human lip motions. In: Proceedings of ICCV 98 (1998)
2. Black, M.J., Yacoob, Y.: Tracking and recognizing rigid and non-rigid facial motions using local parametric models of image motions. In: International Conference on Computer Vision 95, pp. 374–381 (1995)
3. Blanz, V., Vetter, T.: A morphable model for the synthesis of 3d faces. In: SIGGRAPH 1999 Conference Proceedings, pp. 187–194 (1999)
4. Chuang, E., Bregler, C.: Performance driven facial animation using blendshape interpolation. Stanford University Computer Science Technical Report, CS-TR-2002-02 (2002)
5. Chuang, E., Bregler, C.: Mood swings: Expressive speech animation. ACM Transactions on Graphics 24(2), 331–347 (2005)
6. DeCarlo, D., Metaxas, D.: Optical flow constraints on deformable models with applications to face tracking. International Journal of Computer Vision 38(2), 99–127 (2000)
7. Essa, I., Pentland, A.: Facial expression recognition usin a dynamic model and motion energy. In: Proceedings of ICCV 95, pp. 360–367 (1995)
8. Goto, T., Kshirsagar, S., Thalmann, N.M.: Real time facial feature tracking and speech acquisition for cloned head. IEEE Signal Processing Magazine 18(3), 17–25 (2001)
9. Guenter, B., Grimm, C., Wood, D., Malvar, H., Pighin, F.: Making faces. In: SIGGRAPH 98 Conference Proceedings, pp. 55–67 (1998)

10. Joshi, P., Tien, W.C., Desbrun, M., Pighin, F.: Learning controls for blend shape based realistic facial animation. In: Eurographics/SIGGRAPH Symposium on Computer Animation (2003)
11. Kahler, K., Haber, J., Seidel, H.-P.: Reanimating the dead: Reconstruction of expressive faces from skull data. In: SIGGRAPH 2003 (2003)
12. Kalra, P., Mangili, A., Thalmann, N.M., Thalmann, D.: Simulation of facial muscle actions based on rational free form deformations. In: Eurographics' 92, vol. 58, pp. 59–69 (1992)
13. Kass, M., Witkin, A., Terzopoulos, D.: Snakes: Active contour models. International Journal of Computer Vision 1(4), 321–331 (1987)
14. Lee, Y., Terzopoulos, D., Waters, K.: Realistic modeling for facial animation. In: SIGGRAPH' 95 Conference Proceedings, pp. 55–62 (1995)
15. Marschner, S.R., Guenter, B., Raghupathy, S.: Modeling and rendering for realistic facial animation. In: EUROGRAPHICS Rendering Workshop 2000, pp. 98–110 (2000)
16. Oliver, N., Pentland, A., Berard, F.: Lafter: Lips and face tracking. In: Computer Vision and Pattern Recognition '97 (1997)
17. Pighin, F., Szeliski, R., Salesin, D.: Resynthesizing facial animation through 3d model-based tracking. In: International Conference on Computer Vision, pp. 143–150 (1999)
18. Pratt, W.K.: Digital Image Processing, 2nd edn. Wiley Interscience, Chichester (1991)
19. Pyun, H., Kim, Y., Chae, W., Kang, H.W., Shin, S.Y.: An example-based approach for facial expression cloning. In: Eurographics/SIGGRAPH Symposium on Computer Animation (2003)
20. Singh, K., Fiume, E.: Wires: A Geometric Deformation Technique. In: SIGGRAPH' 98 Conference Proceedings, pp. 299–308 (1998)
21. Sloan, P.-P., Rose, C.F., Cohen, M.F.: Shape by example. In: Proceedings of 2001 Symposium on Interactive 3D Graphics, pp. 135–144 (2001)
22. Terzopoulos, D., Waters, K.: Analysis and synthesis of facial image sequences using physical and anatomical models. IEEE Transactions of Pattern Analysis and Machine Intelligence 15(6), 569–579 (1993)
23. Thalmann, N.M., Pandzic, I., Kalra, P.: Interactive facial animation and communication. In: Tutorial of Computer Graphics International '96, pp. 117–130 (1996)
24. Williams, L.: Performance-driven facial animation. In: Proceedings of ACM SIGGRAPH Conference, pp. 235–242. ACM Press, New York (1990)
25. Zhang, L., Snavely, N., Curless, B., Seitz, S.M.: Spacetime faces: High resolution capture for modeling and animation. ACM Transactions on Graphics 23(3), 548–558 (2004)
26. Zhang, Q., Liu, Z., Guo, B., Shum, H.: Geometry-driven photorealistic facial expression synthesis. In: Eurographics/SIGGRAPH Symposium on Computer Animation (2003)

# Predicting Peer Offline Probability in BitTorrent Using Nonlinear Regression

Dongdong Nie[1], Qinyong Ma[2], Lizhuang Ma[1], and Wuzheng Tan[1]

[1] Computer Science & Engineering Department, Shanghai Jiao Tong University, Shanghai
[2] Computer Science & Engineering Department, Zhejiang University, Hangzhou
niedd.mail@gmail.com, mqyray@163.com, ma-lz@cs.sjtu.edu.cn,
tanwuzheng@sjtu.edu.cn

**Abstract.** BitTorrent is a popular and scalable P2P content distribution tool. This study attempts to analyze the factors that affect the offline probability of BitTorrent peer, and express the probability using these factors. We first collect large data set of BitTorrent peers' activities. Then we use nonlinear least-squares regression to determine the probability distribution function for each of the three factors (download percent, download speed, and local time) and the joint probability distribution function of the three factors, and use another large data set to verify the prediction results.

**Keywords:** BitTorrent; Offline; Probability Distribution; Regression.

## 1 Introduction

BitTorrent [1] is a popular and scalable P2P content distribution tool. In the recent years, many research efforts [5, 6, 7, 8] have focused on P2P systems. Some works on the measurements of P2P systems have studied the distributions of peer's session time. Saroiu, et al. [9] present the session durations of Napster and Gnutella. Chu, et al. [10] present the first study of the popularity of files stored and transferred among peers in Napster and Gnutella over month-long periods, and propose that the distribution of session lengths follows a log-quadratic function. Stutzbach, et al. [2, 11] show that peer uptime follows a power-law distribution rather than the commonly assumed Poisson distribution. Besides session time, some studies [3, 9, 10] find that peer's availability varies with the hour of the day. We are inspired by this finding to express offline probability distribution by local time.

If peer's offline probability can be expressed clearly, it would be helpful for BitTorrent to improve its downloading strategy or to implement some interesting functions. In this paper, we try to analyze the factors that affect the offline probability of BitTorrent peer, and describe the probability using these factors. We find that besides uptime, there are still some other important factors: download percent, download speed, and local time. We regard each factor as a random variable. From the large data set of peer activities obtained in a BitTorrent network, we get these variables' values when each peer enters offline state. Based on these values, we get the

L. Ma, R. Nakatsu, and M. Rauterberg (Eds.): ICEC 2007, LNCS 4740, pp. 339–344, 2007.

distribution data for each variable, and determine the expressions to represent these distributions by performing a nonlinear least-squares regression (NLSR) on each distribution data. Then we try to use three main factors (download percent, download speed, and local time) to express the offline probability together, and use another set of BitTorrent log data to verify the expressions.

## 2 Data Set

The data set consists of two parts. The first part, which is called the training set, contains the data that is used for regression analysis. We acquire the training set with the same method as used in [3]. We use an application to acquire the data in four steps. First, it monitors, gathers, and parses the HTML pages of the bt.5qzone.net, a famous BitTorrent website in CERNET (China Education and Research Network), and downloads some new .torrent files randomly. Second, parses the downloaded .torrent file to get corresponding tracker URLs. Third, links to each tracker to get the list of all the peers downloading the files. Fourth, link to each non-firewalled downloading peer, and begin to record its session data. A number of 219063 valid session data was acquired during the period from February 2006 to April 2006. We use this data set to determine the probability distribution function (PDF) of each variable and the joint probability distribution function (JPDF) of three variables.

The second part, which is called the test set, is the BitTorrent tracker log described in [4]. The authors obtained a RedHat torrent's tracker log on a five months long period. The log contains statistics for about 180,000 clients, and it clearly exhibits an initial flash-crowd period with more than 50,000 clients initiating a download in the first five days. We use the filtered 144,196 valid session data as the test set to verify the determined distribution functions.

In the training set and the test set, we only care about the offline data, which is the data related to peer's offline state. The offline data includes the values of the following variables when each peer enters offline state: uptime (equals to session time), download percent, download speed, and local time.

The uptime values can be obtained from the data set directly. A peer's session time is a combination of the time it spends to download the file (the download time) and the additional time it keeps running after the download is complete (the lingering time).

We let a peer's download percent value could be larger than 100%. Its value would exceed 100% if the lingering time is larger than zero. Let $T_d$ be the download time. Let $T_l$ be the lingering time, and set $T_l = 0$ if the download has not be completed. Let $S_d$ be the size of the data downloaded by the peer in $T_d$. Let $S_f$ be the total size of the files. The download percent $P_d$ is calculated as: $P_d = S_d / S_f + T_l / T_d$.

A peer's download speed value is calculated from the last two known sizes of the data downloaded by the peer. The calculated download speed will be zero if the peer has downloaded all the files.

To calculate a peer's local time, we first get the its time zone from its IP address, then converts the recorded offline time to its time zone's corresponding local time.

For the offline data obtained above, we define the following intervals as the analysis domain: uptime is limited to the interval: [0, 1005) minutes, download percent is limited to the interval: [0, 201) percent, and download speed is limit to the interval:

[0, 301500) Bps. The domain covers about 85% of the total offline data. The skipped data covers a large span, while its proportion is small. For instance, the proportion of the sessions with uptimes longer than 1005 minutes is less than 4% of total sessions, but their values covers a large span of time, some peers' uptimes even exceed 100000 minutes. Since peer uptimes follow a power-law distribution, it has some sessions with much longer durations, as well as has a much larger fraction of sessions with short durations. The offline probability of the skipped sessions is very low, so that the limited domain let us concentrate on the sessions with higher offline probabilities, while it has little influence on the sessions with low offline probabilities. For instance, when we compare two peers' offline probabilities, 30% and 10% have much difference, but the difference between 0.01% and 0.03% is little.

The data types of uptime, download percent, and download speed are all float. To facilitate calculation, we divide each variable's domain interval into 100 equal subintervals by rounding to the nearest integer. For instance, uptime's domain interval [0, 1005) is divided into 100 equal subintervals, then the value 3 represents the interval [25, 35). The data type of local time is integer, and the time unit is hour.

## 3  Determine the Distributions of the Variables

Here we first discuss the limitation if we only use the uptime to express peer's offline probability. Consistent with [2], we confirm that the uptime follows a power-law distribution. But we find that offline probability is correlated with other factors. Peer's offline probability varies significantly with its download speed when uptime is fixed. So the accuracy is often limited if we only use uptime to express peer's offline probability. The phenomenon can also be found by the offline probability distribution of download percent described blow. A peer's offline probability would increase suddenly when it just has completed the downloading.

We first get the offline probability distribution of download percent from training set, then attempt to determine its PDF by NLSR. We attempt to use some curve equations to perform the NLSR, and select the equation with best fitting for larger value as its PDF. Let $x_p$ be the download percent. The offline PDF of download percent can be expressed as:

$$y_p = \frac{1}{17.42 \times x_p^{0.93218} + 1.8105} \quad (x_p < 50)$$

$$y_p = \frac{1}{17.42 \times x_p^{0.93218} + 1.8105} + \frac{1}{22.498 \times (x_p - 50)^{1.6413} + 25.6} \quad (x_p \geq 50)$$

(1)

We use the equation to calculate the prediction value, and verify it with the test set. Fig. 1 illustrates the result, in which (a), (b) show the same data; the only difference is that the y-axis in (a) is in log scale. As shown in the figure, a peer's offline probability would increase suddenly when it just has completed the downloading. As can be observed better in (b), the obtained PDF has higher accuracy for larger offline probabilities. It is because of our preference for larger offline probabilities.

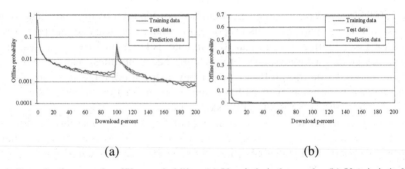

**Fig. 1.** Download percent's offline probability: (a) Y-axis is in log scale; (b) Y-axis is in linear scale

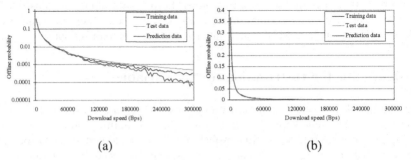

**Fig. 2.** Download speed's offline probability: (a) Y-axis is in log scale; (b) Y-axis is in linear scale

Using the above method, we obtain the PDF of download speed:

$$y_s = \frac{1}{3.1308 \times x_s^{1.3982} + 2.7078} \tag{2}$$

where $x_s$ is the download speed. The result is illustrated in Fig. 2.

Setting $x_t$ as the local time, we obtain the PDF of local time similarly:

$$y_t = 0.043043 - 0.008794 \times \sin(0.23499 \times x_t + 6.4713) + \\ 0.0085267 \times \sin(0.3914 \times x_t + 2.4461) \tag{3}$$

Now we try to use the three variables (download percent, download speed, and local time) to express the offline probability together. The value of the offline probability expressed by three variables together is relative small. Since we prefer larger offline probability, the analysis domain is redefined to the following intervals: download percent is limited to the intervals: [0, 6] & [100, 102] percent, and download speed is limit to the interval: [0, 30150} Bps, while local time is unlimited. Then we perform a multiple least-squares nonlinear regression on the data by the Gauss-Newton method. We obtain the following JPDF:

$$y_p = \frac{1}{2.206 \times x_p^{1.1437} + 0.11516} \quad (x_p < 50)$$

$$y_p = \frac{1}{2.206 \times x_p^{1.1437} + 0.11516} + \tag{4}$$

$$0.037397 + 0.59592 \times \exp(0.60185 - 1.3989*(x_p - 50)) \quad (x_p \geq 50)$$

$$y_s = \frac{1}{1.2357 \times x_s^{1.816} + 2.2582} \tag{5}$$

$$y_t = (0.0021369 + 0.00083506 \times \sin(0.27575 \times x_t + 2.9867) + \tag{6}$$
$$0.00026875 \times \sin(0.5096 \times x_t + 1.3564))$$

$$y = y_p \times y_s \times y_t \tag{7}$$

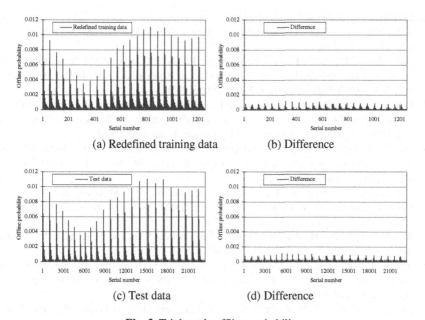

(a) Redefined training data          (b) Difference

(c) Test data          (d) Difference

**Fig. 3.** Triple set's offline probability

The result is illustrated in Fig. 3, in which X-axis is the serial number of the triple (download percent, download speed, local time) set; (a) illustrates the distribution of the redefined training data; (b) illustrates the difference between the prediction data and the redefined training data; (c) illustrates the distribution of the test data; (d) illustrates the difference between the prediction data and the test data.

## 4   Conclusions

This study attempts to predict peer's offline probability in BitTorrent. We first collect large data set of BitTorrent peers' activities. Then we use nonlinear least-squares regression to obtain the probability distribution functions and the joint probability distribution functions for three variables, and compare the prediction values with another large data set. The result shows that the PDFs are relative accurate for larger offline probabilities.

We will collect other popular P2P systems' activity data in the future, and use regression to analyze the offline probabilities of other P2P systems. We will also seek other ways to predict peer's offline probability.

**Acknowledgement.** This work is supported by National Science Foundation of China No.60403044, No. 60573147 and partly funded by the National Key Basic Research and Development Plan of China ("973"Projects)(2006CB303105).

## References

1. BitTorrent: http://www.bittorrent.com/
2. Stutzbach, D., Rejaie, R.: Characterizing Churn in Peer-to-Peer Networks. Technical report CIS-TR-05-03 (2005)
3. Pouwelse, J., Garbacki, P., Epema, D., Sips, H.: The BitTorrent P2P File-Sharing System: Measurements And Analysis. In: Castro, M., van Renesse, R. (eds.) IPTPS 2005. LNCS, vol. 3640, pp. 205–216. Springer, Heidelberg (2005)
4. Izal, M., Urvoy-Keller, G., Biersack, E., Felber, P., Al Hamra, A., Garces-Erice, L.: Dissecting BitTorrent: Five Months in a Torrent's Lifetime. In: Barakat, C., Pratt, I. (eds.) PAM 2004. LNCS, vol. 3015, pp. 1–11. Springer, Heidelberg (2004)
5. Stoica, I., Morris, R., Karger, D., Frans Kaashoek, M., Balakrishnan, H.: Chord: A Scalable Peer-To-Peer Lookup Service for Internet Applications. In: ACM SIGCOMM 2001, San Deigo, CA, pp. 149–160 (2001)
6. Ratnasamy, S., Francis, P., Handley, M., Karp, R., Shenker, S.: A Scalable Content-Addressable Network. In: ACM SIGCOMM 2001, San Diego, CA, pp. 161–172 (2001)
7. Mischke, J., Stiller, B.: Rich and Scalable Peer-to-Peer Search with SHARK. In: AMS'03, pp. 112–122. IEEE Press, Washington (2003)
8. Zhang, C., Krishnamurthy, A., Wang, R.: Brushwood: Distributed Trees in Peer-to-Peer Systems. In: Castro, M., van Renesse, R. (eds.) IPTPS 2005. LNCS, vol. 3640, pp. 47–57. Springer, Heidelberg (2005)
9. Saroiu, S., Gummadi, P., Gribble, S.: A Measurement Study of Peer-to-Peer File Sharing Systems. In: Kienzle, M.G. (ed.) Multimedia Computing and Networking, pp. 156–170. SPIE, San Jose (2002)
10. Chu, J., Labonte, K., Levine, B.: Availability and Locality Measurements of Peer-to-Peer File Systems. In: ITCom: Scalability and Traffic Control in IP Networks, Boston, pp. 310–321 (2002)
11. Stutzbach, D., Rejaie, R.: Towards a Better Understanding of Churn in Peer-to-Peer Networks. Technical Report CIS-TR-04-06 (2004)

# Game Design Guided by Visual Attention

Li Jie and James J. Clark

Centre for Intelligent Machines
McGill University

**Abstract.** Visual attention plays a critical role in game playing. A better understanding of the allocation of visual attention can benefit the design of game scenarios. In this paper we propose to design games in different difficulty levels based on the estimation of attention. We use eye movement information in an analysis of attention. Eye fixation and pursuit conditions are considered separately. We find that the image complexity at eye fixation points and the relative position between pursuit direction and disturbance during pursuit eye movements are significant for attention allocation. This result is applied to the design of an interactive 2D game having two difficulty levels. Player response speeds and scores are compared for each difficulty level of the game.

**Keywords:** game design, visual attention, eye fixation, eye pursuit.

## 1 Introduction

It is well known that computer games have become a very popular and widespread form of entertainment. Now recent studies have shown that computer games are no longer only for entertaining. Some research suggests that games may increase player's attention capacities [1]. Work done by Green and Bavelier found that frequent game players score higher on some attention tasks [2]. Special computer games are also used to help children train their brains to pay attention [3,4] and seniors to improve their memory and attention. It is becoming promising to apply games to health therapy and training.

Undoubtedly visual attention plays a critical role during game playing. Losing games often occur due to player's late noticing or even complete unawareness of important items. A better understanding of visual attention can further improve the design of game scenarios. Studies of visual attention can inform game designers how to attract player's attention (to make games easier) and how to avoid player's attention (to make games harder) under various situations. In this way, games can be designed for different levels of players or specific usages. This brings a new view for game design.

Most current visual attention models ignore top-down influence and focus only on bottom-up information in the processing of natural scenes. The saliency model of attention proposed by Koch, Itti and colleagues used bottom-up information of scenes to indicate the possible locations of attention [5]. It is, however, well known that scene context and task strongly influence attention [6,7,8,9,10,11]. It

L. Ma, R. Nakatsu, and M. Rauterberg (Eds.): ICEC 2007, LNCS 4740, pp. 345–355, 2007.

is even more important to consider top-down factors of attention when estimating attention allocation during games, because attention is more task-relevant and goal-driven for game playing than for free-viewing of scenes.

In this paper, we propose a new way to estimate task-dependent attention allocation based on eye movement information (specifically detecting fixation and pursuit conditions). Combining such eye movement information with image information at eye fixation points, we also provide a simple way to estimate to which extent attention is engaged at a fixation point. Based on the estimation of attention allocation, we show how an interactive computer game can be designed to exhibit different difficulty levels. The game is used to verify our hypotheses concerning attention and also shows the feasibility of applying these ideas to game design.

## 2   Motivation

Reseach on eye movements show that eye movements reflect human thought processes; this led Yarbus to suggest that an observer's thought may be followed to some extent from records of his eye movements [12]. This motivates us to take eye movement information into estimating attention during game play, and to infer top-down influences. Task dependence is a very complex issue, as there are a large number of cognitive tasks that a person can be engaged in, even in an activity as focused as game playing. To simplify the problem we will consider just two rather general classes of task - those that involve having the eye fixed at a specific location and those in which the eye is moving (visual pursuit). As such, we will examine the allocation of attention in each of these two conditions.

Tracking of moving objects with the eye is needed in many different computer games. Conversely, many game situations require the eye be fixed at a given spot, in order to extract information from that spot or to wait for an expected event. Thus, it is necessary, and rewarding, to consider attention based on the specific motion of the eye. Recent studies [13,14] have shown that during pursuit, the allocation of attention in space is found to lead the pursuit direction (i.e. in the direction of object motion). The distance by which attention leads the eye is observed to increase as the pursuit velocity increases. Thus, if we know that the eye is undergoing a pursuit motion we can predict that the attention is most likely to be allocated at some distance ahead of the motion.

In the case of eye fixation, we consider two important aspects. The first is consideration of where the gaze tends to be directed (the fixation point) and the second is consideration of how long the gaze remains at the fixation point (fixation duration). There has been much work done regarding the location of fixation points [15,16,17]. But relatively little research has been aimed at understanding fixation duration during scene viewing. The prediction of the distribution of attention can be markedly different based on different prediction of fixation duration. In this paper, we will explore a way of relating fixation duration to scene complexity. The issue of fixation duration is, in our view, the problem of how sticky attention is "glued" to a fixation point once the fixation point is chosen. The problem has been studied [10,18,19,20,21] and combined into models of reading [22]. But for computational attention models of scenes, it has been neglected. The saliency model of attention relates fixation duration to the saliency value at fixation points [5], incorporating features such as scene luminance [20] and contrast [21]. Fixation duration has also been found to be longer when viewing face images [23] and color photographs [19]. All these studies suggest that fixation duration is influenced by the processing of information presented at the current fixation point. But saliency only tells part of the story. Not only bottom-up but also top-down attentional factors are involved in determining fixation duration. The saliency value may give clues of where attention or the gaze is directed at the beginning of viewing a scene. But once fixation begins, for duration of the fixation, we believe that the processing of the information of image at the fixation point is more important than the raw saliency at the fixation location. In particular, we take as a simple model, that the fixation duration is related to the complexity of the image or scene at the fixation point, as a higher complexity implies that the brain requires a more detailed processing of the visual input to make sense of the scene. For the purposes of computer game design, we hypothesize that local measurements of fixation point scene complexity can be used to predict the stickiness of attention, which will affect the speed at which attention can be shifted away to new targets, and hence will affect reaction times.

Based on these two task-dependent aspects of the attention related to eye movements (i.e. fixation duration and attention during pursuit) we carried out a set of experiments. These experiments tested the effect of (in the fixation case) image complexity on reaction time, and (in the pursuit case) the relative location of targets on reaction time. The results obtained during the experiments were then applied to an interactive 2D computer game to make the game easier or harder through controlling the position of game elements based on our attention models. Consistent results were shown. The idea of designing games, taking into account of attention characteristics during different tasks was demonstrated.

## 3 Methods

### 3.1 Experiment Procedure and Apparatus

The purpose of the first experiment was to detect if image complexity at the fixation point affected the disengagement of attention during fixation and pursuit conditions.

The visual stimuli were generated by a computer and displayed on a screen of a 1280*1024 pixel monitor at a distance of 18 inches (1 degree of visual angle corresponded to approx 30 pixels). Five hundred color images (640*480) from different scene categories (landscape, building, city scene, indoor scene, animal, etc) were used as background. Figure 1 shows some sample images from the 500 images that were shown as background images. At the beginning of each trial, a fixation point of size (0.26*0.26 deg) appeared at the center of the monitor. The background of the monitor was set to be black at this time. After subjects centered their fixations on the fixation point, and felt ready for the experiment, they initiated trials with a key-press. Once subjects triggered the trials, a background image was shown, centered on the display. One small green square of size (0.26*0.26 deg) started to move either rightward or leftward at a speed of 1.4 deg per sec from the center of the background. Subjects were instructed to either pursue the moving square or freely view images. Approximately 2 seconds after the start of every trial, one square object of size (0.65*0.65 deg), either in green or in blue, appeared at random positions inside of images. Subjects were required to react to the color of the square object as soon as possible by pressing corresponding mouse buttons.

**Fig. 1.** Examples of images used as background for the experiment. Each line represents one category of images. From left to Right: city scene, landscape, building, animal, and interior scene.

Six subjects (five males, one female) participated in the experiment. The subjects were all recent graduate students. Data were collected after informed consent was obtained. Experimental sessions lasted for approximately one and a half hours with mandatory three-minute rest periods occurring after approximately every five minutes of data collection. Subjects were given practice in performing the task before collecting experimental data. Subjects had control over when to start a trial through the pressing of a keyboard button. They were seated approximately 18 inches away from the display, and a chin rest was used to minimize head movements. An eye tracker (ISCAN RK-726PCI) was used to record the subjects left eye positions at 240HZ during experiments. Subjects used both eyes to conduct the experiments.

### 3.2   Data Analysis of Eye Positions

At the beginning of every experimental session, we calibrated the eye tracker by having subjects look at a five-point calibration display. Data analysis was carried out on every single trial. By visual inspection of the individual recordings, trials with blinks before the appearance of the flashed square object, missed pursuits, or missed executions were excluded from further analysis. For free viewing trials,

trials were excluded as well if the flashed square object appeared within the same area as previous eye fixation locations. Eye position data were smoothed with a median filter (9 samples).

## 3.3   Entropy of Images

To quantify how much information contained at a fixation point, we used the entropy of the image data in a neighborhood around fixation points. We will refer to this as the information quantity.

A segmentation of the image at the fixation point was first computed [?]. It is a process to classify each image pixel to one of the image parts, and reduces noise. After segmentation, the color pixel data were converted into graylevel. Given the human visual systems "preference" for luminance information, the graylevel values were obtained by the luminance of original images. Entropy was therefore computed for the images based on the luminance values (Y) of the segemented images. Y was obtained according to the following formula. Y = 0.299 R + 0.587 G + 0.114 B.

## 4   Results

### 4.1   For the Free Viewing Condition

The effects of local image entropy in a neighborhood about the fixation area and the global image entropy over the whole image were both checked. Figure 2 show the mean reaction time (to the flashed square object) as a function of the local image entropy at fixation area and image entropy of whole image separately. As expected, we observed the tendency that reaction time increased as the image entropy at local fixation area increased. But for the global image entropy over the whole image, no such tendency was observed. This indicates that the local entropy at the fixation area is potentially one factor related to the time of disengagement of attention at fixation points.

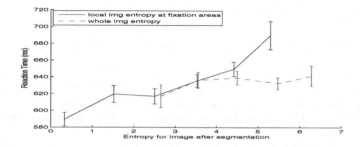

**Fig. 2.** The relationship between the image entropy and reaction time during eye fixation. Error bars represent standard errors of the mean (same for the following figures).

## 4.2   For the Pursuit Condition

The same factors were checked in the pursuit condition. In this case, however, no consistent relationship was found between the image entropy at the eye position and the reaction time. Results are shown in Figure 3. For the case when the flash appeared in front of the pursuit direction, the image entropy of the whole image showed a tendency to affect reaction time. However, this was not found for the case when the flash appeared in the opposite direction as pursuit.

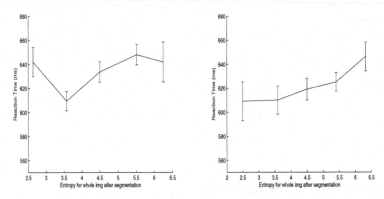

(a) Relationship between image entropy and reaction time. The flash appears behind the pursuit direction.

(b) Relationship between image entropy and reaction time. The flash appears ahead of the pursuit direction.

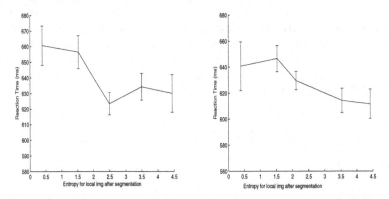

(c) Relationship between local image entropy and reaction time. The flash appears behind the pursuit direction.

(d) Relationship between local image entropy and reaction time. The flash appears ahead of the pursuit direction.

**Fig. 3.** Relationship btw img entropy and reaction time during eye pursuit

Following the experiments described in [13,14], we also checked the subject's reaction time for fixation and pursuit situations separately. For pursuit case, the reaction time was compared under two different conditions. They are where the flashed object appears ahead of the pursuit direction and and where the flashed object appears in the wake of pursuit direction. The results for the comparison of reaction time in these two conditions is shown in Figure 4. From the figure, we can observe that the reaction times for two pursuit cases are significantly different. Reaction times are close to each other for the case of fixation and the case of flash behind the pursuit direction, and significantly larger than when the flash occurs in the direction of pursuit. This result is consistent with what was found in [13,14], where attention was observed to be biased towards the pursuit direction. The bias offset is related to pursuit velocities. The faster the pursuit velocity is, the further ahead attention tends to bias.

We see from these results that the image content at fixation points is more important in affecting attention allocation for fixation than for pursuit. In the pursuit condition, the relative position between the pursuit direction and the visual disturbance is more important than image content.

## 5   Game Application

The results obtained from the previous experiment were applied to an interactive pc game. The game was designed as a normal pc shooter game, except that during the game, eye position information was recorded and analyzed. The eye tracker information was used to determine whether the eye was fixated or was engaged in visual pursuit. This was then used to adjust the strategy employed to present game elements.

The game was designed to exhibit two difficulty levels, hard and easy. For the hard level, enemies were designed to appear at the location of high attentional cost. For the easy levels, enemies were designed to appear at the location with attentional benefit. For the hard level, enemies were displayed when the eye was fixated at a location of image with high entropy, or were presented at a location in the direction opposite to pursuit. For the easy level, enemies were displayed when the eye was fixated at a location of low image entropy, or if the eye was engaged in visual pursuit, the enemies were displayed at a location in the same direction as pursuit.

The game was designed as follows. Four types of enemies appeared during games. They were all shooters, either with bullets, bombs, fireballs, or missiles. Three shooters were displayed right from the beginning of the games. These moved horizontally and shot during moving. They stopped moving temporarily if shot 20 times by players. The player's score was increased by shooting shooters or decreased by being shot. In addition to these three shooters, other enemies would appear continuously. The type of enemies and their locations depended on the eye movement information during playing. When a bomb appeared, it would explode shortly after its appearance. To be protected from the blast, players needed to hide from it.Fireballs would always appear at the right or left bottom corner of the background. They would move horizontally either leftward or rightward, depending on their initial location. To be protected from a fireball, players needed to jump up from the ground. Scores would be deducted if caught

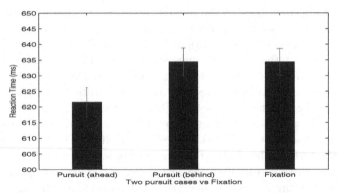

**Fig. 4.** Comparison of reaction time under the pursuit and fixation conditions

**Fig. 5.** One screenshot for the game. The green figures are the three shooters. The blue figure represents players. The red circles show the fixation areas with low and high entropies (low entropy corresponding to easy level, high entropy corresponding to hard level.

by a bomb blast or a fireball. The missile enemy type was used to trigger eye pursuit in the player. This type of enemy flew horizontally at a speed of 4 deg per sec. Players could gain higher scores by pursuing the missile and correctly responding to a number (from 0 to 9) displayed on the missile. The number would appear randomly during the flight of the missile. Players were also allowed to shoot and move horizontally, except while hiding and jumping. The game background was set to images selected from different categories (landscape, city

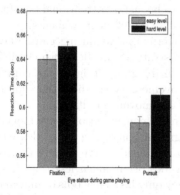
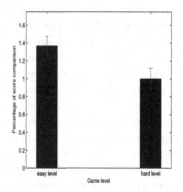

(a) Reaction time for hard and easy levels of the games.

(b) Score comparison for hard and easy levels of the games.Mean score for hard level game is taken to be 1.

**Fig. 6.** Comparison of RT and Scores for hard and easy games

scene, building, animal, etc). Each image background lasted approximately 10 seconds with random numbers of appearance of enemies. A screenshot of the game during play is shown in Figure 5.

The same experimental environment was used in testing the game as in the previous experiment. Five subjects (three females, two males) played this game. Each session of the game lasted approximately six minutes. In total, each subject played the game for approximately three hours. Game levels were alternated randomly for each player without notifying them.

Reaction times and scores were analyzed after the experiment. Figure 6 shows the results. We observed longer reaction times for the hard game and shorter reaction time for the easy game. Statistical significance testing using a Ttest shows significant differences between the reaction times. Also the scores for the two levels of games were significantly different. Higher scores were observed for the easy game and lower scores were observed for the hard game. These indicate that the games were successfully designed into two difficulty levels based on the consideration of attention allocation.

## 6 Discussion and Conclusion

Attention plays a critical role during game playing. A better understanding of attention allocation during different tasks will benefit game design. Based on a model of attention allocation, we can make a game harder by placing important game-relevant items in regions with less attention or we can make a game easier by placing important game-relevant items in regions with more attention. We applied this strategy to an interactive computer game. The test result shows that subjects responded significantly differently to items placed at different attention allocation areas. As expected, for eyes fixated in areas with lower local image entropy, reaction to peripheral targets tends to be faster. Attentional benefit was also associated with items appearing ahead of eye pursuit movements.

Both fixation and pursuit eye motion patterns appear during game playing. Because of the different attention allocation strategies in these two conditions, only considering one type of eye movement during game design is not complete. Our test results separating different eye movement types show the significant differences of reaction time for each type of eye movement situation.

The main contribution of this study is its novel consideration of eye movement types: fixation and pursuit into game design. Although the same idea can be applied to saccade eye movement as well, our consideration is only limited to fixation and pursuit currently, because saccades occur much less than fixation and pursuit, and also once saccades occur, they only last a few tens or hundreds of milliseconds. Results acquired from the experiment were applied to an interactive 2D computer game. Consistent results were shown, which validated the previous psychophysical studies and showed the feasibility of the design idea. Our results suggest that computer game design can benefit from the study of attention, taking into account of different types of eye movements.

**Ethics Approval Disclaimer.** The research presented in this paper involved psychophysical experimentation with human subjects. Prior to carrying out such experimentation, details of the procedures, techniques, and equipment involved in it were approved by the Ethics Review Committee of the Faculty of Education at McGill University.

# References

1. Eriksen, B.A., Eriksen, C.W.: Effects of noise letters upon the identification of a target letter in nonsearch task. Percept. Psychophys. 16, 143V149 (1974)
2. Green, C.S., Bavelier, D.: Action video game modifies visual selective attention. Nature 423, 534V537 (2003)
3. Rueda, M.R., Rothbart, M.K., McCandliss, B.D., Saccomanno, L., Posner, M.I.: From the cover: Training, maturation, and genetic influences on the development of executive attention. PNAS 102, 14931–14936 (2005)
4. Dye, M.W.G., Bavelier, D.: Playing video games enhances visual attention in children. Journal of Vision 4(11), 40a (2004)
5. Itti, L., Koch, C.: A saliency-based search mechanism for overt and covert shift of visual attention. Vision Research 40(10-12), 1489–1506 (2000)
6. Wolfe, J., Cave, K., Franzel, S.: Guided search: An alternative to the feature integration model for visual search. J. Exp. Psychol. Hum. Percept. Perform, 419–433 (1989)
7. Oliva, A., Torralba, A., Castelhano, M.S., Henderson, J.M.: Top-down control of visual attention in object detection. In: IEEE proceedings of the International Conference on Image processing, pp. 253–256. IEEE, Los Alamitos (2003)
8. Land, M.F., Hayhoe, M.: what ways do eye movements contribute to everyday activities? Vision Research, 3559–3565 (2001)
9. Turano, K.A., Geruschat, D.R., Baker, F.H.: Oculomotor strategies for the direction of gaze tested with a real-world activity. Vision Research, 333–346 (2003)

10. Henderson, J.M., Weeks, P.A., Hollingworth, A.: The effects of semantic consistency on eye movements during complex scene viewing. J. Exp. Psychol. Hum. Percept. Perform, 210–228 (1999)
11. Pomplun, M.: Saccadic selectivity in complex visual search displays. Vision Research 12, 1886–1900 (2005)
12. Yarbus, A.F.: Eye Movements and Vision. Plenum Press, New York (1967)
13. van Donkelaar, P., Drew, A.S.: The allocation of attention during smooth pursuit eye movements. Prog. Brain Res. 267–277 (2002)
14. Jie, L., Clark, J.J.: Microsaccadic eye movements during ocular pursuit. Vision Sciences Society Annual Meeting (VSS) 8, 697a (2005)
15. Stiefelhagen, R., Zhu, J.: Head orientation and gaze direction in meetings. In: Conference on Human Factors in Computing Systems, pp. 858–859 (2002)
16. Kayser, C., Nielsen, K.J., Logothetis, N.K.: Fixations in natural scenes: interaction of image structure and image content. Vision Research 16, 2535–2545 (2006)
17. Rajashekar, U., Cormack, L.K., Bovik, A.C.: Image features that draw fixations. In: Proc. IEEE Int. Conf. Image Proc., pp. 313–316 (September 2003)
18. Rayner, K.: Eye movements in reading and information processing: 20 years of research. Psychol. Bull. 372–422 (1998)
19. Henderson, J.M., Hollingworth, A.: Eye movements during scene viewing: an overview. In: Underwood, G. (ed.) Eye Guidance in Reading and Scene Perception, pp. 269–283 (1998)
20. Loftus, G.R.: Picture perception: effects of luminance on available information and information-extraction rate. J. Exp. Psychol. Gen. 342–356 (1985)
21. Loftus, G.R., Nishimoto, T.: Effects of visual degradation on eye-fixation durations, perceptual processing, and long-term visual memory. In: Rayner, K. (ed.) Eye Movements and Visual Cognition: Scene Perception and Reading, pp. 203–226 (1992)
22. Reichle, E.D., Pollatsek, A., Fisher, D.L., Rayner, K.: Toward a model of eye movement control in reading. Psychol. Rev. 125–157 (1989)
23. Guo, K., Mahmoodi, S., Robertson, R.G., Young, M.P.: Longer fixation duration while viewing face images. Experimental Brain Research 1 (2006)
24. Felzenszwalb, P.F., Huttenlocher, D.P.: Efficient graph-based images segmentation. International Journal of Computer Vision 2 (September 2004)

# Dialogs Taking into Account Experience, Emotions and Personality

Anne-Gwenn Bosser[1], Guillaume Levieux[1], Karim Sehaba[2]
Axel Buendia[4], Vincent Corruble[2], Guillaume de Fondaumière[3], Viviane Gal[1],
Stéphane Natkin[1], and Nicolas Sabouret[2]

[1] Conservatoire National des Arts et Métiers, Paris, France
emcedric@cnam.fr
[2] Laboratoire d'Informatique de Paris 6
Université Pierre et Marie Curie – Paris 6, France
firstname.lastname@lip6.fr
[3] Quantic Dream, Paris, France
quantic@quanticdream.com
[4] SpirOps, Paris, France
firstname.lastname@spirops.com

**Abstract.** This paper describes the DEEP project (Dialogs taking into account Experience, Emotions and Personality, adapted to computer games), which started in June 2006. The aim of the project is to provide generic solutions for the integration of autonomous Non Player Characters (NPCs) in next-generation adventure games. DEEP NPCs, equipped with a personality and a believable emotional engine, will use context-based information from the game environment and the player behavior to provide entertaining, rich and relevant dialogs.

**Keywords:** narrative intelligence, interactive narrative, interactive drama, narrative structures, behavior engine, agents, virtual characters, personality model, emotion model, dialog.

## 1 Introduction

In most computer games, especially in solo adventure games, the player immersion quality is directly related to the design of a believable environment. One of the most important constituent of such an environment is its population, the Non-Player Characters (NPCs). These are usually designed through script-level programming. This technique cannot afford the required variability, and can lead to boring, repetitive, or even inconsistent NPCs behavior [9].

In this context, the DEEP project[1] aim is to provide generic solutions for the integration of realistic, autonomous, intelligent and emotional NPCs in next-generation adventure games. The project focuses on providing rich dialog between the player and NPCs. Our approach combines two fundamental research

---

[1] The DEEP project is funded by the French ministries of Culture and Communication (CNC), Research and Industry through the RIAM (Recherche et Innovation en Audiovisuel et Multimédia) network.

L. Ma, R. Nakatsu, and M. Rauterberg (Eds.): ICEC 2007, LNCS 4740, pp. 356–362, 2007.

directions usually seen as difficult to conciliate in academic research : the narrative approach and the autonomous agents approach.

The narrative approach relies on conceptualizing the player experience in the game and asserting the dialog always follows the narrative logic. The other research direction relies on providing an autonomous NPC architecture which allows the design of a wide variety of personalities for virtual characters. The combination of these two directions is identified as the main issue of the project.

This paper describes the scientific challenges faced in the context of the DEEP project and the adopted approaches to solve them. The paper is organized as follows : section 2 defines the DEEP architecture, sections 3 and 4 respectively focus on the narrative model and NPC model. We conclude with the open issues.

## 2   DEEP Architecture

The purpose of the DEEP architecture is to provide NPC dialogs, which are more relevant considering the player experience, and richer through various NPC personalities and an emotional model definition. The dialog engine uses the player and NPC models as a context base for generating the most suitable dialog, according to the current situation. These models are dynamically updated using informations gathered from the game environment. It provides the emotional state and knowledge of each NPC, the player context in the narrative and his expected knowledge.

The general architecture of DEEP is described in figure 1. It relies on three main components: the **Drama Model**, the **NPC Model** and the **Game Controller**.

The **Game Controller** is the game engine component which drives the entire DEEP dialog architecture as well as other aspects of the game-play. Particularly, it manages the **Game State**, which evolves according to the actions of the player or the NPC's behavior.

The **Player Model** is dynamically updated to reflect the player history in the game. It uses a light model of all the possible stories, defined during the game design, the **Narrative Model**.

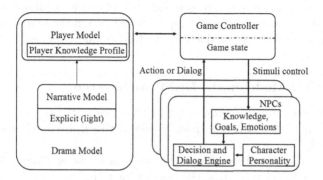

**Fig. 1.** General Architecture

The **Drama Model** results from the narrative approach. The Game Controller uses it to update the game state, and, when necessary, to modify the NPCs knowledge, inducing specific behaviors needed for the narrative.

Events in the game are perceived as stimuli by the **NPC Model**. This model results from the autonomous NPC approach. It triggers a decision process in response to the stimuli, and takes into account NPCs **Personality** and **Emotional** state.

The **Dialog Engine** focuses on providing communication capabilities to the DEEP NPCs. It communicates with the player while selecting topics, nuancing expressions and vocabulary according to each NPC personality and emotional state.

The following two sections gives a more detailed description of the drama model and of the NPC architecture.

# 3   Drama Model

## 3.1   AI in Games

Most of the adventure game designs hypothesize on the player behavior and abilities. For instance, the level design defines, through a mix of topological and logical constraints, the player expected paths and progress in the game [6].

Using this expected behavior, the game designer anticipates a future sequence of events. In order to avoid repetitive dialogs, a NPC will then be programmed as a state automaton providing several different dialogs. This approach reflects the general "Turing test" point of view adopted in most of the games AI [13] : *An intelligent behavior in a game is a behavior which seems to be intelligent considering the current knowledge of the player.*

In the DEEP Project, we formalize this practical approach. We build an explicit model of the player experience, as a game designer or a scenarist would usually implicitly do. The explicit model allows the DEEP architecture to dynamically adapt to the player behavior, providing believable NPC, accurate and relevant from the player perspective.

Building a user model to improve the game design is not a new idea [1] [18] [14], but in these approaches, it is mainly the player as a human being which is modeled. In our very pragmatic approach, we design the model of the player as its avatar in the game, registering its history and experience in the game universe.

## 3.2   The User Model in the DEEP Architecture

We have identified two categories of data to represent the player history in the game, clues and environmental data, stored in **the knowledge base for the user Model**.

In most of the adventure games, the progress of the scenario relies on solving enigma and understanding the current plot. Information is disseminated throughout the game and **clues** are uncovered gradually by the player, very often through dialogs with NPCs. By registering correlated data, we allow the NPC dialog engine to sort out what clues the player is missing for solving the current plot.

This approach is related to Mori and Hoshino's work in which the story is controlled through key actions changing the NPC dialogs [12]. However, in our approach, the dialog is modulated according to the player actions, when variation related to the game environment evolution can be introduced through the NPC emotional model (see section 4).

The model also registers **environmental data**, used by the dialog engine to achieve the immersion in a believable universe. These data are related to the background of the game universe, the player's avatar personal story, or the environment and atmosphere. The NPC dialog engine will use this base for picking dialog elements corresponding to the player experience, thus improving the player immersion in the game.

The user model is also linked to **a light formalization of the scenario**. We propose a player experience model which can be dynamically used to control the NPCs dialogs. Interactive narration models implicitly or explicitly define a partial order of events and plot points, which can be represented as a graph [6]. Our model uses goal nets [3]. We associate plot points with data related to the player progress. At a given step, some of these data are known, maybe known or unknown by the player. A correct progression leads to discard some clues, hide other ones, and use known environmental data to provide realistic dialogs.

Our narrative model is locally defined by the level designer, stamping triggers, clues, environmental datas and defining a partial order between the corresponding events. Using this partial and atomic information, we are able to reconstruct an oriented graph representing the interactive story, only as exhaustive as described by the game designer. By matching this model with the dynamic description of the linear story as witnessed by the player (which is a subset of this graph) we are able to define what kind of knowledge will help the player and communicate it to him through a NPC via the DEEP dialog architecture.

# 4   Emotions and Personality Model

In this section, we explore the structure of emotions and personality information as well as its link with perception, decision and expression. Indeed, the effect of personality and emotions on behavior has been widely studied, whether it concerns a general influence on perception, behavior [10], decision-making and planning [4] or social interaction [8].

Our purpose is to introduce a NPC architecture model allowing the representation of emotions, personality and experience in order to bring flexibility and modularity in the individualized reaction of NPCs. These models must include data related to personality factors, which play an important role in differentiating physiologic and cognitive reactions of each character. They must also process emotion categories, in order to create realistic reactions of the NPC vis-a-vis specific events and to equip each one with appropriate attitudes, particularly in the dialog process. Processing emotions requires also to memorize the previous emotional value of events.

We first present and discuss some emotions and personality models from psychology research. Then, we briefly introduce the principles of our emotional model.

### 4.1 Theoretical Bases

Personality is an important domain of psychology research. Unfortunately, there is no consensus on the definition of personality. Thus, several personality models have been defined. These models consist of a factors set, where each factor is a specific personality property. For example, Eysenck proposes to describe personality based on extraversion and neuroticism, while the *Big-five* model uses five factors: extraversion, agreeableness, conscientiousness, neuroticism and openness [5] [11]. In these models, each personality factor has an impact on the emotions generated from perceived events, and therefore on the character's resulting behavior. By definition, the personality factors are constant over time.

Much work, related to the Cognitive Appraisal theory, proposes various criteria in order to distinguish emotions [16] [15]. These models allow to specify properties and criteria on events which cause emotions. Roseman's model generates seventeen emotions according to a set of criteria [16]. Ortony, Clore and Collins propose an emotional model, named OCC, which cover a vast set of emotional situations [15]. This model became the standard for emotions generation and is used in several works. However the emotional process defined in these models is not complete : the manner in which personality factors influences the feeling of emotions is not defined operationally. Moreover, links between emotions and their intensity, and the intensity levels corresponding to the activation of each emotion are not defined despite their importance confirmed in various experiments [7].

### 4.2 Emotional Model

Our model is based on an explicit representation of personality and emotions, and of each personality factors influence on the sensitivity to emotion categories.

The personality factors are represented by a vector $p$ of $n$ dimension and the emotional state at time $t$ by a vector $e(t)$ with $m$ dimension. $n$ and $m$ are defined according to the used models (for example, $n = 5$ for *Big five* model, $n = 2$ for *Eysenck* model, ...). The influence of each personality factor (let $p_i \in p$) on the sensitivity of each emotional category (let $e_j \in e$) is represented by a function $f(p_i, e_j)$. Thus, a matrix $M_{n*m}$ of functions is formed representing all influences of each personality factor on the all emotional categories. From this matrix, we can calculate the personality-emotions sensitivity. This in turn also influences the decay rate of emotions.

The model updates the emotional state according to the OCC process steps : classification, quantification, interaction and mapping [2]. These steps are started after either each time cycle or stimulus reception.

The architecture of our NPC model is a set of three components :

- *Personality and emotions*: This module identifies the environment events which can affect the NPC. It evaluates their emotional potentials and calculates their influences on the emotions, taking into account the personality and the emotional memory of the NPC.
- *Knowledge and reasoning*: This module makes decisions adapted to the emotional state, personality and active objectives of the NPC. In the DEEP project, we focus on decisions producing dialogs.
- *Behavior*: This module produces emotional behaviors adapted to the situation. It consists in carrying out the knowledge and reasoning module decisions taking into account the current emotional state.

## 5   Conclusion and Open Issues

In this paper, we have described the DEEP project, and how we combine a narrative perspective with an autonomous believable agent approach in order to build an architecture providing rich and versatile NPC dialogs in adventure games. Integrating these two points of view is a challenging task, especially when designing a generic solution ready for industrial use.

The integration of emotions, personality and narratives within the NPC reasoner is the key of the DEEP project success. We are still working on this problem and have to consider several issues.

We have defined an emotional model with strong bases in psychology research. This model represents explicitly personality, emotions, and their interactions. Thus, the updating process of the emotional state is based on the personality factors of a NPC and its previous emotions modified by the last stimuli. Currently, we work on the emotional state influence on the dialog and the decision-making process.

From the narrative perspective, an interesting open issue is the way to deal with the dramatic evolution of the game, in order to extend the capabilities of the dialog engine.

## References

1. Bartle, R.: Hearts, clubs, diamonds, spades: players who suit MUDs. Journal of MUD Research 1(1) (1996)
2. Bartneck, C.: Integrating the occ model of emotions in embodied characters. In: Proceedings of the Workshop on Virtual Conversational Characters: Applications, Methods, and Research Challenges, Melbourne, Australia (November 2002)
3. Cai, Y., Miao, C., Tan, A., Shen, Z.: Fuzzy cognitive goal net for interactive storytelling plot design. In: Proceedings of the ACM SIGGHI Advances in Computer Entertainment (ACE) (2006)
4. Damasio, A.R.: Lérreur de Descartes - la raison des émotions. Odile Jacob (1994)
5. Eysenck, H.J.: The biological basis of personality. In: Thomas, C.C. (ed.), Springfield, IL (1967)
6. Grunvogel, S., Natkin, S., Vega, L.: A new methodology for spatiotemporal Game Design. In: Proceedings of CGAIDE (2004)

7. Izard, C.E., Hembree, E.A., Huebner, R.R.: Infants' emotion expressions to acute pain: Developmental change and stability of individual differences. Developmental Psychology 23, 105–113 (1987)
8. Keltner, D., Haidt, J.: Social functions of emotions. In: Mayne, T., Bonanno, G.A. (eds.) Emotions: Current issues and future directions, ch. 6, pp. 192–213. Guilford Press, New York (2001)
9. Laird, J.E., van Lent, M.: The role of ai in computer games genre. In: Handbook of computer Games study. MIT Press, Cambridge (2005)
10. Marsella, S., Gratch, J.: A step towards irrationality: Using emotion to change belief. In: Proceedings of the 1st International Joint Conference on Autonomous Agents and Multi-Agent Systems, Bologna, Italy (July 2002)
11. McCrae, R.R., John, O.P.: An introduction to the five-factor model and its applications. Journal of Personality 60, 175–215 (1992)
12. Mori, H., Hoshino, J.: Key action technique for digital storytelling. In: Kishino, F., Kitamura, Y., Kato, H., Nagata, N. (eds.) ICEC 2005. LNCS, vol. 3711. Springer, Heidelberg (2005)
13. Natkin, S.: Video Games and Interactive Media, a Glimpse at New Digital Entertainment. In: Peteres, A.K. (ed.) (2006)
14. Natkin, S., Yan, C.: User model in multiplayer mixed reality entertainment applications. In: Proceedings of the ACM SIGCHI International Conference on Advances in Computer Entertainment Technology (ACE) (2006)
15. Ortony, A., Clore, G.L., Collins, A.: The cognitive structure of emotions. Cambridge University Press, Cambridge (1988)
16. Roseman, I.J., Jose, P.E., Spindel, M.: Appraisals of emotion-eliciting events: testing a theory of discrete emotions. Journal of Personality and Social Psychology 59(5), 899–915 (1990)
17. Sehaba, K., Estraillier, P., Lambert, D.: Interactive educational games for autistic children with agent-based system. In: Kishino, F., Kitamura, Y., Kato, H., Nagata, N. (eds.) ICEC 2005. LNCS, vol. 3711, pp. 422–432. Springer, Heidelberg (2005)
18. Szilas, N.: Interactive drama on computer: beyond linear narrative. In: Proceedings of the AAAI Fall Symposium on Narrative Intelligence (1999)

# Marching Bear: An Interface System Encouraging User's Emotional Attachment and Providing an Immersive Experience

Nagisa Munekata, Takanori Komatsu, and Hitoshi Matsubara

Future University-Hakodate
116-2 Kamedanakano, Hakodate 041-8655, Japan
{g3106012,komatsu,matsubar}@fun.ac.jp
http://www.fun.ac.jp

**Abstract.** We developed an interface system called "Marching Bear," where the robot controller's motions were reflected in the motions of certain characters appearing on a computer display. We then conducted a simple experiment to investigate the effectiveness of this interface system to see whether users felt that this interface system was enjoyable. We used a questionnaire and conducted an observation to determine whether users could direct the robot's arms in such a way as to make the character walk. We also investigated the effectiveness of our interface system with two displays, one large, the other small. The results were that most participants felt this system was enjoyable and that they could direct the robot's arms in the way needed to make the character walk. The larger display had a significantly stronger effect on the participants' emotional aspects; they felt that the character had some emotions and that they could communicate with the character well. Therefore, the interface system, Marching Bear, was not only enjoyable for users because of the robot controls, but also this type of interface system may become a users' companion or be perceived as an independent character.

**Keywords:** interface system, emotional aspect, independent character, companion.

## 1 Introduction

Many researchers have developed various video game controllers based on the diversification of video game content and the interest in creating more immersive gameplay. The "Wii Remote" developed by Nintendo [1], "Tatacon" developed by NAMCO [2], and the "EyeToy USB Camera" developed by Sony Computer Entertainment of Europe [3] are three examples of such controllers. The Wii Remote is a remote game controller based on motion sensing technology, and it is specifically designed for many different kinds of video games, including sports, fighting, racing, and shooting games. Tatacon is a drumstick-shaped video game controller where users hold the sticks to beat a drum in time with the music. The EyeToy USB Camera is normally placed on top of a display, and this can detect the bodily movements of

L. Ma, R. Nakatsu, and M. Rauterberg (Eds.): ICEC 2007, LNCS 4740, pp. 363–373, 2007.
© IFIP International Federation for Information Processing 2007

users who play a video game in front of it. These intuitive controllers were developed with the goal of enabling everyone to enjoy playing video games, regardless of their age, gender, or experience at video games. However, at first, it takes some time for users to get accustomed to operating these controllers intuitively so that they pay attention to the controller itself and not the game. The users do not really feel a sense of immersion with the game as long as they are struggling with operating the controller (Figure 1-A).

To solve this problem, some studies have developed a new type of controller using a robot, a so-called robotic user interface (RUI) [4] [5] [6] (Figure 1-B). The RUI is designed to make users feel as if there are no borders between a robot in the real world and a character in the virtual world. A character in the virtual world can be controlled by the motions of a robot used as a controller in the real world. For example, Koizumi et al. developed a hand puppet RUI; its robot controller has a potentiometer and a triaxial acceleration sensor in the robot, which is operated by a user, to detect its motions [7]. This RUI makes the robot in the real world start to vibrate to inform the user that a character has hit one or more obstacles in the virtual world. However, this system was basically designed to satisfy the users' operationalities and functionalities. Therefore, immersive experiences of users are up to the quality of the game content.

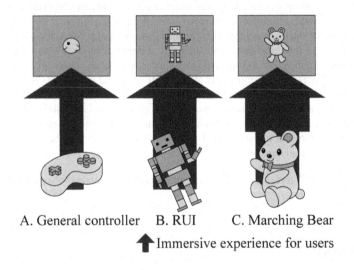

A. General controller    B. RUI    C. Marching Bear

↑ Immersive experience for users

**Fig. 1.** Immersive experience for users

We wanted to develop a system with not only operationality and functionality but also one where users develop a sense of immersion regardless of the game content. We created an interface system using a robot called "Marching Bear." This interface was principally designed to make the user interested in the controlling operations. We hypothesized that the users' interest in the operations would lead them to feel somewhat of an emotional attachment to the interface system itself, and that these feelings would eventually create a strong immersive experience for not only the interface system but also the game content.

## 2 System Overview of Marching Bear

### 2.1 Robot Controller

In our Marching Bear, a stuffed animal like robot is utilized as a controller for users (Figure 2). This robot is a consumer product created by the Iwaya Corporation [7], and it was originally developed to be a communication terminal that connects with IP telephones [8]. The joint configuration of this robot is designed to be similar to a person's upper body: each arm has 2 degrees-of-freedom (DOFs) in the shoulder joint, and the neck has 2 DOFs in a pan-tilt joint. Each joint consists of a pair of servomotors and a joint angle sensor so that the users can directly move these joints using their own hands, and the joint angle values can be measured when they move.

This robot controller was designed like a teddy bear so that users would have a positive impression based on the cute appearance and that this would motivate users to interact with the controller.

**Fig. 2.** IP Robot Phone (by the Iwaya Corporation)

### 2.2 System Configuration

The left figure in Figure 3 shows the overview of the interface system, Marching Bear. This system consists of the robot controller and a virtual bear-like character that appears on a computer display.

Users hold the stuffed animal robot as a controller, and the character on the computer display reflects the users' movements of the robot controller. For example, if the user raises the controller's right–arm, the character's right arm moves. If the user makes the controller's head nod, the character also simultaneously nods its head.

In this system, the virtual character can walk in the virtual world on the computer display only when a user alternates moving the robot controller's arms— as if he or she were leading a toddler by the hands as part of teaching them how to walk. Now think about how we teach toddlers to walk; we do not grab their legs directly; instead,

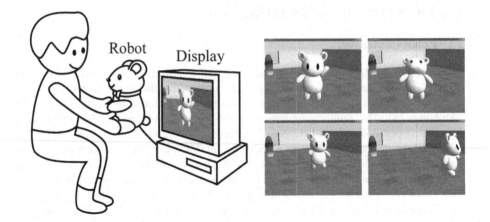

**Fig. 3.** Interface system, Marching Bear (left), and virtual character on the computer display (right)

we get them to walk by leading them by the hands. Thus, we believe that the users' behavior of moving the robots' arms to make it walk indicate that the users regard this robot as an independent character. In this case, these users would have some emotional attachment and feel an immersive experience. However, if users regard this as just a tool for controlling the character, they would grab the robot's legs instead. We believe that grabbing the robot's arms to make it walk, which is an action similar to teaching toddlers to walk, is important for getting users to enjoy controlling the robot.

## 3  Experiment

### 3.1  Overview

We conducted a simple psychological experiment to investigate the effectiveness of this interface system and whether or not users felt that this interface system was enjoyable. We used a questionnaire and conducted an observation to see whether users could move the robot's arms to make the character walk. We also wanted to investigate the effectiveness of different sizes of the virtual character by using a large display and a small one.

### 3.2  Participants

The participants were 20 Japanese university students and university staff members (12 men and 8 women, 22 – 45 years old). All participants had never seen this interface system and an IP Robot Phone. The participants were randomly assigned to the following two groups, i.e., a between-subjects design was used (Figure 4).

 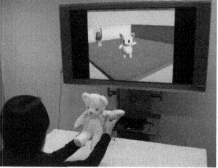

**Fig. 4.** Experimental Scene (Left: Small character group, right: Large character group)

- **Small character group (10 participants):** These participants experienced an interface system with a virtual character in a display that was smaller than the actual robot controller. In this experiment, the virtual character was displayed on a laptop PC's screen, which was 13.3 inches (WXGA, 1280 x 800 pixels), so the actual height of the virtual character was from about 1.5 cm (at the back of the virtual world) to 4.5 cm (at the front of the virtual world).
- **Large character group (10 participants):** These participants experienced a system with a virtual character in a display that was much more similar in size to the actual robot controller. In this experiment, the virtual character was displayed on an LCD monitor's screen, which was 46 inches (WXGA, 1920 x 1080 pixels), so the actual height of the virtual character was from about 5 cm (at the back of the virtual world) to 15.0 cm (at the front of the virtual world).

| 1 | You could understand immediately how to make the bear walk. |
|---|---|
| 2 | You felt sorry for the bear when it hit the wall. |
| 3 | You could move the bear walk around you wanted it to. |
| 4 | You could control the bear's movements completely and intuitively. |
| 5 | The bear has some kinds of emotions. |
| 6 | You felt that you could communicate with the bear well |
| 7 | The movements of the bear were cute. |
| 8 | You enjoyed making the bear move. |
| 9 | You wanted to play with the bear more. |
| 10 | You felt that the bear hated to walk out of this room. |
| 11 | You wanted to take the bear home. |
| 12 | You felt uncomfortable with this stuffed animal robot. |

**Fig. 5.** Questionnaire Used in the Experiment

### 3.3 Procedure

First, an experimenter gave the instruction, "Please feel free to touch and move this stuffed animal robot for ten minutes. If you have any questions about this system, I will answer them after the first three minutes." The experimenter did not mention that moving the controller's arms back and forth makes the character walk. In addition, the experimenter did not inform the participants that the name of this interface system was the "Marching Bear." After a ten-minute trial, all participants were asked to fill in the questionnaire shown in Figure 5. This questionnaire was designed with a five-point likert scale (one point was the worst assessment, and five points was the best). Finally, all participants were interviewed by the experimenter about their impression of playing with the Marching Bear.

## 4    Results

### 4.1    Comparison of the Participants Behaviors

The results of the observation of the users' behaviors indicated that all participants succeeded in making the Marching Bear walk within ten minutes. Five of the participants (small character group: two, large character group: three) succeeded it within three minutes without any help from the experimenter. At first, these five participants focused on moving the robot's legs to make the virtual character walk, and they noticed that the character did not react. Then, they shifted their attention from the legs to the arms, and they eventually noticed how to make this character walk. They reported in their interviews after the experiment that they thought that the character might be able to walk when they saw it at the beginning of the experiment, so they tried to make it walk.

The behaviors of the remaining 15 participants were nearly the same as the first five. At first, they also thought that the character might be able to walk, but they did not show the specific behaviors needed to make the character walk, e.g., they just hugged it or shook its hands. After the first three minutes, they asked the experimenter whether this character could walk or not. The experimenter answered, "It can walk." After this was stated, the participants immediately focused on moving the robot's legs, and eventually, they too noticed how to make the character walk.

### 4.2    Comparison of the Participants' Questionnaires

Figure 6 shows the results of the questionnaire of the two groups. The scores on **Q7, _"The movements of the bear were cute"_**, and **Q8, _"You enjoyed making the bear move"_**, were over four points for both groups (the maximum was five). Thus, most participants of both groups enjoyed playing with the Marching Bear.

The results of an ANOVA revealed significant differences in the answers of four out of the 12 questions between the small character group and the large character group: **Q3, _"You could make the bear walk around as you wanted it to,"_** **Q5, _"The**

| No | Question | Small character | Large character | Significant differences |
|----|----------|-----------------|-----------------|-------------------------|
| 1 | Understand immediately | 2.0 | 1.9 | – |
| 2 | Sorry when it hit the wall | 2.8 | 3.3 | – |
| 3 | Make the bear walk as you wanted it to | 3.3 | 4.1 | p<.05 |
| 4 | Control the bear's movements intuitively | 2.8 | 3.1 | – |
| 5 | The bear has emotions | 1.8 | 2.9 | p<.05 |
| 6 | Could communicate well | 2.1 | 2.8 | p<.10 |
| 7 | Movements were cute | 4.1 | 4.1 | – |
| 8 | Enjoyed making the bear move | 4.2 | 4.4 | – |
| 9 | Wanted to play more | 3.7 | 4.1 | – |
| 10 | The bear hated to be out of this room | 2.7 | 3.0 | – |
| 11 | Wanted to take the bear home | 3.4 | 3.7 | – |
| 12 | Uncomfortable with this robot | 2.1 | 1.4 | p<.05 |

**Fig. 6.** Results of the questionnaires

bear has some kinds of emotions," **Q6,** "You felt that you could communicate withthe bear well," and **Q12,** "You felt uncomfortable with this stuffed animal robot." The results revealed that the participants in the large character group enjoyed their experience significantly more than the ones in the small character group. The comparisons of these four questions are described in the following sections.

### 4.2.1  Q5 and Q6

As already noted, the scores on **Q5, "The bear has some kinds of emotions,"** for participants in the large character group were higher than the ones in the small character group. Specifically, the average score in the small character group was 1.8, while the one in the large character group was 2.9. The results of the ANOVA showed the differences between them were significant $(F(1,18)=7.51$, p<.05 (*)). In addition, for **Q6, "You felt that you could communicate with the bear well,"** the average score in the small character group was 2.1, while the one in the large character group was 2.8. The scores of Q6 were analyzed by a two-factor (character size: small or large) between subjects ANOVA. The results of the ANOVA showed significant tendencies between these scores $(F(1,18)=3.53$, p<.10(+)). These results revealed that participants in the large character group regarded this robot and the virtual character as an independent character that had some emotions, more so than the ones in the small character group.

We thought that the reason for this low score in the small character group was caused by the fact that the size of the virtual character was too small compared to the robot controller. Actually, the height of the virtual character appearing on the computer display was from about 1.5 to 4.5 cm, while the height of the robot controller was about 30 cm. The participants could not understand why their movement of the robot was not clearly reflected in the character appearing on the display.

#### 4.2.2  Q3 and Q4

**Q3, _"You could make the bear walk around as you wanted it to,"_** was a question about the operability of the Marching Bear, as was **Q4, _"You could control the bear's movements completely and intuitively."_** Therefore, Q3 and Q4 were very similar. However, the results of the ANOVA revealed no significant difference in Q4 ($F(1,18)=0.77$, n.s.), but a significant difference was found in Q3 ($F(1,18)=4.43$, p<.05(*)) (Figure 7).

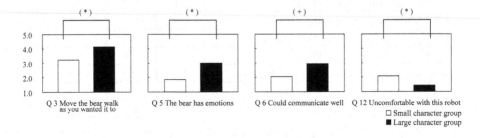

**Fig. 7.** Comparison of scores of questionnaires for small character group and large character group

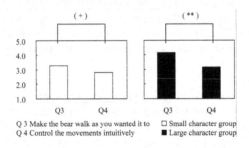

**Fig. 8.** Comparison of scores of questionnaires between Q3 and Q4 in each group

We expected some differences in understanding these two questions between the two groups. Thus, we conducted a statistical analysis to clarify these differences. The scores of Q3 and Q4 were analyzed by a two-factor (question: Q3 or Q4) within subjects ANOVA for each group. The results of the ANOVA showed a significant tendency ($F(1,9) = 5.00$, p<.10(+)) in the small character group and significant differences ($F(1,9) = 11.25$, p<.01(**)) in the large character group (Figure 8). Thus, the participants in the large character group felt that they did not control the Marching Bear but made the Marching Bear walk just as they wanted it to.

We thought that this was because there were differences in utilized keywords between Q3 and Q4. In Q3, the major keywords were "make the bear walk" and "as you wanted it to", while in Q4, they were "control" and "intuitively." Therefore, the keywords in Q3 eventually evoked in the participants an interactive relationship between participants and the Marching Bear, and the keywords in Q4 evoked in them a unilateral relationship between the participants and the Marching Bear.

### 4.2.3  Q8 and Q12

The scores of **Q8, _"You enjoyed making the bear move,"_** in both groups were the highest among all 12 questions. The average score in the small and large character groups was 4.2 and 4.4 point, respectively, with no significant difference between them ($F(1,18)=0.36$, n.s.). Both groups enjoyed playing with the Marching Bear. However, in **Q12, _"You felt uncomfortable with this stuffed animal robot,"_** we found a significant difference between the scores in the small character group and the large character group: 2.1 and 1.4, respectively (Figure 7).

These results show that although the participants in the small character group enjoyed controlling the Marching Bear, they felt more uncomfortable with the stuffed animal robot than the participants in the large character group. This means that the participants in the former group seemed to enjoy controlling this robot as "just a controller." They perhaps felt some annoyance with utilizing a stuffed animal robot just to control a character on a display, and they would have preferred utilizing a more typical game controller.

### 4.3  Summary

We observed the following common phenomena in the small and large character groups based on the results of their questionnaires.

- The participants in both groups (small and large character) discovered how to make the character walk within ten minutes.
- The participants in both group first focused on moving the robot's legs to make the virtual character walk.
- The participants felt that the Marching Bear was cute, and they reported that they enjoyed making this character move around.

The results of the questionnaire from participants in both groups demonstrated the following.

- **Small character group:** The participants in this group saw the Marching Bear as part of a unilateral control relationship more so than the participants in the other group did.
- **Large character group:** The participants felt a stronger emotional attachment and a more immersive experience than the participants in the small character group. They felt that the character had some emotions and that they could communicate with the character well.

Thus, we found that the interface system Marching Bear succeeded in making users interested in the controlling operations. Displaying the virtual character on a larger screen, which could make the participants readily understand their spontaneous actions, would be effective for them to get interest in this system. We thought that these behaviors of the participants might lead to them sustaining their emotional attachment and sense of immersion with this interface system, as we had designed it to do.

# 5   Discussion

## 5.1   Effectiveness of Character's Size

Most participants in the small character group answered that the Marching Bear did not have any emotions but that they enjoyed playing with it as a unilateral controller, much like a typical video game controller. This relationship between the general controller and video games was observed. In this case, when their operating virtual character was suddenly hit by some flying obstacles, most players would react to avoiding these obstacles in the real world. Here, they had some empathy for the virtual character appearing on the display, not the controller.

In the questionnaire, we used the term "the bear," not "Marching Bear," and we did not indicate whether the term "the bear" meant the virtual character or the robot controller. Then, after the experiment, we interviewed the participants in the small character group as to whether they felt the character on the display or the robot controller were cute. Most participants answered that the character on the display was cute and that they were not interested in the stuffed animal robot. Thus, these participants enjoyed using the Marching Bear but paid attention to the virtual character only.

However, participants in the large character group answered during the same interview that both were cute or that they could not choose one. Other interesting phenomena pertaining to this Marching Bear included the virtual character being able to walk based on the user's operational pace, e.g., when the user shook the robot's hands faster, the virtual character could walk faster. However, most participants operated this robot slowly, softly, and gently. These participants reported that they felt sorry for making the bear walk too fast or that it would hurt their arms or that it might be uncomfortable for this robot if they moved it too fast. We observed that one participant groomed the robot's coat, while another adjusted the ribbon on the robot's neck.

Therefore, most participants in the large character group thought that the Marching Bear was a companion or an independent character and that they had a strong emotional attachment to not only the virtual character but also to the stuffed animal robot.

## 5.2   Intuitive Operation

When we teach toddlers how to walk, we do not grab their legs directly because toddlers are not tools, and leading them by the hand to make a toddler walk is quite intuitive for us. However, the results of the experiment showed that both groups' participants first focused on moving the robot's legs to make the virtual character walk. This means that they intuitively thought that moving the robot's legs led to making the character walk. In fact, these behaviors indicated that the participants regarded this robot as just a tool at that time. When they actually moved the robot's legs directly to make the character walk, the robot could not keep a usual posture, e.g., this caused a head-down posture and they handled the robot too roughly. Therefore, participants thought that the Marching Bear was only a tool for the experimental setting.

However, after spending some time with the interactive system, the participants noticed how to make the Marching Bear walk, and then their behavior drastically changed. For example, some participants in the large character group moved the character so that it did not hit the walls in the virtual world. Eventually, these participants regarded the Marching Bear as a companion and independent character. Their behaviors became more gentle and sincere compared to the beginning of the experiment.

## 6  Conclusions

In this study, we developed the interface system, "Marching Bear," where the robot controller's motions are reflected on the motions of certain characters appearing on a computer display. We then conducted an experiment to investigate the effectiveness of the interface system as to whether or not this interface system was enjoyable. A questionnaire was used and an observation conducted as to whether or not users could move the robot's arms to make it walk. We also investigated the effectiveness of the interface system by using a large display and a smaller one. A virtual character was displayed on a laptop PC's display as part of a small character group, or it was displayed on an LCD monitor that enlarged the virtual character as part of a large character group.

The results of the experiments using these two groups demonstrated that the larger character had a much stronger effect on the participants' emotional aspect; they felt that the character had some emotions and that they could communicate with the character well. The robot controls of the interface system Marching Bear was not only enjoyable for the users, we felt that the bear could be a users' companion. The Marching Bear was a success in the sense that it got users interested in the controlling operations.

However, a few participants in the small character group felt effects similar to what most of the participants felt in the large character group, and a few participants in the large character group did not feel such effects. We speculate that the participants' individual differences would account for this phenomenon. Therefore, we are planning to investigate the effects of individual differences on emotional aspects when participants control the Marching Bear.

## References

1. Wii Remote: http://wii.com/
2. TATACON (in Japanese), http://www.bandainamcogames.co.jp/donderpage/
3. EyeToy USB Camera: http://www.eyetoy.com/
4. Sekiguchi, D., Inami, M., Tachi, S.: RobotPHONE:RUI for Interpersonal Communication. In: The proceedings of CHI2001 Extended Abstracts, pp. 277–278 (2001)
5. Johnson, M.P., Wilson, A., Blumberg, B., Kline, C., Bobick, A.: Sympathetic Interface: Using a Plush Toy to Direct Synthetic Characters. In: The proceedings of CHI99, pp. 152–158 (1999)
6. Strommen, E.: When the Interface is a Talking Dinosaur: Leaning Across Media with Acti-Mates Barney. In: The proceedings of CHI98, pp. 288–295 (1998)
7. Koizumi, N., Shimizu, N., Sugimoto, M., Nii, H., Inami, M.: Development of Hand Puppet type Robotic User Interface. Journal of Virtual Reality Society of Japan 11(2), 265–274 (2006) (in Japanese)
8. Sekiguchi, D., Inami, M., Kawakami, N., Tachi, S.: The Design of Internet-Based Robot-PHONE. In: The proceedings of the 14th International Conference on Artificial Reality and Tele-existence 2004, pp. 223–228 (2004)

# Marble Market: Bimanual Interactive Game with a Body Shape Sensor

Kentaro Fukuchi[1] and Jun Rekimoto[2,3]

[1] Graduate School of Information Systems
The University of Electro-Communications
Choufu-shi, Tokyo , JAPAN 182-8585
fukuchi@megaui.net
[2] Interfaculty Initiative in Information Studies,
The University of Tokyo
[3] Interaction Laboratory
Sony Computer Science Laboratories, Inc.
rekimoto@acm.org

**Abstract.** A video game application was developed using SmartSkin, a body shape sensing device. The video game uses a table-sized SmartSkin that can recognize players' arms on the tabletop. Sensor values are translated to a virtual potential field and the system calculates dynamics of game characters on the field.

At most four players can play the game, and the players control many independent game characters displayed on the table using their arms simultaneously.

## 1 Introduction

We developed a multi-player video game that allows users to control many independent game characters simultaneously with player's arms. In order to realize bimanual manipulation on a table-sized input surface, we employed a body shape sensing device based on capacitive sensing, and we introduced a new bimanual interaction technique which we called "bulldozer manipulation". This technique uses an interpolated potential field created by sensor inputs, and calculates physical dynamics of characters on the potential field.

In our game application, the bulldozer manipulation allows users to move more than 10 game characters simultaneously. Players can gather, guide or block game characters with their arms intuitively.

## 2 System Architecture

### 2.1 Sensing Device

We employed SmartSkin[5], a human-body sensing device based on capacitive sensing. This sensor recognizes multiple hand positions and shapes and calculates the distance betwenn the hand and the surface.

SmartSkin consists of grid-shaped electrodes, transmitters, receivers and micro controllers. Figure 3 shows the principle of operation of SmartSkin. The vertical wires are

L. Ma, R. Nakatsu, and M. Rauterberg (Eds.): ICEC 2007, LNCS 4740, pp. 374–380, 2007.
© IFIP International Federation for Information Processing 2007

**Fig. 1.** Table-sized SmartSkin          **Fig. 2.** Two players playing Marble Market

transmitter electrodes, and the horizontal wires are receiver electrodes. When one of the transmitters is excited by a wave signal (of typically several hundred kilohertz), the receiver receives this wave signal because each crossing point (transmitter/receiver pairs) acts as a (very weak) capacitor. The magnitude of the received signal is proportional to the frequency and voltage of the transmitted signal, as well as to the capacitance between the two electrodes. When a conductive and grounded object approaches a crossing point, it capacitively couples with the electrodes, and drains the wave signal. As a result, the received signal amplitude becomes weak. By measuring this effect, it is possible to detect the proximity of a conductive object, such as a human hand.

The time-dividing transmitting signal is sent to each of the vertical electrodes, and the system independently measures values from each of the receiver electrodes. These values are integrated to form two-dimensional sensor values. The right of Figure 5 shows the the integrated sensor values.

The integrated sensor values is similar to a two-dimensional image. The distance between the human body and the sensor corresponds to the luminance of a pixel. Once these values are obtained, algorithms for image processing can be applied to them to recognize gestures.

We used a table-sized SmartSkin that has 8×9 grid cells on a table top, and each cell is 10×10 cm. The resolution of the sensor data is 10 bits (0 – 1,023) and the scan rate is 10 scans per second. A piece of thin white plywood was placed on the grid, and a computer screen was overlaid on it using a projector set above the table (shown in Figure 1). This system provides a touch-panel-like input surface, but can recognize multiple hands of users.

## 2.2  Interaction Techniques

We developed an interaction technique which is called "bulldozer manipulation" with SmartSkin and introduced to our game application.

Fitzmaurice et al. reported that when they provided a pile of colored LEGO blocks and asked subjects to separate them by color, the subjects slid the blocks simultaneously

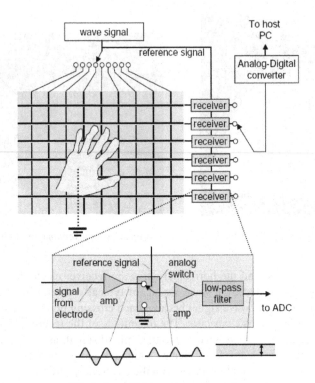

**Fig. 3.** SmartSkin sensor configuration

rather than of picking up and dropping them, using their hands and arms like a 'bulldozer'[2]. Bulldozer manipulation can be performed by physical contact between the objects and the user's hand, and this kind of manipulation was not possible on the input system without physical devices.

In order to simulate the bulldozer manipulation on SmartSkin, the fact that SmartSkin can recognize a shape of the user's arm on the input surface is considered. By capturing the arm shape the system can track the posture of the hands on the input surface so that it can calculate collisions between virtual components and the hands. However, it is difficult to track a hand from a shape data. There are many known techniques to estimate the posture of a hand from video images, but it is not possible to apply these techniques to shape data for the following reasons. First, the posture of the user's arm changes dynamically, but since the shape data from SmartSkin is too simple it is difficult to estimate the motion between the frames, while a video image provides many features such as a texture of the skin. Second, the shape data from SmartSkin represents very limited posture information, and even distinguishing the left and right hand from the data is difficult when the hand only partially touches the input surface. Third, the multi players may touch the input surface simultaneously, but SmartSkin can not distinguish them.

For these reasons, rather than estimating the posture of the hands, bulldozer manipulation was implemented by creating a potential field from the shape data.

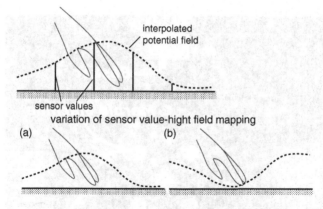

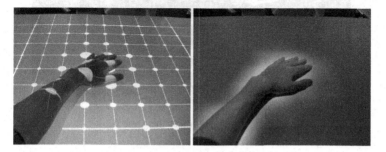

**Fig. 4.** Two methods of creating a potential field

**Fig. 5.** Interpolated sensor values

When a user touches the input surface with his hands, the shapes of the hands are recognized as $8 \times 9$ sensor values. The shape data is smoothed using a bicubic convolution interpolation (Figure 5). This smoothed surface was used as a potential field and the dynamics of objects on the potential field were calculated so that the objects move on the field according to the position and shape of the hands simultaneously. Each object, which is treated as a point mass, rolls on the potential field toward the lower position.

There are two method by which to create a potential field from the sensor values. Figure 4 shows these methods. Method (a) makes the potential high when a hand is close to the surface, which means that an object on the potential field moves away from the hand. In contrast, method (b) makes the potential low when a hand is close to the surface, which means that an object is drawn to the hand. Both methods were tested for bulldozer manipulation, and method (a) was found to be better for this purpose.

## 3 Video Game Application

### 3.1 Game Rules

The game screen is shown in Figure 6. The goal of this game is to bring as many small balls, called *Marbles*, as possible to the player's *Basket*. A *Marble Machine* produces

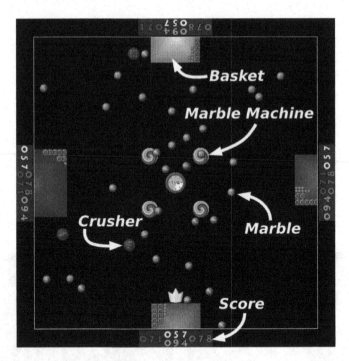

**Fig. 6.** An illustration of the game field

marbles continuously. The Marble Machine sometimes produces large red balls called *Crushers*. Crushers break Marbles. When into a Basket, the Basket looses a quarter of the Marbles already collected. Therefore, players should not collect Crushers, but rather send them toward his opponents' Basket. Marble Machines sometimes provide *Gold Marbles*, which have the value of 50 Marbles, or *Special Marbles*, which bring about some special event.

The player who collected the most Marbles in two minutes wins the game.

### 3.2    Concurrent Manipulation of Many Marbles

Marble Market was exhibited at Sony ExploraScience in Tokyo. In addition, Marble Market was exhibited in a number of open laboratory events, and several visitors played this video game. At both exhibitions, the basic rules of the game were described and the method of moving the Marbles by hand were instructed. However, a detailed description of the techniques of concurrent manipulation was not given. Despite this, the players discovered various techniques by themselves. Through these exhibitions, a number of typical techniques of concurrent manipulation of Marbles were observed.

In order to gather Marbles, the player basically places their of both hands on the table and moves slowly toward his Basket. Many players were observed to place their hands beside a group of Marbles and make them roll on the potential field towards their Basket, following the Marbles with their hands to adjust their direction. Some players formed a funnel in front of their Basket so as to guide Marbles into their basket.

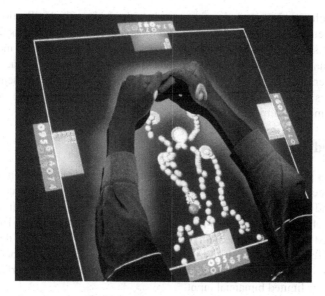

**Fig. 7.** Gathering marbles by arms

The SmartSkin detected not only hands but also arms. When players discovered this, they gathered Marbles more aggressively. Several of them moved their entire arms in the manner of a bulldozer blade. Some players used both arms. Moreover, some players closed off the Marble Machines and Baskets using their arms, as shown in Figure 7. In this way, all of the Marbles from the Marble Machines were guided into their Basket.

These manipulation techniques can be used when a potential increases under a hand. In contrast, when the potential decreases under a hand, as shown in (b) of Figure 4, the following techniques are effective. One technique is simply placing a hand over a Basket to form a potential hole over it, so as to pull in the Marbles rolling near the Basket. The other is putting a hand on a Marble Machine for a while in order to collect the Marbles in the hand, and then to bring them to a Basket by moving the hand slowly.

As mentioned above, techniques by which to gather Marbles differed between the two different potential field. These methods must be evaluated in order to discuss their advantages, but the former method was employed for this application from the observation of the user tests. The former method enables intuitive manipulation, and allows various manipulation, that avoids monotony and makes the game more exciting.

## 4   Discussion

From the observation in the exhibitions, the bulldozer manipulation of Marble Market is easy to learn and effective for concurrent manipulation of many Marbles. As an example of ease of learning, early elementary school children soon learned to control the Marbles using their arms.

On the other hand, in some cases, the behavior of the Marbles was not so intuitive for the players. First, most players moved their hands from the Marble Machines to the Baskets too quickly at first. When the hand is moved quickly, it overtakes the Marbles and the Marbles are accelerated to the opposite side, as described in Section 2.2. In the current implementation, the hand should be moved at the same speed as the Marbles, or placed as shown in Figure 7. This indicates that the potential field method limits bulldozer manipulation. Second, some players pushed the table top surface strongly to block Crushers from entering their Baskets. Since SmartSkin does not sense pressure, this motion is meaningless. However, this observation suggests the use of a pressure sensor for a more intuitive game interface.

## 5   Related Work

Matsushita et al. developed HoloWall[4], an interaction system with an infra-red camera. The system consists of a rear-projection screen and an infra-red camera that is placed behind the screen. The user's arms or hands on the screen is captured by a infraled camera behind the screen. Two-handed interaction was introduced on Holowall, and a shape-based input is implemented, but it is based on a simple collision detection.

DiamondTouch[1] is a multi-user interaction system that accepts concurrent two-handed input. DiamondTouch can identify who is touching the input surface, however it allows a very limited bimanual input.

Jeff Han et al. introduced a multi-touch sensing technique that utilizes an internal reflection in a clear acrylic board[3]. Their system recognizes a contact surface between the acrylic board and the user's fingertips. Since it does not recognize user's body above the board, it is difficult to recognize the whole shape of the arm on the input surface.

## 6   Conclusion

A video game application, Marble Market, was developed that allows bulldozer manipulation to control several characters concurrently. The application uses a SmartSkin sensor to create a potential field from the position and shape data of players' arms and hands, and then the game characters are forced from the field. Marble Market has been exhibited, and various techniques were observed for concurrent manipulation of the characters. From these observations, the bulldozer manipulation is judged to be easy to learn and effective for concurrent manipulation of multiple components.

## References

1. Dietz, P.H., Leigh, D.: DiamondTouch: A Multi-User Touch Technology. In: Proceedings of UIST'01, pp. 219–226 (2001)
2. Fitzmaurice, G.W.: Graspable User Interfaces. PhD thesis, Dept. of Computer Science, University of Toronto (1996)
3. Han, J.Y.: Low-Cost Multi-Touch Sensing Through Frustrated Total Internal Reflection. In: UIST '05: Proceedings of the 18th annual ACM symposium on User interface software and technology, pp. 115–118. ACM Press, New York (2005)
4. Matsushita, N., Rekimoto, J.: HoloWall: Designing a Finger, Hand, Body, and Object Sensitive Wall. In: Proceedings of UIST'97, pp. 209–210 (1997)
5. Rekimoto, J.: SmartSkin: An Infrastructure for Freehand Manipulation on Interactive Surfaces. In: Proceedings of CHI2002, pp. 113–120 (2002)

# Concept and Architecture of a Centaur Robot

Satoshi Tsuda, Yohsuke Oda, Kuniya Shinozaki, and Ryohei Nakatsu

Kwansei Gakuin University, School of Science and Technology
2-1 Gakuen, Sanda, 669-1337 Japan
{amy65823,bhy61926,scbc0052,nakatsu}@ksc.kwansei.ac.jp

**Abstract.** Recently various types of robots are being studied and developed, which can be classified into two groups: humanoid type and animal types. Since each group has its own merits and demerits, a new type of robot is expected to emerge with greater strengths and fewer weaknesses. In this paper we propose a new type of robot called the "Centaur Robot" by merging the concepts of these two types of robots. This robot has a human-like upper body and a four-legged animal-like lower body. Due to this basic architecture, the robot has several merits, including human-like behaviors. It can also walk smoothly and stably even on non-smooth ground. We describe the basic concept of our centaur robot and then explain its hardware and software architectures as well as its merits.

## 1 Introduction

In recent years, various robots are being studied and developed in research institutes and companies that can be classified into two groups: a humanoid robot with two legs [1][2], an animal type robot with four or more legs [3][4][5]. Also a humanoid robot can be classified into those with two legs and those with wheels [6]. Each of these types has its own merits. The design of a humanoid robot with two legs is based on humans and can mimic such human motions as walking. Since this robot's behavior resembles human behavior, it might easily be introduced into society. In the future, such robots are expected to support us in various aspects of our daily life. At the same time, however, its walking capability still lacks stability, and it sometimes falls down, restricting its area of activity. At the same time, quickly returning to a standing position after falling down is a crucial robot capability. Also it does not easily adapt to uneven surfaces. It has difficulty maintaining its balance on ground that is not flat. On the other hand, the merit of an animal type robot is its four legs, which allow it to walk stably even on uneven ground. Since it can also basically stand on three legs, it can adopt to various ground pattern changes. So far, however, the robot has mainly been developed as a pet to which useful applications have rarely been applied. A humanoid robot with wheels for locomotion, which we call a wheel type robot, can move very smoothly and stably on the ground. It rarely falls down. It can even move on slightly uneven ground. On the other hand, it has no ability to move on stairs, which greatly restricts its area of activity since houses usually contain stairs and other types of height differences.

One approach to overcome these problems is to develop new types of robots by merging the strengths of existing robots. In this paper we propose a new type of robot

L. Ma, R. Nakatsu, and M. Rauterberg (Eds.): ICEC 2007, LNCS 4740, pp. 381–388, 2007.

with a human-like upper body and an animal-like lower body that we call a "Centaur Robot." In the following sections, we describe its basic concept and then its detailed software/hardware architectures as well as a prototype we developed.

## 2   Related Works

Recently, especially in Japan, various kinds of robots have been studied and developed, particularly humanoid robots that are expected to support our daily life. For example, HONDA has developed a humanoid robot called ASIMO that has sophisticated walking capability [1]. For animal types of robots, on the other hand, most have been studied and developed as pets instead of supportive robots, including AIBO developed by Sony [3].

Although much research/development continues on humanoid and animal types of robots, little research has integrated these two types for several reasons. One reason is that since there are so many research themes for new functions and improvements for each of these types of robots, researchers have little incentive to concentrate on new types of robots that go beyond humanoid or animal types. Another is that even myths or folktales only contain a few examples of such creatures as centaurs, mermaids, and sphinxes in which humans and animals are integrated. Thus it is rather hard to imagine the functions and application areas that such a new type of robot might have.

Therefore, we developed a centaur robot because we believed by integrating two types of robots we could create a new type of robot with advantages over conventional robots.

## 3   Humanoid Robots

In our work, we are developing a robot that can stably achieve various motions by merging two types of robots: a humanoid and an animal.

There are two approaches for such integration: from the humanoid robot side and from the animal robot side. The former approach tries to realize a four-legged body as well as four-legged walk while maintaining a human-like upper body and achieving human-like motions. On the other hand, the latter approach achieves various human-like motions by adding a human upper body to a four-legged robot. In our study, we chose the former approach and modified the hardware and software of a humanoid robot to realize a centaur robot.

We adopted a humanoid robot developed by Nirvana Technology as a platform robot [7]. This robot has 22 servo motors that can express various human-like motions. Figure 1 shows its appearance, and Table 1 shows its specifications. Figure 2 illustrates the construction of its hardware. The control board, on which a microprocessor SH2 is attached, is connected to the servo motors, a gyro sensor, acceleration sensors, PC, and a battery. The program on the controller can achieve autonomous robot behaviors. At the same time, we can send commands to the robot by PC.

**Fig. 1.** Humanoid robot

**Table 1.** Specifications of humanoid robot

| | |
|---|---|
| Size/Weight | 34 cm/1.7 kg |
| Degree of flexibility | 22 (12 legs, 8 arms, 1 waist, 1 head) |
| CPU | SH2/7047F |
| Motor | KO PDS-2144, FUTABA S3003, FUTABA S3102, FUTABA S3103 |
| Battery | DC6V |

Figure 3 illustrates the software construction. The calculation of the commands necessary to move each motor is carried out each fifteen milliseconds and sent to each servo motor. The instructions to the robot from the PC are first analyzed and based on results go through one of two processes: one command for walking and other commands for other motions. For other commands, the motion data corresponding to the command is read from memory and the control data for each motor is calculated, and then the control data is sent to each servo motor. On the other hand, if the input command is a command for walking, then the real time calculation of the control data for each servo motor is carried out and sent to each servo motor. Calculation consists of three processes: trajectory generation calculation, inverse kinematics calculation, and servo motor angle calculation. In trajectory generation calculation, the position of each ankle studied by observing human walking motion is calculated every fifteen seconds. Then by inverse kinematics calculation the rotation angle of each foot joint is calculated for the same timing. Based on these calculations, finally the angle of each servo motor is calculated. Thus the rotation angle to be achieved for each motor is sent every fifteen milliseconds.

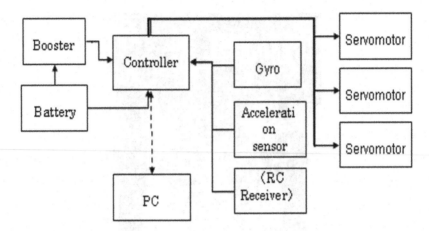

**Fig. 2.** Hardware construction of humanoid robot

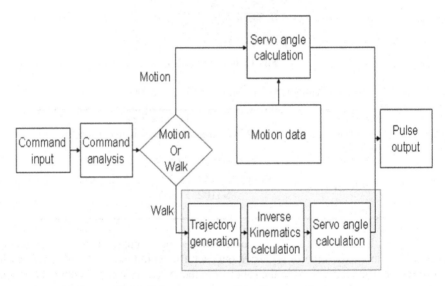

**Fig. 3.** Software construction of humanoid robot

## 4   Centaur Robot

### 4.1   Overview

We developed a centaur robot based on the humanoid robot described in the previous section. We prepared two humanoid robots and used one as a front body. For another robot, we only used its lower body as a back of the centaur robot. Then we connected these two parts by a flat plastic board that functions as the shoulder part. Figures 4 and 5 show the centaur robot's appearance.

**Fig. 4.** Centaur robot

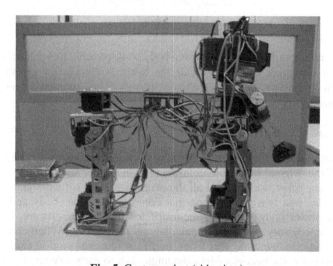

**Fig. 5.** Centaur robot (side view)

## 4.2 Hardware Construction

Now we explain the robot's hardware construction, as illustrated in Figure 6. Apparently for the front the hardware of the original humanoid robot was used, and for the back only the lower body was used. But a comparison of Figs. 3 and 6 shows that this robot's control structure is somewhat different from the original. Two controllers were used for complete control of the robot. One controls the servo motors required for upper body motions. The other controls the servo motors corresponding to the lower body. Since all the sensors are provided for the upper body, the controller corresponding to the upper body manages all sensor feedback. We adopted these two boards for several reasons. One, by using two boards, one of which controls the

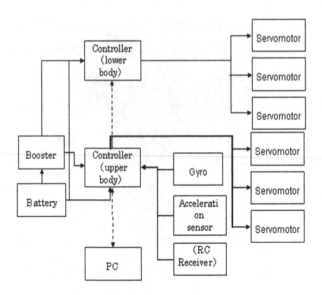

**Fig. 6.** Hardware construction of centaur robot

motions of the upper body and the lower body, it is possible to separately control the behaviors of the upper body as well as the lower body. For the power supply and battery, both controllers are connected to one battery. Also commands from PC are sent to both controllers.

### 4.3  Software Construction

Next, we explain the robot's software construction, as illustrated in Figure 7. The software of the original humanoid controls both the upper and lower bodies together. For the centaur robot, we checked all the original robot's software and separated the software codes into two groups: one that controls the upper body and another that controls the lower body. Thus we reconstructed the whole software. For the upper body, it is unnecessary to carry out calculations for walking. When commands other than a walking command are sent from the PC, it retrieves motion data stored in the memory and sends the necessary rotation angle data to each servo motor. On the other hand software corresponding to the lower body must treat two types of commands as in the case of the original humanoid robot: a command for walking and other commands for additional motions. Also we adopted a method of inserting an arbitrary phase shift between the servo motor control of the front and back legs so that the robot can adopt the most adequate walking motions depending on the walking speed.

By adopting such basic software structure, robot control has the following merits:

(1) The upper and lower body motions can be controlled separately. So far all the motion data developed for achieving various types of humanoid robot motions must be developed to describe the whole body movement. Since the motions of the upper and lower bodies have been separated, we can separately develop two types of motions, and by combining these two types of data, we can generate various kinds of whole body movements for the robot. This idea can easily be applied to the original humanoid robot.

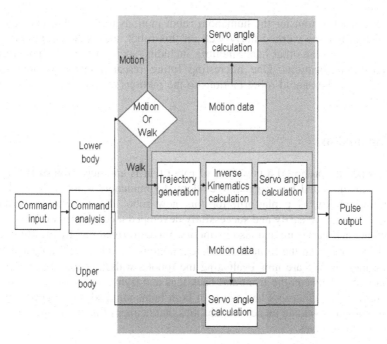

**Fig. 7.** Software construction of centaur robot

(2) The front and back body movements can be separately controlled. Although it seems natural to let the front lower body and back lower bodies perform identical motions, sometimes it is better to control the two bodies by different body motions. Especially in the case of walking and running motions there would be some differences between these two bodies. For example, for trot type walking there should be a $180°$ phase shift between the front and the back legs. In the case of gallop running, the front legs and the back legs should move synchronously.

### 4.4 Evaluation of the Robot

We carried out several experiments to evaluate the motion capability of our centaur robot.

(1) Walking capability

We inserted a phase shift of $180°$ between the walking motion cycle of the front and back legs and confirmed that the robot could move very smoothly by adopting this walking style. In this case the front and back legs move in opposite modes. For example, when the front left leg moves forward, so does the back right leg. Thus this walking style corresponds to trot style walking of animals. By changing the degree of phase shift, the robot can carry out various walking motions such as galloping. We will further study the relationship between phase shift and motion stability/speed.

(2) Capability for other motions

We developed various types of human-like motions for the original humanoid robot [7]. An interesting question is which of these motions could work well on the centaur robot. We tried to transfer the humanoid robot motions to this robot and found that most of the motions worked fairly well on this robot, except bending and twisting type postures. On the other hand, motions including such postures did not work well or needed modifications. One interesting future research theme is automatically transferring the humanoid robot motions to the motions of four legged robot such as this robot.

## 5  Conclusion

In this paper we proposed a new type of robot that is an integration of two types of robots: humanoid and four-legged. We adopted a humanoid robot with two legs and walking capability as a platform for this new robot. By integrating two of the humanoid robots we easily and successfully developed a centaur robot. We described its software and hardware and also its merits. We confirmed that by inserting a phase shift of $180°$ between the front and back leg motions the robot can stably achieve trot walking motion. We are now evaluating the robot's walking capability by changing the phase shift between the front and back legs and trying to determine the optimum phase shift. Since this robot has merits of both humanoid and four-legged robots, we are also going to evaluate its new capabilities that neither of the two type robots could achieve by themselves.

## References

1.  http://www.honda/co.jp/ASIMO/
2.  Friedmann, M., Kiener, J., Petters, S., Thomas, D., von Stryk, O., Sakakmoto, H.: Versatile, high-quality motions and behavior control of humanoid soccer robots. In: Workshop on Humanoid Soccer Robots of the 2006 IEEE International Conference on Humanoid Robots, pp. 9–16 (2006.12)
3.  http://www.jp.aibo.com/
4.  Golubovic, D., Li, B., Hu, H.: A Hybrid Software Platform for Sony AIBO Robots. In: Polani, D., Browning, B., Bonarini, A., Yoshida, K. (eds.) RoboCup 2003. LNCS (LNAI), vol. 3020, pp. 478–486. Springer, Heidelberg (2004)
5.  Kerepesi, A., Kubinyi, E., Jonsson, G.K., Magnusson, M.S., Kiklosi, A.: Behavioural Comparison of Human-Animal (Dog) and Human-Robot (AIBO) Interactions. Behavioural Processes 73(1), 92–99 (2006)
6.  Ishiguro, H., Ono, T., Imai, M., Kanda, T.: Development of an interactive humanoid robot "Robovie" -An interdisciplinary approach. In: Jarvis, R.A., Zelinsky, A. (eds.) Robotics Research, pp. 179–191. Springer, Heidelberg (2003)
7.  Wama, T., Higuchi, M., Sakamoto, H., Nakatsu, R.: Realization of Tai-chi Motion Using a Humanoid Robot. In: Entertainment Computing. LNCS, pp. 14–19. Springer, Heidelberg (2004)

# An Embedded System of Face Recognition Based on ARM and HMM

Yanbin Sun[1,2], Lun Xie[1], Zhiliang Wang[1], and Yi An[2]

[1] Department of Electronic Information Engineering, School of Information Engineering,
University of Science and Technology, Beijing, 100083, China
[2] School of Information, Hebei Polytechic University, Tangshan, Hebei 063009, China
v4lc@sohu.com,
ygao@mail.tsinghua.edu.cn

**Abstract.** Face recognition is important for many applications, including security check-up, judicial administration, visual monitoring and intelligent interaction. Current commercial and research systems use software implementation and require a dedicated computer for the image-processing task--a large, expensive, and complicated-to-use solution. In order to make face recognition ubiquitous, the system complexity, size, and price must be substantially reduced. This paper presents an ARM-based embedded system for face recognition. The float image-pretreatment algorithm was redesigned to enable highly image-pretreatment implementation for ARM9 microprocessor. The system uses a CMOS digital imaging sensor OV7640, a S3C2410A processor and the Linux Operation System for the image processing. A face recognition algorithm based on the HMM is presented. The software can be run in intelligent mobile telephone or PDA directly. This new design is suitable for face detection and recognition, thus making an important step towards low-cost and portable systems.

**Keywords:** embedded system, Linux, HMM, ARM, Face Recognition.

## 1 Introduction

Compared with traditional human identification system, the embedded system of face recognition has many advantages. It's low-cost, simple-to-use, no dedicated image sensor. Face recognition method, which belongs to no-violation and initiatively method, does not interfere the person being identified and does not violate person's privacy, so it's easily accepted.

This paper describes the development of ARM9 embedded system of face recognition, based on the theory of HMM, and presents the design and practice of hardware and software. The system has the functions of image-capturing, face-detecting and face-recognizing. Moreover the float image-pretreatment algorithm is optimized, which increases the system processing speed.

The software of the system can be applied to the mobile phone with the Linux operation system. Thus face images can be captured through the built-in camera and data analyzed. Identification can be accomplished by comparing the result with the face information database.

L. Ma, R. Nakatsu, and M. Rauterberg (Eds.): ICEC 2007, LNCS 4740, pp. 389–394, 2007.
© IFIP International Federation for Information Processing 2007

## 2  System Frame and Design Scheme

This system adopts the S3C2410A microprocessor with the ARM 920T RISC core produced by Samsung. The excellent process ability of S3C2410A microprocessor makes itself the first choice for developing portable devices [1]. To meet the demand of the video capturing of intelligent mobile phone, the system adopts the USB-bus-based video model. The technics concerning the capturing, processing, storing, transmitting of images and HMM algorithm have been used in the system. The system frame is shown in Fig.1.

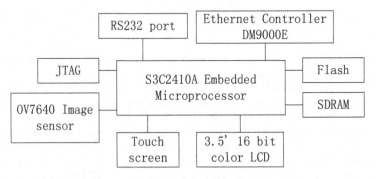

**Fig. 1.** The frame of ARM-based face recognition system

## 3  Image-Preprocessing and Face Recognition Algorithm

The first step of face recognition is to judge whether a face exists in the captured image or video data. If there exists, the following step is to work out the data about the situation and size of the facial organs. All the data makes a specific face, which is to compared with the face database. Through this, identity is recognized [2].

The process of face recognition falls into image preprocessing, face detecting, and face identifying.

### 3.1  Image Preprocessing and Algorithm Optimizing

Human being falls into the yellow, white, brown, and black in skin color. And this system focuses on the recognition of the yellow and white face.

The images from image sensor are presented in RGB method which is not the best model of skin color for computer recognition. Therefore the images are normally transformed from RGB to YUV to be processed. In YUV color model, brightness value can be easily separated and the calculation is simple, so this model is widely used [3,4].

The formula of transforming RGB to YUV is as follows:

$$\begin{bmatrix} Y \\ U \\ V \end{bmatrix} = \begin{bmatrix} 0.299 & 0.587 & 0.114 \\ -0.148 & -0.289 & 0.437 \\ 0.615 & -0.515 & -0.100 \end{bmatrix} \begin{bmatrix} R \\ G \\ B \end{bmatrix} \tag{1}$$

For the lack of floating-point assist-processor of S3C2410A microprocessor, the calculating of the above formula is time-consuming. In order to increase the transforming speed, the floating-point formula is optimized into the formula of integer calculating and shift calculating.

$$\begin{bmatrix} Y \\ U \\ V \end{bmatrix} = \begin{bmatrix} 38 & 74 & 15 \\ -19 & -37 & 61 \\ 79 & -66 & 13 \end{bmatrix} \begin{bmatrix} R \\ G \\ B \end{bmatrix} >> 7 \qquad (2)$$

The experiment proves that this formula greatly increases the transforming speed of the system from RGB to YUV.

The gray images and histograms transformed from the same captured image according to the above formulas are shown in Fig.2.

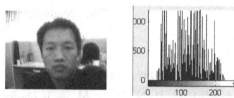

The gray images and histograms transformed from according to the float formula (1)

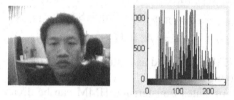

The gray images and histograms transformed from according to the integer formula (2)

**Fig. 2.** Emulating result

From the above data, it is seen that the minor difference between the transforming results of the two formulas has no effect on the following steps.

In the gray image, the value of one point decides whether it is skin location. By a threshold, the gray image can be transformed into two values image, in which 1 is skin location and 0 is not. From the two values image, the initial matrix is worked out by the boundary-based method. Thus a boundary rectangle is decided which covers the skin area. The final output matrix is worked out through area-merging for the initial matrix[2].

## 3.2  Face Detecting and Recognition Based on HMM

Face detecting is to locate the feature areas in the output matrix and separate them. Face recognition is to compare the output feature face with the database. And then the corresponding label of the recognized face is outputted. They are closely related. Face detecting and recognition can be carried out on the base of HMM at the same time [5].

1.   General concept of Hidden Markov Model (HMM)

HMM is a statistic model for feature signals. It consists of Markov chain of hidden, invisible and limited states and a probability density function. Markov chain includes probability distribution function of initial state and probability matrix of transferred state. Probability density function is related with those states.

HMM can be described using parameters as follow:

(1) Element N: it is the states number in the model. Supposing S is state space, and then $S = \{S_1, S_2, \hbar, S_N\}$. The model state at time t is $q_t \in S$, $1 \leq t \leq T$. T is the length of observing serial. The states serial of the model is $Q = \{q_1, q_2, \hbar, q_T\}$.

(2) Element M: it is the possible observed states number in each state. The observed states are marked as $V = \{v_1, v_2, \hbar, v_m\}$ and each observed state is corresponding to one movement state.

(3) States transferring probability distribution $A = \{a_{ij}\}$, in which $a_{ij} = P(q_t = S_j \mid q_{t-1} = S_i)$, $1 \leq i, j \leq N$. The condition is $0 \leq a_{ij} \leq 1$, and
$$\sum_{j=1}^{N} a_{ij} = 1.$$

(4) The observed states probability distribution in state j: $B = \{b_j(k)\}$, $b_j(k) = P(o_t = v_k \mid q_t = S_j)$, $1 \leq j \leq N$, $1 \leq j \leq M$. $o_t$ is observed signal at time t, and observed serail is $O = \{o_1, o_2, \hbar, o_T\}$.

(5) Initial state distribution $\Pi = \{\pi_i\}$, $\pi_i = P(q_i = S_i)$, $1 \leq i \leq N$.

HMM can be abbreviated as $\lambda = \{A, B, \Pi\}$. The input is limited character set $V = \{v_1, v_2, \hbar, v_m\}$, so HMM is named as scattering HMM[6].

2.   HMM for face recognition

According to the types of states transferring, HMM can be divided into ergodic and left-right. The transferring states of ergodic is random, and the state can transferred from itself to any other state. The state of the latter can only transfer from itself to the next.

The distribution of face feature is invariable from top to bottom and from left to right. So face can be modeled by 1D-HMM as is shown in Fig.3.

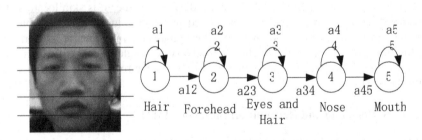

**Fig. 3.** The 1D-HMM for face recognition

3.  Feature values calculating of face image

The width of the face image is defined as W and height as H. Face image is divided into some wrapped blocks. The height of each block is L, and the wrapped depth is P. the total number of the blocks is observing vector T, and $T = (H - L)/(L - P) + 1$. The values of L and P affect the accuracy of recognition.With the increase of P, the recogniton accuracy also increases. The small value of L makes the recognition of the blocks ineffective. The increase of L makes cut feature probability increae. When the P is big, the value of L has no effect on system recognition. Reference [6] has a detaled discussion about the relation among P, L, and HMM.

4.  Training of face HMM

An HMM is built for every face in the face images database, which is trained by 5 different face images of one person. The 2D-DCT transform coefficient vector can form the observing vector series by small-block-dividing method. The HMM parameters will be worked out by training with observing vector series $O = \{o_1, o_2, \hbar, o_T\}$.

First, initialize the HMM $\lambda = \{A, B, \Pi\}$, and work out training data through dividing face image uniformly and from top to bottom. N is the state number of the model, N=6. Observed vector serial concerning every state is used to calculate initial estimate of observed states probability matrix B. The initial values of A and $\Pi$ are worked out of the face model's frame. Then, reestimate the model parameters by the method of maximal similar estimate arithmetic (Baum-Welch estimate arithmetic) , and estimate convergence condition of $P(O|\lambda)$.

The model would be converged when the following formula (3) works. Training iterative process can be finished. Otherwise go on training. C is a given threshold beforehand.

$$|P(O|\lambda^{(k+1)}) - P(O|\lambda^{(k)})| < C (1)$$ (3)

5.  Face recognition

Observed vector serial is worked out from the face image for recognizing by the same method in train process, and its probability is calculated from the face image HMM. The formula is as follows:

$$P(O^T|\lambda^{(k)}) = \max_n P(O^T|\lambda^{(n)})$$ (4)

The face of No. k person corresponding to the face being recognized is identified from the database when formula (4) is sufficed.

The experiment is carried on the face images which are selected from the ORL face database as training unit. The system forms a training vector serial for each face image. The test recognition possibility is high.

The experiment proves this algorithm makes real time treatment feasible, for the algorithm is not easily affected by the changing of facial expressions, strongly resistant to noises, and robust. Further research is needed on another two problems concerning light and gesture.

## 4  Conclusion

The face recognition system based on ARM and HMM has many advantages including small size, less calculating, high speed, and stable performance. So it can satisfy the needs for portable recognition devices. In the coming future, the embedded face recognition system will be widely used in security check-up, ID confirmation, entrance guard system, intelligent attendance check.

**Acknowledgments.** This research was supported in part by grants from 973 Program of Chinese Ministry of Science and Technology (2006CB303101), from the National Natural Science Foundation of China (60573059).

## References

1. Kan, L., Qizheng, L.: Application of Image Gather Based on the S3C2410 Platform And Embedded Linux. CONTROL & AUTOMATION 22(3-2), 125–127,168 (2006)
2. Gong, Y., Sakauchi, M.: Detection of Regions Matching Specified Chromatic Features. Computer Vision and Image Understanding 61(2), 263–269 (1995)
3. Yang, M.H., Kriegman, D.J., Ahuja, N.: Detecting Faces in Images: A Survey. IEEE Transactions on Pattern Analysis and Machine Intelligence 24(1), 34–58 (2002)
4. Nefian, A.V., Hayes, M.H.: Face detection and recognition using Hidden Markov Models. In: Proceedings of the International Conference on Image Processing, pp. 141–145 (1998)
5. Zhiliang, W., Yanling, Z.: An Expert System of Commodity Choose Applied with Artificial Psychology. In: IEEE International Conference on Systems, Man and Cybernetics, pp. 2326–2330 (2001)
6. Samaria, F., Halter, A.: Parameterization of stochastic model for human face identification. In: USA: Proceedings of the second IEEE workshop on application of computer vision (1994)

# Activity Recognition Using One Triaxial Accelerometer: A Neuro-fuzzy Classifier with Feature Reduction

Jhun-Ying Yang[1], Yen-Ping Chen[1], Gwo-Yun Lee[2], Shun-Nan Liou[2], and Jeen-Shing Wang[1]

[1] Department of Electrical Engineering,
National Cheng Kung University,
Tainan 701, Taiwan
[2] Micro Systems Technology Research Laboratories,
Industrial Technology Research Institute,
Tainan 709, Taiwan
jeenshin@mail.ncku.edu.tw

**Abstract.** This paper presents a neuro-fuzzy classifer for activity recognition using one triaxial accelerometer and feature reduction approaches. We use a triaxial accelerometer to acquire subjects' acceleration data and train the neuro-fuzzy classifier to distinguish different activities/movements. To construct the neuro-fuzzy classifier, a modified mapping-constrained agglomerative clustering algorithm is devised to reveal a compact data configuration from the acceleration data. In addition, we investigate two different feature reduction methods, a feature subset selection and linear discriminate analysis. These two methods are used to determine the significant feature subsets and retain the characteristics of the data distribution in the feature space for training the neuro-fuzzy classifier. Experimental results have successfully validated the effectiveness of the proposed classifier.

**Keywords:** Acceleration, activity recognition, feature extraction, linear discriminate analysis, neuro-fuzzy system, triaxial accelerometer.

## 1 Introduction

The development of wearable systems using advanced miniature sensors and wireless technologies has allowed people to issue a command for controlling electric appliances by gestures/activities. Activity recognition is one of the technologies frequently embedded in wearable systems for recognizing human activities or gestures. Nowadays, many researchers have focused on diversifying application domains of human activity recognition in biomedical engineering, medical nursing, and interactive entertainment. Signals for recognition can be obtained from different kinds of detectors. These include electromyography (EMG), audio sensors, image sensors, and accelerometers. Among the aforementioned sensors, accelerometers that can record acceleration data caused by movements and gravity have drawn much attention in the field of activity/gesture recognition [1].

L. Ma, R. Nakatsu, and M. Rauterberg (Eds.): ICEC 2007, LNCS 4740, pp. 395–400, 2007.
© IFIP International Federation for Information Processing 2007

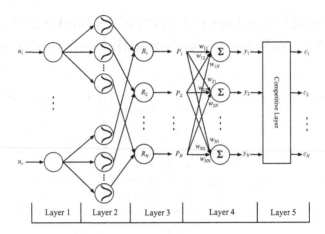

**Fig. 1.** Topology of the neuro-fuzzy classifier

Recently, research studies have proposed a variety of classifiers for activity recognition from acceleration data. These methodologies used to build classifiers include support vector machine (SVM) [4], [6], K-nearest neighbors [4], decision tree, [3], naïve Bayes classifiers [1], [4], hidden Markov models [8], and neural networks [6]. In this paper, we adopt a neuro-fuzzy classifier to recognize human activities using one triaxial accelerometer to acquire a subject's acceleration data. In addition, we compare two different dimensionality reduction methods in our recognition scheme: one is the feature selection method proposed in [2] and the other is linear discriminate analysis (LDA) [5].

The rest of this paper is organized as follows. In section 2, we introduce the structure of a neuro-fuzzy classifier and its construction algorithm. Section 3 presents the detailed information about the proposed recognition strategy, including feature extraction and dimensionality reduction. Section 4 provides the experiment design for validating the effectiveness of the proposed classifier. Finally, conclusions are given the last section.

## 2 Neuro-fuzzy Classifier

In this paper, we adopt a neuro-fuzzy classifier to recognize daily activities from acceleration data. The structure of the neuro-fuzzy classifier is shown in Fig. 1. It contains five layers and the description of the layers is given as follows. **Layer 1**: The nodes in this layer only transmit input values to the nodes of the next layer directly. $\mathbf{u} = [u_1, u_2, ..., u_r]^T$ is the input vector, where $r$ represents the number of elements in the input feature set. **Layer 2**: The nodes represent Gaussian membership functions: $\mu_{M_i^j} = \exp(-(\frac{u_i - m_i^j}{\sigma_i^j})^2)$, where $M_i^j$ is the input fuzzy term set, $m_i^j$ and $\sigma_i^j$ are the center and width of the Gaussian membership function of the $j^{th}$ term of the $i^{th}$ input variable $u_i$. **Layer 3**: The nodes in this layer constitute the antecedents of the fuzzy rule base.

The output of the node is $p_j = \prod_{i=1}^{n} \mu_{M_i^j}$, where $p_j$ is the output function of the $j^{th}$ rule node. **Layer 4**: This is the output layer. The output nodes integrate all the inferred information from Layer 3 with the corresponding singleton values $w_{hj}$ and act as a defuzzifier. $y_h = \sum_{j=1}^{N} w_{hj} p_j$, where $N$ is the number of classes and $\mathbf{y} = [y_1, y_2, ..., y_N]^T$ are the output vector. We set the numbers of the fuzzy rules and output neurons equal to the number of activity classes. The fuzzy rules can be expressed as

$$\text{Rule } j\text{: IF } u_1 \text{ is } M_1^j \text{ and } \cdots \text{ and } u_r \text{ is } M_r^j,$$
$$\textbf{THEN } y_1(k) = w_{1j} p_j \text{ and } \cdots \text{ and } y_N = w_{Nj} p_j. \tag{1}$$

**Layer 5**: This is the competitive layer. Each element in the output vector competes with the others. We set the winner's output be 1 and zeros for the rest outputs.

In general, a clustering technique is appropriate to determine the parameters of the neuro-fuzzy structure. To effectively construct the network structure, we modify the mapping-constrained agglomerative (MCA) clustering algorithm [7] that takes the number of fuzzy rules as the number of clusters in the input and output spaces. The parameters of these clusters including the input centers (**m**), variances (**σ**), and output centers (**W**), can be directly used to construct the neuro-fuzzy classifier. For each cluster, say cluster $\alpha$, the components of $\mathbf{m}_{IO\alpha} = [\mathbf{m}_{I\alpha}, \mathbf{m}_{O\alpha}]^T$ ($\boldsymbol{\sigma}_{IO\alpha} = [\boldsymbol{\sigma}_{I\alpha}, \boldsymbol{\sigma}_{O\alpha}]^T$) denote the centers (variances) in the input space ($I$) and output space ($O$), respectively, and let $z_\alpha$ be the counter representing the number of patterns in cluster $\alpha$. Given a set of training patterns $\mathbf{V} = [\mathbf{u}, \mathbf{y}]^T$, we first assign the initial seed clusters by randomly selecting the data points in the training patterns and then feed the data points as the training patterns. The seed cluster closest to the current data point is defined as the winner cluster. We perform $winner = \arg\min\{\|\mathbf{V} - \mathbf{m}_{IO\alpha}\|\}, \alpha = 1, ..., N$, and update the parameters of the winner cluster: Set the counter of data points $z_{winner} = z_{winner} + 1$. For the input space, set

$$temp\_\mathbf{m}_{Iwinner} = \mathbf{m}_{Iwinner} + \frac{\mathbf{u} - \mathbf{m}_{Iwinner}}{z_{winner}};$$
$$\boldsymbol{\sigma}^2_{Iwinner} = \frac{(z_{winner} - 1)(\sigma^2_{Iwinner} + m^2_{Iwinner}) + \mathbf{u}^2}{z_{winner}} - temp\_\mathbf{m}^2_{Iwinner}; \tag{2}$$
$$\mathbf{m}_{Iwinner} = temp\_\mathbf{m}_{Iwinner}.$$

Similarly, for the output space, set $\mathbf{m}_{Owinner} = \mathbf{m}_{Owinner} + \frac{\mathbf{y} - \mathbf{m}_{Owinner}}{z_{winner}}$. Repeat the above steps until there remains no data to be clustered. The above modified MCA algorithm determines the parameters of **m**, **σ** and **W** by setting $\mathbf{m} = \mathbf{m}_I$, $\boldsymbol{\sigma} = \boldsymbol{\sigma}_I$ and $\mathbf{W} = \mathbf{m}_O$.

## 3  Activity Recognition Strategy

We have developed an effective activity recognition strategy to increase the recognition accuracy and reduce the computational burden of the neuro-fuzzy classifier. First, we cut the raw acceleration sequences into many overlapping windows of the same length and extract features from each window into a feature set.

In order to reduce the dimension of the feature set, we investigate two dimensionality reduction methods in Section 3.2.

## 3.1 Feature Extraction

We extract the features in time domain and frequency domain from each window of the triaxial acceleration data. The time domain features are extracted from the raw data and include mean, correlation between axes, interquartile range, mean absolute deviation, root mean square, standard deviation, and variance. The frequency domain feature is energy calculated as the sum of the squared discrete FFT component magnitudes of the signal in a window [6]. Since we collect signals from a triaxial accelerometer, a total of 24 features (3 axes × 8 features) are calculated from a window of the acceleration data for $x$-axis, $y$-axis, and $z$-axis.

## 3.2 Dimensionality Reduction

In general, the following two approaches are usually used in dimensionality reduction: 1) Selecting the significant features and eliminating irrelative ones to preserve as much of the original information as possible for recognition; and 2) Transforming original feature sets into a lower dimensional feature space with class separability. In this study, we investigate two approaches, a feature subset selection (FSS) [2] and linear discriminate analysis (LDA) [5].

**Feature subset selection.** The FSS is based on common principal components (CPCs) generalized from the principal component analysis (PCA). First, the FSS performs PCA on each class to obtain the CPC loadings [2]. Each row vector in the CPC loadings represents the projection of the corresponding feature of the classes to a lower dimensional common space. Then, a clustering technique is utilized to group the row vectors of the CPC loadings which have similar contribution in the data distribution. We select the points closest to the centers of clusters as the selected features. That is, each data point represents a feature and the number of the selected features equals to the number of clusters.

**Linear discriminate analysis.** The basic concept of the LDA is to seek the most efficient projective direction which minimizes the data distribution in the same class and separates the data distribution in the different classes for discrimination. For this purpose, two scatter matrices are defined: the between-class covariance matrix $S_B$ and the within-class covariance matrix $S_W$. $S_B$ shows the scatter of the expected vectors around the mixture mean:

$$\mathbf{S}_B = \sum_{\alpha=1}^{N} n_\alpha (\mathbf{m}^{(\alpha)} - \mathbf{m})(\mathbf{m}^{(\alpha)} - \mathbf{m})^T, \tag{3}$$

and $S_W$ represents the scatter of samples around their respective class expected vectors:

$$\mathbf{S}_W = \sum_{\alpha=1}^{N} n_\alpha \sum_{i=1}^{n_\alpha} (\mathbf{x}_i^{(\alpha)} - \mathbf{m}^{(\alpha)})(\mathbf{x}_i^{(\alpha)} - \mathbf{m}^{(\alpha)})^T, \tag{4}$$

where $n_\alpha$ is the number of samples in the class $\alpha$, $x_i^{(\alpha)}$ is the $i^{th}$ sample of $\alpha^{th}$ class, $\mathbf{m}^{(\alpha)}$ is the mean vector of the samples in the class $\alpha$, and $\mathbf{m}$ is the mean vector of all the data points. The LDA preserves class separability in a lower dimensional space by finding a unit projective vector $\mathbf{w}$ which maximizes the covariance between classes and minimizes the covariance within class by maximizing the following criterion [5]:

$$J(\mathbf{w}) = \frac{\mathbf{w}^T \mathbf{S}_B \mathbf{w}}{\mathbf{w}^T \mathbf{S}_W \mathbf{w}}. \tag{5}$$

## 4 Experimental Results

The acceleration data was collected using the MMA7260Q triaxial accelerometer on a wearable board. The accelerometer's sensitivity is set from –4.0g to +4.0g and the output signal of the acceleometer is sampled at 100 Hz by a 10-bit ADC.

The classification tasks include eight common domestic activities: walking, running, scrubbing, standing, working at a computer, vacuuming, brushing teeth and sitting. We gathered acceleration data from a single triaxial accelerometer module mounted on the dominant wrist of each subject. All the subjects (seven normal and healthy subjects) were asked to perform each activity for two minutes. We took the window size of 512 with 256 samples overlapped with consecutive windows. A total of 45 windows were obtained from the acceleration data for each activity of one subject.

We utilized a leave-one-subject-out cross-validation procedure to validate the effectiveness of the proposed activity recognition strategy. Six subjects were trained in the recognition scheme and then tested on the subject left out of the training data set. We repeated the same procedure for all the subjects.

The LDA and FSS methods were applied to reduce the dimensionality of the feature space, and then we utilized the lower dimensional feature sets to train and test the proposed neuro-fuzzy classifier. The original feature space was transformed into a new seven-dimensional feature space after performing the LDA. The average cross-validation recognition accuracy achieves 92.86±5.91%. Table 1 shows the confusion matrix that records the number of recognition errors for all the subjects. To compare the performance of the LDA and FSS methods, the FSS method selected seven features from the original 24 features. The average recognition accuracy is

**Table 1.** Confusion matrix for all subjects

| Classified as | Walking | Running | Scrubbing | Standing | Working at a PC | Vacuuming | Brushing teeth | Sitting |
|---|---|---|---|---|---|---|---|---|
| Walking | 304 | 0 | 2 | 0 | 0 | 10 | 0 | 0 |
| Running | 0 | 265 | 0 | 0 | 0 | 1 | 0 | 0 |
| Scrubbing | 0 | 10 | 279 | 0 | 0 | 2 | 16 | 0 |
| Standing | 0 | 0 | 0 | 306 | 0 | 0 | 0 | 0 |
| Working at a PC | 0 | 0 | 0 | 0 | 315 | 0 | 0 | 45 |
| Vacuuming | 11 | 31 | 5 | 9 | 0 | 302 | 0 | 0 |
| Brushing teeth | 0 | 6 | 29 | 0 | 0 | 0 | 299 | 0 |
| Sitting | 0 | 3 | 0 | 0 | 0 | 0 | 0 | 270 |

83.41±5.93%. The LDA method outperforms the FSS method. The recognition results show that the proposed activity recognition strategy can provide satisfactory accuracy by the proposed neuro-fuzzy classifier.

## 5 Conclusions

In this study, we have developed a human activity recognition scheme based on a neuro-fuzzy classifier using acceleration data acquired by a single accelerometer. We employed the modified MCA and two dimensionality reduction methods to construct the neuro-fuzzy classifier. The performances of the proposed classifiers with the FSS and LDA achieve 83% and 93%, respectively. If accuracy is the major concern for building the classifier, the construction algorithm can be associated with optimization techniques to further fine-tune the parameters of the neuro-fuzzy classifiers in improve the overall performance of the classifier.

## References

1. Bao, L., Intille, S.S.: Activity Recognition from User-Annotated Acceleration Data. In: Ferscha, A., Mattern, F. (eds.) PERVASIVE 2004. LNCS, vol. 3001, pp. 1–17. Springer, Heidelberg (2004)
2. Chen, Y.-P., Yang, J.-Y., Liou, S.-N., Lee, G.-Y., Wang, J.-S.: Neural Classifiers for Activity Recognition Using Acceleration Measurements. In: Applied Mathematics and Computation (to appear)
3. Mathie, M.J., Celler, B.G., Lovell, N.H., Coster, A.C.F.: Classification of Basic Daily Movements Using a Triaxial Accelerometer. Medical and Biological Engineering and Computing 42(5), 679–687 (2004)
4. Ravi, N., Dandekar, N., Mysore, P., Littman, M.L.: Activity Recognition from Accelerometer Data. In: Proceedings of the Seventeenth Innovative Applications of Artificial Intelligence Conference, pp. 1541–1546 (2005)
5. Tsymbal, A., Puuronen, S., Pechenizkiy, M., Baumgarten, M., Patterson, D.: Eigenvector-Based Feature Extraction for Classification. In: Proceedings of the Fifteenth International Florida Artificial Intelligence Research Society Conference, pp. 354–358.
6. Wang, S., Yang, J., Chen, N., Chen, X., Zhang, Q.: Human Activity Recognition with User-Free Accelerometers in the Sensor Networks. In: IEEE Int. Conf. Neural Networks and Brain, vol. 2, pp. 1212–1217 (2005)
7. Wang, J.-S., Lee, C.S.G.: Self-Adaptive Neuro-Fuzzy Inference Systems for Classification Applications. IEEE Trans. Fuzzy Systems 10(6), 790–802 (2002)
8. Ward, J.A., Lukowicz, P., Troster, G., Starner, T.E.: Activity Recognition of Assembly Task Using Body-Worn Microphones and Accelerometers. IEEE Trans. Pattern Analysis and Machine Intelligence 28(10), 1553–1567 (2006)

# GFE – Graphical Finite State Machine Editor for Parallel Execution*

David Obdrzalek and Jan Benda

Charles University, Faculty of Mathematics and Physics,
Malostranske namesti 25, 118 00 Prague 1, Czech Republic
david.obdrzalek@mff.cuni.cz, jbe@matfyz.cz

**Abstract.** In this paper we present GFE – the Graphical FSM (Finite State Machine) Editor based on the Grafcet SFC (Sequential Function Chart) model. The GFE takes advantage of automated code generation and provides strong tools for complex control. At the same time it gives a high-level overview of the entire robotic control architecture. A complex control system may be designed, tested and deployed using visual approach. This is particularly useful for education where the students do not have to start always from scratch, or for young robot builders who are not as experienced in low-level programming. Once a control library is implemented for a particular robot, it may be reused and the robot may be programmed using solely graphical approach, because the most complicated part of controller design - the state machine - is automatically generated. This avoids typing errors and allows fast and simple redesign.

**Keywords:** robot control, automatic finite state machine generation, graphical control design.

## 1 Introduction

Robot building is increasingly popular. Even very simple robots are used to do complex jobs in industry and at home. Robots are used in education to demonstrate theoretical algorithmic concepts in real world, or they are even used as a hobby tool to proudly show the author is able to create a movable intelligent toy. Last, but not least, robot-based toys get increasingly more interest by vast public. In all mentioned areas, the users and builders usually do not like to build everything from scratch every time, so they want to reuse whatever possible. Also, the age of robot builders increasingly lowers, and younger authors usually do not have enough experience in programming and so their work is hard. There are numerous tools for such starting roboticians, be it a child or a student, but as any other tool, they have limitations. One of such limitations is quite common: most graphic design tools do not offer the author the freedom to control the

---

* The work was partly supported by the project 1ET100300419 of the Program Information Society of the Thematic Program II of the National Research Program of the Czech Republic.

L. Ma, R. Nakatsu, and M. Rauterberg (Eds.): ICEC 2007, LNCS 4740, pp. 401–406, 2007.

hardware completely and are tied to a specific hardware (e.g. Lego Mindstorms NTX Software [1], Fischertechnik Robo Pro or Lucky Logic [2] etc.), or are too complex for beginners. Some of the tools provide basic blocks, but as the complexity of the system grows, they become to be unmaintainable.

One of the pretty popular tool categories for robotic application uses Finite state machines (FSM). They provide a rich formalism for high level control of robot's processes and strategies. Unfortunately, for practical applications the number of considered states and conditions quickly exceeds the size reasonably maintainable by hand. Moreover, the transcription of a FSM to most programming languages is rarely lucid and easily extensible.

In this paper we present the Graphical Finite State Machine Editor (GFE), a tool for visual design of generalized finite state machines based on the Sequential Function Chart (SFC) model. Compared to a traditional FSM, an SFC chart allows multiple states being active at a time. It also provides means for easy synchronization of parallelly executed branches. The editor allows users to create powerful state machine while using the graphical approach and at the same time allows the user to create low-level functionality for the robotic hardware without losing control of the program because of its complexity.

From within the editor, a function implementing the designed SFC chart in a high-level programming language may be automatically generated. To complete the overall functional control program, basic sensing and control functions have to be linked with the generated code. This set of functions is immutable from the sight of the user and must be created only once for a specific robot hardware. The major advantage of this approach is that no manual edit of code is required when the logic of the chart changes, as only the generated FSM code is affected. Once the input/action library is implemented for a particular robotic platform, the robot may be programmed by a vast public using solely graphical approach. Also, the same user-created control may be used for more hardware platforms without any change, only by replacing the corresponding underlying library. And these are very important features - particularly in the domain of educational robotics.

## 2   The SFC Language

The SFC is a specialized graphical language developed as a tool for design of control automata. It is a subset of the Grafcet norm [3], which (among others) proposes one language for the control system structure - the SFC (Sequential Function Chart). Its intuitive graphical syntax and powerful semantic was taken as the structural basis for the GFE. This section is dedicated to the necessary SFC basics.

The SFC chart has a form of an oriented bi-partitioned graph where two different kinds of nodes are linked using oriented edges:

- *Places* (represented as rectangular blocks in the chart) correspond roughly to the states of an automaton. Each place defines a specific action to be performed by the control program when the place is active. Multiple SFC places may be active at a time. Places active at the beginning of the code execution are called initial and are marked with a double border.

- *Transitions* (represented as thick lines over interconnections) act as conditional expressions that transmit activation within the chart given that all the transition input places are active and the transition condition (a boolean expression) is met. Several transitions may be open at a time.
- *Interconnections* (represented as lines connecting places and transitions) are oriented edges describing the activation flow within the chart.

In a classical deterministic FSM, the network would only branch from a place and only one state may be active at a time. The SFC allows also branching and synchronization for parallel activation of multiple places. This makes it useful for deterministic design of systems with multiple interdependent subsystems and/or asynchronous input events. The available control structures are:

- *Conditioning* (one place connected to multiple transitions): the activation passes from a single input place to one output place (*branching*) or two output places are connected to one input place (*merging*). The flow is determined by the first open transition (see Figure 1).
- *Parallelism* (one transition connected to multiple places): the activation passes through a single transition to all output places (*forking*) or from multiple active places into a single transition (*synchronization*). Prior to opening the transition all the input places connected to the transition must be active (see Figure 2).

**Fig. 1.** Serial branching and merging    **Fig. 2.** Parallel forking and synchronization

## 3    FSM Generation in GFE

Over the years, many formats were proposed for description of the finite state machines (FSM), for example transition graphs, transition tables, SFCs, formal definitions of a FSM as quintuple $\{S, X, Y, d, l\}$ and many others. For our purposes we use the SFC because it allows the FSM designer to naturally work with parallel execution branches without having to withdraw the deterministic FSM model. This is because a well-formed SFC chart maps unambiguously to a deterministic FSM. In this section we describe the automatic creation of an SFC engine.

The state of the entire SFC chart is given by the list of activation numbers of the individual places in the chart (an *activation vector*). To build a SFC engine, the SFC activation rules are applied on the activation vector of the SFC model. The activation vector is implemented using a fixed-length array of activation counters. The SFC engine then consists of a single function that should be periodically called to update the chart state. This function is composed of two sections: the activation update and the place action blocks.

The activation update block contains one conditional block generated for each transition in the chart - the values of input places and the value of the boolean condition are checked to determine if a particular transition is open. If this test succeeds, the transition is opened transferring the activation from the input places (decreasing activation counter) to the output places (increasing the counter).

The second section of the generated function is responsible for performing the actions of the active places. One conditional block is generated for each place to execute the appropriate action if and only if the particular place is active (see the generated code example in Section 5).

## 4    The GFE Output

The presented subset of the SFC language is well suited for description of the control code structure. Unfortunately, the executive part of the SFC is too weak to express every desired action. Many visual control system editors choose to provide the chart designer with access to the low level features of the underlying hardware (see for example the Programming Editor for picaxe [4]). This has two big disadvantages: firstly, programming on the level of hardware control signals is too fine-grained and quickly leads to a high amount of duplicate objects and subsections in the chart, and secondly, programming using low level hardware identifiers is hardly lucid and easy to maintain. Therefore we propose the use of a high level programming language for the actions behind the SFC model and the use of the implementation library for individual low-level hardware operations. The visually edited chart provides easily maintainable structure and a high-level overview of the control actions while the code behind provides powerful, reusable and programmable operations on the hardware.

But how are the individual robot's actions triggered? As stated above, a place in the chart corresponds to an action that should be performed by the control program. In the GFE, the required actions are entered into the text field of each place. When generating the SFC engine, all the place descriptions are treated as control commands and output directly into the resulting engine code. This approach has a great advantage both in easy maintainability and great extensibility as the place actions can range from simple function calls via parameterized function calls with arguments to arbitrarily advanced operations[1]. It relieves the tiring state machine coding from the programmer but still allows to use all the comfortable features of a high-level programming language.

The generated language was chosen to be the C language. This is because of its high penetration in the domain of robotic control systems, great extensibility, portability and a steep learning curve. The C language is widely supported by a

---

[1] We recommend using time-simple operations here because of performance reasons, but it is not a strict dictate. Also, using library calls for low-level functionality instead of coding it in the GFE is highly recommended for maintainability reasons.

broad variety of popular control architectures from small scale RISC microcontrollers to embedded PCs and other portable devices, which enables the same control chart to be used with a wide range of targets. It is also important to note that the choice of C is not binding. Virtually any language could be used, and the GFE may even be enhanced to support custom-defined syntax[2].

## 5   Example

This example is very simple, but even that it demonstrates the principles well. Let us assume the simplest case of a line-following robot. It is equipped with just two sensors (left / right infrared line detectors) and two actuators (left / right engine). The simplest approach directs the robot ahead only stopping individual wheels to keep the black line between the two sensors. When a sensor at one side detects black instead of white surface, the motor at that side is stopped so that the robot turns and the sensor gets off the line (and similarly the other side).

The control code in SFC (see Figure 3 left) is simple and lucid taking advantage of parallel simulation of two independent controllers. The advantage of the presented approach is obvious in comparison with the FSM (see Figure 3 right) isomorphic to the proposed SFC controller.

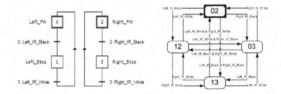

**Fig. 3.** A simple line-follower SFC and a corresponding FSM

The generated SFC engine for this example is shown in Figure 4. The activation vector for the entire SFC chart is represented in a global array initialized by the values of starting activation numbers of the chart's places. The code of the SFC engine consists of two sections: the state update and action execution. In the first section the activation vector is updated following the rules of SFC signal propagation (the GFE_Activated and GFE_Enabled callbacks may be used in the encapsulating control software). The second section is responsible for execution of action code for all active places.

Note how the place and transition captions are turned into function calls. These functions are defined by the capabilities of the target platform and have to be defined in the encapsulating control code. The important fact is that these functions must only be defined once for a particular robotic platform. Once these sensing and control functions are implemented, the robot can be programmed using purely the visual approach.

---

[2] The only required features of the target language are the support for function calls and the support for conditional block execution.

```
int _AV[] = {1, 0, 1, 0};
void GFE_Run() {
    // Perform state update
    if (_AV[0] && Left_IR_Black()) {
        if (!--_AV[0]) GFE_Activated(0, FALSE); // Place 0 lost activation
        if (!_AV[1]++) GFE_Activated(1, TRUE);  // Place 1 gained activation
        GFE_Enabled(1); // Transition 1 may be opened from now on
    }
    if (_AV[1] && Left_IR_White()) { /* ... similar to _AV[0] */ }
    if (_AV[2] && Right_IR_Black()) { /* ... */ }
    if (_AV[3] && Right_IR_White()) { /* ... */ }

    // Perform place actions
    if (_AV[0]) { Left_FW(); }
    if (_AV[1]) { Left_Stop(); }
    if (_AV[2]) { Right_FW(); }
    if (_AV[3]) { Right_Stop(); }
}
```

**Fig. 4.** Code example - the generated SFC engine for the line-follower robot

## 6  Conclusion

In this paper we presented the GFE (Graphical FSM Editor) as a tool for visual design of generalized Finite State Machines based on the Grafcet SFC model. The GFE is intended for use by robot builders and users who want to concern on controlling the robot and not wasting time by implementing control state machine and low-level functionality every time anew.

The editor supports automatic generation of the SFC code to be included into a control system written in the C language. This allows an inexperienced user, given with a predefined set of control and sensing functions, to design, deploy and execute a complete control system using only visual approach. The major advantage of this approach is that no manual edit of code is required when the logic of chart changes, as only the generated SFC engine is affected. The editor also has great educational potential: once the action/input library is implemented for a particular robot, it may be programmed by a vast public using solely graphical approach.

## References

1. Lego, Mindstorms NTX Software, http://mindstorms.lego.com/
2. Fischertechnik, Robo Pro, Lucky Logic,
   http://www.fischertechnik.com/html/computing-software.html
3. International Electrotechnical Commission, IEC 1131-3: Programmable Controllers
   - Part3: Programming Languages, IEC 1131-3 (1993)
4. Crocodile Technology, Programming Editor,
   http://www.rev-ed.co.uk/picaxe/progedit.htm

# Media Me: Body and Personal Media Interaction

Owen Noel Newton Fernando[1], Imiyage Janaka Prasad Wijesena[1],
Adrian David Cheok[1], Ajith Parakum Madurapperuma[2],
Lochandaka Ranathunga[2], Mei Gangwen[1], Miyuru Dayarathna[2],
Srinivasan Mariappan[1], and Lee Rui Jie Jerome[1]

[1] Mixed Reality Lab, National University of Singapore, Singapore
[2] Faculty of Information Technology, University of Moratuwa, Sri Lanka
contact@mixedrealitylab.org
http://www.mixedrealitylab.org

**Abstract.** "Media Me" is a media interactive art work which comments on the bidirectional relationship between people and the media through the use of a realtime video mosaic. The elements of the video mosaic could be personal, cultural, historical, and educational. This research can be considered as a combination of creativity, art, and digital entertainment as well as an extension of personal media broadcasting. It comments on the growing trend of personal broadcasting and social media.

**Keywords:** Video mosaic, interactive media, human-media interaction.

## 1 Introduction

Television has been the mass media for broadcasting media content for a long time. However, developments in broadband internet and social networks have made it possible for individuals to use their own personal media as broadcast media. For example, "YouTube" allows individuals to submit personal videos for public viewing. From the previous concept of a few broadcast channels, now we have millions of channels broadcast by individuals. This has led Time Magazine to announce the person of the year in 2006 [1] as "you", to highlight the revolution in personal media that has developed.

As an artistic reflection on new personal media, Media Me is an interactive video installation that displays a captured image of a person as a video mosaic [2] [3] made of hundreds of videos. We literally turn the body into videos, which artistically represent the revolution in personal media. Videos are continuously arranged in realtime to form a mosaic representation of the background to provide meaningful contents, such as cultural and historical media. When no image is captured by the system, Media Me activates and reflects the media itself by creating a mosaic of cultural and historical content.

Media Me can be considered as a new form of personal media where a person can create and broadcast her own customized contents as image elements. For the current version of Media Me, we have used religion, cultural, and historical movies of Sri Lanka to create a meaningful video Mosaic. This system can also

L. Ma, R. Nakatsu, and M. Rauterberg (Eds.): ICEC 2007, LNCS 4740, pp. 407–410, 2007.

(a) National Heritage of Sri Lanka

(b) Buddhism in Sri Lanaka

**Fig. 1.** Mosaic created by the system

be used for educational purposes in an interactive way, for example exploring national heritage of Sri Lanka. We are also extending the system for various other cultures.

In Figure 1(a) the face (foreground) and the background mosaic are constructed with video clips showing national heritage of Sri Lanka. Similarly, Figure 1(b) shows mosaic constructed with videos of Buddhism in Sri Lanka. The background videos are randomly selected and arranged by the system. The system analyzes each area of the foreground and selects a video clip that can substitute that area. As shown in the Figure 1, some level of colour correction is applied to the foreground video clips to attain a more natural look and feel.

## 2   System Overview

The image of the person, who stands in front of the blue screen, is captured by the camera. In the system initialization process the average colour of the background is computed and it is used to remove the background from the extracted video frame. The foreground is segmented to rectangular areas and average colour of each of them is calculated. The average colour is used to find a matching video clips from the video database. The video clips in the database are pre-analyzed and organized based on their average color. Since the system has only a finite number of videos, some amount of colour correction is applied to the selected video clips in order to attain the realistic look and feel. The background of the original video is removed and replaced with larger tiled set of videos. These videos are randomly selected from a video database. Finally, the background and the foreground are combined to create the mosaic. An electronic projector projects the final video mosaic onto a large screen right before the person. The full system architecture is shown in Figure 2.

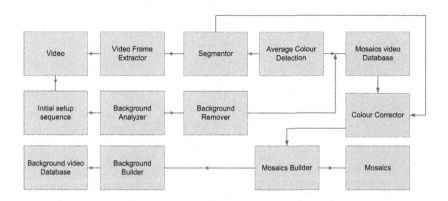

**Fig. 2.** Media Me: System Architecture

# 3   Conclusion

Computing technologies are increasingly being used to support new forms of entertainment and creativity. Creativity, art, and digital entertainment systems provide futuristic new media forms. Media Me[1] is a media interactive art work which comments on the bidirectional relationship between people and the media through the use of a realtime video mosaic. It also provides the means to educate the masses while entertaining them. This will also bring new ways of communication between people and media, and new forms of social, educational, and cultural interaction.

**Acknowledgments.** Media Me is funded by Singapore Science Center. This project is installed in the iSpace at Singapore Science center to allow visitors to obtain a novel experience in entrainment and social communication.

# References

1. Time Magazine Website (December 13, 2006)
   http://www.time.com/time/magazine/article/0,9171,1569514,00.html
2. Mackay, W., Pagani, D.: Video mosaic: laying out time in a physical space. In: MULTIMEDIA '94. Proc. of the second ACM Int. Conf. on Multimedia, California, USA, pp. 165–172 (1994)
3. Klein, A.W., Grant, T., Finkelstein, A., Cohen, M.F.: Video mosaics. In: NPAR '02. Proc. of the 2nd Int. symposium on Non-photorealistic animation and rendering, Annecy, France, pp. 21–29 (2002)

---

[1] Web: http://mediame.mixedrealitylab.org

# Background Subtraction Using Running Gaussian Average and Frame Difference

Zhen Tang, Zhenjiang Miao, and Yanli Wan

Institute of Information Science,
Beijing JiaoTong University, Beijing 100044, P.R. China
{06120376,zjmiao}@bjtu.edu.cn,
wanlili3646@sohu.com

**Abstract.** Background Subtraction methods are wildly used to detect moving object from static cameras. It has many applications such as traffic monitoring, human motion capture and recognition, and video surveillance. It is hard to propose a background model which works well under all different situations. Actually, there is no need to propose a pervasive model; it is a good model as long as it works well under a special situation. In this paper, a new method combining Gaussian Average and Frame Difference is proposed. Shadow suppression is not specifically dealt with, because it is considered to be part of the background, and can be subtracted by using an appropriate threshold. At last, a new method is raised to fill small gaps that the detected foreground or the moving objects may contain.

## 1 Introduction

Background Subtraction is the first and impotent step in many computer vision applications such as moving object detection, people tracking, traffic monitoring, video surveillance and video semantic annotation. In order to robustly track the moving object, an accurate, reliable and flexible background model is required. As raised in paper [1], a good background model must have the following features: high precision; with the two meanings of accuracy in shape detection and reactivity to changes in time; flexibility in difference lighting conditions; and efficiency in order to provided in real-time. Many background subtraction methods have been proposed in the past decades including Running Gaussian Average , Temporal Median Filter , Mixture of Gaussians , Kernel Density Estimation (KDE) , Kalman Filter , and Cooccurence of Image Variations . These methods are either too time consuming (like GMM with online EM algorithm) or too space consuming (like Temporal Median Filter proposed in [3]). Running Gaussian Average is a simple method to describe a background, and it can get a real-time performing. But the shortcoming is it is not a so accurate one. Many methods have been proposed to improve the performing of this method. Koller et al. in [4] remarked that the model should be selectively updated. Sumer Jabri et al. in [5] combined this method with edge information to improve the quality and reliability of the results. In this paper, we combine this method with frame difference method, and

L. Ma, R. Nakatsu, and M. Rauterberg (Eds.): ICEC 2007, LNCS 4740, pp. 411–414, 2007.

we propose a new method to fill small gaps that the foreground or the moving objects may contain. In shadows and ghosts suppression aspect, R. Cucchiara et al. in [1] [6] proposed some effective methods, and got good results. In this paper, we consider shadows as part of the background based on the assumption that the shadow is not strong, so we can eliminate it using an appropriate threshold during the background updating period.

The rest of the paper is organized as follows. In section 2, Running Gaussian Average method is summarized. Frame difference method is discussed in detail in section 3. Then the experiment results and conclusion are discussed.

## 2   Running Gaussian Average Model and Frame Difference

As described by Wren et al. in [2] [5], the background is modeled based on ideally fitting a Gaussian probability density (pdf) on the last $n$ pixel's value. For each pixel, a running average $m_t$ and a standard deviation $\sigma_t$ are maintained for each color channel. A difference image $D_t$ is derived by subtracting the running average from a new coming frame. After a confidence normalization step for every color channel, the image is changed into gray scale and then a binary mask $B^c_t$ is derived.

The Frame Difference Method [7] is based on the fact that these is nearly no variation of background in consecutive two or three frames. So the moving objects can be simply extracted by the difference of the current frame and the previous frame. In order to eliminate the ghost in the difference images, an intersection step is performed on the consecutive two binarilized difference images. After the above procedure, a binary mask $B^f_t$ is derived.

## 3   The Combination of the Two Methods

The motivation of combining the two methods is that the masks witch we get above can compensate each other. So we integrate $B^f_t$ with $B^c_t$ and get a more reliable one:

$$B_t = \begin{cases} 0 & B^c_t + B^f_t < 0 \\ B^c_t + B^f_t & 0 \le B^c_t + B^f_t \le 255 \\ 255 & B^c_t + B^f_t > 255 \end{cases} \quad (1)$$

Sometimes $B_t$ has some small gaps or even big holes after filtering the noises, so we employ the following steps to fill the gaps and holes.

step1: filling small gaps

A 3×3 or 5×5 window is employed to remove the small gaps [7]. We set each foreground pixel at the center of the window, and if there are more than half of the foreground pixels contained in the window, then we will fill the gaps within the window. This method is effective to the small gaps, but it is helpless with the big holes. Then step2 is performed.

step2: filling big holes

Actually, holes are part of foreground regions, but misplaced as the background. In order to check if a background pixel is misplaced or not, we employed a larger 25×25 window. Set each background pixel at the center of the window, and check if there are enough foreground pixels at each direction of eight directions (north, south, east, west, northeast, northwest, southeast and southwest), if there are, then this pixel belongs to the foreground, and we give it the value 255.

## 4  Experiment Results and Conclusions

In our experiment, the proposed method is compared with the running Gaussian average and the frame difference, and the results are shown in Fig.1.

From the experimental results, we can see that, the result of the running Gaussian average $B^c_t$ is no so satisfied, many pixels of the moving object is wrongly detected; the edge of the object is not consecutive too. The frame difference has a better result $B^f_t$, but is also has some gaps and holes, which should be removed from the masks. The result of the proposed method is shown in Fig.1. (c), which is more accurate and reliable. Fig.1. (d) is the result after filling the gaps and holes.

But when a moving object stops, it will be quickly incorporated into the background. This may result in object losing when used to object tracking application. And how to further eliminate the noise is also a challenging problem.

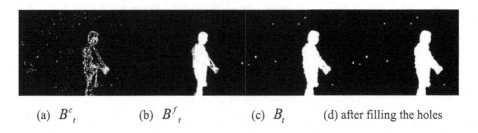

(a) $B^c_t$        (b) $B^f_t$        (c) $B_t$        (d) after filling the holes

**Fig. 1.** Experiment results

## Acknowledgments

This work is supported by National 973 Key Research Program 2006CB303105, National 973 Key Research Program 2004CB318110 and University Key Research Fund 2004SZ002.

## References

1. Cucchiara, R., Piccardi, M., Prati, A.: Detecting Moving Objects, Ghost, and Shadows in Video Streams. IEEE Transactions on Analysis and Machine Intelligence 25(10), 1337–1342 (2003)
2. Wren, C., Azarhayejani, A., Darrell, T., Pentland, A.P.: Pfinder: real-time tracking of the human body. IEEE Trans. on Pattern Anal. And Machine Intell. 19(7), 780–785 (1997)
3. Lo, B.P.L., Velastin, S.A.: Automatic congestion detection system for underground platforms. In: Proc. ISIMP2001, pp. 158–161 (May 2001)
4. Koller, D., Weber, J., Huang, T., Ma, J., Ogasawara, G., Rao, B., Russell, S.: Towards Robust Automatic Traffic Scene Analysis in Real-time. In: Proc. ICPR'94, pp. 126–131 (November 1994)
5. Jabri, S., Durie, Z., Wechsler, H., Rosenfield, A.: Detection and Location of People in Video Images Using Adaptive Fusion of Color and Edge Information. In: icpr, 15th International Conference on Pattern Recognition (ICPR'00), vol. 4, p. 4627 (2000)
6. Cucchiara, R., Grana, C., Piccardi, M., Prati, A.: Detection Objects, Shadows and Ghosts in Video Streams by Exploiting Color and Motion Information. In: 11th International Conference on Image Analysis and Processing, pp. 360–365 (September 26-28, 2001)
7. Zang, Q., Klette, R.: Robust Background Subtraction and Maintenance. In: Proceedings of the 17th International Conference on Pattern Recognition, Cambridge, UK, pp. 90–93 (2004)

# Playing and Cheating in Ambient Entertainment

Anton Nijholt

University of Twente, Human Media Interaction
PO Box 217, 7500 AE Enschede, The Netherlands
anijholt@cs.utwente.nl

**Abstract.** We survey ways to extract information from users interacting in ambient intelligence entertainment environments. We speculate on the use of this information, including information obtained from physiological processes and brain-computer interfacing, in future game environments.

**Keywords:** Entertainment computing, nonverbal interaction, cheating.

## 1 Introduction

In future Ambient Intelligence (AmI) environments we assume intelligence embedded in the environment, its objects (furniture, mobile robots) and its virtual, sometimes visualized agents (virtual humans). These environments support the human inhabitants or visitors of these environments in their activities and interactions by perceiving them through their sensors (proximity sensors, cameras, microphones, etc.). Support can be reactive, but also and more importantly, pro-active and unobtrusive, anticipating the needs of the inhabitants and visitors by sensing their behavioral signals and being aware of the context in which they act [1].

Health, recreation, sports and playing games are among the needs inhabitants and visitors of smart environments will have. Sensors in these environments can detect and interpret nonverbal activity and can give multimedia feedback to invite, stimulate, guide, advise and engage. Activity can aim at improving physical and mental health (well-being), but also at improving capabilities related to a profession (ballet, etc.), recreation (juggling, etc.), or sports (fencing, etc.). Fun, just fun, to be achieved from interaction can be another aim of such environments.

For many of these (envisioned) applications, the nonverbal interactions with the environment are important and need to be recognized and interpreted. And, rather than having a rather regulated process of turn taking as in dialogue systems, in these applications the main flow of events is continuous, rather than segmented.

In this paper we look at nonverbal interaction in ambient entertainment applications. How is the environment going to use such information? For example, in an entertainment game, will the environment use this information to make the experience more attractive for the user, providing him or her with more chances, or should the environment be in competition with the user and employ all information that can be derived from the user's behavior to win? In the latter case, the human gamer may try to hide his or her intentions in order to mislead the environment.

L. Ma, R. Nakatsu, and M. Rauterberg (Eds.): ICEC 2007, LNCS 4740, pp. 415–420, 2007.

Information that can be taken into account is physiological information, including information obtained from measuring brain activity (brain-computer interfacing). Again, this knowledge can be used to adapt the interaction with the user in a particular entertainment game situation. And, in a situation where we really compete with the computer we need to be aware that the computer is using this information against us. Can we control our nonverbal behavior, our physiological processes and our brain activity in such a way that we can mislead the computer?

## 2  Dance, Music, Sports, and Fitness

Entertainment, health, sports, and leisure applications using information and communication technology often require and encourage physical body movements and often applications are designed for that reason. In our research we look at bodily and gestural interaction with game and leisure environments that are equipped with sensors (cameras, microphones, touch, and proximity sensors) and application-dependent intelligence (allowing reactive and proactive activity). Interpretation of the bodily interaction, requiring domain-dependent artificial intelligence, needs to be done by the environment and the agents that maintain the interaction with the human partner. In the display of reactive and pro-active activity embodied virtual agents play an important role. Virtual agents can play the role of teacher, coach, partner or game opponent. Hence, there are, among others, a virtual therapist that helps patients to recover from injuries [2], a Tai Chi training master [3], and a shadow boxer [4].

We have designed applications in which our ideas about nonverbal and bodily interaction have been implemented [5,6,7]. We looked at the design, implementation and evaluation of a virtual dancer that invites a visitor to dance with her, a conductor that guides musicians in their playing, and a virtual trainer that helps a user or patient in his exercises. In the applications there is a continuous interaction between an embodied agent and a human partner. Rather than have the more traditional verbal interaction supported by nonverbal communication, here the main interaction is nonverbal. Speech and language, when present at all, have a supporting role. In these applications there is multimodal analysis of a user's activities.

## 3  Learning to Know the User

In AmI environments user profiles are maintained. The profile will continuously be adapted by new information made available by the user (not necessarily with the aim to have its profile updated). Our environments perceive a user's activities and use that information to learn about the user (and adapt and extend his profile).

In order to learn about the user, his or her personality, his or her 'human values' and attitudes, questionnaires have been designed. In [8] it is remarked that "Personality represents those characteristics of the person that account for consistent patterns of feeling, thinking, and behaving." Without doubt, in face-to-face interaction, our interaction behavior does not only depend on our own personality, but also on the personality characteristics that we try to derive from the behavior of our partner in the interaction and that we attribute to our interaction partner or to the profile we made up from already available information about our interaction partner.

Questionnaires that aim to measure personality are well-known. They depend on models of personality theory (trait theory, personal construct theory, psychodynamic theory, etc.). In educational environments it is not unusual to take into account personality characteristics and associated questionnaires in order to be able to match learning styles with tutoring strategies, and the display of feedback. Using a user's scores on personality dimensions in order to adapt a game is an unexplored area of game and entertainment research. When we know that a particular user has a high score on curiosity, creativity and untraditional (high scores on Openness), we can make use of that. Similarly, it also helps if we know that a user is cynical, rude and uncooperative (low scores on Agreeableness).

Many other questionnaires exist. Apart from personality we can look at questionnaires that measure intelligence and emotional intelligence. Moreover there are questionnaires that aim to measure the values a user has. A good example is the so-called Human Values Scale [9] and in particular how it is used in the context of recommender systems [10]. There are also questionnaires that aim at extracting information that is more directly related to educational, game, and entertainment situations [11]. Hence, we can look at decision-making style questionnaires where thoroughness, control, hesitancy, social resistance, perfectionism, idealism and instinctiveness are among the issues that are assessed, and we can look at questionnaires where we can look at a players willingness to empathize with other personality characters in a game (see e.g. the empathy questionnaire [12].

Summarizing, to answer the question what the environment can learn about the user, we can look at demographic information that has been collected, information about the user that can be generated from 'external' sources (email content and communication, web page visits, Skype, device use, etc.), information about the context (what behavior can be expected), and information that can be obtained from filled-in forms and questionnaires that tell us about intelligence, personality, emotional intelligence, and more specialized questionnaires that help us to anticipate gaming styles, and decision making behavior. Obviously, it is far from natural to ask people to fill in questionnaires.

## 4  Learning from Behavior in the Entertainment Environment

Although information about the entertainment gamer can be obtained through questionnaires, as mentioned in the previous section, this is a rather unnatural way and we can not expect that people are willing to spend time before starting to play.

There are also possibilities to obtain information about the user by hiding the questionnaires in a playful interaction with the user. For example, in [13] an attempt is made to score personality by means of an informal conversation where elements of the traditional questionnaires are merged into the conversation by the computer. Interesting is also the approach in [14], where music preferences are correlated with personality dimensions. This approach fits in a framework correlating personality dimensions and behavior that occurs in everyday life.

In AmI environments we have the technology to capture human behavior in everyday life. In our ambient entertainment view the same technology is available and we can either assume that behavior of a particular user or visitor of our ambient entertainment environment already carries a user profile that has been generated from the user's behavior in the past, or we can assume that during a possibly playful interaction with the environment a profile can be obtained and can be used by the environment to adapt to the user's characteristics.

What can we learn from behavioral information captured by cameras, microphones and other types of sensors? In [15] results are reported from short observations of expressive behavior. Observations include the assessment of relationships, distinguishing anxious and depressed people from normal people, predicting judges' expectations for a trial outcome, determining political views of television newscasters, etc. Personality judgments from 'thin slices of behavior' and their accuracy are also discussed in [16]. An example where real-time behavioral analysis is done by a computer can be found in [17]. Here a participant is invited in front of a video camera for about 30 seconds. After that a personality profile is generated.

## 5  Playing with Behavioral Information

### 5.1  Taking into Account Involuntary User Responses

In the examples mentioned earlier we have bodily interaction with the computer system. Input to an entertainment environment can be based on conscious decisions made by the human. This is usually the case when keyboard, mouse or joystick is used. Behavioral signals and patterns during activities provide (additional) information about the tasks that a user wants to perform, the way they should be performed and the user's appreciation of task, performance, and context. Sensing and understanding these signals is an important issue in 'human computing' [1] and it makes human computing an important area of research for entertainment computing. This kind of input is not always consciously provided by a user and is sometimes beyond the control of the user. Behavioral signals also provide information about the affective state of the user and this information is useful to adapt the environment (more or less control by the user, other challenges, etc.) to the user.

More information about the affective state of the user of an entertainment environment can be obtained by collecting and interpreting information obtained from measuring physiological processes and brain activity. Physiological cues are obtained from, for example, respiration, heart rate, pulse, skin temperature and conductance, perspiration, muscle action potentials and blood pressure [18,19]. Unfortunately, this information can mostly not be obtained unobtrusively. Finally, we should mention measured brain activity. Again, measuring brain activity, e.g. by using an EEG cap, can provide information about the affective state of the user (frustration, engagement, etc.) and this can be used to dynamically adapt the interface to the user and provide tailored feedback.

### 5.2  User Control of 'Involuntary' Responses

Playing against a computer is not fair. The computer knows about our affective state and can decide to use it or to communicate it to our (virtual) opponents or team players in the environment who can use it to their advantage. On the other hand, apart from adapting the environment, the computer can also make the  human player aware of his affective state so that he can make an attempt to control it since it can decrease own performance and give away unwanted information to other players in the game.

In games and sports opponents can be misled. We can as well try to mislead or tease our virtual and human partners who play in a computer-controlled environment. One step further is that we have entertainment games where misleading the computer is an essential part of the game. A simple example is playing soccer against a humanoid robot and the robot's aim is to win rather than to offer its human partner an enjoyable experience. In such a situation misleading means for example making feints. But also, trying to look more tired than we really are and all other kinds of misleading behavior that we can think of. In our virtual dancer installation human dancers sometimes try to tease the virtual dancer by acting unexpected and then look how she reacts. In other environments we may want to hide our intentions from the computer by controlling our facial expressions (e.g., in a poker game with a computer that can observe us). Once we know that our non-human opponent is receptive for our behavioral, physiological or brain processes, we need to cheat in order to obtain more satisfaction from the entertainment game. Game research in this direction is rare, but it is well-known that people can learn to control, up to a certain level, these processes. Research and development in among others brain-computer interfacing makes clear that interesting new types of entertainment in which ideas described above can be incorporated will become available in the future [20,21].

## 6  Conclusions

We looked at ways to provide the computer in an entertainment environment with as much information about ourselves and our preferences as possible. In particular we looked at ways for a computer to extract this information automatically from our behavior. We also looked at the computer as our opponent rather than as provider of enjoyable experiences. We then prefer to mislead the computer and hide information about our affective state or even control and manipulate our behavioral, physiological and brain processes so that we consciously provide the computer with misinformation allowing us to become the 'winner' in smart entertainment environments.

## References

1. Pantic, M., Pentland, A., Nijholt, A., Huang, T.: Human Computing and Machine Understanding of Human Behavior: A Survey. In: Pantic, M., et al. (ed.) AI for Human Computing. LNCS (LNAI), vol. 4451, pp. 47–71. Springer, Heidelberg (2007)
2. Babu, S., Zanbaka, C., Jackson, J., Chung, T-O., Lok, B., Shin, M.C., Hodges, L.F.: Virtual Human Physiotherapist Framework for Personalized Training and Rehabilitation. In: Graphics Interface 2005, Victoria, British Columbia, Canada (2005)

3. Chua, P.T., Crivella, R., Daly, B., Hu, N., Schaaf, R., Ventura, D., Camill, T., Hodgins, J., Pausch, R.: Training for Physical Tasks in Virtual Environments: Tai Chi. In: IEEE Virtual Reality 2003, pp. 87–94. IEEE Computer Society Press, Washington, DC (2003)

4. Höysniemi, J., Aula, A., Auvinen, P., Hännikäinen, J., Hämäläinen, P.: Shadow boxer: a physically interactive fitness game. In: Third Nordic Conference on Human-Computer interaction (NordiCHI '04), vol. 82, pp. 389–392. ACM Press, New York (2004)

5. Reidsma, D., van Welbergen, H., Poppe, R., Bos, P., Nijholt, A.: Towards Bi-directional Dancing Interaction. In: Harper, R., Rauterberg, M., Combetto, M. (eds.) ICEC 2006. LNCS, vol. 4161, pp. 1–12. Springer, Heidelberg (2006)

6. Bos, P., Reidsma, D., Ruttkay, Z., Nijholt, A.: Interacting with a Virtual Conductor. In: Harper, R., Rauterberg, M., Combetto, M. (eds.) ICEC 2006. LNCS, vol. 4161, pp. 25–30. Springer, Heidelberg (2006)

7. Ruttkay, Z., Zwiers, J., van Welbergen, H., Reidsma, D.: Towards a Reactive Virtual Trainer. In: Gratch, J., Young, M., Aylett, R., Ballin, D., Olivier, P. (eds.) IVA 2006. LNCS (LNAI), vol. 4133, pp. 292–303. Springer, Heidelberg (2006)

8. Pervin, L.A., John, O.P.: Personality: theory and research. John Wiley and Sons, Chichester (2001)

9. Schwartz, S.H.: A Proposal for Measuring Value Orientations across Nations; The Hebrew University of Jerusalem (2003)

10. Guzmán, J., González, G., De La Rosa, J.L., Castán, J.: Human Values Scale: Modeling the Human Values Scale in Recommender Systems: A first approach. In: López, B., Meléndez, J., Radeva, P., Vitriá, J. (eds.) Artificial Intelligence Research and Development, vol. 131, pp. 405–412. IOS Press, Amsterdam (2005)

11. Douse, N.A., McManus, I.C.: The Personality of Fantasy Game Players. British Journal of Psychology 84(4), 505–509 (1993)

12. Davis, M.H.: Measuring individual differences in empathy: Evidence for a multidimensional approach. J. of Personality and Social Psychology 44, 113–126 (1983)

13. Bodewitz, M.J.: Measuring personality by means of a computer dialog. MSc. thesis, HMI, University of Twente (2004)

14. Rentfrow, P.J., Gosling, S.D.: The Do Re Mi's of Everyday Life. J. of Personality and Social Psychology 84(6), 1236–1256 (2003)

15. Ambady, N., Rosenthal, R.: Thin slices of expressive behavior as predictors of interpersonal consequences: A meta-analysis. Psychological Bulletin 111(2), 256–274 (1992)

16. Borkenau, P., Mauer, N., Riemann, R., Spinath, F.M., Angleitner, A.: Thin slices of behavior as cues of personality and intelligence. J. of Personality and Social Psychology 86, 599–614 (2004)

17. Bechinie, M., Grammer, K.: Charisma Cam: A prototype of an intelligent digital sensory organ for virtual humans. In: Rist, T., Aylett, R., Ballin, D., Rickel, J. (eds.) IVA 2003. LNCS (LNAI), vol. 2792, pp. 212–216. Springer, Heidelberg (2003)

18. Picard, R.W., Vyzas, E., Healey, J.: Toward machine emotional intelligence: Analysis of affective physiological state. IEEE Transactions on Pattern Analysis and Machine Intelligence 23(10), 1175–1191 (2001)

19. Picard, R.W., Daily, S.B.: Evaluating affective interactions: Alternatives to asking what users feel. In: Human Factors in Computing Systems. Workshop on Innovative Approaches to Evaluating Affective Interfaces, Portland, OR, (April 2-7, 2005)

20. Gilleade, K., Dix, A., Allanson, J.: Affective Videogames and Modes of Affective Gaming: Assist Me, Challenge Me, Emote Me. In: DIGRA'2005, Vancouver, Canada (2005)

21. Nijholt, A., Tan, D.: Playing with your Brain: Brain-Computer Interfaces and Games. In: Bernhaupt, R., Tscheligi, M. (eds.) Proceedings ACE (International Conference on Advances in Computer Entertainment Technology), pp. 305–306. ACM Press, New York (2007)

# Selfish Search on Playing Shogi

Takeshi Ito

Department of Computer Science,
University of Electro-Communications, Tokyo, Japan
ito@cs.uec.ac.jp

## 1 Introduction

If a human faces a complex problem with a large number of potential solutions and calculations, he will not always act logically. In gamble, public lottery, etc., we see a mechanism by which a bookmaker makes a profit probable. There the chances of winning are always overestimated by the human player. For example, in public lottery, some people are allured by ungrounded rumors (such as "it is the turn of the sales store to win"). Other people take superstitious actions grounded on fortune-telling. A fully different example of irrational human decision making in games can be found in the domain of the imperfect information and the chance gambling game Mahjong. A recent study [1] evaluating game records of internet Mahjong concluded that some amateur players treat a professional's remark like a proverb and believe it blindly in spite of a lack of evidence to support the proposition.

Not only in games of chance, but also in combinatorial game like Chess, Shogi (Japanese Chess) or Go, a human decision is mostly not necessarily founded on rational thinking. Many players are tending to select a candidate move intuitively based on their knowledge and experience. The study of Chess by De Groot is a famous example [2]. In previous work, we conducted mental experiments in the domain of Shogi and replicated De Groot's research on the human intuitive thinking process in the domain of Shogi [3,4,5,6].

Computer programs perform the decision-making tasks in combinatorial games such as Shogi in a quite different from human players. Here we have two opposing systems that deserve further research.

First, human experience cannot be treated as intuitive knowledge. So, we have to address the human search process in another way than by heuristics only. Second, the computer is arriving at a (best) move by the virtue that its search process is based on a rigidly structured search. In computer Shogi, the technique of finding the best move happens by the alpha-beta game-tree search. It is based on an evaluation function that is widely used. The approach is known as "a search driven system" [7].

Computer Shogi avoided incorporating human heuristics as much as possible (since intuition is considered to be more important than experience), and has developed the technology for searching deeply, fast and wide [8]. In the last decade we see that Shogi programs are becoming stronger with the progress of the hardware technology. The playing strength of the top class Shogi programs is said to roughly equal the strength of 6-dan amateur players. It reaches the level of professional players [9].

However, strong Shogi programs play sometimes moves which are perceived of as *unnatural* by human players. As mentioned above, a significant difference exists

L. Ma, R. Nakatsu, and M. Rauterberg (Eds.): ICEC 2007, LNCS 4740, pp. 421–426, 2007.

between the decision-making process of humans and computers. A reason is that computer programs, in spite of playing strongly, suffer from intuition. Their style of play may be uninteresting and not useful to study for a human player. This might be so because a player does not understand the meaning of the move played by the computer. Some programs are able to display a part of their search log to show the 'meaning' of a particular move. However, since the move decision process is not presented completely, it may remain unintelligible as a whole, and the human player cannot understand it.

In order to show a decision-making process in a form understandable to a human, it is necessary to clarify the thought process that human players are performing. In this article, we show what kind of search process is carried out in the human thought process which generates a move when playing Shogi.

Based on interviews with human expert players and verbal protocol data of human players of various levels, we will discuss in particular the "mechanism of prediction" peculiar to human players.

## 2   Some Results from Psychological Experiments

### (1)  Reducing the set of candidate moves to a few moves

Figure 1 expresses the average number of moves mentioned as candidate moves at the time of determining the next move and making the human being to think freely on the next move [6]. In the figure we see that the amateur 1-DAN (middle level players) raised many candidate moves. In average they still arrived at five whereas there are only three candidate moves. Since the problem given here is the position where a legal move exceeds 100 hands from tens hands, it turns out that a part of mere lawful hand is examined.

Considering the problem that a hand with pieces easily exceeds the number of 100 moves, it turns out that players are bound to examine only a part of the legal moves.

It is assumed that human players cannot consider many matters in parallel. Moreover, a human does not count all legal moves and so it differs in this respect from a computer. In practice it turned out that the human search process is particularly

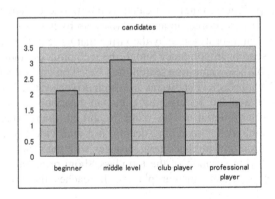

**Fig. 1.** Average number of the candidate move on next move test

used for candidate moves when only a few moves exist. The move chosen is then evaluated by intuition.

**(2) Predict in linear**

Given the problem as shown in Figure 2. By the time it had to choose a next move the Shogi player under consideration was made to utter his decision-making process; the contents were recorded and analyzed [6].

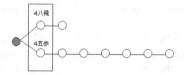

**Fig. 2.** A problem of next move test experiments

Figures 3-6 express by a search tree the move at which a player of a certain Shogi strength predicted the next move of Figure 2. Although there is a great difference in the contents of thought, it turned out that the form of a search tree has the almost same form. And, although there are some branches with candidate moves, the tree predicts almost linearly.

We believe that a move generation system for mimicking the thought processes of a human Shogi Player who advances and arrives at the point doing so linearly. In computer Shogi, the candidate moves are all the legal moves, and a game tree is constituted from a prediction by assuming all legal moves by Black and White. The

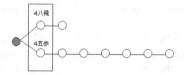

**Fig. 3.** A search tree of novice

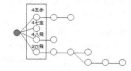

**Fig. 4.** A search tree of middle level player

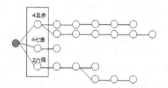

**Fig. 5.** A search tree of club player

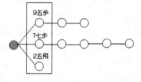

**Fig. 6.** A search tree of professional player

program searches by the MIN-MAX method using a static evaluation function which assesses the advantage or disadvantage of the position. However, it is clear that a human does not do MIN-MAX calculation like a computer. A human player predicts almost linearly. He starts at the intuitively proper move, and predicts to confirm whether the future position becomes really good for himself.

## 3  Selfish Search Based on Psychological Restrictions

As seen in Section 2, a candidate move is extracted and then the search process peculiar to a human being is made. The process predicts linearly and is called "Selfish Search". So it is different from the search by a computer. We believe that this "selfish prediction" is a thought process that is peculiar to a human. It is bounded by psychological restrictions by the human being. The range of the target problem is narrow. If a problem is counted in all its possibilities, it is also possible that all the cases are performing a comprehensive search like a computer. For example, if it is a game with comparatively narrow search space such as TIC-TAC-TOE (e.g., by summarizing the symmetrical position or eliminating the move in which it loses simply), it will be possible to narrow the search space sharply. Analogously, a human will also count all the possibilities, and he will try to deduce a conclusion. However, the difficult games (the game of Go, Shogi, Chess, etc.) which have been played for a long time have a search space in which a human cannot search easily. In the large game tree of such a search space, a human gives up all searching, performs a "selfish search" within the limits which focus on some moves. He then can assume by "intuition", and is considered to determine a next move. Figure 7 expresses the number and speed of the prediction in relation to Shogi skill. The graph is from the result of an above-mentioned psychological experiment. According to this figure, it turns out that the speed of searching becomes quickly, so that the Shogi skill becomes high, and the number of searching is increasing according to it. However, the speed which a top professional player searches is about ten moves per minute. The space which can be searched within a limited time is considered to be about at most some hundred moves. Thus, it can be said that there is a psychological limit in a human's search speed.

Besides, a comparison of the search tree described by (2) in Section 2 shows that a human is performing as few linear predictions of a branch as possible. Furthermore, a human never calculates MIN-MAX-search for the all search trees with generating parallel branches from a certain node. The human advances by one reading at a time; many linear prediction results are compared simply, and a next move is determined so that it may become a straight line by a certain fixed view. In other words, a human can say that he is poor at performing a parallel prediction, and that he can perform only sequential predictions.

Such "a limit of searching speed" and "a limit of parallel search ability" are limits of functional calculation abilities of the human. I call this limit "psychological restrictions". If it thinks as mentioned above, it can be said that human thought is bound and prescribed by these psychological restrictions. "Selfish Search" which the human player is performing can be considered to be the optimized thought method in the "psychological restrictions" of the human.

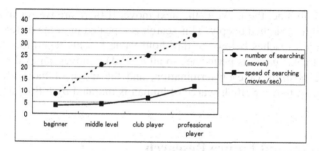

**Fig. 7.** Number and speed of searching for the strength on Shogi

## 4  Proposal of Selfish Search System

In advance of this selfish Search system, I have developed the knowledge driven Shogi system (HIT: Human Intuitive Thought) imitating human intuitive thought [10]. This system can generate a move by describing the intuitive knowledge which the expert of Shogi has in the form of a production rule, without searching. In HIT, a score is first given to all the legal moves by the production rule prepared beforehand. About 400 production rules are given to HIT now. By applying these rules, a score is given to all the legal moves Based on the given scores, the moves are sorted. The move which has the highest score is generated as a candidate move. A next move is determined by performing selfish prediction as shown in Figure 9 using the candidate move generated by HIT.

As shown in Figure 8, if a position is given, a score will be given to all the legal moves by HIT, and it will sort sequentially from a higher rank. It will become a candidate move if the higher lank of candidate move and within threshold α. If the

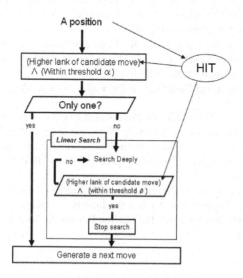

**Fig. 8.** Selfish Search Algorithm

candidate is only one, the move is the next move. If there are two or more candidate moves, it will be searched deeply. This search is repeated until the difference between candidate moves reaches below the threshold value $\beta$. This repetition realizes linear search. This linear search is performed to all candidate moves, an evaluation function estimates the position of each termination, and the move of most a high score is chosen as a next move. Selfish search of human is imitated by following the series of procedure.

## 5  Conclusion and Future Research

This article investigated the main characteristics of human search. The concept of "selfish search" was introduced to describe the decision-making process of a human player. We explained that "selfish search" is based on psychological restrictions. Moreover, we considered a function of "selfish search" in the middle stage of a game and formulated on adequate learning process.

Future research will address a knowledge-driven type of a computer-aided design using "selfish search" in combination with a learning-support system for human players.

## References

[1]  Totsugeki-Tohoku: Science of the Mah-jongg, Kodansha (2004)
[2]  de Groot, A.D.: Thought and Choice in Chess. Mouton Publishers, The Hague, The Netherlands (1965)
[3]  Ito, T.: A Cognitive Processes on Playing Shogi. In: Game Programming Workshop in Japan '99, pp. 177–184 (1999)
[4]  Ito, T., Matsubara, H., Grimbergen, R.: Cognitive Science Approach to Shogi Playing Processes (1) –Some Results on Memory Experiments. Information Processing Society of Japan Journal 43(10), 2998–3011 (2002)
[5]  Ito, T., Matsubara, H., Grimbergen, R.: Cognitive Science Approach to Shogi Playing Processes (2) –Some Results on Next Move Test Experiments. Information Processing Society of Japan Journal 45(5), 1481–1492 (2004)
[6]  Ito, T.: The Thought and Cognition on the Verbal Data of Shogi Experts, IPSJ SIG-GI-12-2, pp.9–15 (2004)
[7]  Ito, T.: Thinking of Computers vs Professional Players –Contemporary and Future of Computer Shogi. In: Game Programming Workshop in Japan 2005, pp. 40–47 (2005)
[8]  Takizawa, T.: A Success of the Computer Shogi of the New Feeling by "Full Search" and Learning, and an Influence of the High-speed Algorithm. IPSJ Magazine 47(8), 875–881 (2006)
[9]  Takizawa, T.: Contemporary Computer Shogi. IPSJ SIG-GI-16-1, pp.1–8 (May 2006)
[10]  Ito, T.: A Shogi Program that Applies the Intuitive Thinking of Experts -HIT (Human Intuitive Thought) Shogi Project. Information Processing Society of Japan Journal 46(6), 1527–1532 (2005)

# The Effects of Network Loads and Latency in Multiplayer Online Games*

Jin Ryong Kim, Il Kyu Park, and Kwang Hyun Shim

Digital Content Research Division
Electronics and Telecommunications Research Institution
Daejeon, Republic of Korea
{jessekim,xiao,shimkh}@etri.re.kr

**Abstract.** In this work, we performed variety of tests to see the effects of network loads and latency in multiplayer online games. We applied hierarchical load testing architecture using large scale virtual clients to find out the bottlenecks of the game servers. We also investigated the effect of latency on multiplayer online games. We controlled network game packets (i.e. packet delay, packet drop rate, packet duplication rate, packet reordering rate) to see the impact on real-time multiplayer games.

**Keywords:** Load tests, multiplayer games, MMOG tests, P2P-based tests, network game tests, mean opinion score.

## 1 Introduction

Recent technologies in broadband network and 3D rendering have made it possible to provide high quality and large scaled 3D online games. Advances in 3D graphics hardware and rendering software technologies enabled people to enjoy realistic 3D games. The increase in residential broadband Internet connections encouraged the popularity of multiplayer online games.

However, the growth in the popularity of interactive multiplayer network games has increased the importance of a better understanding of the effects of network loads and network latency. In massively multiplayer online games (MMOG), large scales of players enter single virtual world concurrently and interact with each other. MMOG are very large distributed applications and shares very large states. However, one of the main issues in MMOG is how to handle massive amount of network packets. Most of MMOGs have client-server based network architecture. That is, the server has to process all the network and I/O. The overhead of handling all the communication among clients through the server can result in long delays and a large amount of consumed networking resources. Thus, the server can be a single point of failure.

In peer-to-peer multiplayer online games, handling the real-time interaction among peers is one of the main challenging issues. Many games such as first person shooters (FPS), casual sports games, and racing games adopt peer-to-peer architecture along

---

* This work is funded by MIC of Korea and the project number is 2006-S-044-01.

L. Ma, R. Nakatsu, and M. Rauterberg (Eds.): ICEC 2007, LNCS 4740, pp. 427–432, 2007.

with client-server architecture. It is because they have high requirements in maintaining the consistency of the virtual world. In this case, the latency is the main issue. Most online games have low bit-rate requirements, sending frequent but small packets. They require prompt response from tens to hundreds msec. They are very sensitive in delayed packets and require very low thresholds in latency depending on the genre of the games.

## 2  Related Work

A lot of research work has been done on testing and analyzing multiplayer online games. Fritsch et al. [1] illustrated the effect of latency and network limitations on MMORPGs. They conducted and analyzed different combinations of user actions using Everquest 2 [2]. Dick et al. [3] measured the effect of latency on performance in multiplayer games using GOS and MOS methodologies. The authors introduced the subject MOS and the objective game outcome score as a normalized metric for multiplayer games. They analyzed that various multiplayer games behave differently under the same network conditions. Pantel et al. [4] analyzed the impact on real-time multiplayer games using car racing simulation. They concluded that a delay of more than 100 ms should be avoided for a racing game. The authors mentioned that a delay up to 50 ms is uncritical for a car-racing game. They believed that dead-reckoning has the drawback that the prediction error exponentially increases with increasing network delays. Beigeder et al. [5] illustrated the effects of loss and latency on user performance in Unreal Tournament 2003 [6]. In their work, they discovered that the first person shooting (FPS) game players can notice latencies over 100 ms.

## 3  Approach

### 3.1  Load Tests Methodology

A load testing architecture for MMOG should be able to create hundreds to thousands loads to ensure the stability of the servers. In order to perform load tests on MMOG, we present a hierarchical load testing methodology [7].

Figure 1 illustrates a hierarchical load testing methodology for MMOG. It consists of master host, a number of agent hosts and virtual clients on their agent host. In this methodology, we put one master host to manage a number of agent hosts. The number of agent hosts can be increased constantly in parallel and create as many virtual clients as up to their hardware performance. The virtual clients can connect with servers and create actual loads and they are controlled by a master host via their agent host.

The master host controls its agent hosts and deliver event packets to agent hosts. The master host exists as an application entity and manages overall load test.

One or more agent hosts communicate with a master host. They actually interpret received commands from a master host and manage their virtual clients. The roles of agent hosts are to create, control, remove or monitor their virtual clients. The virtual clients are the replacement of actual client application and they are controlled by a master host. The virtual clients enter the virtual game worlds by connecting to the server. They join the game and interact with each other.

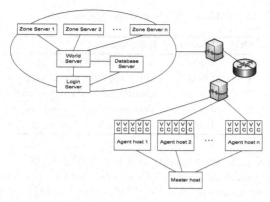

**Fig. 1.** Hierarchical load testing architecture

## 3.2 Peer-to-Peer Based Tests Methodology

In peer-to-peer network game tests, we set virtual network environment for each client host to get their own network environment. For networking factors, we controlled packet delay, packet drop probability, packet duplication and packet reordering rate. We selected one peer-to-peer based multiplayer online game: online FPS game.

Figure 2 illustrates the network topology for our sample games. The roles of the servers are to manage the client connections, login information, and manage the game channels and game rooms. Once the game players get together in a game room, each game player connects up with other peers. Within the peers, one becomes the master host (server) and others become slave hosts (clients). This game application uses TCP/IP for the client-server mode and UDP/IP for the peer-to-peer mode.

To find out the effect of network latency in multiplayer online games, we used the Mean Opinion Score (MOS). The MOS is the arithmetic mean of all the individual

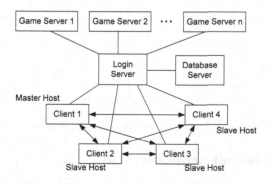

**Fig. 2.** Hybrid network topology in typical peer-to-peer network games

**Table 1.** The Mean Score Opinion Values

| MOS | Quality | Impairment |
|-----|---------|------------|
| 5 | Excellent | No noticeable impairments |
| 4 | Good | Minor impairment noticeable |
| 3 | Fair | Clearly impaired environment |
| 2 | Poor | Very annoying environment |
| 1 | Bad | Unacceptable environment |

scores, and can range from 1 (worst) to 5 (best). The MOS provides a numerical indication of the perceived quality of received media after compression and/or transmission. In our case, we used the MOS values in [3]. The MOS values for peer-to-peer based tests are illustrated in Table 1.

## 4   Experiment

### 4.1   MMOG Load Tests

The purpose of this test is to find out the bottleneck point when the large number of virtual clients communicates with the server in the same time. In this experiment, we set the virtual clients to send 1Kbye packets to the server in every one second. The number of virtual clients increased from 500 to 3,000 and the location of the virtual clients were widely distributed in the virtual world. We measured round trip time (delay) for each case.

Figure 3 is the results of this test. In this test, the round trip delay is constantly increased when the number of virtual clients is increased. The memory of the server remained stable but the network and CPU usage has been increased constantly.

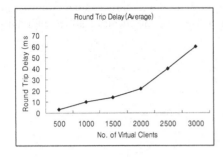 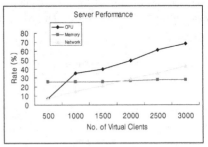

**Fig. 3.** Round trip delay and server performance for large scale packet transmission test

### 4.2   Peer-to-Peer Network Environment Tests

The purpose of this test is to find out the bottleneck point when we controlled the network environment factors. As illustrated in Figure 7, we set two scenarios: (a) controlling network packets in master client, (b) controlling network packets in slave client.

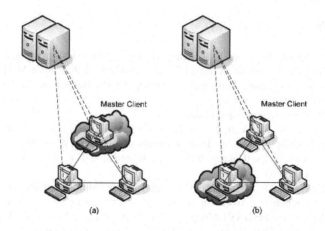

**Fig. 4.** Hybrid network topology for peer-to-peer based multiplayer games. (a) Scenario 1, (b) Scenario 2

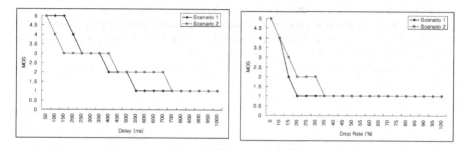

**Fig. 5.** Packet delay and packet drop tests for scenario 1 and 2

Figure 5 is the result of packet delay and drop tests. In this figure, we noticed that the game players can play without noticeable impairments when the delay is under 200 msec for scenario 1 and under 100 msec for scenario 2. We also found out that the game players can notice the impairments when the packet drop rate is over 10%.

We also carried out the packet duplication test, but the game content was not affected at all.

## 5 Conclusion

In this work, we performed variety of tests on both MMOG and peer-to-peer based multiplayer online games to find out the effects of network loads and network latency. We used a hierarchical load testing architecture to test the performance of the servers in MMOG. We also carried out peer-to-peer based tests by changing network factors (packet delay, packet drop rate, and packet duplication). For this test, we used MOS values. In results, we noticed that packet delay of 100 ms and packet drop rate of 10% are the critical points for peer-to-peer multiplayer online games, especially FPS games.

# References

1. Fritsch, T., Ritter, H., Schiller, J.: The effect of latency and network limitations on MMORPGs: A field study of Everquest 2. In: Proceedings of the Fourth ACM Network and System Support for Games (NetGames) Workshop, Hawthorne, NY. ACM Press, New York (October 10-11, 2005)
2. Everquest2: http://www.everquest2.com
3. Dick, M., Wellnitz, O., Wolf, L.: Analysis of factors affecting players performance and perception in multiplayer games. In: Proceedings of the Fourth ACM Network and System Support for Games (NetGames) Workshop, Hawthorne, NY. ACM Press, New York (October 10-11, 2005)
4. Pantel, L., Wolf, L.: On the impact of delay on real-time multiplayer games. In: Proceedings of the ACM International Workshop on Network and Operating System Support for Digital Audio and Video (NOSSDAV), Miami, pp. 23–29. ACM Press, New York (May 2002)
5. Beigbeder, T., Coughlan, R., Lusher, C., Plunkett, J., Agu, E., Claypool, M.: The effects of loss and latency on user performance in Unreal Tournament 2003. In: Proceedings of ACM Network and System Support for Games Workshop (NetGames), Portland, OR, pp. 144–151. ACM Press, New York (September 2004)
6. Unreal Tournament (2003), http://www.unrealtournament.com/ut2003
7. Lim, B., Kim, J., Shim, K.: Hierarchical load testing architecture using large scale virtual clients. In: Proceedings of IEEE International Conference on Multimedia and Expo 2006 (ICME 2006), Toronto, Ontario, Canada (July 9-12, 2006)

# Design for Debate in Robotics: Questioning Paradigms in a Techno-social Discourse

Wouter Reeskamp and Katrien Ploegmakers

Department of Industrial Design, University of Technology Eindhoven,
P.O. Box 513, 5600 MB Eindhoven, The Netherlands
wouter@studiosophisti.nl, katrien@kaasdesign.nl

**Abstract.** 'Design for Debate' is an emerging approach in the domain of design. This paper proposes a more pragmatic application. A workshop was developed and conducted with experts in the field of social robotics. Concepts for affective robots were visualized to provoke out-of-the-box thinking. During eight workshops, robotic professionals questioned their paradigms.

**Keywords:** Design for Debate, Critical Design, Social Robotics, Paradigms, Design Parameters, Workshop.

## 1 Introduction

'Design for Debate' has been introduced in academic circles by Tony Dunne and Bill Gaver [1] by describing their vision of an 'artist-designer' as a creator of what they call 'value fiction'. They advocate that a critical professional can create design proposals to explore and question a two-sided story that comes along with development of a future techno-society. What they propose is design-centred fiction meant to challenge the meaning of these paradigms, and think beyond in terms of social values that are interesting to address.

'Design for Debate' hasn't been explicitly defined, but based on interviews [2] and work of Dunne [3] we derive the following aspects.
Design for Debate is a way to start discussion in society at large
Design for Debate is focussed on the meaning of future scenarios, mostly in relation with emerging technologies
Design for Debate makes use of designers' visualisation skills to make abstract concepts tangible and discussable
Design for Debate is value-centred instead of fact-centred
Discussion within Design for Debate is meant to question values of the future, but doesn't necessarily seek answers

### 1.1 Applying 'Design for Debate'

The study set-up was different compared to 'Design for Debate' in that respect it did not aim at society at large, but at a techno-social professional discourse. Fundamentally the people who are giving shape to the future techno society. Another difference was that

L. Ma, R. Nakatsu, and M. Rauterberg (Eds.): ICEC 2007, LNCS 4740, pp. 433–436, 2007.

we intended not only to raise questions, but also to capture given reactions. Our method therefore aims at challenging other designers to rethink the values and meanings of their visions on future society. You could say that it's less of a research tool and more a method of out-of-the-box thinking. We chose the domain of 'Affective Robotics' (also known as Personal or Social Robotics) since this field is, in terms of design and social conventions still, very much under development.

## 2  Study Set-Up

### 2.1  Mapping Design Parameters

When discussing a topic as broad as robotics in a cross-cultural setting, discussions can become too comprehensive and therefore superficial. To prevent this, we created a framework from parameters of affective robot design and herewith outlined the topics of our interest. We focused on two questions: 'What 'appearance' parameters are useful stimuli to create the notion of an affectionate experience with an object?' and 'What 'behavior' parameters are necessary to create and maintain an affectionate experience with an object?' This resulted in twelve topics (Table 1). It is not an all-embracing framework; it just contains a dozen topics we think are of importance, when developing a social robot.

We created two parameter-models (Fig. 2), one on appearance and one on behavior. Each parameter-model addresses six topics. To stage a discussion about the twelve topics we defined scales ranging from one extreme to another.

**Table 1.** The twelve design parameters

| Appearance | Behavior |
|---|---|
| Shape | Obedience |
| Tactility | Functionality |
| Face | Learning capabilities |
| Body language | Specialization |
| Sound | Intelligence |
| Temperature | Stickiness |

### 2.2  Developing Provoking Concepts

To have the right type of discussion with professionals, it is crucial to let them think beyond paradigms familiar to them in their everyday practice. The approach we propose with 'Design for Debate' is to challenge the participants with extreme, thought-provoking concepts to bring visions and relations out into the open. In our case we proposed six affective robots in scenarios, all technical and social more or less feasible, but still ambivalent in their characteristics.

An important premise is the mixture of extremes to make sure that discussion is not dogmatically heading in one direction. We used two (physical) parameter-models systematically to generate the design proposals. This interlinked the parameters with the concepts used to provoke the discussion. (Fig.1).

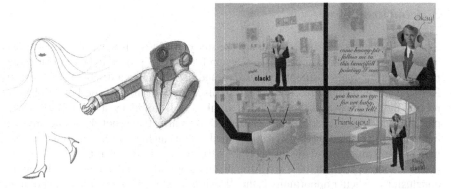

**Fig. 1.** Babe-bot concept: When wearing the special suit, a beautiful lady/man, whom you cannot see but can clearly hear and feel, will guide you through the museum

## 2.3  Workshop Participants

As input for our design-research we staged a debate with Dutch and Japanese parties involved in research, development and design of robots for affection. Eight workshops were done to make this (virtual) debate possible. The participants were industrial companies including Sony, Philips Research and R2R, academic institutes like the Robotics Department of Osaka University, Nirvana Technologies, ATR, AIST and the Designed Intelligence group of the University of Technology Eindhoven.

## 2.4  Chair Discussions

From each concept product-drawings and a user-scenario were shown and the parameter-models were set according to the design proposal. The models were used after each concept presentation to provoke a discussion with the participants (Fig.2), by asking questions such as: 'What parameter do you think makes this a strong concept?' and 'which parameter would you suggest to change in order to create a robot that is more affective?' The aim was not to assess the designs as such, yet to trigger the developers to think and react on possibilities in the field of robotics beyond those they are familiar with.

**Fig. 2.** Workshop participants (Japanese and Dutch) adjust the parameter-models

## 3  Conclusion

Since we had eight sessions to compare our study in 'Design for Debate', a solid idea of its value has arisen. Our approach in 'Design for Debate' proved to be of great value in pinpointing the main assumptions, visions and paradigms in a discourse of 'Affective Robotics'. E.g. a senior researcher said in discussion on the 'Mystic-bot' "A ball as a robot? Before this workshop I didn't think a ball could be a robot". Or when a participant claimed regarding the 'Babe-bot': "An affective robot should be physical", but during the discussion this was questioned. "You can have affection for a person you met in the virtual world of internet, so why not for a virtual robot?" (Fig.1) As a research tool it proved to be more difficult, since opinions tend to be too varied to draw conclusions. A better opportunity is that 'Design for Debate' offers a starting point for a creative process. It can serve as a 'vehicle of communication'; it sets certain definitions and it sparks imagination. And since it makes use of knowledge and wisdom of people it is less time-consuming then literature or scientific research, without leading to superficial results. But due to the subjective nature it is simply not appropriate for reproducible study. 'Design for Debate' cán be of value to set an agenda for these research topics.

## 4  Discussion

Currently discussion on 'Design for Debate' is mainly arising in the discourse of design research, though we foresee its value in commercial context as well. Due to its practical nature, orientating research can be done in a relative short time-span. Moreover the results are often inspiring and can be a catalyst in following creative processes. Due to its open yet focused principle we think it is especially relevant to address complex problems where social, technological, psychological and economic factors are intertwined.

## References

1. Dunne, A., Gaver, W.: The Pillow: Artist-Designers in the Digital Age. In: CHI97 (1997)
2. Debatty, R.: Interview with Anthony Dunne (2007),
   http://www.we-make-money-not-art.com
3. Dunne, A., Raby, F.: Design Noir: The secret life of electronic objects, August BirkHauser (2001)

# Extracting Realistic Textures from Reference Spheres

Zuoyong Zheng, Lizhuang Ma, and Zhou Zeng

Department of Computer Science, Shanghai Jiaotong University
200240 Shanghai, China
oliver.zheng@sjtu.edu.cn, ma-lz@cs.sjtu.edu.cn,
bluecourse@china.com

**Abstract.** This paper proposes a method for extracting realistic textures from real-world reference spheres. The BRDF parameters of fundamental materials, as well as a material weight map for the sphere are obtained through a non-linear optimization process. The material weight map can be used as a conventional texture for relighting. With the BRDF models recovered, the real and natural appearances of 3D objects can be reproduced under novel lighting and viewing directions.

**Keywords:** BRDF, Material Weight, Texture Mapping, Realistic Rendering.

## 1 Introduction and Related Works

Realistic rendering is one of the research areas developing rapidly in computer graphics literature in recent years, and the representation of true materials in the scene plays an important role, which can be described using BRDF (Bi-directional Reflectance Distribution Function). To express complex spatially-varying appearances of real world objects, H. Lensch, J. Kautz et. al [1] developed a image-based method for recovering material properties, using a Splitting-Reclustering-Fitting iteration. D. B. Goldman, B. Curless et. al [2] assumed each object point comprises predetermined number of materials blended at different proportions, and recovered the BRDF parameters, normals at each point, as well as the material weight map using a non-linear overall optimization. W. Matusik, H. Pfister et al [3] sampled over 100 spheres applied PCA to express any possible BRDF as a linear combination of dimension-reduced vectors.

Inspired by D.B.Goldman's algorithm [2], we proposed an improved algorithm to recover BRDF models of fundamental materials, as well as their corresponding material weight map. The material weight map reflects color variations everywhere on the object, and BRDF models express overall reflectance properties. They can be used as a special kind of texture to achieve dynamic re-lighting easily.

## 2 Principle

To recover the fundamental material weight map and BRDF models, an objective function is formulated [2]:

$$Q(\alpha, \gamma) = \sum_{l,p,c} (I_{l,p,c} - \sum_{m} \gamma_{p,m} f_c(n_p, L_l, v, \alpha_m))^2 \tag{1}$$

L. Ma, R. Nakatsu, and M. Rauterberg (Eds.): ICEC 2007, LNCS 4740, pp. 437–440, 2007.
© IFIP International Federation for Information Processing 2007

where the subscript $p$ denotes pixel index, $c$ color component (RGB), $m$ material index, $l$ light index, and $I_{l,p,c}$ represents the intensity of pixel $p$ under the illumination of the light source at location $l$ (in this paper, "pixel intensity" is replaced by "radiance"). $\gamma_{p,m}$ denotes the weight of material $m$ for pixel $p$ (actually it means object point corresponding to the pixel $p$); The function $f_c$ is actually the reflectance model, and can also be considered as an imaging formulation, where $n_p$ denotes the normal at point $p$, $L$ the light source parameters (intensity / direction), $v$ the viewpoint, and $\alpha_m$ the BRDF parameter set for material $m$. $f_c$ is actually the product of light intensity and BRDF, where BRDF model takes the form of Isotropic Ward [4]:

$$BRDF(\theta_i, \theta_r, \sigma) = \frac{\rho_d}{\pi} + \frac{\rho_s}{\sqrt{\cos\theta_i \cos\theta_r}} \frac{\exp[-\tan\sigma^2 / \beta^2]}{4\pi\beta^2} \qquad (2)$$

where $\rho_d$ and $\rho_s$ represents the diffuse and specular coefficient, respectively, and $\beta$ denotes material roughness. $\rho_d$ and $\rho_s$ has three independent values at color channel $c$, so they are 3x1 vectors. In this paper, BRDF models in objective function (1) have total 14 parameters to solve because we assume two fundamental materials. In addition, $\theta_i$, $\theta_r$ and $\sigma$ represents the angle between the normal and the incident, reflected and halfway vector. These geometrical parameters actually take the form of $n_p$, $L_l$ and $v$ in (1).

The material weight $\gamma_{p,m}$ implies that each object point $p$ is composed of several materials. We realize that there exists a natural relation between the material weight map and the real texture, and that conventional texture mapping technologies can be applied to map the material weights to other 3D models. So, we proposed a method for extracting real textures from spherical reference spheres, including the material weight maps and BRDF models. After mapping the material weights as a texture map to 3D objects, the BRDF models recovered is used to render them, finally reaching the approximately same appearance as the sampled materials.

## 3   Implementation

All original images were photographed in a closed space surrounded by a piece of black curtain (Fig. 1). The camera used is Canon EOS 5D with a 200 mm lens and a remote control system, and was fixed on a tripod. A 5W halogen bulb was mounted on a metallic arm whose position was controlled precisely by a computer.

We use the calibration toolbox developed by Bouguet [5] to obtain the internal and external parameters of the camera; the radiance response curve of the camera was

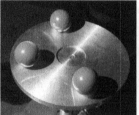

**Fig. 1.** Experiment setup

recovered by Debevec and Malik's method [6], which can be used to synthesize a single high dynamic image from a group of low dynamic ones.

The lighting directions were determined by the highlight peaks on three table tennises which were prayed with shiny green paint (Fig. 1). The light intensity was calculated easily by means of a piece of Lambert gray card with diffuse albedo 18%.

We use the camera response curve to synthesize HDRIs for each of the lighting directions. After removing the invalid pixels not belonging to the sampled spheres or in the attached shadows, we calculated geometrical parameters $\theta_i$, $\theta_r$ and $\sigma$ in Ward model using the known camera parameters and light positions.

To estimate the initial diffuse coefficients, pixels in specularity were filtered firstly. The remainder imaging points may be considered to be consistent with Lambertian and their single diffuse coefficient was averaged to form the initial values. Then, the initial diffuse coefficient of each pixel was transformed into HSV space and the V component was dropped. By means of K-means clustering according to (cos(2*PI*H), sin(2*PI*H), S), each pixel falls into either of two groups. If pixel $p$ is grouped into material $m1$, $\gamma_p$ is $(\gamma_{p,m1}, 0)$, otherwise $(0, \gamma_{p,m2})$. Each group actually corresponds to a specific kind of material. Subsequently, we optimize the initial specular coefficients using Levenberg-Marquardt algorithm, using the objective function in formula (1).

By far, the optimization for BRDF parameters and material weight forms an iteration procedure. Holding BRDF parameters constant, the material weights $\gamma_p$ are optimized; while holding material weight constant, the BRDF parameters are optimized. This alternate iteration will terminate until the objective function converges.

## 4   Experiment Results

In this experiment, seven lighting direction was selected. A marble and a wooden striped sphere were selected as samples. According to the steps described in section 3, we eventually obtain a material weight map of the valid region of the spheres, and 14 parameters of two BRDF model. The results are shown in Fig. 2, and rendered objects shown in Fig. 3:

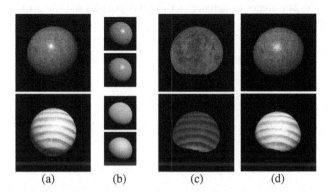

(a)              (b)              (c)              (d)

**Fig. 2.** Experiment result: (a) source images (b) material reference spheres rendered using recovered BRDF parameters (c) material weight maps for two sampled spheres, where the weights of the two materials are encoded in R/G channel, and channel B denotes the shading $(1-\gamma_{p,m1}-\gamma_{p,m2})$ (d) restored spheres rendered using material weight maps and BRDF models

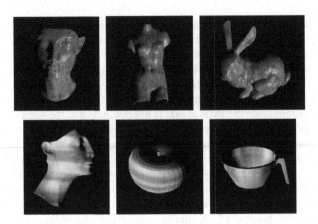

**Fig. 3.** Realistic rendering with the materials of the marble and wooden sphere

# References

1. Lensch, H.P., Kautz, J., Goesele, M., Heidrich, W., Seidel, H.P.: Image-Based Reconstruction of Spatial Appearance and Geometric Detail. ACM Trans. Graphics 22(2), 234–257 (2003)
2. Goldman, D.B., Curless, B., Hertzmann, A., Seitz, S.M.: Shape and Spatially-Varying BRDFs From Photometric Stereo. In: Proc. of the Tenth IEEE International Conference on Computer Vision (ICCV 2005), pp. 341–348. IEEE Computer Society Press, Los Alamitos (2005)
3. Matusik, W., Pfister, H., Brand, M., McMillan, L.: Efficient Isotropic BRDF Measurement. In: Proc. Eurographics Symp. Rendering: 14th Eurographics Workshop Rendering, pp. 241–248 (2003)
4. Ward, G.: Measuring and modeling anisotropic reflection. In: Computer Graphics (SIGGRAPH '94 Proceedings), pp. 239–246 (1994)
5. http://www.vision.caltech.edu/bouguetj/calib_doc/index.html
6. Debevec, P.E., Malik, J.: Recovering high dynamic range radiance maps from photographs. In: Proc. of the 24th annual conference on Computer graphics and interactive techniques, pp. 369–378 (1997)

# Application and Research on Affection Model Based on Bayesian Network

Lin Shi, Zhiliang Wang, and Zhigang Li

[1] P.O. BOX 135, University of Science and Technology, Beijing 100083, China
[2] Computer Center, Tangshan College, Tangshan, Hebei 063000, China
{pattiesl,lzghello}@126.com,
wzl@263.net

**Abstract.** It needs not only intelligence but also emotion for the computer to realize harmonious human computer interaction, which is one of the research focuses in the field of computer science. This paper proposes a hierarchical approach to represent personality, affection and emotion, using Bayesian Network to affection model and show emotion via virtual human's facial expression. The affection model was applied to an affective HCI system, proved to be simple, effective and stable.

## 1 Hierarchical Model of the Virtual Human

### 1.1 Instruction of the Hierarchical Model

We construct a hierarchical model: The Personality-affection-emotion model. Based on OCEAN model in psychology field, We classify human's personality into five dimensions:[1] Openness, Conscientiousness, Extraversion, Agreeableness, and Neuroticism; each factor corresponds to one dimension in the personality space[2], and each dimension is closely-related with facial expression and affection representation. We classify affection into positive and negative [3] adopting the most popular classification of basic emotions: happiness, surprise, fear, sadness, disgust, and anger, in addition, we add a neutral emotion. Corresponding to emotions, we use Ekman's theory, six basic facial expressions[4][5][6] and another neutral facial expression.

### 1.2 Extension of the AIML Tag

We take the chatting robot ALICE as our virtual human, which is based on AIML (Artificial Intelligence Markup Language) Technology. When inputs a question, it will produce a relative answer. There are detailed descriptions about AIML in literature[7]. In order to endow ALICE with emotion, we add an emotion tag to represent her response emotion. There are seven emotion tags corresponding to seven basic emotions mentioned above. For example(5% probability of sad, 95% probability of happy):

L. Ma, R. Nakatsu, and M. Rauterberg (Eds.): ICEC 2007, LNCS 4740, pp. 441–444, 2007.

```
<category>
<pattern>How are you doing nowadays?</pattern>
<template><emo name="happiness" prob="95">
<emo name="sadness" prob="5"> Everything is running smoothly.
</template>
</category>
```

## 2  Construction of the Affection Model Based on Bayesian Network

As Fig.1 shows, we construct an affection model based on Bayesian network involving two parent nodes and one child node, one corresponding model for each personality factor of the OCEAN model. Of course, user can combine any two or several factors arbitrarily .For example, user can totally constructs such a personality: 20% openness and 80% Neuroticism, the value range of "Current Affection $A_c$" and "Response Affection $A_r$" in Fig.1 is either positive or negative. Initial value of $A_c$ depends on different personality. $A_r$ is extracted from

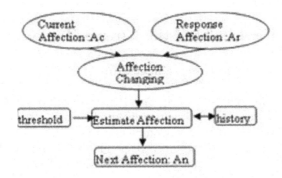

**Fig. 1.** Affection model for each personality

the emotion tags of ALICE's answer. There are different conditional transition probabilities for each personality $\pi$ to decide next affection. The probability represents affective process.

We get the conditional probability for the changing of affection $P(A_n|A_c, A_r)$ after training to ALICE with different personality. Once the conditional transition probability and prior probability $P(e_i)$ are given, a possible affection can be definite according to the following formula:

$$P(A_n) = BBN(A_c, A_r, \pi) = P(A_n|A_c, A_r)P(e_i) \tag{1}$$

$P(A_n)$ decides the affection change. When $P(A_n) > k$(a threshold, $0 \leq k \leq 1$ ), we choose $A_n$ as the next affection state. Otherwise, hold the previous affection state. The history preserves $P(A_n)$ for the next computation.

## 3   Conversion from Affection to Emotion

When the next affection state is certain, it's necessary to choose qualifying emotion response to control the virtual human's facial expression. There are three key factors deciding the emotion state: ALICE's response emotion $e_r$ , current affection $A_n$ (output of the affection model) and the previous emotion state, defined as $e_p$.

The first key factor can be easily controlled by adding emotion tags in ALICE's answers when we establish AIML database. The second key-factor is the output of the affection model. As for positive affection and negative affection, we defined emotion state transition probability matrix respectively and experientially. More users testing the system can certainly optimize these values, getting more believable results. Formula (2) shows how to get the next emotion state $e_n$:

$$P(e_n) = \Gamma A_n(Ex(e_p), Ex(e_r))P(e_r) \tag{2}$$

$\Gamma A_n$ denotes the transition probability matrix of affection $A_n$. $Ex(e_r)$ denotes the corresponding expression. we also set a threshold $s, (0 \leq s \leq 1)$ .Only if $P(e_n) \geq s$ ,the emotion state changes to $e_n$ , otherwise , it will remain unchanging.

## 4   Results

We hypothesize Personality:70% Openness, 30% Neuroticism, affection is positive. So we can get $\Gamma A_n$ experientially.

$$\Gamma A_n = \begin{bmatrix} 0.8 & 0.2 & 0.05 & 0.05 \\ 0.6 & 0.2 & 0.1 & 0.1 \\ 0.7 & 0.05 & 0.05 & 0.2 \\ 0.3 & 0.05 & 0.15 & 0.3 \end{bmatrix}$$

The user and virtual human play roles as student and teacher respectively; Four basic emotions , m1,m2,m3,m4 denotes happiness, angry, sadness and neutral respectively; And there's a regulation if the maximal probability is 10% bigger than the second maximal probability, then don't consider the influence of the latter.The threshold $s = 0.5$, virtual teacher's emotion is $e_r$ .The followings are results of the experiment based on the above assumption:

(1) An happy conversation. Input :"Good morning Ms Yang!", virtual teacher is influenced by positive emotion, after training and testing lots of times, we can get the corresponding probability: $P(e_r) = [0.8\ 0.05\ 0.1\ 0.05]^T$ ,according to the proposed formula for the emotion probability, we can get the results:

$P(e_n) = \Gamma A_n \cdot P(e_r) = [0.6525\ 0.505\ 0.5775\ 0.2775]^T$

After some judges, the next emotion is happiness. Then choose the facial expression corresponding to happiness according to $Ex(e_p)$ .The system result is as left part of Fig.2 shows.

(2)An unhappy conversation. Input :"Ms Yang, I forgot doing my homework yesterday!", virtual teacher is influenced by negative emotion, after training and testing lots of times, we can get the corresponding probability: $P(e_r) = [0.05\ 0.5\ 0.2\ 0.25]^T$ , according to the proposed formula for the emotion probability, we can get the results:

$$P(e_n) = \Gamma A_n \cdot P(e_r) = [0.1125\quad 0.175\quad 0.12\quad 0.145]^T$$

After some judges, the next emotion is anger. Then choose the facial expression corresponding to anger according to $Ex(e_p)$ .The system result is as right part of Fig.2 shows.

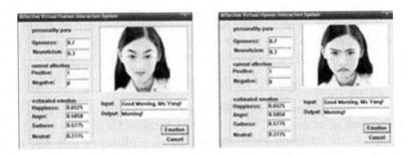

**Fig. 2.** Affective HCI System Interface, Emotion is happiness and anger

**Acknowledgments.** Work supported by Chinese National Nature Science Foundation (No.60573059) and by Foundation of University of Science and Technology Beijing.

# References

1. Costa, P.T., McCrae, R.R.: Normal personality assessment in clinical practice. The NEO personality inventory, Psychological Assessment (1992)
2. Chen, M., Luo, J., Dong, S.: ATOM-A task oriented multi-channel interface structure model. Journal of Computer-Aided Design & Computer Graphics, 61–67 (1996)
3. Deng, L., Zheng, R.: Affect Variables and Mental Health in College Students. Chinese Mental Health Journal 18, 58–60 (2004)
4. Li, D., Guo, D.: The Study of Self-Organization in Emotional System. Advances in Psychological Science 12(4), 512–518 (2004)
5. Morishima, S.: Realtime Face Analysis and Synthesis Using Neural Network. In: Neural Networks for Signal Processing X, pp. 13–22. IEEE Press, Los Alamitos (2000)
6. Suzuki, K., Yamada, H., Hartono, P., Hashimoto, S.: Modeling of Interrelationship between Physical Feature of Face and Its Impression. In: Proc. The First Int'l Symposium on Measurement, Analysis and Modeling of Human Functions, pp. 310–315 (2001)
7. Xue, W., Shi, Z., Gu, X., Wang, Z.: The Research of Emotional Interaction System Based on Agent. Computer Engineering and Applications 38(19), 6–8 (2002)

# A Survey on Projector-Based PC Clustered Distributed-Rendering Large Screen Displays and Techniques

Munjae Song[1] and Seongwon Park[2]

[1] Institute for Graphic Interfaces, 3rd Fl, Ewha-Sk Telecom Bldg. 11-1
Daehyun-dong, Seodaemun-gu, Seoul 120-750, Korea
mjsong@igi.re.kr
[2] Graduate School of Information, Yonsei University, 134 Sinchon-Dong,
Seodaemun-Gu, Seoul, Korea
seongwon@yonsei.ac.kr

**Abstract.** Large screen display systems are common display systems nowadays. Especially projector-based PC cluster large screen display systems share most of large screen display system market and they are main research topics today. A lot of researchers research on cluster algorithms, computation power improvements, high performance graphic rendering technologies, high speed buses, networks, and HCIs. Also, remarkable research results are being published by technical leading groups. Whereas, following groups who want research on large screen display have difficulties even to build a test system. Unfortunately, there are not enough information to build large screen display systems. In this paper, we survey on projector-based PC cluster large screen display technologies that use distributed rendering.

**Keywords:** Large screen display, Tiled display, PC cluster, Projector-based, Distributed rendering.

## 1 Introduction

The projector-based PC cluster large screen display technology has a dramatic improvement a past decade. It has few advantages, and its advantages make PC clustered systems are popular. Next are the advantages of PC clustered large screen display systems.

- PC performance is improving very fast. Current CPUs have multiple cores and acceleration functions for vector calculation, e.g. MMX, 3D NOW and SIMD. Almost every PC is equipped with high-performance graphic cards having multiple rendering pipelines, programmable Shaders, and sometimes multiple GPUs.
- Using COTS (Commercial Off-The-Shelf) systems lowers system cost by cutting down prices and increasing product stability. Projector-based PC cluster large screen display systems which use COTS devices are widely used because they are low-price and reliable system.

L. Ma, R. Nakatsu, and M. Rauterberg (Eds.): ICEC 2007, LNCS 4740, pp. 445–449, 2007.

- There is a number of PC clustering open/free software which has abilities to customize and improve for building large screen display systems.

Nowadays, many researchers use seamless projector-based PC clustered distributed large screen display systems. We include our surveys, experiences of building large screen display systems. We believe this paper will help research groups who want build a projector-based PC clustered distributed large screen display system. Especially, we focus on research groups that research with large screen display systems, but do not want research on large screen display system deeply.

## 2    Cluster Software

In this section we survey cluster software, discriminating large screen display software. The cluster software has two types. One is image-based streaming software, another is distributed rendering software. Table 1 shows advantages and shortcomings of two types of large screen display software.

**Table 1.** Comparison table of large screen display software

| Type | Advantages | Shortcomings |
|------|-----------|--------------|
| Image-based streaming software | - Do not consider that update scene graph, timer, random number, and user input | - Dedicate network devices for wide bandwidth<br>- Clients do not use their resource |
| Distributed rendering software | - Typical network device<br>- Clients use their resource and master has small loads<br>- Handle big and complex data with distributed system | - Difficulties of update scene graph, timer, random number, and user input |

### 2.1    Image Based Streaming Software

There are a lot of image based streaming software, but in this section, check remarkable software. TeraVision [19], SAGE [8][23] and Juxta View[10] are remarkable research results.

### 2.2    Distributed Rendering Software

Following, we review remarkable distributed rendering software, some of them are open source and others are commercial products. Open source software are flexible but commercial products do not need additional development and are stable. Good classifications of distributed rendering software can be found in [27], [18]. Remarkable distributed rendering softwares are CAVE[15], VR juggler [3], Syzygy [24], Jinx [25], OpenSG [22], Chromium [6], NAVER [17], Nova [32][29].

## 3   Hardware Devices

Projector-based PC cluster large screen display system needs special hardware devices[33][7]. For example, projectors[2][4][16], graphic cards[14] [31], projector stages[28] [20] [30], and screens are needed for building large screen display systems.

## 4   Software Requirements

Some projector-based large screen displays need several features. These features are not essential functions but, make improve large screen display system's quality better. For example, edge-blending[12][11][5][13], NLDC (NLDC) [20][21][1][9]and Frame-lock. Fig. 1 shows implementation process with software features.

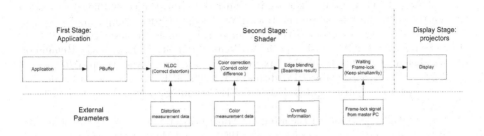

**Fig. 1.** Flow chart of implementation process

## 5   Conclusion

Large screen display systems are common display systems today. Especially projector-based PC cluster large screen displays are most popular large screen display systems. Projector-based systems are more useful for making seamless large screen display systems than multi-monitor systems. This paper shows a guide to build projector-based PC clustered large screen display systems. We believe this paper is useful to understand building projector-based large screen display systems.

**Acknowledgments.** This work was supported by the IT RD program of MIC/ IITA.[2005-S-604-02, Realistic Virtual Engineering Technology Development].

## References

1. van Baar, J., Willwacher, T., Rao, S., Raskar, R.: Seamless Multi-Projector Display on Curved Screens. In: Deisinger, J., Kunz, A. (eds.) Eurographics Workshop on Virtual Environments (EGVE), pp. 281–286. ACM Press, New York (2003)
2. Barco: http://www.barco.com

3. Bierbaum, A., Just, C., Hartling, P., Meinert, K., Baker, A., Cruz-Neira, C.: VR Juggler: A Virtual Platform for Virtual Reality Application Development. In: Proceedings of the Virtual Reality 2001 Conference, Yokohama, Japan, pp. 215–222. IEEE Computer Society, Los Alamitos (2001)
4. Christie Digital Systems, Inc., http://www.christiedigital.com
5. Hereld, M., Judson, I.R., Stevens, R.L.: Introduction to Building Projection-based Tiled Display Systems. IEEE Computer Graphics and Applications 20, 22–28 (2000)
6. Humphreys, G., Houston, M., Ng, R., Frank, R., Ahern, S., Kirchner, P.D., Klosowski, J.T.: Chromium: A Stream Processing Framework for Interactive Graphics on Clusters of Workstations. In: Proceedings of ACM SIGGRAPH 2002, San Antonio, Texas, pp. 693–702 (2002)
7. INFITEC GmbH: http://www.infitec.net
8. Jeong, B., Jagodic, R., Renambot, L., Singh, R., Johnson, A., Leigh, J.: Scalable graphics architecture for high-resolution displays. In: IEEE Information Visualization Workshop 2005, Minneapolis, MN, USA (2005)
9. Johnson, T., Gyarfas, F., Skarbez, R., Quirk, P.: Multi Projector Image Correction on the GPU. In: Poster presentation at Workshop on Edge Computing Using New Commodity Architectures (EDGE). Chapel Hill, North Carolina (2006)
10. Krishnaprasad, N.K., Vishwanath, V., Venkataraman, S., Rao, A.G., Renamhot, L., Leigh, J., Johnson, A.E.: Juxtaview: A tool for interactive visualization of large imagery on scalable tiled displays. In: 2004 IEEE International Conference on Cluster Computing, pp. 411–420. IEEE Computer Society Press, Los Alamitos (2004)
11. Li, K., Chen, Y.: Optical Blending for Multi projector Display Wall Systems. In: 12th Lasers and Electro-Optics Society 1999 Annual Meeting (LEOS '99), pp. 281–282. IEEE Press, Los Alamitos (1999)
12. Majumder, A., Stevens, R.: Perceptual Photometric Seamlessness in Tiled Projection-Based Displays. ACM Transactions on Graphics 24, 118–139 (2005)
13. Mayer, T.: New Options and Considerations for Creating Enhanced Viewing Experiences. Computer Graphics 31, 32–34 (1997)
14. NVIDIA corporation: http://www.nvidia.com
15. Pape, D., Cruz-Neira, C., Czernuszenko, M.: CAVE Users Guide (1997), http://www.evl.uic.edu/pape/CAVE
16. Matsushita Electric Industrial Co. Ltd., http://panasonic.co.jp
17. Park, C., Ahn, S.C., Kwon, Y.-M., Kim, H.-G., Ko, H.: Gyeongju VR Theater: A Journey into the Breath of Sorabol. Presence 12, 125–139 (2003)
18. Raffin, B., Soares, L., Ni, T., Ball, R., Schmidt, G.S., Livingston, M.A., Staadt, O.G., May, R.: PC clusters for virtual reality. In: IEEE Virtual Reality Conference(VR2006), pp. 215–222. IEEE Computer Society, Los Alamitos (2006)
19. Singh, R., Jeong, B., Renambot, L., Johnson, A., Leigh, J.: TeraVision: a Distributed, Scalable, High Resolution Graphics Streaming System. In: Cluster Computing, 2004 IEEE International Conference. IEEE CNF, pp. 391–400 (2004)
20. Raskar, R., Browny, M.S., Yang, R., Chen, W.-C., Welch, G., Towles, H., Sealesy, B., Fuchs, H.: Multi-projector displays using camera-based registration. In: IEEE Visualization, IEEE CNF, San Fransisco, CA, USA, pp. 161–522 (1999)
21. Raskar, R., van Baar, J.: Low-Cost Multi-Projector Curved Screen Displays. In: International Symposium Scociety for Information Display (SID) (2005)
22. Reiners, D.: Opensg: A scene graph system for flexible and efficient reltime rendering for virtual and augmented reality applications. Dissertation, TU Darmstadt, Germany (2002)

23. Renambot, L., Rao, A., Singh, R., Jeong, B., Krishnaprasad, N., Vishwanath, V., Chandrasekhar, V., Schwarz, N., Spale, A., Zhang, C., Goldman, G., Leigh, J., Johnson, A.: Sage: the scalable adaptive graphics environment. In: WACE 2004, Nice, France (2004)
24. Schaeffer, B., Goudeseune, C.: Syzygy: Native PC Cluster VR. In: IEEE VR Conference, Los Angeles, CA, USA, pp. 15–22. IEEE Computer Society, Los Alamitos (2003)
25. Soares, L.P., Zuffo, M.K.: Jinx: an X3D Browser for VR Immersive Simulation Based on Clusters of Commodity Computers. In: Ninth international conference on 3D Web technology, Monterey, California, USA, pp. 79–86. ACM Press, New York (2004)
26. SGI: http://www.sgi.com
27. Streit, A., Christie, R., Boud, A.: Understanding next-generation vr: classifying commodity clusters for immersive virtual reality. In: 2nd international conference on Computer graphics and interactive techniques in Australasia and South East Asia, pp. 222–229. ACM Press, New York (2004)
28. Surati, R.J.: A Scalable Self-Calibrating Technology for Seamless Large-Scale Displays. PhD thesis, Department of Electrical Engineering and Computer Sceince, Massachussetts Institute of Technology (1999)
29. VISIONMAX International LTD: http://www.visionmaxint.com
30. Li, Z., Varshney, A.: Calibrating Scalable Multi-projector Display Using Camera Holography Trees. In: Seventh Annual Symposium on Immersive Projection Technology (IPT 2002), Orlando, FL. IEEE Computer Society Press, Los Alamitos (2002)
31. 3Dlabs Inc., http://workstation.3dlabs.com
32. 3Digm Inc., http://www.3digm.com
33. 3D PERCEPTION: http://www.3d-perception.com/

# Automated Personal Authentication Using Both Palmprints

Xiangqian Wu[1], Kuanquan Wang[1], and David Zhang[2]

[1] School of Computer Science and Technology,
Harbin Institute of Technology (HIT), Harbin 150001, China
{xqwu,wangkq}@hit.edu.cn
[2] Biometric Research Centre, Department of Computing,
Hong Kong Polytechnic University, Kowloon, Hong Kong
csdzhang@comp.polyu.edu.hk

**Abstract.** To satisfy personal interests, different entertainment computing should be performed for different people (called personal entertainment computing). For personal entertainment computing, the personal identity should be first automatically authenticated. This paper proposes a novel approach for automated personal authentication by using both palmprints. The experimental results show that the fusion of the information of both palmprints can dramatically improve the authentication accuracy.

## 1 Introduction

The different people have different interests. To meet personal interests, different entertainment computing should be performed for different people (called personal entertainment computing). For example, the cyber pets should act different to meet different interests and the robots should provide different services to different people. To conduct personal entertainment computing, the personal identity should be first automatically authenticated. The palmprint is a relatively new biometric feature used for automated personal authentication [1, 2, 3, 4, 5]. Many algorithms have been developed for palmprint recognition in the last several years [4, 5, 6]. All of these algorithms only use sole palmprint of each person for authorization and the accuracies are not high enough to meet some applications. To improve the accuracy, this paper uses both palmprints of each person for authentication. In the following sections, the preprocessing technique described in [5] is used to crop the central part of the image, which is $128 \times 128$, for analysis.

## 2 Feature Extraction and Matching

Let $I$ denote a palmprint image and $G_\sigma$ denote a 2D Gaussian filter with the variance $\sigma$. The palmprint is first filtered by $G_\sigma$ as below:

$$I_f = I * G_\theta \tag{1}$$

where $*$ is the convolution operator.

L. Ma, R. Nakatsu, and M. Rauterberg (Eds.): ICEC 2007, LNCS 4740, pp. 450–453, 2007.

Then the difference of $I_f$ in the horizontal direction is computed as following:

$$D = I_f * b \tag{2}$$

$$b = [-1, 1] \tag{3}$$

where $*$ is the convolution operator.

Finally, the palmprint is encoded according to the sign of each pixel of $D$:

$$C(i,j) = \begin{cases} 1, & \text{if } D(i,j) > 0; \\ 0, & \text{otherwise.} \end{cases} \tag{4}$$

$C$ is called DiffCode of the palmprint $I$. The size of the preprocessed palmprint is $128 \times 128$. Extra experiments shows that the image with $32 \times 32$ is enough for the DiffCode extraction and matching. Therefore, before compute the DiffCode, we resize the image from $128 \times 128$ to $32 \times 32$. Hence the size of the DiffCode is $32 \times 32$. Fig. 1 shows some examples of DiffCode.

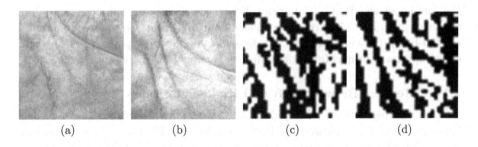

(a)                    (b)                    (c)                    (d)

**Fig. 1.** Some examples of DiffCodes. (a), (b) are the original palmprint and (c),(d) are their DiffCodes.

The matching score of two DiffCodes $C_1$ and $C_2$ is then defined as below:

$$S(C_1, C_2) = 1 - \frac{\sum_{i=1}^{32} \sum_{j=1}^{32} (C_1(i,j) \otimes C_2(i,j))}{32 \times 32} \tag{5}$$

Actually, $S(C_1, C_2)$ is the percentage of the places where $C_1$ and $C_2$ have the same values. Obviously, $S(C_1, C_2)$ is between 0 and 1 and the larger the matching score, the greater the similarity between $C_1$ and $C_2$. The matching score of a perfect match is 1. Because of imperfect preprocessing, there may still be a little translation between the palmprints captured from the same palm at different times. To overcome this problem, we vertically and horizontally translate $C_1$ a few points to get the translated $C_1^T$, and then, at each translated position, compute the matching score between $C_1^T$ and $C_2$. Finally, the final matching score is taken to be the maximum matching score of all the translated positions.

## 3   Score Fusion

Denote $x_1$ and $x_2$ as the scores obtained from the left palmprints matching and right palmprints matching between two persons, respectively. To obtain the final matching score $x$, we fuse these two scores by following simple strategies, which need not any prior knowledge or training.

$S_1$: *Maximum Strategy:*

$$x = \max(x_1, x_2) \tag{6}$$

$S_2$: *Minimum Strategy:*

$$x = \min(x_1, x_2) \tag{7}$$

$S_3$: *Product Strategy:*

$$x = \sqrt{x_1 x_2} \tag{8}$$

$S_4$: *Sum Strategy:*

$$x = \frac{x_1 + x_2}{2} \tag{9}$$

## 4   Experimental Results And Analysis

We employed the PolyU Palmprint Database [7] to test our approach. This database contains 7752 grayscale images captured from 386 different palms by a CCD-based device. From this database, we can get 3701 pairs (right and left) of palmprints captured from 193 different persons to test the approach.

### 4.1   Difference Between Left and Right Palmprints

To fuse the features of both palmprint, we should investigate the difference between them. If the palmprints from the right and left hands of same persons are very similar, the fusion cannot improve the performance much. To investigate this, two types of matching are conducted on the database: 1) Each palmprint is matched against all of the palmprints from different persons; 2) Each left palmprint is matched against the right palmprints of the same person. The score distributions of these two types of matchings are plotted in Fig. 2. This figure shows that the difference between the right and left palmprints of the same persons is close to that of the palmprints from different persons. Hence, the left and right palmprints of the same person are independent. So they can be fused to improve the authentication accuracy.

### 4.2   Accuracy Tests

To evaluate the accuracies of the different fusion strategies, each pair of palmprints in the database is matched with the other pairs. The ROC curve of each strategy is plotted in Fig. 3 and the EER of them are listed in Table 1. This figure and table also demonstrate that each fusion strategy can improve the authentication accuracy. The Sum and Product strategies are the best ones, which can decrease the EER from about 0.2% (left palmprints) or 0.3% (right palmprints) to 0.03%.

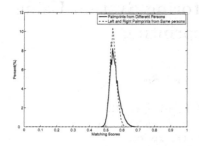 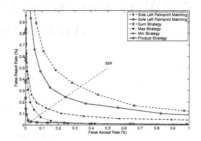

**Fig. 2.** The matching score distributions    **Fig. 3.** ROC curves of different strategies

**Table 1.** EER of different strategies

| Strategy | Sole Left Palmprint | Sole Right Palmprint | Sum | Maximum | Minimum | Product |
|---|---|---|---|---|---|---|
| EER | 0.326% | 0.243% | 0.0319% | 0.080% | 0.137% | 0.0313% |

## 5  Conclusions

For conducting personal entertainment computing, this paper authenticates people automatically using palmprints of both hand, which can dramatically improve the authentication accuracy.

## Acknowledgements

This work is partially supported by the NSFC (No. 60441005), the Key-Project of the 11th-Five-Year Plan of Educational Science of Hei Longjiang Province, China (No. HZG160), the Science and Technology Project of the Education Department of Hei Longjiang Province (No. 11523026) and the Development Program for Outstanding Young Teachers in Harbin Institute of Technology.

## References

1. Zhang, D.: Palmprint Authentication. Kluwer Academic Publishers, Dordrecht (2004)
2. Wu, X., Zhang, D., Wang, K.: Palmprint Recognition. Scientific Publishers, China (2006)
3. Duta, N., Jain, A., Mardia, K.: Matching of palmprint. Pattern Recognition Letters 23, 477–485 (2001)
4. Han, C., Chen, H., Lin, C., Fan, K.: Personal authentication using palm-print features. Pattern Recognition 36, 371–381 (2003)
5. Zhang, D., Kong, W., You, J., Wong, M.: Online palmprint identification. IEEE Transactions on Pattern Analysis and Machine Intelligence 25, 1041–1050 (2003)
6. Wu, X., Wang, K., Zhang, D.: Palm-line extraction and matching for personal authentication. IEEE Transactions on Systems, Man, and Cybernetics—Part A: Systems and Humans 36, 978–987 (2006)
7. PolyU Palmprint Palmprint Database:
http://www.comp.polyu.edu.hk/~biometrics/

# A TV Commercial Monitoring System Using Audio Fingerprinting

Seungjae Lee and Jin S. Seo

Digital Contents Research Division, ETRI,
161 Gajeong-dong, Yuseong-gu, Daejon, Korea
{seungjlee,jsseo}@etri.re.kr

**Abstract.** In this paper, we describe an audio fingerprinting-based commercial monitoring system for TV broadcasting. The goal of the commercial monitoring is to identify commercials being broadcasted and find out the time duration. If there are similar commercials in the fingerprint database, we sometimes have trouble in determining which commercial has been broadcasted. To solve this problem, we propose the partial distance comparison method which identifies commercials and discriminates them from background music. Experimental results show that the proposed method improves commercial-identification performance by discriminating different versions of the same commercial.

## 1 Introduction

Audio fingerprinting is a technology which identifies an unknown audio with audio features, and it has a lot of applications including filtering for file-sharing services, automated monitoring for broadcasting stations, audio recognition through mobile network, etc [1]. In this paper, we proposed an audio fingerprinting-based commercial monitoring system which exactly identifies commercials when similar commercials are in the fingerprint database.

Similar commercials are produced by adding a new part, removing or replacing some parts of the original. Consequently, they have the same part, and we need to discriminate similar commercials. If all commercials have prior information such as title, we can classify them and use their information to identify the correct commercial. However, we can not get all information in advance, and there are sometimes errors in prior information. Therefore, we bind similar commercials by searching the fingerprint database when we create and update it. Based on those bindings, we can find candidate commercials and identify the broadcasted commercial by comparing partial distances.

## 2 System Overview

The proposed system is composed of recording server, searching server, and monitoring server as shown in Fig. 1. In recording server, the proposed system records broadcasting signal. In searching server, we search candidate commercials by using the extracted fingerprints from the recorded signal. In monitoring server, the system informs us the monitoring result among the candidate commercials.

L. Ma, R. Nakatsu, and M. Rauterberg (Eds.): ICEC 2007, LNCS 4740, pp. 454–457, 2007.
© IFIP International Federation for Information Processing 2007

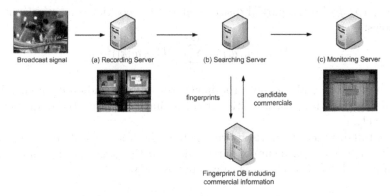

**Fig. 1.** The Commercial Monitoring System

## 2.1   Audio Feature

In commercial monitoring, the selection of audio feature determines the efficiency and the robustness of the system. Among previous work [2,3], we use normalized spectral subband centorids[3] as audio feature because of the robustness against compression, equalization, random start, time-scale modification, and linear speed change. Instead of the original overlap ratio, we overlap 87.5% in order to get a fine time resolution. For each frame, 16 normalized spectral centroids are extracted, and 94 frames are used for the identification.

A set of commercials to be monitored is collected in advance, and then, the fingerprint database is generated based on the extracted features and their prior information such as title. At the same time, each commercial is searched in the present database in order to find similar commercials and bind them. We also make an index for the fingerprint database using K-D tree for a fast search.

## 2.2   Candidate Commercials

After extracting fingerprints from the recorded audio signal, we collect N sets of candidate positions in the database by searching the index tree using N successive fingerprints of the extracted fingerprints. Then, based on the sequential relationship among the N sets of candidate positions, the duplicated ones are removed and the unique set is obtained.

For the unique set, the Euclidean distance between the extracted fingerprints and the fingerprints in the database is calculated for 94 frames to collect candidate commercials. If there are commercials below the fixed threshold, we make a list and sort it by the time duration in descending order, and deliver it to the monitoring server. If not, we examine the next $N$ successive fingerprints.

## 2.3   Decision and Time Verification

In monitoring server, we determine the title and the time duration of the broadcasted commercial by using partial distance comparison and time verification.

Let $D_{part}(p_i, q_i)$ be the partial distance at the $i$th position, and it is expressed as follows:

$$D_{part}(p_i, q_i) = \sum_{k=0}^{15} (p_i[k] - q_i[k])^2 \tag{1}$$

where $p_i[k]$, $q_i[k]$, and $k$ denote the fingerprint of the candidate commercial in the database, the fingerprint of the broadcasting signal, and the frequency bin, respectively.

In partial distance comparison, we calculate the absolute difference $D_{comp}$ between the left normalized sum of partial distance $D_{left}$ and the right normalized sum of partial distance $D_{right}$ is calculated as follows:

$$D_{comp} = |D_{left} - D_{right}| = \frac{1}{M-m} \left| \sum_{i=m}^{M-1} D_{part}(p_i, q_i) - \sum_{i=M}^{2M-m} D_{part}(p_i, q_i) \right| \tag{2}$$

where $M$ and $m$ denote the middle point of total frames to be compared and the number of frames to be skipped. We reject the first $m$ frames and the last $m$ frames to minimize an error caused by the boundaries between commercials. For the sorted candidate commercials, this comparison is continued until the $D_{comp}$ is below the fixed threshold. If found, the time verification is performed. If not, new candidate commercials are collected by using the next $N$ fingerprints.

In time verification, the start and the end position are determined by finding the minimum position of the sum of $K$ partial distances. We use a 87.5% overlap ratio with 375.1ms frame, then the time resolution would be about 46.4ms.

## 3   Experimental Results

We made a fingerprint database from 1266 commercials. There are about 40% commercials which have similar commercials. The length of commercial is 5, 10, 15, 20, 30, or 60 sec. The test signal, which had been recorded from 2 different broadcasting stations, is about 12 hours, and it has 288 commercial appearances. Out of them, 269 commercials were in the fingerprint database at first, and 19 commercials were updated to it. We used 2.4GHz CPU and 2G memory. An average processing time for broadcasting signal of an hour is about 6 minutes. Table 1. shows the experimental results.

In the first experiment, without the partial distance comparison, the monitoring were performed by using the minimum Euclidean distance of candidate

**Table 1.** The Commercial Monitoring Results

| Test set | # of commercials | # of detection | # of false positive | # of false negative |
|---|---|---|---|---|
| 1 | 288 | 269(21) | 31 | 1 |
| 2 | 288 | 288 | 13 | 1 |

commercials. We exactly found 269 commercials, but there were 21 cases that needed the postprocessing to discriminate similar commercials. Moreover, some of false positive cases were occurred due to the audio similarity of a TV program and a commercial.

In the second experiment, we updated 19 commercials which are not in the database but in the test signal and tested the monitoring system with the partial comparison. As we expected, 288 commercials were detected without the postprocessing and false positive cases were decreased. However, there were still some false positive cases and a false negative case.

The false negative case had been occurred because of the overlap between the recorded broadcasting files. The false positive cases had resulted from the silence and noise-like sound of some commercials. To overcome this limitation, the monitoring system need some video features.

## 4 Conclusion

In this paper, we examined the commercial monitoring system for TV broadcasting. In commercials, there are a lot of similar commercials by adding a new part, removing or replacing some parts of the original commercial. As a result, we need to exactly discriminate each broadcasted commercial, and it is important due to business reasons. The proposed system introduces a commercial monitoring method based on the partial distance comparison whose discrimination performance was confirmed by experiments with real broadcasting signal.

## Acknowledgement

This work was supported by the IT RD program of MIC/IITA. [2007-S-017-01, Development of user-centric contents protection and distribution technology]

## References

1. Haitsma, J., Kalker, T.: A highly robust audio fingerprinting system. In: Proceedings of International Symposium on Music Information Retrieval (October 2002)
2. Cano, P., Battle, E., Kalker, T., Haitsma, J.: A review of algorithms for audio fingerprinting. In: Proceedings of International Workshop on Multimedia Signal Processing (December 2002)
3. Seo, J.S., Jin, M., Lee, S., Jang, D., Lee, S., Yoo, C.D.: Audio fingerprinting based on normalized spectral subband centorids. In: Proceedings of IEEE International Conference on Acoustics, Speech and Signal Processing, vol. III, pp. 213–216. IEEE Computer Society Press, Los Alamitos (2005)

# Player Immersion in the Computer Game Narrative

Hua Qin[1], Pei-Luen Patrick Rau[1], and Gavriel Salvendy[2]

[1] Department of Industrial Engineering, Tsinghua University, Beijing 100084, China
[2] School of Industrial Engineering, Purdue University, West Lafayette, IN 47907, U.S.A
qinh03@mails.tsinghua.edu.cn

**Abstract.** The main characteristics of the computer game narrative are interactive and nonlinear, so this study proposes a questionnaire aim at studying player immersion in the computer game narrative. To evaluate the questionnaire, a survey was conducted on the Internet. After factor analysis and reliability test, an instrument for measuring player immersion were obtained. This instrument not only can be applied to the computer game narrative, it also ca be used to measure user experience in story-oriented virtual reality.

## 1 Introduction

Involvement in media such as novels, movies, computer games and virtual reality has been described as an experience of feeling deeply engaged with the medium. In the research of those fields, many terms have been developed to try to account for these experiences, such as flow, cognitive absorption (CA), presence and immersion [1,2,3,4,5]. These terms — flow, cognitive absorption, presence and immersion — have some overlap in studies, but in game research, immersion is a widely used term. In game worlds, players can see, hear and manipulate the environment, just as they do in the real world. This provides the player with a strong visceral and cognitive belief in what is experienced in the virtual context as physical reality. Ermi and Mäyrä [6] believed that immersion more clearly connotes the mental processes involved in the game. In addition, in the computer game industry, the term immersion is widely used [6,7,8]. Thus, the term immersion describing players totally submerged in their fictional surroundings is appropriate. Researchers consider immersion, like flow, to also be a multi-dimensional concept [2,6,7]. They attempt to interpret the depth or representation of the immersion in the field of the game. Table 1 summarizes the dimensions of engagement experience including flow, cognitive absorption, presence and immersion.

For the computer game narrative, one of the characteristics that make it different from traditional narratives is interactivity. Interaction is a form of participating actively in the narrative. Therefore, gamers are not only the audience, but also players and narrators. They have intense subjective experience in listening, watching and acting. Another characteristic of the computer game narrative is its nonlinear structure. The relationship between independent events is causality, not a fixed sequence. These characteristics determine that players will have different experiences

Commonly, general dimensions of engaging experience mainly include challenge, skill, time distortion, concentration, control and so on [3,7,9,10,13,15]. As for games,

L. Ma, R. Nakatsu, and M. Rauterberg (Eds.): ICEC 2007, LNCS 4740, pp. 458–461, 2007.

**Table 1.** Dimensions of engaging experience

| Author | Engaging Experience | Application | Dimensions |
|---|---|---|---|
| Csikszentmihalyi [9] | Flow | Human psychology | 1. Focused concentration; 2. Merging of activity and awareness; 3. Perceived control; 4. Time distortion; 5 Loss of self-consciousness |
| Hoffman & Novak [10] | Flow | A computer-mediated environments | 1. Consumer learning; 2. Perceived behavioral control (or confidence); 4. Exploratory behavior; 5. Positive subjective experiences; 6. Distortion in time perception |
| Chou & Ting [11] | Flow | Online computer game | 1. Concentration; 2. Playfulness; 3. Distortion in time perception; 4. Telepresence; 5. Exploratory behavior |
| Skadberg & Kimmel [12] | Flow | Browsing a website | 1. Enjoyment; 2. Lost track of time; 3. Telepresence |
| Pace [13] | Flow | Web information seeking activities | 1. Duration; 2. Frequency and intensity; 3. Joy of discovery; 4. Reduced awareness of irrelevant factors; 5. Distorted sense of time; 6. Merging of action and awareness; 7. Sense of control; 8. Mental alertness; 9. Telepresence |
| Sweetser and Wyeth [14] | Flow | Game player experience | 1. Concentration; 2. Challenge; 3. Skills; 4. Control; 5. Clear goals; 6. Feedback; 7. Immersion; 8. Social interaction |
| Agarwal, Sambamarthy, and Stair [15] | Cognitive absorption | Information technology | 1 Control; 2. Attention focus; 3. Curiosity; 4. Intrinsic interest; 5. Computer; 6. Playfulness; 7. Ease of use |
| Agarwal and Karahanna [5] | Cognitive absorption | Information technology | 1. Temporal dissociation; 2. Focused immersion; 3. Heightened enjoyment; 4. Control; 5. Curiosity |
| Witmer and Singer [3] | Presence and immersion | Virtual environment | 1. Presence: *Control; *Sensory; *Distraction; *Realism 2. Immersion: *Tendency to become involved in activities; *Tendency to maintain focus on current activities; *Tendency to play video games |
| Brooks [7] | Immersion | Narrative in virtual reality and other interfaces | 1. Time; 2. Context; 3. Participation |
| Brown and Cairns [2] | Immersion | Game | 1. Emotional involvement; 2. Transportation to different place; 3. Attention; 4. Control and autonomy |
| Ermi and Mäyrä [6] | Immersion | Gameplay experience | 1. Sensory immersion; 2. Challenge-based immersion; 3. Imaginary immersion |

some studies have also focused on these factors including concentration, playfulness, and control [6,11,14]. Because this study attempts to evaluate player immersion in the computer game narrative, the researchers consider that comprehending the structure and content of the story is a precondition of immersion. Only by understanding the content and structure of a series of events the players can make a plan or reason out a strategy for the next steps. Failure to comprehend the story may lead to failure to play [16]. Another aspect for studying player immersion in the computer game narrative is emotion. Therefore, a questionnaire for this study added items of story comprehension and emotion besides general dimensions of engaging experience. The questionnaire was composed of 30 items. In order to examine the reliability and validity of the questionnaire, a survey was conducted on a website.

## 2  Measuring Player Immersion

The whole procedure of the survey see figure 1. A questionnaire constructed of 30 questions or items was conducted on a website. There were 340 participants and 309 of respondents were effective. About 70% of the respondents were students. The ages of 93.85% of the subjects were from 20 to 30, and 95.47% had higher than undergraduate education levels. Only 36% of the participants had played games no more than 5 years. The participants supplied their personal information and brief information about their experience with computer games. Then the participants were asked to imagine a familiar game with a story frame to some degree while answering the 30 questions. The following steps were factor analysis including Exploratory Factor Analysis (EFA) and Confirmatory Factor Analysis (CFA) to find and confirm the structural characteristics of the questionnaire. The aim is to obtain an optimal and simple model. The 309 data were divided into two parts for the two factor analyses. Then reliability and validity of the instrument were tested. The results showed that original questionnaire was constructed of six dimensions and the 30 items were changed into 18 items. The reliability test was also satisfactory.

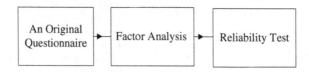

**Fig. 1.** The procedure of the survey

## 3  Discussion

The genres of computer games are diversiform and narratives differ in thousands of ways, so it is difficult to find a general measurement from the design aspects. However, most of computer games at present are story-oriented. This study considered that the degree of player immersion in the story could reflect the computer game narrative. Therefore, a questionnaire based on players' perception, cognition, motion and emotion at the beginning of, in the course of and after playing the games were proposed to measure player immersion.

At present, most studies only consider the computer game narrative as one aspect of computer games. There are nearly no systematical systems for measuring the game narrative. This study explores this field through empirical methods. The instrument proposed in this study provides a starting point for future theoretical research.

# References

1. Csikszentmihalyi, M.: Flow: The Psychology of Optimal Experience. Harper and Row, New York (1990)
2. Brown, E., Cairns, P.: A grounded investigation of game immersion. In: CHI 2004, ACM Conference on Human Factors in Computing, pp. 1297–1300. ACM Press, New York (2004)
3. Witmer, B.G., Singer, M.J.: Measuring presence in virtual environments: A presence questionnaire. Presence, Teleoperators and Virtual Environments 7(3), 225–240 (1998)
4. McMahan, A.: Immersion, engagement, and presence: A method for analyzing 3-D video games. In: Wolf, M.J.P., Perron, B. (eds.) The Video Game Theory Reader, New York, pp. 67–86 (2003)
5. Agarwal, R., Karahanna, E.: Time flies when you're having fun: cognitive absorption and beliefs about information technology usage. MIS Quarterly 24(4), 665–694 (2000)
6. Ermi, L., Mäyrä, F.: Fundamental components of the gameplay experience: analyzing immersion. In: Castell, S., Jenson, J. (eds.) Changing Views: Worlds in Play. Selected Papers of the 2005 Digital Games Research Association's Second International Conference, pp. 15–27 (2005)
7. Brooks, K.: There is nothing virtual about immersion: Narrative immersion for VR and other interfaces (2003), Retrieved (May 25, 2007) from http://alumni.media.mit.edu/ brooks/storybiz/immersiveNotVirtual.pdf
8. Cairns, P., Cox, A., Berthouze, N., Dhoparee, S., Jennett, C.: Quantifying the experience of immersion in games. In: Cognitive Science of Games and Gameplay workshop at Cognitive Science 2006, Vancouver (2006)
9. Csikszentmihalyi, M.: The flow experience and its significance for human psychology. In: Csikszentmihalyi, M., Csikszentmihalyi, I.S. (eds.) Optimal Experience: Psychological Studies of Flow in Consciousness. Cambridge University Press, Cambridge, MA (1988)
10. Hoffman, D.L., Novak, T.P.: Marketing in hypermedia computer-mediated environments: conceptual foundations. Journal of Marketing 60(7), 50–68 (1996)
11. Chou, T.J., Ting, C.C.: The role of flow experience in Cyber-Game Addiction. Cyber Psychology and Behavior 6(6), 663–675 (2003)
12. Skadberg, Y.X., Kimmel, J.R.: Visitors' flow experience while browsing a website: Its measurement, contributing factors and consequences. Computers in Human Behavior 20(3), 403–422 (2004)
13. Pace, S.: A grounded theory of the flow experiences of Web users. Int. J. Human-Computer Studies 60(3), 327–363 (2004)
14. Sweetser, P., Wyeth, P.: GameFlow: A model for evaluating player enjoyment in games. ACM Computers in Entertainment 3(3), 1–24 (2005)
15. Agarwal, R., Sambamurthy, V., Stair, R.: Cognitive absorption and the adoption of new information technologies. Presented at the Academy of Management Annual Meeting, Boston (1997)
16. Tavinor, G.: Video games, fiction, and emotion. In: Proceedings of the Second Australasian Conference on Interactive Entertainment, Sydney, Australia (2005)

# Music Video Viewers' Preference Evaluation Criteria and Their Characteristics

Maiko Kamata and Michiaki Yasumura

Graduate School of Media and Governance, Keio University.
5322 Endo, Fujisawa-shi, Kanagawa-ken, Japan
{kamata,yasumura}@sfc.keio.ac.jp

**Abstract.** This study investigated music video viewers' characteristics and their preference evaluation criteria. We had detailed interviews based on the evaluation grid method with ten participants. All participants watch music videos frequently. Our participants could be divided into following two types: (1) *Singer-based type* viewers: they emphasized the importance of the singer(s) singing the song in their preference evaluation criteria. (2) *Image-based type* viewers: they insisted that the images were the high-priority parameters in their preference evaluation. It is noteworthy that their preference criteria and viewing style were affected by whether they prefer Japanese or English songs.

**Keywords:** music video, viewer, preference evaluation, detailed interviews.

## 1 Introduction

Music video has been supporting today's music industry in terms of promotion and entertainment. Today, music video is a well-known media and is available on television, DVD, and the internet. Viewers with experienced-eyes naturally demand for more attractive music videos. Thus, it is crucial for music video designers to create music videos that meet viewers' expectations. Under the current circumstance, a study that approaches the insight of viewers surely offers the key to a development of entertainable music video making methodology.

In this study, we carried out a case study interview with frequent music video viewers and investigated relationships between their preference evaluation criteria and participants' characteristics. We believe that this study provides an opportunity to deepen our understandings of viewers. Moreover, we also aim to develop music video making methodology. Our discussion will help music video designers to carry out their work with their target viewers in mind.

## 2 Previous Work

Our previous work discussed characteristics of viewers' favorite music videos by using the k-means clustering analysis. As a result, we found that there were three types of viewers' favorite music videos. The results indicated that the primary reason

L. Ma, R. Nakatsu, and M. Rauterberg (Eds.): ICEC 2007, LNCS 4740, pp. 462–465, 2007.

that viewers favored the music videos were: (1) auditory-leading type: they liked music and singer; (2) visual-leading type: they were amazed by the imaging technique; (3) synergic type: they got favorable impressions overall. This result suggests the important factors to be included in attractive music videos [1].

However, we have not revealed who prefer which type of music video. In other words, it is still not clear that what kind of personality appreciates what kinds of music videos. Against this backdrop, this paper is intended as an investigation of this relationship between viewers' personality and their favorite music videos.

## 3  Interview Methods

We had detailed interviews based on the evaluation grid method with ten undergraduate students. The evaluation grid method is a detailed interview method that is used for clarifying participants' concrete evaluation criteria towards a certain object [2].

We first asked participants to write down titles of their favorite music videos on cards. Next, participants were asked to line up the cards from their most favorite to least favorite on a table. Then, we pointed pairs of cards and asked them why they prefer one over another. These procedures enabled participants to express their specific evaluation criteria easily. Each session took forty to fifty minutes to complete.

**Table 1.** Participants Details. The participants in this interview were all Japanese students from our University. Six males and four females, age 19 to 23 (*mean*: 21.4, *Standard Deviation*: 1.29). They all watch music videos more than one time per week. We also asked them their favorite music category (Japanese or English or both) and oversea experience.

| ID | AGE | SEX | FREQUENCY they watch | MUSIC they like | OVERSEA experience (6month+) |
|----|-----|-----|----------------------|-----------------|------------------------------|
| A | 21 | F | 1-2 / per week | English | Yes |
| B | 20 | F | 2-3 / per week | English | No |
| C | 22 | M | 1-2 / per week | Japanese | Yes |
| D | 23 | M | 2-3 / per week | Japanese | No |
| E | 22 | M | 2-3 / per week | Mainly Japanese | No |
| F | 22 | F | 2-3 / per week | Mainly English | Yes |
| G | 19 | F | 1-2 / per week | English | Yes |
| H | 21 | M | 2-3 / per week | Japanese | No |
| I | 22 | M | 2-3 / per week | Japanese | No |
| J | 23 | M | 2-3 / per week | English | Yes |

## 4  Results of the Interview

In this survey, the most fundamental preference criterion for our participants was either the singer or the image of music video. Although most of them value both criteria, they give great importance on one. Here, we divided participants into two types in order to investigate viewers' characteristics closely according to their preference criteria.

## (1) *Singer-Based Type*

The ultimate evaluation criterion for the participant A, C, D, H and I were the singer(s) who sang the song. In fact, almost all of their favorite music videos were of their favorite singer(s). Their primary purpose of watching music videos is to expose their favorite singers.

## (2) *Image-Based Type*

We categorized participant B, E, F, G, and J as the image-based type. It is notable that most of the image-based viewers were with experience of residing outside of Japan over six months. One exception, B, aspired to go abroad and now she is currently preparing for her staying in an English-spoken country. Overall, the image-based type viewers were interested in music in general and invested a good deal of time to experience various styles of music videos. They often contact media that provides to a broad range of music videos such as the internet radios and music-only TV programs.

It is worth arguing that there were radical differences between the singer-based and image-based types on the following four points:

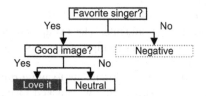

**Fig. 1.** Singer-based Type Preference Evaluation

(a) **Music**: the singer-based viewers tend to prefer Japanese pop songs whereas the image-based viewers were passionate listeners of the English songs.

**Fig. 2.** Image-based Type Preference Evaluation

**Table 2.** Cross-Classification of Preference on Music by Types. Fisher's exact significance probability was p=0.103 (>.10) and did not recognise a statistical association between their preference on music and evaluation type. Although we could not confirm the association statistically, we can read a certain tendency from this table.

|  | Singer-Based | Image-Based | Total |
|---|---|---|---|
| J-Pop | 4 | 1 | 5 |
| English | 1 | 4 | 5 |
| Total | 5 | 5 | 10 |

(b) **Purpose**: the singer-based viewers watch music videos because they consider music videos as a tool to admire their favorite singers. On the other hand, the main purposes for the image-based viewers were to enrich their listening experience or gathering information. This fact gave us a clue to explain why the singer-based preferred the *audio-leading type* and the image-based preferred the *visual-leading type* music videos.

(c) **Media**: the singer-based viewers first encounter shortened or edited music videos by hit charts TV programs. When they are motivated to see more, they purchase music video DVD or go to the singer's website to be satisfied. On the other, the image-based only watch full-length music videos by the internet radios and all-music TV channels.

(d) **Viewing experience:** the singer-based viewers had narrow experience and dedicated their time for their favorite singers. Meanwhile, the image-based had vast experience and found pleasure in getting acquainted with attractive images.

One interpretation of these clear contrasts is that viewers' preference on music (i.e. Japanese pop or English) affects on their viewing style. People prefer Japanese pop naturally access Japanese media and get used to it which usually offers edited versions of music videos. In contrast, participants who favored English songs exposed to western-based media which brings full-length viewing experience. This is probably the reason for good agreement between viewers' preference on music and preference criteria and their viewing styles.

# 5 Conclusion

In this paper, we explored relationships between viewers' personality and their preference criteria of music videos. We found that the most significant evaluation criterion was either the singer or the image of the music video. We also recognized remarkable differences between viewers of the singer-based and the image-based type. It seems reasonable to assume that viewers' viewing style and preference evaluation were closely related to their preference of music.

Taken together, we suggest music video designers to identify their main viewers' type and concentrate on fulfilling their expectation. In addition, viewers' media-cultural background deserves careful attention because it is a key factor that cultivates viewers' preference evaluation.

## Acknowledgements

Authors would like to thank all of our participants and Professor Makoto Arisawa of Content Engineering Lab in Keio University for his support of this study.

## References

1. Kamata, M., Furukawa, K.: Three Types of Viewers' Favorite Music Videos. In: Proc. of the International Conference on Advances in Computer Entertainment Technology 2007, Salzburg, Austria, pp. 196–199 (2007)
2. Sanui, J., Inui, M.: Phenomenological Approach to the Evaluation of Places: A study on the construct system associated with place evaluation. Journal of architecture, planning and environmental engineering. Transactions of AIJ 367, 15–22 (1986)

# Virtual Consumption: Using Player Types to Explore Virtual Consumer Behavior

Penny Drennan[1] and Dominique A. Keeffe[2]

[1] Faculty of Information Technology, Queensland University of Technology
[2] Faculty of Business, Queensland University of Technology
{p drennan, d.keeffe}@qut.edu.au

**Abstract.** As virtual economies begin to interact more with real world economies, it is important to consider the in-game activities that players engage in, which create and transfer game currency. Specifically, we examine products and services that players offer to each other within MMORPGs. We use Bartle's taxonomy of player types to illustrate the different behavioral approaches players have in consuming these products and services. We introduce the term virtual consumption to describe these in-game exchanges and highlight the need for further research into this phenomenon.

**Keywords:** player types, virtual consumption, consumer behavior.

## 1 Introduction

There is a growing body of research that explores the intersection between real and virtual world economies [2, 6]. However, there have been few attempts to explore virtual consumption, which is the way that players behave while consuming in-game products and services. As real world and game economies converge and the scale of game economies increases, it is imperative to investigate the services that are offered in virtual worlds, and the behavior of players in virtual (i.e. in-game) consumption situations. This paper explores how Bartle's taxonomy of player types can be used to investigate virtual consumer behavior within the context of Massively Multi-player Online Role-Playing Games (MMORPGs). We begin by providing details about Bartle's taxonomy, followed by a brief introduction to the domain of consumer behavior. Next, we illustrate the concept of virtual consumption in an MMORPG. Finally, we propose ways that players might engage in virtual consumption situations, based on their predominant approach to MMORPGs, as described by Bartle. Finally, we outline further work aimed at exploring virtual consumption in more depth.

## 2 Player Types

While there are many studies exploring player behavior and motivation in MMORPGs [4, 9], Bartle provides the most well known and comprehensive categorization of player types [1]. He outlines four categories of behavior based on two axes of playing style. These axes

L. Ma, R. Nakatsu, and M. Rauterberg (Eds.): ICEC 2007, LNCS 4740, pp. 466–469, 2007.

identify the focus of the player's attention (world-oriented versus player-oriented) and describe the way the player approaches the game (action versus interaction). The intersecting axes thus form four distinct player types: killers, socializers, achievers, and explorers. Bartle has since extended this taxonomy by adding a third axis, describing behavior as either implicit or explicit for each of the four player categories outlined above [1]. However, we believe that the four original player types provide scope for an initial exploration of virtual consumer behavior, without presupposing certain types of behavior.

## 3   Traditional Consumer Behavior

Given that virtual worlds are both psychologically unique and the setting for a range of different player behaviors, we propose that virtual worlds provide the ideal environment to investigate consumer (mis)behavior because they allow players (or "consumers") to behave in a way that is realistic but uninhibited by social norms. Traditionally, consumer behavior is described as the "study of the processes involved when individuals or groups select, purchase, use or dispose of products, services, ideas or experiences to satisfy needs and desires" [8]. Consumers can engage in a range of behaviors as a response to their satisfaction or dissatisfaction with what they have purchased. However, consumers do not always behave appropriately, especially when they are dissatisfied with their purchase. One of the most extreme negative behavioral responses a consumer can engage in is retaliation, which is an aggressive behavior engaged in with the intention of getting even [5]. These behaviors can be overt or covert and include verbal or physical abuse, theft, creating a cost/loss, vandalism, and trashing [5]. All retaliatory behavior is motivated by a desire to correct inequity (whether real or psychological): it's a case of 'You got me. I got you back. Now we're even' [5, 7]. While traditional research is conducted using real life consumption situations, we propose that consumers will engage in a similar range of behaviors in virtual worlds. It is vital that we investigate virtual consumption as virtual economies meet real world economies.

## 4   Consumption in MMORPGs

MMORPGs promote consumption that is specific to the story and fantasy elements of its specific environment. For instance, studies of *Guild Wars* [3] indicate that players sometimes act as merchants by providing a range of goods for sale to other players. The items that they offer are the same goods offered by merchant non-player characters (NPCs), so these players do not offer a unique virtual service. However, transactions between players and player merchants shave the margins, providing lower costs and allowing players to sell items for higher prices than they can get from NPCs. Usually player merchants are higher level characters, who have gathered a large collection of items from different areas throughout the game. Similarly, other high level players will offer to act as "runners" to lower level characters. This means that they offer to quickly and safely take players through difficult sections of the game in return for game currency. Successful runners are required to be familiar with the section of the game that they are providing the service for, as well as being equipped with the skills to safely navigate the area [3].

## 5 Player Types in Virtual Consumption

We propose that players will approach virtual consumption situations differently depending on their dominant player type. We can examine Bartle's taxonomy of player types in light of virtual consumer behavior, by considering how each player type might act in a virtual consumption situation. Both positive and negative consumer behavior can be demonstrated by all four player types. However, we believe that retaliatory consumer behavior is more likely to be shown by killers and socializers. Conversely, achievers and explorers are more likely to *provide* than *consume*.

First, we suggest that socializers will be motivated to create and maintain positive consumption relationships with other players. When socializers experience highly satisfactory consumption situations, they are most likely to engage in positive consumer behavior, such as helping service providers or advocating on behalf of the service provider. Further, socializers would be keen to develop a closer relationship with their service provider and attempt to salvage the unsatisfactory consumption situations by using their communication skills. This might result in the player negotiating with or complaining to the service provider. A dissatisfied socializer is unlikely to engage in retaliation against a service provider. However, socializers may be motivated to retaliate against service providers if they perceive that a member of their social network has been adversely affected and is in need of support or intervention.

Second, we propose that killers are motivated to extract maximum value from their consumption experiences without regard for future interactions. A merely satisfactory experience will not prompt any particular behavior from a killer; they have received what they need from the interaction and are not likely to expend further energy prolonging the experience. However, it is when consumption situations are unsatisfactory that killers might begin to display the overt behavior that characterizes this player type. When killers are dissatisfied, we propose that they will engage in negative behaviors that are disproportionate to the event that caused them. This retaliatory behavior can escalate (depending on the situation) into verbally abusive fighting. Of all player types, killers are most likely to engage in retaliation as they perceive that there is a lack of consequence engendered by the anonymity in most MMORPGs.

Finally, achievers and explorers are less likely to engage in the extreme behavior demonstrated by socializers and killers due to their focus on the world. We suggest this is because they are the players most likely to *provide* products and services to other players by virtue of their world focus. Achievers are likely to have the necessary skills to complete difficult areas of the game with panache, making them candidates to offer running services. Explorers are also likely to be competent runners, as they have knowledge of quicker and safer routes through difficult parts of the game. Further, explorers are likely to be player merchants because they may have discovered artifacts in areas of the MMORPG that other players have not yet accessed. These world-focused skills put achievers and explorers in a position where they are more likely to *provide* rather than *consume*.

## 6   Conclusions and Future Work

This paper demonstrated how Bartle's taxonomy of player types could be meaningfully applied to virtual consumption. We have explored the concept of traditional consumer behavior and how it may be mirrored in virtual worlds. We also examined possible classification of consumer behavior, by exploring Bartle's taxonomy of player types as an organizing framework. Given this preliminary exploration, there are many directions in which future work can progress. We believe that observing players will allow us to access more information about player motivations and their responses to specific consumption situations. These player studies will develop a corpus of evidence illuminating virtual consumption in MMORPGs.

## References

1. Bartle, R.A.: Designing Virtual Worlds, 1st edn. New Riders Publishing, Indianapolis, Indiana (2003)
2. Castronova, E.: Virtual Worlds: A First-Hand Account of Market and Society on the Cyberian Frontier. CESifo Working Paper Series No. 618 (2001)
3. Drennan, P.: An Ethnographic Study of Player Behaviour in MMORPGs. Unpublished doctoral dissertation, University of Queensland, Australia (2007)
4. Ducheneaut, N., Yee, N., Nickell, E., Moore, R.J.: 'Alone together?' exploring the social dynamics of massively multiplayer online games. In: ACM Conference on Human Factors in Computing Systems (CHI 2006), pp. 407–416. ACM, New York (2006)
5. Huefner, J.C., Hunt, H.K.: Consumer retaliation as a response to dissatisfaction. Journal of Consumer Satisfaction, Dissatisfaction and Complaining Behavior 47, 107–117 (2000)
6. Malaby, T.: Parlaying Value: Capital in and beyond Virtual Worlds. Games & Culture 1, 141–162 (2006)
7. Skarlicki, D.P., Folger, R.: Retaliation in the workplace: The roles of distributive, procedural, and interactional justice. Journal of Applied Psychology 82, 434–443 (1997)
8. Solomon, M.R., Dann, S., Dann, S., Russell-Bennett, R.: Consumer Behaviour: Buying, Having, Being. 1st edn. Pearson Education, Frenchs Forest, NSW (2007)
9. Yee, N.: Motivations of Play in Online Games. Journal of CyberPsychology and Behavior 9, 772–775 (2007)

# Codebook Design of Keyblock Based Image Retrieval

Hui Liu and Cai-ming Zhang

School of Computer Science & Technology, Shangdong Economic Univ.,
Ji'nan, Shandong Province, 250014

**Abstract.** This paper presents an image retrieval method based on keyblocks combing with interest points, furthermore the generation of codebook is also utilized to enhance the retrieval performance, where the balance between the retrieved precision and time cost can decide the codebook size of this CBIR system. Finally, the proposed method is compared with the method that only depends on interest points or keyblocks.

**Keywords:** CBIR, keyblocks, codebook, retrieved precision.

## 1 Introduction

Content-based image retrieval (CBIR) is currently a very important research area on multimedia applications. In order to overcome the deficiencies of global feature, a series of ROI based methods has been proposed[1]. The typical systems are Blobworld system[2] of University of California, Berkeley and SIMPLIcity system[3] of Pennsylvania State University, etc. But only the gray information is considered in these systems, which is not reasonable and has difference with human visual perception.

The target of detecting all interest points is to extract the most representative points in an image. Moravec published a paper in 1977 which mentioned corners detection[4].Now we can receive above interest points detection result by use of Harris Corner method[5], which shows that most points distribute on the border of idiographic object in image.

But we have found that interest points mainly extract features distributing on the edge of objects, instead of paying attention to the placid parts of image, especially to big proportional images, which makes us neglect those idiographic objects inevitably.

In this paper, we propose an efficient method based on the composition of interest points and keyblocks to solve the feature representation problem, which has more comprehensive consideration to object border and local region of image.

## 2 Keyblock Generation

In this section, we present this method to generate many keyblocks (the construction of keyword-like image feature segments) of image and combining these keyblocks with interest points during the course of image retrieval. Here we use clustering algorithms to generate keyblocks.

L. Ma, R. Nakatsu, and M. Rauterberg (Eds.): ICEC 2007, LNCS 4740, pp. 470–474, 2007.

## 2.1  Keyblock Generation for Each Semantic Class

For each semantic class, a corresponding codebook (consists of the set of selected keyblocks) is generated. Each keyblock in these codebooks will retain its original pixel intensity values and will also carry a class label corresponding to the type of geographic feature it represents.

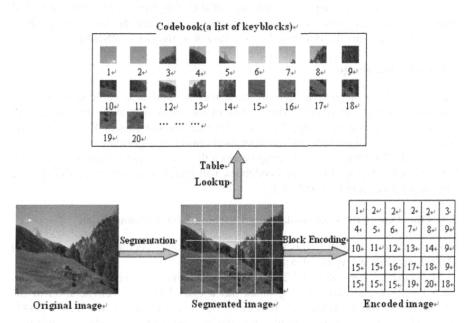

**Fig. 1.** General procedure for image encoding

Automatic method[6] is used in keyblock selection: For each semantic class, domain experts are asked to provide some training images to initiate the standard keyblock generation procedure presented as followed:

Let $C=\{c_1, \dots, c_i, \dots, c_N\}$ be the "codebook" of keyblocks representing the images, where $N$ is the codebook size and $c_i$ ($1 \leq i \leq N$) are the keyblocks. Let $F$ be a mapping:

$$F : R^k \rightarrow C=\{c_1, \dots, c_i, \dots, c_N | c_i \in R^k,\}$$

where $R^k$ is the Euclidean space of dimension $k$. Given a sequence $T =\{t_1, \dots, t_j, \dots, t_i | t_j \in R^k \}$, the mapping $F$ gives rise to a partition of $T$ which consists of $N$ cells $P=\{p_1, \dots, p_i, \dots, p_N\}$, where $p_i=\{t_i | t \in T, F(t)=\tilde{c_i}\}$ For a given distortion function $d(t_j, c_i)$, which is the distance between the input $t_j$ and output code $c_i$ (for example, the Euclidean distance), an optimal mapping should satisfy the following conditions:

—*Nearest Neighbor Condition*: For each $p_i$, if $t \in p_i$, then $d(t, c_i) \leq d(t, c_j)$, for all $j \neq i$.

—*Centroid Condition*: For a given partition $P$, the optimal code vectors satisfy:

$$c_i = \frac{\sum_{t \in p_i} t}{k_i}, \ 1 \leq i \leq N, \text{ where } k_i \text{ is the cardinality of } p_i$$

The purpose of this stage is to assign semantic meaning to each keyblock, since domain knowledge can be imported. There are a variety of clustering algorithms[7.etc.] available which can be applied to data sets of different types. Two commonly-used algorithms that can serve as the basis for this approach are the *Generalized Lloyd Algorithm* (GLA) and the *Pairwise Nearest Neighbor Algorithm* (PNNA) [8].

### 2.2  Codebook Merge

The codebooks generated in 2.1 are now merged into a larger codebook. This codebook comprises keyblocks with a range of meanings and can be directly used in image encoding and decoding. However, because the component keyblocks come from different training sets, and unsupervised clustering algorithms may have been employed in 2.1, there may be overlap between the boundaries of clusters centered on the keyblocks. The quality of this codebook will therefore be improved through the fine-tuning process in following 2.3.

### 2.3  Fine-Tuning the Codebook Using Learning Vector Quantization

Fine-tuning is performed in this section by using learning vector quantization (LVQ) algorithms [Kohonen et al. 1995].

The codebook generated in 2.2 will be used as the initial codebook for this process. Each keyblock and each training block has a class label. In each iteration of the clustering algorithm, updates are performed on those two data items (keyblocks) $c_i$ and $c_j$ which are nearest to a training input (training block) $t$. This update is performed when one of these data items belongs to the correct class while the other belongs to an incorrect class, and $t$ falls within an update zone defined around the mid-plane of cluster boundaries formed by $c_i$ and $c_j$. Assuming that $d_i$ and $d_j$ are the distances of $t$ from $c_i$ and $c_j$, respectively, this update zone is defined as the region where $min(d_i d_j, d_j d_i) \ \square \ T$, with $T$ being a threshold with a typical value between 0.5 and 0.7.

At this point, each image is a two-dimensional array of codebook keyblock indices. It can also be considered as a list of keyblocks similar in format to a text document defined by a list of keywords. We can reconstruct the image to test whether the codebook was properly selected (see Fig.1).

## 3  Similarity Calculation

In this paper we carry out similarity calculation based on histogram model usually used in information retrieval, which is a vector model with special form. Suppose D={$d_j$}is a database which contains n images, and K={$k_i$} is a codebook which contains t codewords, the calculation method is described in [9].We can adjust the value of weight appropriately in terms of out understanding of images during the course of image retrieval, in order to receiving the result we need.

## 4 Experiments and Result

In order to test our method, we select 5 categories images (automobile, animal, plane, ship, architecture) from COREL[10] database, which is classified by high-level semantics (defined by a large group of human observers as standard ground truth). Then we collect 100 images from each category randomly as the query set and denote the query set as $QS =\{ I_1 ,..., I_{100} \}$. These demonstration images constitute 500 times query in total. We choose the first 20 most similar images as retrieval results each time.

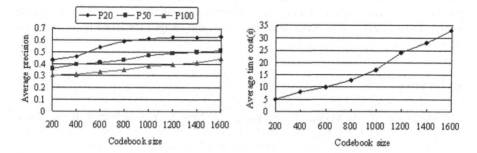

**Fig. 2.** Precision and time cost for different codebook sizes

### 4.1 Determining the Size of the Codebook

To determine the size of the codebook, different numbers of clusters have been selected and evaluated. Considering that the value of $k$, i.e. the maximum number of the expanded codewords is related with $N$, i.e. the size of the codebook. A retrieved image is considered a match if it belongs to the same category of the query image. The average precisions within the top 20(50,100) images are shown in Fig.2 (a), and retrieval time costs for different codebook sizes are given in Fig.2(b).

### 4.2 Performance of Experiments

As to each kind of images, its average Normal Precision is the average value of 5 query results, the same to average Normal Recall, as shown in Table 1:

**Table 1.** The retrieval results for different $\omega$ value

| Images | Average Normal Precision (%) | | | Average Normal Recall (%) | | |
|---|---|---|---|---|---|---|
| | $\omega_1=1,$ $\omega_2=0$ | $\omega_1=0,$ $\omega_2=1$ | $\omega_1=0.5,$ $\omega_2=0.5$ | $\omega_1=1,$ $\omega_2=0$ | $\omega_1=0,$ $\omega_2=1$ | $\omega_1=0.5,$ $\omega_2=0.5$ |
| Automobile | 85.3 | 77.5 | 70.5 | 69.2 | 65.1 | 60.8 |
| Animal | 84.1 | 80.2 | 65.7 | 71.3 | 62.5 | 59.3 |
| Plane | 82.2 | 72.6 | 74.1 | 75.8 | 70.5 | 55.1 |
| Ship | 79.8 | 76.1 | 74.7 | 62.7 | 70.1 | 62.4 |
| Architecture | 83.0 | 81.8 | 79.3 | 70.4 | 63.3 | 66.9 |

The performance of experiments shows that the instance where $\omega_1=1$ and $\omega_2=0$, which considers the similarity of keyblocks containing interest points plays best, which indicates that the keyblacks which interest points exist on make up the shortcoming of information only from edges. Furthermore, the variability of $\omega$ increases the flexibility of retrieval.

# 5 Conclusion

The goal is to use keyblock analysis module by constructing codebook to increase the capability of the interest points analysis module by Harris for queries where the placid parts of image was important and carry out similarity calculation based on histogram model. Experiment results have shown some of the images retrieved by this system improved.

# References

1. Xiangyang, W., Hongying, Y., Fengli, H.: A New Regions-of-Interest Based Image Retrieval Using DWT. In: Proceedings of ISCIT2005, pp. 127–130 (2005)
2. Carson, C.: Blobworld: Image segmentation using expectation-maximization and its applications to image querying. IEEE Trans. on Pattern Analysis and Machine Intelligence 24(8), 1026–1038 (2002)
3. Wang, J.Z., Li, J., Wiederhold, G.: SIMPLIcity: Semantics-sensitive integrated matching for picture libraries. IEEE Trans. Pattern Analysis and Machine Intelligence 23(9), 947–963 (2001)
4. Moravec, H.P.: Towards automatic visual obstacle avoidance. IJCAI, 584 (1977)
5. Harris, C.: A combined corner and edge detector. In: 4th ALVEY vision conference, pp. 147–151 (1988)
6. Zhu, L., Rao, A., Zhang, A.: Theory of Keyblock-Based Image Retrieval. ACM Transactions on Information Systems 20(2), 224–257 (2002)
7. Zhang, T.: An Efficient Data Clustering Method for Very Large Databases. In: ACM SIGMOD International Conference on Management of Data, Montreal, pp. 103–114 (1996)
8. Zhu, I.: keyblock: an approach for content-based image retrieval. ACM multimedia, 157–166 (2000)
9. Liu, H., Ma, J.: Research on Image Retrieval based on Interest Points and Keyblocks. Journal of Computational Information Systems 3(4), 1679–1685 (2007)
10. Corel stock photo library, Ontario. Corel, Canada.

# Template Based Image Mosaics

Yoon-Seok Choi, Bon-Ki Koo, and Ji-Hyung Lee

CG Research Team, Digital Content Research Division,
Electronics and Telecommunications Research Institute,
161 Gajeong-dong, Yuseong-gu, Daejeon, 305-350, Replublic of korea
{ys-choi,bkkoo,ijihyung}@etri.re.kr

**Abstract.** We propose an image mosaic method based on tile template. Compared with a conventional mosaic which is comprised of the circle or the square tiles, our approach uses the arbitrary shaped tiles. But an arbitrary shaped tile leaves the excessive gap between tiles in the mosaic construction. Then the gap makes it difficult to preserve the fine detail of an original image. Our approach controls overlap between tiles to minimize the gap by using the mask technique and adopts stackable technique to represent the fine detail of a source image automatically.

**Keywords:** Non Photorealistic Rendering, Mosaic Rendering, Image Mosaic.

## 1 Introduction

Non photorealistic rendering is the general term for rendering techniques that use various painting materials such as pen, oil, watercolor, and so on. Several studies have been made on the simulated mosaic in the field of non photorealistic rendering. Mosaic is an art technique which produces an art work by assembling the pattern or the form of a tile, a marble, the paper, and the flat glass to the plane canvas.

This paper shows a mosaic rendering method using the various shaped tiles including circle or rectangle tiles.

## 2 Previous Work

In mosaic rendering, several research were proposed including the colored paper mosaics [1], photomosaics [2], the square tile [3], and so on. According to the method for determining the shape, the color, the location, and the orientation of a tile, mosaic rendering produces the various images.

Seo [1] proposed mosaic effects of color-paper. Seo could express a hand-made mosaic effect by using the texture as well as the torn-paper effect. Photomosaics [2] made mosaics from photographs instead of solid colored tiles and arranged small images in a rectangular grid. From a distance, small images are seen together as a large image. Hausner [3] decided the location of square tiles by using the centroidal voronoi diagram and varied the orientations of the tiles

L. Ma, R. Nakatsu, and M. Rauterberg (Eds.): ICEC 2007, LNCS 4740, pp. 475–478, 2007.

using the direction field. He generated random square tiles on the image plane and then rearranged them iteratively until the area of tiles is maximized to preserve input image edges. Dobashi *et al.* [4] tried to improve Hausner's approach by using the different tile shapes. Park [5] suggested an algorithm using multi-layered photomosaic with stackable tiles which are independent, rotatable and non-rectangular in shape, such as coins, dishes, and so on.

A template refers to the part in which the tile image shows up in a screen. The shapes of templates might be more free than a circle or a square. We explain our approach which generates mosaic image based on a template of a tile with mask control and stackable tiles.

## 3   Template Based Image Mosaics

To produce mosaic, we use three types of masks: edge, energy, and write masks. The edge and energy masks are necessary for preserving the edge of an original image and representing a beauty of margin respectively. The energy mask is generated based on the light intensity value of image. The edge mask includes edge information generated by edge detection algorithm. When rendering process positions a tile in a segment, which is the divided area of an image, the write mask informs whether the segment is vacant or not. If it is vacant the mask stores the information which target image is filled with the tile. The edge and energy masks operate analogously to the write mask. The mosaic production has two steps. In the first step, the empty space of an image is filled with a tile. In the second step, the expression of an image is improved by piling up a tile with a multi-layer. Fig 1 shows the process to produce a mosaic image.

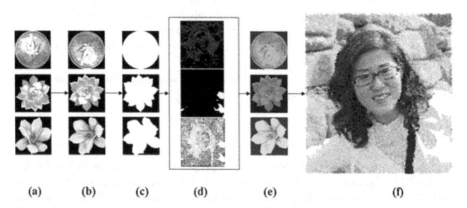

(a)        (b)        (c)        (d)        (e)                    (f)

**Fig. 1.** Process diagram (a) various shaped tiles (b) rotated tiles (c) templates of tiles (d) edge, energy, and write masks (e) colored tiles (f) final image

### 3.1   Tile Alignment

First of all, the write mask with the the equal size to that of the target mosaic is set up as 0. To generate multi-angled tiles, we use flood filling method. The flood filling method searched repeatedly space and decided a good position to locate a tile while rotating a tile with comparing a template of a tile with three types of masks. Whenever a space is filled with tiles, the space of write mask which is corresponding to the filled space is set to 1. In order to minimize gap between tiles, the size of a tile can be reduced. The positions of tiles are determined through a comparison between the template extracted from the tiles and the masks. The filling process is repeated until there is no space for tile filling.

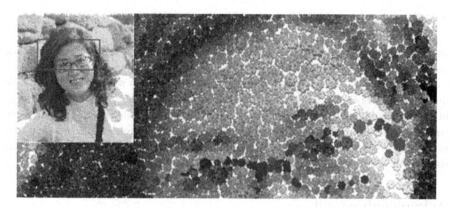

**Fig. 2.** Fine details using stackable tiles

**Fig. 3.** Template based Mosaics Rendering: Source image, tile, and the result

## 3.2  Detail Enhancement with Stackable Tiles

We applied a conventional photomosaic algorithm and merged it with a shadow effect as Park's approach [5]. Comparing original image with a colored tile with the RGB value, we decided the inappropriate position of each tile. In this case, the edge mask which is used in the previous step was not used. For improving the fine details of mosaic image, stackable tiles are used (Fig. 2).

## 4  Conclusion and Future Work

In this paper, we tried to generate mosaic image based on a template of tile using mask control and stackable tiles. The three types of masks are produced based on the source image and tiles are aligned through comparison with the masks. These masks control not only the positions of the tiles but also the sizes of them. Finally in order to enhance images expression we adopted stackable tiles. However, as to the overlay control through the mask control, the gap minimization between tiles is limited. Two dimension nesting problem is from now on applied for resolving the gap minimization problem between the tiles.

## Acknowledgement

This work was supported by the IT R&D program of MIC/IITA. [2005-S082-02, Development of Non-Photorealistic Animation Technology]

## References

1. Seo, S., Park, Y., Kim, S., Yoon, K.: Colored Paper Mosaic Rendering. In: SIG-GRAPH '01: Proceedings of Conference on Sketches and Abstaracts and Applications, p. 157 (2001)
2. Silverts, R., Hawley, M.: Photomosaics. Henry Holt, New York (1997)
3. Alejo, H.: Simulating Decorative Mosaics. In: SIGGRAPH '01: Proceedings of the 28th annual conference on Computer graphics and interactive techniques, pp. 573–580 (2001)
4. Yoshinori, D., Toshiyuki, H., Henry, J., Tomoyuki, N.: A method for creating mosaic images using voronoi diagrams. In: EUROGRAPHICS '02: Proceedings Annual Conference of the European Association for Computer Graphics (2002)
5. Park, J.: The Coinage Project #1: "Time Is Money". Leonardo 38(2), 124 (2005)

# Author Index

# Lecture Notes in Computer Science

Sublibrary 1: Theoretical Computer Science and General Issues

For information about Vols. 1– 4431
please contact your bookseller or Springer

Vol. 4600: H. Comon-Lundh, C. Kirchner, H. Kirchner (Eds.), Rewriting, Computation and Proof. XVI, 273 pages. 2007.

Vol. 4599: S. Vassiliadis, M. Berekovic, T.D. Hämäläinen (Eds.), Embedded Computer Systems: Architectures, Modeling, and Simulation. XVIII, 466 pages. 2007.

Vol. 4598: G. Lin (Ed.), Computing and Combinatorics. XII, 570 pages. 2007.

Vol. 4596: L. Arge, C. Cachin, T. Jurdziński, A. Tarlecki (Eds.), Automata, Languages and Programming. XVII, 953 pages. 2007.

Vol. 4595: D. Bošnački, S. Edelkamp (Eds.), Model Checking Software. X, 285 pages. 2007.

Vol. 4590: W. Damm, H. Hermanns (Eds.), Computer Aided Verification. XV, 562 pages. 2007.

Vol. 4588: T. Harju, J. Karhumäki, A. Lepistö (Eds.), Developments in Language Theory. XI, 423 pages. 2007.

Vol. 4583: S.R. Della Rocca (Ed.), Typed Lambda Calculi and Applications. X, 397 pages. 2007.

Vol. 4580: B. Ma, K. Zhang (Eds.), Combinatorial Pattern Matching. XII, 366 pages. 2007.

Vol. 4576: D. Leivant, R. de Queiroz (Eds.), Logic, Language, Information and Computation. X, 363 pages. 2007.

Vol. 4547: C. Carlet, B. Sunar (Eds.), Arithmetic of Finite Fields. XI, 355 pages. 2007.

Vol. 4546: J. Kleijn, A. Yakovlev (Eds.), Petri Nets and Other Models of Concurrency – ICATPN 2007. XI, 515 pages. 2007.

Vol. 4545: H. Anai, K. Horimoto, T. Kutsia (Eds.), Algebraic Biology. XIII, 379 pages. 2007.

Vol. 4533: F. Baader (Ed.), Term Rewriting and Applications. XII, 419 pages. 2007.

Vol. 4528: J. Mira, J.R. Álvarez (Eds.), Nature Inspired Problem-Solving Methods in Knowledge Engineering, Part II. XXII, 650 pages. 2007.

Vol. 4527: J. Mira, J.R. Álvarez (Eds.), Bio-inspired Modeling of Cognitive Tasks, Part I. XXII, 630 pages. 2007.

Vol. 4525: C. Demetrescu (Ed.), Experimental Algorithms. XIII, 448 pages. 2007.

Vol. 4514: S.N. Artemov, A. Nerode (Eds.), Logical Foundations of Computer Science. XI, 513 pages. 2007.

Vol. 4513: M. Fischetti, D.P. Williamson (Eds.), Integer Programming and Combinatorial Optimization. IX, 500 pages. 2007.

Vol. 4510: P. Van Hentenryck, L.A. Wolsey (Eds.), Integration of AI and OR Techniques in Constraint Programming for Combinatorial Optimization Problems. X, 391 pages. 2007.

Vol. 4507: F. Sandoval, A. Prieto, J. Cabestany, M. Graña (Eds.), Computational and Ambient Intelligence. XXVI, 1167 pages. 2007.

Vol. 4501: J. Marques-Silva, K.A. Sakallah (Eds.), Theory and Applications of Satisfiability Testing – SAT 2007. XI, 384 pages. 2007.

Vol. 4497: S.B. Cooper, B. Löwe, A. Sorbi (Eds.), Computation and Logic in the Real World. XVIII, 826 pages. 2007.

Vol. 4494: H. Jin, O.F. Rana, Y. Pan, V.K. Prasanna (Eds.), Algorithms and Architectures for Parallel Processing. XIV, 508 pages. 2007.

Vol. 4493: D. Liu, S. Fei, Z. Hou, H. Zhang, C. Sun (Eds.), Advances in Neural Networks – ISNN 2007, Part III. XXVI, 1215 pages. 2007.

Vol. 4492: D. Liu, S. Fei, Z. Hou, H. Zhang, C. Sun (Eds.), Advances in Neural Networks – ISNN 2007, Part II. XXVII, 1321 pages. 2007.

Vol. 4491: D. Liu, S. Fei, Z.-G. Hou, H. Zhang, C. Sun (Eds.), Advances in Neural Networks – ISNN 2007, Part I. LIV, 1365 pages. 2007.

Vol. 4490: Y. Shi, G.D. van Albada, J. Dongarra, P.M.A. Sloot (Eds.), Computational Science – ICCS 2007, Part IV. XXXVII, 1211 pages. 2007.

Vol. 4489: Y. Shi, G.D. van Albada, J. Dongarra, P.M.A. Sloot (Eds.), Computational Science – ICCS 2007, Part III. XXXVII, 1257 pages. 2007.

Vol. 4488: Y. Shi, G.D. van Albada, J. Dongarra, P.M.A. Sloot (Eds.), Computational Science – ICCS 2007, Part II. XXXV, 1251 pages. 2007.

Vol. 4487: Y. Shi, G.D. van Albada, J. Dongarra, P.M.A. Sloot (Eds.), Computational Science – ICCS 2007, Part I. LXXXI, 1275 pages. 2007.

Vol. 4484: J.-Y. Cai, S.B. Cooper, H. Zhu (Eds.), Theory and Applications of Models of Computation. XIII, 772 pages. 2007.

Vol. 4475: P. Crescenzi, G. Prencipe, G. Pucci (Eds.), Fun with Algorithms. X, 273 pages. 2007.

Vol. 4474: G. Prencipe, S. Zaks (Eds.), Structural Information and Communication Complexity. XI, 342 pages. 2007.

Vol. 4459: C. Cérin, K.-C. Li (Eds.), Advances in Grid and Pervasive Computing. XVI, 759 pages. 2007.

Vol. 4449: Z. Horváth, V. Zsók, A. Butterfield (Eds.), Implementation and Application of Functional Languages. X, 271 pages. 2007.

Vol. 4448: M. Giacobini (Ed.), Applications of Evolutionary Computing. XXIII, 755 pages. 2007.

Vol. 4447: E. Marchiori, J.H. Moore, J.C. Rajapakse (Eds.), Evolutionary Computation, Machine Learning and Data Mining in Bioinformatics. XI, 302 pages. 2007.

Vol. 4446: C. Cotta, J. van Hemert (Eds.), Evolutionary Computation in Combinatorial Optimization. XII, 241 pages. 2007.

Vol. 4445: M. Ebner, M. O'Neill, A. Ekárt, L. Vanneschi, A.I. Esparcia-Alcázar (Eds.), Genetic Programming. XI, 382 pages. 2007.

Vol. 4436: C.R. Stephens, M. Toussaint, D. Whitley, P.F. Stadler (Eds.), Foundations of Genetic Algorithms. IX, 213 pages. 2007.

Vol. 4433: E. Şahin, W.M. Spears, A.F.T. Winfield (Eds.), Swarm Robotics. XII, 221 pages. 2007.

Vol. 4432: B. Beliczynski, A. Dzielinski, M. Iwanowski, B. Ribeiro (Eds.), Adaptive and Natural Computing Algorithms, Part II. XXVI, 761 pages. 2007.